Lecture Notes in Computer Science 15280

Formal Methods

Subline of Lecture Notes in Computer Science

More information about this series at https://link.springer.com/bookseries/558

Alexandre Madeira · Alexander Knapp
Editors

Software Engineering and Formal Methods

22nd International Conference, SEFM 2024
Aveiro, Portugal, November 6–8, 2024
Proceedings

Springer

Editors
Alexandre Madeira
Campus Gualtar
University of Aveiro
Aveiro, Portugal

Alexander Knapp
University of Augsburg
Augsburg, Germany

ISSN 0302-9743 ISSN 1611-3349 (electronic)
Lecture Notes in Computer Science
ISBN 978-3-031-77381-5 ISBN 978-3-031-77382-2 (eBook)
https://doi.org/10.1007/978-3-031-77382-2

This Springer imprint is published by the registered company Springer Nature Switzerland AG
The registered company address is: Gewerbestrasse 11, 6330 Cham, Switzerland

Preface

The SEFM conference series aims to bring together researchers and practitioners from academia, industry, and government, to advance the state of the art in formal methods, to facilitate their uptake in the software industry, and to encourage their integration within practical software engineering methods and tools. The topics covered range from formal modelling, specification, and design in software development over safety-critical, fault-tolerant, and secure systems to real-time, hybrid, and cyber-physical systems and quantum computing.

This volume contains the papers presented at SEFM 2024, the 22nd International Conference on Software Engineering and Formal Methods, held on November 6–8, 2024 in Aveiro, Portugal.

Following the call for papers, there were 82 announced submissions of which 14 were retracted or not submitted in time. The remaining submissions were each single-blindly reviewed independently by three reviewers, and this was followed by a lively online discussion amongst the reviewers. Based on the reviewing results, the Programme Committee decided to accept 23 regular research papers for presentation at the conference and publication in this volume. The editors thank the members of the Programme Committee and the additional reviewers for their reviews and discussions. We also thank all authors for their submissions, whether accepted or not, and hope that they will keep contributing to future editions of this conference series.

Continuing the practise established with last year's edition of SEFM, paper submissions could be accompanied by artefacts to be evaluated against the EAPLS badging scheme. The artefact evaluation serves to enable future researchers to effectively build on and compare with previous work. The Artefact Evaluation Committee awarded the *Available* badge to 10 artefacts, the *Functional* badge to 5 artefacts, and the *(Functional and) Reusable* badge to 4 artefacts. We thank the members of the Artefact Evaluation Committee, chaired by Marie-Christine Jakobs, for their work.

The programme also includes three invited talks: Luís Soares Barbosa (INESC TEC and University of Minho, Portugal) on "Paraconsistency for the working software engineer"; Paula Herber (Universität Münster, Germany) on "Formal Verification of Cyber-physical Systems using Domain-Specific Abstractions"; and John van de Wetering (University of Amsterdam, Netherlands) on "Picturing Quantum Software". We thank the three keynote speakers for their insights.

Associated with the main SEFM 2024 conference there were four workshops: DataMod, ReacTS, Ibex, and CIFMA. We thank all organisers of these associated events for contributing to the success of SEFM and the Workshop Chair, José Proença, for the coordination. The event was supported by the FCT, the Portuguese funding agency for Science and Technology, at CIDMA with the project UIDB/04106/2020 (https://doi.org/10.54499/UIDB/04106/2020).

We would like to thank the SEFM Steering Committee and their chair, Antonio Cerone, for their guidance and support; José Proença for managing the web site; Springer's Lecture Notes in Computer Science team for their support, and EasyChair for providing the reviewing infrastructure.

September 2024

Alexandre Madeira
Alexander Knapp

Organization

Programme Committee Chairs

Alexander Knapp	University of Augsburg, Germany
Alexandre Madeira	University of Aveiro, Portugal

Artefact Evaluation Committee Chair

Marie-Christine Jakobs	LMU Munich, Germany

Steering Committee

Radu Calinescu	University of York, UK
Antonio Cerone	Nazarbayev University, Kazakhstan
Rocco De Nicola	IMT—School for Advanced Studies Lucca, Italy
Gwen Salaün	Grenoble Alpes University, France
Marjan Sirjani	Mälardalen University, Sweden
Bernd-Holger Schlingloff	Fraunhofer FOKUS and Humboldt University of Berlin, Germany
Ming Chai	Beijing Jiaotong University, China

Programme Committee

Luis S. Barbosa	University of Minho, Portugal
Mario Bravetti	University of Bologna, Italy
Radu Calinescu	University of York, UK
Taolue Chen	Birkbeck, University of London, UK
Alcino Cunha	University of Minho, Portugal
Carla Ferreira	Universidade NOVA de Lisboa, Portugal
João Ferreira	University of Lisbon, Portugal
Adrian Francalanza	University of Malta, Malta
Hubert Garavel	Inria, France
Mario Gleirscher	University of Bremen, Germany
Marie-Christine Jakobs	LMU Munich, Germany
Christian Johansen	Norwegian University of Science and Technology, Norway
Daniela Kaufmann	TU Wien, Austria
Alexander Knapp (Co-chair)	University of Augsburg, Germany
Burcu Kulahcioglu Ozkan	Delft University of Technology, Netherlands
Alexandre Madeira (Co-chair)	University of Aveiro, Portugal
Manuel A. Martins	University of Aveiro, Portugal

Marjan Mernik	University of Maribor, Slovenia
Charles Morisset	Newcastle University, UK
Stephan Merz	Inria Nancy, France
Renato Neves	University of Minho, Portugal
Rocco De Nicola	IMT—School for Advanced Studies Lucca, Italy
Peter Ölveczky	University of Oslo, Norway
Jovanka Pantovic	University of Novi Sad, Serbia
Carlos Pombo	University of Buenos Aires, Argentina
José Proença	University of Porto, Portugal
Gwen Salaün	Université Grenoble Alpes, France
Augusto Sampaio	Federal University of Pernambuco, Brazil
Marjan Sirjani	Mälardalen University, Sweden
Ana Sokolova	University of Salzburg, Austria
Pierre-Yves Schobbens	University of Namur, Belgium
Meng Sun	Peking University, China
Bernardo Toninho	Universidade Nova de Lisboa and NOVA-LINCS, Portugal
Ionut Tutu	Romanian Academy, Romania
Tim Willemse	Eindhoven University of Technology, Netherlands

Artefact Evaluation Committee

Zsófia Ádám	Budapest University of Technology and Economics, Hungary
Alessio Coltellacci	Inria, France
Simon Dierl	TU Dortmund, Germany
Jan Haltermann	Carl von Ossietzky University of Oldenburg, Germany
Marie-Christine Jakobs (Chair)	LMU Munich, Germany
Marek Jankola	LMU Munich, Germany
Joabe Jesus	University of Pernambuco, Brazil
Eduard Kamburjan	University of Oslo, Norway
Bjørnar Luteberget	SINTEF Digital, Norway
Agustín Eloy Martinez Suñé	Universidad de Buenos Aires, Argentina
James Ortiz	University of Namur, Belgium
Cedric Richter	Carl von Ossietzky University of Oldenburg, Germany
Martin Tappler	TU Wien, Austria

Additional Reviewers

Misael Alpizar Santana
Hernán Gagliardi
Pedro Antonino
Dušan Gajić
Simón Emmanuel Gutiérrez Brida
Letterio Galletta
Lorenzo Bacchiani
Leandro Gomes
Giovanni Bacci
Calum Imrie

José Bernardo Barros
Omar Inverso
Mario Benevides
Bruno Lopes
Giovanni Bernardi
Stefan Marksteiner
Davide Bresolin
Zahra Moezkarimi
Marco Carbone
Cosimo Perini Brogi
Pablo Castro
Ivan Prokić
Claudia Chirita
Germán Regis
Matteo Cimini
Jurriaan Rot
Mihai Codescu
Wendelin Serwe
Diana Costa
Adenilso Simao
Gabriele Costa
Simone Soderi
Maximiliano Cristia
Jorge Sousa Pinto
Jovana Dedeic
Ioannis Stefanakos
Kavan Fatehi
Muhammad Waseem Anwar
Daniel Figueiredo
Jasmine Xuereb
Maria João Frade
Hengjun Zhao
Nils Froleyks

Local Organisation

Juliana Cunha University of Aveiro, Portugal
Alexandre Madeira University of Aveiro, Portugal
Manuel Martins University of Aveiro, Portugal
Renato Neves University of Minho, Portugal
José Proença University of Porto, Portugal

Picturing Quantum Software (Invited Talk)

John van de Wetering

University of Amsterdam, Amsterdam, Netherlands
john@vdwetering.name

Abstract. Quantum software is the code that runs on a quantum computer. I'll give a brief overview of what this means, as well as a trifecta of important challenges in this area: efficient compilation, verification, and classical simulation of quantum programs. Then, I'll discuss some of the ways we've been attacking these problems in recent years, using a number of techniques based on graph rewriting and the ZX calculus.

Contents

Invited Talks

Contributed Papers

Invited Talks

Formal Verification of Cyber-Physical Systems Using Domain-Specific Abstractions

Paula Herber[1,2(✉)], Julius Adelt[1(✉)], and Philip Tasche[2(✉)]

[1] University of Münster, Einsteinstr. 62, 48149 Münster, Germany
{paula.herber,julius.adelt}@uni-muenster.de
[2] University of Twente, Enschede, The Netherlands
p.b.h.tasche@utwente.nl

Abstract. Cyber-physical systems have become ubiquitous in our daily lives, and their complexity continually evolves to unprecedented levels. In addition to their heterogeneity and interaction with a physical environment, we see a tremendous increase in the use of learning to make autonomous decisions in dynamic environments. These developments pose significant challenges for ensuring safety and resilience of cyber-physical systems. Formal methods have the potential to guarantee such properties under all circumstances. However, they are expensive and severely suffer from scalability issues. To improve scalability and applicability of formal methods, it is highly desirable to exploit domain-specific knowledge. In this paper, we summarize some of our recent efforts towards reusable specification and more scalable verification of cyber-physical systems using domain-specific abstractions. In particular, we present our ideas to use domain-specific abstractions to provide 1) reusable semantics encodings that enable us to automatically transform domain-specific system design languages such as SystemC or Simulink into a formal representation, and 2) reusable specification mechanisms for contracts and invariants that can be used for deductive verification of safety and resilience of reactive, hybrid, and learning systems. We discuss promising results and open problems, and identify challenges for future work.

Keywords: Formal Specifications · Cyber-Physical Systems · Deductive Verification · Reusability · Abstraction

1 Introduction

Cyber-physical systems (CPS) typically consist of a discrete controller (cyber part) and a technical environment (physical part). Hardware and software are typically deeply intertwined in these systems. CPS surround us in our everyday lives and range from home appliances over cars and airplanes to critical infrastructure such as water or energy supply systems. The complexity of these

A. Madeira and A. Knapp (Eds.): SEFM 2024, LNCS 15280, pp. 3–21, 2025.
https://doi.org/10.1007/978-3-031-77382-2_1

systems is steadily increasing as they are integrated into increasingly dynamic environments, while the functional demands continue to grow. Further, in the era of self-driving vehicles and autonomous distributed control systems, cyber-physical systems increasingly use machine learning techniques to make control decisions. At the same time, these systems are often safety-critical. For example, an autonomous robot could harm pedestrians or a reactor could overheat.

To ensure safety and resilience of cyber-physical systems for all possible input scenarios, formal methods are highly desirable. However, there are three major barriers that impede the application of formal methods for cyber-physical systems: First, they require a formal model, which is often difficult to establish. The formalization of informally defined system models requires a high level of expertise and manual effort, in particular for cyber-physical systems, which are typically heterogeneous, i.e., they combine hardware and software, discrete and continuous behavior, and take autonomous decisions with learning components. Second, formal verification does not scale well. Existing formal verification techniques either rely on automatic analysis techniques such as model checking, which suffer from the state space explosion problem, or they require manual effort to guide the verification process, for example, in deductive verification. While deductive verification is a powerful approach to establish a system's safety under all circumstances, it heavily relies on the user to define assertions, contracts, and invariants. Third, and finally, there is a lack of abstractions for the safe integration of learning components that ensure safety and resilience even in the presence of disruptions, but do not impede the performance of learning.

In this invited paper, we summarize our recent efforts to overcome these problems. In particular, we discuss how *domain-specific abstractions* can be used for reusable specification and more scalable verification of cyber-physical systems. Our key ideas are to use domain-specific abstractions to provide 1) reusable semantics encodings that enable us to automatically transform domain-specific system design languages such as SystemC or Matlab Simulink into a formal representation, and 2) reusable specification mechanisms for contracts and invariants that can be used for deductive verification of reactive, hybrid, and intelligent systems. In our recent work, we have presented reusable semantics encodings to enable the deductive verification of two industrially used system design languages, namely SystemC and Simulink [2,25,38]. Furthermore, we have presented reusable specification mechanisms, namely a *reachable abstract states invariant* (RASI), which abstractly captures reachable states in reactive hardware/software systems [37,38], and *reusable specification patterns* for safe integration of learning components in autonomous CPS [1,2] and for defining resilience [3]. Both specification mechanisms are based on domain-specific abstractions, and significantly reduce the manual effort required for deductive verification of safety and resilience with well-established deductive verification tools, i.e., the interactive theorem prover KeYmaera X [12] for hybrid systems and the auto-active verifier VerCors [6] for concurrent systems. We summarize our main results, and discuss challenges and open problems.

2 Preliminaries

To cope with the ever-increasing complexity of CPS, model-based development has become more and more wide-spread during the last two decades. This has several advantages, ranging from early-design space exploration, over increased quality, reusability, and maintainability, to automated code generation. In CPS design, model-based development is often achieved by using system design languages, which enable analysis and simulation during the whole development process with executable system models. Two industrially widely used system design languages for CPS are SystemC [21] and MATLAB/Simulink [27]. SystemC is control-flow oriented and widely used for the design of integrated hardware/software systems, Simulink is data-flow oriented and widely used for modeling and simulation of dynamic systems. In this section, we briefly introduce SystemC and Simulink. Furthermore, we briefly introduce the deductive verification tools VerCors [6] and KeYmaera X [12] together with the underlying formalisms.

2.1 SystemC

SystemC is a system-level design language and a framework for hardware/software co-simulation. The semantics of SystemC is informally defined in an IEEE standard [21]. It is implemented as a C++ class library, which provides language elements for the description of hardware and software, and allows for modeling of both hardware and software components on various levels of abstraction. It also features an event-driven simulation kernel. A SystemC design consists of a set of communicating processes, triggered by events and interacting through channels. Modules and channels represent structural information. SystemC also introduces an integer-valued time model with arbitrary time resolution. Figure 1a shows an excerpt of a SystemC `Robot` module, which we have also used as an illustrating example in [38]. In this example, a `sensor` method (which is executed within an `SC_THREAD` process) periodically reads the distance to an obstacle `dist` from a sensor. If the distance falls below a given threshold `MIN_DIST`, the sensor process triggers an obstacle detected event `od` with a zero time delay (which will trigger a control process not shown here). The execution of SystemC designs is controlled by a non-preemptive scheduler. Processes suspend themselves using `wait` statements, and resume execution when an event they are waiting for is triggered or a timing delay given in the `wait` statement expires. Like typical hardware description languages, SystemC supports the notion of delta-cycles, which impose a partial order on parallel processes.

2.2 Simulink

MATLAB/Simulink [27] is a data-flow oriented modeling language, which extends classical block diagrams with means to model dynamic systems, e.g., differential equations and complex mathematical functions. With that, it enables the design and simulation of hybrid systems. The basic building blocks in Simulink are blocks, which belong to one or more of several groups, e.g.,

```
SC_MODULE(Robot) {
    sc_event od;
    void sensor() {
      int dist = 0;
      while(true) {
        wait(2, SC_MS);
        dist = read_sensor(dist);
        if(dist < MIN_DIST)
          od.notify(SC_ZERO_TIME);
    }
    SC_CTOR(Robot) {
      SC_THREAD(sensor);
};
```

(a) SystemC Example [38]

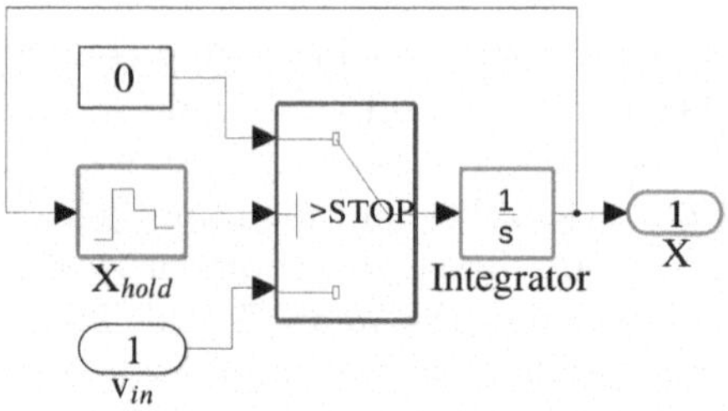

(b) Simulink Example [2]

Fig. 1. Example SystemC and Simulink Models

direct feed-through, time-discrete, time-continuous, and control-flow blocks. Signals connect blocks and may carry discrete or continuous values.

Figure 1b shows a small example, which models the dynamics of a simple vehicle. The position X of the vehicle is computed by continuously integrating over either the input velocity v_{in} if the vehicle is moving, or over 0 if it passed a *STOP* position. The red switch block switches between these two behaviors, and is controlled by a discrete controller, in this example simply modeled by a blue zero order hold block, which samples the position of the vehicle at discrete sample times and tells the switch if it has reached its *STOP* position.

To model learning in dynamic systems, Mathworks provides a reinforcement learning (RL) toolbox [28] for Simulink. The RL toolbox provides an RL agent block, which samples observations and rewards and chooses actions in fixed intervals. Thus, it can be used to replace manually designed controllers with a controller that learns to dynamically choose actions that maximize a reward function. RL is a class of machine learning methods for learning in a trial and error approach by interacting with an environment through actions [36]. The mathematical basis for most RL algorithms are Markov decision processes (MDPs) [36]. An MDP is a tuple (S, A, R, p), where S is a set of possible states, A a set of possible actions, $R \subset \mathbb{R}$ a set of rewards, and p a probability distribution, which defines the probability of reaching successor states from a given state with a given action. In an MDP, an agent and an environment interact in discrete time steps. At each step t, the agent receives a current state $s_t \in S$ from the environment and chooses an action $a_t \in A$ to interact with it. The environment reacts with a new state $s_{t+1} \in S$ resulting from the action and a numeric reward $r_{t+1} \in R$. The goal of a RL algorithm is to optimize the reward over time by learning a policy $\pi(a|s)$ that determines which actions to take in which states.

2.3 VerCors and the Prototypal Verification Language PVL

The VerCors program verifier [6] is an auto-active deductive verifier for concurrent programs, which means that after providing annotations, no interaction

```
class ErrorCount{
  int cnt; boolean active;
  resource lock_invariant() = Perm(cnt, 1) ** cnt >= 0;
  ensures Perm(active, 1) ** active;
  ErrorCount(){   {= Perm(active, 1) ** Perm(cnt, 1) =}
    active = true; {= Perm(active, 1) ** active ** Perm(cnt, 1) =}
    cnt = 0;       {= ... ** Perm(cnt, 1) ** cnt == 0 =}
  }                {= Perm(active, 1) ** active =}
  requires err > 0 ** Perm(active, read) ** active;
  void add(int err){ {= ... =}
    lock(this);      {= ... ** Perm(cnt, 1) ** cnt >= 0 =}
    cnt = cnt + err; {= ... ** Perm(cnt, 1) ** cnt > 0 =}
    unlock(this);    {= ... =}
} }
```

Fig. 2. Example PVL Program

with the user is required. VerCors supports several input languages such as Java, OpenCL, OpenMP and the Prototypal Verification Language PVL. It enables modular reasoning about method contracts that consist of pre- and postconditions, specified with the `requires` and `ensures` keywords, respectively. To cope with concurrent memory accesses, VerCors uses permission-based separation logic, which means that we must explicitly specify the read and write permissions of each variable. In the example shown in Fig. 2, an error counter defines a shared variable `cnt`, which may be increased by several processes. Initially, the constructor sets the variable `cnt` to zero and `active` to `true`, and other processes will only work on it if the `active` flag has already been set. To synchronize concurrent accesses, VerCors supports locks, which are associated with a `lock_invariant` that must be established whenever the lock is released. A lock can also store permissions that must be returned to the lock upon release. In the example, the `lock_invariant` is defined as `Perm(cnt, 1) **` $cnt \geq 0$, which means that the lock stores write permission for `cnt`, i.e., no process can access `cnt` without holding the lock. Additionally, a process can assume $cnt \geq 0$ when acquiring the lock and must ensure the same when releasing it using `unlock`.

2.4 KeYmaera X and the Differential Dynamic Logic d$\mathcal{L}$

The differential dynamic logic (d$\mathcal{L}$) [32] is a logic for formally specifying and reasoning about properties of hybrid systems, which are modeled as hybrid programs. Hybrid programs are built from the following syntax: $\alpha; \beta$ is a sequential composition of two hybrid programs α and β. α^* is a non-deterministic repetition. $x := e$ is a discrete assignment of term e to variable x. $x := *$ assigns a non-deterministically chosen value to x. $\alpha \mathbin{++} \beta$ is a non-deterministic choice. $?\mathcal{Q}$ is a test formula. $\mathit{if}(\mathcal{Q})\{\alpha\}\mathit{else}\{\beta\}$ is syntactic sugar for $\{?\mathcal{Q}; \alpha{+}{+}?\neg\mathcal{Q}; \beta\}$. $\{x_1' = \eta_1, \dots, x_n' = \eta_n \;\&\; \mathcal{Q}\}$ is a continuous evolution, where variables x_i evolve with differential equations $x_i' = \eta_i$ while an evolution domain $\mathcal{Q}$ is satisfied. d$\mathcal{L}$ provides modalities $[\alpha]\phi$ and $\langle\alpha\rangle\phi$ for reasoning about reachable states. Safety specifications are expressed as $\mathit{pre} \rightarrow [\alpha]\mathit{post}$ and can be verified using the interactive theorem prover KeYmaera X [12]. Proofs in KeYmaera X are based on the d$\mathcal{L}$ sequent calculus, which applies inference rules to simplify d$\mathcal{L}$ formulas

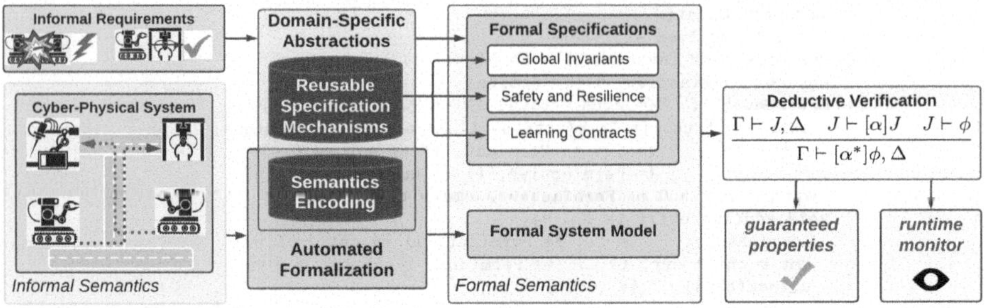

Fig. 3. Overall Approach

into subgoals. In KeYmaera X, proofs are automatically stored in tactics, which can be rerun and customized. For simple models, or subgoals of a larger proof, the theorem prover is often able to find solutions automatically.

3 Domain-Specific Abstractions for CPS Verification

An underlying key concept of our research over the last decade has been to use domain-specific abstractions to define reusable specifications that precisely yet abstractly capture typical patterns in a given domain, and thus enable us to tailor formal verification to these patterns. For example, in reactive embedded systems, where concurrent processes interact through events, an abstraction that captures the process and event states while abstracting from underlying data is highly useful to verify the correct interplay between processes. In hybrid systems, where a (potentially intelligent) discrete controller controls a technical environment that evolves continuously, an abstraction that captures the effect of the controller's action on the system's evolution between discrete sampling steps is well-suited to scale up formal verification.

Our overall approach for reusable and scalable formal CPS verification is shown in Fig. 3. We start with an informally defined *Cyber-Physical System* model and an informal description of its *Informal Requirements.* We assume that the CPS is modeled in an industrial design language such as SystemC or Simulink. Please note that from such a model, an implementation is often generated automatically via code generation in existing model-driven design processes, or the CPS model serves as a golden reference model. Thus, it is crucial to verify the correctness of this model for the construction of safe and resilient systems.

At the heart of our approach shown in Fig. 3, we propose *Domain-Specific Abstraction. Domain-Specific Abstraction* provides us with *Reusable Specification Mechanisms*, which can be used to systematically derive *global invariants*, formal specifications of *Safety and Resilience*, and *Learning Contracts* that describe safe actions of learning components. Furthermore, the *Domain-Specific Abstractions* can also be used to define *Semantics Encodings*, i.e., encodings of the execution semantics of informally defined system design languages. These encodings can be used to define *Automated Formalizations*, which transform a given informal CPS model, e.g., a SystemC design or Simulink model, into a formal system model. The result of the *Domain-Specific Abstraction* together with the *Automated Formalization* is a formal representation of the system under verification and its requirements. Our existing transformations from SystemC to VerCors (VeSUV[1]) [38] and from Simulink to d$\mathcal{L}$ (Simulink2d$\mathcal{L}$[2]) [25] are examples for such an *Automated Formalization.* VeSUV enables us to derive a program in the Prototypal Verification Language (PVL) from a given SystemC design fully automatically, and Simulink2d$\mathcal{L}$ enables us to derive a formal representation in differential dynamic logic (d$\mathcal{L}$) from a given Simulink model fully automatically. This gives us access to existing well-established tools for *Deductive Verification*, for example, the auto-active verifier VerCors [6] or the interactive theorem prover KeYmaera X [12]. Such tools enable us to use deductive inference rules such as loop induction to verify that given properties hold in all reachable system states. This is possible even for unbounded state spaces, for example, even for an arbitrarily repeated control loop or a parameterized system if we provide the necessary assertions, invariants and contracts. *Deductive verification* results in *guaranteed properties*, i.e., properties that are satisfied for all possible system executions. Additionally, tools such as VerCors and KeYmaera X can also be used to verify individual components with respect to their contract, and KeYmaera X also supports the automated generation of *runtime monitors*, which can be used to enforce contracts for unverified components at runtime.

A major challenge in deductive verification is the enormous cost that is required to manually define the necessary formal specifications that define the system behavior, contracts, assertions, and invariants. Our key idea to reduce this cost is to use *Domain-Specific Abstraction* to define *Semantics Encodings* and *Reusable Specification Mechanisms*, as explained in the following sections.

4 Encoding of Informal Execution Semantics Using Domain-Specific Abstractions

For informal system models, we use domain-specific abstractions to encode the informally defined execution semantics in an existing formally well-defined language. From these semantics encodings, we derive transformation rules for relevant language constructs. We also encode predefined models for key components of the language definition that capture its execution semantics, e.g., the scheduler and event mechanism for SystemC. Based on our semantics encodings, we then develop fully automatic transformations from industrially used system design languages into well-defined formal models. Our approach has three major advantages: First, with our semantics encodings, we define formal semantics for

[1] https://vercors.ewi.utwente.nl/vesuv/.
[2] https://github.com/EmbSys-WWU/Simulink2dL.

```
1  void run() {
2    lock(m);
3    while (true) {
4      m.event_state[TIMEOUT] = 2;
5      m.process_state[0] = TIMEOUT;
6      while (m.process_state[0] != RUNNABLE
7       || m.event_state[TIMEOUT] != OCCURED) {
8        unlock(m);
9        lock(m);
10     }
11     dist = read_sensor();
12     if (dist < MIN_DIST) {
13       m.event_state[OD] = DELTA_DELAY;
14     }
15   }
16   unlock(m);
17 }
```

(a) Encoding of the Sensor Process

```
while (true) {
  lock(this);
  immediate_wakeup();
  reset_events_no_delta();
  if (no_process_ready()) {
    reset_occurred_events();
    int d = min_advance(event_state);
    advance_time(d);
    wakeup_after_wait();
    reset_all_events();
  }
  unlock(this);
}
```

(b) Encoding of the Scheduler

Fig. 4. SystemC Encoding in PVL [38]

informally defined industrial system design languages. Second, the transformation into formal models is performed fully automatically, which means that we spare the designer the tedious task of creating a formal model. Third, we gain access to existing and thus mature and sophisticated verification tools. In the following, we briefly summarize the key ideas of our encoding of SystemC for deductive verification with VerCors and our encoding of Simulink in d$\mathcal{L}$.

4.1 Encoding SystemC for Deductive Verification with VerCors

To support deductive verification of SystemC designs using VerCors, we have defined an automated transformation from SystemC into the Prototypal Verification Language PVL, which uses an encoding of the SystemC execution semantics that exploits domain-specific abstractions [38]. To encode a given SystemC design in PVL, we translate each process into a PVL thread, and also translate all shared data and functions into PVL syntax. To capture the execution semantics of SystemC, we provide a predefined abstract encoding of the SystemC scheduler and events. We use a global lock to encode SystemC's non-preemptive scheduling semantics, i.e., that each process is executed without preemption until it voluntarily gives up control with a wait statement. We associate this global lock with global invariants, such as the reachable abstract states invariant (RASI). Since these invariants must be established whenever the lock is released, they are guaranteed to hold at any possible interleaving point between processes.

Figure 4a shows how we encode the *sensor* process from Fig. 1a in PVL. We encode any SystemC process as a PVL thread and implement its process logic in its `run` method. The thread starts by acquiring the global lock (l. 2) and ends by releasing it (l. 16). This ensures that only one process is executed at a time, as the SystemC scheduling semantics prescribes. The *sensor* eventually gives up control by waiting for 2 ms. We encode this (ll. 4–10) by creating a dedicated timeout event and setting its notification delay to 2 (assuming a time

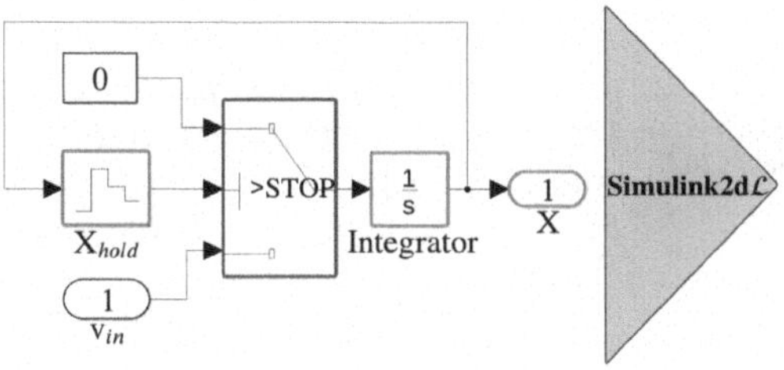

$$
\begin{aligned}
&pre \rightarrow [\{\\
&\ \{?clk \geq t_S; X_{hold} := X; clk := 0;\\
&++?clk < t_S;\}\\
&\ v_{in} := *; ?(v_{min} \leq v_{in} \& v_{in} \leq v_{max});\\
&\ \{?X_{hold} > STOP;\\
&\quad \{X' = 0, clk' = 1 \,\&\, clk \leq t_S\}\\
&++\,?X_{hold} \leq STOP;\\
&\quad \{X' = v_{in}, clk' = 1 \,\&\, clk \leq t_S\}\}\\
&\}*]\, post
\end{aligned}
$$

Fig. 5. Simple Vehicle in Simulink and d$\mathcal{L}$ [2]

resolution of 1 ms). The process then waits for the scheduler to notify this timeout event. Until then, the process releases the global lock to let other processes execute. To check when the timeout has passed, it reacquires and releases the lock in a busy wait. As PVL considers arbitrary interleavings, this encoding covers all interleavings possible in the SystemC design. As shown in this example, we encode the process and event states using global arrays `event_state` and `process_state` and use the global lock to synchronize processes according to the SystemC semantics. Any remaining program logic can be transformed in a straight-forward manner. Once the two milliseconds are over, the scheduler will notify the timeout event and the process will become runnable again. The *sensor* then checks whether the distance of some obstacle is closer than a given minimal distance and if it is, notifies the obstacle detected event `od` by setting its event state to `DELTA_DELAY`. The triggering of timed events and processes is taken care of by an abstract implementation of the scheduler in PVL, which is shown in Fig. 4b. Note that the methods used in the scheduler model are not implemented but abstractly specified by their postconditions, which provides us with a powerful domain-specific abstraction, as we can completely abstract from their implementation. For further details, we refer to [38].

4.2 Encoding Simulink in the Differential Dynamic Logic

Our encoding of Simulink in d$\mathcal{L}$ maps the semantics of hybrid Simulink models into the differential dynamic logic [25,26]. Based on this mapping, we have defined an automated transformation from Simulink into d$\mathcal{L}$ [2,25].

As shown in our small example in Fig. 1b, a hybrid Simulink model may contain discrete, continuous, and control flow blocks. Figure 5 shows how this example is encoded in d$\mathcal{L}$. We encode discrete blocks, like the zero-order hold block, as discrete assignments that are only executed whenever we reach the sample time, that is, whenever the global simulation clock is equal to the sample time t_S. We encode continuous blocks, like the integrator, as continuous evolutions, in this example $X' = 0$ and $X' = v_{in}$. This means that the time-derivative of X is either 0 or v_{in}, and X is continuously evolved as long as the evolution domain is satisfied. In our example, the evolution domain is $clk \leq t_S$,

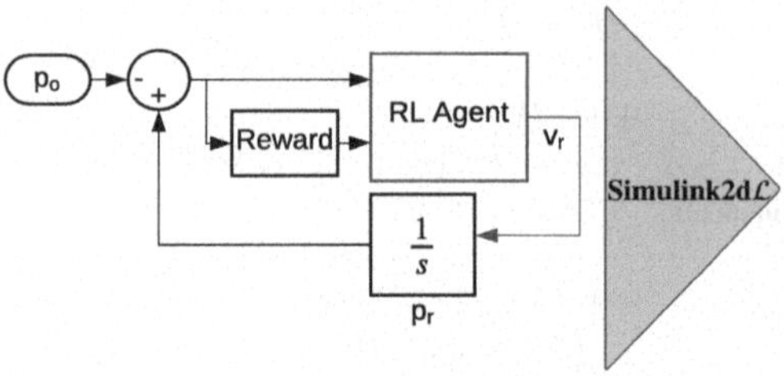

$$
\begin{aligned}
&pre \rightarrow [\{\\
&\quad p_o := *; ?(p_o \geq p_{o,\mathtt{MIN}} \ \&\ p_o \leq p_{o,\mathtt{MAX}});\\
&\quad \{?c_{\mathtt{rl}} \geq t_{\mathtt{S}}; c_{\mathtt{rl}} := 0; v_r := *; ?(HC);\\
&\quad ++?c_{\mathtt{rl}} < t_{\mathtt{S}};\}\\
&\quad \{t' = 1, p_r' = v_r, {c_{\mathtt{rl}}}' = 1 \ \&\ c_{\mathtt{rl}} \leq t_{\mathtt{S}}\}\\
&\}^*]\, post
\end{aligned}
$$

Fig. 6. Simple RL Robot in Simulink and d$\mathcal{L}$

i.e., we can evolve the differential equations until we reach the sample time. We encode control flow blocks, like the switch block, as test formulas, in this case with $X_{hold} > STOP$ and $X_{hold} \leq STOP$, together with a non-deterministic choice $++$ between the guarded alternatives. To model the overall simulation loop, we use a non-deterministic repetition ($*$), which means that the discrete assignments and continuous evolutions can be executed arbitrarily often. Inputs like the input velocity v_{in} are also modeled by discrete assignments, where an arbitrary value is assigned from the given signal range. In our full formalization we also provide an over-approximation of numerical errors, nested control flow, and a number of other block types. For further details, we refer to [25].

CPS increasingly use machine learning techniques to make good control decisions in unexpected situations. In [2], we have presented an extension of our transformation from Simulink to d$\mathcal{L}$ to support reinforcement learning (RL) agent blocks. To integrate RL agents safely into the transformation, we proposed to define the safe behavior of RL agents with hybrid contracts (HC), which specify assumptions on inputs and guarantees on outputs. Contracts replace agents during transformation, enabling us to abstract from their implementation for the verification of the whole system. To ensure that the RL agent adheres to its contract at run-time, we automatically generate runtime monitors from the contract, which are used as a shield ensuring that only safe actions are chosen.

Figure 6 shows an illustrating example of a simple intelligent robot where the velocity v_r is chosen by an RL agent depending on the distance to the position p_o of a moving obstacle. The position of the robot p_r is calculated again using an integrator. In the d$\mathcal{L}$ model, the input position p_o is captured by a non-deterministic assignment together with a constraining test, i.e., an arbitrary value from the given input range can be assigned at any time. The integrator block that models the position p_r of the robot is captured by a continuous evolution $p_r' = v_r$. The agent selects a velocity as an action (v_r), which is restricted by the hybrid contract, in discrete sampling steps, i.e., whenever the time since the last decision $c_{\mathtt{rl}}$ reaches the sample time $t_{\mathtt{S}}$. Otherwise, it does nothing.

In this example, a crucial property is that the distance to the moving obstacle never falls below a safety threshold, i.e., $[\alpha]p_o - p_r > \theta_{\mathtt{MIN}}$. A hybrid contract to ensure that the actions of the RL agent are always safe with respect to this property is $HC \equiv p_o - p_r - v_r \cdot t_{\mathrm{S}} - v_{o,\mathtt{MAX}} \cdot t_{\mathrm{S}} > \theta_{\mathtt{MIN}}$, which ensures that the velocity of the robot is always chosen such that the current distance plus the maximal movement of the robot and the obstacle towards each other is still greater than the minimal safety threshold.

Please note that the way we capture the interplay between discrete and continuous behavior, the abstraction of input signals, and the way we capture intelligent components can all be viewed as domain-specific abstractions, i.e., we exploit domain-specific knowledge to provide reusable semantics encodings.

5 Reusable Specification Mechanisms

Our semantics encodings of SystemC in PVL and of Simulink in d$\mathcal{L}$ enable us to capture the semantics of an informally defined, industrially used system design language with a formally well-defined language. The resulting automated transformations from SystemC to PVL and from Simulink to d$\mathcal{L}$ enable us to use the auto-active deductive verifier VerCors respectively the interactive theorem prover KeYmaera X to formally verify the correctness of a given system model for all possible input scenarios for an unbounded time, and even for unbounded system parameters. However, the verification itself is not fully automated. The designer needs to specify invariants and assumptions, making the formal verification process quite expensive in terms of manual effort and required expertise. While domain-specific abstractions have helped us to capture the semantics of SystemC and Simulink precisely yet concisely, they can also help us to define reusable specification mechanisms.

5.1 Reachable Abstract States Invariant for Reactive Hardware/Software Systems

In our encoding of the SystemC semantics, we capture the states of processes and events in global arrays. What we often need for the verification of global safety properties in embedded or cyber-physical systems is knowledge about the currently executed process and recently occurred events. For example, we may want to verify that the sensor values really indicate a close obstacle if the *obstacle detected* event occurs. However, such global properties are difficult to prove with modular reasoning. While it is one of the major strengths of auto-active verifiers such as VerCors to enable modular verification by using local reasoning, where we consider each method separately, this also means that we do not have knowledge about global process and event states within the proof of one method. To overcome this problem and to ease the verification of global properties, we have defined a reusable specification mechanism called the reachable abstract states invariant (RASI) in [38].

```
resource global_invariant() =
  ...
  /* >>> Abstract state space <<< */
  ** ( (process_state == [-1, -1] && event_state == [-3, -3, -3]
        && sensor.pc == 0 && controller.pc == 0)
     || (process_state == [0, -1] && event_state == [2, -3, -3]
        && sensor.pc == 1 && controller.pc == 0)
     || (process_state == [-1, 2] && event_state == [-3, -3, -3]
        && sensor.pc == 0 && controller.pc == 1)
     || ... )
  /* >>> Global properties <<< */
  ** (event_state[2] > -2 ==> sensor.dist < MIN_DIST) // when sensor notifies od
  ** (event_state[2] == -2 ==> sensor.dist < MIN_DIST); // when od occurs
```

Fig. 7. Reachable Abstract States Invariant Example [38]

The idea behind the RASI is to capture the part of the global program state that is relevant for proving a given property, and abstract from the rest. It consists of a disjunction of abstract states, given by the valuations of a subset of tracked variables. Figure 7 shows an example from [38] for our example SystemC robot design in which program counters, process and event states are tracked and all data variables are abstracted. This allows us to reason about global properties, like "process X can only become runnable if event A has been notified" or "event B can only be notified if process Y is in some specific state", while avoiding a state space explosion induced by data and input variables. Since finding an appropriate level of abstraction and generating the state space can be difficult tasks, we automate this process using abstract interpretation and abstraction refinement. We describe the automation of the RASI generation in [37].

We have demonstrated the applicability and effectiveness of our semantics encoding of SystemC together with the RASI by deductively verifying several crucial properties of a simple robot, a producer-consumer example, and an automotive control system with anti-lock braking system and anti-slip regulation (ABS) in [37,38]. Previously, the verification of the ABS was not possible with existing approaches based on model checking, due to its enormous state space. In our experiments, all designs were parameterized, that is, we have verified the designs for arbitrary distances for the obstacle detection, for arbitrary buffer sizes, and an arbitrary slack. We have successfully verified both local properties - for example that the control algorithm of the ABS system behaves as specified - and global safety properties, for example that each control cycle of the ABS is completed within a given maximum time. Of course, this was at the price of manual invariant definitions, but thanks to the powerful reasoning techniques of VerCors and the RASI, we only needed very few manually defined invariants.

5.2 Reusable Contract Patterns for Safe Integration of Learning

To increase reusability and to reduce the manual effort for deductive verification, we have defined a reusable specification mechanism for Simulink and the d$\mathcal{L}$ [1], namely reusable patterns for hybrid contracts. What we exploit there is the (domain-specific) observation that hybrid contracts often look very similar for similar applications. For example, for many systems where a discrete controller (possibly a reinforcement learning controller) is embedded into a continuous control systems, so-called threshold properties are crucial. Our hybrid contract pattern for threshold properties is shown in the first two rows of Table 1. The first row provides a pattern for a safety property where the controller should keep a safety-critical variable always below or above a given threshold $var_{sc} \sim \theta$ (with $\sim \in \{<, \leq, =, \geq, >\}$). To verify such properties, we always need to ensure that at the time where we take a discrete control *action*, the current value of the controlled variable var_{sc} plus the worst case reaction *wcreaction* of the overall system in its current *state* still is within the given threshold θ for a specified time frame, e.g., the sample time t_S. We have shown that this pattern can be applied to a variety of case studies [1]. For example, for an autonomous robot that moves in a factory with moving obstacles, we ensure that a minimal safety distance is maintained even if the robot and moving obstacles move towards each other with maximum velocity within the current sample time. In an adaptive cruise control system, the follower car chooses the acceleration such that the distance to the leader car is still greater than its maximum braking distance within the next sample time, even if the leader stops moving.

Beside the threshold pattern, we have also defined a recovery pattern and a resilience pattern, which are also shown in Table 1. The recovery pattern can be used for properties where we want to show that if a given threshold is violated due to a disruption, the system returns to a safe state within a given time limit $t_{R,MAX}$. The resilience pattern can be used for systems that can choose between several service levels to deal with disruptions. With this pattern, a system can still choose higher service levels if we are sufficiently far from a given threshold, but needs to choose a degraded service level if not. This pattern can also be applied to the autonomous robot to ensure that it stops if opponents are too close but can drive with higher velocities if there is sufficient room around it.

We have also shown that invariants can be derived from the contract patterns above with little additional effort. To demonstrate the applicability of our

Table 1. Range, Recovery and Resilience Contract Patterns [1]

Threshold Property	$pre \rightarrow [\alpha]\ var_{sc} \sim \theta$
Threshold Contract	$var_{sc} \sim \theta \rightarrow var_{sc} + wcreaction(, action, t_S) \sim \theta$
Recovery Property	$pre \rightarrow [\alpha]\ (t - t_{D,LAST} > t_{R,MAX} \rightarrow var_{sc} \sim \theta)$
Recovery Contract	$\neg(var_{sc} \sim \theta_{MIN}) \rightarrow var_{sc} + wcreaction(, action, t_R) \sim \theta$
Threshold Contract	$var_{sc} \sim \theta \rightarrow var_{sc} + wcreaction(, action, t_S) \sim \theta$
Resilience Property	$pre \rightarrow [\alpha]\ var_{sc} \sim \theta \wedge act \geq serv_{deg}$
Full Service Contract	$var_{sc} \sim \theta \pm \Delta_{suff} \rightarrow \begin{array}{l} var_{sc} + wcreaction(, action, t_S) \sim \theta \\ \wedge\ action \geq service_{deg} \end{array}$
Degraded Service	$\neg(var_{sc} \sim \theta) \rightarrow action = service_{deg}$

approach, we have applied the patterns to an intelligent temperature control system, a water tank, the autonomous robot, an adaptive cruise control and an intelligent water distribution system, and have successfully verified crucial properties within a few person days. For further details, we refer to [1].

5.3 Reusable Specification of Resilience in Autonomous Systems

A crucial property of intelligent or learning systems is resilience, i.e., the system's capability to adapt and maintain its correct functioning in the presence of changes and disruptions [24]. To verify such resilience properties for autonomous hybrid systems deductively, we have introduced several reusable specification mechanisms in [3]. First, we have extended our concept of *Service Levels* to formalize the system's adaptive response to stressors. This means, for example, that we describe graceful degradation using a degraded service level together with safety thresholds that are still maintained under stress. Second, we have introduced reusable *Stressor Patterns.* They are designed to capture various disturbances and changes, ranging from discrete or continuous *noise* over timed *delays* to complete *failures.* In our definition, stressors strictly extend the possible behavior of components with non-determinism. This facilitates easy integration of stressors into existing d$\mathcal{L}$ models. Furthermore we avoid the need to provide probability distributions, which are often not available or hard to obtain. Third and finally, to verify autonomous hybrid systems under different stress levels, we have proposed reusable *Observer Patterns*, which may never change the system's behavior but are used to passively capture the dynamic effects of stressors and stress intensity on the system.

Figure 8 shows an example where our stressor and observer patterns together with two different service levels are used to describe resilience of an autonomous RL robot towards sensor noise. It uses our *discrete noise* stressor pattern, which simply adds a non-deterministically chosen discrete noise η to sensor inputs. Further stressor patterns for continuous noise (e.g., drift of a robot or leak of a tank), failures, and delays, are defined in [3]. The observer pattern used in this example systematically tracks the current stress and the system state whenever the noise is higher than a given threshold for low stress η_{low}. If such a disruption occurs, the point of time of the high stress is stored in t_{hs} and the highly stressed sensor value in d_{hs}. The service levels in this example are defined such that the robot stops or maintains an evasion distance if it has never been put under high stress ($t_{hs} = -1$), and maintains a safe stopping distance if it has been put under high stress ($t_{hs} \geq 0$).

To demonstrate the applicability of our approach, we have defined several resilience properties for an intelligent water distribution system and an autonomous robot in a factory setting. Both case studies are closely inspired by existing Simulink models provided by Mathworks. We have again deductively verified these properties using the interactive theorem prover KeYmaera X within a few person days. For further details, we refer to [3].

$$
\begin{array}{rl}
 & [\{ \\
\text{Sensor } +\eta: & \eta_{old} := \eta; \eta := *; d_s := ||\vec{p_r}, \vec{p_a}|| + \eta; \\
\text{Observer:} & if(\eta > \eta_{low} \wedge \eta_{old} \leq \eta_{low})\{t_{hs} := t; d_{hs} := ||\vec{p_r}, \vec{p_a}||\}; \\
\text{RL Agent:} & if(c_r \geq t_s)\ \{\ c_r := 0; \vec{v_r} := *; ?(HC);\ \} \\
\text{Plant:} & ...\{t' = 1, c_r' = 1, \vec{p_r}' = \vec{v_r} \,\&\, c_r \leq t_s\}... \\
 & \}^*] \\
\text{Service:} & (t_{hs} = -1 \rightarrow (\vec{v_r} \geq \vec{v}_{min,r} \wedge ||\vec{p_r}, \vec{p_a}|| > \theta_{evade} \vee ||\vec{v_r}|| = 0)) \wedge \\
 & (t_{hs} \geq 0 \rightarrow (\vec{v_r} \geq \vec{v}_{min,r} \wedge ||\vec{p_r}, \vec{p_a}|| > \theta_{stop} \vee ||\vec{v_r}|| = 0))
\end{array}
$$

Fig. 8. RL Robot Example with Noise [3]

6 Related Work

There exists a broad body of work on reusability in deductive verification. For example, in [7,15,23,35] contracts are used for software verification. Techniques to enable proof reuse have been incorporated in many verification systems, including KeY [4] and KeYmaera X [31], e.g., by reusing proofs as lemmas or developing reusable proof tactics. An overview over the reuse of specifications, intermediate representations, and verification tools is given in [14]. However, these approaches address reusability from a perspective of building proofs technically, and not from an application or domain-specific point of view. They do not address the question how specifications or contracts specified for one application can be reused for similar applications in a given domain. The same holds for the broad spectrum of approaches for automated invariant generation, for example, [20,34]: they tend to focus on technology for building proofs and not on leveraging knowledge about the application [14]. Some application-specific specification patterns have been proposed for complex verification problems, for example, for structured arrays in [13], or for the parallel prefix sum in [35]. In [10], a contract-based approach to analyze systems from various application domains is proposed, in [15], abstract method calls for structured reuse are proposed, and in [23], the reuse of proofs for variants of software product lines. However, to the best of our knowledge, none of the existing approaches systematically explores domain-specific abstractions to define reusable specification mechanisms.

In the last decade, a variety of approaches have been proposed for the formal verification of systems that are modeled in industrially used design languages like SystemC [21] or Simulink [27]. For example, transformations from SystemC into formal representations are proposed in [11,16–19,22]. However, all of these approaches rely on model checking at some point, and although they implicitly exploit domain-knowledge, they do not explicitly base these transformations on domain-specific abstractions. There also exists a number of approaches to enable formal verification for Simulink. The Simulink Design Verifier [29] provides means to use model checking and abstract interpretation, and in [5,33], transformations from Simulink into the input languages of various verification tools are proposed. However, they are only applicable for purely discrete systems, and their scalability is limited. Approaches for the formal analysis of hybrid Simulink models have been presented, for example, in [8,9,30,39]. However, all of these approaches either do not scale well, or the property specification and the verification process require a very high level of expertise.

7 Open Problems

Although there can be seen quite some progress on the reusable specification and scalable verification of cyber-physical systems during the last decades, there remain a lot of open challenges. The major challenges that need to be solved to enable scalable formal verification of industrial-sized cyber-physical systems are, in our opinion:

1. **Improve reusability of formal specifications.** Both our semantics encodings and the reusable specification mechanisms we have presented increase the reusability of formal specifications and have the potential to reduce the required manual effort for deductive verification processes. However, the results so far are preliminary in the sense that we only have looked at a few design languages and case studies, and the use of the specification mechanisms still requires a high level of expertise. It remains a major challenge to define reusable specification mechanisms for other languages and system classes, to find ways to generalize our initial ideas on how to exploit domain-specific knowledge, and to reduce the required expertise.
2. **Further reduce the specification effort.** While the semantics encodings we have presented enable fully automated transformations from informally defined models into (abstract) formal representations, the use of the reusable specification mechanisms and also the deductive verification process itself still require a significant amount of manual effort. It is one of the major challenges to reduce this effort. A potential road towards this could be to exploit symbolic artificial intelligence techniques and large language models to find good abstractions and formal specifications automatically.
3. **Go beyond qualitative safety properties.** So far, we have only considered qualitative properties. Even though we have also considered resilience, we have basically reduced the desired resilience properties to safety properties by defining (discrete) service levels and ensuring varying safety properties on each service level. For modern cyber-physical systems, also security properties such as confidentiality and integrity, and quantitative properties such as the resilience and performance in the presence of uncertainty play an important role. It remains an open question whether the domain-specific abstractions discussed here could also be transferred to such properties.

8 Conclusion

In this paper, we have summarized our main results and contributions on using domain-specific abstractions for reusable specification and scalable formal verification of cyber-physical systems. We have shown that domain-specific abstractions are a valuable tool both for the formalization and automated transformation of informally defined system descriptions into formal models as well as for providing the formal specifications that are necessary for scalable deductive verification. For the former, we use semantics encodings, which precisely yet abstractly capture the execution semantics of informally defined design languages. For the latter, we have presented three reusable specification mechanisms: First, a reachable abstract states invariant, which enables us to verify global properties by using local reasoning together with abstract knowledge about the reachable state space in reactive and concurrent systems. Second, we have presented reusable contract patterns for defining safe actions of reinforcement learning components that control a continuous environment. Third, we have presented specification patterns for verifying resilience, namely service levels and stressor and observer patterns.

In future work, we plan to investigate the trade-off between fine- and coarse-granular abstractions, and their effect on the precision and permissiveness of formal specifications. We plan to derive guidelines for the specification of domain-specific abstractions. Furthermore, we plan to exploit symbolic execution and symbolic artificial intelligence techniques to generate abstractions automatically.

References

1. Adelt, J., Brettschneider, D., Herber, P.: Reusable contracts for safe integration of reinforcement learning in hybrid systems. In: Bouajjani, A., Holík, L., Wu, Z. (eds.) ATVA 2022. LNCS, vol. 13505, pp. 58–74. Springer, Cham (2022). https://doi.org/10.1007/978-3-031-19992-9_4
2. Adelt, J., Liebrenz, T., Herber, P.: Formal verification of intelligent hybrid systems that are modeled with simulink and the reinforcement learning toolbox. In: Huisman, M., Păsăreanu, C., Zhan, N. (eds.) FM 2021. LNCS, vol. 13047, pp. 349–366. Springer, Cham (2021). https://doi.org/10.1007/978-3-030-90870-6_19
3. Adelt, J., Mensing, R., Herber, P.: Reusable specification patterns for verification of resilience in autonomous hybrid systems. In: Platzer, A., Rozier, K.Y., Pradella, M., Rossi, M. (eds.) FM 2024. LNCS, vol. 14934, pp. 208–228. Springer, Cham (2024). https://doi.org/10.1007/978-3-031-71177-0_14
4. Ahrendt, W., et al.: The KeY platform for verification and analysis of Java programs. In: Giannakopoulou, D., Kroening, D. (eds.) VSTTE 2014. LNCS, vol. 8471, pp. 55–71. Springer, Cham (2014). https://doi.org/10.1007/978-3-319-12154-3_4
5. Araiza-Illan, D., Eder, K., Richards, A.: Formal verification of control systems properties with theorem proving. In: International Conference on Control. IEEE (2014)
6. Armborst, L., et al.: The VerCors verifier: a progress report. In: Gurfinkel, A., Ganesh, V. (eds.) CAV 2024. LNCS, vol. 14682, pp. 3–18. Springer, Cham (2024). https://doi.org/10.1007/978-3-031-65630-9_1
7. Beckert, B., Klebanov, V.: Proof reuse for deductive program verification. In: International Conference on Software Engineering and Formal Methods, pp. 77–86. IEEE (2004)
8. Chen, M., et al.: MARS: a toolchain for modelling, analysis and verification of hybrid systems. In: Hinchey, M.G., Bowen, J.P., Olderog, E.-R. (eds.) Provably Correct Systems. NMSSE, pp. 39–58. Springer, Cham (2017). https://doi.org/10.1007/978-3-319-48628-4_3

9. Chutinan, A., Krogh, B.H.: Computational techniques for hybrid system verification. IEEE Trans. Autom. Control **48**(1), 64–75 (2003)
10. Cimatti, A., Dorigatti, M., Tonetta, S.: OCRA: a tool for checking the refinement of temporal contracts. In: International Conference on Automated Software Engineering. IEEE (2013)
11. Cimatti, A., Narasamdya, I., Roveri, M.: Software model checking SystemC. IEEE Trans. Comput.-Aided Des. Integr. Circuits Syst. **32**(5) (2013)
12. Fulton, N., Mitsch, S., Quesel, J.-D., Völp, M., Platzer, A.: KeYmaera X: an axiomatic tactical theorem prover for hybrid systems. In: Felty, A.P., Middeldorp, A. (eds.) CADE 2015. LNCS (LNAI), vol. 9195, pp. 527–538. Springer, Cham (2015). https://doi.org/10.1007/978-3-319-21401-6_36
13. Genestier, R., Giorgetti, A., Petiot, G.: Sequential generation of structured arrays and its deductive verification. In: Blanchette, J.C., Kosmatov, N. (eds.) TAP 2015. LNCS, vol. 9154, pp. 109–128. Springer, Cham (2015). https://doi.org/10.1007/978-3-319-21215-9_7
14. Hähnle, R., Huisman, M.: Deductive software verification: from pen-and-paper proofs to industrial tools. In: Steffen, B., Woeginger, G. (eds.) Computing and Software Science. LNCS, vol. 10000, pp. 345–373. Springer, Cham (2019). https://doi.org/10.1007/978-3-319-91908-9_18
15. Hähnle, R., Schaefer, I., Bubel, R.: Reuse in software verification by abstract method calls. In: Bonacina, M.P. (ed.) CADE 2013. LNCS (LNAI), vol. 7898, pp. 300–314. Springer, Heidelberg (2013). https://doi.org/10.1007/978-3-642-38574-2_21
16. Herber, P.: The RESCUE approach – towards compositional hardware/software co-verification. In: International Conference on Embedded Software and Syst (ICESS). IEEE (2014)
17. Herber, P., Fellmuth, J., Glesner, S.: Model checking SystemC designs using timed automata. In: International Conference on Hardware/Software Codesign and System Synthesis, pp. 131–136. ACM (2008)
18. Herber, P., Hünnemeyer, B.: Formal verification of SystemC designs using the BLAST software model checker. In: ACESMB@ MoDELS, pp. 44–53 (2014)
19. Herdt, V., Große, D., Drechsler, R.: Formal verification of SystemC-based designs using symbolic simulation. In: Enhanced Virtual Prototyping, pp. 59–117. Springer, Cham (2021). https://doi.org/10.1007/978-3-030-54828-5_4
20. Hoder, K., Kovács, L., Voronkov, A.: Invariant generation in vampire. In: Abdulla, P.A., Leino, K.R.M. (eds.) TACAS 2011. LNCS, vol. 6605, pp. 60–64. Springer, Heidelberg (2011). https://doi.org/10.1007/978-3-642-19835-9_7
21. IEEE Standards Association: IEEE Std. 1666-2011, Open SystemC Language Reference Manual. IEEE Press (2011). https://standards.ieee.org/ieee/1666/4814/
22. Jaß, L., Herber, P.: Bit-precise formal verification for SystemC using satisfiability modulo theories solving. In: Götz, M., Schirner, G., Wehrmeister, M.A., Al Faruque, M.A., Rettberg, A. (eds.) IESS 2015. IAICT, vol. 523, pp. 51–63. Springer, Cham (2017). https://doi.org/10.1007/978-3-319-90023-0_5
23. Knüppel, A., et al.: Using abstract contracts for verifying evolving features and their interactions. In: Ahrendt, W., Beckert, B., Bubel, R., Hähnle, R., Ulbrich, M. (eds.) Deductive Software Verification: Future Perspectives. LNCS, vol. 12345, pp. 122–148. Springer, Cham (2020). https://doi.org/10.1007/978-3-030-64354-6_5
24. Laprie, J.C.: From dependability to resilience. In: IEEE/IFIP International Conference on Dependable Systems and Networks (DSN), pp. G8–G9 (2008)

25. Liebrenz, T., Herber, P., Glesner, S.: Deductive verification of hybrid control systems modeled in Simulink with KeYmaera X. In: Sun, J., Sun, M. (eds.) ICFEM 2018. LNCS, vol. 11232, pp. 89–105. Springer, Cham (2018). https://doi.org/10.1007/978-3-030-02450-5_6
26. Liebrenz, T., Herber, P., Glesner, S.: A service-oriented approach for decomposing and verifying hybrid system models. In: Arbab, F., Jongmans, S.-S. (eds.) FACS 2019. LNCS, vol. 12018, pp. 127–146. Springer, Cham (2020). https://doi.org/10.1007/978-3-030-40914-2_7
27. MathWorks: MATLAB Simulink. www.mathworks.com/products/simulink.html
28. MathWorks: Reinforcement Learning Toolbox. https://www.mathworks.com/products/reinforcement-learning.html
29. MathWorks: Simulink Design Verifier. https://www.mathworks.com/products/simulink-design-verifier.html
30. Minopoli, S., Frehse, G.: SL2SX translator: from simulink to SpaceEx models. In: International Conference on Hybrid Systems: Computation and Control, pp. 93–98. ACM (2016)
31. Mitsch, S., Platzer, A.: The KeYmaera X proof IDE: concepts on usability in hybrid systems theorem proving. In: Workshop on Formal Integrated Development Environment. Theoretical Computer Science, vol. 240, pp. 67–81 (2017)
32. Platzer, A.: Differential dynamic logic for hybrid systems. J. Autom. Reason. **41**(2), 143–189 (2008)
33. Reicherdt, R., Glesner, S.: Formal verification of discrete-time MATLAB/Simulink models using boogie. In: Giannakopoulou, D., Salaün, G. (eds.) SEFM 2014. LNCS, vol. 8702, pp. 190–204. Springer, Cham (2014). https://doi.org/10.1007/978-3-319-10431-7_14
34. Rodríguez-Carbonell, E., Kapur, D.: Automatic generation of polynomial invariants of bounded degree using abstract interpretation. Sci. Comput. Program. **64**(1), 54–75 (2007)
35. Safari, M., Oortwijn, W., Joosten, S., Huisman, M.: Formal verification of parallel prefix sum. In: Lee, R., Jha, S., Mavridou, A., Giannakopoulou, D. (eds.) NFM 2020. LNCS, vol. 12229, pp. 170–186. Springer, Cham (2020). https://doi.org/10.1007/978-3-030-55754-6_10
36. Sutton, R.S., Barto, A.G.: Reinforcement Learning: An Introduction, 2nd edn. The MIT Press, Cambridge (2018)
37. Tasche, P., Herber, P., Huisman, M.: Automated invariant generation for efficient deductive reasoning about embedded systems. In: International Conference on Software Engineering and Formal Methods – SEFM 2024 (2024)
38. Tasche, P., Monti, R.E., Drerup, S.E., Blohm, P., Herber, P., Huisman, M.: Deductive verification of parameterized embedded systems modeled in SystemC. In: Dimitrova, R., Lahav, O., Wolff, S. (eds.) VMCAI 2024. LNCS, vol. 14500, pp. 187–209. Springer, Cham (2024). https://doi.org/10.1007/978-3-031-50521-8_9
39. Zou, L., Zhan, N., Wang, S., Fränzle, M.: Formal verification of Simulink/Stateflow diagrams. In: Finkbeiner, B., Pu, G., Zhang, L. (eds.) ATVA 2015. LNCS, vol. 9364, pp. 464–481. Springer, Cham (2015). https://doi.org/10.1007/978-3-319-24953-7_33

Paraconsistency for the Working Software Engineer (Extended Abstract)

Luís Soares Barbosa(✉)

INESC TEC and Department Informatics, Minho University, Braga, Portugal
lsb@di.uminho.pt

Abstract. Modelling complex information systems often entails the need for dealing with scenarios of inconsistency in which several requirements either reinforce or contradict each other. This lecture summarises recent joint work with Juliana Cunha, Alexandre Madeira and Ana Cruz on a variant of transition systems endowed with positive and negative accessibility relations, and a metric space over the lattice of truth values. Such structures are called *paraconsistent* transition systems, the qualifier stressing a connection to paraconsistent logic, a logic taking inconsistent information as potentially informative. A coalgebraic perspective on this family of structures is also discussed.

To the memory of Newton da Costa, in the year of his death at the age of 94, on 16 April 2024.

1 A Scenario

Age-related macular degeneration (AMD) is a disease of the macula, the central part of the eye responsible for vision, consensually recognised as the leading cause of vision loss in western countries in people aged over 55 years. It is a multifactorial disease, with a complex pathophysiology, for which onset and progression different risk factors, environmental and genetic, contribute. The disease being multifactorial, its progression is still not well understood. For example, the rate of progression is different between patients, often with similar profiles, and even between the two eyes of the same patient.

Large epidemiological studies have helped understanding AMD risk factors and pathophysiology. Typically, the data obtained from such studies refers not only to the genetics of the cohort, but also to deep phenotyping analysis performed in both healthy controls and participants with AMD. The latter resorts to multimodal imaging techniques, from near-infrared capture to spectral-domain

This work was financed by FCT, the Portuguese Foundation for Science and Technology, within the project IBEX, with reference PTDC/CCI-COM/4280/2021.

A. Madeira and A. Knapp (Eds.): SEFM 2024, LNCS 15280, pp. 22–30, 2025.
https://doi.org/10.1007/978-3-031-77382-2_2

optical coherence tomography. All patients had both eyes classified in a central reading centre and graded into 5 stages of disease severity status.

This data is very rich, but, at the same time, highly heterogeneous. Heterogeneous not only with respect to origins, formats and time span, but also in what concerns its assessment by different expert teams. The latter is the crucial observation here. Actually, the evidence level assigned to each data factor (e.g. in an image) as an enabler for a specific future development of the disease may vary from an expert to another, often leading to contradicting conclusions. Data consolidation becomes even more complex if a temporal dimension is introduced allowing for comparative assessments of patients along a time axis of several years. Indeed, potentially contradicting medical judgements on what dictates the evolution of AMD cannot be swept under the carpet.

An effective inference framework to explore AMD data requires the ability to reason about contradictory, or even inconsistent data in a sound and effective way. Each piece of data, as well as all sorts of (empirical) relationships among them, can be assigned a pair of weights, a positive and a negative one. Informally, the positive weight captures the degree of effectiveness (*confidence*) and the negative weight captures the degree of impossibility (*absence*) of a particular judgement on data or a relationship. The framework will thus be able to capture both vagueness, whenever both weights sum less than 1, as usual e.g. in fuzzy systems, and potential inconsistency, when their sum exceeds 1. This labelling is crucial to data classification, but requires suitable logics to take them into consideration in the inference process. Such is the purpose of the research line discussed in this talk.

2 Paraconsistency in Computer Science

Actually, the world of data, pervasive to all natural and artificial ecosystems, is a mined field. Not only the values and structure of data changes from one computation to another, but also the logic under which this information needs to be understood changes as well (e.g. from classical to probabilistic, from fuzzy to linear). On the other hand, informational states may exhibit potentially inconsistent (or partially consistent) data, reflecting the diversity of judgements (e.g. from different domain experts). Moreover, it may be linked by both positive transitions (witnessing e.g. the existence of a computational step, or its cost, or its probability, etc.) and negative transitions (recording whatever prevents such a step to occur, and also possibly expressed as a specific weight). Finally, the weights of such transitions are, in most cases, non-complementary, opening an inference arena encompassing both classical, vague and even (controlled forms of) inconsistent reasoning.

This motivates the qualifier *paraconsistent* used in our title. The word is borrowed from the work on paraconsistent logic [12,13,19], a branch of logic which accommodates inconsistency in a controlled way, treating inconsistent information as potentially informative. Although extremely expressive, such logics are still under studied and lack suitable computational support.

But what do we mean by *accommodating inconsistency* in logical reasoning? Indeed, absence of contradiction is considered core within the method of Science, out of which only nonsense prevails. However, as briefly shown above, reality entails the need to be able to deal with contradictory scenarios. Paraconsistency, in such a setting, is the study of logical systems in which the presence of a contradiction does not imply triviality. This means, logics in which the simultaneous presence of an assertion and of its negation does not always trivialize the conclusions. Recall that trivialization occurs when every statement in the theory can be proved, i.e. becomes a theorem. The principle according to which any statement can be proven from a contradiction is know as the principle of explosion, a hallmark of all forms of classical logic. Paraconsistency, on the other hand, takes consistency as a primitive, independent notion, therefore separating the concept of contradiction from that of deductive triviality, and, as a result, inconsistency from contradiction, and, dually, consistency from absence of contradiction.

Exploring formal ways to deal with logical theories which may be inconsistent but not trivial has a long tradition in Logic and Philosophy. The idea that denying the law of noncontradiction would lead to still meaningful, although non-Aristotelian logics, appeared in the 1910's in the independent work of Jan Łukasiewicz [37] and Nicolai Vasiliev [40], later formalised, by the middle of the century, by Stanislaw Jaśkowski whose main interest was in the study of empirical theories including contradictory assumptions [33] (see also [21] for a broader discussion). In 1958 Newton da Costa seminal paper [18] went behind the propositional level of previous works. The influence of the so-called Brazilian school was remarkable. Quickly the topic attracted larger attention, and the original scope broadened out[1]. In an interview for a video documentary [43] in 2019, da Costa summed up his programme as follows: *I decided to do it the other way round: mathematics with contradictions. Existence in mathematics means anything but the absence of contradiction. Contradictions begin to appear at the edges of mathematics. There are always problems.* To a large extent, current work from this initial trend is known as LFI (the *logic of formal inconsistency* [12] which is endowed with a syntactic annotation, in the form a unary operator, to express the fact that a sentence is consistent.

In 1990, *Mathematical Reviews* added a new entry, 03B53, called *Paraconsistent Logic*, later expanded to *Logics admitting inconsistency (paraconsistent logics, discussive logics, etc.)*. But the real, unexpected impact was on applications. Actually, a bit surprisingly, applications quickly emerged ranging from Philosophy of Science [5,39], to Mathematics [28,29,44], from Economics [45], to the Foundations of Quantum Mechanics [14,20,27,31].

In Computer Science this family of logics found application in reasoning models [7,17], namely in the context of AI, but also in other domains from databases [3] and semantics of concurrency [9,34] to quantum computation [1,

[1] As da Costa shared in an interview [43], the qualifier paraconsistent, expressing a logic *at the side of consistency*, was suggested to him by Peruvian logician Francisco Miró-Quesada in 1976.

15]. A metodological perspective on paraconsistency in systems modelling, and further applications are addressed in a 2016 book significantly entitled *Towards Paraconsistent Engineering* [2].

3 Paraconsistent Transition Systems and Their Logics

The work reported in this talk emerged in the context of software formal modelling. The original motivation comes from the domain of many-valued logics to deal with informational contexts in which the classical bivalent distinction is not enough, in particular when facing the need to capture vagueness or uncertainty. Residuated lattices, adding a commutative monoidal structure to a complete lattice such that the monoid composition has a right adjoint, the residue, provide the semantic universe for such logics. A suitable choice of the lattice carrier, which stands for the set of truth values, does the job—a typical example being the real $[0, 1]$ interval. Reference [11] explores, in a systematic way, the modal extensions of many-valued logics whose Kripke frames are defined over (variants of) residuated lattices.

This is not yet, however, the whole picture. In a number of modelling scenarios, as the one outlined in Sect. 1, there is a need to deal simultaneously with what could be called *positive* and *negative* accessibility relations, one weighting the possibility of a transition to be present, the other weighting the possibility of being absent. In the concrete contexts we are interested in, such weights are not complementary, and thus both relations must be explicitly incorporated in the Kripke frame.

Assume, for example that weights for both transitions come from a residuated lattice over the real $[0, 1]$ interval. Then, jointly, the two accessibility relations in the frame express

- *inconsistency*, when the positive and negative weights are contradictory, i.e. they sum to some value greater than 1 (cf, the upper triangle filled in grey in the figure below).
- *vagueness*, when the sum is less than 1 (cf, the lower, periwinkle triangle);
- *strict consistency*, when the sum is exactly 1, which means that the measures of the factors enforcing or preventing a transition are complementary, corresponding to the red line in the figure.

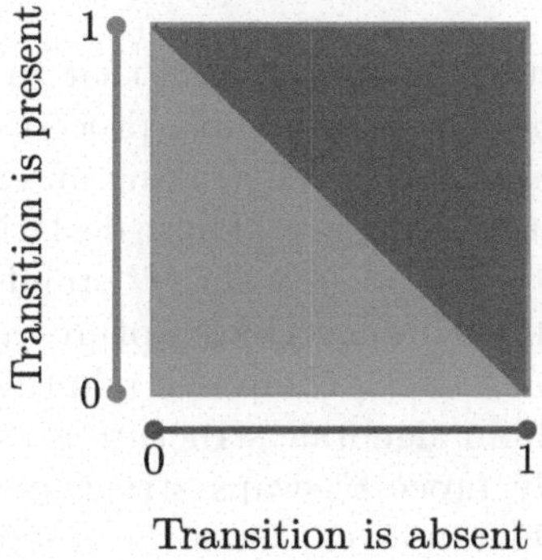

Choosing a residuated lattice A to weight transitions, we have defined in a serie of papers starting with reference [23], the notion of a *paraconsistent transition system* over A by explicitly considering a *positive* and a *negative* accessibility relation, taking weights from that common universe. Equivalently, a transition between two states can be regarded as weighted by a pair of values. In a similar way, the valuation of a proposition in a state is a pair of (not necessarily complementary) values capturing, respectively, the degree upon which it may be considered to hold or to fail. A *distance* between two such weights needs to be computed, namely to assess the level of vagueness or inconsistency in a given transition. As a smooth generalization of the example above, this is taken into account by a suitable metric over the carrier of A.

Not only the algebraic structure underlying such systems, but also the generated modal logic, as a generalization of Belnap's four-valued logic [8], were developed in [22]. Later in [25] this was extended to the multi-modal case, thus giving rise to a *structured specification logic* [42] equipped with specific versions of the standard structured specification operators *à la CASL* [38]. This offers to the working software engineer the (formal) tools to specify such systems in a compositional way. Technically, the price to be paid to support this move consists of framing the logic as an institution [30]. Most recent results, including suitable notions of simulation and bisimulation, appear in references [24,26], the later providing a detailed overview to the whole approach.

Applications to typical computing scenarios were discussed in [17], on reactive graphs, and [4], on noise analysis in quantum circuits. Current research efforts address the scenario sketched in Sect. 1, and the implementation of a devoted reasoning engine able to represent data and data relationships from weighted, but opposing, points of view.

4 A Coalgebraic Perspective

The final part of this talk will propose a different perspective over the semantic structures and logics underlying the concept of *paraconsistent transition system*. Over time, coalgebra theory [32,41] emerged as the right mathematics to express and reason about any sort of state-based, transition system. As an illustrative example, among many others, the reader is referred to the extensive work by F. Bartels, A. Sokolova and E. de Vink [6] on a coalgebraic rendering of probabilistic transition systems.

To take a more elementary example, recall that to define an inductive data structure one essentially specifies its 'assembly process'. For example, one builds a sequence in a data domain D, either by taking an empty list or by adjoining a fresh element to an existing sequence. Thus, declaring a sequence data type yields a function $\zeta : \mathbf{1} + D \times U \longrightarrow U$, where U stands for the data type being defined. The structured domain of function ζ captures a signature of *constructors* ($nil : \mathbf{1} \longrightarrow U$, $cons : D \times U \longrightarrow U$), composed additively. The whole procedure resembles the way in which an algebraic structure is defined.

Reversing the 'assembly process' swaps structure from the domain to the codomain of the arrow, which now captures the result of a 'decomposition' or 'observation' process. In the example this is performed by the familiar *head* and *tail selectors* joined together into

$$\alpha : U \longrightarrow \mathbf{1} + D \times U$$

which either returns a token $*$, when observing an empty sequence, or its decomposition in the top element and the remaining tail.

This reversal of perspective also leads to a different understanding of what U may stand for. The product $D \times U$ captures the fact that both the head and the tail of a sequence are selected (or *observed*) simultaneously. In fact, once one is no longer focused on how to construct U, but simply on what can be observed of it, finiteness is no longer required: both finite or infinite sequences can be observed through the process above. Therefore, U can be more accurately thought of as a *state space* of a machine generating a finite or infinite sequence of values of type D. Elements of U, in this example, can no longer be distinguished by construction, but should rather be identified when generating the same sequence. That is to say, when it becomes impossible to distinguish them through the observations allowed by the 'shape' structuring the codomain of α.

Function α above is an example of a *coalgebra*. Its ingredients are: a carrier U (intuitively the state space of a transition system), the *shape* of allowed observations, technically a functor $\mathcal{F}(X) = \mathbf{1} + D \times X$, and the observation *dynamics* given by function α, *i.e.* the machine itself. Formally, a $\mathcal{F}$-coalgebra is a pair $\langle U, \alpha \rangle$ consisting of an object U and a map $\alpha : U \longrightarrow \mathcal{F}\, U$. The latter maps states to structured collections of successor states. By varying $\mathcal{F}$, *i.e.* the shape of the underlying transitions, one may capture a large class of semantic structures used to model computational phenomena as (more or less complex) transition systems. Going even further, $\mathcal{F}$ is not restricted to be an endofunctor in *Set*, the category of sets and functions.

A morphism between two $\mathcal{F}$-coalgebras, $\langle U, \alpha \rangle$ and $\langle V, \beta \rangle$, is a map h between carriers U and V which preserves the dynamics, *i.e.* such that $\beta \cdot h = \mathcal{F}\, h \cdot \alpha$. As one would expect, $\mathcal{F}$-coalgebras and their morphisms form a category $C_{\mathcal{F}}$ where both composition and identities are inherited from the host category C.

This sets Coalgebra as a suitable mathematical framework for the study of dynamical systems in both a *compositional* and *uniform* way. The qualifier *uniform* requires some extra explanation: coalgebraic concepts (*i.e.* models, constructions, logics, and proof principles) are parametric on, or *typed* by, the functor that characterises the underlying transition structure.

This applies to the semantic structures, their morphisms and notions of (observational) equivalence, but also to the modal logics that are systematically derived, again, from the underlying functor. The literature on what is now called coalgebraic logic is vast [16,35,36]. Modalities, and therefore modal reasoning, also acquires a shape.

We will play this exercise for paraconsistent transition systems, with their double positive/negative weights. A first characterization, in the category of sets and set-theoretic functions, will be refined to the (finite, deterministic) case in which the set of states form a vector of (pairs of) weights, generalising the construction proposed in reference [10]. The coalgebraic methodology, as remarked above, provides a semantics for our systems induced by the unique morphism to the final coalgebra, a canonical notion of observational equivalence, and specific modal logic. This will provide an insightful comparison with our previous results and may pave the way for a more systematic study of paraconsistent transition systems.

References

1. Agudelo, J.C., Carnielli, W.A.: Paraconsistent machines and their relation to quantum computing. J. Log. Comput. **20**(2), 573–595 (2010)
2. Akama, S. (ed.): Towards Paraconsistent Engineering. Intelligent Systems Reference Library, Springer, Cham (2016)
3. de Amo, S., Carnielli, W.A., Marcos, J.: A logical framework for integrating inconsistent information in multiple databases. In: Eiter, T., Schewe, K.-D. (eds.) FoIKS 2002. LNCS, vol. 2284, pp. 67–84. Springer, Heidelberg (2002). https://doi.org/10.1007/3-540-45758-5_5
4. Barbosa, L.S., Madeira, A.: Capturing qubit decoherence through paraconsistent transition systems. In: Chiba, S., Cong, Y., Boix, E.G. (eds.) Companion Proceedings of the 7th International Conference on the Art, Science, and Engineering of Programming, Programming 2023, Tokyo, Japan, March 13-17, 2023, pp. 109–110. ACM (2023)
5. Barrio, E., Re, B.D.: Paraconsistency and its philosophical interpretations. Australas. J. Log. **15**(2), 151–170 (2018)
6. Bartels, F., Sokolova, A., de Vink, E.P.: A hierarchy of probabilistic system types. Theor. Comput. Sci. **327**(1–2), 3–22 (2004)
7. Baskent, C.: Public Announcements, Topology and Paraconsistency. In: Informal Proceedings of LOFT Conference 2014. HAL-01094782, Bregen, Norway (2014)
8. Belnap, N.D.: A Useful Four-Valued Logic, pp. 5–37. Springer Netherlands, Dordrecht (1977)
9. Bergstra, J.A., Middelburg, C.A.: Contradiction-tolerant process algebra with propositional signals. CoRR **abs/1508.06899** (2015). http://arxiv.org/abs/1508.06899
10. Bonchi, F., Bonsangue, M.M., Boreale, M., Rutten, J.J.M.M., Silva, A.: A coalgebraic perspective on linear weighted automata. Inf. Comp. **211**, 77–105 (2012). https://doi.org/10.1016/j.ic.2011.12.002
11. Bou, F., Esteva, F., Godo, L., Rodríguez, R.O.: On the minimum many-valued modal logic over a finite residuated lattice. J. Logic Comput. **21**(5), 739–790 (2009). https://doi.org/10.1093/logcom/exp062
12. Carnielli, W., Coniglio, M.E., ao Marcos, J.: Logics of Formal Inconsistency. In: Handbook of Philosophical Logic, vol. 14, pp. 1–93. Springer (2007)
13. Carnielli, W., Coniglio, M.E.: Paraconsistent Logic: Consistency, Contradiction and Negation, Logic, Epistemology, and the Unity of Science Series, vol. 40. Springer (2016)
14. Chiara, M.L.D., Giuntini, R.: Paraconsistent quantum logics. Found. Phys. **19**, 891–904 (1989)
15. Chiara, M.L.D., Giuntini, R.: Paraconsistent ideas in quantum logic. Synth. **125**(1–2), 55–68 (2000)
16. Cîrstea, C., Kurz, A., Pattinson, D., Schröder, L., Venema, Y.: Modal logics are coalgebraic. Comput. J. **54**(1), 31–41 (2011)

17. Costa, D., Figueiredo, D., Martins, M.A.: Relation-changing models meet paraconsistency. J. Log. Algebraic Methods Program. **133**, 100870 (2023)
18. da Costa, N.: Nota sôbre o conceito de contradição (in portuguese with english summary). Anuário da Sociedade Paranaense de Matemática **1** (1958)
19. da Costa, N.: On the theory of inconsistent formal systems. Notre Dame J. Formal Logic **15**, 497–510 (1974)
20. da Costa, N., Doria, F.A.: Undecidability and incompleteness in classical mechanics. Int. J. Theor. Phys. **30**, 1041–1073 (1991)
21. da Costa, N., Doria, F.A.: On jaśkowski's discussive logic. Stud. Logica. **54**(4), 33–60 (1995)
22. Cruz, A., Madeira, A., Barbosa, L.S.: A logic for paraconsistent transition systems. In: Indrzejczak, A., Zawidzki, M. (eds.) Proceedings of the 10th International Conference on Non-Classical Logics. Theory and Applications, NCL 2022, Łódź, Poland, 14-18 March 2022. EPTCS, vol. 358, pp. 270–284 (2022)
23. Cruz, A., Madeira, A., Barbosa, L.S.: Paraconsistent transition systems. In: Nantes-Sobrinho, D., Fontaine, P. (eds.) Proceedings 17th International Workshop on Logical and Semantic Frameworks with Applications, LSFA 2022, Belo Horizonte, Brazil (hybrid), 23-24 September 2022. EPTCS, vol. 376, pp. 3–15 (2022)
24. Cunha, J., Madeira, A., Barbosa, L.S.: Stepwise development of paraconsistent processes. In: David, C., Sun, M. (eds.) Theoretical Aspects of Software Engineering - 17th International Symposium, TASE 2023, Bristol, UK, July 4-6, 2023, Proceedings. LNCS, vol. 13931, pp. 327–343. Springer (2023)
25. Cunha, J., Madeira, A., Barbosa, L.S.: Structured specification of paraconsistent transition systems. In: Hojjat, H., Ábrahám, E. (eds.) Fundamentals of Software Engineering - 10th International Conference, FSEN 2023, Tehran, Iran, May 4-5, 2023, Revised Selected Papers. LNCS, vol. 14155, pp. 1–17. Springer (2023)
26. Cunha, J., Madeira, A., Barbosa, L.S.: Paraconsistent transition structures: compositional principles and a modal logic. Mathematical Structures in Computer Science (2024 (in print))
27. Filho, J.S.: Paraconsistent annotated logic in analysis of physical systems: Introducing the paraquantum $h\psi$ factor of quantization. J. Mod. Phys. **2**(11), 1397–1409 (2011)
28. Filho, J.S.: An introduction to paraconsistent integral differential calculus: with application examples. Appl. Math. **5**(6) (2014)
29. Goertzel, B.: Paraconsistent foundations for quantum probability. CoRR abs/2101.07498 (2021). https://arxiv.org/abs/2101.07498
30. Goguen, J.A., Burstall, R.M.: Institutions: abstract model theory for specification and programming. J. ACM **39**(1), 95–146 (1992)
31. ao I. Silva Filho, J.: Undulatory theory with paraconsistent logic (part i): quantum logical model with two wave functions. J. Quantum Inf. Sci. **6**(3) (2016)
32. Jacobs, B.: Introduction to Coalgebra: Towards Mathematics of States and Observation, Cambridge Tracts in Th. Comp. Sc., vol. 59. Cambridge Univ. Press (2016)
33. Jaskowski, S.: Propositional calculus for contradictory deductive systems (communicated at the meeting of march 19, 1948). Studia Logica Int. J. Symbolic Logic **20**(2), 143–160 (1969)
34. Kamide, N.: Paraconsistent sequential linear-time temporal logic: Combining paraconsistency and sequentiality in temporal reasoning. Rep. Math. Logic **52**, 3–44 (2017)
35. Kupke, C., Pattinson, D.: Coalgebraic semantics of modal logics: An overview. Theor. Comput. Sci. **412**(38), 5070–5094 (2011)

36. Kurz, A., Palmigiano, A., Venema, Y.: Coalgebra and logic: A brief overview. J. Log. Comput. **20**(5), 985–990 (2010)
37. Łukasiewicz, J.: O zasadzie sprzeczności u Arystotelesa (On the principle of contradiction in Aristotle). Polska Akademia Umiejętności (1910)
38. Mossakowski, T., Haxthausen, A.E., Sannella, D., Tarlecki, A.: Casl - the common algebraic specification language: Semantics and proof theory. Comput. Artif. Intell. **22**(3–4), 285–321 (2003)
39. Priest, G.: Paraconsistency and dialetheism. In: Gabbay, D.M., Woods, J. (eds.) The Many Valued and Nonmonotonic Turn in Logic, Handbook of the History of Logic, vol. 8, pp. 129–204. Elsevier (2007)
40. Raspa, V.: Thinking About Contradictions: The Imaginary Logic of Nikolai Aleksandrovich Vasiliev. Springer Verlag, Cham, Switzerland (2017)
41. Rutten, J.J.M.M.: Universal coalgebra: a theory of systems. Theor. Comput. Sci. **249**(1), 3–80 (2000)
42. Sannella, D., Tarlecki, A.: Foundations of Algebraic Specification and Formal Software Development. Monographs in Theoretical Computer Science. An EATCS Series, Springer (2012)
43. Severo, F.: The spirit of contradiction (2019), https://www.youtube.com/watch?v=8gKKabtLA_U&t=10s
44. de Souza, E.G., Costa-Leite, A., Dias, D.H.B.: On a paraconsistentization functor in the category of consequence structures. J. Appl. Non-Classical Logics **26**(3), 240–250 (2016)
45. Test, R.R.: The cost of consistency: Information economy in paraconsistent belief revision. South American Journal of Logic **1**(2), 461–480 (2015)

Contributed Papers

User-Guided Verification of Security Protocols via Sound Animation

Kangfeng Ye(✉), Roberto Metere, and Poonam Yadav

University of York, York, UK
{kangfeng.ye,roberto.metere,poonam.yadav}@york.ac.uk

Abstract. Current formal verification of security protocols relies on specialized researchers and complex tools, inaccessible to protocol designers who informally evaluate their work with emulators. This paper addresses this gap by embedding symbolic analysis into the design process. Our approach implements the Dolev-Yao attack model using a variant of CSP based on Interaction Trees (ITrees) to compile protocols into animators – executable programs that designers can use for debugging and inspection. To guarantee the soundness of our compilation, we mechanised our approach in the theorem prover Isabelle/HOL. As traditionally done with symbolic tools, we refer to the Diffie-Hellman key exchange and the Needham-Schroeder public-key protocol (and Lowe's patched variant). We demonstrate how our animator can easily reveal the mechanics of attacks and verify corrections. This work facilitates security integration at the design level and supports further security property analysis and software-engineered integrations.

Keywords: Interaction Trees · CSP · Sound Animation · Formal Verification · Code Generation · Security Protocols

1 Introduction

The application of formal verification to security protocols has brought clear benefits and provable guarantees of several security properties. Examples are: *authentication*, the process of verifying a claimed identity of a user, device, or other entity in a computer system [1]; *handover*, the passing on of responsibilities of a particular post by the outgoing guard to the incoming guard [2]; *privacy* of data and devices against outside threats, spyware, and subversion [3]; *access control*, determining who is allowed to access certain data, applications, and resources, and in what circumstances [4]. The above properties increased the global trust towards popularly adopted protocols, as TLS [5,6].

A range of tools have been developed or applied to automatically analyse the security properties of protocols, such as FDR [7], Isabelle [8], Maude-NPA [9], AVISPA [10], ProVerif [11], Tamarin-prover [12]. They have demonstrated useful tools for the discovery of attacks to otherwise unknown vulnerabilities [3,4,13], for the identification of missing or weak assumptions [1], for the proposal of fixes or improvements to protocols [1,13,14], and for the guarantee of correctness [2]. These works were carried out by formal verification and security researchers with

A. Madeira and A. Knapp (Eds.): SEFM 2024, LNCS 15280, pp. 33–51, 2025.
https://doi.org/10.1007/978-3-031-77382-2_3

solid knowledge of formal specification and verification and experience with particular verification tools. So, the approaches used in these works are *not* obviously accessible by other users, such as security protocol designers. The general procedure for the application of these approaches starts with a complete security protocol, followed by protocol modelling in a formal specification language, verification using a tool, and finally concludes with a verification report (problems, fixes, suggestions, etc.) to be sent to the protocol designers or standard organisers. This procedure is usually *non-iterative* or *each iteration takes a very long time* because designers do not actively participate in this verification loop.

Several studies [14–17] have investigated a formal and accessible technique, *animation*, to general designers or engineers. Here, an animation of a formal specification model is an executable computer program implemented in programming languages such as C++, Java, or Haskell. It provides user interfaces to allow users to interact with the encoded model. This allows users to inspect the model's behaviour by interactively choosing what the model is allowed to do and observing its response. The animation approach differs from *testing* as animation is used even if an implementation does not exist (yet). A significant problem with the above-mentioned studies is that the animation is *not* guaranteed to be sound, that is, they provide no guarantees that all the traces of an animation unequivocally correspond to traces of the original specification. Soundness becomes an essential aspect if we apply animations to the security of protocols, as one needs to prove that a counterexample or an attack found in the animation must reflect a problem in the original protocol specification.

Our main idea to provide the required soundness is to use Interaction Trees [18] (ITrees) where a formal specification can be associated with an abstract and also executable denotational semantics [19]. Animation models interactions of reactive systems with their environment through events. We use ITrees as coinductive tree structures to construct denotational and operational semantics, enabling both reasoning and implementation. Using ITrees, Foster et al. [20] gave semantics to a version of CSP process algebra [21,22], called ITree-based CSP, and mechanised it in Isabelle/HOL [8] to allow automatic generation of Haskell code from a CSP model for animation. This has been applied in [23] to animate control software in robotics and demonstrate functional correctness through manual interaction. The animation is thus sound thanks to ITree's executable semantics and Isabelle's code generator [24], which translates executable ITree definitions in the source HOL logic to target functional languages (such as Haskell). The translation preserves semantic correctness using higher-order rewrite systems [25]. Soundness is not a formally proved property for animation, but the simple and unbroken link from operational semantics of CSP, to (corecursive) definitions of CSP operators in ITrees, and to the final Haskell code through equational logic-based code generator (all in Isabelle/HOL) ensures its soundness. As a result, we do not need to test the generated Haskell code to check its correctness, which can largely save effort in software engineering. ITree-based CSP is not expressive than other process algebras such as standard CSP and Pi calculus, but its executable nature makes it more suitable for the development of accessible techniques, like animation. We apply ITree-based CSP to go beyond

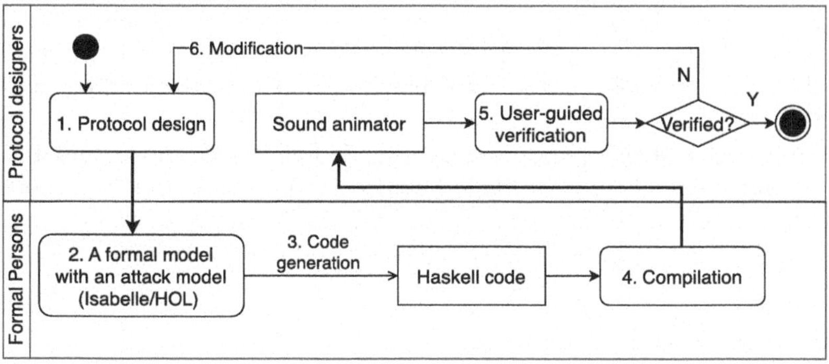

Fig. 1. User-guided verification workflow via sound animation.

functional correctness to obtain sound animation for the security properties of protocols and extend the animator to automatically check reachability and feasibility. We emphasise that interactivity and automation not only provide verified security insights at the early stages of the protocol design, but they do so while releasing the burden of having to know additional formal languages. This is a significant step toward the accessibility required by designers and other wider stakeholders.

One workflow that our approach supports is *interactive*, as shown in Fig. 1, where protocol designers can use the animator to carry out user-guided verification. We call this workflow *lightweight verification* because the animation is sound but may not be exhaustive. Through our animator, the designer can (1) manually explore the protocol by interacting with the animator, (2) automatically explore the exhaustive event space up to specified steps,[1] (3) automatically check the reachability of a set of particular events, or (4) test the feasibility of a specified sequence of events or trace. In this way, the animator is indeed a *verified model checker*. We call it *user-guided* because users can choose to manually explore some steps first (to get to their interesting interaction points, or *intermediate* interactions) and then start automatic verification,[2] which is different from usual model checkers which automatically explore the whole state space from initial states.

Our technical contributions are summarised as follows: (1) we propose a framework to model security protocols using ITree-based CSP, which is suitable not only for animation presented in this paper but also for theorem proving in the future; (2) we extend the animator from manual-only exploration to automatic reachability check and feasibility check; (3) we model two security protocols, the Needham-Schroeder public key protocol (NSPK) [26] and Diffie-Hellman key

[1] This is due to the memory consumption and exploration time constrains. In practice, a protocol run is normally finished in finite steps.

[2] The illustrations of user-guided verification can be found online at https://github.com/RandallYe/Animation_of_Security_Protocols.

exchange protocol (DH) [27]; and (4) we generate animators and use them to demonstrate attacks and verify patched versions. All definitions in this paper are mechanised and show an icon (🔗) that links to the corresponding repository artefacts[3].

The remainder of this paper is organised as follows. We review related work in Sect. 2, introduce ITrees and ITree-based CSP in Sect. 3, and then model and animate the Needham-Schroeder and the Diffie-Hellman protocols in Sects. 4 and 5 respectively. Finally, in Sect. 6, we conclude and discuss future work.

2 Related Work

NSPK [26] is an important yet simple protocol aiming to establish secure communication between two parties over an insecure network with the help of a trusted third party who securely distributes pre-registered public keys. Lowe used CSP and the model checker FDR to find a man-in-the-middle attack in the protocol (NSPK) and proposed a fix [13] (NSLPK). Then, the two versions of the protocol became widely studied examples in the formal verification of security protocols by many researchers using different tools. Paulson [28] used the inductive approach in Isabelle/HOL. Schneider [29] used CSP hand proofs to analyse the protocol and considered more about cryptographic equations. Cremers et al. [30] developed operational semantics for security protocols and analysed both versions. Blanchet et al. [31] used ProVerif, and Meier [32] used Tamarin-prover to analyse the protocols.

DH [27,33] is another important protocol on which many authenticated key agreement protocols are based . DH protocol does not include authentication, making it vulnerable to man-in-the-middle attacks. It is usually combined with other authentication protocols, such as DSA or RSA. ProVerif has been applied to verify various DH-based protocols [34], and Tamarin is also applied [12].

All these studies used model checking or theorem proving for verification and were conducted by researchers. Instead, in our approach, protocol designers (indeed, anyone after a short training) can verify the protocols using animation.

Kazmierczak et al. [15] developed an animator for Z specifications and used it to explore and test models. They regard animation as a lightweight formal method. Dutle et al. [17] proposed an approach to manually translate formally verified models to Java code, which allows the animation of the formal specifications. Miller et al. [14] implemented an emulator, written in C++, to experiment with 5G authenticated key establishment procedures. Boichut et al.'s SPAN [16], written in OCaml and Tcl/Tk, is an animation tool for the specification language used in AVISPA. It can find the attack in NSPK. However, the soundness guarantee is the most significant difference of our work from SPAN and the other. Additionally, our approach is more flexible and accessible to extend (for example, to support different attack models) and maintained because animators are automatically generated from CSP specifications.

[3] Available in the repository shown above. We assume basic knowledge of Isabelle/HOL from interested readers to understand these definitions and theorems.

Our work is based on [20,23], and applies to the modelling and animation of security protocols. Additionally, we extended the animator command line interface from manual-only exploration to combined manual, random, and automatic exploration with reachability and feasibility checks.

3 ITree-Based CSP

This section briefly introduces interaction trees and the ITree-based CSP processes and operators, with their semantics omitted here for brevity. A complete account of the semantics is in [20,23].

Interaction trees (ITrees) [18] are a data structure for modelling reactive systems interacting with their environment through events. They are potentially *infinite* and defined as coinductive trees in Isabelle/HOL.

```
codatatype ('e, 'r) itree =
Ret 'r | Sil "('e, 'r) itree" | Vis "'e ⇸ ('e, 'r) itree"
```

ITrees are parameterised over two types: `'e` for events (E), and `'r` for return values or states (R) . Three possible interactions are provided: (1) $\mathit{Ret}\, x$: termination with a value x of type R returned, denoted as $\checkmark_x$; (2) $\mathit{Sil}\, P$: an internal silent event, denoted as τP for a successor ITree P; or (3) $\mathit{Vis}\, F$: a choice among several visible events represented by a partial function F of type $E \nrightarrow (E, R)\mathit{itree}$ $E \nrightarrow (E, R)\mathit{itree}$.

In [20,23], deterministic CSP processes are given executable semantics using ITrees. Determinism is inherent in ITrees since we use a partial function to model events and their continuations. The CSP operators, therefore, cannot introduce nondeterminism. We summarise the processes and operators in both traditional (that is, the CSP presented in most literature like [21,22]) and ITree-based CSP in the first and second columns in Table 1 where †-marked operators block the events that will lead to nondeterminism in their counterparts in standard CSP, for the sake of determinism. The semantics of $\Box$, $\backslash$, and $\triangle$ operators follows the maximal progress assumption [20,23] that τ has the highest priority, *Ret* has higher priority, and then *Vis* events have lower priority.

In addition to nondeterminism, there are some other differences between the two versions of CSP. First, standard CSP processes are stateless, and values are passed between processes only through communication or parameters. In contrast, ITree-based processes are stateful, so they could return values, such as $\checkmark_v$, and then pass in variables in sequential composition. Second, sequential composition $P \fatsemi Q$ in ITrees is defined through a monadic bind operator [20]. With the monadic do notation, we can write a sequential composition like $\mathsf{do}\{x \leftarrow \mathit{inp}\, c\, S;\ P(x)\}$ denoting the process accepts input values from set S on channel c and records the value in the variable x, then passes the value of x to $P(x)$. Finally, ITree-based CSP provides the tail-recursive iteration *iterate* and its special infinite *loop*. In standard CSP, this is implemented using recursion.

4 Needham-Schroeder Public Key Protocol

NSPK [26] is used to establish mutual authentication between two parties (such as Alice and Bob) over an insecure or public network using asymmetric encryption. Alice and Bob do not know each other's public keys and use a trusted server (S) to distribute them on request. The protocol is illustrated in Fig. 2 where a sequence of seven messages is shown on the left, and the interaction between A (Alice), B (Bob), and S is displayed on the right.

In this protocol, A and B are assumed to know the public key of S, which is used to verify messages from S that are digitally signed using the private key of S. Among the seven messages, four of them are used by A (or B) to request the public key of B (or A) from S in Message 1 (or 4) and by S to return the B's (or A's) public key pk_B (or pk_A) to A (or B) in Message 2 (or Message 5), which is

Table 1. Processes and operators in standard CSP and ITree-based CSP.

Standard	ITree-based	Description
τ	τ	Invisible event.
$Skip$ or ✓	skip (or $\mathsf{Ret}()$)	Skip: terminate immediately, and return a unit type ().
	$\mathsf{Ret}\ v$	Return: terminate immediately and return value v.
$Stop$	stop	Deadlock: refuse any interaction without a state change.
$c \rightarrow P$	$\mathtt{do}\{\mathsf{outp}\ c\ ();\ P\}$	Prefix: synchronise on channel c, then behave like P.
$c!v \rightarrow P$	$\mathtt{do}\{\mathsf{outp}\ c\ v;\ P\}$	Output: synchronise on channel c with value v, and then behave like P.
$c?x \rightarrow P(x)$	$\mathtt{do}\{x \leftarrow \mathsf{inp}\, c\, \mathbb{U};\ P(x)\}$	Input: accept an input of any value (of type T) on channel c, record it in x, and then behave like $P(x)$.
$c?x : S \rightarrow P(x)$	$\mathtt{do}\{x \leftarrow \mathsf{inp}\, c\, S;\ P(x)\}$	Restricted input: It is similar to input but only accepts the values from set S.
$b\ \&\ P$	$\mathtt{do}\{\mathsf{guard}\ b;\ P\}$	Guarded process: behave like P if b is true or deadlock
$P \Box Q$	$P \Box Q^{\dagger}$	External choice: offer the environment a choice of the first events of P and Q, then behave accordingly.
$P \sqcap Q$		Internal choice: nondeterministic choice between P and Q without offering the environment a choice.
$P;\ Q$	$P \mathbin{⨟} Q$	Sequential composition: behave like P initially, and behave like Q if P terminates.
$P \triangle Q$	$P \triangle Q^{\dagger}$	Interrupt: behave like P, but offer the environment a choice of the initial events of Q at any time until P terminates. If one of these events is performed, Q takes over and behaves accordingly.
$P \Theta_E Q$	$P \llbracket E \rhd Q$	Exception:behave like P until P performs an event from set E, at that point, then behave like Q.
$P \parallel_E Q$	$P \parallel_E Q^{\dagger}$	Parallel composition: P and Q run simultaneously, synchronise on the events in E, progress independently on the events not in E, and terminate if both terminate.
$P \mathbin{\vert\vert\vert} Q$	$P \mathbin{\vert\vert\vert} Q^{\dagger}$	Interleave: equal to $P \parallel_{\emptyset} Q$ where P and Q always progress independently on any event.
$P \setminus E$	$P \setminus E^{\dagger}$	Hiding: behave like P except that the events from E become internal.
$P\llbracket c \leftarrow d \rrbracket$	$P\llbracket \rho \rrbracket^{\dagger}$	Renaming: rename the event c in P to d, or a relation ρ in ITrees.
Recursive functions, omitted here	$\mathsf{iterate}\ b\ P\ s$	Tail-recursive iteration: continue to execute P while the condition $b\ s$ holds and otherwise terminates and returns the current state s.
$I(s) = P;\ I(s')$	$\mathsf{loop}\ P$	Infinite loop, equal to $\mathsf{iterate}\, b\ P\ s$ where $b\ s$ is always true.

1. $A \rightarrow S: (A,B)$
2. $S \rightarrow A: \{\!|(pk_B,B)|\!\}^d_{sk_S}$
3. $A \rightarrow B: \{\!|(na,A)|\!\}^a_{pk_B}$
4. $B \rightarrow S: (B,A)$
5. $S \rightarrow B: \{\!|(pk_A,A)|\!\}^d_{sk_S}$
6. $B \rightarrow A: \{\!|(na,nb)|\!\}^a_{pk_A}$
7. $A \rightarrow B: \{\!|nb|\!\}^a_{pk_B}$

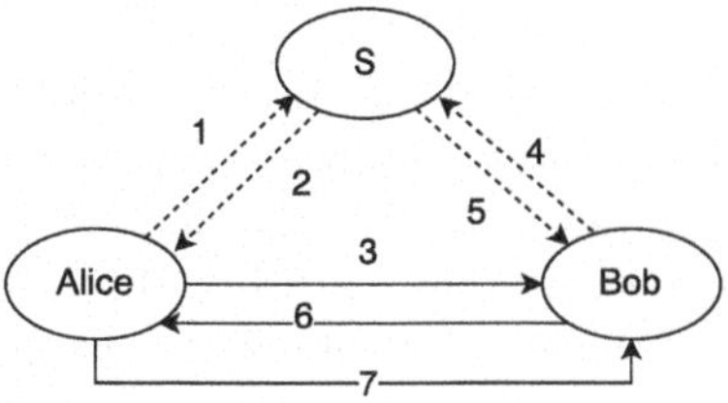

Fig. 2. Needham-Schroeder public key protocol

signed using a private key sk_S of S. These messages are for *public key retrieve.* In the other three messages, A sends B Message 3 composed of her nonce (na) and identity (A) and encrypted using B's public key pk_B. B replies A Message 6 composed of na and his nonce (nb) and encrypted using A's public key pk_A, and finally, A confirms to B that she knows nb in Message 7. The other three messages are for *authentication.*

This protocol's security goals include the secrecy or confidentiality of Alice's and Bob's nonces (that is, na and nb) along with mutual authentication. This protocol, named NSPK7 here, is well-known to be vulnerable to a man-in-the-middle attack [13]. Most researchers studied a simplified 3-message version, NSPK3, where the public key retrieve messages are omitted because communications with the trusted server are assumed to be secure (through a secure channel). We also use model NSPK3 and show how our animation can detect the attack automatically. Before showing that, we need to introduce the network and attack models that characterise the Dolev-Yao analysis.

Network Model. Alice and Bob communicate through an insecure network (at the top of Fig. 3), which is under the attacker's control. Thus, Alice and Bob send and receive messages to and from the attacker (the diagram in the middle). In CSP, we use parallel composition to model communication (the diagram at the bottom).

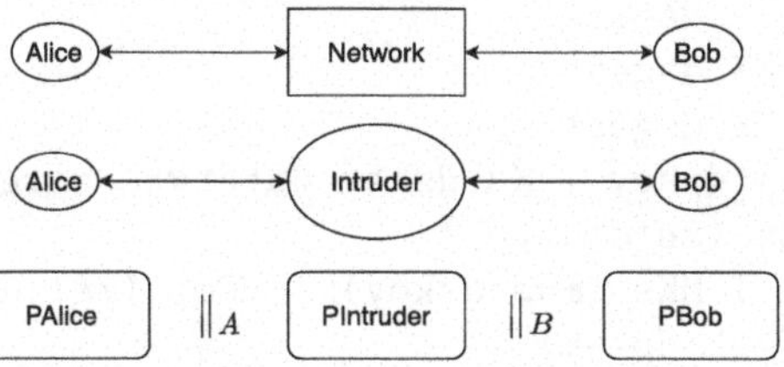

Fig. 3. Network model.

Attack Model. We consider the Dolev-Yao model [35] for symbolical verification of security protocols where the attacker or intruder controls the entire network and can intercept, delete, modify, delay, inject, and build new messages from the current knowledge but is limited by the (perfect black-box) cryptography that the intruder cannot decrypt a message without knowing its key and forge a signature. As such, the intruder can augment their knowledge offline by applying inference rules to any pieces of knowledge he already has. Such rules are defined in Fig. 2 where K denotes its current knowledge. Rules are divided into two groups: *break-down* ($\vdash_{\Downarrow}$) rules, what messages can be derived from K using member, unpairing, decryption, and digital signature verification rules, and *build-up* ($\vdash_{\Uparrow}$) rules, what messages can be built up from K using member, pairing, and encryption, and digital sign rules.

Table 2. Intruder message inference rules.

Name	Premise	Break down	Build up
Member	$m \in K$	$K \vdash_{\Downarrow} m$	$K \vdash_{\Uparrow} m$
Pairing	$m \in K \wedge m' \in K$		$K \vdash_{\Uparrow} (m, m')$
Unpairing	$(m, m') \in K$	$K \vdash_{\Downarrow} m$ and $K \vdash_{\Downarrow} m'$	
Encryption/Sign	$m \in K \wedge k \in K$		$K \vdash_{\Uparrow} \{m\}_k$
Decryption/Verify	$\{m\}_k \in K \wedge k^{-1} \in K$	$K \vdash_{\Downarrow} m$	

We note that the encryption and decryption inference rules suit asymmetric, symmetric, and digital signatures. Symmetric encryption uses a single key for encryption and decryption (its inverse $k^{-1} = k$). Asymmetric encryption uses a public key for encryption and a private key for decryption (so $k^{-1^{-1}} = k$). A digital signature uses a private key to sign a message and a public key to verify authenticity.

Modelling of NSPK3. Below, we define a variety of data types used in this protocol.

```
datatype dagent = Alice | Bob | Intruder
datatype dnonce = N dagent
datatype dpkey = PK dagent
datatype dskey = SK dagent
datatype dkey = Kp dpkey | Ks dskey datatype dmsg = MAg
(ma:dagent) | MNon (mn:dnonce)
| MKp (mkp:dpkey) | MKs (mks:dskey) | MCmp (mc1:dmsg) (mc2:dmsg) |
MEnc (mem:dmsg) (mek:dpkey)
```

The enumeration `dagent` contains three considered agents. Each agent is associated with a nonce of type `dnonce` using a constructor `N`, a public key of type `dpkey` using a constructor `PK`, and a private key of type `dskey` using a constructor `SK`. Both public keys and private keys are of a type `dkey` using different constructors `Kp` and `Ks`. All messages for communication on channels are of type dmsg, including agent's identities of type dagent (with the constructor MAg), nonces (with MNon), public keys (with MKp), private keys (with MKs), compound of two messages (with MCmp), and asymmetric encryption (with MEnc). We note ma, mn, etc., in the definition of dmsg are functions used to extract corresponding elements from a message of type dmsg. For example, ma has a type dmsg⇒dagent which returns the agent identity Alice encoded in a message like MAg Alice. We also introduce the symbols $\langle m_1, m_2 \rangle$ and $\{\!|m|\!\}^a_k$ for the compound MCmp m1 m2 and the encryption MEnc m k. We also use $\langle m_1, m_2, m_3 \rangle$ for $\langle m_1, \langle m_2, m_3 \rangle \rangle$.

Inspired by [13] , we declare signals to specify and verify properties.

```
datatype dsig = StartProt dagent dagent dnonce dnonce
| EndProt dagent dagent dnonce dnonce
| ClaimSecret (sag:dagent) (sn:dnonce) (sp: "ℙ dagent")
```

Using ClaimSecret A na {B}, for example, the agent A claims its nonce na only known to B. We use StartProt or EndProt A B na nb to signal A starts or finishes a protocol run with B using their nonces na and nb.

Message Inferences. In Isabelle, we define a function break_sk for the break-down rules in Table 2 to derive a list of messages from a given list and supplied set (sks) of private keys for decryption, for the sake of implementation in Haskell.

```
fun break_sk::"dmsg list ⇒ dskey set ⇒ dmsg list" where
break_sk [] sks = [] |
break_sk ⟨m1, m2⟩#xs sks = remdups
  (break_sk [m1] sks @ break_sk [m2] sks @ break_sk xs sks) |
break_sk {|m|}^a_(PK k)#xs sks = if SK k ∈ sks then
  insert {|m|}^a_(PK k) (remdups (break_sk [m] sks @ break_sk xs sks))
  else insert {|m|}^a_(PK k) (break_sk xs sks) |
break_sk m#xs sks = insert m (break_sk xs sks)
```

For a compound message ($\langle m1, m2 \rangle$ in the head of a list), the unpairing rule in Fig. 2 is applied: recursively break-down m1, m2, and also the tail xs, concatenate (@) them together with the duplicates removed by remdups. For asymmetric encryption, the decryption rule is applied depending on whether the corresponding private key (SK k) is in sks or not, where insert is a list function to insert an element into a list if it does exist in the list or ignore it. We apply the member rule for other messages (using the pattern match m#xs). We also define breakm xs be break_sk xs (extract_skey xs) where extract_skey extracts private keys from the list xs of messages.

For the build-up rules, the resulting messages could be very large or infinite by, for example, applying the pairing and encryption rules alternately. Dealing with these large sets of messages will take space in memory and computation time. For the sake of animation, we limit the number of times these rules will be applied in the definition build_n below where build_n xs ks nc ne l is used to build up messages from a given list xs of messages, a list ks of public keys, the number nc of applications of the pairing rule, the number ne of applications of the encryption rule, and the maximum length `l` of built messages. However, this will not impact the correctness of protocols verified with appropriate parameters. For example, for NSPK3 or NSPK7, `nc`, `ne`, and `l` could be 1, 1, and 2.

```
fun build_n ::"dmsg list⇒dpkey list⇒nat⇒nat⇒nat⇒dmsg list"
where build_n xs ks 0 0 l = xs |
build_n xs ks (Suc nc) 0 l =
    (build_n (union (pair2 xs xs l) xs) ks nc 0 l) |
build_n xs ks 0 (Suc ne) l =
    (build_n (union  (enc_1 xs ks) xs) ks 0 ne l) |
build_n xs ks (Suc nc) (Suc ne) l = (List.union
    (build_n (union (pair2 xs xs l) xs) ks nc (Suc ne) l)
    (build_n (union (enc_1 xs ks) xs) ks (Suc nc) ne l))
```

The pattern matches on line 2, lines 3 and 4, 5 and 6, and 7–9 above correspond to the member build-up rule, the pairing rule, the encryption rule, and both pairing and encryption rules in Fig. 2. We define the function `pair2 xs ys l` to pair each element `x` from `xs` with each element `y` from `ys` to form a list of new compound messages $\langle \mathtt{x}, \mathtt{y} \rangle$ if `x` and `y` are not the same, and the length of the new message does exceed `l`. The pairing definition on lines 3 and 4 denotes the application of the pairing rule once and then builds up using the pairing rule for one less time (`nc`) on the union (on the list) of the first application result (`pair2 xs xs l`) and `xs`. The function `enc_1 xs ks` aims to build up messages by encrypting each message in `xs` using every public key in `ks`.

Channels. We define all channels grouped in a type `Chan` for communicate below.

```
datatype Chan =
env :: dagent×dagent
send, recv, hear, fake :: dagent×dagent×dmsg
leak :: dmsg sig :: dsig terminate :: unit
```

The channel `env` is used for the environment to request an authentication between two agents. The channels `send`, `recv`, `hear`, and `fake` are for communication between agents in the form of a source agent, a destination agent, and a message. The `leak` channel indicates a secret known by the intruder. The `sig` channel signals a particular point (modelled as a signal) reached. The `terminate` channel is used to terminate the protocol run.

Processes. We model Alice as an initiator using the standard syntax for simplicity.

$$
\begin{aligned}
&\mathit{Initiator}(A, na) \mathrel{\widehat{=}} \mathit{env}!A?B \rightarrow \mathit{sig}!(\mathtt{ClaimSecret\ A\ na\ \{B\}}) \rightarrow \\
&\quad \mathit{send}!A!\mathit{Intruder}!\{\!|\langle \mathtt{MNon\ na}, \mathtt{Mag\ A} \rangle|\!\}^{a}_{\mathtt{PK\ B}} \rightarrow \\
&\quad \mathit{recv}!\mathit{Intruder}!A?m : \{ nb : \mathit{dnonce} \bullet \{\!|\langle \mathtt{MNon\ na}, \mathtt{MMon\ nb} \rangle|\!\}^{a}_{\mathtt{PK\ A}} \} \rightarrow \\
&\quad \mathit{sig}!(\mathtt{StartProt\ A\ B\ na\ nb}) \rightarrow \mathit{send}!A!\mathit{Intruder}!\{\!|\mathtt{MNon\ nb}|\!\}^{a}_{\mathtt{PK\ B}} \rightarrow \\
&\quad \mathit{sig}!(\mathtt{EndProt\ A\ B\ na\ nb}) \rightarrow \mathit{terminate} \rightarrow \mathsf{skip}
\end{aligned}
$$

The *Initiator* has Two Parameters: A for the agent identity and na for a nonce of A. The *Initiator* first waits for the environment's input on channel `env`, where B is the counterpart for the mutual authentication. Then it signals a `ClaimSecret` that na of A is only known to B; it sends Message 3 in Fig. 2 to the public network (that is, the Intruder) and receives Message 6 from `Intruder` using a restricted set of messages; it signals a `StartProt` for A to run the protocol with B using `na` and `nb` where `nb` is extracted from `m` using `mn (mc2 (mem m))`; it sends Message 7 (`nb`); then it signals a `EndProt` for A to finish the protocol run with B using `na` and `nb`; and finally the `Initiator` terminates.

Similarly, we model Bob as a responder.

$$
\begin{aligned}
& \mathit{Responder}(B, nb) \mathrel{\widehat{=}} \\
& \quad \mathit{recv}!\mathit{Intruder}!B?m : \{na : \mathit{dnonce};\ A : \mathit{dagent} \bullet \{\!|\langle \texttt{MNon na}, \texttt{MAg A}\rangle|\!\}^{a}_{\texttt{PK B}}\} \rightarrow \\
& \quad \mathit{sig}!(\texttt{ClaimSecret B nb \{A\}}) \rightarrow \mathit{sig}!(\texttt{StartProt B A na nb}) \rightarrow \\
& \quad \mathit{send}!B!\mathit{Intruder}!\{\!|\langle \texttt{MNon na}, \texttt{MMon nb}\rangle|\!\}^{a}_{\texttt{PK A}} \rightarrow \\
& \quad \mathit{recv}!\mathit{Intruder}!B?m : \{\{\!|\texttt{MNon nb}|\!\}^{a}_{\texttt{PK B}}\} \rightarrow \\
& \quad \mathit{sig}!(\texttt{EndProt B A na nb}) \rightarrow \mathit{terminate} \rightarrow \textsf{skip}
\end{aligned}
$$

The na and A are extracted from the received message m using `ma (mc2 (mem m))` and `mn (mc1 (mem m))`. Given its identity I, nonce ni, a list k of knowledge, and a list s of secrets, we model Intruder below.

$$
\begin{aligned}
& \mathit{PIntruder0}(I, ni, k, s) \mathrel{\widehat{=}} \\
& \quad (\mathit{hear}?\_!\mathit{Intruder}?m \rightarrow \mathit{PIntruder0}(I, ni, \texttt{breakm(insert m k)}, s)) \ \Box \\
& \quad \left(\Box\, A : \mathit{dagent};\ m : \mathit{build\_n}(k) \bullet \mathit{fake}!\mathit{Intruder}!A!m \rightarrow \mathit{PIntruder0}(I, ni, k, s)\right) \Box \\
& \quad \left(\Box\, m : \texttt{filter } (\lambda \texttt{x. member k x) s} \bullet \mathit{leak}!m \rightarrow \mathit{PIntruder0}(I, ni, k, s)\right) \Box \\
& \quad (\mathit{terminate} \rightarrow \texttt{skip})
\end{aligned}
$$

The process models the following behaviours of the intruder: it can hear a message m from any agent (_) and learn new knowledge (`breakm(insert m k)`) from m; it can fake all the messages which can be built up from its knowledge; it can leak a message m if m is in both k and s (by `filter (λx. member k x) s`), that is, a secret known to the intruder; and it can terminate. This process models an active attacker. We can simply remove its capability of faking messages (so no need to build up messages) to model a passive attacker. In this process, if a secret is leaked, it continues to offer the `leak!m` event. This is not an incorrect behaviour. But it will result in more traces in the animator later having interleaving `leak` events (so it is more challenging to explore the traces using animation). We introduce the processes below to restrict each secret from being leaked only once.

$$
\begin{aligned}
& \mathit{PLeakOnce}(\mathit{secrects}) \mathrel{\widehat{=}} \mathop{|||}\ s : \mathit{secrets} \bullet \mathit{leak}!s \rightarrow \mathit{skip} \\
& \mathit{PIntruder1}(I, ni, k, s) \mathrel{\widehat{=}} \\
& \quad \Big(\mathit{PIntruder0}(I, ni, k, s) \parallel_{\mathit{LkEvents}(s)} \mathit{PLeakOnce}(s)\Big) \, [\![\mathit{TermEvent} \rhd \mathit{skip}
\end{aligned}
$$

PLeakOnce is an indexed interleaving and it `leak`s each secret s in *secrets* once. *PIntruder*1 uses the parallel composition to restrict *PIntruder*0 for the `leak` event where *LkEvents*(s) is a set of `Leak` events for all secrets s. We also use the exception operator to allow the composition to be terminated by a `terminate` event.

The initial knowledge of the intruder includes the identities and public keys of all the agents and a private key of the intruder. The secrets of NSPK3 are the nonces *na* and *nb* in Fig. 2.

```
definition InitKnows =
  AllAgentsLst @ AllPKsLst @ [MNon (N Intruder), MKs (SK
Intruder)]
definition AllSecrets = removeAll (MNon (N Intruder)) AllNoncesLst
```

The behaviour of the intruder *PIntruder* is defined below with `hear` and `fake` events renamed to `send` and `recv` according to a relation *nameMapI*.

$$PIntruder2 \mathrel{\widehat{=}} PIntruder1\ \texttt{Intruder (N Intruder) InitKnows AllSecrets}$$
$$PIntruder \mathrel{\widehat{=}} PIntruder2[\![nameMapI]\!]$$

In NSPK3, Alice plays the initiator role, and Bob plays the responder role. Their behaviours are the instantiation of `Initiator` and `Responder`, respectively.

```
definition PAlice = Initiator Alice (N Alice)
definition PBob = Responder Bob (N Bob)
```

Finally, the NSPK3 protocol is modelled below where *TermEvent* contains only the `terminate` event, and *ABIEvents* contains the events for communication between Alice, Bob, and Intruder including the `terminate` event.

$$NSPK3 \mathrel{\widehat{=}} (PAlice \parallel_{TermEvent} PBob) \parallel_{ABIEvents} PIntruder$$

In modelling NSPK3, protocol designers provide the protocol specification (Fig. 2), the security goals (secrecy and authenticity), and the attack model specification. Then formal methods researchers model them with an implemented attack model in ITree-based CSP in Isabelle/HOL and generate an animator to the designers. In our model, message types, message inference, channels, and the process `PIntruder` are general infrastructure and can be reused for other protocols. And the processes `Initiator` and `Responder` are specific for this protocol.

Animation. After NSPK3 is modelled in Isabelle, we can (soundly) generate Haskell code and compile it into an executable program using the `animate_sec` command, which we also implement to animate security protocols using ITrees.

In Fig. 4, we show the first interaction of the model with its environment: the lines starting with `Events` are produced by the model or the animator and

```
1  Starting ITree Animation...
2  Events:
3   (1) Env [Alice] Bob;
4   (2) Env [Alice] Intruder;
5   (3) Recv [Bob<=Intruder] {<N Intruder, Alice>}_PK Bob;
6   (4) Recv [Bob<=Intruder] {<N Intruder, Intruder>}_PK Bob;
7  [Choose: 1-4]: 1 Env_C (Alice,Bob)
8  Events:
9   (1) Recv [Bob<=Intruder] {<N Intruder, Alice>}_PK Bob;
10  (2) Recv [Bob<=Intruder] {<N Intruder, Intruder>}_PK Bob;
11  (3) Sig ClaimSecret Alice (N Alice) (Set [ Bob ]);
```

Fig. 4. First interaction with the NSPK3 animator.

describe all enabled events, and the lines beginning with `[Choose: 1-n]` represents a user's choice of enabled events from number 1 to n. Initially, there are four enabled events: the first two events on lines `3-4` are due to `PAlice` to get a request from the environment on which principal to establish a session for Alice, and the other two events on lines `5-6` represent the (fake) messages sent by the intruder to Bob. These messages are built up using the intruder's initial knowledge (because no message is heard by now). After one event (the first event in this case) is chosen on line `7`, then the model accepts the request on the `Evn` channel, and three events are enabled to allow users to interact further. This is the default way to explore the protocol manually.

Additionally, the animator provides five extra ways to exhaustively (`Auto`) or randomly (`Rand`) explore the event space up to specified steps or check the reachability of a set of particular events while monitoring the reachability of other events using both exhaustive (`AReach`) or random search (`RReach`), or check the feasibility of a specified sequence of events.

We use `AReach 15 %Terminate%` to search all possible traces for a successful protocol termination, and many traces are found. We use `AReach 15 %Leak N Bob%` to automatically search the possible violation of the *secrecy* for the nonce of Bob. Only one trace is shown in Fig. 5. This is the man-in-the-middle attack [13]. Similarly, we checked the authenticity of Alice and Bob and found that Alice's authenticity was not violated, but Bob's authenticity was violated in six traces.

Our animation can also check whether a given trace is feasible. For example, we can check whether a particular trace for the successful establishment of the mutual authentication between Alice and Bob is feasible.

During the manual exploration or automatic check, the animated protocol often deadlocks (that is, no further enabled events). This happens because we model only one protocol run (instead of an infinite number of sessions) for both Alice and Bob. If, for example, a message faked by the intruder interferes with the standard protocol run for Alice or Bob, they will wait for the next message, which may never be possible. This modelling of one protocol run using a single initiator role for Alice and a single responder role for Bob will not affect whether

```
AReach 15, %Leak N Bob%
Reachability by Auto: 15
  Events for reachability check: ["Leak N Bob"]
  Events for monitoring: []
*** These events ["Leak N Bob"] are reached! ***
Trace: [Env [Alice] Intruder, Sig ClaimSecret Alice (N Alice) (Set
      [ Intruder ]), Send [Alice=>Intruder] {<N Alice, Alice>}_PK Intruder
      , Recv [Bob<=Intruder] {<N Alice, Alice>}_PK Bob, Sig ClaimSecret
      Bob (N Bob) (Set [ Alice ]), Sig StartProt Bob Alice (N Alice)
      (N Bob), Send [Bob=>Intruder] {<N Alice, N Bob>}_PK Alice, Recv [Alice
      <=Intruder] {<N Alice, N Bob>}_PK Alice, Sig StartProt Alice Intruder
      (N Alice) (N Bob), Send [Alice=>Intruder] {N Bob}_PK Intruder, ]
```

Fig. 5. Violation of secrecy for the nonce of Bob.

an attack exists and could be found according to Lowe [13]. He proved that if there is an attack in the NSPK protocol, the attack must be in this simple version. So, if NSPK3 is secure, then the general NSPK is also secure.

NSLPK3. In Lowe's corrected protocol [13], B's identity is additionally appended to Message 6 in Fig. 2 to stop the intruder from replaying this message from B to A because A expects this message from the intruder (with whom A is told to establish the authentication in the attack) but it is from B. We changed the message sent in `Responder` to $\{\!\!\{\langle \texttt{MNon na}, \texttt{MMon nb}, \texttt{MAg B}\rangle\}\!\!\}^{a}_{\texttt{PK A}})$ and our animation could not find such an attack.

NSPK7. For the original NSPK7 shown in Fig. 2, Alice and Bob do not know each other's public key. They retrieve the public keys from a server. So a new agent `Server` is added to `dagent`. The server uses its private key to sign messages and sends them to Alice and Bob, who know the server's public key. So we add a new type of message, `MSig`, in `dmsg`, denoted as $\{\!\!\{m\}\!\!\}^{d}_{k}$.

```
datatype dagent = Alice | Bob | Intruder | Server
datatype dmsg = ... | MSig (msd:dmsg) (msk:dskey)
```

1. $A \rightarrow B: g^{na}$
2. B computes $k_B = g^{na^{nb}}$
3. $B \rightarrow A: g^{nb}$
4. A computes $k_A = g^{nb^{na}}$
5. $A \rightarrow B: \{\!\!\{s\}\!\!\}^{s}_{k_A}$
6. B decrypts it using k_B to get s

(a) Original DH protocol

1. $A \rightarrow B: \langle \{\!\!\{g^{na}\}\!\!\}^{d}_{sk_A}, pk_A \rangle$
2. B uses received pk_A to verify the message and gets g^{na}; B computes $k_B = g^{na^{nb}}$
3. $B \rightarrow A: \{\!\!\{g^{nb}\}\!\!\}^{d}_{sk_B}$
4. A initially knows pk_B and verifies the message and gets g^{nb}; A computes $k_A = g^{nb^{na}}$
5. $A \rightarrow B: \{\!\!\{s\}\!\!\}^{s}_{k_A}$
6. B decrypts it using k_B to get s

(b) DH with digital signature

Fig. 6. Diffie-Hellman key exchange protocol

We also assume Alice and Bob use a private network to communicate with the server so the intruder cannot intercept the messages. For this purpose, we add two secure channels `send_s` and `recv_s` in `Chan`. The intruder does not know Alice and Bob's public keys and uses these secure channels to get them. Our animation shows that NSPK7 is vulnerable to the same man-in-the-middle attack.

5 Diffie-Hellman Key Exchange Protocol

The Diffie-Hellman (DH) [27] protocol aims to establish a shared secret between two agents using agreed information over an insecure network. Then they can use the secret to encrypt further messages or derive encryption keys. DH is based on modular exponentiation $g^a \,\mathsf{mod}\, p$ where g is the base, a is the power or exponent, and p is the modulus. Both parties publicly (that is, the intruder also knows) agree to use g and p. The a is private and only known to the agent who owns it.

We illustrate the original protocol (DH) in Fig. 6a, which is vulnerable to the man-in-the-middle attack, and a variant (DHDS) [36] of the protocol in Fig. 6a that uses the digital signature to tackle the attack where the modulus p part is omitted. The general procedure of a DH protocol run includes (1) both A and B send g^{na} and g^{nb} (where na and nb are their private nonces) to each other, (2) they compute $k_A = g^{nb^{na}}$ and $k_B = g^{na^{nb}}$, and so $k_A = k_B$ (that is, they get a shared secret), and (3) A sends a secret (symmetrically) encrypted by k_A, and then B can use the same k_B to decrypt it. In DHDS, A knows B's public key and expects a message from B that is signed using B's private key. The intruder cannot forge B's digital signature without knowing B's private key.

In Isabelle, we add three types of messages in `dmsg`: `MSEnc` for symmetric encryption, `MExpg` for the base g, and `MModExp` for modular exponentiation with corresponding annotations: $\{\!|m|\!\}^s_k$, g, and $(g_m)^b$

```
datatype dmsg = ... | MSEnc (msem:dmsg) (msek:dmsg)
| MExpg | MModExp (mmem:dmsg) (mmee:dnonce)
```

For the implementation (in `breakm`) of the decryption break-down rule in Fig. 2, an encrypted message $\{\!|m|\!\}^s_k$, when the key k is a `MModExp` like $g^{na^{nb}}$, can be decrypted only if g^{na} and nb are known, or g^{nb} and na are known, or g, na, and nb are all known.

For the build-up rule, we implement functions `mod_exp1` and `mod_exp2` to compose messages (from a list of nonces) that are resulted by applying modular exponentiation up to once and twice.

We use the animation to find an attack in the original DH by automatic reachability check of the `terminate` event. One counterexample (among several) is shown in Fig. 7 where the encrypted secret (`PK Alice`) is leaked, but Bob believes he gets the encrypted message from Alice. The trace shows that the intruder establishes a shared key ($g^{ni^{na}}$) with Alice and a shared key ($g^{ni^{nb}}$) with Bob where ni, na, and nb denote `N Intruder`, `N Alice`, and `N Bob`. The secret (`PK Alice`) sent by Alice is decrypted by the Intruder (using the shared

```
*** These events ["Terminate"] are reached! ***
Trace: [Send [
    Alice=>Intruder] g^N Alice, Send [Bob=>Intruder] g^N Bob, Recv [Alice
    <=Intruder] g^N Intruder, Recv [Bob<=Intruder] g^N Intruder, Send
     [Alice=>Intruder] {PK Alice}^S_g^N Intruder^N Alice, Leak PK Alice
    , Recv [Bob<=Intruder] {PK Alice}^S_g^N Bob^N Intruder, Terminate, ]
```

Fig. 7. One trace of the violation of secrecy in the original DH.

key with Alice), and then the Intruder re-encrypts the secret using the shared key with Bob. Bob finally decrypts it and believes it is from Alice. This is the man-in-the-middle attack.

We also used the animation to check DHDS and found only two traces of the successful termination, neither of which would leak the secret. This concludes that DHDS is secure for the attack.

6 Conclusion and Future Work

In this paper, we presented a novel approach to automatically generate sound animation in the Dolev-Yao attack model, arguably the most adopted model for symbolic analysis for security protocols. We implement our analysis in ITree-based CSP in Isabelle, to support verification guided by users. Our animator is a verified model checker, able to check reachability using automatic exhaustive or random search. Additionally, it supports interactive exploration and feasibility checks, which are usually not provided by model checkers.

We showcased our approach with two traditional case studies, the Needham-Schroeder protocol and the Diffie-Hellman key exchange protocol. We model them in five variants (in total) and verify such variants via the generated animators. Once the animator is generated, it can be used by users who do not need to know the formal language (Isabelle). Our animator can find the attacks in the flawed variants and guarantee these attacks do not exist in the revised variants.

Improvements to our current approach can take several directions. One future work is to develop a general framework to combine different features implemented in the examples, such as asymmetric and symmetric encryption, digital signature, and modular exponentiation. We will also introduce a hash function. Another improvement is to support a multiple (or possibly infinite) number of sessions, as our model for each agent supports only one. This might be done by implementing a CSP operator similar to the replicate operator from the *pi*-calculus (e.g., as implemented in ProVerif). Also, our current approach supports the workflow illustrated in Fig. 1, where formal researchers are still required to model security protocols. We can create a domain-specific language (DSL) for the modelling of security protocols, then automate the transformation from the DSL to ITree-based CSP. The ambitious and challenging aim here is to fully automatize the workflow and allow protocol designers to carry out user-guided verification without *any* involvement of formal verification experts.

Our work has many potential applications. Our future interests include the verification of security protocols used in 5G or 6G networks, particularly in the areas with new architectures, such as Open-RAN, or with resource-constrained devices typical, for example, in edge computing, using physical layer security. Security analysis in such may require flexible attack models.

Finally, animation has certain limitations in terms of enumerable and finite data types such as agents, keys, nonces, and messages, as well as intensive space and computation time requirements to infer messages for the intruder, which is mitigated by imposing the number of times a build-up rule can be applied in `build_n`. It means animation can only verify a protocol with finite agents and bounded message inference in a finite number of interactions or steps. These are due to the executable nature of animation. They, however, are not the limitations of ITrees and ITree-based CSP. We can use general *datatypes* or *codatatypes* and inductive sets in Isabelle/HOL to define (infinite) inferred messages. Such a model can be verified using theorem proving based on the operational and denotational semantics of ITree-based CSP [20]. This, however, creates a hole between models for theorem proving and for animation, which can be filled by using functional algorithm and data refinement in Isabelle's code generation (thanks to its equational logic). This is part of our future work to integrate theorem proving and animation together.

Acknowledgements. The EPSRC and DSIT support this work through the Communications Hub for Empowering Distributed Cloud Computing Applications and Research (CHEDDAR) under grants EP/X040518/1, EP/Y037421/1 and EP/Y019229/1. We thank Prof. Jim Woodcock and Dr. Simon Foster for their various discussions on this work and helpful suggestions.

References

1. Basin, D., Dreier, J., Hirschi, L., Radomirovic, S., Sasse, R., Stettler, V.: A formal analysis of 5G authentication. In: Proceedings of the 2018 ACM SIGSAC Conference on Computer and Communications Security. CCS '18, New York, NY, USA, Association for Computing Machinery, pp. 1383–1396 (2018)
2. Peltonen, A., Sasse, R., Basin, D.: A comprehensive formal analysis of 5G handover. In: Proceedings of the 14th ACM Conference on Security and Privacy in Wireless and Mobile Networks. WiSec '21, New York, NY, USA, Association for Computing Machinery, pp. 1–12 (2021)
3. Arapinis, M., Mancini, L., Ritter, E., Ryan, M., Golde, N., Redon, K., Borgaonkar, R.: New privacy issues in mobile telephony: fix and verification. In: Proceedings of the 2012 ACM Conference on Computer and Communications Security. CCS '12, New York, NY, USA, Association for Computing Machinery, pp. 205–216 (2012)
4. Akon, M., Yang, T., Dong, Y., Hussain, S.R.: Formal analysis of access control mechanism of 5G core network. In: Proceedings of the 2023 ACM SIGSAC Conference on Computer and Communications Security. CCS '23, New York, NY, USA, Association for Computing Machinery, pp. 666–680 (2023)
5. Bhargavan, K., Blanchet, B., Kobeissi, N.: Verified models and reference implementations for the TLS 1.3 standard candidate. In: 2017 IEEE Symposium on Security and Privacy (SP), IEEE (May 2017)

6. Basin, D., Cremers, C., Dreier, J., Sasse, R.: Tamarin: verification of large-scale, real world. cryptographic protocols. IEEE Secur. Priv. Mag. **20**(3), 24–32 (2022)
7. Gibson-Robinson, T., Armstrong, P., Boulgakov, A., Roscoe, A.W.: FDR3 - a modern refinement checker for CSP. In: Tools and Algorithms for the Construction and Analysis of Systems, pp. 187–201 (2014)
8. Nipkow, T., Wenzel, M., Paulson, L.C.: Isabelle/HOL: a proof assistant for higher-order logic. Springer (2002). https://doi.org/10.1007/3-540-45949-9
9. Escobar, S., Meadows, C., Meseguer, J.: A rewriting-based inference system for the NRL Protocol Analyzer and its meta-logical properties. Theoret. Comput. Sci. **367**(1–2), 162–202 (2006)
10. Armando, A., et al.: The AVISPA Tool for the Automated Validation of Internet Security Protocols and Applications, pp. 281–285. Springer, Berlin Heidelberg (2005). https://doi.org/10.1007/11513988_27
11. Blanchet, B.: Modeling and verifying security protocols with the applied pi calculus and proverif. Found. Trends Priv. Secur. **1**(1-2), 1–135 (2016)
12. Basin, D., Cremers, C., Dreier, J., Sasse, R.: Symbolically analyzing security protocols using tamarin. ACM SIGLOG News **4**(4), 19–30 (2017)
13. owe, G.: Breaking and fixing the Needham-Schroeder Public-Key Protocol using FDR. In: Margaria, T., Steffen, B. (eds.) Tools and Algorithms for the Construction and Analysis of Systems. TACAS 1996. Lecture Notes in Computer Science, vol. 1055. Springer, Berlin, Heidelberg (1996). https://doi.org/10.1007/3-540-61042-1_43
14. Miller, R., Boureanu, I., Wesemeyer, S., Newton, C.J.P.: The 5G key-establishment stack: in-depth formal verification and experimentation. In: Proceedings of the 2022 ACM on Asia Conference on Computer and Communications Security. ASIA CCS '22, New York, NY, USA, Association for Computing Machinery, pp. 237–251 (2022)
15. Kazmierczak, E., Winikoff, M., Dart, P.W.: Verifying model oriented specifications through animation. In: 5th Asia-Pacific Software Engineering Conference (APSEC '98), 2-4 December 1998, Taipei, Taiwan, ROC, IEEE Computer Society, pp. 254–261 (1998)
16. Boichut, Y., Genet, T., Glouche, Y., Heen, O.: Using animation to improve formal specifications of security protocols. In: 2nd Conference on Security in Network Architectures and Information Systems (SARSSI 2007), pp. 169–182 (2007)
17. Dutle, A.M., Muñoz, C.A., Narkawicz, A.J., Butler, R.W.: Software Validation via Model Animation. In: Blanchette, J., Kosmatov, N. (eds.) Tests and Proofs. TAP 2015. Lecture Notes in Computer Science, vol. 9154. Springer, Cham (2015). https://doi.org/10.1007/978-3-319-21215-9_6
18. Xia, L.y., et al.: Interaction trees: representing recursive and impure programs in Coq. Proc. ACM Program. Lang. **4**(POPL), 1–32 (2019)
19. Xia, L.y.: Executable Denotational Semantics with Interaction Trees. PhD thesis, University of Pennsylvania (2022)
20. Foster, S., Hur, C.K., Woodcock, J.: Formally verified simulations of state-rich processes using interaction trees in Isabelle/HOL. In Haddad, S., Varacca, D., eds.: 32nd International Conference on Concurrency Theory (CONCUR 2021). Volume 203 of Leibniz International Proceedings in Informatics (LIPIcs)., Dagstuhl, Germany, Schloss Dagstuhl – Leibniz-Zentrum für Informatik, 20:1–20:18 (2021)
21. Hoare, C.A.R.: Communicating Sequential Processes. Prentice-Hall Int. (1985)
22. Roscoe, A.W.: Understanding Concurrent Systems. Texts in Computer Science. Springer (2011)

23. Ye, K., Foster, S., Woodcock, J.: Formally verified animation for RoboChart using interaction trees. J. Logical Algebraic Methods Program. **137**, 100940 (2024)
24. Haftmann, F., Nipkow, T.: Code generation via higher-order rewrite systems. In: Blume, M., Kobayashi, N., Vidal, G., (eds.) Functional and Logic Programming, 10th International Symposium, FLOPS 2010, Sendai, Japan, April 19-21, 2010. Proceedings. Volume 6009 of Lecture Notes in Computer Science., Springer pp. 103–117 (2010). https://doi.org/10.1007/978-3-642-12251-4_9
25. Mayr, R., Nipkow, T.: Higher-order rewrite systems and their confluence. Theoret. Comput. Sci. **192**(1), 3–29 (1998)
26. Needham, R.M., Schroeder, M.D.: Using encryption for authentication in large networks of computers. Commun. ACM **21**(12), 993–999 (1978)
27. Diffie, W., Hellman, M.: New directions in cryptography. IEEE Trans. Inf. Theory **22**(6), 644–654 (1976)
28. Paulson, L.C.: Mechanized proofs of security protocols: needham-schroeder with public keys. Technical report, University of Cambridge (1997)
29. Schneider, S.: Using CSP for protocol analysis: The Needham-Schroeder Public-Key Protocol. Technical report (February 1997)
30. Cremers, C., Mauw, S.: Operational semantics of security protocols, pp. 66–89. Springer, Berlin Heidelberg (2005). https://doi.org/10.1007/11495628_4
31. Blanchet, B., Smyth, B., Cheval, V., Sylvestre, M.: ProVerif 2.05: Automatic Cryptographic Protocol Verifier, User Manual and Tutorial (2023)
32. Meier, S.: Advancing automated security protocol verification. PhD thesis (2013)
33. Merkle, R.C.: Secure communications over insecure channels. Commun. ACM **21**(4), pp. 294–299 (1978)
34. Küsters, R., Truderung, T.: Using ProVerif to analyze protocols with diffie-hellman exponentiation. In: 2009 22nd IEEE Computer Security Foundations Symposium pp. 157–171 (2009)
35. Dolev, D., Yao, A.: On the security of public key protocols. IEEE Trans. Inf. Theory **29**(2), 198–208 (1983)
36. Diffie, W., Van Oorschot, P.C., Wiener, M.J.: Authentication and authenticated key exchanges. Des. Codes Crypt. **2**(2), 107–125 (1992)

A Policy Framework for Regulating External Calls in Smart Contracts

Margherita Renieri(✉) and Letterio Galletta

IMT School for Advanced Studies Lucca, Lucca, Italy
{margherita.renieri,letterio.galletta}@imtlucca.it

Abstract. Smart contracts, functioning autonomously within blockchain ecosystems, obviate the necessity for central oversight. Typically programmed in Solidity, these contracts interact with others on Ethereum via external calls that allow a contract to invoke a function of another contract. However, external calls lack mechanisms to ensure that the called code satisfies some predefined behavioral policies. In this paper, we propose a formal framework to specify and enforce security policies to address this issue. Specifically, we present a core calculus for smart contracts equipped with constructs for specifying policies at the code level, allowing for monitoring and enforcing desired behaviors. We provide the formal semantics of this calculus and describe how our approach can be used to detect and prevent flash loan-based arbitrage scenarios.

Keywords: Security policies · Decentralized Finance · Arbitrage Attacks

1 Introduction

Smart contracts are computer programs deployed and executed within a blockchain environment. On the Ethereum blockchain, they are commonly written in the Solidity language and compiled into the EVM bytecode. The definition of a smart contract in Solidity looks like a class in any OOP language: contracts have an internal mutable state and a set of functions to manipulate it. These public functions can be invoked by users directly through transactions or other contracts through the external calls mechanism. Although this mechanism is powerful in enabling interactions between smart contracts, it provides no means to ensure that the invoked code satisfies some predefined behavioral policies. This is even more critical when we pass the address of a smart contract as an argument to a function that, in turn, invokes a function within the passed contract, so letting the caller control the code that is actually executed. For example, a contract `Bank` may implement a function `calculateInterest(RateProvider pro)` by invoking the function `getCurrentRate()` on the parameter `pro` of type `RateProvider` to obtain the current rate of a given crypto-asset in exchange for some fees. The trustworthiness of the computation depends on the

A. Madeira and A. Knapp (Eds.): SEFM 2024, LNCS 15280, pp. 52–69, 2025.
https://doi.org/10.1007/978-3-031-77382-2_4

code of `getCurrentRate()`. Relying on external code could have severe security consequences as many attacks on smart contracts exploit external calls to run attacker-controlled code, e.g., reentrancy attacks [8,12].

To address this issue, we propose a methodology to specify and enforce security policies at contract code level, inspired by Schneider [14] and Kozen [10]. The methodology involves (1) extending the programming language with constructs for expressing security policies to guard pieces of code; and (2) introducing inside the semantics of the language mechanisms to check that the code is compliant with such policies at run-time.

More precisely, we start from TinySol [4], a core calculus for smart contracts, and we extend it with a policy framing construct $\phi[S]$ for guarding the execution of statements S with a developer-defined policy ϕ. Intuitively, a policy ϕ is a predicate that specifies the set of program executions that are acceptable. The predicate ϕ is a pair (re, E), where re is a regular expression and E is an assertion (boolean expression). The regular expression re predicates on the *execution history*, namely the sequence of function calls made by the contract. While the expression E predicates on the state of the computation, i.e., the values of contract and function variables. Since the values of these variables will be only known at run-time, we allow them to occur also inside re. These variables will be bound to concrete values while evaluating re against the execution history. We define the semantics of TinySol as a transition system that describes the result of a computation (the reaching state), and that keeps track of the sequence of function calls performed at run-time together with their actual parameters (the *history*). Moreover, we define a run-time procedure to check when the execution satisfies the policies of a contract. This procedure works as follows: given a policy $\phi = (re, E)$, we first obtain a symbolic automaton from re that accepts all the histories that may be compliant for some assignment of variables occurring in re; then, we evaluate the assertion E to check its validity. A history is compliant if it passes both these checks, otherwise it is not, and the execution is reverted.

In the rest of the paper, we proceed as follows. We provide some background information and motivations for our work in Sect. 2. Section 3 presents the formalization of our methodology. Section 4 shows our use cases on DeFi protocols. Section 5 compares our work with the relevant literature, and Sect. 6 concludes and discusses future work.

2 Background and Motivation

Decentralized Finance (DeFi) is an innovative financial system built on blockchain technology, utilizing smart contracts to enable decentralized trading, lending, and investment. While Ethereum is a dominant platform, DeFi ecosystems have also developed on other platforms like Solana. However, DeFi is characterized by significant fragmentation and inefficiencies, with prices for identical financial instruments varying considerably across different venues and each venue responding inconsistently to market movements. These discrepancies offer profitable opportunities for speculative actions to manipulate the price of assets to take some advantage or to cause damage to other users.

Flash loans are financial instruments that allow users to borrow crypto-assets without needing up-front collateral, leveraging the atomicity of blockchain transactions. This atomicity ensures that the entire transaction either completes successfully or is aborted. Intuitively, they work as follows. At the beginning of a transaction, a user requests a loan of some crypto-assets to a DeFi service offering flash loans. The user performs various financial operations with the borrowed crypto-assets, including arbitrage, collateral swaps, etc., that can be completed within the scope of a single transaction. At the end of the transaction, the user pays back the loan plus a small fee. If the user cannot repay the loan, the transaction fails and reverts: all actions taken during the transaction are undone as if they never happened. This mechanism is risk-free for the lending contract and it is possible due to the Ethereum Virtual Machine's (EVM) ability to revert state changes. Qin et al. [13] provide a detailed introduction to flash loans, their common uses, and potential attacks facilitated by them.

Listing 1.1 shows a prototypical implementation of a `flashLoan` function, similar to the one of Aave protocol [1].

```
function flashLoan(receiverAddress, asset, amount, params):
    // Calculate fees for the asset
    // Check if there is enough liquidity
    if liquidity[asset] < amount:
        raise error "Insufficient liquidity"

    // Update the liquidity to reflect the loan
    liquidity[asset] -= amount

    // Transfer the assets to the receiver
    transfer(asset, receiverAddress, amount)

    // Execute the operation in the receiver contract
    if not receiverAddress.executeOperation(asset, amount, fee, msg.sender,
         params):
        raise error "FlashLoan execution failed"

    // Collect the borrowed amount plus fee
    totalDebt = amount + fee

    // Check if receiver has enough tokens to repay the loan
    receiverBalance = getBalance(receiverAddress, asset)
    if receiverBalance < totalDebt:
        raise error "Insufficient token balance to repay the loan"

    transferFrom(receiverAddress, self, totalDebt, asset)
    liquidity[asset] += totalDebt

    // Emit the flash loan event
    emit FlashLoan(receiverAddress, asset, amount, fee)
```

Listing 1.1. Code of a `flashloan` function.

The function above allows a calling smart contract to borrow an asset, execute arbitrary code using that asset via the external call mechanism, and then return the borrowed amount with a small fee. The parameter `receiverAddress` specifies the contract that receives the borrowed assets and executes a custom code via the function `executeOperation` called within the `flashLoan` function. The parameter `asset` contains the address of the asset to be borrowed, while `amount` specifies its quantity. The parameter `params` provides additional data required by the receiver contract for its operations. Once the fees for the borrowed asset are calculated and some sanity checks verify that the pool has enough liquidity, the requested assets are transferred to the receiver contract. Then, the function `flashLoan` invokes the external function `executeOperation`, passing as parameters the borrowed asset, the amount, the requested fees, the caller's address (`msg.sender`), and additional parameters. The receiver contract returns true to signal successful execution; otherwise, the transaction raises an error. After the receiver contract executes its code, it must repay the borrowed amount plus the fees. When the debt is paid back to the lending contract, the liquidity pool is updated to reflect the repayment, restoring the previous amount of crypto-assets.

Flash loans offer several financial opportunities for price attacks and speculative actions, including arbitrage. Milionis et al. [11] provide an in-depth analysis of arbitrage focusing on the differences between Automated Market Maker[1] (AMM) and market prices. Based on their strategies, arbitrageurs can be classified into opportunistic and myopic. The first category waits for larger mispricings, hoping for greater future gains rather than immediate profits, and prefers missing opportunities for faster, more short-term focused arbitrageurs. The second one, on the other hand, aims to maximize immediate profit: users execute trades that make a profit by buying (or selling) crypto-assets from an AMM if their price, adjusted for fees, is below (or above) the market one, and then selling (or buying) them to another AMM at the market price. The generic flow of flash loan-based arbitrage transactions of a myopic arbitrageur is the following: the user borrows some crypto-assets through a flash loan on a AMM and uses the loaned amount to execute a series of exchanges with other AMMs. She generates profits from the price discrepancies between the assets.

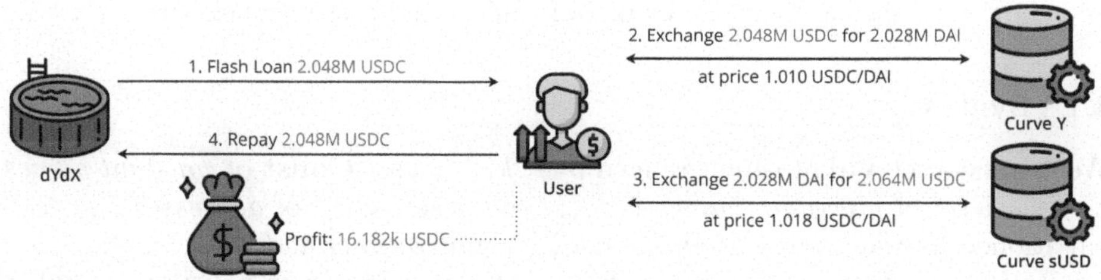

Fig. 1. High-level execution of a flash loan-based arbitrage transaction: (1) flash loan requested to the dYdX liquidity pool; (2) swap exchange from USDC to DAI in the AMM Curve Y; (3) swap exchange from DAI to USDC in the AMM Curve sUSD;(4) repay the flash loan.

Figure 1 illustrates the steps of a flash loan-based arbitrage involving the liquidity pool dYdX and the two AMMs, CurveY and Curve sUSD. The transaction

[1] A financial instruments that allow users to exchange crypto-assets (tokens).

dated back to July 31, 2020,[2] the arbitrageur borrowed 2.048 million USDC,[3] executed two exchanges, one from USDC to DAI[4] from Curve Y, and the other one in the opposite directions from Curve sUSD. At the end of them, she paid its debt with dYdX but realized a profit of 16.182 thousand USDC.

Arbitrage, while beneficial for synchronizing asset prices across different DeFi markets, can be exploited to perform attacks on the market as described above. The capability of composing DeFi protocols through external calls is essential due to the interconnected nature of DeFi platforms. However, this composability not only facilitates chained trading and arbitrage opportunities but also introduces opportunities for malicious actors. Therefore, regulating external calls through robust policies is imperative to mitigate potential attacks and maintain market integrity. Here, we propose history-based policies as a means to regulate how the various protocols are composed, enforcing good behavior among the involved parties. More precisely, our policy framework addresses security concerns by analyzing transaction patterns and protocol interactions to identify potential vulnerabilities and proactively strengthen defenses against malicious activities. Protecting the invocation of the function `executeOperation` with a policy ϕ in the function `flashLoan` enables us to identify and potentially mitigate profitable unwanted scenarios like the one described above (see Sect. 4).

3 TinySol with Policies

In this section, we introduce the core calculus for smart contracts, building upon the work of Bartoletti et al. [4]. First, we present the syntax and semantics of the enriched language, with a particular focus on the introduced policy component (Sects. 3.1 and 3.2). Following this, we formalize the execution of transactions using a labeled transition system (LTS). Finally, we review symbolic automata and show how we use them to define our policy checking mechanism (Sect. 3.3).

3.1 Syntax

We assume a set **Val** of *values* ranged by $v, k, \ldots$, a set **Const** of *constant names* $x, y, \ldots$, a set of *procedure names* $\mathtt{f}, \mathtt{g}, \ldots$. and a set **Addr** of *addresses* $\mathcal{X}, \mathcal{Y}, \ldots$, partitioned into *account addresses* $\mathcal{A}, \mathcal{B}, \ldots$ and *contract addresses* $\mathcal{C}, \mathcal{D}, \ldots$. As a notation, we write sequences in bold, e.g.$\boldsymbol{v}$ is a sequence of values, while ϵ denotes the empty sequence. We use $n, n', \ldots$ to range over $\mathbb{N}$, and $b, b', \ldots$ to range over boolean values.

In TinySol, a *contract* is a finite set of terms of the form $\mathtt{f}(\boldsymbol{x})\{S\}$, where S is a *statement*. Each term $\mathtt{f}(\boldsymbol{x})\{S\}$ is a contract function, where $\mathtt{f}$ is its name,

---

[2] Its address is 0xf7498a2546c3d70f49d83a2a5476fd9dcb6518100b2a731294d0d7b9f79f754a.

[3] USD Coin is a digital currency entirely backed by U.S. dollar assets: each USDC token represents a tokenized U.S. dollar, with a value closely mirroring that of one U.S. dollar.

[4] DAI is an Ethereum stablecoin that maintains a value close to USD using supply-controlling smart contracts, regulated by MakerDAO's MKR token holders.

$\boldsymbol{x}$ are its formal parameters (omitted when empty), and S is the function body. Moreover, we represent the internal state of a contract as a key-value store, formally, a partial function from keys $k \in \mathbf{Val}$ to values $v \in \mathbf{Val}$.

The syntax of TinySol is in Fig. 2. Many statements (Fig. 2, left) are standard in common imperative languages, so we only comment on the most relevant: `throw` raises an uncatchable exception, rolling-back the state; $\mathcal{X}.\mathtt{f}(\boldsymbol{v})\$n$ implements the external call mechanism calling the function `f` of the contract at address $\mathcal{X}$, passing the arguments $\boldsymbol{v}$, and transferring n units of currency to $\mathcal{X}$; $\phi[S]$ executes the statements S guarded by the policy ϕ, aborting the execution if the history generated by S is not compliant with ϕ.

Also, the expressions (Fig. 2, right) are quite standard. We assume all the usual constants, arithmetic, logic, and cryptographic operators. Peculiar of TinySol is the expression $!k$ that evaluates to *true* if the key k is bound in the contract store, *false* otherwise. Then, the expression $?k$ looks up the value of the key k in the contract store. Finally, the expression $E_1.E_2$ evaluates E_1 to produce the address of a contract $\mathcal{X}$ and then evalutes E_2 in that address.

A *policy* ϕ (Fig. 2, left) is a pair (re, E) where re is a regular expression that represents the sequence of function invocations, and E is a boolean expression. The regular expression syntax is standard: $\cdot$ denotes concatenation, + choices, and * zero or more repetitions. The alphabet is represented by patterns *patt* capturing function invocation and may contain variables. More precisely, $\mathcal{C}.\mathtt{f}(\boldsymbol{v})$ denotes an invocation to the function `f` of the contract with address $\mathcal{C}$ with argument $\boldsymbol{v}$; whereas $x.\mathtt{f}(\boldsymbol{v})$ is a call to function `f` with argument $\boldsymbol{v}$ where x is a placeholder for the address of the contract the function belongs to; $\mathcal{C}.\mathtt{f}(\boldsymbol{x})$ denotes a call where the arguments are variables; finally, $x.\mathtt{f}(\boldsymbol{x}')$ is a call where the address and the arguments are denoted by variables. The variables occurring in a pattern can be used by the expression E to express some conditions. These variables will be bound to concrete values while checking the policy compliance.

Finally, we assume a mapping Γ from addresses to contracts that we use to retrieve the definition of a contract. In order to allow for a uniform treatment of account and contract addresses, we require that $\Gamma(\mathcal{A}) = \{\mathtt{f}_{\mathtt{skip}}()\{\mathtt{skip}\}\}$ for all account addresses $\mathcal{A}$. Also, we use the following syntactic sugar: we write $\mathcal{X}.\mathtt{f}(\boldsymbol{v})$ to denote a call $\mathcal{X}.\mathtt{f}(\boldsymbol{v})\$n$, when there is no money transfer (i.e., $n = 0$). We write `if` E `then` S for `if` E `then` S `else skip`.

3.2 Semantics

We formalize the execution of TinySol contracts by providing operational semantics for both transactions and function contracts. In our semantics, the execution of a transaction is not deterministically started by a user account, and it triggers the execution of a contract function. A successful transaction results in a change of the blockchain state. We first present the semantics of TinySol statements and then the semantics of transactions. Note that our policy mechanism is activated during statement execution but affects transaction semantics since the corresponding transaction is reverted when a policy is violated.

S ::=	statement
$\texttt{skip}$	skip
$\mid \texttt{throw}$	exception
$\mid E{:=}E'$	store update
$\mid S; S'$	sequence
$\mid \texttt{if}\ E\ \texttt{then}\ S\ \texttt{else}\ S'$	conditional
$\mid \texttt{while}\ E\ \texttt{do}\ S$	loop
$\mid \phi[S]$	security policy
$\mid E_0.\texttt{f}(\boldsymbol{E_1})\$E_2$	call
$\phi ::= (re, E)$	policy
re ::=	regular expression
$patt$	basic event
$\mid \epsilon$	empty string
$\mid re \cdot re$	sequential composition
$\mid re + re$	choice
$\mid re^\star$	iteration

E ::=	expression
v	value
$\mid x$	const name
$\mid \mathcal{X}$	address
$\mid \texttt{op}\ \boldsymbol{E}$	operator
$\mid ?E$	key lookup
$\mid !E$	key bound?
$\mid E_1.E_2$	context
$patt$ ::=	function calls
$\mathcal{C}.\texttt{f}(\boldsymbol{v})$	ground
$\mid x.\texttt{f}(\boldsymbol{v})$	addr. variable
$\mid \mathcal{C}.\texttt{f}(\boldsymbol{x})$	arg. variables
$\mid x.\texttt{f}(\boldsymbol{x'})$	addr. and arg. variables

Fig. 2. Syntax of the language.

Statements. The semantics of a contract is given in terms of a transition system where configurations have the form:

$$\langle S, \sigma, \rho, \eta \rangle$$

where S is the sequence of statements to be executed; σ is the starting state; ρ is the variable environment; η is the history recording the sequence of function calls, made during the execution.

In detail, a *blockchain state* σ: **Addr** $\rightarrow$ (**Val** $\rightharpoonup$ **Val**) is a map from addresses to key-value stores. A key-value store is, in turn, a partial function from keys to values and represents the internal state of a smart contract. We use brackets to represent finite maps, e.g., $\{{}^{v_1}/_{x_1}, \cdots, {}^{v_n}/_{x_n}\}$ maps x_i to v_i, for $i \in 1..n$. As usual, when a key k is not bound to any value in $\sigma\,\mathcal{X}$, we write $\sigma\,\mathcal{X}\,k = \bot$. We postulate that for each address, there exists the distinct key `balance` recording the balance of that address. Moreover, when we refer to the key of an address $\mathcal{X}$, we use the notation $\mathcal{X}.k$ and call it a qualified key. Consequently, we write $\sigma(\mathcal{X}.k)$ for $\sigma\mathcal{X}k$. Below, we use the auxiliary operators $\sigma + \mathcal{X} : n$ and $\sigma - \mathcal{X} : n$ on states, to, respectively, increase/decrease the `balance` of $\mathcal{X}$ of n currency units:

$$\sigma \circ \mathcal{X} : n \;=\; \sigma\{{}^{(\sigma\mathcal{X}\,\texttt{balance})\,\circ\, n}/_{\mathcal{X}.\texttt{balance}}\} \qquad (\circ \in \{+, -\})$$

A variable environment ρ: **Const** $\rightharpoonup$ **Val** is a partial function from constant name to values used to provide values to function parameters (that once assigned cannot be changed) and to special names such as `value` and `sender` used inside the body of functions.

A history η is a sequence of function calls given by the following grammar:

$$\eta ::= \epsilon \mid \mathcal{X}.\mathtt{f}\,(\boldsymbol{v}) \mid \eta \cdot \eta$$

where ϵ is the empty history, $\mathcal{X}.\mathtt{f}\,(\boldsymbol{v})$ denotes the invocation of the function `f` of the contract with address $\mathcal{X}$ passing the values $\boldsymbol{v}$ as arguments.

We give the operational semantics of statements in a big-step style, where transitions have the form

$$\langle S, \sigma, \rho, \eta \rangle \xrightarrow{\mathcal{X}} \langle \sigma', \eta' \rangle$$

meaning that the statement S executed in the contract $\mathcal{X}$, in the state σ, with environment ρ, and history η terminates and produces the final state σ' and history η'. Note that our semantics is parameterized by the contract address in which the evaluation is taking place.

Figure 3 shows the semantics of expressions where we use `op` to denote syntactic operators and op for their semantic counterparts. The semantics of expression results in a value and its definition is quite standard: the environment ρ is used to evaluate constant names x, while the state σ is used to evaluate keys in $!\,E$ and $?E$. The semantics of $E_1.E_2$ first evaluates E_1 within a contract with address $\mathcal{X}$ producing an address $\mathcal{Y}$, then evaluates E_2 within the contract $\mathcal{Y}$. Note that expressions have no side effects, and all the semantic operators are *strict*, i.e. their result is $\perp$ if some operand is $\perp$.

The semantics of statements is in Fig. 4, and it is mostly standard, except for the last two rules. The rule [Policy] evaluates the policy framing $\phi[S]$ construct: it executes the statement S that (if it terminates) produces a state σ' and a history η'; then, it checks that η' is compliant with the policy ϕ through the predicate $\eta' \vDash_{\sigma',\rho,\mathcal{X}} \phi$ defined in Sect. 3.3. If the history meets the policy, the computation results in the pair $\langle \sigma', \eta' \rangle$, otherwise it is aborted.

The rule [Procedure call] handles a procedure call $E_0.\mathtt{f}\,(\boldsymbol{E}_1)\$E_2$ within the contract $\mathcal{X}$. The premise of the rule requires that (i) E_0 evaluates to an address $\mathcal{Y}$; (ii) E_2 evaluates to a non-negative number n, not exceeding the balance of $\mathcal{X}$; (iii) the contract at $\mathcal{Y}$ has a procedure named `f` with formal parameters $x_1 \cdots x_h$; (iv) $\boldsymbol{E}_1$ evaluates to a sequence of values of length h. If all these conditions hold, then the procedure body S is executed in a state where $\mathcal{X}$'s balance is decreased by n, $\mathcal{Y}$'s balance is increased by n, and in an environment where the formal parameters are bound to the actual ones, and the special names `sender` and `value` are bound, respectively, to $\mathcal{X}$ (the caller) and n (the value transferred to $\mathcal{Y}$). Executing S may affect both the store of $\mathcal{X}$ and, in case of procedure calls, also the store of other contracts.

Transactions. A *transaction* T is a term of the form $\mathcal{A} \xrightarrow{n} \mathcal{C} : \mathtt{f}\,(\boldsymbol{v})$, where $\mathcal{A}$ is the address of the caller, $\mathcal{C}$ is the address of the called contract, `f` is the

$$[\![v]\!]^{\mathcal{X}}_{\sigma,\rho} = v \qquad [\![x]\!]^{\mathcal{X}}_{\sigma,\rho} = \rho\, x \qquad [\![\mathcal{Y}]\!]^{\mathcal{X}}_{\sigma,\rho} = \mathcal{Y} \qquad [\![\mathbf{op}\boldsymbol{E}]\!]^{\mathcal{X}}_{\sigma,\rho} = \mathrm{op}\,[\![\boldsymbol{E}]\!]^{\mathcal{X}}_{\sigma,\rho} \qquad [\![E_1.E_2]\!]^{\mathcal{X}}_{\sigma,\rho} = [\![E_2]\!]^{[\![E_1]\!]^{\mathcal{X}}_{\sigma,\rho}}_{\sigma,\rho}$$

$$[\![?E]\!]^{\mathcal{X}}_{\sigma,\rho} = \sigma\,\mathcal{X}\,([\![E]\!]^{\mathcal{X}}_{\sigma,\rho}) \qquad [\![!E]\!]^{\mathcal{X}}_{\sigma,\rho} = \begin{cases} \mathit{true} & \text{if } [\![E]\!]^{\mathcal{X}}_{\sigma,\rho} \neq \bot \text{ and } \sigma\,\mathcal{X}\,([\![E]\!]^{\mathcal{X}}_{\sigma,\rho}) \neq \bot \\ \mathit{false} & \text{if } [\![E]\!]^{\mathcal{X}}_{\sigma,\rho} \neq \bot \text{ and } \sigma\,\mathcal{X}\,([\![E]\!]^{\mathcal{X}}_{\sigma,\rho}) = \bot \end{cases}$$

Fig. 3. Semantics of expressions.

$$\frac{}{\langle \mathtt{skip}, \sigma, \rho, \eta\rangle \xrightarrow{\mathcal{X}} \langle \sigma, \eta\rangle}\,[\text{SKIP}] \qquad \frac{[\![E]\!]^{\mathcal{X}}_{\sigma,\rho} = k \quad [\![E']\!]^{\mathcal{X}}_{\sigma,\rho} = v}{\langle E{:=}E', \sigma, \rho, \eta\rangle \xrightarrow{\mathcal{X}} \langle \sigma\{{}^{v}/_{\mathcal{X}.k}\}, \eta'\rangle}\,[\text{UPDATE}]$$

$$\frac{[\![E]\!]^{\mathcal{X}}_{\sigma,\rho} = b \quad b \in \{\mathit{true}, \mathit{false}\}}{\langle \mathtt{if}\ E\ \mathtt{then}\ S_{\mathit{true}}\ \mathtt{else}\ S_{\mathit{false}}, \sigma, \rho, \eta\rangle \xrightarrow{\mathcal{X}} \langle S_b, \eta'\rangle}\,[\text{CONDITION}] \qquad \frac{\langle S_0, \sigma, \rho, \eta\rangle \xrightarrow{\mathcal{X}} \langle \sigma', \eta'\rangle}{\langle S_0; S_1, \sigma, \rho, \eta\rangle \xrightarrow{\mathcal{X}} \langle \sigma', \eta'\rangle}\,[\text{SEQUENCE}]$$

$$\frac{[\![E]\!]^{\mathcal{X}}_{\sigma,\rho} = \mathit{false}}{\langle \mathtt{while}\ E\ \mathtt{do}\ S, \sigma, \rho, \eta\rangle \xrightarrow{\mathcal{X}} \langle \sigma, \eta\rangle}\,[\text{WHILE FALSE}] \qquad \frac{[\![E]\!]^{\mathcal{X}}_{\sigma,\rho} = \mathit{true} \quad \langle S, \sigma, \rho, \eta\rangle \xrightarrow{\mathcal{X}} \langle \sigma', \eta'\rangle}{\langle \mathtt{while}\ E\ \mathtt{do}\ S, \sigma, \rho, \eta\rangle \xrightarrow{\mathcal{X}} \langle \sigma', \eta'\rangle}\,[\text{WHILE TRUE}]$$

$$\frac{\langle S, \sigma, \rho, \eta\rangle \xrightarrow{\mathcal{X}} \langle \sigma', \eta'\rangle \quad \eta' \vDash_{\sigma',\rho,\mathcal{X}} \phi}{\langle \phi[S], \sigma, \rho, \eta\rangle \xrightarrow{\mathcal{X}} \langle \sigma', \eta'\rangle}\,[\text{POLICY}]$$

$$\frac{\begin{array}{lll} [\![E_0]\!]^{\mathcal{X}}_{\sigma,\rho} = \mathcal{Y} & \mathtt{f}(\boldsymbol{x})\{S\} \in \Gamma(\mathcal{Y}) & \eta' = \eta :: \mathcal{Y} : f(v) \\ [\![\boldsymbol{E_1}]\!]^{\mathcal{X}}_{\sigma,\rho} = \boldsymbol{v} & \sigma' = \sigma - \mathcal{X} : n + \mathcal{Y} : n & \langle S, \sigma', \rho', \eta'\rangle \xrightarrow{\mathcal{X}} \langle \sigma'', \eta''\rangle \\ [\![E_2]\!]^{\mathcal{X}}_{\sigma,\rho} = n & \rho' = \{{}^{\mathcal{X}}/_{\mathtt{sender}}, {}^{n}/_{\mathtt{value}}, {}^{\boldsymbol{v}}/_{\boldsymbol{x}}\} & \end{array}}{\langle E_0.\mathtt{f}(\boldsymbol{E_1})\$E_2, \sigma, \rho, \eta\rangle \xrightarrow{\mathcal{X}} \langle \sigma'', \eta''\rangle}\,[\text{PROCEDURE CALL}]$$

Fig. 4. Semantics of statements.

called procedure, n is the value transferred from $\mathcal{A}$ to $\mathbb{C}$, and $\boldsymbol{v}$ is the sequence of actual parameters. We formalize the execution of a transaction T through a transition system where configurations have the form $\langle \sigma, \eta\rangle$ describing the blockchain state where T takes place producing a new configuration $\langle \sigma', \eta'\rangle$. Executing the transaction causes the execution of the contract function $\mathtt{f}$. The call of $\mathtt{f}$ is defined by the following rules:

$$\frac{\begin{array}{c} \mathtt{f}(\boldsymbol{x})\{S\} \in \Gamma(\mathbb{C}) \quad \sigma\,\mathcal{A}\,\mathtt{balance} \geq n \\ \langle S, \sigma - \mathcal{A} : n + \mathbb{C} : n, \{{}^{\mathcal{A}}/_{\mathtt{sender}}, {}^{n}/_{\mathtt{value}}, {}^{\boldsymbol{v}}/_{\boldsymbol{x}}\}, \eta\rangle \xrightarrow{\mathbb{C}} \langle \sigma', \eta'\rangle \end{array}}{\langle \sigma, \eta\rangle \xrightarrow{\mathcal{A} \xrightarrow{n} \mathbb{C}:\mathtt{f}(\boldsymbol{v})} \langle \sigma', \eta'\rangle}\,[\text{Tx1}]$$

$$\frac{\begin{array}{c} \mathtt{f}(\boldsymbol{x})\{S\} \in \Gamma(\mathbb{C}) \\ \big(\sigma\,\mathcal{A}\,\mathtt{balance} < n \quad \text{or} \quad \langle S, \sigma - \mathcal{A} : n + \mathbb{C} : n, \{{}^{\mathcal{A}}/_{\mathtt{sender}}, {}^{n}/_{\mathtt{value}}, {}^{\boldsymbol{v}}/_{\boldsymbol{x}}\}, \eta\rangle \not\rightarrow\big) \end{array}}{\langle \sigma, \eta\rangle \xrightarrow{\mathcal{A} \xrightarrow{n} \mathbb{C}:\mathtt{f}(\boldsymbol{v})} \langle \sigma, \eta\rangle}\,[\text{Tx2}]$$

Rule [Tx1] handles the case where the transaction is successful: this happens when $\mathcal{A}$'s balance is at least n, and the procedure call terminates in a non-error state, meaning that all policies defined in $\mathtt{f}$ are satisfied. Note that n units of currency are transferred to $\mathbb{C}$ *before* starting to execute $\mathtt{f}$, and that the names $\mathtt{sender}$

and `value` are set, respectively, to $\mathcal{A}$ and n. Instead, [Tx2] applies either when $\mathcal{A}$'s balance is not enough, or the execution of `f` fails (this also covers the case when `f` does not terminate or during the execution of the function body is not compliant with all the policies of function `f`). In these cases, T does not alter the state $\langle \sigma, \eta \rangle \xrightarrow{\mathsf{T}} \langle \sigma, \eta \rangle$.

We naturally extend the semantics above when we have a sequence of transactions $[\mathsf{T}_1, \mathsf{T}_2, \cdots, \mathsf{T}_n]$, formally:

$$\langle \sigma_0, \eta_0 \rangle \xrightarrow{\mathsf{T}_1} \langle \sigma_1, \eta_1 \rangle \xrightarrow{\mathsf{T}_2} \langle \sigma_2, \eta_2 \rangle \cdots \xrightarrow{\mathsf{T}_n} \langle \sigma_n, \eta_n \rangle$$

Note that erroneous transactions occur in the execution of the sequence $[\mathsf{T}_1, \mathsf{T}_2, \cdots, \mathsf{T}_n]$ does not effect the semantics, since rule [Tx2] leaves the state and the history unchanged.

3.3 Checking Policies

In this section, we describe how we ensure that a history η complies with a policy $\phi = (re, E)$. Intuitively, our verification procedure consists of two steps: (*i*) we check that η belongs to the language of re, by transforming re into a symbolic automaton; (*ii*) we evaluate the assertion E in the current state and check that it evaluates to true. If both steps succeed, η complies with ϕ, otherwise, it does not. Below, we first review the basic notions of symbolic regular expressions and automata [16], and then we detail the two steps above.

Symbolic automata are generalizations of finite automata where the alphabet is a Boolean algebra, and transitions are labeled by predicates over such algebra. This allows symbolic automata to operate over infinite alphabets, such as the set of rational numbers, while retaining the decidability properties of their finite counterparts. Similarly, symbolic regular expressions are a generalization of regular expressions operating over a Boolean algebra.

An *effective Boolean algebra* $\mathcal{A}$ is a tuple

$$(\mathfrak{D}, \Psi, [\![\_]\!], \top, \bot, \vee, \wedge, \neg) \tag{1}$$

where $\mathfrak{D}$ is a (possibly infinite) set of *domain elements*; Ψ is a set of *predicates* over $\mathfrak{D}$ closed under the logical connectives $\vee, \wedge, \neg$; the component $[\![\_]\!] : \Psi \to 2^{\mathfrak{D}}$ is a *denotation function* such that $[\![\top]\!] = \mathfrak{D}$, $[\![\bot]\!] = \emptyset$, and $\forall \psi_1, \psi_2 \in \Psi, [\![\psi_1 \vee \psi_2]\!] = [\![\psi_1]\!] \cup [\![\psi_2]\!]$, and $[\![\neg \psi_1]\!] = \mathfrak{D} \setminus [\![\psi_1]\!]$. Moreover, when $[\![\psi_1]\!] \neq \emptyset$, then the predicate ψ_1 is *satisfiable*. We require that checking satisfiability is decidable.

Example 1 (Linear Integer Arithmetic). As an example of effective Boolean algebra, consider $(\mathbb{Z}, \Psi, [\![\cdot]\!], \bot, \top, \vee, \wedge, \neg)$, where $\mathbb{Z}$ is the set of integer numbers. The set Ψ contains all quantifier-free formulas on integer linear arithmetic, namely, formulas such as $\psi_{>0}(x) \triangleq x > 0$ and $\psi_{\text{odd}}(x) \triangleq x\%2 = 1$. Given a formula ψ, $[\![\psi]\!]$ denotes the set of integer satisfying it; $\bot, \top, \vee, \wedge, \neg$ represent the always false, true predicates and the standard logical connectives. It is noteworthy that satisfiability is decidable for such a Boolean algebra. Indeed, given a formula ψ, the interpretation function $[\![\psi]\!]$ can use an SMT solver for checking the satisfiability and model generation. For example, $[\![\psi_{>0}(x)]\!]$ is true if there exists an integer x such that $x > 0$, and $[\![\psi_{\text{odd}}(x)]\!]$ is true if there exists an integer x such that $x\%2 = 1$. Boolean operations allow for the combination and manipulation of these predicates within algebra.

Given an effective Boolean algebra $(\mathfrak{D}, \Psi, [\![\_]\!], \top, \bot, \vee, \wedge, \neg)$, a *symbolic regular expression* is defined as follows:

- The constants ε and $\emptyset$ are symbolic regular expressions denoting the languages $\{\varepsilon\}$ and $\emptyset$, respectively.
- Any predicate $\psi \in \Psi$ is a symbolic regular expression that accepts the language defined as $\mathcal{L}(\psi) = [\![\psi]\!]$.
- Given symbolic regular expressions sre_1 and sre_2, the expressions $sre_1 + sre_2$, $sre_1 \cdot sre_2$, and sre_1^* are symbolic regular expressions.

Elements of $\mathfrak{D}$ are *characters*. A *word* over $\mathfrak{D}$ is a sequence $a_1 \dots a_m$, where $a_i \in \mathfrak{D}$, $i = 1, \dots, m$. If $m = 0$, then we have the *empty* word, denoted by ε. The set of all words over $\mathfrak{D}$ is denoted by $\mathfrak{D}^\star$. Any language defined by a symbolic regular expression is a *symbolic regular language*.

A *symbolic nondeterministic finite automaton with epsilon transitions*, *s-ϵNFA* is a quintuple

$$\mathcal{N} = (\mathcal{A}, Q, \Delta, I, F)$$

where the alphabet $\mathcal{A}$ is an effective Boolean algebra; Q is a finite set of *states*; $\Delta \subseteq Q \times (\Psi \cup \{\epsilon\}) \times Q$ is a finite set of *transitions*; $I \subseteq Q$ is the set of *initial states*; and $F \subseteq Q$ is the set of *final states*. The language of $\mathcal{N}$, denoted by $\mathcal{L}(\mathcal{N})$ is the set of words $w \in \mathfrak{D}^\star$ such that either $w = \varepsilon$ or $w = a_0 \dots a_k$ and there exist a sequence of transitions $(q_i, \psi_i, q_{i+1}) \in \Delta$ and $a_i \in [\![\psi_i]\!]$ for $i \in [0, k]$, with $q_0 \in I$ and $q_k \in F$.

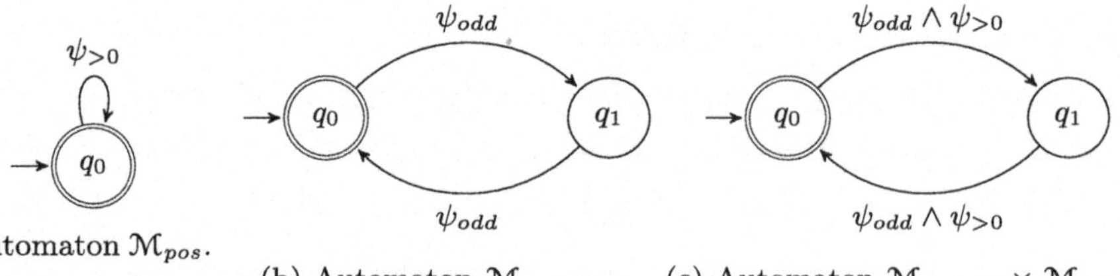

(a) Automaton $\mathcal{M}_{pos}$. (b) Automaton $\mathcal{M}_{ev/odd}$. (c) Automaton $\mathcal{M}_{ev/odd} \times \mathcal{M}_{pos}$.

Fig. 5. Symbolic automata built on the Boolean algebra of Example 1.

Example 2. Consider again the Boolean algebra of Example 1. Figure 5 illustrates three examples of *s-ϵNFAs*, $\mathcal{M}_{\text{pos}}$, $\mathcal{M}_{\text{ev/odd}}$, and $\mathcal{M}_{\text{ev/odd}} \times \mathcal{M}_{\text{pos}}$, built on this algebra and where $\psi_{>0}(x) \wedge \psi_{\text{odd}}(x)$ denote the formula from Example 1.

The automaton $\mathcal{M}_{\text{pos}}$ accepts all strings consisting only of positive numbers, while $\mathcal{M}_{\text{ev/odd}}$ accepts all strings of even length consisting only of odd numbers. For example, $\mathcal{M}_{\text{ev/odd}}$ accepts the string $2, 4, 6, 2$ (we separate characters with a comma for clarity, but the comma is not in the language) and rejects the strings $2, 4, 6$ and $51, 26$. The automaton $\mathcal{M}_{\text{ev/odd}} \times \mathcal{M}_{\text{pos}}$ is obtained by the product of $\mathcal{M}_{\text{pos}}$ and $\mathcal{M}_{\text{ev/odd}}$, and accepts the language $\mathcal{L}(\mathcal{M}_{\text{pos}}) \cap \mathcal{L}(\mathcal{M}_{\text{ev/odd}})$.

Tamm and Veanes [16] proved that we can apply the counterpart of Thompson's construction [17,20] to a symbolic regular expression to derive an *s-ϵNFA*. For further details on symbolic regular expressions and automata, we refer the interested reader to [16].

Now we define $\mathcal{P} = (\mathfrak{D}, \Psi, [\![\_]\!], \top, \bot, \vee, \wedge, \neg)$ the Boolean algebra for our policies, as follows:

- $\mathfrak{D}$ is the set of ground patterns generated by the first production *patt* of Fig. 2, namely, $\mathfrak{D} = \{p \in \mathit{patt} \mid p = \mathcal{C}.\mathtt{f}(\boldsymbol{v})\}$.
- Ψ is the set of pattern predicates defined as follows. For each pattern $p \in \mathit{patt}$ we introduce a predicate $\psi_p(x) \triangleq x = p$ that holds when the argument x (a ground pattern from $\mathfrak{D}$) matches p for some substitution θ of variables in p. Therefore, we define the set of predicates $\Psi = \{\psi_p \mid \psi_p \text{ for } p \in \mathit{patt}\}$ and we close it under logical connectives $\vee, \wedge, \neg$.
- for each pattern predicate ψ_p, $[\![\psi_p]\!] = \{q \mid \psi_p(q) \text{ holds for some } \theta\}$.

We note that the Boolean algebra $\mathcal{P}$ is effective because $[\![\psi_p]\!] \neq \emptyset$ is decidable. Indeed, at least two approaches exist to check the satisfiability of a pattern predicate ψ_p. The first approach involves a straightforward matching between the argument x (a ground pattern) and the pattern p, finding a possible assignment to the variables of p that makes them syntactically equal.

The second approach instead involves encoding our Boolean algebra in the theory of the uninterpreted function with equality and using a standard SMT solver to check satisfiability.

To ensure that a history η complies with a policy $\phi = (re, E)$ within the contract $\mathcal{X}$ and in the state σ', in symbols $\eta' \vDash_{\sigma', \rho, \mathcal{X}} \phi$, we proceed as follows. First, we transform re into a symbolic regular expression predicating on the pattern of the policy and build the corresponding *s-ϵNFA* $\mathcal{N}$.

Proposition 1 of [16] ensures that the *s-ϵNFA* accepts the same language of the symbolic regular expression. Then we check if the history η' belongs to the language $\mathcal{L}(\mathcal{N})$: this means that if there exists a sequence of transitions $q_0 \xrightarrow{p_1} \dots \xrightarrow{p_n} q_f$ for $\eta' = p_1 \dots p_n$ where each transition is possible for some substitution θ_i. Therefore, η' belongs to the language $\mathcal{L}(\mathcal{N})$ holds for some $\theta' = \theta_1 \dots \theta_n$. Then, we evaluate the assertion $[\![E]\!]_{\sigma', \rho \cdot \theta'}$ in the state σ' and in the environment ρ extended with the substitution θ' and check that it evaluates to true. If all the steps above succeed, η' complies with ϕ, otherwise, it does not: when the history η' does not belong to the language of $\mathcal{N}$ ($\eta' \notin \mathcal{L}(\mathcal{N})$) or E evaluates to false, the execution is aborted because of a policy violation.

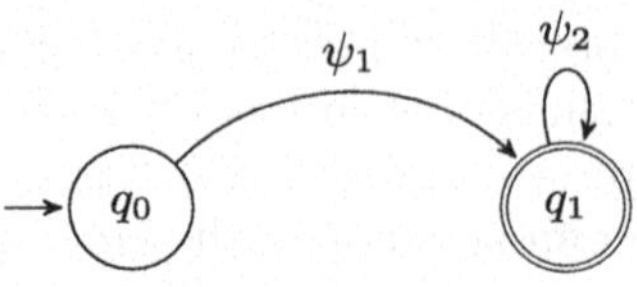

Fig. 6. Automaton $\mathcal{N}$ for the symbolic regular expression *sre* of Example 3.

Example 3. Consider a policy $\phi = (re, E)$ where $re = x.\mathtt{f}_1(y) \cdot z.\mathtt{f}_2(w)^\star$ and $E = (y > 0 \wedge w = 13)$. We first transform re into a symbolic regular expression sre as follows: take the predicates $\psi_1 = x.\mathtt{f}_1(y)$ and $\psi_2 = z.\mathtt{f}_2(w)$, then $sre = \psi_1 \cdot \psi_2^\star$ by simply lifting the patterns of re in the corresponding predicates. From this symbolic regular expression, we build the corresponding automaton $\mathcal{N}$ shown in Fig. 6. Given a history $\eta = c.\mathtt{f}_1(18) \cdot d.\mathtt{f}_2(13) \cdot d.\mathtt{f}_2(13)$, it is easy to check that $\eta \in \mathcal{L}(\mathcal{N})$ with variables assignment $\theta = \{y \mapsto 18, x \mapsto c, z \mapsto d, w \mapsto 13\}$, so η satisfies re. Then, we evaluate E in a state σ and environment ρ extended with θ, namely $[\![E]\!]_{\sigma,\rho\cdot\theta} = (y > 0 \wedge w = 13)$ that evaluates to true. Therefore, history η is compliant with the policy ϕ.

4 Detecting Arbitrage

This section shows how our policy framework can prevent the arbitrage shown in Fig. 1 and illustrates how our policy checking mechanism works. We introduce a policy to protect the call to `executeOperation()` in Listing 1.1 for detecting sequences of function calls that may indicate the attempt of an arbitrage. The idea is that our policy detects sequences of invocations to the swap method to transfers of tokens in opposing directions involving the same token types and different AMMs. The policy will be parametric on the contracts performing the transfers and on the types of tokens. Below, we denote with `User`, `dYdX`, `CurveY`, and `CurvesUSD` the addresses of the contracts involved in Fig. 1 and with `Flash` the address of the contract created by the user implementing the `executeOperation` function. Moreover, we use τ_a and τ_b to indicate the token types USDC and DAI, respectively. Also, we assume that the market price for token types τ_a and τ_b is provided by an Oracle contract with address `O`. Assume `User` requests a `loan` of 2048 million tokens of type τ_a and invokes the `flashLoan` function of Listing 1.2 passing the address of `Flash` as first parameter:

```
function executeOperation(
  asset, amount, fee, address, memory
) {
  // First Swap on CurveY
  CurveY.swap(User, USDC, DAI, 2048M);

  // Get New Token Balance after the first swap
  uint256 toBalance = IERC20(DAI).balanceOf(address(this));
  require(toBalance > 0, "Swap on CurveY failed to return any tokens");

  // Second Swap on CurvesUSD
```

```
CurvesUSD.swap(User, DAI, USDC, 2028M);

// Get New Token Balance after the second swap
uint256 finalBalance = IERC20(USDC).balanceOf(address(this));
require(finalBalance > 0, "Swap on CurvesUSD failed to return any tokens");

// Ensure that final balance is enough to repay the loan with fee
require(finalBalance >= amount.add(fee), "Arbitrage trade did not return
     enough tokens to repay the loan");
```

Listing 1.2. Function implementing an arbitrage to be used with `flashLoan`.

The execution of `flashLoan()` results in the following sequence of calls:

1. $\texttt{dYdX.balance()}$
2. $\texttt{dYdX.transfer}(\tau_a, \texttt{Flash}, \texttt{loan})$
3. $\texttt{Flash.executeOperation()}$
4. $\texttt{CurveY.swap}(\texttt{User}, \tau_a, \tau_b, \texttt{amount}_1)$
5. $\texttt{CurvesUSD.swap}(\texttt{User}, \tau_b, \tau_a, \texttt{amount}_2)$
6. $\texttt{Flash.payback(dYdX)}$

First, the `dYdX` contract performs some sanity checks, during these checks, it invokes the `dYdX.balance()` function. Then, the requested amounts of tokens are transferred to the contract `Flash` via a call to $\texttt{dYdX.transfer}(\tau_a, \texttt{Flash}, \texttt{loan})$. This transfer of tokens is followed by the invocation of `executeOperation()` of the `Flash` contract that executes the two swaps: the first swap concerns $\texttt{amount}_1$ (2048 million) of tokens of type τ_a to acquire $\texttt{amount}_2$ (2028 million) tokens of type τ_b on `CurveY` ($\texttt{CurveY.swap}(\texttt{User}, \tau_a, \tau_b, \texttt{amount}_1)$). Then, the function performs the reverse swap on `CurvesUSD` ($\texttt{CurvesUSD.swap}(\texttt{User}, \tau_b, \tau_a, \texttt{amount}_2)$). After these swaps, the `Flash` contract repays its debt to the `dYdX`, including additional fees, via the call to the function `Flash.payback(dYdX)`.

```
// Execute the operation in the receiver contract
φ { if not receiverAddress.executeOperation(asset, amount, fee, msg.sender,
   params):
   raise error "FlashLoan execution failed" }
```

Listing 1.3. Policy introduction in the `flashloan`.

We prevent the execution of the arbitrage by enclosing the call to the function `executeOperation` inside a policy framing construct. The amended line of code of the `flashLoan` function is shown in Listing 1.3. The policy ϕ blocks the execution when it detects a sequence of swaps of opposing directions involving the same token types across different AMMs (steps 4 and 5 of the flow described above), that AMMs have a different token ratio, and that the token price significantly differs from their market price provided by the oracle O. Formally, the policy $\phi = (re, E)$ is defined as follows:

$$
\begin{aligned}
re =& a.\texttt{swap}(x, y, z) \cdot b.\texttt{swap}(x', z', y') \\
E =& (a \neq b \wedge x = x' \wedge \frac{a.y}{a.z} = \frac{b.z'}{b.y'} \wedge \left|\frac{a.y - \texttt{O}.y}{a.z - \texttt{O}.z}\right| \leq \epsilon \wedge \left|\frac{b.z' - \texttt{O}.z'}{b.y' - \texttt{O}.y'}\right| \leq \epsilon)
\end{aligned}
$$

where the regular expression re detects the sequence of the two consecutive swaps, while the assertion E holds when the involved AMMs are different ($a \neq b$), the calling contract is the same ($x = x'$), the ratio between the exchanged token is the same ($\frac{a.y}{a.z} = \frac{b.z'}{b.y'}$), and the ratio of the difference between the exchanged tokens of the AMMs and the market price of each asset as given by contract Oracle O to is below a small threshold ϵ. Note that in the assertion E we assume that the amount of the token type y exchanged through a swap on the AMM a is accessed using the syntax $a.y$. We use the same syntax for the other token types and AMMs, and for accessing the market price of each token type via the oracle O. We first transform re into the symbolic regular expression $\psi_1 \cdot \psi_2$ where $\psi_1 = a.\texttt{swap}(x, y, z)$ and $\psi_2 = b.\texttt{swap}(x', z', y')$, and then build the corresponding automaton $\mathcal{A}$ shown in Fig. 7. Given $\eta = \texttt{CurveY.swap}(\texttt{User}, \tau_\mathsf{a}, \tau_\mathsf{b}, \texttt{amount}_1) \cdot \texttt{CurvesUSD.swap}(\texttt{User}, \tau_\mathsf{b}, \tau_\mathsf{a}, \texttt{amount}_2)$, it is easy to check that $\eta \in \mathfrak{L}(\mathcal{A})$ with variables assignment $\theta = \{a \mapsto \texttt{CurveY}, b \mapsto \texttt{CurvesUSD}, x \mapsto \texttt{User}, x' \mapsto \texttt{User}, y \mapsto \tau_\mathsf{a}, z \mapsto \tau_\mathsf{b}, y' \mapsto \tau_\mathsf{b}, z' \mapsto \tau_\mathsf{a}\}$. Then, we evaluate E in a state σ and environment ρ extended with θ, namely $[\![E]\!]_{\sigma,\rho\cdot\theta}$, that evaluates to false because the ratio of between the exchanged tokens ($\frac{\texttt{CurveY}.\tau_\mathsf{a}}{\texttt{CurveY}.\tau_\mathsf{b}} \neq \frac{\texttt{CurvesUSD}.\tau_\mathsf{a}}{\texttt{CurvesUSD}.\tau_\mathsf{b}}$) differs. Indeed, as shown in Fig. 1, the price ratio for CurveY is 1.010 USDC/DAI, while for CurvesUSD is 1.918 USDC/DAI. This discrepancy confirms the attempt of an arbitrage, so the history η is not compliant with the policy ϕ, and the execution of flashLoan is reverted.

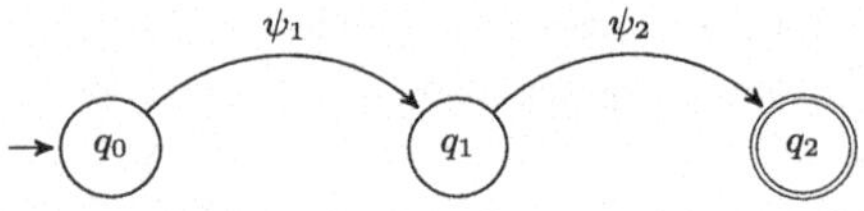

Fig. 7. Automaton $\mathcal{A}$ for the policy preventing flash-loan-based arbitrages.

5 Related Work

We compare our work with the relevant literature. Over the past few decades, the formalism of symbolic automata has been extensively studied [6,7,16], and applied to solve different verification tasks. Here, we rely on the results of Tamm and Veanes in [16] concerning the theory of symbolic regular languages and on the relation between symbolic automata and symbolic regular expression. To the best of our knowledge, this is the first paper that uses symbolic automata to express and enforce security policy following Schneider [14].

To formally present our policy mechanism, we extend TinySol, the minimal calculus for the Solidity contract introduced by Bartoletti et al. [4]. We enhanced the language by introducing a way to express policy over the execution history and the construct of policy framing to enforce them. Moreover, we extended the semantics accordingly and defined a procedure for checking policies at run-time.

The concept of history-based policies has been explored in previous works, notably by Skalka and Smith [15] and Bartoletti et al. [2,3]. Skalka and Smith [15] combine type and effect systems with model-checking to extract a history expression from the code automatically and to verify that a higher-order program satisfies a policy ϕ. Their approach allows the static enforcement of history- and stack-based security mechanisms. Bartoletti et al. [2] uses a similar mechanism to express access control policies over resources and to verify that objects and resources are created and manipulated according to such policies. The main difference between these papers and ours is that their verification procedure occurs statically and on the code of programs, whereas our verification occurs at run-time. In particular, their verification procedures require the code of the whole program or at least an abstract description of the behavior of all called functions, given in terms of types and effects. Here, we do not have this assumption, so we can easily deal with open-world scenarios like DeFi, where a contract can be called by other unknown contracts.

Several papers address price manipulation vulnerabilities in DeFi and propose detection tools for smart contracts, such as DeFiRanger [21], DeFiScanner [19], DeFiTainter [9], BLOCKEYE [21], and FlashSyn [5]. DeFiRanger [21] builds a cash flow tree (CFT) from Ethereum transaction data to reflect token transfers and accounts, giving a DeFi meaning to blockchain transactions. Wang et al. [19] uses taint analysis to uncover price manipulation vulnerabilities in DeFi protocols. BLOCKEYE [18] performs automated and accurate real-time attack detection of Ethereum-based DeFi protocols by symbolic reasoning techniques. FlashSyn [5] automatically synthesizes adversarial transactions exploiting DeFi protocols via flash loans, overcoming complex DeFi logic and search space challenges with a synthesis-via-approximation technique. Unlike the above papers, our work focuses on formal verification, ensuring run-time security by validating histories produced by smart contract execution. This methodology guarantees the absence of security violations during execution, setting it apart from existing solutions. Finally, Zhou et al. in [22] introduced a method based on analyzing internal transactions to detect and prevent attacks within DeFi platforms. They emphasize policy enforcement and vulnerability management amidst DeFi's composability, especially concerning arbitrage scenarios utilizing external calls. Although the goal of this paper is similar to ours, their focus is primarily on automated revenue extraction through trading strategies. In contrast, our smart contract calculus emphasizes formal methods and run-time verification for robust policy enforcement and vulnerability management.

6 Conclusion

In this paper, we introduced a formal framework for specifying and enforcing security policies to regulate external calls in smart contracts. We enhanced TinySol, a core calculus for smart contracts, by incorporating constructs that allow developers to specify their policies at the code level, and a run-time verification mechanism to check that the called code is compliant with the policy.

In future work, we plan to study how our mechanism can be implemented. We envisage two possible directions: implementing the policy checking mechanism inside the EVM or encoding it directly within Solidity. Moreover, we want to explore other profitable scenarios within the DeFi ecosystem that could leverage our policy framework to prevent speculative actions. Finally, we will study if we can verify that an external call satisfies the policies up-front the transaction without actually running it.

Acknowledgments. Work partially supported by projects SERICS (PE00000014) and PRIN AM∀DEUS (P2022EPPHM) under the MUR National Recovery and Resilience Plan funded by the European Union - NextGenerationEU.

References

1. Aave Documentation V3: Flash loans (2023). https://docs.aave.com/developers/guides/flash-loans. Accessed Aug 2024
2. Bartoletti, M., Degano, P., Ferrari, G.L.: History-based access control with local policies. In: Sassone, V. (ed.) FoSSaCS 2005. LNCS, vol. 3441, pp. 316–332. Springer, Heidelberg (2005). https://doi.org/10.1007/978-3-540-31982-5_20
3. Bartoletti, M., Degano, P., Ferrari, G., Zunino, R.: Local policies for resource usage analysis. ACM Trans. Program. Lang. Syst. **31**(6), 23:1–23:43 (2009)
4. Bartoletti, M., Galletta, L., Murgia, M.: A minimal core calculus for solidity contracts. In: Pérez-Solà, C., Navarro-Arribas, G., Biryukov, A., Garcia-Alfaro, J. (eds.) DPM/CBT -2019. LNCS, vol. 11737, pp. 233–243. Springer, Cham (2019). https://doi.org/10.1007/978-3-030-31500-9_15
5. Chen, Z., Beillahi, S.M., Long, F.: FlashSYN: flash loan attack synthesis via counter example driven approximation. In: Proceedings of the IEEE/ACM 46th International Conference on Software Engineering, pp. 1–13 (2024)
6. Drews, S., D'Antoni, L.: Learning symbolic automata. In: Legay, A., Margaria, T. (eds.) TACAS 2017. LNCS, vol. 10205, pp. 173–189. Springer, Heidelberg (2017). https://doi.org/10.1007/978-3-662-54577-5_10
7. Fisman, D., Frenkel, H., Zilles, S.: Inferring symbolic automata. Logic. Methods Comput. Sci. **19** (2023)
8. Fáwọlé, J.: A broad overview of reentrancy attacks in solidity contracts (2023). https://www.quicknode.com/guides/ethereum-development/smart-contracts/a-broad-overview-of-reentrancy-attacks-in-solidity-contracts. Accessed Aug 2024
9. Kong, Q., Chen, J., Wang, Y., Jiang, Z., Zheng, Z.: Defitainter: detecting price manipulation vulnerabilities in DeFI protocols. In: Proceedings of the 32nd ACM SIGSOFT International Symposium on Software Testing and Analysis, pp. 1144–1156 (2023)
10. Kozen, D.: Language-based security: invited lecture. In: Kutyłowski, M., Pacholski, L., Wierzbicki, T. (eds.) MFCS 1999. LNCS, vol. 1672, pp. 284–298. Springer, Heidelberg (1999). https://doi.org/10.1007/3-540-48340-3_26
11. Milionis, J., Moallemi, C.C., Roughgarden, T.: Automated market making and arbitrage profits in the presence of fees. arXiv preprint arXiv:2305.14604 (2023)
12. OWASP Project: Reentrancy attack (2024). https://owasp.org/www-project-smart-contract-top-10/2023/en/src/SC01-reentrancy-attacks.html. Accessed Aug 2024

13. Qin, K., Zhou, L., Livshits, B., Gervais, A.: Attacking the DeFi ecosystem with flash loans for fun and profit. In: Borisov, N., Diaz, C. (eds.) FC 2021. LNCS, vol. 12674, pp. 3–32. Springer, Heidelberg (2021). https://doi.org/10.1007/978-3-662-64322-8_1
14. Schneider, F.B.: Enforceable security policies. ACM Trans. Inf. Syst. Secur. (TISSEC) **3**(1), 30–50 (2000)
15. Skalka, C., Smith, S.: History effects and verification. In: Chin, W.-N. (ed.) APLAS 2004. LNCS, vol. 3302, pp. 107–128. Springer, Heidelberg (2004). https://doi.org/10.1007/978-3-540-30477-7_8
16. Tamm, H., Veanes, M.: Theoretical aspects of symbolic automata. In: Tjoa, A.M., Bellatreche, L., Biffl, S., van Leeuwen, J., Wiedermann, J. (eds.) SOFSEM 2018. LNCS, vol. 10706, pp. 428–441. Springer, Cham (2018). https://doi.org/10.1007/978-3-319-73117-9_30
17. Thompson, K.: Programming techniques: regular expression search algorithm. Commun. ACM **11**(6), 419–422 (1968)
18. Wang, B., et al.: Blockeye: hunting for DeFI attacks on blockchain. In: 2021 IEEE/ACM 43rd International Conference on Software Engineering: Companion Proceedings (ICSE-Companion), pp. 17–20. IEEE (2021)
19. Wang, D., et al.: Towards a first step to understand flash loan and its applications in DeFI ecosystem. In: Proceedings of the Ninth International Workshop on Security in Blockchain and Cloud Computing, pp. 23–28 (2021)
20. Watson, B.W.: A taxonomy of finite automata construction algorithms. Computing Science Notes, Technische Universiteit Eindhoven (1993)
21. Wu, S., et al.: Defiranger: detecting DeFI price manipulation attacks. IEEE Trans. Depend. Secure Comput. 1–15 (2023)
22. Zhou, L., Qin, K., Cully, A., Livshits, B., Gervais, A.: On the just-in-time discovery of profit-generating transactions in DeFI protocols. In: 2021 IEEE Symposium on Security and Privacy (SP), pp. 919–936. IEEE (2021)

Exploiting Assumptions for Effective Monitoring of Real-Time Properties Under Partial Observability

Alessandro Cimatti[1], Thomas M. Grosen[2](✉), Kim G. Larsen[2], Stefano Tonetta[1], and Martin Zimmermann[2]

[1] Fondazione Bruno Kessler, Trento, Italy
{cimatti,tonettas}@fbk.eu

[2] Aalborg University, Aalborg, Denmark
{tmgr,kgl,mzi}@cs.aau.dk

Abstract. Runtime verification of temporal properties over timed sequences of observations is crucial in various applications within cyber-physical systems ranging from autonomous vehicles over smart grids to medical devices. In this paper, we are addressing the challenge of effectively predicting the failure or success of properties in a continuous real-time setting. Our approach allows predictions to exploit assumptions on the system being monitored and supports predictions of non-observable system behaviour (e.g. internal faults). More concretely, in our approach properties are expressed in Metric Interval Temporal Logic (MITL), assumptions on the monitored system are specified in terms of Timed Automata, and observations are to be provided in terms of sequences of timed constraints. We present an assumption-based runtime verification algorithm and its implementation on top of the real-time verification tool UPPAAL. We show experimentally that assumptions can be effective in anticipating the satisfaction/violation of timed properties and in handling monitoring properties that predicate over unobservable events.

Keywords: Assumption-based runtime verification · Real-Time · MITL · Timed Automata

1 Introduction

The problem of monitoring timed properties has gained significant attention due to its crucial role in ensuring the correctness and reliability of real-time systems. The runtime verification of temporal properties over timed sequences of observations is crucial in various applications ranging from cyber-physical systems

T.M. Grosen, K.G. Larsen, and M. Zimmermann have been supported by DIREC - Digital Research Centre Denmark. A. Cimatti and S. Tonetta have been supported by the PNRR project FAIR - Future AI Research (PE00000013), under the Italian NRRP MUR program funded by the NextGenerationEU.

A. Madeira and A. Knapp (Eds.): SEFM 2024, LNCS 15280, pp. 70–88, 2025.
https://doi.org/10.1007/978-3-031-77382-2_5

including autonomous vehicles and beyond. While different solutions for runtime verification of timed temporal properties have been presented [4–6,20,22], some challenges remain to be addressed, in particular extending these solutions with prognosis and diagnosis capabilities. More specifically, we are here interested in effectively predicting in advance the failure of properties and in handling partially observable systems.

In the discrete-time setting, these challenges have been addressed with Assumption-Based Runtime Verification (ABRV) [12–15]. ABRV uses assumptions about the behavior of the system to predict the future behavior of the system and to relate observable and non-observable variables. These assumptions can be derived, for example, from models produced during the system design, or from the data collected from the system in operation. Exploiting assumptions, the monitor can anticipate the detection of property failures. Moreover, the specification is no more limited to the interface of black box systems as in traditional runtime verification, but can be extended to constrain also the internal non-observable parts (such as, for example, internal faults).

In ABRV, the output of the monitor has four possible values:

- $\top$ (Satisfied): given the sequence of observations, the system satisfies the specified temporal properties under the given assumption.
- $\bot$ (Violated): this value indicates that the observed behavior of the system violates the specified temporal property, under the given assumption.
- $\times$ (Out-of-model): the observed behavior violates the assumptions, i.e., there is no run of the assumption compatible with the observations.
- *?* (Unknown): given the current observations and assumption, it is not possible to determine definitively whether the property is satisfied or violated.

Here, we enhance the monitoring of timed systems with assumptions. We define and solve the problem of ABRV for timed properties for the following setting:

- The *properties* to be monitored are specified in Metric Interval Temporal Logic (MITL), which allows for the expression of temporal properties over timed words, making it suitable for real-time systems.
- The *assumptions* about the system are specified in terms of Timed Automata which relate observable events with non-observable events, locations, and clocks.
- The *observations* are specified in terms of sequences of timed constraints which predicate over the assumption automaton defining the set of its runs that are compatible with the observations.

Like in the discrete-time case, the assumption allows the monitor to give a $\top$ or $\bot$ verdict even if the property contains future operators and non-observable events. For example, suppose we monitor the MITL property $\varphi = F_{[0,10]} a \wedge G_{[0,20]} \neg b$ (expressing that there is an a in the first ten units of time, but no b in the first 20 units of time) and we assume that the system satisfies the property $\psi = G_{[0,1]} \neg b \wedge G(a \rightarrow G_{[0,10]} \neg b)$ (expressing that there is no b in the first unit of time and no a is followed by a b within ten units of time). Then, the monitor can output a $\top$ verdict even before time 20, for instance at time 10 when b is false in the interval $[0, 10]$ and a is true at time 10. Further, it can even give the verdict $\top$ if b is not observable, e.g., when a is true at time 0 and 10.

One of our main contributions is a rich definition of observations that take into account both data and time uncertainty. As in [15], the observations are represented by formulas that can capture the uncertainty on data. For example, $\neg a$ means that a is not seen but b can be true or false. The approach is further extended to have uncertainty on time, taking into account potential errors in the timestamps with which the monitor receives data from the system. This is represented in the observations with time intervals that are associated to observation formulas. Thus, for example, we can say that a is seen in an interval $[6, 7]$ but we do not know exactly when. Finally, we concatenate these pairs of formulas and time intervals to form complex observation patterns. For example, the sequence $o = (a, [0, 0], !)(\neg a, [0, 7], *)(a, [6, 7], !)(\neg a, [6, 16], *)(a, [15, 16], !)$ says that we see three a's, one at time 0, another in the interval $[6, 7]$, and a final one in the interval $[15, 16]$ and that we do not know anything about b (intuitively, an observation with an ! ($*$) indicates exactly one occurrence (zero or more occurrences)). If the system satisfies the assumption ψ from above, we can conclude at time 16 that the property φ is true despite the uncertainty about time and b.

We propose a *zone-based online* algorithm that at any time provides a monitoring verdict saying if the property is satisfied or violated given the assumption and a sequence of observations. We implemented the algorithm on top of UPPAAL and show the feasibility of the approach. Especially, we demonstrate how the assumptions can be effective in anticipating the satisfaction/violation of timed properties and in handling properties that predicate over unobservable events. We also report on the influence of unobservable events on the response-time, the time it takes to compute a verdict when given a new observation.

2 Preliminaries

The set of natural numbers (excluding zero) is $\mathbb{N}$, we define $\mathbb{N}_0 = \mathbb{N} \cup \{0\}$, the set of non-negative rational numbers is $\mathbb{Q}_{\geq 0}$, and the set of non-negative real numbers is $\mathbb{R}_{\geq 0}$. The powerset of a set S is denoted by 2^S.

Timed Words. A timed word over a finite alphabet Σ is a pair $\rho = (\sigma, \tau)$ where σ is a nonempty word over Σ and τ is a sequence of non-decreasing non-negative real numbers of the same length as σ. Timed words may be finite or infinite. In the latter case, we require $\limsup \tau = \infty$, i.e., time diverges. The set of finite timed words is denoted by $T\Sigma^*$ and the set of infinite timed words by $T\Sigma^\omega$. We also represent a timed word as a sequence of pairs $(\sigma_1, \tau_1)(\sigma_2, \tau_2)\dots$. If $\rho = (\sigma_1, \tau_1)(\sigma_2, \tau_2)\cdots(\sigma_n, \tau_n)$ is a finite timed word, we denote by $\tau(\rho)$ the total time duration of ρ, i.e., τ_n. We lift this to languages $L \subseteq T\Sigma^*$ by defining $\tau(L) = \sup_{\rho \in L} \tau(\rho)$, which can be infinite.

If $\rho_1 = (\sigma_1^1, \tau_1^1)\dots(\sigma_n^1, \tau_n^1)$ is a finite timed word, $\rho_2 = (\sigma_1^2, \tau_1^2)(\sigma_2^2, \tau_2^2)\dots$ a finite or infinite timed word, and $t \in \mathbb{R}_{\geq 0}$ then the concatenation $\rho_1 \cdot_t \rho_2$ is defined iff $t \geq \tau(\rho_1)$. Then, we define $\rho_1 \cdot_t \rho_2 = (\sigma_1, \tau_1)(\sigma_2, \tau_2) \cdots$ such that

$$\sigma_i = \begin{cases} \sigma_i^1 & \text{if } i \leq n \\ \sigma_{i-n}^2 & \text{else} \end{cases} \quad \text{and} \quad \tau_i = \begin{cases} \tau_i^1 & \text{if } i \leq n \\ \tau_{i-n}^2 + t & \text{else.} \end{cases}$$

We lift this definition to sets $L_1 \subseteq T\Sigma^*$ and $L_2 \subseteq T\Sigma^* \cup T\Sigma^\omega$ via

$$L_1 \cdot_t L_2 = \{\rho_1 \cdot_t \rho_2 \mid \rho_1 \in L_1 \text{ and } \rho_2 \in L_2\},$$

provided we have $t \geq \tau(L_1)$.

Timed Automata. A timed Büchi automaton (TBA) $\mathcal{B} = (Q, Q_0, \Sigma, C, \Delta, \mathcal{F})$ consists of a finite alphabet Σ, a finite set Q of locations, a set $Q_0 \subseteq Q$ of initial locations, a finite set C of clocks, a finite set $\Delta \subseteq Q \times Q \times \Sigma \times 2^C \times G(C)$ of transitions with $G(C)$ being the set of clock constraints over C, and a set $\mathcal{F} \subseteq Q$ of accepting locations. A transition (q, q', a, λ, g) is an edge from q to q' on input symbol a, where λ is the set of clocks to reset and g is a clock constraint over C. A clock constraint is a conjunction of atomic constraints of the form $c \sim n$, where c is a clock, $n \in \mathbb{N}_0$, and $\sim \in \{<, \leq, =, \geq, >\}$.

A state of $\mathcal{B}$ is a pair (q, v) where q is a location in Q and $v \colon C \to \mathbb{R}_{\geq 0}$ is a valuation mapping clocks to their values. For any $d \in \mathbb{R}_{\geq 0}$, $v+d$ is the valuation $x \mapsto v(x) + d$. A run of $\mathcal{B}$ from a state (q_0, v_0) over a timed word $(\sigma_1, \tau_1)(\sigma_2, \tau_2) \cdots$ is a sequence of steps $(q_0, v_0) \xrightarrow{(\sigma_1,\tau_1)} (q_1, v_1) \xrightarrow{(\sigma_2,\tau_2)} (q_2, v_2) \xrightarrow{(\sigma_3,\tau_3)} \cdots$ where for all $i \geq 1$ there is a transition $(q_{i-1}, q_i, \sigma_i, \lambda_i, g_i)$ such that $v_i(c) = 0$ for all c in λ_i and $v_i(c) = v_{i-1}(c) + (\tau_i - \tau_{i-1})$ otherwise, and g_i is satisfied by the valuation $v_{i-1} + (\tau_i - \tau_{i-1})$. Here, we use $\tau_0 = 0$. Given a run r, we denote the set of locations visited infinitely many times by r as $\mathrm{Inf}(r)$. A run r of $\mathcal{B}$ is accepting if $\mathrm{Inf}(r) \cap \mathcal{F} \neq \emptyset$. The language of $\mathcal{B}$ from a starting state (q, v), denoted $L(\mathcal{B}, (q, v))$, is the set of all timed words with an accepting run in $\mathcal{A}$ starting from (q, v). We define the language of $\mathcal{B}$, written $L(\mathcal{B})$, to be $\bigcup_q L(\mathcal{B}, (q, v_0))$, where q ranges over all locations in Q_0 and where $v_0(c) = 0$ for all $c \in C$.

Proposition 1 ([2]). *For all TBA $\mathcal{B}$, $\mathcal{B}'$ there is a TBA $\mathcal{B} \otimes \mathcal{B}'$ with $L(\mathcal{B} \otimes \mathcal{B}') = L(\mathcal{B}) \cap L(\mathcal{B}')$. The set of states of $\mathcal{B} \otimes \mathcal{B}'$ is $Q \times Q' \times \{0, 1\}$, where Q and Q' are the sets of states of $\mathcal{B}$ and $\mathcal{B}'$, respectively.*

Logic. We use Metric Temporal Interval Logic (MITL) to formally express properties to be monitored; these are subsequently translated into equivalent TBA which we use in our monitoring algorithm. The syntax of MITL formulas over a finite alphabet Σ is defined as

$$\varphi ::= p \mid \neg\varphi \mid \varphi \vee \varphi \mid X_I \varphi \mid \varphi \, U_I \varphi$$

where $p \in \Sigma$ and I ranges over non-singular intervals over $\mathbb{R}_{\geq 0}$ with endpoints in $\mathbb{N}_0 \cup \{\infty\}$. Note that we often write $\sim n$ for $I = \{d \in \mathbb{R} \mid d \sim n\}$ where $\sim \in \{<, \leq, \geq, >\}$, and $n \in \mathbb{N}$. We also define the standard syntactic sugar

$\texttt{true} = p \vee \neg p$, $\texttt{false} = \neg\texttt{true}$, $\varphi \wedge \psi = \neg(\neg\varphi \vee \neg\psi)$, $\varphi \rightarrow \psi = \neg\varphi \vee \psi$, $F_I\varphi = \texttt{true}\ U_I\varphi$, and $G_I\varphi = \neg F_I\neg\varphi$.

The semantics of MITL is defined over infinite timed words. Given such a timed word $\rho = (\sigma_1, \tau_1)(\sigma_2, \tau_2)\cdots \in T\Sigma^\omega$, a position $i \geq 1$, and an MITL formula φ, we inductively define the satisfaction relation $\rho, i \models \varphi$ as follows:

- $\rho, i \models p$ iff $p = \sigma_i$.
- $\rho, i \models \neg\varphi$ iff $\rho, i \not\models \varphi$.
- $\rho, i \models \varphi \vee \psi$ if $\rho, i \models \varphi$ or $\rho, i \models \psi$.
- $\rho, i \models X_I\varphi$ iff $\rho, (i+1) \models \varphi$ and $\tau_{i+1} - \tau_i \in I$.
- $\rho, i \models \varphi\ U_I\psi$ iff there exists $k \geq i$ s.t. $\rho, k \models \psi$, $\tau_k - \tau_i \in I$, and $\rho, j \models \varphi$ for all $i \leq j < k$.

We write $\rho \models \varphi$ whenever $\rho, 1 \models \varphi$. The language $L(\varphi)$ of an MITL formula φ is the set of all infinite timed words that satisfy φ.

Theorem 1 ([3,9]). *For each MITL formula φ there exists a TBA $\mathcal{B}$ such that $L(\varphi) = L(\mathcal{B})$.*

Example 1. Figure 1 illustrates the above theorem providing a TBA for the formula $F_{[0,10]}a \wedge G_{[0,20]}\neg b$ and its negation.

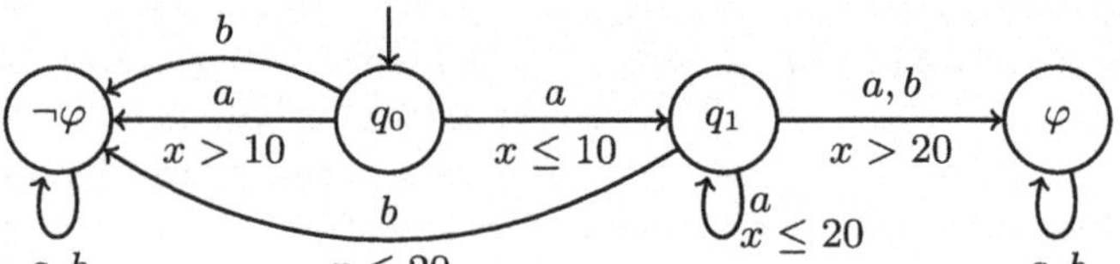

Fig. 1. A TBA for the language of the formula $\varphi = F_{[0,10]}a \wedge G_{[0,20]}\neg b$ and its negation: If location φ ($\neg\varphi$) is accepting then it accepts $L(\varphi)$ ($L(\neg\varphi)$).

3 Monitoring Under Assumptions

Monitoring timed properties [6,20] requires to determine whether every extension of a finite observation (a finite timed word) satisfies a given property (yielding the verdict $\top$), whether every extension violates the property (yielding the verdict $\bot$), or neither is true (yielding the verdict *?*). Monitoring under assumptions involves two changes over the classical monitoring framework.

Firstly, the assumption itself: In its most general form, it is a set $A \subseteq T\Sigma^\omega$ of infinite timed words. Intuitively, A contains the executions we assume to be possibly generatable by the system we are monitoring. Hence, every execution that is not in A does not need to be taken into account when determining a verdict, i.e., the assumption refines verdicts. However, this also means that our assumption can be invalidated if we observe an execution prefix that is not consistent with our assumption. This requires a new verdict, denoted by $\times$. In this case, the assumption needs to be refined as it does not match our observation.

Secondly, we allow inexact observations: In the classical setting, we observe a finite timed word $(\sigma_1, \tau_1) \cdots (\sigma_n, \tau_n)$ and reason about its possible extensions. Hence, we implicitly presume that no other events occurred between time 0 and τ_n and that the timepoints are exact. In the following, we allow for some imperfect information about the observation. In the most general form, an observation is then a set $O \subseteq T\Sigma^*$ of finite timed words. Intuitively, O contains those words that are consistent with our (imperfect) observation.

Example 2. Consider the property "$F_{[0,10]}a \wedge G_{[0,20]}\neg b$" of Example 1. Monitoring this property on a timed word, a conclusive verdict is given in the following cases:

- The property is false at any time in the interval $[0, 20]$ a "b" is observed;
- The property is false after time 10 if "a" was not previously observed;
- The property is true after time 20 if "b" was not previously observed and "a" was observed in the interval $[0, 10]$.

Consider now the assumption "$G_{[0,1]}\neg b \wedge G(a \rightarrow G_{[0,10]}\neg b)$" which corresponds to the TBA in Fig. 2. Then, if "a" was observed in the interval $[0, 10]$, as soon as we see another "a" within the interval $[10, 20]$ and no b was observed before, we can conclude that the property is true. On the other hand, if a "b" is observed at time 0, then the observation violates the assumption.

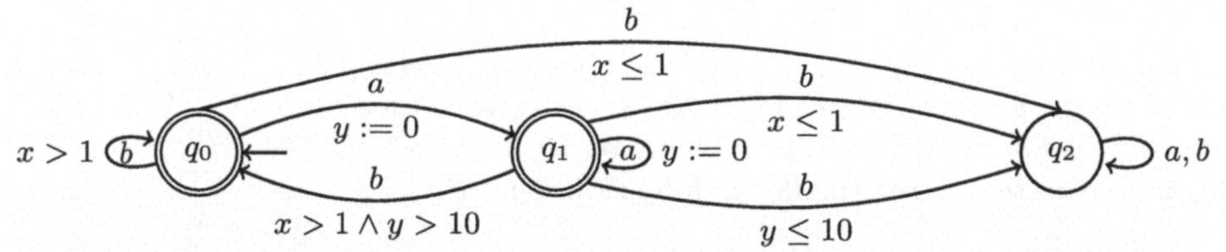

Fig. 2. A TBA for the language of the formula $G_{[0,1]}\neg b \wedge$ G(a $\rightarrow G_{[0,10]}\neg b)$ with accepting locations q_0 and q_1.

Example 3. Let us consider again the property "$F_{[0,10]}a \wedge G_{[0,20]}\neg b$" but now we observe "$a$" with uncertainty on the timestamps and "b" is unobservable. For example, we observe "a" at time 0, another time in the interval $[6, 7]$ and a final time in the interval $[15, 16]$, and now is time 30. The words that are consistent with these observations have the form $\rho_0(a, 0)\rho_1(a, t_1)\rho_2(a, t_2)\rho_3$ where

- $t_1 \in [6, 7]$ and $t_2 \in [15, 16]$,
- ρ_0 is a (possibly empty) finite timed word $(b, 0) \cdots (b, 0)$,
- ρ_1 is a (possibly empty) finite timed word $(b, t_{1,1}) \cdots (b, t_{1,n_1})$ with $t_{1,j} \in [0, t_1]$ for all $1 \leq j \leq n_1$,

- ρ_2 is a (possibly empty) finite timed word $(b, t_{2,1}) \cdots (b, t_{2,n_2})$ with $t_{2,j} \in [t_1, t_2]$ for all $1 \leq j \leq n_2$, and
- ρ_3 is a (possibly empty) finite timed word $(b, t_{3,1}) \cdots (b, t_{3,n_3})$ with $t_{3,j} \in [t_2, 30]$ for all $1 \leq j \leq n_3$.

Without assumptions we cannot have any conclusive verdict, because we do not know if a "b" occurred before timepoint 20 or not. But with the assumption from the previous example, we can conclude at time 16 that the property is true:

- ρ_0 must be empty, as there cannot be a b within the first unit of time.
- ρ_1 must be empty, as there cannot be a b for ten units of time after the a at timepoint 0 and $t_1 \leq 7 \leq 10$.
- ρ_2 must be empty, as there cannot be a b for ten units of time after the a at timepoint t_1 and $t_2 \leq 16 \leq t_1 + 10$.
- ρ_3 cannot contain a b with timestamp $t_{3,j} \leq 20$, as this would imply that a b has occurred less than ten units of time after the a at t_2.

Thus, under the assumption, we can make a definitive verdict, which we could not without the assumption.

In the following, we formalize this intuition. To develop the theory as general as possible, we allow real timepoints in the observations. Later, when we are concerned with algorithms, we will restrict ourselves to rational inputs. In the same spirit, we begin with a very abstract definition of monitoring under assumptions. Later, we will explain how to represent the property, the assumption, and the observation finitely.

Definition 1. *Let $\mathbb{B}_4 = \{\top, \bot, ?, \times\}$. Given a property $\varphi \subseteq T\Sigma^\omega$ of infinite timed words, an assumption $A \subseteq T\Sigma^\omega$, a nonempty observation $O \subseteq T\Sigma^*$, and a current time instant $t \geq \tau(O)$, the function $\mathcal{V}\colon (2^{T\Sigma^\omega} \times 2^{T\Sigma^\omega}) \to (2^{T\Sigma^*} \times \mathbb{R}_{\geq 0}) \to \mathbb{B}_4$ evaluates to a verdict with the following definition:*

$$\mathcal{V}(\varphi, A)(O, t) = \begin{cases} \times & \text{if } O \cdot_t T\Sigma^\omega \cap A = \emptyset, \\ \top & \text{if } O \cdot_t T\Sigma^\omega \cap A \neq \emptyset \text{ and } O \cdot_t T\Sigma^\omega \cap A \subseteq \varphi, \\ \bot & \text{if } O \cdot_t T\Sigma^\omega \cap A \neq \emptyset \text{ and } O \cdot_t T\Sigma^\omega \cap A \subseteq T\Sigma^\omega \setminus \varphi, \\ ? & \text{otherwise.} \end{cases}$$

$\mathcal{V}(\varphi, A)(O, t)$ is undefined when $t < \tau(O)$.

In the following, we present an algorithm computing $\mathcal{V}$ in the setting where

- the property φ and its complement is accepted by a TBA (this covers in particular the case of φ being given in MITL due to Theorem 1),
- the assumption A is given by a TBA, and
- the observation O is given by a sequence of pairs of time-intervals and propositional formulas over the locations, the clock constraints, and the alphabet of the assumption automaton.

We begin by introducing the assumption and observations. The former is given by a TBA, which we typically denote by $\mathcal{A}$ to distinguish it from other TBA. Thus, let $\mathcal{A} = (Q, Q_0, \Sigma, C, \Delta, \mathcal{F})$ be a TBA, i.e., Q is the set of locations, Σ is the alphabet, and C is the set of clocks. Recall that $G(C)$ denotes the clock constraints over C, i.e., conjunctions of atomic constraints of the form $c \sim n$, where $c \in C$ is a clock, $n \in \mathbb{N}_0$, and $\sim \in \{<, \leq, =, \geq, >\}$. Let ϕ be a propositional formula over the set $\Sigma \cup Q \cup G(C)$ of propositions (which is infinite!), let $\sigma \in \Sigma$, and let (q, v) be a state of $\mathcal{A}$. We define $\sigma, (q, v) \models \phi$ as follows:

- For $\sigma' \in \Sigma$, $\sigma, (q, v) \models \sigma'$ iff $\sigma' = \sigma$.
- For $q' \in Q$, $\sigma, (q, v) \models q'$ iff $q' = q$.
- For $g \in G(C)$, $\sigma, (q, v) \models g$ iff g is satisfied by v.
- The semantics of Boolean connectives is defined as usual.

An $\mathcal{A}$-observation is a finite sequence $o = (\phi_1, I_1, m_1) \cdots (\phi_n, I_n, m_n)$ where the ϕ_j are propositional formulas over $\Sigma \cup Q \cup G(C)$, the I_j are bounded intervals of $\mathbb{R}_{\geq 0}$ (which may overlap), and the multiplicities m_j are in $\{!, *\}$. It defines the language $\mathcal{C}_{\mathcal{A}}(o) \subseteq T\Sigma^*$ of (consistent) finite timed words $(\sigma_1, \tau_1) \cdots (\sigma_{n'}, \tau_{n'})$ such that there is a prefix

$$r = (q_0, v_0) \xrightarrow{(\sigma_1,\tau_1)} (q_1, v_1) \xrightarrow{(\sigma_2,\tau_2)} \cdots \xrightarrow{(\sigma_{n'-1},\tau_{n'-1})} (q_{n'-1}, v_{n'-1}) \xrightarrow{(\sigma_{n'},\tau_{n'})} (q_{n'}, v_{n'})$$

of a run of $\mathcal{A}$ with $q_0 \in Q_0$, $v_0(c) = 0$ for all $c \in C$, and there is a function $h\colon \{1, 2, \ldots, n'\} \to \{1, 2, \ldots, n\}$ such that

1. $h(1) \leq h(2) \leq \cdots \leq h(n')$,
2. for every $j \in \{1, 2, \ldots, n\}$ with $m_j =!$, there is a unique $j' \in \{1, 2, \ldots, n'\}$ such that $h(j') = j$ (i.e., observations with an ! must appear exactly once, observations with an $*$ may appear zero or more times),
3. $\tau_j \in I_{h(j)}$ for all $j \in \{1, 2, \ldots, n'\}$, and
4. $\sigma_j, (q_j, v_j) \models \phi_{h(j)}$ for all $j \in \{1, 2, \ldots, n'\}$.

Thus, a finite sequence of such formulas and intervals yields a language of finite timed words, those that are consistent with the formulas and intervals.

Example 4. Let us continue Example 3 and let $\mathcal{A}$ be the assumption automaton shown in Fig. 2. Consider the $\mathcal{A}$-observation

$$o = (a, [0, 0], !)(\neg a, [0, 7], *)(a, [6, 7], !)(\neg a, [6, 16], *)(a, [15, 16], !)(\neg a, [0, 30], *).$$

Then, as argued in Example 3, $\mathcal{C}_{\mathcal{A}}(o)$ is the language

$$\{(a, 0)(a, t_1)(a, t_2)(b, t_{3,1}) \cdots (b, t_{3,n_3}) \mid \\ t_1 \in [6, 7], t_2 \in [15, 16], \text{ and } t_2 + 10 < t_{3,1} \leq \cdots \leq t_{3,n_3} \leq 30\}.$$

For example, given the run prefix (we ignore the clock x as it is never reset and thus is always equal to the timestamp on the transition leading to a state)

$$r = (q_0, y = 0) \xrightarrow{(a,0)} (q_1, y = 0) \xrightarrow{(a,6)} (q_1, y = 0) \xrightarrow{(a,15)} (q_1, y = 0)$$

we can define h as follows: $h(1) = 1, h(2) = 3, h(3) = 5$. For the run prefix

$$r = (q_0, y = 0) \xrightarrow{(a,0)} (q_1, y = 0) \xrightarrow{(a,6)} (q_1, y = 0) \xrightarrow{(b,15)} (q_2, y = 9) \xrightarrow{(a,16)} (q_2, y = 10)$$

we can define the function h as follows: $h(1) = 1, h(2) = 3, h(3) = 4, h(4) = 5$. Finally, the run prefix

$$r = (q_0, y = 0) \xrightarrow{(a,0)} (q_1, y = 0) \xrightarrow{(a,6)} (q_1, y = 0) \xrightarrow{(a,15)} (q_2, y = 9) \xrightarrow{(a,16)} (q_2, y = 10)$$

is the prefix of a run of $\mathcal{A}$ but it is not compatible with the observation o. In fact, any h satisfying the conditions 1), 3), and 4) should assign $h(3) = 5$ and $h(4) = 5$ violating condition 2).

Remark 1. We have $\tau(\mathcal{C}_{\mathcal{A}}((\phi_1, I_1, m_1) \cdots (\phi_n, I_n, m_n))) \leq \sup I_n$ by definition.

4 A Zone-Based Monitoring Algorithm

In this section, we present an algorithm computing the monitoring function $\mathcal{V}$. To this end, we first need to introduce some notation for TBA and zones to represent subsets of states of TBA, which may be uncountable. Recall that we have defined the theory of monitoring under assumptions with respect to arbitrary, i.e., real, timepoints. However, as we are now dealing with algorithms, we have to restrict ourselves to rational inputs (which are finitely representable). Thus, we say that an $\mathcal{A}$-observation $(\phi_1, I_1, m_1) \cdots (\phi_n, I_n, m_n)$ is rational, if each I_j is an interval over $\mathbb{R}_{\geq 0}$ with rational endpoints.

For the monitoring algorithm, we use – as is standard in analysing timed automata models – symbolic states being pairs (q, Z) of locations and zones. A zone is a finite conjunction of constraints of the form $x \sim t$ and $x - x' \sim t$ for clocks x, x', constants $t \in \mathbb{Q}_{\geq 0}$, and $\sim \in \{<, \leq, =, \geq, >\}$. Given two zones Z and Z' over a set C of clocks, and a set $\lambda \subseteq C$ of clocks, we define the following operations on zones (which can be efficiently implemented using the DBM data-structure [8]):

- $Z[\lambda] = \{v \mid \exists v' \models Z \text{ s.t. } v(x) = 0 \text{ if } x \in \lambda, \text{ otherwise } v(x) = v'(x)\}$
- $Z^{\nearrow} = \{v \mid \exists v' \models Z \text{ s.t. } v = v' + d \text{ for some } d \in \mathbb{R}_{\geq 0}\}$
- $Z \wedge Z' = \{v \mid v \models Z \textit{ and } v \models Z'\}$.

To describe our algorithm, we first define the set of states of a TBA from where it is possible to reach an accepting location infinitely many times in the future, i.e., those states from which an accepting run is possible. This is useful, because if processing a finite timed word leads to such a state, then the timed word can be extended to an infinite one in the language of the automaton, a notion that underlies Definition 1. Given a TBA $\mathcal{B} = (Q, Q_0, \Sigma, C, \Delta, \mathcal{F})$, the set of states with nonempty language is:

$$S^{ne}_{\mathcal{B}} = \{(q, v) \mid q \in Q, v \in C \to \mathbb{R}_{\geq 0} \text{ s.t. } L(\mathcal{B}, (q, v)) \neq \emptyset\}.$$

Proposition 2 ([20]). *$S^{ne}_{\mathcal{B}}$ can be computed using a zone-based algorithm.*

We continue by capturing the set of states of a TBA that can be reached by processing a finite timed word. In the following definition, we write $(q_0, v_0) \xrightarrow{\rho}_{\mathcal{B}} (q_n, v_n)$ for a finite timed word $\rho = (\sigma, \tau) \in T\Sigma^*$ to denote the existence of a finite sequence of states

$$(q_0, v_0) \xrightarrow{(\sigma_1,\tau_1)} (q_1, v_1) \xrightarrow{(\sigma_2,\tau_2)} \cdots \xrightarrow{(\sigma_n,\tau_n)} (q_n, v_n)$$

where for all $1 \le i \le n$ there is a transition $(q_{i-1}, q_i, \sigma_i, \lambda_i, g_i)$ such that $v_i(c) = 0$ for all c in λ_i and $v_{i-1}(c)+(\tau_i - \tau_{i-1})$ otherwise, and g is satisfied by the valuation $v_{i-1} + (\tau_i - \tau_{i-1})$, where we use $\tau_0 = 0$. Given a TBA $\mathcal{B}$, a finite timed word $\rho \in T\Sigma^*$, and a time-point $t \in \mathbb{R}_{\ge 0}$ with $t \ge \tau(\rho)$, the set of possible states a run over ρ starting from initial states of $\mathcal{B}$ can end in after time t has passed is

$$\mathcal{T}_{\mathcal{B}}(\rho, t) = \bigcup_{q_0 \in Q_0} \{(q, v + (t - \tau(\rho))) \mid (q_0, v_0) \xrightarrow{\rho}_{\mathcal{B}} (q, v)\},$$

where v_0 is the clock valuation mapping every clock to 0. We call $\mathcal{T}_{\mathcal{B}}(\rho, t)$ the reach-set of $\mathcal{B}$ over (ρ, t). The above definition is adapted from [20] to take into account the time that has passed since the last observation, i.e., the input t.

Next, we lift this definition to sets $L \subseteq T\Sigma^*$ of finite words via

$$\mathcal{T}_{\mathcal{B}}(L, t) = \bigcup_{\rho \in L} \mathcal{T}_{\mathcal{B}}(\rho, t),$$

assuming $t \ge \tau(L)$. Otherwise, $\mathcal{T}_{\mathcal{B}}(L, t) = \emptyset$ by convention.

We now show how to compute reach-sets using zones. First, we use the zone operations introduced above to compute the successor states of an input letter with a given target location. Fix a TBA $(Q, Q_0, \Sigma, C, \Delta, \mathcal{F})$. For a symbolic state (q, Z), a letter $\sigma \in \Sigma$ and target location $q' \in Q$, we define

$$\mathrm{Post}((q, Z), \sigma, q') = \{(q', Z') \mid (q, q', \sigma, \lambda, g) \in \Delta, Z' = (Z^{\nearrow} \wedge g)[\lambda]\},$$

being the set of states one can reach by taking a σ-transition at some point in the future from (q, Z) with q' as target-location. Using Post we can compute the successor states of a time-uncertain letter/target location (σ, q', I), where $\sigma \in \Sigma$, $q' \in Q$ and $I \subseteq \mathbb{R}_{\ge 0}$ is a time interval with rational endpoints. For this, we extend zones with an additional clock *time* just recording time since system start. The successors of a symbolic state (q, Z) are

$$\mathrm{Succ}((q, Z), (\sigma, q', I)) = \{(q', Z') \mid (q', Z'') \in \mathrm{Post}((q, Z), \sigma, q'), Z' = Z'' \wedge \mathit{time} \in I\}$$

and the successors of a set of symbolic states S are

$$\mathrm{Succ}(S, (\sigma, q', I)) = \bigcup_{(q,Z) \in S} \mathrm{Succ}((q, Z), (\sigma, q', I)).$$

Now, our main technical lemma below exploits the above to effectively compute reach-sets. More precisely, given a rational $\mathcal{A}$-observation o (i.e., the TBA $\mathcal{A}$

represents the assumption), we can compute the reach-set of the set $\mathcal{C}_{\mathcal{A}}(o)$ in the product $\mathcal{B} \otimes \mathcal{A}$, for any given TBA $\mathcal{B}$, i.e., we compute the words consistent with the observation o in the TBA $\mathcal{A}$ (the assumption), while the reach-set of that language is computed in $\mathcal{B}\otimes\mathcal{A}$ (this will later be the product of the property (or its negation) and the assumption).

Lemma 1. *Fix TBA $\mathcal{A}, \mathcal{B}$. There is a zone-based online algorithm computing*

$$\mathcal{T}_{\mathcal{B}\otimes\mathcal{A}}(\mathcal{C}_{\mathcal{A}}((\phi_1, I_1, m_1)\cdots(\phi_n, I_n, m_n)), t)$$

for every rational observation $(\phi_1, I_1, m_1)\cdots(\phi_n, I_n, m_n)$, and every $t \in \mathbb{Q}_{\geq 0}$ with $t \geq \sup I_n$.

Proof. Let $o^i = (\phi_1, I_1, m_1)\cdots(\phi_i, I_i, m_i)$, and let us denote by $S^i_{\mathcal{B}\otimes\mathcal{A}}$ the set $\mathcal{T}_{\mathcal{B}\otimes\mathcal{A}}(\mathcal{C}_{\mathcal{A}}(o^i))$ of successors of o^i in $\mathcal{B}\otimes\mathcal{A}$. We will show inductively in i, that $S^i_{\mathcal{B}\otimes\mathcal{A}}$ can be obtained effectively using zone operations. For the base case $i = 0$, we note that $\mathcal{C}_{\mathcal{A}}(o^0) = \{\varepsilon\}$, thus $\mathcal{T}_{\mathcal{B}\otimes\mathcal{A}}(\mathcal{C}_{\mathcal{A}}(o^0))$ is the set of initial states of $\mathcal{B}\otimes\mathcal{A}$, which is clearly effectively representable using zones.

For the inductive case, let us assume that $S^{i-1}_{\mathcal{B}\otimes\mathcal{A}}$ is effectively computable using zone operations. Now consider consider (ϕ_i, I_i, m_i). Given that Σ, $Q_{\mathcal{A}}$ and $Q_{\mathcal{B}}$ are finite, ϕ_i is equivalent to a finite disjunction of simple formulas of the form $\psi_{i,j} = \sigma_{i,j} \wedge q^a_{i,j} \wedge g_{i,j}$, where $\sigma_{i,j} \in \Sigma$, $q^a_{i,j} \in Q_{\mathcal{A}}$, and $g_{i,j} \in G(C_{\mathcal{A}})$. Now in the case $m_i =!$, the set of successors of $\psi_{i,j}$ is simply

$$S^i_{\mathcal{B}\otimes\mathcal{A}} = \bigcup_j \bigcup_{q^b\in Q_{\mathcal{B}}} \bigcup_{k\in\{0,1\}} \mathrm{Succ}(S^{i-1}_{\mathcal{B}\otimes\mathcal{A}}, (\sigma_{i,j}, (q^b, q^a_{i,j}, k), I_i)) \wedge g_{i,j}.$$

In the case $m_i = *$, $S^i_{\mathcal{B}\otimes\mathcal{A}}$ is the least fixed-point $\mathbf{X}$, satisfying the equality

$$\mathbf{X} = S^{i-1}_{\mathcal{B}\otimes\mathcal{A}} \cup \bigcup_j \bigcup_{q^b\in Q_{\mathcal{B}}} \bigcup_{k\in\{0,1\}} [\mathrm{Succ}(\mathbf{X}, (\sigma_{i,j}, (q^b, q^a_{i,j}, k), I_i)) \wedge g_{i,j}.]$$

Given the upper bounds of the interval I_i, the least fixed-point will be found in a finite number of iterations of the right-hand-side of the above equation (starting from the empty set).

The above inductive proof provides in an obvious manner the basis for an effective online construction of the sets $\mathcal{T}_{\mathcal{B}\otimes\mathcal{A}}(\mathcal{C}_{\mathcal{A}}(o^i))$. □

Now, we are able to present our algorithm to compute $\mathcal{V}$ for a property φ (given by two TBA $\mathcal{B}_\varphi$ and $\mathcal{B}_{\neg\varphi}$ such that $L(\mathcal{B}_\varphi) = L(\varphi)$ and $L(\mathcal{B}_{\neg\varphi}) = L(\neg\varphi)$) and an assumption A (given by a TBA $\mathcal{A}$): Given $o = (\phi_1, I_1, m_1)\cdots(\phi_n, I_n, m_n)$ (a rational observation) and $t > \sup I_n$, do the following:

1. Compute $\mathcal{T}_{\mathcal{A}}(\mathcal{C}_{\mathcal{A}}(o), t)$. If it is nonempty (which is the case iff $\mathcal{C}_{\mathcal{A}}(o)$ is nonempty), but has an empty intersection with $S^{ne}_{\mathcal{A}}$, then return $\times$. This checks whether there is some finite word that is consistent with the observation and can be extended to satisfy the assumption. If this is not the case, then the assumption was wrong.

2. Compute $\mathcal{T}_{\mathcal{B}_{\neg\varphi}\otimes\mathcal{A}}(\mathcal{C}_{\mathcal{A}}(o), t)$. If it has an empty intersection with $S^{ne}_{\mathcal{B}_{\neg\varphi}\otimes\mathcal{A}}$, then return $\top$: If there is a finite word consistent with the observation that can be extended to satisfy the assumption, but no such extension satisfies the complement of the property, then every such extension must satisfy the property. Hence, we can return $\top$.
3. Compute $\mathcal{T}_{\mathcal{B}_{\varphi}\otimes\mathcal{A}}(\mathcal{C}_{\mathcal{A}}(o), t)$. If it has an empty intersection with $S^{ne}_{\mathcal{B}_{\varphi}\otimes\mathcal{A}}$, then return $\perp$: If there is a finite word consistent with the observation that can be extended to satisfy the assumption, but no such extension satisfies the property, then every such extension must satisfy the complement of the property. Hence, we can return $\perp$.
4. Return *?*. Otherwise, there is both a finite word that is consistent with the observation that can be extended to satisfy the property and a finite word that is consistent with the observation that can be extended to satisfy the complement of the property. Consequently, we return *?*.

Theorem 2. *The algorithm described above computes* $\mathcal{V}(\varphi, A)$.

As argued above, our algorithm can be implemented using zones: both the reach-sets and the sets of nonempty states can be computed using zones, zones are closed under intersection, and can be tested effectively for emptiness [7].

Furthermore, our algorithm is online in the following sense: The set of nonempty states only needs to be computed once for each of the three automata and the symbolic states capturing

$$\mathcal{T}_{\mathcal{A}}(\mathcal{C}_{\mathcal{A}}((\phi_1, I_1, m_1)\cdots(\phi_n, I_n, m_n)(\phi_{n+1}, I_{n+1}, m_{n+1})), t')$$

can be computed from the symbolic states capturing

$$\mathcal{T}_{\mathcal{A}}(\mathcal{C}_{\mathcal{A}}((\phi_1, I_1, m_1)\cdots(\phi_n, I_n, m_n)), t),$$

as evident from the proof of Lemma 1. The same is true for the reach-sets in the other two automata $\mathcal{B}_{\neg\varphi}\otimes\mathcal{A}$ and $\mathcal{B}_{\varphi}\otimes\mathcal{A}$.

Remark 2. Our algorithm requires TBA both for the property *and* its complement, but TBA are in general not closed under complementation [2]. For the important case of MITL properties, such automata always exist, as MITL is closed under negation and can be translated into equivalent TBA (Theorem 1).

5 Evaluation

We implemented our assumption-based online monitoring algorithm described in Sect. 4 by extending the UPPAAL tool component MoniTAal[1], thereby demonstrating how the use of assumptions and unobservable events can enhance monitoring capabilities. In the following, we report on two proof-of-concept cases.

[1] https://github.com/DEIS-Tools/MoniTAal.

Task Sequence. We first experiment with a system under monitoring that produces a finite sequence of events $a_1, \ldots, a_k$. Each a_i, with $1 \leq i < k$, is followed by a_{i+1} with a time within the interval $[l_i, u_i]$. The assumption is formalized by the TBA shown in Fig. 3. The domain is parameterized on k, and the l_i and u_i. Further, depending on the experiment, not all the a_i will be observable. We consider the bounded response property $G(a_1 \rightarrow F_{[0,B]} a_k)$. Suppose that we observe a timed word $(a_1, t_1) \cdots (a_k, t_k)$. If for some j in the range $1 < j \leq k$, we have $t_j + \sum_{j \leq i < k} u_i \leq B + t_1$, then the verdict at time t_j is $\top$. On the other hand, if $t_j + \sum_{j \leq i < k} l_i > B + t_1$, then the verdict at time t_j is $\bot$. As a corner case, if $\sum_{1 \leq i < k} u_i \leq B$ or $\sum_{1 \leq i < k} l_i > B$, the verdict is respectively $\top$ and $\bot$ at time 0, since all words of the assumption respectively satisfy and violate the property. We run several experiments to show the effect of the assumption and study the scalability under a sequence of unobservable events.

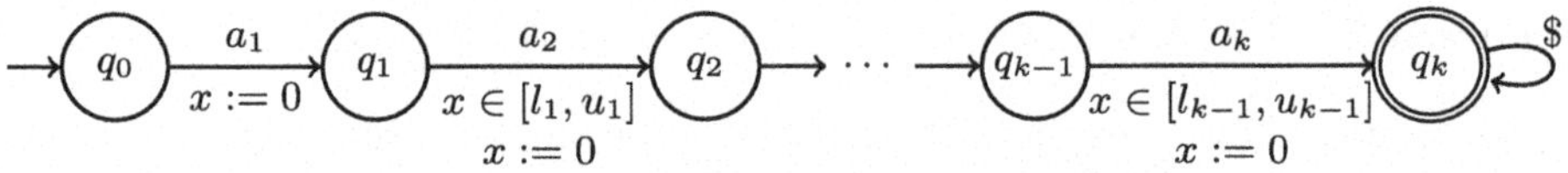

Fig. 3. A TBA representing the assumption for the bounded response example.

First we show how unobservable events can affect the response-time, the time between receiving an event and outputting a verdict. We pick $k = 100$ and $l_i = 50$ and $u_i = 100$ for all i. The events $\{a_i \mid i \in \{21, \ldots, 40\} \cup \{61, \ldots, 80\}\}$ are unobservable within the interval $[0, 10000]$. In Fig. 4 we see that for each consecutive unobservable event, the response time grows linearly. This is due to the reach-set growing. Nevertheless, the reach-set shrinks when an observable event is received. The minimum response time is 4583 nanoseconds (ns), the maximum is 115926 ns and the average is 24753 ns. For reference, if we monitor 5000 consecutive unobservable events, the maximum response time is 32 ms.

To show the effect of the assumption, we monitor the bounded response property $G(a_1 \rightarrow F_{[0,675]} a_{10})$ a thousand times, with and without the assumption where $l_i = 50$ and $u_i = 100$ for all i. The observed words are random, but within the assumption. The results in Table 1 show that verdicts are computed earlier with the assumption than without. Without the assumption the earliest verdicts were in 33 cases $\bot$ after observing a_9, while with the assumption we saw a $\top$ or $\bot$ verdict in 522 cases before observing a_{10}.

Thus, when monitoring a live system in an online setting (compared to evaluating a log history), a verdict can be reached earlier, because of the restrictions the assumption inhibits. Furthermore, we demonstrate in this case how unobservable events can affect the size of the reach-set, as the number of words that are consistent with an observation can increase with the number of consecutive unobservable events. This in turn affects the response-time.

Conveyor Belt Example. This example represents a conveyor belt that moves an item through different stations, where the item is processed according to some

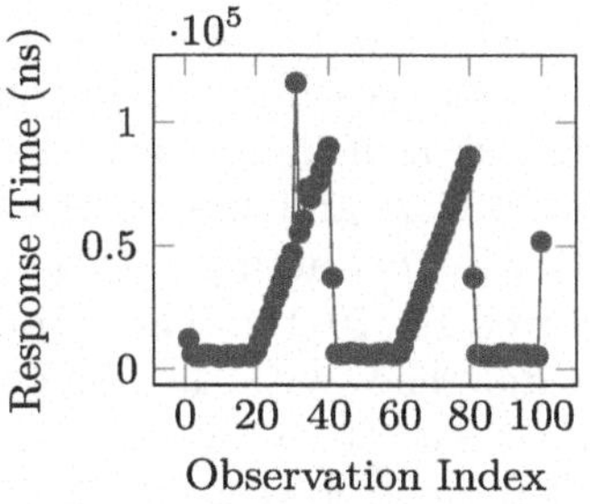

Fig. 4. Response time of the monitoring implementation, when monitoring the task sequence example with $\{a_i \mid i \in \{21, \ldots, 40\} \cup \{61, \ldots, 80\}\}$ being unobservable.

Table 1. Verdict distribution for monitoring the task sequence example a thousand times with $k = 10$, $B = 675$, $l_i = 50$ and $u_i = 100$ for all i, with and without assumption. Each row specifies the number of times each verdict is given after an observation.

Observation	Verdicts					
	No Assumption			With Assumption		
	$\top$	$\bot$	?	$\top$	$\bot$	?
a_5	0	0	1000	0	0	1000
a_6	0	0	1000	0	1	999
a_7	0	0	1000	17	15	967
a_8	0	0	1000	81	90	796
a_9	0	33	967	165	153	478
a_{10}	0	457	510	246	232	0

task. The task in the nominal case takes between 8 and 10 times units. However, if the process is faulty, it finishes earlier and takes between 7 and 9 time units: it may sometimes complete correctly on time, but it may in other cases stop too early. The fault can happen at any time and is permanent. Our assumption automaton is shown in Fig. 5. Our monitoring property is simply $G\neg fault$.

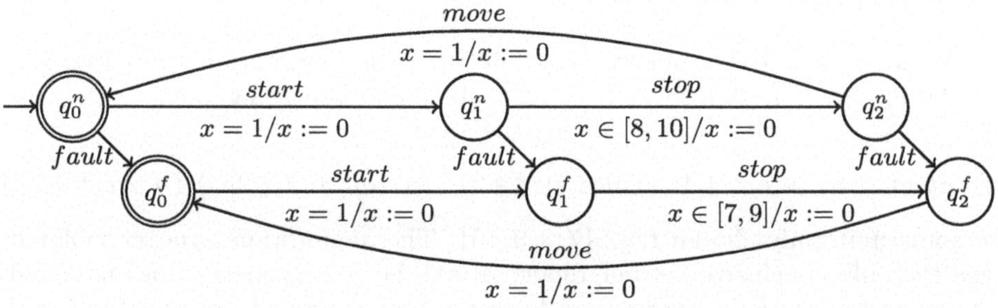

Fig. 5. A TBA representing the assumption for the conveyor belt example.

Consider that we observe the events *start*, *stop*, and *move* with precise information on the time. If the *stop* signal happens less than 8 time units after *start*, we detect a violation of the property. If instead *stop* happens between 8 and 9 time units, we cannot say if there was a fault or not.

Suppose now that we have uncertainty on the time of the observations like in the following observation sequence:

$$(start, [1, 1], !)(fault, [1, 11], *)(stop, [8, 10], !)(fault, [8, 11], *)(move, [9, 11], !)$$
$$(fault, [9, 12], *)(start, [10, 12], !)(fault, [11, 22], *)(stop, [16, 18], !)$$

The first *stop* happens at a time between 8 and 10, thus between 7 and 9 time units after the first *start*. This is compatible with both a nominal (with *stop* occurring between times 9 and 10) and a faulty execution (with *stop* occurring between times 8 and 9): after the first stop, we do not know if there was a fault.

The second *start* happens in the time interval $[10, 12]$ and has the same uncertainty: it is consistent with the nominal behavior if *start* actually occurred in $[11, 12]$ and with a faulty behavior if *start* occurred in $[10, 11]$. The second stop happens in the time interval $[16, 18]$. Thus, the difference with the previous start is between 4 and 8 time units. This seems compatible with a nominal delay ($[8, 10]$). However, from the reasoning done above, if there were no fault the second start would have occurred in the interval $[11, 12]$ and the second *stop* would have occurred in the interval $[19, 22]$, which is not compatible with the observation. Thus we can conclude there was a fault.

Table 2. Distribution of verdicts when monitoring 1000 random words of the conveyor belt assumption. Each column shows the number of times a conclusive verdict is given after observing the pattern a number of times. The longest run had 24 repetitions of the pattern before a verdict is given.

Repetitions	1	2	3	4	5	6	7	8	9	10	11
#Verdicts	251	185	125	121	90	47	48	31	24	20	13
Repetitions	12	13	14	15	16	17	18	19	20	24	
#Verdicts	13	9	4	5	4	2	2	2	3	1	

We monitored the property $G\neg fault$ with the assumption from Fig. 5 by simulating the conveyor belt with an unbounded repeating pattern $\rho_1 \cdot_{\tau(\rho_1)} \rho_2 \cdot_{\tau(\rho_1)+\tau(\rho_2)} \cdots$ with each ρ_i having the form

$$(fault, [0,1], *), (start, 1, !), (fault, [1, t_i{+}2], *), (stop, [t_i, t_i{+}2], !), (move, t_i{+}2, !)$$

for some uniformly chosen $t_i \in \{7, 8, 9, 10\}$. The assumption is never violated, thus the only conclusive verdict reported is $\perp$ i.e. the property does not hold. The pattern essentially randomly selects whether *stop* is observed after 7, 8, 9 or 10 time units after *start*. Since 7 is only possible after a fault, there is a 1 in 4 chance, per repetition, of violating the property. The results in Table 2 show that in 251 out of 1000 cases a definitive verdict is given after observing the pattern once, and that the longest is 24 repetitions.

With this example, we see how an assumption makes it possible to monitor properties over unobservable events. Without an assumption, reasoning about unobservable behaviour would not be possible for such a property.

6 Related Work

Our automata-based monitoring of finite words against specifications over infinite words follows the seminal work of Bauer et al. [6], who presented monitoring algorithms for LTL and timed LTL. Their algorithm for timed LTL is based on clock regions [2], while we follow the approach of Grosen et al. [20] and use clock zones [8], whose performance is an order of magnitude faster. Also, they translated timed LTL into event-clock automata, which are less expressive than the timed Büchi automata (TBA) used both by Grosen et al. [20] and here. This approach has also been applied to monitoring under delayed observations [17].

As our algorithms work with TBA, we also support MITL specifications, as these can be compiled into TBA. The monitoring problem for MITL has been investigated before. Baldor et al. showed how to construct a monitor for dense-time MITL formulas by constructing a tree of timed transducers [4]. Ho et al. split unbounded and bounded parts of MITL formulas for monitoring, using traditional LTL monitoring for the unbounded parts and permitting a simpler construction for the (finite-word) bounded parts [22].

There is also a large body of work on monitoring with finite-word semantics. Roşu et al. focussed on discrete-time finite-word MTL [28], while Basin et al. proposed algorithms for monitoring real-time finite-word properties [5] and compared different time models. Donzé et al. [16] focussed on monitoring a quantitative semantics for STL, a variant of MTL with predicates over real-valued signals. André et al. consider monitoring finite logs of parameterized timed and hybrid systems [31]. Finally, Ulus et al. described monitoring timed regular expressions over finite words using unions of two-dimensional zones [29,30].

The contribution of this paper is focused on extending the monitoring of timed properties with assumptions, framing the problem as defined in [12–15] for the discrete-time setting. Assumptions were first used in [23] for extending the monitoring of LTL with predictive capabilities. In [32], the assumption for predictive RV is computed applying static analysis to the monitored program. Pinisetty et al. further extend the predictive RV idea to support RV of timed properties [25], where the *a priori knowledge* is also expressed as a timed property. As in [15], we adopt a four-valued semantics for timed properties and we support partial observability. Besides the complexity of moving from discrete to dense time semantics, the ABRV framework is extended with a rich notion of observations that take into account uncertainty on the time.

The research of partial observability in Discrete-Event Systems is usually connected with diagnosability [26] and predictability [18,19]. These notions have been extended to timed systems (see, e.g., [10,11]). Moreover, they are related to monitorability, an important topic in RV and other related fields [1,24,27], which has been studied taking into account assumptions in [21].

7 Conclusion

In this paper, we extended runtime verification of timed properties with assumptions. These are used for anticipating or predicting a property failure or success, as well as for considering partial observability of the monitored system. A key contribution is to enable runtime verification to consider an observation sequence that has uncertainty on both the states/events and on the timing information.

We provided an effective zone-based algorithm to compute the states that can be reached with such an observation sequence considering a property specified in MITL and an assumption as a TBA. Thus, such a computation can be used for online monitoring of timed properties under assumptions. The algorithm was implemented on top of UPPAAL and experimented with a few examples to show the feasibility of the approach.

For future work, further investigation is needed to check the scalability of the approach and to apply and optimize it to real-world case studies.

References

1. Aceto, L., Achilleos, A., Francalanza, A., Ingólfsdóttir, A., Lehtinen, K.: An operational guide to monitorability. In: Ölveczky, P.C., Salaün, G. (eds.) SEFM 2019. LNCS, vol. 11724, pp. 433–453. Springer, Cham (2019). https://doi.org/10.1007/978-3-030-30446-1_23
2. Alur, R., Dill, D.L.: A theory of timed automata. Theor. Comput. Sci. **126**(2), 183–235 (1994). https://doi.org/10.1016/0304-3975(94)90010-8
3. Alur, R., Feder, T., Henzinger, T.A.: The benefits of relaxing punctuality. J. ACM **43**(1) (1996)
4. Baldor, K., Niu, J.: Monitoring dense-time, continuous-semantics, metric temporal logic. In: Qadeer, S., Tasiran, S. (eds.) RV 2012. LNCS, vol. 7687, pp. 245–259. Springer, Heidelberg (2013). https://doi.org/10.1007/978-3-642-35632-2_24
5. Basin, D., Klaedtke, F., Zălinescu, E.: Algorithms for monitoring real-time properties. In: Khurshid, S., Sen, K. (eds.) RV 2011. LNCS, vol. 7186, pp. 260–275. Springer, Heidelberg (2012). https://doi.org/10.1007/978-3-642-29860-8_20
6. Bauer, A., Leucker, M., Schallhart, C.: Monitoring of real-time properties. In: Arun-Kumar, S., Garg, N. (eds.) FSTTCS 2006. LNCS, vol. 4337, pp. 260–272. Springer, Heidelberg (2006). https://doi.org/10.1007/11944836_25
7. Bellman, R.: Dynamic Programming. Princeton University Press, Princeton (1957)
8. Bengtsson, J., Yi, W.: Timed automata: semantics, algorithms and tools. In: Desel, J., Reisig, W., Rozenberg, G. (eds.) ACPN 2003. LNCS, vol. 3098, pp. 87–124. Springer, Heidelberg (2004). https://doi.org/10.1007/978-3-540-27755-2_3
9. Brihaye, T., Geeraerts, G., Ho, H.-M., Monmege, B.: MightyL: a compositional translation from MITL to timed automata. In: Majumdar, R., Kunčak, V. (eds.) CAV 2017. LNCS, vol. 10426, pp. 421–440. Springer, Cham (2017). https://doi.org/10.1007/978-3-319-63387-9_21
10. Cassez, F., Grastien, A.: Predictability of event occurrences in timed systems. In: Braberman, V., Fribourg, L. (eds.) FORMATS 2013. LNCS, vol. 8053, pp. 62–76. Springer, Heidelberg (2013). https://doi.org/10.1007/978-3-642-40229-6_5
11. Cassez, F., Tripakis, S.: Fault diagnosis of timed systems. In: Communicating Embedded Systems, pp. 107–138. Wiley, New York (2013)
12. Cimatti, A., Tian, C., Tonetta, S.: Assumption-based runtime verification with partial observability and resets. In: Finkbeiner, B., Mariani, L. (eds.) RV 2019. LNCS, vol. 11757, pp. 165–184. Springer, Cham (2019). https://doi.org/10.1007/978-3-030-32079-9_10
13. Cimatti, A., Tian, C., Tonetta, S.: NuRV: a nuXmv extension for runtime verification. In: Finkbeiner, B., Mariani, L. (eds.) RV 2019. LNCS, vol. 11757, pp. 382–392. Springer, Cham (2019). https://doi.org/10.1007/978-3-030-32079-9_23

14. Cimatti, A., Tian, C., Tonetta, S.: Assumption-based runtime verification of infinite-state systems. In: Feng, L., Fisman, D. (eds.) RV 2021. LNCS, vol. 12974, pp. 207–227. Springer, Cham (2021). https://doi.org/10.1007/978-3-030-88494-9_11
15. Cimatti, A., Tian, C., Tonetta, S.: Assumption-based runtime verification. Formal Methods Syst. Des. **60**(2), 277–324 (2022)
16. Donzé, A., Ferrère, T., Maler, O.: Efficient robust monitoring for STL. In: Sharygina, N., Veith, H. (eds.) CAV 2013. LNCS, vol. 8044, pp. 264–279. Springer, Heidelberg (2013). https://doi.org/10.1007/978-3-642-39799-8_19
17. Fränzle, M., Grosen, T.M., Larsen, K.G., Zimmermann, M.: Monitoring real-time systems under parametric delay. arXiv:2404.18282 (2024). https://doi.org/10.48550/ARXIV.2404.18282. Accepted for publication at iFM 2024
18. Genc, S., Lafortune, S.: Predictability of event occurrences in partially-observed discrete-event systems. Automatica **45**(2), 301–311 (2009). https://doi.org/10.1016/j.automatica.2008.06.022
19. Genc, S., Lafortune, S.: Predictability in discrete-event systems under partial observation. IFAC Proc. Vol. **39**(13), 1461–1466 (2006). https://doi.org/10.3182/20060829-4-CN-2909.00243
20. Grosen, T.M., Kauffman, S., Larsen, K.G., Zimmermann, M.: Monitoring timed properties (revisited). In: Bogomolov, S., Parker, D. (eds.) FORMATS 2022. LNCS, vol. 13465, pp. 43–62. Springer, Cham (2022). https://doi.org/10.1007/978-3-031-15839-1_3
21. Henzinger, T.A., Saraç, N.E.: Monitorability under assumptions. In: Deshmukh, J., Ničković, D. (eds.) RV 2020. LNCS, vol. 12399, pp. 3–18. Springer, Cham (2020). https://doi.org/10.1007/978-3-030-60508-7_1
22. Ho, H.-M., Ouaknine, J., Worrell, J.: Online monitoring of metric temporal logic. In: Bonakdarpour, B., Smolka, S.A. (eds.) RV 2014. LNCS, vol. 8734, pp. 178–192. Springer, Cham (2014). https://doi.org/10.1007/978-3-319-11164-3_15
23. Leucker, M.: Sliding between model checking and runtime verification. In: Qadeer, S., Tasiran, S. (eds.) RV 2012. LNCS, vol. 7687, pp. 82–87. Springer, Heidelberg (2013). https://doi.org/10.1007/978-3-642-35632-2_10
24. Peled, D., Havelund, K.: Refining the safety–liveness classification of temporal properties according to monitorability. In: Margaria, T., Graf, S., Larsen, K.G. (eds.) Models, Mindsets, Meta: The What, the How, and the Why Not? LNCS, vol. 11200, pp. 218–234. Springer, Cham (2019). https://doi.org/10.1007/978-3-030-22348-9_14
25. Pinisetty, S., Jéron, T., Tripakis, S., Falcone, Y., Marchand, H., Preoteasa, V.: Predictive runtime verification of timed properties. J. Syst. Softw. **132**, 353–365 (2017). https://doi.org/10.1016/j.jss.2017.06.060
26. Sampath, M., Sengupta, R., Lafortune, S., Sinnamohideen, K., Teneketzis, D.: Diagnosability of discrete-event systems. IEEE Trans. Autom. Control **40**(9), 1555–1575 (1995). https://doi.org/10.1109/9.412626
27. Sistla, A.P., Žefran, M., Feng, Y.: Monitorability of stochastic dynamical systems. In: Gopalakrishnan, G., Qadeer, S. (eds.) CAV 2011. LNCS, vol. 6806, pp. 720–736. Springer, Heidelberg (2011). https://doi.org/10.1007/978-3-642-22110-1_58
28. Thati, P., Roşu, G.: Monitoring algorithms for metric temporal logic specifications. Electron. Notes Theor. Comput. Sci. **113**, 145–162 (2005). https://doi.org/10.1016/j.entcs.2004.01.029, Proceedings of the Fourth Workshop on Runtime Verification (RV 2004)

29. Ulus, D., Ferrère, T., Asarin, E., Maler, O.: Timed pattern matching. In: Legay, A., Bozga, M. (eds.) FORMATS 2014. LNCS, vol. 8711, pp. 222–236. Springer, Cham (2014). https://doi.org/10.1007/978-3-319-10512-3_16
30. Ulus, D., Ferrère, T., Asarin, E., Maler, O.: Online timed pattern matching using derivatives. In: Chechik, M., Raskin, J.-F. (eds.) TACAS 2016. LNCS, vol. 9636, pp. 736–751. Springer, Heidelberg (2016). https://doi.org/10.1007/978-3-662-49674-9_47
31. Waga, M., André, É., Hasuo, I.: Model-bounded monitoring of hybrid systems. ACM Trans. Cyber Phys. Syst. **6**(4), 30:1–30:26 (2022). https://doi.org/10.1145/3529095
32. Zhang, X., Leucker, M., Dong, W.: Runtime verification with predictive semantics. In: Goodloe, A.E., Person, S. (eds.) NFM 2012. LNCS, vol. 7226, pp. 418–432. Springer, Heidelberg (2012). https://doi.org/10.1007/978-3-642-28891-3_37

A Formal Modeling Language for Smart Contracts

Adele Veschetti(✉), Richard Bubel, and Reiner Hähnle

Department of Computer Science, TU Darmstadt, Darmstadt, Germany
{adele.veschetti,richard.bubel,reiner.haehnle}@tu-darmstadt.de

Abstract. Smart contracts codify real-world transactions and automatically execute the terms of the contract when predefined conditions are met. This paper proposes SmartML, a modeling language for smart contracts that is platform independent and easy to comprehend. We detail its formal semantics and type system with a focus on its role in addressing security vulnerabilities. We show along a case study, how SmartML prevents reentrancy attacks, illustrating its efficacy in reinforcing the reliability and security of smart contracts within decentralized systems.

1 Introduction

Distributed ledger technologies are realized as a peer-to-peer network, where each node independently maintains and updates an identical record of all transactions, known as a ledger. To establish consensus on the accuracy of a single ledger copy, a consensus algorithm is employed. The most popular design for distributed ledgers employs blockchains, which are immutable lists with built-in integrity and security guarantees. These assurances, coupled with a consensus algorithm, establish the trustworthiness of distributed ledgers.

A central aspect for the usefulness of blockchains is their capability to store programs, so-called smart contracts, and their (dormant) runtime state in between transactions. Smart contracts formalize agreements between parties, such as resource exchange protocols, with the expectation of providing tamper-proof storage for security-critical assets. Despite this promise, widely-used smart contract languages are often complex, rendering them susceptible to unforeseen attacks. At the same time, in blockchain systems, rectifying errors post-transaction is nearly impossible. Both aspects together make it of paramount importance to ensure the correct functionality of smart contracts *before* deployment. The fact that correctness of smart contracts is relevant in practice is substantiated by the vast number of security vulnerabilities [8] and (partially successful) attacks such as DAO [20], the latter causing damage of 50 million USD worth of Ether.

In consequence, there is a strong motivation for formal specification and verification of smart contracts, despite the effort involved, with a variety of

This work is funded by the ATHENE project "Model-centric Deductive Verification of Smart Contracts".

A. Madeira and A. Knapp (Eds.): SEFM 2024, LNCS 15280, pp. 89–106, 2025.
https://doi.org/10.1007/978-3-031-77382-2_6

approaches [8,13,17,22]. However, to be feasible and economical in practice, the effort for specification and verification of smart contracts must be as small as possible. This is the focus of our work.

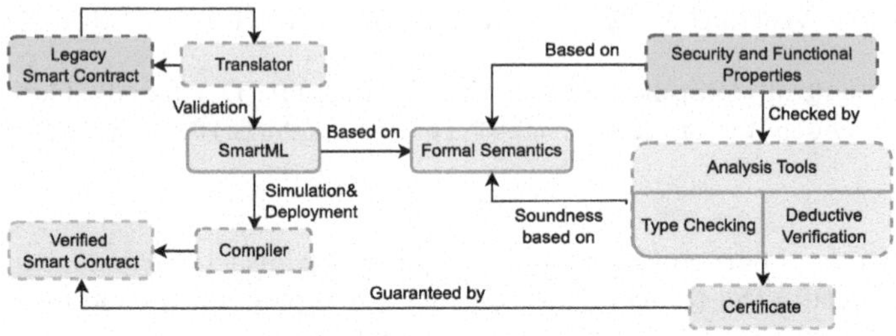

Fig. 1. Overview of the SmartML framework

We propose SmartML, a platform-independent modeling framework (see Fig. 1) for smart contracts that enables formal verification and certification of the absence of well-defined classes of vulnerabilities.

One main objective is to develop a modeling language that is easy to comprehend to support validation and verification. For comprehensibility we aim at a balance between ease-to-use and explicit behavior (for example, explicit transaction handling). Comprehensibility also requires a well-defined (and designed) semantics that provides definite answers. This is achieved by providing a formal semantics which is also the backbone for verification of smart contract behavior, forming the basis for sound analyses like type checking, static analysis, and deductive verification, ensuring security and functional correctness.

To summarize, SmartML aims to meet the following requirements: (i) easier validation of smart contracts through clear and precise modeling; (ii) the ability to execute SmartML and thus to simulate its effects, as well as the possibility to compile into native code such as the Ethereum Virtual Machine; (iii) support for analyzing legacy smart contracts via translation into SmartML.

Regarding the latter, we present a sound type system to prevent reentrancy in smart contracts by regulating the flow of interactions between functions. Using type checking we can avoid unintended recursive calls, reducing the risk of reentrancy vulnerabilities, but still permitting safe reentrant calls. This achieves increased overall security of smart contracts by maintaining strict control over their execution flow without being overly restrictive and limiting functionality.

The paper is organized as follows. Section 2 contains an overview of smart contracts and reentrancy attacks to make the paper self-contained. The SmartML modeling language, along with its semantics, is detailed in Sect. 3. The formal definition of reentrancy security is given in Sect. 4, while Sect. 5 presents the type system for safe reentrancy. Section 6 provides examples to illustrate the discussed concepts. A comparative analysis of our proposal with existing literature is in Sect. 7, while Sect. 8 summarizes key findings and explores potential avenues for future research.

2 Background

2.1 Smart Contracts

Blockchain technology facilitates a distributed computing architecture, wherein transactions are publicly disclosed and participants reach consensus on a singular transaction history, commonly referred to as a ledger [9]. Transactions are organized into blocks, timestamped, and made public. The cryptographic hash of each block makes altering published blocks highly challenging.

Among the applications of blockchains, smart contracts stand out. These automated, self-executing contracts redefine traditional agreements, offering efficiency and transparency in various industries. A smart contract is essentially a computer program delineated by its source code. It has the capability to automatically execute the terms of a distinct agreement expressed in natural language if certain conditions are met. Typically crafted using high-level languages, smart contracts are then compiled to bytecode and encapsulated in self-contained entities deployable on any node within a blockchain.

Smart contracts can be developed and deployed on various blockchain platforms, such as NXT [5], Ethereum [3], and Hyperledger Fabric [4]. Each platform offers distinct features, including specialized programming languages, contract code execution, and varying security measures.

2.2 Reentrancy

One of the most common vulnerabilities of smart contracts is the reentrancy attack: it initiates a recursively called procedure facilitating the transfer of funds between two smart contracts, a vulnerable contract $\mathcal{C}$ and a malicious contract $\mathcal{A}$. The attacker places a call to the vulnerable contract with the aim of transferring funds to $\mathcal{A}$. Contract $\mathcal{C}$ verifies whether the attacker possesses the requisite funds and, upon confirmation, proceeds to transfer the funds to contract $\mathcal{A}$. Upon receipt of the funds, contract $\mathcal{A}$ activates a callback function, which subsequently invokes contract $\mathcal{C}$ again *before the balance update occurs.* Reentrancy attacks can be categorized into three forms, each with distinct characteristic:

1. *Single Reentrancy Attack*: Here the vulnerable function that the attacker recursively calls is the same as the one being exploited.
2. *Cross-function Attack*: These occur when a vulnerable function shares state with another function that yields a desirable outcome for the attacker.
3. *Cross-contract Attack*: It takes place when the state from one contract is invoked in another contract before it is fully updated.

Specifically, cross-function reentrancy refers to a vulnerability in smart contracts where an external call is made to another function within the same contract before the completion of the first function's state changes. In other words, during the execution of one function, an external call is initiated to a *different* function within the *same* contract, potentially leading to unexpected or malicious behavior. Identifying this form of reentrancy attack is challenging: In complex protocols many combinations occur, making it practically impossible to manually test every possible outcome. Spotting cross-contract vulnerability is also challenging, because it involves interactions between multiple smart contracts, making it hard to foresee the execution sequence and potential vulnerabilities.

One way to avoid certain reentrancy vulnerabilities is to adhere to the Checks-Effects-Interactions Pattern [24]. This approach suggests that a smart contract should initially perform necessary checks (Checks), subsequently modify its internal state (Effects), and *only then* interact with other smart contracts, some of which could be potentially malicious. By following this pattern, a reentrant call becomes indistinguishable from a call initiated after the completion of the initial call. This is because, in both cases, the contract's state is already finalized and secure. However, while the Checks-Effects-Interactions pattern is a crucial guideline for avoiding reentrancy vulnerabilities within a *single* contract, it may not provide sufficient protection against cross-contract or cross-function reentrancy attacks. The inherent complexity of these attacks, combined with the nature of smart contract interactions, requires a more comprehensive approach.

3 SmartML

A SmartML program is a sequence of contract declarations and algebraic data type (ADT) definitions. Combining contract and immutable ADT declarations provides a flexible and suitably abstract approach to smart contract modeling.

The selection of language features of SmartML resulted from a comprehensive, detailed, and systematic analysis of the commonalities and differences among existing smart contract languages. Putting a strong focus on security through static analysis and deductive verification, SmartML employs a formal semantics to ensure the unambiguous meaning of its operations. The modeling language is also equipped with a type system designed to address crucial security aspects like safe reentrancy. Listing 1 shows a simple smart contract written in SmartML.

```
contract C {
 int n ;
 constructor(int val) {
  this.n = val;
 }
 int m(int x) {
  return n+x;
 }
}
```

Listing 1: SmartML Code

3.1 Syntax

The grammar of SmartML is shown in Table 1. We use the following syntactic conventions: C, D refer to contract names; A, L, K, M represent ADT declarations, contract declarations, constructor and method declarations, respectively; n stands for ADT function declarations; d indicates ADT expressions; f, g denote fields; m stands for method declarations; s, e, v, and τ cover statements, expressions, values, and types, respectively, while local variables are denoted by x. We use the overline symbol ($\overline{f}$) to represent a (possibly empty) sequence of elements $f_1, \ldots, f_n$ and square brackets [ ] to indicate optional elements.

The set of all local program variables is called $\textsf{ProgVars}$. For ease of presentation, we assume that each local program has a unique name. The set of program variables $\textsf{ProgVars}$ includes the special variable $\textbf{this}_C$ for each contract type C. If the context is clear the subscript C is omitted.

Table 1. The syntax of SmartML.

P	$::= \overline{A}\ \overline{L}$	(program)
A	$::= \textbf{datatype}\ adt\ \{\textbf{constructor}\{\overline{fn} :: \overline{adt}\}\ \overline{F}\}$	(datatype)
F	$::= \tau_n\ n(\overline{\tau}\ \overline{w})\ \{d\}$	(ADT function)
d	$::= \textbf{if}\ (c)\ \{\ e\ \}\ \textbf{else}\ \{\ e\ \} \mid \textbf{return}\ e \mid n(\overline{w})$	(ADT expression)
	$\mid \textbf{switch}\ e\ \{\textbf{case}\ e :\ d;\ \textbf{default} :\ d\}$	
L	$::= \textbf{contract}\ C\ [\textbf{extends}\ D]\ \{\overline{f} : \overline{\tau}_f; K; \overline{M}\}$	(contract)
K	$::= \textbf{constructor}([\overline{g} : \overline{\tau}_g,]\ \overline{f} : \overline{\tau}_f)\ \{[\textbf{super}(\overline{g});]\ \textbf{this}.\overline{f} = \overline{f}\}$	(constructor)
M	$::= \tau_m\ m(\overline{\tau}\ \overline{v})\ \{s\}$	(method)
s	$::= \textbf{if}\ (e)\ \{s\}\ [\textbf{else}\ \{s\}] \mid \textbf{while}(e)\ \{s\} \mid \textbf{let}\ v := rhs\ \textbf{in}\ s$	(statement)
	$\mid \textbf{assert}(e) \mid v := rhs \mid v := v.m(\overline{v}) \mid v.m(\overline{v}) \mid \textbf{return}\ [e]$	
	$\mid \textbf{throw}\ e \mid \textbf{try}\ s_0\ \textbf{abort}\ \{s_1\}\ \textbf{success}\ \{s_2\} \mid s_1; s_2$	
e	$::= v \mid e_1\ \textsf{op}\ e_2 \mid e_1\ \textsf{bop}\ e_2$	(expression)
v	$::= x \mid !v \mid v.f \mid \textbf{true} \mid \textbf{false} \mid d \mid \textbf{this}_C$	(value)
rhs	$::= e \mid \textbf{new}\ C(\overline{v})$	(right-hand side)
$\textsf{op}$	$::= + \mid - \mid \times \mid \div$	(arithmetic operator)
$\textsf{bop}$	$::= \leq \mid \geq \mid \&\& \mid \mid\mid \mid = \mid \neq$	(boolean operator)

An ADT definition consists of a sequence of function definitions. ADT expressions include **if–then–else**, **return**, **switch**-constructs, and function calls.

A contract declaration introduces a contract C, which may extend a contract D. Contract C has fields $\overline{f}$ with types $\overline{\tau_f}$, a constructor K and methods $\overline{m}$. The set of all contract types (names) is called $\textsf{Contract}$, the set of all fields is called $\textsf{Field}$. The constructor initializes the fields of a contract C. Its structure is determined by the instance variable declarations of C and the contract it extends: the parameters must match the declared instance variables, and its body must include a call to the super class constructor for initializing its fields with parameters $\overline{g}$. Subsequently, an assignment of the parameters $\overline{f}$ to the new fields with the same names as declared in C is performed. A method declaration introduces a method named m with return type τ_m and parameters $\overline{v}$ having types $\overline{\tau}$. Most statements are standard; for instance, $v := rhs$ and $v := v.m(\overline{v})$ denote assignments, and $\textbf{assert}(\textsf{e})$ ensures that a condition holds: If the expression e evaluates to **true**, executing an assertion is like executing a skip. On the other hand, if the expression evaluates to **false**, it is equivalent to throwing an error. Expression syntax is standard, however, for field access $v.f$, we restrict v to $\textsf{\textbf{this}}_C$. For ease of presentation, we assume that method invocations pass only local variables as arguments.

This article focuses on contract and statement definitions. Consequently, we do not detail the semantics and type system related to ADT definitions.

3.2 Semantics

We describe the semantics of SmartML in the style of structural operational semantics (SOS) [16]. SOS defines a transition system whose nodes are configurations that represent the current computation context, including call stack, memory, and program counter.

To formally define configurations we need a notion of computation state. Intuitively, each state assigns to program variables and contract fields[1] their current value. It is characteristic of smart contracts to distinguish between *volatile* memory and *persistent* memory, where the former stores temporary information produced during computation of a self-contained task (also called a *transaction*) while the latter is information that may influence the execution of subsequent transactions and is thus stored on the blockchain.

Definition 1. (Domain and State). *The set of semantic values* D *is called* domain. *For each contract type, ADT or primitive type* τ *there is a domain* $\mathsf{D}^\tau \subseteq \mathsf{D}$. *A* state *is a pair* (s_v, s_p) *of* volatile memory s_v *and* persistent *memory* s_p *where*

- *volatile memory is a mapping* $s_v : \mathsf{Var} \to \mathsf{D}$ *from program variables to their domain* D*;*
- *persistent memory is a mapping* $s_p : \mathsf{D}^{\mathsf{Contract}} \to (\mathsf{D}^{\mathsf{Field}} \to \mathsf{D})$, *which assigns to each contract its own persistent memory (where* $\mathsf{D}^{\mathsf{Contract}} := \bigcup_{C \in \mathsf{Contract}} \mathsf{D}^C$*).*

We can now define a *configuration*, which forms the context wherein SmartML operates and that is modified by the execution of a SmartML program.

Definition 2. (Configuration). *A* configuration *is a quintuple*

$$\{\overbrace{c_0}^{\textit{contract}}, \overbrace{\overline{contrs}}^{\textit{call stack}}, \overbrace{(s_v, s_p)}^{\textit{state}}, \overbrace{trans}^{\textit{rollback persistent memory}}, \overbrace{m_0 \mapsto cnt_0}^{\textit{continuation}}\}$$

consisting of:

- *The current active contract* $c_0 \in \mathsf{D}^{\mathsf{Contract}}$*;*
- *the call stack* $\overline{contrs} = c_1[s_1, m_1, cnt_1] \circ \cdots \circ c_n[s_n, m_n, cnt_n]$, *where each argument triple of the current caller* c_i *contains the state* s_i *in which* c_i *was suspended, the method* m_i *from where the call originated, and the remaining code* cnt_i *to be executed by* c_i*;*
- *the current state* $\sigma_0 = (s_v^0, s_p^0)$*;*

[1] *State variables* in Solidity terminology.

- $\overline{trans}$ *is a sequence of persistent memories* $s_{p_1}, \ldots, s_{p_k}$*; in case of a revert the system reverts back to the first state* s_{p_1} *in the sequence*
- *the continuation* $m_0 \mapsto cnt_0$*, i.e. the remaining code* cnt_0 *to be executed next in the scope of the currently active method* m_0.

Table 2 shows selected SOS rules, while the complete semantics can be found in the extended version of the paper [23].

We start with the assignment rule [E-Assign]. It is applicable in a state (s_v^0, s_p^0) when the first statement of a continuation is an assignment with a program variable x on the left side and a type-compatible *side-effect free* expression e on the right side. The code following the assignment is matched by r. Execution of the assignment leads to an updated configuration, whose continuation is just r with the assignment removed and its effect reflected in the updated volatile store s_v', which is identical to s_v^0 except for the value of program variable x. The value of $s_v'(x)$ is equal to the value of the assignment's right hand side e evaluated in the original state (s_v^0, s_p^0).

Rule [E-MethodCall (w/o Trans)] defines the effect of an internal method invocation that does not open a new transaction. The invocation **this**.$n(\bar{e})$ of method n on the current contract leads to the following configuration changes:

- When returning without a revert/error from the call, execution must continue with the code after the invocation statement. Hence, we record the current context on the call stack. This involves pushing a record on the stack which is composed of (i) the caller c_0, (ii) the volatile memory s_v^0, (iii) the currently executed method m_0, (iv) the continuation r to be executed upon return of the call (the program counter). The current contract remains the active contract instance, but the called method n becomes now the active method, whose body is executed next.
- The volatile storage s_v' accessible to the called method n consists initially only of the values passed as arguments ($[\![\bar{e}]\!]_{(s_v^0, s_p^0)}$).
- As no new transaction is opened (and the current one not closed), the list of transactions remains unchanged.

Method invocations embedded in a **try−abort−success** statement open a new transaction. The **try−abort−success** statement provides the means for appropriate error handling in case of a failed transaction. The semantics for a method invocation that opens a new transaction [E-MethodCall (w/ Trans)] is similar to the previous rule, but we have to extend the list of transactions by recording the current persistent store s_p^0 so we can revert the state in case of an abort. The continuation put on the call stack still contains the **try−abort−success**, but with the actual invocation statement replaced by an anonymous marker '?'.

Finally, we have a look at one of the rules for returning from a method invocation in the context of a **try−abort−success** statement. We focus on the rule [E-MethodCall (ReturnFromTry II)] for a failed transaction. In that case, we have to revert the persistent storage back to the state before opening the transaction, i.e., instead of continuing execution in s_p^0, we continue with the persistent storage s_p^1. The code executed next is the body of the **abort**-clause, where its pattern variable v is bound to the thrown error e.

Table 2. Selected rules for the SmartML SOS semantics

[E-ASSIGN]

$$\frac{v_e = [\![e]\!]_{(s_v^0, s_p^0)} \quad e \text{ side-effect free} \quad s'_v = s_v^0[x \leftarrow v_e]}{(c_0, \overline{contrs}, (s_v^0, s_p^0), \overline{trans}, m_0 \mapsto x := e; r) \leadsto (c_0, \overline{contrs}, (s'_v, s_p^0), \overline{trans}, m_0 \mapsto r)}$$

[E-METHODCALL (W/O TRANS)]

$$\frac{s'_v = [\bar{a} \leftarrow [\![\bar{e}]\!]_{(s_v^0, s_p^0)}] \quad \bar{e} \text{ side-effect free} \quad n(\overline{\tau a})\{body_n\}}{(c_0, \overline{contrs}, (s_v^0, s_p^0), \overline{trans}, m_0 \mapsto \textbf{this}.n(\bar{e}); r) \leadsto (c_0, [c_0[s_v^0, m_0, r], \overline{contrs}], (s'_v, s_p^0), \overline{trans}, n \mapsto body_n)}$$

[E-METHODCALL (W/ TRANS)]

$$\frac{s'_v = [\bar{a} \leftarrow [\![\bar{e}]\!]_{(s_v^0, s_p^0)}] \quad \bar{e} \text{ side-effect free} \quad n(\overline{\tau a})\{body_n\}}{(c_0, [\overline{contrs}], (s_v^0, s_p^0), \overline{trans}, m_0 \mapsto \textbf{try } u.n(\bar{e}) \textbf{ abort } \{cb\} \textbf{ success } \{st\}; r) \leadsto (c_u, [c_0[s_v^0, \textbf{try ? abort } \{cb\} \textbf{ success } \{st\}, r], \overline{contrs}], (s'_v, s_p^0), [s_p^0, \overline{trans}], n \mapsto body_n)}$$

[E-METHODCALL (RETURNFROMTRY II)]

$$\frac{v = [\![e]\!]_{(s_v^0, s_p^0)}}{(c_0, [c_1[s_v^1, \textbf{try ? abort } \{cb\} \textbf{ success } \{st\}, r], \overline{contrs}], (s_v^0, s_p^0), [s_p^1, \overline{trans}], m_0 \mapsto \textbf{throw } e) \leadsto (c_1, \overline{contrs}, (s_v^1, s_p^1), \overline{trans}, m_1 \mapsto cb(v); r)}$$

4 Formalisation of Reentrance Safety

We define different versions of reentrance safety for a given SmartML contract C. First we define what we mean by a reachable configuration.

Definition 1. (Reachable Configuration). *We call a configuration cfg* reachable *(for a given smart contract C) if it can be derived in a finite number of SOS steps from an initial configuration of the form $\{c_0, [], (s_v^0, s_p^0), s_p^0, m_0 \mapsto cnt_0\}$.*

We say that a reentrance is *present* in the execution of a method m of a contract instance c_0 (of type C) if the invocation of m (i) starts a transaction, in other words, it is not an internal call; (ii) contains a call to a method n of a different contract d as well as (iii) a subsequent call to some method of c_0 before returning from the call to n. This is formalized as follows:

Definition 2. (Rentrance). *Given a reachable configuration for a contract c_0 of type C of the form $cfg := \{c_n, [cs_0 \circ \cdots \circ cs_{n-1}], (s_v^n, s_p^n), s_p^0, m_n \mapsto cnt_n\}$ with $cs_r := c_r[s_v^r, m_r, cnt_r]$. A* reentrance is present *in cfg iff the formula*

$$\exists i, k, j. \overbrace{(i \neq j \rightarrow (c_i = c_j \wedge m_i = m_j \wedge i < k < j \wedge c_k \neq c_i))}^{\mathsf{reentrantMatrix}(cfg, i, k, j)}$$

holds.

The following definition introduces the concept of *strict reentrance safety* which guarantees that no reentrant calls occur within the smart contract.

Definition 3. (Strict Reentrance Safety). *A smart contract* c_0 *of type* C *is* strictly reentrance safe *iff for all reachable configurations cfg, the formula* $\neg(\exists k, j.\mathsf{reentrantMatrix}(cfg, 0, k, j))$ *holds.*

The definition above can only be satisfied by contracts that do not invoke other contracts, thus remaining entirely self-contained. However, if no modifications are made to fields of reentrant contracts after a call, then reentrancy is still considered to be *safe*. Such a more liberal notion of reentrance safety can be defined using the function Fields, which returns the names of the fields of a contract. We call the resulting notion *non-modifying reentrance safety*.

Definition 4. (Non-modifying Reentrance Safety). *A smart contract* c_0 *of type* C *is* non-modifying reentrance safe *when for all reachable configurations cfg, for all* j, k *such that* $\mathsf{reentrantMatrix}(cfg, 0, k, j)$ *holds, it follows that for all* $l > k$*:*

$$c_l = c_0 \wedge \mathsf{Fields}(c_0) \cap \mathsf{Fields}(c_l) = \emptyset \ .$$

Smart contracts may contain fields that are inessential for preventing reentrancy vulnerabilities. Let us call such fields *irrelevant* and denote them as the set IrrelevantFields. Irrelevant fields do not contain critical assets, such as balance and flag variables that play a vital role in guarding against reentrancy attacks. Unlike balances and flags, variables in IrrelevantFields are not involved in fund management or in controlling a contract's execution flow. While irrelevant fields may influence a contract's behavior or store data, their modification after external calls is unlikely to introduce reentrancy vulnerabilities. By focusing solely on relevant fields we can establish a more liberal and practically applicable definition of reentrancy safety.

Definition 5. (Modifying Reentrance Safety). *A smart contract* c_0 *of type* C *is* modifying reentrance safe *when for all reachable configurations cfg, for all* j, k *such that* $\mathsf{reentrantMatrix}(cfg, 0, k, j)$ *holds, it follows that for all* $l > k$*:*

$$c_l = c_0 \wedge \mathsf{Fields}(c_0) \cap \mathsf{Fields}(c_l) \subseteq \mathsf{IrrelevantFields} \ .$$

The set of irrelevant fields can be specified by trusted user annotations. However, it may also be derived from specifications, for instance, if fields are not constrained/used by invariants of a contract or if parts of the invariant are not needed to verify a contract's methods. In our type system, we will consider the modifying reentrance safety definition of reentrancy as it offers a balanced approach between security and flexibility. Considering the strict reentrance safety definition would be too restrictive, as it blocks all reentrant calls, even those that are harmless. Likewise, non-modifying reentrance safety, which disallows any reentrant call that modifies contract fields, would impose unnecessary limitations without adding security benefits.

5 Asserting Safe Reentrancy

To ensure safe reentrancy for SmartML contracts, we present a type system preventing unsafe reentrancy, while permitting provably safe reentrant calls.

5.1 Contract Locations and Field Access

To implement the *Modifying Reentrancy Safety* policy (see Definition 5), we must ensure that the contract does not access any relevant fields after an external call. Thus, we have to collect all memory locations in the persistent memory (in other words, the memory locations for fields of contract instances) to which read and write accesses may occur within a given sequence of statements. To represent these locations, we introduce symbolic values that refer to contract instances. These play the role of the values assigned to program variables or fields. Further, we need to represent memory locations to which values can be assigned. These memory locations are either program variables or the fields of contracts.

Definition 6. (Contract Identities, Locations). *The set* CID *contains for each contract type* $C \in \mathsf{Contract}$ *infinitely many symbolic constants* κ *of type* C *(disjoint from program variables) that represent a* contract identity *(i.e., the semantic value of* κ *are the objects in* D^C*). We use* CID^τ *for the set of all contract identities of type* τ*. We permit aliasing, i.e., two contract identity symbols* $\kappa_1, \kappa_2 \in \mathsf{CID}$ *may refer to the same contract identity. A* contract location *is a pair* $(c, f) \in \mathsf{CID} \times \mathit{Field}$*. The set of all contract locations is called* $\mathsf{ContractLoc}$*. The set of all memory locations* MemLoc *is defined as* $\mathsf{MemLoc} := \mathsf{ProgVars} \cup \mathsf{ContractLoc}$.

To determine whether a reentrancy might be problematic, tracking read and write access to fields is mandatory. To model field accesses, we define a function $\mathsf{Loc} : \mathsf{CID} \times (\mathsf{Statement} \cup \mathsf{Expression}) \to 2^{\mathsf{ContractLoc}}$ that collects all persistent memory locations accessed by a statement or expression p in the context of contract c. Function Loc is defined inductively on the syntactic structure of p:

$$\mathsf{Loc}(c,p) = \begin{cases} \{(c,f)\} \cup \mathsf{Loc}(c,e) & \text{if } p \equiv [\mathtt{this}.f \ := \ e] \\ \{(c,f)\} & \text{if } p \equiv [\mathtt{this}.f] \\ \dots & \\ \mathsf{Loc}(c,s_1) \cup \mathsf{Loc}(c,s_2) & \text{if } p \equiv [s_1; s_2] \\ \mathsf{Loc}(c, \boldsymbol{mbody}(C,m)) & \text{if } p \equiv [\mathtt{this}.m(\overline{v})],\ C \text{ type of } c \\ \{(c,f) \mid f \in \boldsymbol{fields}(C)\} & \text{if } p \equiv [d.m(\overline{v})],\ d \neq \mathtt{this},\ C \text{ type of } c \end{cases}$$

Loc makes use of the lookup functions ***fields*** and ***mbody***, whose complete definitions can be found in the extended version of the paper [23].

5.2 Blocking Unsafe Reentrancy via Locks

The goal of the type system is to prevent reentrant calls by using a locking mechanism. Upon invocation of a function from another contract, or a function within the same contract that modifies its fields, that function is considered locked, ensuring exclusive access and preventing reentrancy vulnerabilities.

A typing judgment has the shape $\Gamma; \Delta; \mathcal{S}; \mathcal{L} \vdash^{\mathsf{this_c}}_{\mathsf{m}} s \Rrightarrow \Gamma'; \Delta'; \mathcal{S}'; \mathcal{L}'$ with input context $(\Gamma; \Delta; \mathcal{S}; \mathcal{L})$, caller reference $\mathtt{this}_c$, executing method $\mathtt{m}$, statement s to be typed, and output context $(\Gamma'; \Delta'; \mathcal{S}'; \mathcal{L}')$. The presence of a set of contract locations $\mathcal{L}$ is justified, because an expression can change the object references that determine reentrancy. An empty context slot is represented by symbol $\varnothing$.

Context slot Γ is a *data typing environment*, mapping program variables and fields x to their types. We write $\Gamma, x : \tau$ for the *data typing environment* Γ' that is equal to Γ except that it maps x to type τ. The possible types τ are:

$$\tau := \texttt{int} \mid \texttt{bool} \mid \texttt{string} \mid \texttt{address} \mid \mathit{adt} \mid \mathit{cnt} \mid \mathit{stm}$$

where $\mathit{cnt} \in \mathsf{Contract}$, adt is the type name of an ADT and stm types a *statement*.

Context slot Δ contains pairs $\langle \kappa, m \rangle$, where κ is a contract identity and m is a locked method of the contract. We use set notation to add and remove elements.

To improve precision, it is useful to keep track of aliasing. For this we need bookkeeping of contract identities in memory. Partial state functions are used to track assignments to contract-typed memory locations. We can then use partial states $\mathcal{S}$ to compute an over-approximation for the aliasing relation.

Definition 7. (Partial State). *A* partial state *function* $\mathcal{S} : \mathsf{MemLoc} \rightharpoonup 2^{\mathsf{CID}}$ *maps memory locations to a set of contract identities. Partial states are undefined for memory locations that are not declared as a contract type.*

We write $\mathcal{S} + [ml \mapsto K]$ *the partial state function that results from* $\mathcal{S}$ *by adding the mapping from memory location* ml *to the set of contract instances* K.

We define the initial partial state function $\mathcal{S}_{\mathsf{init}}$ *that maps each memory location* ml *of contract type* τ *exactly to* CID^{τ}.

For example, $\mathcal{S}(ml) = \{\kappa_1, \kappa_2\}$ means that the value of ml is one of the contract identities κ_1 or κ_2. Two memory locations ml_1, ml_2 are possibly aliased if $\mathcal{S}(ml_1) \cap \mathcal{S}(ml_2) \neq \emptyset$.

The context $\mathcal{L}$ is a multiset that contains all memory locations accessed by the body of the method undergoing type checking. We use standard multiset notation for operations on $\mathcal{L}$. In this notation, elements in $\mathcal{L}$ take the form $(\kappa, f)^n$, indicating that element (κ, f) has multiplicity n.

Table 3 shows selected typing rules (more are in the paper's extended version [23]). The symbol <: denotes the usual object subtyping relation.

To verify that a smart contract C has safe reentrancy, we begin with rule [Cnt-Ok]. This rule creates a new contract identity κ for C, and initiates type checking for each of its methods. Next, rule [Mth-Ok] validates the well-typedness of each method of C. Here, the multiset $\mathcal{L}$ is initialized for the remaining type-checking process to the result of applying function Loc to the method's body.

First, for each rule the output context for $\mathcal{L}$ is determined by *excluding* the memory locations accessed by the involved statement as calculated by Loc.

We split the rule for assignment statements into two cases depending on whether the assigned variable is of contract type, because we need to track the locations of contract references. Hence, in rule [Assign-Cnt], the output context $\mathcal{S}$ is updated depending on whether e is a memory location or a complex expression. For a memory location, we update v to $\mathcal{S}(e)$, otherwise, we safely approximate the range of values by the set of all contract identities of corresponding type.

Table 3. Selected typing rules for SmartML

[Succ]

$$\frac{\Gamma; \Delta; \mathcal{S}; \mathcal{L} \vdash^{\mathsf{this}_c}_{\mathsf{m}} s_1 : stm \Rrightarrow \Gamma_1; \Delta_1; \mathcal{S}_1; \mathcal{L}_1 \quad \Gamma_1; \Delta_1; \mathcal{S}_1; \mathcal{L}_1 \vdash^{\mathsf{this}_c}_{\mathsf{m}} s_2 : stm \Rrightarrow \Gamma_2; \Delta_2; \mathcal{S}_2; \mathcal{L}_2}{\Gamma; \Delta; \mathcal{S}; \mathcal{L} \vdash^{\mathsf{this}_c}_{\mathsf{m}} s_1; s_2 : stm \Rrightarrow \Gamma_2; \Delta_2; \mathcal{S}_2; \mathcal{L}_2}$$

[Assign]

$$\frac{\Gamma \vdash v : \tau \quad \tau \neq cnt \quad \Gamma \vdash e : \tau' \quad \tau' <: \tau}{\Gamma; \Delta; \mathcal{S}; \mathcal{L} \vdash^{\mathsf{this}_c}_{\mathsf{m}} v := e : stm \Rrightarrow \Gamma; \Delta; \mathcal{S}; \mathcal{L} \setminus \mathsf{Loc}(\mathcal{S}(\mathtt{this}_c), v := e)}$$

[Assign-Cnt]

$$\frac{\Gamma \vdash v : cnt \ \Gamma \vdash rhs : cnt \quad (rhs \in \mathsf{MemLoc} \Rightarrow \mathsf{Mod} = \mathcal{S}(e)) \vee (rhs \text{ is complex expr} \Rightarrow \mathsf{Mod} = \mathsf{CID})}{\Gamma; \Delta; \mathcal{S}; \mathcal{L} \vdash^{\mathsf{this}_c}_{\mathsf{m}} v := rhs : stm \Rrightarrow \Gamma; \Delta; \mathcal{S} + [v \mapsto \mathsf{Mod}]; \mathcal{L} \setminus \mathsf{Loc}(\mathcal{S}(\mathtt{this}_c), v := rhs)}$$

[If-Else]

$$\frac{\Gamma \vdash e : \mathtt{bool} \quad \Gamma; \Delta; \mathcal{S}; \mathcal{L} \vdash^{\mathsf{this}_c}_{\mathsf{m}} s_i : stm \Rrightarrow \Gamma_i; \Delta_i; \mathcal{S}_i; \mathcal{L}_i \quad \text{for } i \in \{1, 2\}}{\begin{array}{l}\Gamma; \Delta; \mathcal{S}; \mathcal{L} \vdash^{\mathsf{this}_c}_{\mathsf{m}} \mathtt{if}\ (e)\ \{s_1\}\ \mathtt{else}\ \{s_2\} : stm \Rrightarrow \\ \qquad \Gamma_1 \cup \Gamma_2; \Delta_1 \cup \Delta_2; \mathcal{S}_1 \cup \mathcal{S}_2; \mathcal{L} \setminus (\mathcal{L}_1 \cup \mathcal{L}_2 \cup \mathsf{Loc}(\mathcal{S}(\mathtt{this}_c), e))\end{array}}$$

[Call-Safe]

$$\frac{\begin{array}{c}\Gamma \vdash v : cnt \quad \boldsymbol{mtype}(cnt, m_v) = \overline{\tau} \longrightarrow \tau_0 \quad \Gamma \vdash \overline{u} : \overline{\tau} \\ \Gamma, \boldsymbol{fields}(v); \Delta; \mathcal{S} \vdash \boldsymbol{mbody}(cnt, m_v)\ ok \quad \langle \mathcal{S}(v), m_v \rangle \cap \Delta = \varnothing \\ \mathcal{L} \subseteq \mathsf{IrrelevantFields} \ \vee\ (\mathcal{S}(v) = \mathcal{S}(\mathtt{this}_c) \ \wedge\ \mathsf{Loc}(\mathcal{S}(v), \boldsymbol{mbody}(cnt, m_v)) \subseteq \mathsf{IrrelevantFields})\end{array}}{\Gamma; \Delta; \mathcal{S}; \mathcal{L} \vdash^{\mathsf{this}_c}_{\mathsf{m}} v.m_v(\overline{u}) : stm \Rrightarrow \Gamma; \Delta; \mathcal{S}; \mathcal{L} \setminus \mathsf{Loc}(\mathcal{S}(\mathtt{this}_c), v.m_v(\overline{u}))}$$

[Call]

$$\frac{\begin{array}{c}\Gamma \vdash v : cnt \quad \boldsymbol{mtype}(cnt, m_v) = \overline{\tau} \longrightarrow \tau_0 \quad \Gamma \vdash \overline{u} : \overline{\tau} \\ \Gamma, \boldsymbol{fields}(v); \Delta \cup \{\langle \mathcal{S}(\mathtt{this}_c), m \rangle\}; \mathcal{S} \vdash \boldsymbol{mbody}(cnt, m_v)\ ok \quad \langle \mathcal{S}(v), m_v \rangle \cap \Delta = \varnothing\end{array}}{\Gamma; \Delta; \mathcal{S}; \mathcal{L} \vdash^{\mathsf{this}_c}_{\mathsf{m}} v.m_v(\overline{u}) : stm \Rrightarrow \Gamma; \Delta \cup \{\langle \mathcal{S}(v), m_v \rangle\}; \mathcal{S}; \mathcal{L} \setminus \mathsf{Loc}(\mathcal{S}(\mathtt{this}_c), v.m_v(\overline{u}))}$$

[Mth-Ok]

$$\frac{\begin{array}{c}c = \mathtt{contract}\ C\ \mathtt{extends}\ D\ \{\ldots\} \quad \boldsymbol{mtype}(D, m) = \overline{\tau} \longrightarrow \tau_0 \quad \Gamma \vdash \overline{v} : \overline{\tau} \quad \mathcal{L} = \mathsf{Loc}(\mathcal{S}(\mathtt{this}_c), s) \\ \Gamma, \overline{v} : \overline{\tau}; \Delta; \mathcal{S} + [\overline{v} \mapsto \overline{\mathsf{CID}}]; \mathcal{L} \vdash^{\mathsf{this}_c}_{\mathsf{m}} s : stm \Rrightarrow \Gamma'; \Delta'; \mathcal{S}'; \mathcal{L}'\end{array}}{\Gamma; \Delta; \mathcal{S} \vdash m(\overline{v})\{s\}\ ok}$$

[Cnt-Ok]

$$\frac{\begin{array}{c}\boldsymbol{fields}(D) = \overline{g} : \overline{\tau}_g \qquad \mathtt{constructor}(\overline{g} : \overline{\tau}_g, \overline{f} : \overline{\tau}_f)\{\mathtt{super}(\overline{g});\ \mathtt{this}.\overline{f} = \overline{f}\} \\ ctx \vdash m_1(\overline{v}_1)\{s_1\}\ ok; \quad \cdots \quad ctx \vdash m_n(\overline{v}_n)\{s_n\}\ ok \\ \kappa\ fresh \text{ contract identity and } ctx := \overline{g} : \overline{\tau}_g, \overline{f} : \overline{\tau}_f; \varnothing; \mathcal{S}_{\mathsf{init}} + [\mathtt{this}_c \mapsto \kappa]\end{array}}{\vdash \mathtt{contract}\ C\ \mathtt{extends}\ D\ \{\ \overline{f} : \overline{T}_f;\ \mathtt{constructor}(\overline{f}, \overline{g});\ m_1; \ldots; m_n\}\ ok}$$

Rule [Succ] is straightforward. The outputs of [If-Else] are the union of the outputs of each branch. This prevents reentrancy, but we possibly over-approximate the contracts' current locations when contract assignments are involved.

Rules [Call-Safe] and [Call] prevent reentrancy. Rule [Call-Safe] checks the *safe* method calls. There are two scenarios when a call is considered safe: (i) A call to a method within the same contract that leaves the contract's relevant field variables unaltered and thus satisfies $\mathsf{Loc}(\mathcal{S}(v), \boldsymbol{mbody}(cnt, m_v)) \subseteq \mathsf{IrrelevantFields}$. This check is crucial for preventing cross-function reentrancy. (ii) One can ensure that all checks or updates on the contract's relevant fields were completed before initiating the call itself. This is achieved by checking that the multiset $\mathcal{L}$ contains only irrelevant fields. In this way, we are sure that no pending access to the contract's relevant fields occur after the call. Both call rules ensure that the targeted method is currently unlocked by examining whether Δ contains a possible alias of the caller v by checking condition $\langle \mathcal{S}(v), m_v \rangle$.[2] Since, for the moment, we work on a closed-world assumption, we are able to check the body of the called method including the callee method in the set Δ. This prevents potentially dangerous reentrant calls to that specific method, ensuring that the method cannot be invoked again while it is already being executed. The [Call] rule adds the known aliases of v to the encountered memory locations, whereas rule [Call-Safe] does not, because it proved accesses to be safe.

We show adequacy of the type system through two fundamental properties: type preservation, which ensures that the types are maintained throughout evaluation, and progress, which guarantees that well-typed programs do not get stuck during execution. The proofs can be found in [23].

Recall from Sect. 3.2 that $cfg[s] \rightsquigarrow cfg'[s']$ means a statement s in an SOS configuration cfg is reduced to a statement s' in configuration cfg'.

Theorem 1. (Type Preservation). *Let* $c = \texttt{contract}\ C\ \texttt{extends}\ D\ \{\ldots\}$ *be a contract with* $\vdash c\ \mathsf{ok}$, *s a statement of c. If* $\Gamma; \Delta; \mathcal{S}; \mathcal{L} \vdash s : stm \Rrightarrow \Gamma'; \Delta'; \mathcal{S}'; \mathcal{L}'$ *and* $cfg[s] \rightsquigarrow cfg'[s']$, *then* $\exists\, \Gamma_1, \Delta_1$ *such that* $\Gamma \subseteq \Gamma_1$, $\Delta \subseteq \Delta_1$ *and* $\Gamma_1; \Delta_1; \mathcal{S}; \mathcal{L} \vdash s' : stm \Rrightarrow \Gamma'; \Delta'; \mathcal{S}'; \mathcal{L}'$.

Theorem 2. (Progress). *If* $\Gamma; \Delta; \mathcal{S}; \mathcal{L} \vdash s : stm \Rrightarrow \Gamma'; \Delta'; \mathcal{S}'; \mathcal{L}'$ *for statement s, then for any configuration cfg there exists s' such that* $cfg[s] \rightsquigarrow cfg'[s']$.

The next theorem ensures reentrancy prevention, and thus that SmartML contracts are *modifying reentrant safe.*

Theorem 3. (Reentrancy Security). *Any smart contract that can be typed as* $\vdash \texttt{contract}\ C\ \texttt{extends}\ D\ \{\ldots\}\ \mathsf{ok}$ *is modifying reentrance safe.*

6 Reentrancy Mitigation

6.1 Case Study

This section illustrates the power of SmartML's type system for preventing reentrancy attacks. We analyze two SmartML contracts to show how the type system enforces secure execution flow, effectively eliminating the possibility of reentrancy. Listing 2 presents the Store contract, while Listing 3 presents the code of the Attacker. The code features a cross-function reentrancy attack, where the attacker attempts to withdraw more funds than permitted by invoking the transfer function within its receive function. We describe the code of the listings.

The Store contract is in Listing 2, except the constructor which follows the usual pattern. The withdraw function checks the balance of the caller and performs the internal call **this** \$bal.transfer(**sender**). An example of an external call

[2] As a contract might be associated with multiple locations, by a slight abuse of notation we identify $\langle \mathcal{S}(v), m_v \rangle$ with $\langle \kappa_1, m_v \rangle, \ldots, \langle \kappa_n, m_v \rangle$, where $\mathcal{S}(v) = \{\kappa_1, \ldots, \kappa_n\}$.

```
1 contract Store {
2  ListAddress addr; ListInt balances;
3  withdraw() {
4   int bal = 0;
5   int idx = addr.indexOf(addr,sender);
6   if (idx != −1) {bal = balances.get(idx);}
7   assert(bal > 0);
8   this $bal.transfer(sender);
9  }
10 bool transfer(address addr) {
11  try addr$⟨amount⟩.receive();
12  abort { return false; }
13  success {
14   balances.set(idx,0);
15   return true;
16  }
17 }}
```

Listing 2: Store contract

```
1 contract Attacker {
2  int balance;
3  Store s;
4  constructor() {
5   this.balance = 1;
6   this.s = new Store();
7  }
8  bool attack() {
9   try s$balance.deposit();
10  abort{ return false; }
11  success{
12    try s.withdraw();
13    abort{ return false; }
14    success{ return true; }
15  }}
16 bool receive() {
17  balance=balance+⟨amount⟩;
18  try s$⟨amount⟩.transfer(address(this));
19  abort{ return false; }
20  success{ return true; }
21 }}
```

Listing 3: Attacker

with resource consumption is in line 11 of the function transfer. Lines 11–16 show transaction handling using a **try–abort–success** statement, allowing developers detailed control over nested transactions in SmartML. For lack of space, we do not show the deposit function, which adds the resource specified by the caller to the correct address. In Listing 3, the attack function deposits and then tries to withdraw funds from the store. The notation s$balance.deposit() is used to explicitly indicate the amount of money being deposited. When funds are received, the receive function increases the balance and recursively triggers another withdrawal. Thus draining the Store's funds by repeatedly invoking transfer.

Our type system effectively blocks the repetitive call by leveraging the set Δ. Specifically, when the type system evaluates whether the transfer function of the Store contract can be invoked within the receive function of the Attacker, the derivation process encounters a failure. This occurs because $\textbf{this}_{\text{Store}}$ and store are aliased, meaning they share the same partial state. Consequently, the type system detects a conflict as it attempts to verify that the set Δ does not include $\langle \mathcal{S}(\text{store}), \text{transfer} \rangle$ (recall the convention in footnote 2). This conflict indicates a potential reentrancy vulnerability, leading the type system to block the operation and thereby ensuring the security of the contract execution (see Fig. 2).

$$\times$$

$$\{\langle \mathcal{S}(\mathbf{this}_{\mathrm{Att}}), \mathsf{attack}\rangle, \langle \mathcal{S}(\mathbf{this}_{\mathrm{Store}}), \mathsf{withdraw}\rangle, \langle \mathcal{S}(\mathbf{this}_{\mathrm{Store}}), \mathsf{transfer}\rangle\} \cap \langle \mathcal{S}(\mathsf{store}), \mathsf{transfer}\rangle = \varnothing$$

$$\{\langle \mathcal{S}(\mathbf{this}_{\mathrm{Att}}), \mathsf{attack}\rangle, \langle \mathcal{S}(\mathbf{this}_{\mathrm{Store}}), \mathsf{withdraw}\rangle, \langle \mathcal{S}(\mathbf{this}_{\mathrm{Store}}), \mathsf{transfer}\rangle\} \vdash^{\mathbf{this}_{\mathrm{Att}}}_{\mathsf{receive}} \mathsf{store.transfer()}$$

$$\ldots$$

$$\{\langle \mathcal{S}(\mathbf{this}_{\mathrm{Att}}), \mathsf{attack}\rangle, \langle \mathcal{S}(\mathbf{this}_{\mathrm{Store}}), \mathsf{withdraw}\rangle\} \vdash^{\mathbf{this}_{\mathrm{Store}}}_{\mathsf{transfer}} \mathsf{att.receive()} \Rrightarrow \{\langle \mathcal{S}(\mathbf{this}_{\mathrm{Att}}), \mathsf{attack}\rangle, \langle \mathcal{S}(\mathbf{this}_{\mathrm{Store}}), \mathsf{transfer}\rangle, \langle \mathcal{S}(\mathbf{this}_{\mathrm{Store}}), \mathsf{transfer}\rangle\}$$

$$\ldots$$

$$\{\langle \mathcal{S}(\mathbf{this}_{\mathrm{Att}}), \mathsf{attack}\rangle\} \vdash^{\mathbf{this}_{\mathrm{Store}}}_{\mathsf{withdraw}} \mathbf{this}_{\mathrm{Store}}\mathsf{.transfer(amount,index)} \Rrightarrow \{\langle \mathcal{S}(\mathbf{this}_{\mathrm{Att}}), \mathsf{attack}\rangle, \langle \mathcal{S}(\mathbf{this}_{\mathrm{Store}}), \mathsf{withdraw}\rangle\}$$

$$\ldots$$

$$\varnothing \vdash^{\mathbf{this}_{\mathrm{Att}}}_{\mathsf{attack}} \mathsf{store.withdraw()} \Rrightarrow \{\langle \mathcal{S}(\mathbf{this}_{\mathrm{Att}}), \mathsf{attack}\rangle\}$$

$$\ldots$$

Fig. 2. Type derivation for the example (relevant checks and changes to Δ only)

6.2 Safe Reentrancy

While a complete ban on reentrancy seems like a simple solution, it is overly restrictive and reduces the functionality and interoperability of smart contracts. For this reason, our type system has been carefully designed as a safeguard against unsafe reentrant calls while permitting those considered to be secure. A key feature is the ability to verify that all necessary checks and field updates are completed before making a call to an external contract. When such a call satisfies the non-interference condition, it is considered safe. Such calls are not added to the set Δ of locked method calls. Thus, this approach to designing our type system serves a dual purpose: it effectively prevents reentrancy attacks while enabling the execution of safe calls, finding a middle ground that avoids unnecessary restrictions.

7 Related Work

Various smart contract languages address reentrancy vulnerabilities using different methods. Scilla [18,19] is an intermediate language for verified smart contracts, relying on communicating automata and Coq for proving contract properties. Scilla avoids reentrancy by removing the call-and-return paradigm in contract interactions. However, their approach is not compositional in the sense that it fails to block cross-contract reentrancy. Obsidian [11] and Flint [17] are two smart contract languages that enhance contract behavior comprehensibility with typestate integration. Obsidian includes a dynamic check for object-level reentrancy, whereas Flint lacks a reentrancy check. Like Scilla, both languages lack compositionality, i.e. fail to block cross-contract reentrancy, even though both incorporate a linear asset concept to prevent certain attacks.

SeRIF [10] detects reentrancy based on a trusted-untrusted computation model using a type system with trust labels for secure information flow. It spots cross-contract reentrancy without blocking every reentrant call. However, we avoid a control flow type system, maintaining flexibility and expressiveness without imposing constraints on program structure. Nomos [12] adopts a security enforcement strategy grounded in session types. The linearity of session types does not fully address reentrancy, hence, the paper employs the resources monitored by these session types as a safeguard. This approach ensures that attackers cannot gain authorization to invoke a contract that is currently in use, eliminating all forms of reentrancy, even safe reentrancy. In contrast, our approach permits safe tail reentrancy calls. SolType [21] is a refinement type system for Solidity that prevents over- and under-flows in smart contracts. While the type system is very powerful concerning arithmetic bugs in smart contracts, it does not provide a safety guarantee against reentrancy.

Move [7] is a smart contract language used in platforms like Libra/Diem [2], Aptos [1], and Sui [6]. Its static type system with linear types prevents improper duplication or deletion of resources such as tokens. While Move's linear types enhance security during execution, SmartML prioritizes pre-deployment modeling and correctness, offering platform-independent analysis of contract behavior.

Oyente [15] is a bug finding tool with no soundness guarantees, based on symbolic execution. While symbolic execution is a powerful generic technique for discovering bugs, it does not guarantee to explore all program paths (resulting in false negatives). SECURIFY [22] is a tool for analyzing Ethereum smart contracts by checking for compliance a nd violation patterns based on dependency graphs.

Both tools, focus on one or two contracts, and thus, sequences and interleavings of function calls from multiple contracts are often ignored. In contrast, our approach guarantees security against cross-contract reentrancy attacks.

Several tools use formal verification to analyze contracts, like VERISOL [13] which is a highly automated formal verifier for Solidity. It not only generates proofs, but also identifies counterexamples, ensuring smart contracts align with a state machine model including access control policies. Solythesis [14] is a source-to-source Solidity compiler that takes a smart contract and a user-specified invariant as its input and produces an instrumented contract that rejects all transactions that violate the invariant. These tools focus on single contract safety, so they lack the ability of compositional verification.

8 Conclusion and Future Work

We presented a platform-independent modeling framework for smart contracts. SmartML offers a comprehensive approach to formally specify and verify smart contracts, mitigating the inherent complexities and vulnerabilities that can expose security-critical assets to unforeseen attacks. SmartML complements the state-of-the-art by providing a structured and abstract representation of contracts. This facilitates understanding and analysis.

A formal operational semantics and a type system for safe reentrancy checks further establishes a robust foundation for expressing and verifying functional correctness as well as security properties of smart contracts.

We are currently developing a translator from existing smart contract languages to SmartML (and back). In the immediate future we aim to relax the closed-world condition regarding reentrancy prevention, allowing for an adaptable approach without compromising security. We are also developing a deductive verification and static analysis tool, with the aim of proving the absence of relevant classes of security vulnerabilities and functional correctness of smart contracts. Finally, we will conduct experiments on the usability of SmartML to evaluate comprehension of SmartML programs.

References

1. Aptos Blockchain. Official Website. https://aptos.dev/en
2. Diem Blockchain. Official Website. https://www.diem.com/en-us/
3. Ethereum. Official Website. https://ethereum.org/
4. Hyperledger Fabric. Official Website. https://www.hyperledger.org/projects/fabric
5. NXT. Official Website. https://nxt.org/
6. Sui Foundation. Official Website. https://sui.io/about
7. The Move Language. https://move-book.com/reference/
8. Abdellatif, T., Brousmiche, K.L.: Formal verification of smart contracts based on users and blockchain behaviors models. In: NTMS, pp. 1–5. IEEE (2018)
9. Bashir, I.: Mastering Blockchain. Packt Publishing (2017)
10. Cecchetti, E., Yao, S., Ni, H., Myers, A.C.: Compositional security for reentrant applications. In: SP, pp. 1249–1267. IEEE (2021)
11. Coblenz, M., et al.: Obsidian: typestate and assets for safer blockchain programming. arXiv preprint arXiv:1909.03523 (2019)
12. Das, A., Balzer, S., Hoffmann, J., Pfenning, F., Santurkar, I.: Resource-aware session types for digital contracts. In: 34th IEEE Computer Security Foundations Symposium, CSF 2021, pp. 1–16. IEEE (2021). https://doi.org/10.1109/CSF51468.2021.00004
13. Lahiri, S.K., Chen, S., Wang, Y., Dillig, I.: Formal specification and verification of smart contracts for azure blockchain. arxiv preprint arXiv:1812.08829 (2018)
14. Li, A., Choi, J.A., Long, F.: Securing smart contract with runtime validation. In: PLDI, pp. 438–453. ACM (2020)
15. Luu, L., Chu, D.H., Olickel, H., Saxena, P., Hobor, A.: Making Smart Contracts Smarter. In: CCS, pp. 254–269. ACM (2016)
16. Plotkin, G.D.: A structural approach to operational semantics. J. Log. Algebraic Methods Program. **60–61**, 17–139 (2004)
17. Schrans, F., Hails, D., Harkness, A., Drossopoulou, S., Eisenbach, S.: Flint for safer smart contracts. arxiv preprint arXiv:1904.06534 (2019)
18. Sergey, I., Kumar, A., Hobor, A.: Scilla: a smart contract intermediate-level language. arXiv preprint arXiv:1801.00687 (2018)
19. Sergey, I., Nagaraj, V., Johannsen, J., Kumar, A., Trunov, A., Hao, K.C.: Safer smart contract programming with Scilla. Proc. ACM Program. Lang. **3**(OOPSLA), 185:1–185:30 (2019). https://doi.org/10.1145/3360611
20. Siegel, D.: Understanding the DAO attack (2023). https://www.coindesk.com/learn/understanding-the-dao-attack/
21. Tan, B., Mariano, B., Lahiri, S.K., Dillig, I., Feng, Y.: SolType: refinement types for arithmetic overflow in solidity. Proc. ACM Program. Lang. **6**(POPL), 1–29 (2022)

22. Tsankov, P., Dan, A., Drachsler-Cohen, D., Gervais, A., Buenzli, F., Vechev, M.T.: Securify: practical security analysis of smart contracts. arXiv preprint arXiv:1806.01143 (2018)
23. Veschetti, A., Bubel, R., Hähnle, R.: SmartML: towards a modeling language for smart contracts. arXiv preprint arXiv:2403.06622 (2024)
24. Wöhrer, M., Zdun, U.: Smart contracts: security patterns in the ethereum ecosystem and solidity. In: IWBOSE@SANER, pp. 2–8. IEEE (2018)

Symbolic Execution for Precise Information Flow Analysis of Timed Concurrent Systems

Jonas Becker-Kupczok(✉) and Paula Herber

Computer Science Department, University of Münster, Münster, Germany
{jonas.becker-kupczok,paula.herber}@uni-muenster.de

Abstract. Information flow analysis (IFA) is a powerful technique for verifying confidentiality and integrity. This is highly desirable for embedded systems, where security violations can lead to significant economic damages or even loss of human life. Unfortunately, if shared bus architectures are used, classical IFA that do not consider timing behavior will always classify the whole system as insecure. In this paper, we present an approach to regain precision in IFA for timed systems that concurrently execute processes using a cooperative scheduler. Our key idea is to extend a classical IFA approach based on program dependence graphs with a symbolic execution together with abstract interpretation to precisely yet abstractly capture data, control, timing, and event dependencies between processes. While this increases the cost of the analysis, the gain in precision leverages IFA even for concurrent systems with time-shared bus architectures as they are widely used, for example, in the automotive industry. We have implemented our approach for the system level description language SystemC, and demonstrate its applicability with a case study that uses a general-purpose input/ouput (GPIO).

Keywords: Information Flow Analysis · Symbolic Execution · Timing · Concurrency · Embedded Systems · SystemC

1 Introduction

Embedded systems are ubiquitous in today's everyday life, and they are often used in safety- and security-critical applications, e.g. in cars or pacemakers. This makes it crucial to protect them against malevolent attacks. In particular, it is highly desirable to prevent attackers from gaining access to critical functionality such as the brakes of a car, or to sensitive information, such as those collected in medical devices. One way of ensuring confidentiality or integrity is performing an information flow analysis (IFA) to verify non-interference between high (i.e. confidential or untrusted) inputs and low (i.e. public or critical) outputs. However, embedded systems are typically heavily time-dependent and concurrent, which makes the analysis challenging. Approaches for IFA of such systems exist, but usually suffer loss of precision or require manual effort and high expertise.

In this paper, we present an approach to regain precision in IFA for timed systems that concurrently execute processes using a cooperative scheduler. To

A. Madeira and A. Knapp (Eds.): SEFM 2024, LNCS 15280, pp. 107–125, 2025.
https://doi.org/10.1007/978-3-031-77382-2_7

achieve this, we exploit that in systems which use a cooperative scheduler, such as in the system level design language SystemC, all statements between a thread gaining and voluntarily relinquishing control form an atomic block. Our key ideas are twofold: First, we use a symbolic execution where we abstract from selected data variables using abstract interpretation but keep track of the states of most processes, events, and other scheduling-relevant information. With that, we gain a safe overapproximation of all possible interleavings, but eliminate spurious information flow from interleavings that are precluded by the systems timing behavior. We store the result as a newly defined thread interleaving graph (TIG). We use this graph similarly to a control flow graph (CFG), precisely extracting inter-process data dependencies with a definition reachability analysis. Second, we combine these dependencies with inter-process control dependencies as well as regular intra-process dependencies to construct a SystemC dependence graph (SysCDG), which precisely captures data, control, timing, and event dependencies within a SystemC design.

To illustrate our approach, we present an example where three processes communicate trusted and untrusted information via a shared bus architecture. We demonstrate the steps that are necessary to construct the TIG and SysCDG, and to analyze the information flow. To demonstrate the regain in precision of our approach compared to a classical IFA, we perform the analysis with and without considering timing behavior. The untrusted information that is fed into the example system is part of the backwards slice of the critical output with classical IFA, but not with our IFA that is refined with a symbolic execution. Thus, our approach can prove the system to be secure, while disregarding the timing information inevitably results in a false positive. To demonstrate the applicability of our approach, we also analyze a more complex example based on a general purpose input/output (GPIO) implementation.

The rest of this paper is structured as follows: In Sect. 2, we introduce IFA, symbolic execution, and SystemC. In Sect. 3, we present our motivating example. We introduce our approach to regain precision in IFA for timed concurrent systems in Sect. 4, before presenting experimental results in Sect. 5. We discuss related work in Sect. 6, and conclude in Sect. 7.

2 Background

In this section, we introduce the necessary background to understand the remainder of this paper, namely IFA, symbolic execution, and SystemC.

2.1 Information Flow Analysis

The goal of information flow analysis (IFA) is to find all those program locations (particularly all inputs) that can influence the execution of a given program location (usually an output). This information can be used to analyze properties such as non-interference [12] which can be used to establish confidentiality or integrity of information.

```
1       if (x <= 10)
2           x *= 2;
3       else
4           x = 3 * (x - 10);
5       print(x);
```

Listing 1. Example for a symbolic execution

IFA can be carried out using security type systems [42] or program dependence graphs (PDGs) [20]. Both techniques generally have the same precision [31]. A PDG contains a node for every program location in a method and edges for all possible influences between program locations. These edges are typically induced by data and control dependencies. The PDG can then be used to compute the backwards slice [43] of any output, i.e. the set of all nodes from which there exists a path in the PDG to the output node (the slicing criterion).

2.2 Symbolic Execution with Abstract Interpretation

Symbolic execution is the execution of a program with symbolic values [25]. This allows the simulation of many executions with different inputs or non-deterministic choices in one or few passes. Classical symbolic execution uses symbolic values that are calculated from terms and expressions in the program. We use a more general definition where symbolic values can be anything from concrete values over the results of abstract interpretations [4] (e.g. interval analyses) to completely unknown.

These symbolic values kept by the execution form an abstracted state of the system. Whenever it reaches a point where the next step cannot unambiguously be determined from the abstracted state, the execution branches, continuing with every possibility independently.

Consider the example in Listing 1. Suppose that the execution stores an interval of the possible values that `x` might have at any given time, and that prior to reaching the code in the example, that interval is $[0, \infty)$. As this interval does not suffice to rule out any of the two branches of the if statement, the execution itself branches and considers both possibilities independently. For the then branch, the interval is first updated to $[0, 10]$ to reflect that the if condition must be true and then to $[0, 20]$ according to the calculation in line 2. For the else branch, the interval is similarly updated first to $(10, \infty)$ and then to $(0, \infty)$. Thus, the execution results in two different states with regards to `x`. It is then up to the execution whether or not to combine these states into a generalization of both (i.e. $\texttt{x} \in [0, \infty)$) or continue forward from both states independently.

If instead of $[0, \infty)$ the interval at the beginning is $(12, 42)$, then the analysis only needs to explore the else branch, leading to $\texttt{x} \in (6, 96)$. On the other hand, if the execution completely abstracts from the value of `x`, both branches have to be explored but also directly lead to the same resulting state, because the only value that is changed differently between them is abstracted away.

2.3 SystemC

SystemC is a system-level design language and a framework for HW/SW co-simulation. The semantics of SystemC is informally defined in an IEEE standard [21]. It is implemented as a C++ class library, which provides language elements for the description of hardware and software, and allows for modeling of both hardware and software components on various levels of abstraction. It also features an event-driven simulation kernel, which enables the simulation of the design. A SystemC design consists of a set of communicating processes, triggered by events or timing delays and interacting through channels.

Like typical hardware simulators, SystemC models concurrency by imposing a partial order on parallel processes using delta-cycles: During simulation, the scheduler works in phases. In the evaluation phase a ready process is selected non-deterministically and executed until it terminates or reaches a wait-statement. This is repeated until no more processes are ready, in which case the scheduler switches to the update/notify phase. There, values written to signals or channels during the previous evaluation phase become visible to other processes. At the end of the update/notify phase, a delta delay passes. This is a special unit of simulation time which is treated as greater than zero but smaller than any real delay. Each passage of a delta delay constitutes one delta cycle. Afterwards, if no process is ready, simulation time is increased to the earliest point where any process becomes ready. Finally, a new evaluation phase is started.

In essence, this means that threads only yield control voluntarily and are executed atomically between waits. We will make use of this fact in our approach. This makes it suitable specifically for SystemC, but similar properties can also be assumed for other languages that use a cooperative scheduler.

3 Motivating Example

To illustrate our approach, we use a simplified version of a shared bus connecting an electronic control unit (ECU, lines 5–15) to the diagnosis interface (lines 16–23) and the pump system (lines 24–30) of an insulin pump (see Listing 2). The ECU reads information from an untrusted WiFi module (line 7) and a trusted sensor (line 10), and alternatingly writes this information on the bus (lines 8 & 11). In this scenario, the (safety-critical) pump system should never receive the untrusted information. These three components are modeled as individual processes (instantiated in the constructor, lines 31–35), which are synchronized by properly timing their accesses to the bus: Between two writes, the ECU waits for 2 ns (lines 9 & 13), forming a 4 ns cycle. The diagnosis process mimics this cycle, but offset by 1 ns. This ensures that it always reads the bus (line 19) 1 ns after the untrusted information has been written by the ECU. The pump system on the other hand does not wait for some time, but for an event to be triggered (line 26). This is done by the ECU after writing the trusted information, with a delay of 1 ns (line 12). Taken together, this ensures that within any 4 ns cycle, the ECU first writes untrusted information on the bus, the diagnosis process then reads that information, after which the ECU overwrites the untrusted with

```
SC_MODULE(InsulinPump) {
  sc_signal<int> bus;
  sc_event event;

  void ecu() {
    while (true) {
      int data = wifiIn();
      bus.write(data);
      wait(2, SC_NS);
      data = sensorIn();
      bus.write(data);
      event.notify(1, SC_NS);
      wait(2, SC_NS);
    }
  }
  void diagnosis() {
    wait(1, SC_NS);
    while (true) {
      int read = bus.read();
      display(read);
      wait(4, SC_NS);
    }
  }
  void pump() {
    while (true) {
      wait(event);
      int read = bus.read();
      ctrlPump(read);
    }
  }
  SC_CTOR(InsulinPump) {
    SC_THREAD(ecu);
    SC_THREAD(diagnosis);
    SC_THREAD(pump);
  }
}
```

Listing 2. Motivating example of an insulin pump.

trusted information which is finally read by the pump system. Thus, no untrusted information flows to the pump, and the system is secure.

However, a timing and event insensitive analysis may find the opposite: Without these sensitivities, any syntactically possible interleaving between the processes would have to be considered. This includes, e.g., the interleaving where the pump runs after the ECU writes the untrusted information but before its second part can overwrite it with trusted information. In this case, untrusted information would in fact flow to the pump. Since such time-shared architectures are common in embedded systems, avoiding this imprecision is highly desirable. In the following, we present our approach to that goal.

4 Precise IFA for Timed Concurrent Systems

To leverage symbolic execution for precise IFA of timed concurrent systems, we have to overcome two problems. First, classical IFA that are agnostic to timing synchronizations often induce a high loss of precision in time-shared bus architectures, as they classify the whole bus as insecure. Second, event sensitivities may introduce control dependencies that are difficult to compute statically, as they depend on the current state of the concurrent execution, including scheduling and timing behavior. In our motivating example, anything that happens within `pump` is dependent on the event being notified by `ecu`. This does not cause any problematic information flow in this case, but must be accounted for in general.

Our key ideas to overcome these problems are twofold. First, to cope with the loss of precision that is induced by timing-agnostic IFA, we eliminate spurious information flow from interleavings that are precluded by the systems timing behavior using a symbolic execution. Second, we model any triggers that cause

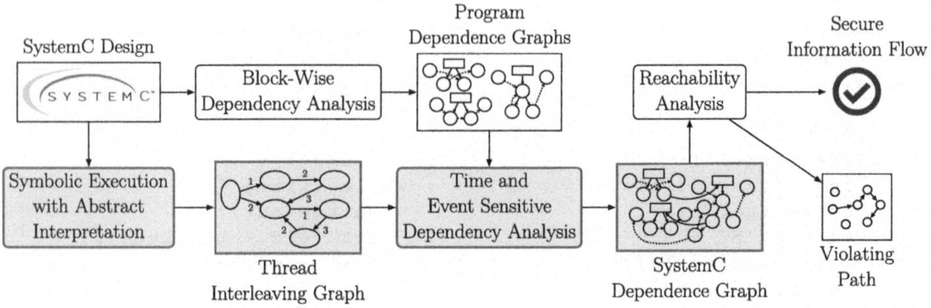

Fig. 1. Visualization of our approach. Our contributions are highlighted in blue. (Color figure online)

the execution of code blocks (e.g. events) with global variables. These trigger variables are considered to be written at (e.g.) notify statements and to be read when the corresponding block is actually executed. With that, a subsequent dependence analysis precisely integrates these inter-process control dependencies.

Our overall approach is shown in Fig. 1. For a given SystemC design, we compute all possible interleavings using a symbolic execution which may (or may not) abstract from parts of the state such as all data variables except process, event, and scheduling variables. This provides us with a safe but precise overapproximation of possible interleavings. The non-preemptive scheduler of SystemC aids us in this by allowing us to split each process into atomic blocks. The result is a thread interleaving graph (TIG) which works similar to a CFG and can – combined with PDGs for the respective blocks, obtained with established techniques – be used to compute inter-block data dependencies with a definition reachability analysis. Inter-block control, timing, and event dependencies can be integrated into this analysis by modeling block and event triggers as global variables. Finally, we gain a SystemC dependence graph (SysCDG) that precisely captures all data, control, timing, and event dependencies of the system. IFA can be performed on this SysCDG with a classical reachability analysis.

4.1 Symbolic Execution for Thread Interleavings

The first step in our analysis is to find all possible interleavings of the concurrent system. Importantly, it is not necessary to find the exact set of all truly possible interleavings, but any safe overapproximation will suffice. However, the smaller the overapproximation, the more precise the overall analysis will be.

Exploiting the non-preemptive scheduler of SystemC, we only consider interleavings between atomic blocks of code, separated by wait statements. Still, the exact set of interleavings is not computable in general and expensive to compute even in most computable cases, which is why we perform a symbolic execution. To provide a compromise between precision and computational effort, the granularity of that execution can be varied depending on the available resources and

Algorithm 1. Symbolic Execution for Thread Interleavings

```
Input: Set of (abstract) initial states S_0
Output: TIG (V, E) with nodes V and edges E
V ← ∅                                          ▷ set of reached states, i.e. TIG nodes
E ← ∅                                          ▷ set of state transitions, i.e. TIG edges
W ← ∅                                          ▷ worklist of states
for s ∈ S_0 do
    W ← W ∪ {s}                                ▷ add initial states to worklist
end for
while W ≠ ∅ do
    s ∈ W, W ← W \ {s}                         ▷ take state from worklist
    if s ∉ V then                              ▷ ignore if already visited
        V ← V ∪ {s}                            ▷ add to set of reached states
        if evaluationPhasePossiblyDone(s) then
            T ← possibleSchedulerTransitions(s)    ▷ find scheduler transitions
            E ← E ∪ T                          ▷ add to set of state transitions
            W ← W ∪ {s' | ∃i : (s, s', i) ∈ T} ▷ add reached states to worklist
        end if
        for p ∈ possiblyReadyProcesses(s) do
            T ← possibleProcessTransitions(s, p)   ▷ find process transitions
            E ← E ∪ T                          ▷ add to set of state transitions
            W ← W ∪ {s' | ∃i : (s, s', i) ∈ T} ▷ add reached states to worklist
        end for
    end if
end while
return (V, E)
```

the required precision. In particular, we can use arbitrary levels of abstraction for different variables or other parts of the state. The abstraction level may range from concrete values over symbolic constraints or intervals [4] to completely abstract. We define an abstracted state in SystemC as follows.

Definition 1 (Abstracted State). *Let P be the set of all processes, V the set of all variables, E the set of all events, and C the set of all primitive channels. Let T be the set of all possible delays for timed waits and notifications, including the delta delay Δ. An abstracted state is a tuple $s = (s_v, s_e, s_u, s_p, s_l)$, with*

- *s_v an abstract variable assignment mapping each $v \in V$ into $dom(v)$, where $dom(v)$ is the abstract domain of v,*
- *s_e an abstraction of pending events, mapping each $e \in E$ to a set of possible event states $\subseteq \{\texttt{idle}\} \cup (\{\texttt{pending}\} \times T)$,*
- *s_u an abstract set of update requests, mapping each $c \in C$ into $\{\texttt{idle}, \texttt{pending}, \texttt{unknown}\}$,*
- *s_p an abstraction of process states, mapping each $p \in P$ to a set of possible process states $\subseteq \{\texttt{done}, \texttt{ready}\} \cup (\{\texttt{wait}\} \times (E \cup T))$,[1] and*

[1] SystemC allows for more complex process states, e.g. waiting for one or all of several events or combining waiting for events with a timeout. We omit this in the definition, but our prototypical implementation can handle such complex process states.

– s_l *an abstraction of program locations, mapping each* $p \in P$ *to a set of possible current locations with stack traces* $\subseteq L \times \{L^n | n \in \mathbb{N}\}$ *where* L *uniquely identifies one expression.*

Concrete values/domains are a possible abstractions in the sense of this definition. The most relevant part of the state to keep track of is that influencing scheduler decisions, e.g. what event or time which process is currently waiting for or which expression is next to be evaluated in each process. This may also include values influencing whether or not wait or notify statements are reached at all, such as the current size of a blocking FIFO queue (as done in e.g. [41]).

For our motivating example, the abstract state keeps s_e, s_u, s_p, and s_l concrete, but completely abstracts from all variable values except those storing instances of modules, channels, or events (i.e. `this`, `bus`, `bus.change`, and `event`).

As is common with symbolic executions, whenever the considered state is too abstract to determine the exact result of a control or scheduling decision, it forks and takes all possible paths. Specifically, whenever more than one process is ready to be executed at any given time, all options are evaluated independently – thus capturing all possible interleavings of atomic blocks. Algorithm 1 shows a pseudocode representation of this practice in our symbolic execution.

This finally results in a graph, consisting of (abstracted) reachable states as nodes and transitions between these states as edges, where each edge corresponds either to the execution of exactly one atomic block or to an advancement of simulation time by the scheduler (potentially by just one delta cycle). We call this graph the thread interleaving graph (TIG), and define it as follows.

Definition 2 (Thread Interleaving Graph). *A thread interleaving graph consists of a set of nodes* V *and a set of labeled, directed edges* $E \subseteq V \times V \times I$ *for some set of label information* I. *Every* $s \in V$ *represents an (abstracted) state of the system. Every edge* $e \in E$ *represents an atomic state transition by the system, e.g. the evaluation of one atomic block or the passage of some time. The label provides additional information, e.g. for identifying the atomic block.*

Figure 2 shows a slightly simplified TIG for our motivating example. After the initialization phase, where every process is called once in non-deterministic order, a stable cycle emerges. Crucially, the diagnosis interface and pump only read during their second respective atomic blocks, not during initialization. Note that the TIG is not always technically a graph, as multiple edges with differing labels may exist between the same nodes. This does not impact our analysis.

4.2 Block-Wise Dependency Analysis

Independent of the symbolic execution, we construct PDGs for all atomic blocks, capturing their internal (intra-block) dependencies. This can be done with established techniques, as described in Sect. 2.1. The choice of the specific technique used does not impact our further analysis, as long as all dependencies are captured (the more precise, the better). This allows for the employment of advanced techniques, such as those for context [19] or object sensitivity [14].

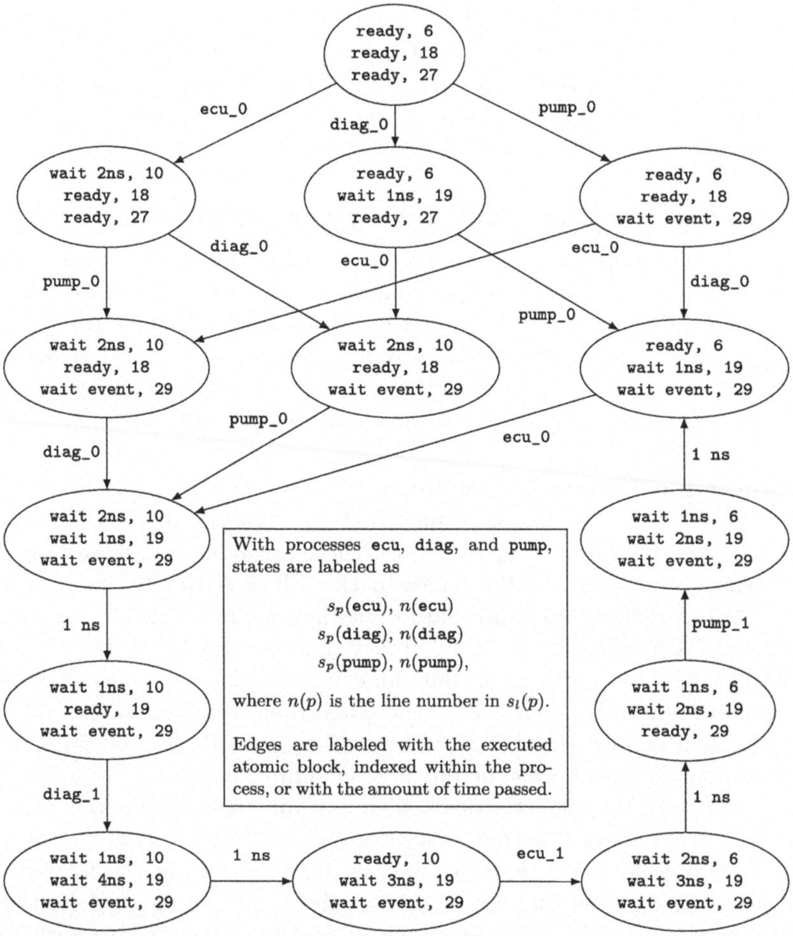

Fig. 2. Simplified TIG for our motivating example. Some states and transitions caused by technical details and not relevant for the example are omitted.

However, we do have two technical requirements for the PDGs. First, we require that for every piece of code which is not directly control dependent on other code within the same PDG, there is an entry node on which that code is considered to be control dependent.

The second requirement concerns the reading and writing of variables which may be written respectively read in other blocks. For any variable that may be read during a block without also being written first, the PDG for that block must contain an in node for that variable. Conversely, for any variable that may be written during a block and which may be read outside that block (e.g. a global variable or a local variable that is still in scope after a wait statement), the PDG must contain a corresponding out node. Whenever the variable is read respectively written at a node, that node must be connected to the corresponding in respectively out node if it might not be overwritten in between.

These entry, in, and out nodes will serve as the connecting points between PDGs when we are integrating them during our time and event sensitive dependency analysis, as described in the following section.

4.3 Time and Event Sensitive Dependency Analysis

At this step in our approach, we combine the intra-block dependencies captured in the PDGs with inter-block dependencies which can be obtained from the TIG, resulting in a SystemC dependence graph (SysCDG) precisely capturing all dependencies. We first explain how to obtain inter-block data dependencies in Sect. 4.3.1 and then how to extend that approach to inter-block control dependencies (including timing and event dependencies) in Sect. 4.3.2.

4.3.1 Inter-block Data Dependencies

The TIG is similar, though somewhat dual to a CFG: In a CFG, the nodes correspond to code statements, which are the equivalent of our atomic blocks, which in turn correspond to the edges in the TIG. With this insight, we can use the TIG to precisely compute data dependencies between atomic blocks by resorting to a simple definition reachability analysis: Every variable for which there exists an in respectively an out node in the PDG for a block is treated as being read respectively written at the corresponding edge in the TIG. Each out node is then connected with an edge to every in node for the same variable whose TIG edge is reached by the out node's definition.

This approach also correctly deals with variables which may or may not be written in a given block: In that case, the PDG for that block contains both an in and an out node for that variable, and an edge from the former to the latter. During the definition reachability analysis, all incoming definitions are connected to the in node and then replaced by the out node. However, due to the edge between the two nodes, any reading reached by the new definition still transitively "remembers" its dependencies on the old definitions.

4.3.2 Inter-block Control Dependencies

With regards to control dependencies, one key difference between the TIG and a CFG adds some difficulty: Whereas in a CFG, the effects of a control decision are local (i.e. the branching occurs directly at the point where the decision is made), this is not the case in the TIG. For example, if an event is notified with a timed delay, the effects of that notification only become visible in the TIG after the delay has passed, which allows other blocks to be potentially executed in between. This means that inter-block control dependencies cannot be determined using the established, post-dominance based approach, and a new solution is required.

In SystemC, an atomic block can be triggered in three different ways. The first is that the block appears after another block in the same process, separated by a wait statement. In this case, execution of the wait statement triggers

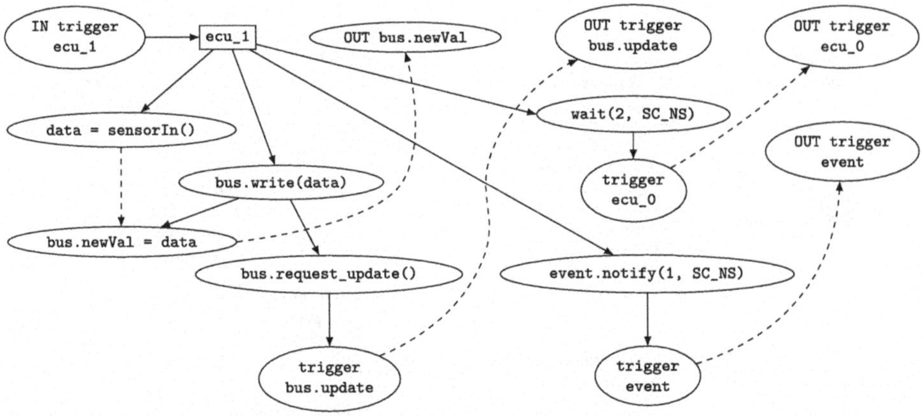

Fig. 3. Simplified PDG for the second atomic block of the ECU process (lines 10–13 in Listing 2). Solid edges mark control dependencies, dashed ones data dependencies. Some technical nodes not relevant for the example are omitted.

the execution of the second block, at such time as prescribed by the statement. The second is that a block may be (statically or dynamically) sensitive on an event which is notified in another block. In this case the execution of the notify statement triggers the execution of the sensitive block. These two ways are not mutually exclusive, because a wait statement can specify an event (with or without a timeout), making the following atomic block dynamically sensitive on that event. The third way is that calls to `request_update` on primitive channels from the SystemC standard library cause the function `update` to be invoked on them at the end of the current delta cycle.

We deal with the dependencies induced by such triggers by treating triggered blocks, update requests, and notified events as written variables, which are read when the triggered block, requested update or notified event is actually called. Specifically, for every trigger/request/notification, the PDG for the block during which it takes place will contain an out node for that trigger/request/notification. When an event is actually called, the notification variable is considered to be read (leading to the creation of a corresponding in node) and trigger variables for all blocks possibly sensitive on that event at that time are considered to be written (creating corresponding variable out nodes). Note that a safe but precise over-approximation of these blocks can easily be obtained from the symbolic execution. Whenever an atomic block or update is started, the corresponding trigger/request variable is considered to be read, and the entry node of that block is considered to be control dependent on the created in node.

This way, inter-block control, timing, and event dependencies are translated into inter-block data dependencies, which can be dealt with as described above. They do however require some special treatment for the definition reachability analysis: Because atomic blocks can require several triggers (e.g., two events must both be called for a block to be triggered), later "writes" to these variables do not

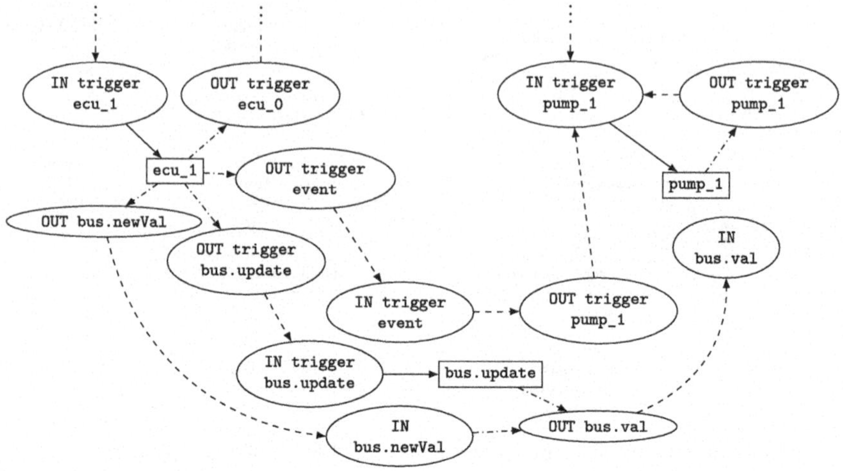

Fig. 4. Simplified excerpt from the SysCDG, focusing on the writing and reading of trusted information. Only in, out, and entry nodes of the respective PDGs are shown. Dash-dotted edges illustrate transitive dependencies.

kill the reachability of earlier writes. Instead, reachability is killed whenever such a variable is read, because the start of an atomic block consumes its trigger(s).

Interestingly, this approach allows us to also capture timing dependencies: The trigger or notification caused by a timed wait or notification statement is dependent on the parameters of that statement as well as (transitively) the entry node of the block containing that statement. Together, these specify the exact timing at which the trigger comes into effect. These dependencies are transitively spread to the entry nodes of the ultimately triggered blocks, meaning any observable behavior resulting from these blocks can also be traced back to the parameters and the block. If they are influenced by secret information and the observable behavior is public, this security violation is found by the analysis.

Figure 3 shows a simplified PDG for the second atomic block of the ECU process (lines 10–13 in Listing 2). Figure 4 shows an excerpt of the SysCDG, illustrating how inter-block data and control dependencies are introduced between the PDGs for the individual transitions. E.g., it can be seen that the data read from the sensor by the ECU influences the new value of the bus (Fig. 3), which then in turn influences the actual value of the bus after the update (Fig. 4), but also that whether or not some code is executed relies only on whether or not its predecessor is executed, not on the data.

4.3.3 Reachability Analysis on SystemC Dependence Graph

Once the SysCDG is constructed, established techniques can be used to perform the IFA on it. Typically, this means simple reachability analyses to find the backwards slices of public or critical outputs. More elaborate approaches are also possible, e.g. if the PDGs make use of summary edges [19] or declassification or to further increase precision with the use of path conditions [39].

In the case of our example, we are mainly interested in the backwards slice of `ctrlPump(read)` (line 28) in the process `pump`. Within the PDG for the second atomic block of that process (not included in this paper), this node is first control dependent on the entry node and second data dependent on the in node for `bus.val` via `read = bus.read()`.

From there on, we can track the dependencies in the SysCDG (see Fig. 4): The entry node is dependent on the corresponding trigger in node, which in turn is (firstly) dependent on the event being notified in `ecu_1`. This is of course dependent on that block being executed (i.e. its entry node), but not on any data which may be read or written. Secondly, the trigger in node is also control dependent on trigger out nodes of `pump_1` and (not shown in Fig. 4) `pump_0`. However, none of these dependencies lead to any input.

The in node for `bus.val` however can, via `bus.update`, be traced back to the out node for `bus.newVal` of `ecu_1`, which in turn depends on the data obtained at `data = sensorIn()` (see Fig. 3). This is the only input that `ctrlPump(read)` is dependent on. Since both are meant to deal with trusted information (i.e. they have the same security level), this constitutes no security breach.

It is important to note that `data = wifiIn()` cannot influence `ctrlPump (read)`, because the data flow that originates at it is killed at the `bus.update` after `ecu_1`. This can only be established by the analysis because the symbolic execution determined that the pair of `ecu_1` and `bus.update` must always happen between `ecu_0` and `pump_1`, and in that order.

5 Evaluation

To evaluate our approach, we have prototypically implemented it in Java for SystemC[2]. For comparison, apart from our motivating example, we also ran our analysis on some variants of it as well as on a more complex example based on a general purpose input/output (GPIO). The results are shown in Table 1. For each example, it displays the number nodes in the TIG, the numbers of nodes and edges in the SysCDG, the number of nodes in the backwards slice of the slicing criterion, the percentage of these nodes in the SysCDG, the result of the analysis, the ground truth of whether the example is secure, and the total time the analysis took[3] in milliseconds.

In the context of the symbolic execution, our implementation currently only distinguishes between concrete variables, for which the exact determined value is kept at all times, and abstract variables, for which it is assumed that they could have any possible value at any time. The implementation also currently requires that whenever a wait or notify statement is reached, all parameters of

---

[2] A reproduction package including the implementation and all examples discussed in this paper can be found at https://doi.org/10.5281/zenodo.12584236.

[3] Executed with Java 21 on an AMD Ryzen 9 5900X with 6.5 GB of RAM available to the JVM and without use of parallelization in the analysis.

Table 1. Results of running our analysis on some different examples.

Example	TIG # nodes	SysCDG # nodes	SysCDG # edges	backwards slice # nodes	backwards slice % nodes	secure analysis	secure truth	ms
Motivating Example	20	273	351	67	24.5	yes	yes	68
Timing Agnostic	28	663	1053	374	56.4	no	no[a]	30
Timing Leak	24	338	457	128	37.9	no	no	15
Change Dependent	32	413	543	183	44.3	no	no	16
GPIO Based	235	8256	10770	3062	37.1	yes	yes	193

[a]While the motivating example is secure but classified as insecure by classical IFA (false positive), the modifications make it insecure. A timing agnostic analysis would not be able to differentiate this example from the unmodified one, thus having to report a false positive.

that statement are determined. For our motivating example, only the variables storing the `bus` (and its `value_changed_event`), the `event`, and the module instance (`this`) are concrete, all other variables are abstract.

For ease of implementation, the PDGs are built directly during the analysis, one executed expression at a time without any advanced IFA techniques. Context sensitivity in the sense of [19] is achieved by treating any subsequent execution of an expression as a new program location with its own PDG node, instead of with the more elegant approach from the same paper. This heavily inflates the size of the SysCDG, but does not impact its precision. E.g., for our motivating example, we determined that roughly 70% of nodes in the SysCDG are duplicates of the remaining 30% of nodes, just for other transitions. For our larger GPIO based example discussed below, roughly 90% of nodes are duplicates that could likely be avoided by implementing more advanced IFA techniques.

In the end, the analysis of our motivating example leads to a SysCDG consisting of 273 nodes and 351 edges. The backwards slice of the critical output in line 30 of Listing 2 contains 67 of these nodes, or 24.5%. As expected, the nodes corresponding to the trusted input in line 10 of the listing are contained within the slice, whereas those corresponding to the untrusted input in line 7 are not. This shows that our analysis correctly identifies the example as secure.

To further demonstrate the increase in precision, we also ran our analysis on a variant of the motivating example where every wait statement has been replaced by `wait(SC_ZERO_TIME)`, effectively allowing any interleaving of processes. This mimics what would be yielded by an approach without any sensitivity towards timing based synchronization but otherwise identical precision. For this timing agnostic variant of our example, the SysCDG consists of 663 nodes and 1053 edges in total, with the backwards slice of the critical output containing 374 of these nodes or roughly 56.4%. In contrast to the unmodified example, this backwards slice does contain nodes corresponding to both the trusted as well as the untrusted input. Thus, the system would be falsely classified as insecure.

To demonstrate the soundness of our approach, we also modified our example such that the critical output is either time or event dependent on the untrusted input. For the former modification, the notification delay of the event notification in line 12 of the running example is changed to 0.75 ns or 1.25 ns, depending on the untrusted input. This does not impact the timing based synchronization, but the point in time at which the critical output takes place. For the latter modification, instead of waiting for a dedicated event, `pump` waits for the `value_changed_event` of `bus` (twice, so that it skips the untrusted bus cycle). This may seem secure on first glance, however (with standard configurations) the `value_changed_event` is only notified during `bus.update` if the bus's value actually changes. Thus, the critical output may not be executed at all if the trusted and untrusted information happen to be the same in one cycle. Our analysis correctly identifies both examples as insecure.

Finally, to demonstrate the applicability of our approach to a more complex example, we replaced the bus with a modified version of a GPIO implementation by MetaMorph Inc., a company that develops embedded systems. In this example, the ECU is split into two processes, one for the (untrusted) WiFi module and one for the (trusted) sensor, but both still using the same bus. For its analysis, we again abstract from most variables, except for those storing module, channel or event instances, similar to our motivating example. However, we do keep track of some boolean values which control the state of the GPIO. We also abstract from all events on which no process is ever sensitive. With these abstractions, our analysis finds 235 reachable abstracted states, leading to a SysCDG with 8256 nodes and 10770 edges. The backwards slice of the critical output (`ctrlPump`) contains the value written by the sensor, but not that written by the WiFi module, proving that the system does ensure integrity.

6 Related Work

There are numerous approaches for IFA on concurrent systems. Many of the recently developed ones are based on rely/guarantee reasoning [3,30,32,37] or separation logics [6,7,23], and as such require at least some manual effort with a high degree of expertise for most non-trivial cases. Among other approaches [6,8,10,15,27,29], they also often ensure the absence of timing leaks. However, they achieve this by prohibiting branching or synchronization on high values. Graph-based approaches, e.g. [11,26,33], can be fully automated, but at the cost of losing precision and higher computational effort. Also, none of the aforementioned approaches take timing based synchronization into account.

[34] presents a type system for information flow control in UPPAAL timed automata that takes non-determinism and clocks of timed systems into account. However, the approach is specifically tailored to the semantics of UPPAAL timed automata and cannot easily be transferred to other (and more expressive) languages such as SystemC. While they define timed commands to enforce information flow control, they also do not provide means for IFA in existing systems.

Symbolic execution has been successfully combined with IFA [1,5,9,35,36,40]. However, these approaches do not take timing and concurrency into account.

There exist several approaches to enable the analysis and formal verification for SystemC. Some of them rely on a transformation of SystemC designs into some sort of state machine [13,17,22], or they use process algebras, petri-nets or a C representation for the verification of SystemC designs [2,16,24,28]. In [18], the authors present an approach to verify SystemC designs using symbolic simulation and partial order reduction. In [22,38], the authors present a combination of induction and bounded model checking to formally verify SystemC designs. However, all of these approaches target the verification of safety properties, and do not take security properties into account.

To the best of our knowledge, symbolic execution has not yet been combined with IFA to regain precision for timed concurrent systems.

7 Conclusion

In this paper, we have proposed a new approach to leverage IFA for timed concurrent systems using symbolic execution. To the best of our knowledge, this is the first approach to precisely take timing based synchronization into account in PDG-based IFA. In addition, our approach also captures timing based side channel leaks. We demonstrated the applicability of our approach to hardware/-software co-designs by providing a prototypical implementation for SystemC and showing how in our case studies, it avoids the false positives of timing agnostic approaches without reporting false negatives.

Currently, our approach still needs some manual effort to find a good level of abstraction for the symbolic execution. The usage of heuristics, preliminary (classical) dependency analyses or artificial intelligence may make this unnecessary for many or most cases, warranting research in that direction.

Future work may also improve the scalability of our analysis. One possible approach for that goal could be to identify components of a system that communicate via timing synchronized channels, and restricting the precise analysis to those components while using less precise but cheaper (e.g. graph-based) approaches for their interaction with other parts of the system.

Another interesting avenue for future work would be to integrate path conditions [39] into our analysis. These conditions capture semantic information that is otherwise usually lost in PDG-based IFA. Our symbolic execution could enable a cheap collection of path conditions, so a combination of these approaches might yield fruitful symbiotic effects.

References

1. Chattopadhyay, S., Beck, M., Rezine, A., Zeller, A.: Quantifying the information leakage in cache attacks via symbolic execution. ACM Trans. Embed. Comput. Syst. **18**(1), 7:1–7:27 (2019)
2. Cimatti, A., Narasamdya, I., Roveri, M.: Software model checking SystemC. IEEE Trans. Comput.-Aided Des. Integr. Circuits Syst. **32**(5), 774–787 (2013)

3. Coughlin, N., Smith, G.: Rely/guarantee reasoning for noninterference in non-blocking algorithms. In: IEEE Computer Security Foundations Symposium, CSF, pp. 380–394 (2020)
4. Cousot, P., Cousot, R.: Abstract interpretation: a unified lattice model for static analysis of programs by construction or approximation of fixpoints. In: ACM Symposium on Principles of Programming Languages, pp. 238–252 (1977)
5. Davidson, D., Moench, B., Ristenpart, T., Jha, S.: FIE on firmware: finding vulnerabilities in embedded systems using symbolic execution. In: USENIX Security Symposium, pp. 463–478 (2013)
6. Eilers, M., Dardinier, T., Müller, P.: CommCSL: proving information flow security for concurrent programs using abstract commutativity. Proc. ACM Program. Lang. **7**(PLDI), 1682–1707 (2023)
7. Ernst, G., Murray, T.: SecCSL: security concurrent separation logic. In: Dillig, I., Tasiran, S. (eds.) CAV 2019. LNCS, vol. 11562, pp. 208–230. Springer, Cham (2019). https://doi.org/10.1007/978-3-030-25543-5_13
8. Focardi, R., Gorrieri, R., Martinelli, F.: Real-time information flow analysis. IEEE J. Sel. Areas Commun. **21**(1), 20–35 (2003)
9. Fowze, F., Choudhury, M., Forte, D.: Eisec: exhaustive information flow security of hardware intellectual property utilizing symbolic execution. In: Asian Hardware Oriented Security and Trust Symposium, AsianHOST, pp. 1–6 (2022)
10. Gerking, C., Schubert, D., Bodden, E.: Model checking the information flow security of real-time systems. In: Engineering Secure Software and Systems - International Symposium, ESSoS. vol. 10953, pp. 27–43 (2018)
11. Giffhorn, D., Snelting, G.: A new algorithm for low-deterministic security. Int. J. Inf. Sec. **14**(3), 263–287 (2015)
12. Goguen, J.A., Meseguer, J.: Security policies and security models. In: 1982 IEEE Symposium on Security and Privacy, pp. 11–20 (1982)
13. Habibi, A., Moinudeen, H., Tahar, S.: Generating finite state machines from SystemC. In: Design, Automation and Test in Europe (DATE), pp. 76–81 (2006)
14. Hammer, C., Snelting, G.: An improved slicer for java. In: ACM SIGPLAN-SIGSOFT Workshop on Program Analysis For Software Tools and Engineering, PASTE, pp. 17–22 (2004)
15. Hecker, M., Bischof, S., Snelting, G.: On time-sensitive control dependencies. ACM Trans. Program. Lang. Syst. **44**(1), 2:1–2:37 (2022)
16. Herber, P., Hünnemeyer, B.: Formal verification of SystemC designs using the BLAST software model checker. In: ACESMB@ MoDELS, pp. 44–53 (2014)
17. Herber, P., Pockrandt, M., Glesner, S.: STATE – a SystemC to timed automata transformation engine. In: ICESS (2015)
18. Herdt, V., Le, H.M., Große, D., Drechsler, R.: Verifying SystemC using intermediate verification language and stateful symbolic simulation. IEEE Trans. Comput-Aided Des. Integr. Circuits Syst. **38**(7), 1359–1372 (2018)
19. Horwitz, S., Reps, T.W., Binkley, D.W.: Interprocedural slicing using dependence graphs. ACM Trans. Program. Lang. Syst. **12**(1), 26–60 (1990)
20. Hsieh, C.S., Unger, E.A., Mata-Toledo, R.A.: Using program dependence graphs for information flow control. J. Syst. Softw. **17**(3), 227–232 (1992)
21. IEEE Standards Association: IEEE Std. 1666–2011, Open SystemC Language Reference Manual. IEEE Press (2011)
22. Jaß, L., Herber, P.: Bit-precise formal verification for SystemC using satisfiability modulo theories solving. In: International Embedded Systems Symposium (IESS) (2015)

23. Karbyshev, A., Svendsen, K., Askarov, A., Birkedal, L.: Compositional non-interference for concurrent programs via separation and framing. In: Principles of Security and Trust - International Conference, POST, vol. 10804, pp. 53–78 (2018)
24. Karlsson, D., Eles, P., Peng, Z.: Formal verification of SystemC designs using a petri-net based representation. In: Design, Automation and Test in Europe (DATE), pp. 1228–1233 (2006)
25. King, J.C.: Symbolic execution and program testing. Commun. ACM **19**(7), 385–394 (1976)
26. Krinke, J.: Context-sensitive slicing of concurrent programs. In: ACM SIGSOFT Symposium on Foundations of Software Engineering, FSE, pp. 178–187 (2003)
27. Lanotte, R., Maggiolo-Schettini, A., Troina, A.: Time and probability-based information flow analysis. IEEE Trans. Softw. Eng. **36**(5), 719–734 (2010)
28. Man, K.L., Fedeli, A., Mercaldi, M., Boubekeur, M., Schellekens, M.P.: SC2SCFL: automated SystemC to SystemCFL translation. In: Embedded Computing Systems: Architectures, Modeling, and Simulation, pp. 34–45 (2007)
29. Mantel, H., Sabelfeld, A.: A generic approach to the security of multi-threaded programs. In: IEEE Computer Security Foundations Workshop (CSFW), pp. 126–142. IEEE Computer Society (2001)
30. Mantel, H., Sands, D., Sudbrock, H.: Assumptions and guarantees for compositional noninterference. In: IEEE Computer Security Foundations Symposium, CSF, pp. 218–232 (2011)
31. Mantel, H., Sudbrock, H.: Types vs. PDGs in information flow analysis. In: Logic-Based Program Synthesis and Transformation: International Symposium, LOPSTR, pp. 106–121 (2013)
32. Murray, T.C., Sison, R., Engelhardt, K.: COVERN: a logic for compositional verification of information flow control. In: IEEE European Symposium on Security and Privacy, EuroS&P, pp. 16–30 (2018)
33. Nanda, M.G., Ramesh, S.: Interprocedural slicing of multithreaded programs with applications to Java. ACM Trans. Program. Lang. Syst. **28**(6), 1088–1144 (2006)
34. Nielson, F., Nielson, H.R., Vasilikos, P.: Information flow for timed automata. In: Aceto, L., Bacci, G., Bacci, G., Ingólfsdóttir, A., Legay, A., Mardare, R. (eds.) Models, Algorithms, Logics and Tools. LNCS, vol. 10460, pp. 3–21. Springer, Cham (2017). https://doi.org/10.1007/978-3-319-63121-9_1
35. Phan, Q., Malacaria, P., Tkachuk, O., Pasareanu, C.S.: Symbolic quantitative information flow. ACM SIGSOFT Softw. Eng. Notes **37**(6), 1–5 (2012)
36. Ryan, K., Gregoire, M., Sturton, C.: SEIF: augmented symbolic execution for information flow in hardware designs. In: International Workshop on Hardware and Architectural Support for Security and Privacy, HASP, pp. 1–9 (2023)
37. Schoepe, D., Murray, T., Sabelfeld, A.: VERONICA: expressive and precise concurrent information flow security. In: IEEE Computer Security Foundations Symposium, CSF, pp. 79–94 (2020)
38. Schwan, S., Herber, P.: Optimized hardware/software co-verification using the UCLID satisfiability modulo theory solver. In: International Conference on Enabling Technologies: Infrastructure for Collaborative Enterprises, WETICE, pp. 225–230 (2020)
39. Snelting, G.: Combining slicing and constraint solving for validation of measurement software. In: Static Analysis, International Symposium, SAS, vol. 1145, pp. 332–348 (1996)

40. Subramanyan, P., Malik, S., Khattri, H., Maiti, A., Fung, J.M.: Verifying information flow properties of firmware using symbolic execution. In: Design, Automation and Test in Europe Conference and Exhibition, DATE, pp. 337–342 (2016)
41. Tasche, P., Monti, R.E., Drerup, S.E., Blohm, P., Herber, P., Huisman, M.: Deductive verification of parameterized embedded systems modeled in SystemC. In: Verification, Model Checking, and Abstract Interpretation, pp. 187–209 (2024)
42. Volpano, D., Irvine, C., Smith, G.: A sound type system for secure flow analysis. J. Comput. Secur. **4**(2–3), 167–187 (1996)
43. Weiser, M.D.: Program slicing. IEEE Trans. Softw. Eng. **10**(4), 352–357 (1984)

Validating Traces of Distributed Programs Against TLA$^+$ Specifications

Horatiu Cirstea[1], Markus A. Kuppe[2], Benjamin Loillier[1], and Stephan Merz[1(✉)]

[1] University of Lorraine, CNRS, Inria, LORIA, Nancy, France
stephan.merz@loria.fr
[2] Microsoft Research, Redmond, USA

Abstract. TLA$^+$ is a formal language for specifying systems, including distributed algorithms, that is supported by powerful verification tools. In this work we present a framework for checking if traces of distributed programs are compatible with high-level specifications written in TLA$^+$. The problem is reduced to a constrained model checking problem, realized using the TLC model checker. Our framework consists of an API for instrumenting Java programs in order to record traces of executions, of a collection of TLA$^+$ operators that are used for relating those traces to specifications, and of scripts for running the model checker. Crucially, traces only contain updates to specification variables rather than full values, and developers may choose to trace only certain variables. We have applied our approach to several distributed programs, detecting discrepancies between the specifications and the implementations in all cases. We discuss reasons for these discrepancies, best practices for instrumenting programs, and how to interpret the verdict produced by TLC.

1 Introduction

Distributed systems are at the heart of modern cloud services and they are known to be error-prone, due to phenomena such as message delays or failures of nodes and communication networks. Applying formal methods during the design and development of these systems can help increase the confidence in their correctness and resilience. For example, the TLA$^+$ [18] specification language and verification tools have been successfully used in industry [20,24] for designing distributed algorithms underlying modern cloud systems. TLA$^+$ and similar specification formalisms are most useful for describing and analyzing systems at high levels of abstraction, but they do not provide much support for validating actual implementations of these systems. Although TLA$^+$ supports a notion of refinement, formally proving a chain of refinements from a high-level design of a distributed algorithm to an actual implementation would be a daunting task, complicated by the fact that standard programming languages do not provide explicit control of the grain of atomicity of the running program. In

This work was partly supported by a grant from Oracle Corporation.

A. Madeira and A. Knapp (Eds.): SEFM 2024, LNCS 15280, pp. 126–143, 2025.
https://doi.org/10.1007/978-3-031-77382-2_8

this work, we instead present a lightweight approach to validating distributed programs against high-level specifications that relies on recording finite traces of program executions and leveraging the TLA$^+$ model checker TLC [29] for comparing those traces to the state machine described in the TLA$^+$ specification. Although this approach does not provide formal correctness guarantees, even when the TLA$^+$ specification has been extensively verified, we have found it very useful for discovering and analyzing discrepancies between the runs of distributed programs and their high-level specifications. We have thus been able to discover serious bugs that had gone undetected by more traditional quality assurance techniques.

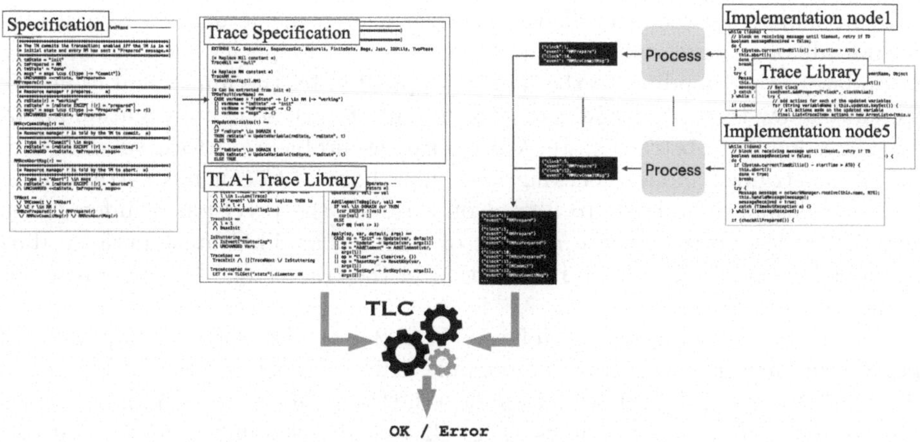

Fig. 1. Overview of trace validation.

Figure 1 summarizes the approach. The starting point consists of a distributed Implementation and of the Specification, written in TLA$^+$, it is supposed to implement. We have designed a Trace Library that facilitates the instrumentation of Java programs in order to record information on how program operations correspond to transitions described in the TLA$^+$ specification, including updates of its variables. Executing the instrumented programs produces traces in JSON format that are aggregated into a single file. We also provide a TLA$^+$ Trace Library that helps write a Trace Specification, extending the original specification. The model checker TLC is then used to check the program trace against the trace specification. Although our trace library was developed for Java, the overall approach can easily be adapted to any other imperative language. We also implemented a few features in TLC that support our approach.

Because the traces record the evolution of the state of the TLA$^+$ specification, our approach is easiest to apply when the specification exists prior to building the implementation, the implementor is familar with it, and uses it as a blueprint when writing the code. However, we have also used the approach in order to "reverse engineer" a TLA$^+$ specification from an existing distributed program and better understand its operation. Trace validation can also help ensure that the specification and implementation remain in sync over time because it is easy to apply it again in case of changes to the specification or the implementation.

The main problem when instrumenting a program is to identify suitable "linearization points" at which the program completes a step that corresponds to an atomic transition of the high-level state machine. Basic guiding principles are to log an event when shared state has been updated, such as when sending or receiving messages, performing operations on locks or on stable data storage. Feedback from trace validation can help with adapting the instrumentation in order to take into account differences in the grain of atomicity between the specification and the implementation, as discussed later. Because data representation generally differs between the TLA$^+$ specification and the actual program, it may be difficult or impractical to compute the value of a specification variable (or its update) corresponding to the data manipulated by the implementation. We therefore allow traces to be incomplete and only record some information about the corresponding abstract state. We reduce the problem of trace validation to one of constrained model checking and show how TLC can reconstruct missing information. This leads to a tradeoff between the precision of information recorded in the trace and the amount of search that TLC must perform during model checking. Too little information in the trace may also jeopardize the verdict of validation.

The paper is organized as follows: Sect. 2 provides some background on TLA$^+$ and introduces our running example. Our approach to instrumentation is described in Sect. 3. In Sect. 4 we formalize the trace validation problem, describe how we realized the approach using TLC, and discuss our experience with it. Section 5 discusses related work, and Sect. 6 concludes the paper and presents some perspectives for future work.

2 Background

2.1 TLA$^+$ Specifications

TLA$^+$ [18] is a specification language based on Zermelo-Fraenkel set theory and linear-time temporal logic that has found wide use for writing high-level specifications of concurrent and distributed algorithms. It emphasizes the use of mathematical descriptions based on sets and functions for specifying data structures. In TLA$^+$, the state space of a system is represented using variables, and formulas are evaluated over *behaviors*, i.e., sequences of states that assign values to variables. Algorithms are described as state machines whose specifications are written in the canonical form $Init \wedge \Box[Next]_{vars} \wedge L$. In this formula, *Init* is a state predicate describing the possible initial states of the system, *Next* represents the next-state relation, usually written as the disjunction of actions describing the possible state transitions, *vars* is a tuple containing all state variables that appear in the specification, and L is a temporal formula asserting liveness and fairness assumptions. A state predicate is a formula of first-order logic that is evaluated over single states. A transition predicate (or, synonymously, action) is a first-order formula that may contain unprimed and primed occurrences of variables. Such a formula is evaluated over a pair of states, with unprimed variables referring to the values before the transition and primed variables to the values after the transition. The formula $[Next]_{vars}$ holds of a pair of states $\langle s, t \rangle$ if either *Next* holds of $\langle s, t \rangle$ (and therefore the pair represents an actual step of the system) or the tuple *vars* evaluates to the same value in the two states (and the pair represents a stuttering step). Systematically allowing for stuttering steps enables the refinement of a specification S by another specification I written at a lower level of abstraction to be represented as the validity of the implication $I \Rightarrow S$. The complementary property L is used to express fairness assumptions and is at the basis of verifying liveness properties of algorithms. Since in this work we analyze finite traces of programs, we ignore liveness properties and are interested in finite behaviors, i.e., sequences $s_0 \ldots s_n$ of states such that *Init* holds of s_0 and $[Next]_{vars}$ holds for all pairs $\langle s_i, s_{i+1} \rangle$ for $i \in 0 \,..\, n-1$.

As a running example for this paper, Fig. 2 contains an excerpt of the TLA+ specification of the well-known Two-Phase Commit protocol where a transaction manager (TM) helps a set of resource managers (RMs) reach agreement on whether to commit or abort a transaction: the RMs send messages indicating that they are prepared to commit, while the TM listens for such messages and based on the votes of the participants broadcasts a commit or an abort message. This specification is part of a collection of example TLA+ modules.[1] The module first declares a constant parameter `RM` that represents the set of RMs and four variables representing the control states of the RMs (represented as a function with domain `RM`) and of the TM, the set of RMs that have declared their preparedness to carry out the transaction, and the set of messages that have been sent during the protocol. The initial state of the system is described by the predicate `TPInit`: every RM is in state `"working"`, the TM in state `"init"`, and the sets of prepared RMs and of messages are empty. The following operators define actions that describe individual state transitions. For example, `RMPrepare(r)` represents an RM `r` declaring its preparedness to carry out the transaction by moving to control state `"prepared"` and adding a corresponding message to the set of messages `msgs`. The action `TPNext` corresponds to the next-state relation of the state machine, defined as the disjunction of the previously defined actions, and formula `Spec` represents the overall specification. The TLA+ tools, including the model checker TLC and the proof assistant TLAPS [2], can be used to verify properties of the specification, including the invariant `Consistent` that RMs must agree about committing or aborting a transaction.

[1] https://github.com/tlaplus/Examples/tree/master/specifications/transaction_commit.

```
CONSTANT RM
VARIABLES rmState, tmState, tmPrepared, msgs
vars ≜ ⟨rmState, tmState, tmPrepared, msgs⟩
Messages ≜ [type : {"Prepared"}, rm : RM] ∪ [type : {"Commit", "Abort"}]
TPInit ≜
   ∧ rmState = [r ∈ RM ↦ "working"] ∧ tmState = "init"
   ∧ tmPrepared = {} ∧ msgs = {}
RMPrepare(r) ≜
   ∧ UNCHANGED ⟨tmState, tmPrepared⟩ ∧ rmState[r] = "working"
   ∧ rmState' = [rmState EXCEPT ![r] = "prepared"]
   ∧ msgs' = msgs ∪ {[type ↦ "Prepared", rm ↦ r]}
RMRcvCommitMsg(r) ≜
   ∧ UNCHANGED ⟨tmState, tmPrepared, msgs⟩ ∧ [type ↦ "Commit"] ∈ msgs
   ∧ rmState' = [rmState EXCEPT ![r] = "committed"]
RMRcvAbortMsg(r) ≜ ...
TMRcvPrepared(r) ≜
   ∧ UNCHANGED ⟨rmState,tmState,msgs⟩ ∧ tmPrepared' = tmPrepared ∪ {r}
   ∧ tmState = "init" ∧ [type ↦ "Prepared", rm ↦ r] ∈ msgs
TMCommit ≜
   ∧ UNCHANGED ⟨rmState, tmPrepared⟩ ∧ tmState = "init" ∧ tmPrepared = RM
   ∧ tmState' = "done" ∧ msgs' = msgs ∪ {[type ↦ "Commit"]}
TMAbort ≜ ...
TPNext ≜
   ∨ TMCommit ∨ TMAbort
   ∨ ∃ r ∈ RM : ∨ RMPrepare(r) ∨ TMRcvPrepared(r)
                ∨ RMRcvCommitMsg(r) ∨ RMRcvAbortMsg(r)
Spec ≜ TPInit ∧ □[TPNext]_vars
Consistent ≜
   ∀ r1,r2 ∈ RM: ¬(rmState[r1] = "aborted" ∧ rmState[r2] = "committed")
```

Fig. 2. TLA+ Specification of Two-Phase Commit.

2.2 Java Implementation

A possible Java implementation of the resource managers is presented in Fig. 3. Only a simplified version of the main method is shown, the auxiliary methods are faithful Java translations of the actions in the TLA+ specification.[2]

An RM is identified by a `name` and uses a `network` (manager) to send and receive messages. Once it completes its task (represented by method `working`), it sends a message to the TM indicating that it is prepared to commit and waits for a reply. The method `handleMessage` causes the transaction to be committed or aborted, according to the decision received from the TM. If no reply is received before the `RECEIVE_TIMEOUT`, the RM resends its prepared message to the TM.

[2] The full implementation is available at https://github.com/lbinria/TwoPhase.

```java
public class ResourceManager {
  String name, tmName;
  ResourceManagerState state;
  NetworkManager network;
  public void run() throws IOException {
     working();
     while (true) {
        sendPrepared();
        try {
           Message message = network.receive(name, RECEIVE_TIMEOUT);
           handleMessage(message);
           return;
        } catch (TimeOutException e) {}
} } }
```

Fig. 3. Java implementation of the RM of the Two-Phase Commit protocol.

3 Instrumenting Distributed Programs

Our objective in this work is to check traces of program executions against a TLA$^+$ specification of the algorithm the program is expected to implement. In order to obtain such traces (in JSON format), we instrument implementations, registering changes made to specification variables and logging them to a file, together with a timestamp. Section 4 describes the structure of TLA$^+$ trace specifications used to process the traces generated in this way.

The main class of the Java library we designed, TLATracer, essentially provides two methods: `notifyChange` for tracking variable updates, and `log` used to produce one log entry in the trace file that reflects all the variable changes recorded with `notifyChange` since the last call to `log` (or since the start of the process if `log` was never called before).[3]

```java
void notifyChange(String var, List<String> path,
                  String op, List<Object> args);
long log(String eventName, Object[] args, long clockValue);
```

Updates to variables are tracked using the method `notifyChange`, which allows the programmer to specify an update to several fields (identified using the `path` argument) of the TLA$^+$ variable `var` by applying the operation `op` to the old field value and the arguments `args`. Our library supports operations such as updating the variable by a new value, adding or removing a value to or from a set or bag (multi-set) etc. In its general form, the `log` method records the variable changes as well as the name and optionally the parameters of the corresponding TLA$^+$ action. The time when the log has been performed is used as a timestamp for the

[3] The library available at https://github.com/lbinria/trace_validation_tools/ offers more convenience methods to track variable changes and log events.

corresponding entry. The library provides different types of clocks (in-memory, file-based or server-based) that can be used with the tracer, in which case the argument need not be indicated explicitly, but it should be specified when the implementation uses a logical clock. The library currently supports scalar logical clocks but vector clocks can easily be added.

For example, in the `sendPrepared` method, an RM sets its state to `"prepared"` and sends a corresponding message to the TM (lines 2 and 6, respectively):[4]

```
1 void sendPrepared()  {
2   state = ResourceManagerState.PREPARED;
3   tracer.notifyChange("rmState", {name}, "Update", {"prepared"});
4   tracer.notifyChange("msgs", {}, "Add", {"type":"Prepared", "rm":name});
5   tracer.log("RMPrepare", {name});
6   networkManager.send(new Message(name, tmName, "Prepared", 0));
7 }
```

The remaining lines are used for tracing purposes. Line 3 records the change of the entry corresponding to the RM executing `sendPrepared` (i.e. `this.name`) of the TLA$^+$ variable `rmState` to the new value `"prepared"`. Similarly, line 4 indicates that a message of type `"Prepared"` from the current RM is added to the set `msgs`. Finally, in line 5 these changes are logged as corresponding to the TLA$^+$ action `RMPrepare` with the current RM as parameter. For an RM named `"rm-0"`, the above code produces the following log entry in JSON format:


```
{ "clock": 4,
  "rmState": [ { "op": "Update", "path": ["rm-0"], "args": ["prepared"] } ],
  "msgs": [ { "op": "Add", "path": [],
              "args": ["type":"Prepared","rm":"rm-0"] } ],
  "event": "RMPrepare", "event_args": ["rm-0"] }
```


It should be noted that it is possible to trace updates to only a subset of specification variables. Similarly, indicating the name and the arguments of the TLA$^+$ action is optional. For example, the size of the value of a variable might be prohibitively large, or the value might simply be unknown, for example because the implementation handles encrypted values. In the above example, either or both calls to `notifyChange` could have been omitted. As discussed in Sect. 4, the model checker will fill in suitable values for variables omitted from tracing. However, providing more detailed information can lead to more efficient validation and strengthen confidence in the results.

The library also provides Python scripts for merging the trace files produced by different processes and for validating the resulting trace using TLC.

4 Checking Program Traces Against TLA$^+$ Specifications

Having obtained a log from an execution of the distributed program, we must check if this log matches some behavior of the TLA$^+$ state machine specification

[4] We take some syntactic liberties, such as writing `{...}` instead of `List.of(...)`.

that the program is expected to implement. We define the problem more formally, explain how we realize trace validation, report our experience with this approach, and discuss some technical aspects of trace validation.

4.1 The Trace Validation Problem

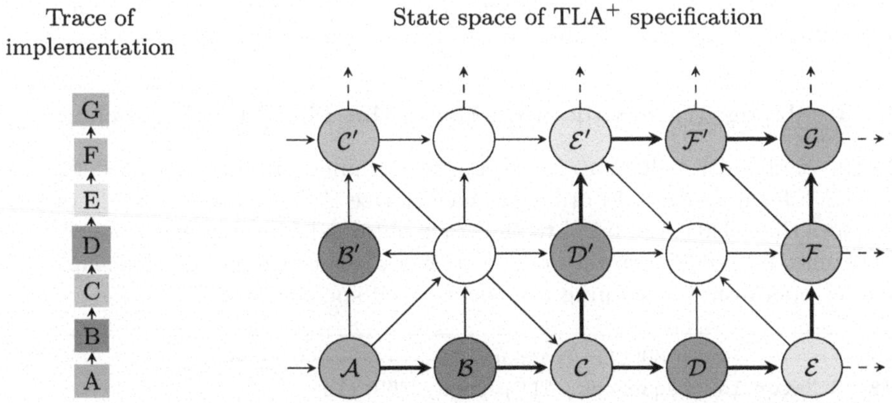

Fig. 4. Trace validation as a search for paths in the state space.

Our problem can be stated as follows. Let $\mathcal{S}$ be the set of finite behaviors that satisfy the specification *Spec*, and let $\mathcal{T}$ be the set of finite behaviors represented by the trace, with arbitrary values assigned to variables whose values are not recorded. The trace is compatible with the specification if $\mathcal{S} \cap \mathcal{T} \neq \emptyset$. Note in particular that we do not check for refinement of the high-level specification by the trace, expressed as $\mathcal{T} \subseteq \mathcal{S}$: this condition would be too strong in the presence of non-deterministically chosen values for variables not recorded in the trace.

Figure 4 illustrates the idea. On the left-hand side, the chain of nodes represents the trace obtained from the instrumented program. The graph on the right-hand side represents the state space of the TLA+ specification, and we must check if the trace can be matched to some path in the state space. The first node of the trace must correspond to some initial state of the graph: in our example, we assume that this is the case for the state labeled $\mathcal{A}$ in the lower left-hand corner. Then, we try to match at least one successor of an already matched state with the corresponding successor in the trace. There may be several matching states, in particular due to incomplete information about variable values: in the example, we assume that two successors of state $\mathcal{A}$ match the second node of the trace. On the other hand, the state labeled $\mathcal{C}'$ in the left-hand column of the state space does not have a successor matching the node labeled D in the trace. Overall, the trace of the example is compatible since there is at least one path in the state space that matches the trace, cf. the two paths indicated by thick arrows.

The problem is actually a little more subtle: atomic steps of the implementation need not match precisely those of the specification but may correspond to zero or several steps of the TLA$^+$ specification. We explain how we reduce the problem to one of constrained model checking and how we realize it using the TLC model checker. In general, the programmer is in charge of tracking the correspondence between the event names in the trace and the actions in the specification as well as that between the names of the logged variables and those from the specification. In the specific case presented in the next section, these correspondences are one to one and could be automatically generated.

4.2 Realizing Trace Validation Using the TLC Model Checker

The set $\mathcal{S}$ of finite behaviors satisfying the original specification is defined by the TLA$^+$ formula *Spec*. In order to characterize the intersection $\mathcal{S} \cap \mathcal{T}$ of finite behaviors that also correspond to the trace obtained from the execution, we add constraints to *Spec*. Concretely, our framework provides a module `TraceSpec` that provides operators for defining the constrained specification.

```
------------------- MODULE TraceSpec -------------------
EXTENDS Naturals, Sequences, TLC, Json, IOUtils
VARIABLE l
Trace ≜ ndJsonDeserialize(IOEnv.TRACE_PATH)
IsEvent(e) ≜
  ∧ l ∈ 1 .. Len(Trace) ∧ l' = l + 1
  ∧ "event" ∈ DOMAIN Trace[l] => Trace[l].event = e
  ∧ UpdateVariables(Trace[l])
```

The module declares a variable `l` that will denote the number of the current line of the trace. The definition of the operator `Trace` causes the JSON representation of the trace to be internalized as a sequence of records whose fields correspond to the entries of the log file. The operator `IsEvent(e)` encapsulates processing the current line of the trace and generating the constraints imposed by it. It requires that `l` is a valid index into the trace. The trace may explicitly indicate the event corresponding to the current transition by including an `"event"` field, in which case the operator checks for the expected value. (Any event parameters indicated by the entry are taken into account below.) The operator increments the variable `l` and computes new values for the variables recorded in the current line of the trace, by evaluating the operator `UpdateVariables`:

```
UpdateVariables(ll) ≜
  ∧ "rmState" ∈ DOMAIN ll =>
       rmState' = UpdateVariable(rmState, "rmState", ll)
  ∧ ...  \* similar lines for variables tmState, tmPrepared, msgs
```

That operator is defined as a conjunction that checks for each variable of the original specification if a corresponding entry exists in the current line of the trace and, if so, determines the new value of the variable from that entry.

The operator `UpdateVariable` is predefined in our framework and computes the new value from the value of the first argument (i.e., the unprimed variable) and the operator to be applied according to the trace. For example, the JSON entry

```
"rmState": [ { "op": "Update", "path": ["rm-0"], "args": ["prepared"] } ]
```

will give rise to the TLA+ value

```
[rmState EXCEPT !["rm-0"] = "prepared"]
```

representing the function `rmState` with the value at argument `rmState["rm-0"]` replaced by `"prepared"`. A single update in the JSON trace may correspond to changes to several parts of a complex value such as a function or a record. Predefined TLA+ operators exist for the different operators that our framework currently supports, and this can be smoothly extended, both in the instrumentation library and at the TLA+ level, should additional operators be desirable.

For every action of the original specification, we then construct a similar action of the trace specification by conjoining the predicate `IsEvent`. For example, the action of the trace specification corresponding to the `TMCommit` action of the specification of the two-phase commit protocol is defined as

```
IsTMCommit ≜ IsEvent("TMCommit") ∧ TMCommit
```

Because TLC evaluates formulas from left to right, the effect of these definitions is to first update state variables based on the information in the trace and then evaluate the action predicate of the underlying specification. This evaluation checks that the predicate is satisfied while non-deterministically generating suitable values for any variables left open in the trace. For actions that take arguments, we define the constrained action such that any parameters provided in the trace indicate the instance of the original action that may occur:

```
IsTMRcvPrepared ≜
  ∧ IsEvent("TMRcvPrepared")
  ∧ IF "event_args" ∈ DOMAIN Trace[l] ∧ Len(Trace[l].event_args) >= 1
      THEN TMRcvPrepared(Trace[l].event_args[1])
      ELSE ∃ r ∈ RM : TMRcvPrepared(r)
```

The overall next-state relation `TraceNext` is defined as the disjunction of these actions. Writing the trace specification for a given algorithm specification is systematic and could be automated in most cases, except when `TraceNext` may include disjuncts corresponding to action composition as discussed in Sect. 4.3.

TLC evaluates the action `TraceNext` from the current state in order to compute all possible successor states. Even if no such state can be found (as in the case of state C in the leftmost column of Fig. 4), there may still exist matching behaviors elsewhere in the state space. Therefore, we should not direct TLC to check for deadlocks of the constrained specification. It would also be inappropriate to verify the liveness property `◇(l >= Len(Trace))`, which would not hold for incomplete prefixes of the constrained state space. On the other hand, checking the invariant `□(l < Len(Trace))` will cause TLC to output a behavior of the original specification that matches the trace if such a behavior exists. However, no useful information will be provided when the trace cannot be matched, i.e., when trace validation fails. Instead, we may observe that the length of the longest path in the constrained state space corresponds to the diameter of the graph,[5] which suggests defining the predicate

```
TraceAccepted ≜ TLCGet("stats").diameter - 1 = Len(Trace)
```

as the postcondition to check for determining success of trace validation. If the postcondition is violated, $\mathcal{S}$ does not contain any behavior whose prefix of appropriate length is in $\mathcal{T}$, i.e., matches the log of the execution. Because there is not a single behavior explaining this failure, TLC cannot generate a counter-example. However, it can generate a maximal finite behavior in $\mathcal{S}$ that corresponds to the log but cannot be extended further. The *hit-based breakpoint* feature of the TLA$^+$ debugger [17] can be used to halt state-space exploration when the diameter reported by TLC is attained, and the user can then step back and forth in the state space in order to understand the discrepancy. The extended version of this paper [1] contains a more detailed discussion.

Regardless of whether we use a property or a postcondition, trace validation might incorrectly accept a trace if the trace provides incomplete information. A particularly extreme case would be a trace that does not log any variable updates or action occurrences and only provides the length of a finite execution.

4.3 Analyzing Discrepancies

We have used trace validation for several case studies: besides the two-phase commit protocol presented here, we experimented with a distributed key-value store ensuring snapshot isolation [7] whose specification was taken from the standard collection of TLA$^+$ specifications [19], the distributed termination detection algorithm EWD 998 [4,15] from the same collection, two existing implementations of the Raft consensus algorithm [22], and the Microsoft Confidential Consortium Framework [11]. In all cases, trace validation quickly identified executions of the distributed implementations that could not be matched to the high-level specification. In the following, we identify several reasons for such discrepancies.

Implementation Shortcuts. The implementation of the Two-Phase Commit protocol could use a counter to store the number (rather than the identities) of the RMs from which a `"Prepared"` message was received, and it could check if all RMs are prepared to carry out the transaction by simply comparing the counter value to the number of resource managers. Such an implementation will work correctly as long as no messages are lost. However, if some RM resends the `"Prepared"` message due to a timeout, the TM might count it twice and then commit prematurely. We found this kind of implementation error to be reliably detected using trace validation.

Overly Strict Specifications. The implementation [16] of the token-based distributed termination detection algorithm EWD 998 allowed a node to send an

[5] The presence of the line counter `l` excludes cycles in the constrained state space.

ordinary (non-token) message to itself, which was ruled out in the specification. Again, trace validation quickly discovered this mismatch, which can be resolved by adapting either the specification or the implementation.

Mismatch of the Grain of Atomicity. Mainstream programming languages do not provide atomic transactions encapsulating several updates, so the choice of when to log an action corresponding to the TLA+ specification requires consideration. Transitions that modify shared state such as sending or receiving network messages, acquiring or releasing global locks or committing state to stable storage are natural candidates. In most cases, we found it not too difficult to identify suitable points in the code for instrumentation, but the choices are important for trace validation to be meaningful.

It frequently happens that the implementation takes steps that are invisible at the level of the abstract state space. In our Two-Phase Commit running example, sent messages are (permanently) stored in a set, so resending a message due to a timeout conceptually corresponds to a stuttering step of the specification. However, when the implementation resends, say, a `"Prepared"` message, it should not log an `RMPrepare` step because such a step is not allowed to take place when the RM is already in state `"prepared"`. For this example, one can either choose to omit logging an action when a message is resent or only log the new (in fact unchanged) variable values but no action. The fact that TLA+ specifications are insensitive to stuttering steps is helpful in such situations.

An implementation may also combine two or more separate steps of the TLA+ specification into a single transition. For example, in Raft implementations, nodes may update their term upon receiving an AppendEntries request for a higher term, whereas the two actions of updating the term and appending entries are distinguished in the Raft specification. In such cases, one may instrument the implementation such that it logs two transitions in succession. Alternatively, one may add an explicit disjunct to the next-state relation of the TLA+ specification used for trace validation, making use of the TLA+ action composition operator $A \circ B$, support for which has recently been added to TLC. Doing so is a way of explicitly documenting optimizations of the implementation with respect to the specification.

4.4 Experience with Trace Validation

Overall, we and the engineers we worked with found it quite straightforward to instrument existing code, notably when the TLA+ specification was used as a guideline for writing the implementation. The instrumentation library presented in Sect. 3 with corresponding TLA+ operators shown in Sect. 4.2 was found helpful but not strictly necessary: in fact, it was not used in all of our case studies. Writing the trace specification is generally systematic and straightforward.

The most significant case study to which we applied trace validation occurred in the context of reverse engineering a formal specification for a Raft-inspired consensus algorithm implemented within the Confidential Consortium Framework (CCF). The starting point was a specification written after analyzing the source code, which was then corrected and amended through trace validation based on an existing test suite that exercises non-trivial system behavior. Model checking the resulting specification revealed serious violations of key safety properties. The counterexamples obtained in this way were translated into new tests, which confirmed previously unknown problems with the implementation. After addressing these issues at the specification level, corresponding updates to the implementation were made. To ensure ongoing consistency between the specification and its implementation, trace validation is now part of CCF's continuous integration pipeline. A detailed analysis of our experiences with formally verifying CCF, including trace validation, is discussed in a separate paper [12].

We also leveraged trace validation when implementing the distributed termination detection algorithm EWD 998, starting from its preexisting TLA$^+$ specification. The algorithm is based on a token-passing scheme for detecting when global termination has occurred; its implementation consists of about 500 lines of code. Its specification includes an action for atomically passing the token from one node to its neighbor. The implementation is based on asynchronous message passing, and sending and receiving the token was logged as two separate transitions. Moreover, the implementation sends the token as soon as local termination occurs, whereas the specification has a separate action for termination detection. Trace validation pointed out both discrepancies, which are instances of differences in the grain of atomicity. Once these discrepancies were fixed by having the implementation log both termination detection and token sending, but not token receiving, the issue mentioned previously of a node possibly sending an ordinary message to itself was detected. Finally, it was found that the nodes continued to pass the token even after all nodes except for the initiator had terminated, which corresponded to an implementation error. Since then, thousands of traces have been successfully validated, and we are now confident that the implementation is indeed correct.

4.5 Implementation Aspects

Our approach to instrumentation is flexible with regard to the detail of information recorded in the trace: only a subset of variables needs to be included in the trace, and names and parameters of corresponding TLA$^+$ actions may or may not be given. Less information in the trace increases the potential degree of non-determinism in the trace specification and may lead to a combinatorial explosion during model checking. To some extent, this problem can be alleviated using different exploration strategies. TLC's default breadth-first search (BFS) ensures shortest-length counter-examples and is most informative for debugging. However, depth-first search (DFS) constrained by the length of the trace can be more efficient because checking can be stopped as soon as some behavior of the expected length has been found.

We report in Fig. 5 the numbers of distinct states explored with BFS/DFS by TLC for several valid traces that contain more or less information; a single figure indicates that BFS and DFS generate the same number of states. We consider traces for the Two-Phase Commit protocol for 4, 8, 12, and 16 RMs. For the Key-Value Store we consider 4, 8 or 12 agents accessing a store with a maximum

Instance	length	VEA	V	VpEA	EA	E
TP, 4 RMs	17	19	211/35	19	48/22	246/58
TP, 8 RMs	33	35	8k/73	35	640/42	22k/695
TP, 12 RMs	73	74	∞/209	74	11k/86	2.5M/27k
TP, 16 RMs	90	91	∞/270	91	205k/107	∞/557k
KV, 4a, 10k, 20v	109	111	∞/158	13k/149	111	∞/35k
KV, 8a, 10k, 20v	229	231	∞/317	18k/307	231	∞/176k
KV, 12a, 10k, 20v	295	297	∞/423	678k/411	297	∞/300k
KV, 4a, 20k, 40v	131	133	∞/298	∞/285	133	∞/9.9M
KV, 8a, 20k, 40v	249	251	∞/1164	∞/1146	251	∞
KV, 12a, 20k, 40v	308	310	∞/552	∞/538	310	∞

Fig. 5. Number of distinct states explored for valid traces of Two-Phase Commit (TP) and Key-Value Store (KV), for various degrees of precision (1hr timeout).

of either 10 keys and 20 values or 20 keys and 40 values. The column headings indicate the kind of information that was recorded in the traces: all variables and the events with their arguments (VEA), just the variables (V), the variables and some events (VpEA), only the events with their arguments (EA) or only event names (E). For Two-Phase Commit, VpEA records only the events of the TM, for Key-Value Store, only the start and end of transactions are logged.

As expected, tracing full information for variables and the events requires exploring the least number of states. Logging only the variables or only the event names quickly leads to state-space explosion that makes trace validation infeasible. However, recording well-chosen partial information is sufficient for limiting the state space. For the Key-Value Store, logging events and their arguments is enough because they uniquely determine the corresponding variable values. For Two-Phase Commit, logging the events of the RMs is unnecessary.

Besides an exponential growth of the number of states, too imprecise logs may even lead to erroneous traces being accepted because the model checker may be able to infer suitable values that do not correspond to the actual ones. Nevertheless, such traces, which require little instrumentation, can still be useful at early stages of validation for finding issues. For instance, validating a trace containing only the event names for 16 RMs takes a considerable amount of time but the bug concerning the implementation using counters mentioned in Sect. 4.3 can still be detected with such a trace in less than a minute.

5 Related Work

The verification of execution traces against high-level properties or specifications has a long history in formal methods. Havelund [10] introduced runtime verification as a lightweight method for checking that a system's execution trace conforms to its high-level specification. Runtime verification typically involves the generation of a monitor from the specification, which consumes the trace events to check conformance [6]. Howard et al. [13] verified execution traces directly against the system's high-level specification. Their work also demonstrated that it was feasible to use standard model checkers (ProB and Spin) to check execution traces against these specifications, a technique that we also employ. However, they did not consider distributed programs that require the use of (centralized or distributed) clocks for preserving causality, and they did not consider traces with incomplete information.

Tasiran et al. [25] were the first to extract and validate traces obtained from a hardware simulator against a TLA$^+$ spec, demonstrating the practical applicability of trace validation. The adoption of TLA$^+$ among distributed system practitioners, spurred by Newcombe et al. [20], and the formalization of trace validation as a refinement check by Pressler [23], caused trace validation to be applied to real-world distributed systems. For instance, Davis et al. [3] applied the technique to MongoDB, discovering a non-trivial implementation bug. However, they faced challenges in consistently logging the implementation state, and aligning different grains of atomicity, which we attribute to them not leveraging TLA$^+$'s non-determinism to infer implementation state, and action composition to align atomicity. Niu et al. [21] also validated traces of Zookeeper, ensuring that its implementation corresponds to its spec. Similarly, Wang et al. [28] revealed several implementation bugs by replaying TLA$^+$ behaviors against instrumented implementations. Furthermore, the work by Wang et al. serves as an example of the challenges of aligning the grains of atomicity, illustrated by the authors asserting two bugs in a widely used and well-established specification [22]. We contend that these are, in fact, common TLA$^+$ modeling patterns and can be handled with action composition. Nevertheless, all efforts found non-trivial bugs in real-world systems by comparing implementation traces to high-level TLA$^+$ behaviors, a testament to the effectiveness of this approach.

To facilitate a closer alignment between high-level specifications and their actual implementations, Hackett et al. [9] and Foo et al. [8] proposed extensions to PlusCal, an algorithmic language whose translator serves as a front-end to TLA$^+$. These aim at adding sufficient detail to specifications for code generation and enabling the generation of runtime monitors, respectively. Despite these advancements, the requirement for implementation-level shims may impede widespread industry adoption. Moreover, the projection from a global state machine, which is a common modeling pattern, to node-local state machines prevent the verification of global properties by monitors. Yet, both approaches still translate specifications written in their PlusCal extensions into TLA$^+$, allowing users to leverage all of the existing verification tools.

Notions of testing implementations against formal specifications, such as input-output conformance [26] are related to work on trace validation in that they also help establishing confidence in the correctness of implementations. A main difference is that in these approaches, implementations are considered black boxes that admit certain observations at the interfaces, whereas we assume having access to the implementation code. A similar remark holds for techniques of active learning of state machines [27]. Although we only have anecdotal evidence, we observed that programmers find it quite easy to instrument their code, and that they will apply the necessary engineering judgment to overcome mismatches between the grains of atomicity of the specification and the implementation.

6 Conclusion

Formal verification techniques are known to be most effective for specifications written at high levels of abstraction where the size of state spaces (for model checking) and the complexity of invariants (for deductive verification) are manageable. High-level specifications can serve as guidelines for programmers when implementing an algorithm, and in some cases it may even be possible to generate code from a sufficiently detailed specification. Model-based testing is a collection of techniques that rely on formal specifications for generating test cases, aiming at coverage guarantees or at exploring parts of the state space deemed interesting based on an analysis of the specification.

In this paper we described an approach for relating traces of the executions of a distributed program to the state machine described by a high-level specification written in TLA$^+$. Our purpose with this approach is to identify discrepancies that can be analyzed using the TLC model checker in order to determine if they are due to an error in the implementation, a restrictive specification, or an artefact due to a mismatch in the grains of atomicity. Although the technique does not provide formal correctness guarantees, mainly due to the necessary decisions on when to log an event corresponding to an atomic action, we have found it to be surprisingly effective for finding serious bugs in implementations that had previously been validated using traditional quality assurance techniques.

We are certainly not the first to suggest that trace validation can be worthwhile for relating high-level specifications and programs. Original aspects, to the best of our knowledge, are our ability to handle different grains of atomicity, and that we do not require all specification variables or events to be traced in the log; instead, we use a model checker to reconstruct missing information. This leads to a tradeoff between the amount of detail included in the trace, the increase of the search space for model checking, and the reliability of the verdict. Our experiments suggest that it is enough to trace a suitably chosen subset of variables and/or events. We implemented a library of Java methods and TLA$^+$ operators to support collecting traces but their use is not strictly essential for applying our technique. In fact, the EWD 998 and the CCF case studies used ad-hoc code instrumentations for generating the logs.

We contribute industry-grade support for trace validation by implementing action composition, depth-first search, and debugging of trace validation in the TLC model checker and the TLA$^+$ debugger. This support enabled not only the successful adoption of trace validation by the previously mentioned CCF project but also by the etcd project [5], a widely-used distributed key-value store. Both projects verify that their implementations in C++ and Go, respectively, adhere to their TLA$^+$ specifications. We have exclusively used the explicit-state model checker TLC in our experiments. In principle, symbolic model checkers such as TLA$^+$'s Apalache tool [14] could also be used, but we suspect that the overhead of generating and evaluating constraints would be prohibitive in comparison to explicit-state model checking, in particular when the degree of non-determinism is low, as is the case when recording sufficiently informative traces.

At the moment, we exploit random variations in implementation parameters such as message delays or failures in order to generate meaningful traces of the program to be analyzed. In future work, we intend to use the TLA$^+$ specification in order to be able to steer executions towards "interesting" parts of the state space. We also intend to study the feasibility of applying trace validation online during the execution of the program or even of using the technique as a run-time monitor to block unsafe transitions of the implementation.

References

1. Cirstea, H., Kuppe, M.A., Loillier, B., Merz, S.: Validating traces of distributed programs against TLA$^+$ specifications. arXiv:2404.16075 [cs.DC] (2024)
2. Cousineau, D., Doligez, D., Lamport, L., Merz, S., Ricketts, D., Vanzetto, H.: TLA$^+$ Proofs. In: Giannakopoulou, D., Méry, D. (eds.) FM 2012. LNCS, vol. 7436, pp. 147–154. Springer, Heidelberg (2012). https://doi.org/10.1007/978-3-642-32759-9_14
3. Davis, A.J.J., Hirschhorn, M., Schvimer, J.: eXtreme modelling in practice. Proc. VLDB Endowment **13**(9), 1346–1358 (2020)
4. Dijkstra, E.W.: EWD 998: Shmuel Safra's version of termination detection. http://www.cs.utexas.edu/users/EWD/ewd09xx/EWD998.PDF (1987)
5. etcd project. TLA+ specification and trace validation for raft library: a brief guide. https://github.com/etcd-io/raft/tree/main/tla (2024)
6. Falcone, Y., Havelund, K., Reger, G.: A tutorial on runtime verification. Eng. Depend. Softw. Syst. **34**, 141–175 (2013)
7. Fekete, A.: Snapshot Isolation. In: Liu, L., Özsu, M.T. (eds.) Encyclopedia of Database Systems, pp. 2659–2664. Springer US, Boston, MA (2009).https://doi.org/10.1007/978-0-387-39940-9_346
8. Foo, D., Costea, A., Chin, W.-N.: Protocol conformance with choreographic PlusCal. In: David, C., Sun, M. (eds.) Theoretical Aspects of Software Engineering: 17th International Symposium, TASE 2023, Bristol, UK, July 4–6, 2023, Proceedings, pp. 126–145. Springer Nature Switzerland, Cham (2023).https://doi.org/10.1007/978-3-031-35257-7_8
9. Hackett, F., Hosseini, S., Costa, R., Do, M., Beschastnikh, I.: Compiling distributed system models with PGo. In: Proceedings of the 28th ACM International Conference on Architectural Support for Programming Languages and Operating Systems, vol. 2, pp. 159–175, Vancouver BC Canada. ACM (2023)
10. Havelund, K.: Using Runtime Analysis to Guide Model Checking of Java Programs. In: Havelund, K., Penix, J., Visser, W. (eds.) SPIN 2000. LNCS, vol. 1885, pp. 245–264. Springer, Heidelberg (2000). https://doi.org/10.1007/10722468_15
11. Howard, H., et al.: Confidential Consortium Framework: secure multiparty applications with confidentiality, integrity, and high availability. Proc. VLDB Endowment **17**(2), 225–240 (2023)
12. Howard, H., Kuppe, M.A., Ashton, E., Chamayou, A., Crooks, N.: Smart casual verification of CCF's distributed consensus and consistency protocols. arXiv:2406.17455 [cs.DC] (2024)

13. Howard, Y., Gruner, S., Gravell, A., Ferreira, C., Augusto, J.C.: Model-based trace-checking. arXiv:1111.2825 [cs] (2011)
14. Konnov, I., Kukovec, J., Tran, T.-H.: TLA+ model checking made symbolic. Proc. ACM Program. Lang., 3(OOPSLA) (2019)
15. Konnov, I., Kuppe, M., Merz, S.: Specification and verification with the TLA+ Trifecta: TLC, Apalache, and TLAPS. In: Margaria, T., Steffen, B. (eds.) Leveraging Applications of Formal Methods, Verification and Validation. Verification Principles: 11th International Symposium, ISoLA 2022, Rhodes, Greece, October 22–30, 2022, Proceedings, Part I, pp. 88–105. Springer International Publishing, Cham (2022).https://doi.org/10.1007/978-3-031-19849-6_6
16. Kuppe, M.A.: Implementing a TLA+ specification: EWD998Chan. https://github.com/tlaplus/Examples/pull/75 (2023)
17. Kuppe, M.A.: The TLA+ debugger. In: Masci, P., Bernardeschi, C., Graziani, P., Koddenbrock, M., Palmieri, M., editors, Software Engineering and Formal Methods. SEFM 2022 Co-located Workshops, vol. 13765, pp. 174–180. Springer, Cham (2023).https://doi.org/10.1007/978-3-031-26236-4_15
18. Lamport, L.: Specifying Systems. Mass, Addison-Wesley, Boston (2002)
19. Lamport, L., et al.: TLA+ examples. https://github.com/tlaplus/examples/
20. Newcombe, C., Rath, T., Zhang, F., Munteanu, B., Brooker, M., Deardeuff, M.: How Amazon Web Services uses formal methods. Commun. ACM **58**(4), 66–73 (2015)
21. Niu, Z., Dong, L., Zhu, Y., Chen, L.: Verifying zookeeper based on model-based runtime trace-checking using TLA+. In: Proceedings of the 7th International Conference on Cyber Security and Information Engineering, pp. 13–18, Brisbane QLD Australia. ACM (2022)
22. Ongaro, D., Ousterhout, J.: In search of an understandable consensus algorithm. In: 2014 USENIX Annual Technical Conference, pp. 305–319, Philadelphia, PA (2014). USENIX Association
23. Pressler, R.: Conjunction capers: a TLA+ truffle. https://conf.tlapl.us/2020/ (2020)
24. Schultz, W., Zhou, S., Dardik, I., Tripakis, S.: Design and analysis of a logless dynamic reconfiguration protocol. In: Bramas, Q., Gramoli, V., Milani, A., editors 25th International Conference Principles of Distributed Systems (OPODIS 2021), vol. 217 of LIPIcs, pp. 26:1-26:16, Strasbourg, France (2021). Schloss Dagstuhl - Leibniz-Zentrum für Informatik
25. Tasiran, S., Yu, Y., Batson, B., Kreider, S.: Using formal specifications to monitor and guide simulation: verifying the cache coherence engine of the Alpha 21364 microprocessor. In: Proceedings of the 3rd IEEE Workshop on Microprocessor Test and Verification, Common Challenges and Solutions (2002)
26. Tretmans, J.: Test generation with inputs, outputs and repetitive quiescence. Softw. Concepts Tools **17**(3), 103–120 (1996)
27. Vaandrager, F.W.: Model learning. Commun. ACM **60**(2), 86–95 (2017)
28. Wang, D., Dou, W., Gao, Y., Wu, C., Wei, J., Huang, T.: Model checking guided testing for distributed systems. In: Proceedings of the Eighteenth European Conference on Computer Systems, pp. 127–143, Rome Italy. ACM (2023)
29. Yu, Y., Manolios, P., Lamport, L.: Model Checking TLA+ Specifications. In: Pierre, L., Kropf, T. (eds.) CHARME 1999. LNCS, vol. 1703, pp. 54–66. Springer, Heidelberg (1999). https://doi.org/10.1007/3-540-48153-2_6

Partially-Observable Security Games for Attack-Defence Analysis in Software Systems

Narges Khakpour[1(✉)] and David Parker[2]

[1] Newcastle University, Newcastle NE1 7RU, UK
narges.khakpour@newcastle.ac.uk
[2] University of Oxford, Oxford OX1 2JD, UK
david.parker@cs.ox.ac.uk

Abstract. Given the presence of residual vulnerabilities in software systems, it is critical to apply suitable countermeasures in order to minimize the likelihood of an attack. In this paper we propose a formal approach, based on stochastic games, to threat analysis and synthesis of defence strategies for protecting systems with vulnerabilities. Crucially, we support analysis under partial observation, where some of the attacker's activities are unobservable or undetectable by the defender. We construct a one-sided partially observable security game and transform it into a perfect game, for which formal analysis is feasible. We prove that this transformation is sound for a sub-class of security games and a subset of objectives specified in the temporal logic rPATL. We implement our approach and evaluate it by applying it to a real-life example.

1 Introduction

In today's increasingly complex software systems, many vulnerabilities still remain in the system after being discovered due to factors such as the lack of a patch or knowledge to fix them, cost considerations, or organizational preferences for availability and usability over security [31]. Threat modelling is as a widely-used technique for specifying, discovering and analyzing security weaknesses in order to assess and manage the security of systems with vulnerabilities [18].

A wide range of models and languages has been proposed for threat modelling and analysis (see [18,22] for a survey). Attack graph-based [28] and attack tree-based [32] approaches are among the most common. While attack trees have received a lot of attention in the past, they are often constructed manually or semi-automatically, which is a challenge when developing automated online analysis techniques. In contrast, attack graphs can be generated fully automatically using formal approaches, such as model checking [28] or logic-based reasoning [27], making them a suitable candidate for automated analysis.

The opposing objectives and dependent strategies of attack and defence make them well-suited for *game-based* threat analysis, enabling us to model the interactions between the attacker and the defender to construct effective defences

A. Madeira and A. Knapp (Eds.): SEFM 2024, LNCS 15280, pp. 144–161, 2025.
https://doi.org/10.1007/978-3-031-77382-2_9

and assess threats. Game theory has been applied to analyze security in different research communities in recent years [2,13,14] (see [25] for a survey).

However, most of the research achievements in this area are based on the hypothesis that both players have full observation of the opponent's moves, which is unrealistic in practice. This is because it is not always possible to observe all the attacker's activities; many vulnerabilities and malicious activities cannot be detected due to factors such as the high overhead of monitoring, expensive security controls, or ineffective security mechanisms.

In this paper, we propose an approached based on *stochastic games*, under *partial observation*, for the analysis of attack-defence scenarios in systems with vulnerabilities and the automatic synthesis of defence strategies. We employ attack graphs for the automatic construction of attack scenarios, and build on stochastic modelling and verification with games [12] for security analysis, which provides formal assurance for systems operating in uncertain environments.

We define the semantics of attack graphs in terms of Symbolic Markov Decision Processes, which specify the attacker's behaviour. We specify defences as a set of rules, triggered as a reaction to an attack or as a preventive action to stop potential future attacks. A *fully observable* (also called *perfect*) stochastic two-player game is then constructed from the attacker's and defender's behaviour, in which each player has full observation of the other players' actions. This allows us to analyze attack-defence scenarios and synthesize defence strategies using existing formal verification methods and tools. We specify attacker or defender objectives in the temporal logic rPATL (Probabilistic ATL with Rewards) [12] and use the stochastic game verification tool PRISM-games [23].

To support reasoning under partial observation, we define a *partially observable one-sided security game* (PO-security game). This provides partial observation of the attacker's behaviour but, on the other hand, assumes that the attacker has full observation of the defender's actions. This type of game, where one player has full observation and the other has partial observation, is called a *one-sided partially observable game* [11]. Note that, if the defender wins in this one-sided game setting, they will also win in a setting where the attacker has only partial observation [10]. While the formal verification community has studied analysis under partial observation and presented theoretical results (e.g., [3,8–10]), progress on developing practical methods for stochastic games under partial observation has been very limited, even for the simpler one-sided case [7].

To analyze a PO-security game, we transform it into a perfect game and then analyze the resulting model with PRISM-games. We prove that this transformation is sound for a subclass of security games called ODT (Observable Defence Triggers) security games and a subset of rPATL properties (called observable step-unbounded defence objectives). This means that a synthesized strategy for the defender in the resulting perfect security game is a valid strategy for the defender in the original PO-security game.

We implement a prototype tool to support the proposed approach and evaluate it through application to a real-life case study. Our experimental results demonstrate that transforming a PO-security game significantly enhances the performance of our analysis and can serve as a promising technique for reducing the state space when dealing with large attack graphs.

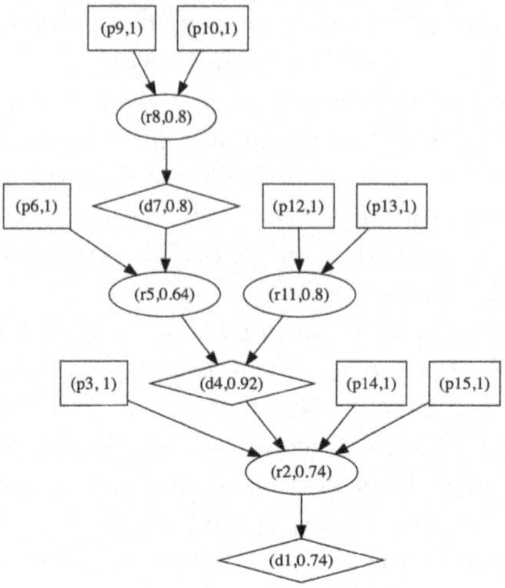

Node	Label
p3	plycent03_has_weak_cpu
p6	plycent02_access_ssh_plycent03
p9	has_access_to_plycent02
p10	vul_cve-2018-7566_exists_on_plycent02
p12	has_access_ssh_to_plycent03
p13	attacker_located_on_internet
p14	plycent03_offers_ssh
p15	vul_cve-2018-5390_exists_on_plycent03
d1	plycent03_is_down
d4	gained_ssh_access_to_plycent03
d7	has_root_exec_code_priv_on_plycent02
r2	perform_remote_DOS
r5	perform_multi-hop_access
r8	tamper_memory
r11	directly_access_to

Fig. 1. An Example Attack Graph

The contributions of this paper are: (i) constructing a security game from an attack graph and the defender's behaviour; (ii) introducing partially observable security games and an approach for their analysis; and (iii) applying it to a real-life case study. The paper is organized as follows. Section 2 presents preliminaries on stochastic games. Section 3 constructs a fully observable security game, and Sect. 4 discusses PO-security games. We present the evaluation in Sect. 5, discuss related work in Sect. 6, and conclude in Sect. 7. Formal proofs can be found in an extended version of this paper [20].

2 Preliminaries

2.1 Attack Graphs

An attack graph shows strategies that can be taken by an attacker to reach its *final goal*. It comprises three types of nodes: (a) *condition nodes*, depicted as rectangles, show the *primitive capabilities* that an attacker has, (b) *derived nodes*, represented by diamonds, are associated with *derived capabilities* gained through attack actions, and (c) *rule nodes*, represented by ellipses, show actions. Figure 1 shows an attack graph where the label of a node is of the form (id, p): id is the node identifier and p is the probability of reaching that node. The table gives a description of each node identifier. When the prerequisites of a rule (i.e. its predecessor nodes) in the attack graph are satisfied, it is activated and leads to its consequence (i.e., its successor node) with a probability.

The attack graph in Fig. 1 describes an attack scenario where the attacker's goal is to take the system plycent03 down. The attacker is located on the internet and has direct access to the system plycent02, which has a vulnerability that can lead to memory tampering. They also have access to the SSH service offered by plycent03, which suffers from the vulnerability vul_cve-2018-5390 that can be exploited to perform a DoS attack. The attacker can directly access the SSH service on plycent03 (via the path r11 and r2), or indirectly via exploiting the vulnerability on plycent02 (via the path r8, r5, and r2). Once the attacker gains access to the SSH service of plycent03, they can exploit its vulnerability to perform a Denial of Service (DoS) attack.

From the system description and the attack goal, we generate an attack graph using MulVAL (Multihost, Multistage Vulnerability Analysis) [27], similar to [21]. MulVAL is a logic programming-based system to automatically build attack scenarios. The logical attack graph produced by MulVAL relies on the method proposed in [31] to calculate a cumulative security metric called AGP (Attack Graph-based Probabilistic Metric) that shows the likelihood of an attacker reaching a specific derived node in the attack graph from an entry point, considering the causality among attack steps. The probability of an attack depends on the attacker's resources, skills, attack success rate, etc. We use the scores provided by the Common Vulnerability Scoring System (CVSS)[1] and domain experts to initialize the scores for primitive and rule nodes. CVSS is a vulnerability database that provides different scores to measure the severity and exploitability of vulnerabilities.

2.2 Probabilistic Model Checking

Probabilistic model checking is an approach to formal verification and strategy synthesis for probabilistic systems, including for stochastic games [12,29]. Let $\mathbb{P}_X$ be the set of all discrete probability distribution functions over the set X, $V = \langle v_1, \ldots, v_n \rangle$ be a vector of variables, $\mathcal{D}_{v_i}$ be the domain of a variable v_i, and $\mathcal{D}_V = \prod_{i=1}^{n} \mathcal{D}_{v_i}$. A *valuation* $\boldsymbol{\nu}$ of V is a tuple $\langle \boldsymbol{\nu}_1, \ldots, \boldsymbol{\nu}_n \rangle \in \mathcal{D}_V$, and we denote the i-th value of $\boldsymbol{\nu}$ by $\boldsymbol{\nu}(v_i)$ for $1 \leq i \leq n$.

Our modelling approach uses *Symbolic Markov Decision Processes* (SMDPs), a high-level description of a Markov Decision Process (MDP) in a similar form to the modelling language of the PRISM [24] and PRISM-games [23] tools.

Definition 1 (Symbolic Markov Decision Process). *A* Symbolic Markov Decision Process *(SMDP) is a tuple* $\mathrm{M} = \langle V, \boldsymbol{\nu}_0, \Sigma, \delta \rangle$ *where* $V = \langle v_1, \ldots, v_n \rangle$ *is a tuple of variables,* $\boldsymbol{\nu}_0 \in \mathcal{D}_V$ *gives the initial conditions on the variables,* Σ *is a finite non-empty set of actions, and* δ *is a finite set of probabilistic transitions* $\langle \phi, \sigma, \mathcal{P}_U \rangle$ *where* $\phi \subseteq \mathcal{D}_V$ *is a predicate on* V *which guards the transition,* $\sigma \in \Sigma$ *is an action and* $\mathcal{P}_U \in \mathbb{P}_U$ *is a discrete probability distribution over the set* U *of update functions of the form* $u : \mathcal{D}_V \mapsto \mathcal{D}_V$*, defined as a set of assignments.*

SMDP M starts in its initial state. A transition can fire if its guard is satisfied and, when fired, the variables are updated with the probabilities corresponding to its update functions. The semantics of M is an MDP $\overline{\mathrm{M}} = \langle V, S, s_0, \Sigma, \overline{\delta} \rangle$

[1] https://www.first.org/cvss/.

where $S \subseteq \mathcal{D}_V$ is a set of states, $s_0 = \boldsymbol{\nu}_0$ is the initial state and $\overline{\delta} : S \times \Sigma \rightarrow \mathbb{P}_S$ is a (partial) transition function defined as follows:

$$\overline{\delta} = \{\langle\langle s, \sigma\rangle, f(U, s)\rangle \mid \exists \delta = \langle \phi, \sigma, \mathcal{P}_U\rangle \in \delta, s \models \phi\}$$
$$f(U, s) = \begin{cases} \langle t, p\rangle & u \in U, t = u(s), p = \mathcal{P}_U(u) \\ \text{undef} & \text{otherwise} \end{cases}$$

Definition 2 (Two-Player Stochastic Game). *Let* $\overline{\mathrm{M}_1} = \langle V_1, S_1, s_{1,0}, \Sigma_1, \overline{\delta}_1\rangle$ *and* $\overline{\mathrm{M}_2} = \langle V_2, S_2, s_{2,0}, \Sigma_2, \overline{\delta}_2\rangle$ *be two MDPs specifying two players' behaviour. A (turn-based) stochastic two-player game is a tuple* $\mathcal{G} = \langle P, V, S, s_0, \Sigma, \mathsf{sch}, \Delta\rangle$ *where* $P = \{1, 2\}$ *is the set of players,* V *is a vector of state variables over* $V_1 \cup V_2 \cup \{t\}$*,* $S \subseteq \mathcal{D}_V$ *is the set of states,* s_0 *is the initial state,* $\Sigma = \Sigma_1 \cup \Sigma_2$ *is the set of actions,* $\mathsf{sch} : S \rightarrow P$ *is a scheduler and* $\Delta = \{\langle\langle \boldsymbol{\nu}, \sigma\rangle, \mathcal{P}_S\rangle\}$ *is a (partial) transition function defined as follows.*

Let $\boldsymbol{\nu}_{\downarrow V_i}$ *be the projection of* $\boldsymbol{\nu}$ *onto the variables in* V_i*. Let* $(\boldsymbol{\nu} \downarrow_{V_i})\backslash x$ *denote a tuple obtained by setting the subtuple* V_i *in* $\boldsymbol{\nu}$ *to* x*, and* $\overline{\delta}_i(x, \sigma)(x')$ *represent the probability of a transition from state* x *to state* x' *with action* σ *according to* $\overline{\delta}_i$*. The probability of a transition from* $\mathcal{P}_S$ *in state* $\boldsymbol{\nu}$ *with the active player* i *to a state* $\boldsymbol{\nu}'$ *by performing action* σ *is:*

$$\mathcal{P}_S(\boldsymbol{\nu}') = \begin{cases} p & \boldsymbol{\nu}_{\downarrow\{t\}} = i \\ & \wedge\ \exists x.\ \overline{\delta}_i(\boldsymbol{\nu}_{\downarrow V_i}, \sigma)(x) = p \wedge \boldsymbol{\nu}' = (((\boldsymbol{\nu} \downarrow_{V_i})\backslash x) \downarrow_{\{t\}})\backslash \mathsf{sch}(\boldsymbol{\nu}) \\ 0 & \text{otherwise} \end{cases}$$

Informally, the transition function in Definition 2 says that a state with active player i is updated to a new state $\boldsymbol{\nu}'$ in which the active player's state $\boldsymbol{\nu}_{\downarrow V_i}$ is updated to x with probability p, the other player's local substate remains unmodified and the active player is updated according to the scheduler function. We represent the game by $\overline{\mathrm{M}_1} \mid\mid \overline{\mathrm{M}_2}$ and partition the game's states into sets S_1 and S_2, controlled by each of the two players. Furthermore, $\Sigma(s)$ denotes the actions that can be performed in state $s \in S$. We also annotate games with *reward structures* $\xi : \Sigma \rightarrow \mathbb{R}_{\geq 0}$, which can be used to model rewards or costs.

Given a game $\mathcal{G}$ and an objective ψ, the goal of strategy synthesis is to synthesize strategies for (coalitions of) players to be able to win the game. A strategy informally determines the optimal action that should be performed by the coalition in each state to achieve its objective. The objective ψ is specified using the temporal logic rPATL (probabilistic alternating-time temporal logic with rewards). This logic allows us to express quantitative properties of the games, e.g., to ensure that the probability of an event's occurrence meets some threshold (for example: "can the defender protect the network in such a way that the probability of the system being compromised by the attacker is less than 0.1?"). rPATL is a branching-time logic and contains state formulas ϕ and path formulas ψ. The syntax is given by the following grammar:

$$\phi := \top \mid \alpha \mid \neg\phi \mid \phi \wedge \phi \mid \langle\langle C\rangle\rangle \mathsf{P}_{\bowtie p}[\psi] \mid \langle\langle C\rangle\rangle \mathsf{R}^{\xi}_{\bowtie x}[\mathsf{F}\phi]$$
$$\psi := \mathsf{X}\,\phi \mid \phi_1 \mathsf{U}^{\leq k} \phi_2 \mid \phi_1 \mathsf{U} \phi_2$$

where α is an atomic proposition, C is a coalition of players, $\bowtie \in \{<, \leq, >, \geq\}$, $p \in [0, 1]$, $x \in \mathbb{R}$, $k \in \mathbb{N}$ and ξ is a reward structure.

The operators X ("next"), $\mathsf{U}^{\leq k}$ ("bounded until"), U ("until") and F ("eventually") are the standard temporal operators. Informally, $\langle\langle C \rangle\rangle \mathsf{P}_{\bowtie p}[\psi]$ states that the coalition C has a strategy to ensure that the path formula ψ will be satisfied with a probability meeting the bound $\bowtie p$, regardless of the strategies of other players. Similarly, $\langle\langle C \rangle\rangle \mathsf{R}^{\xi}_{\bowtie x}[\mathsf{F}\phi]$ means that C has a strategy guaranteeing that the expected reward ξ accumulated until reaching a state where ϕ is true satisfies $\bowtie x$. We write $s \models \phi$ to indicate that state s of $\mathcal{G}$ satisfies the formula ϕ, and write $\mathcal{G} \models \phi$, if $s_0 \models \phi$. Further, $\mathsf{Sat}(\phi) = \{s \in S \mid s \models \phi\}$ denotes the set of states satisfying ϕ. We refer the reader to [12] for the full semantics of rPATL. In this paper, we use PRISM-games [23] to synthesize strategies for players according to objectives specified in rPATL.

3 Fully-Observable Security Games

We construct a perfect (fully observable) two-player stochastic security game between the attacker and defender, where the attacker's goal is to gain a specific capability, and the defender tries to prevent the attacker from doing so. In such a turn-based stochastic game, each player independently chooses an action in every round, and a player's action is fully observable by the opponent, i.e., the attacker and the defender have perfect observation of each other's moves.

Attacker Behaviour. We follow a similar approach to [30] to formalize an attack graph where the state of an attacker is represented using a set of Boolean variables, each corresponding to the attacker holding either a primitive capability (box node) or a derived capability (diamond node). Initially, the attacker only holds the primitive capabilities and has no derived capabilities. A transition corresponds to the attacker performing an action by applying a rule σ and, when it is triggered (i.e., the rule prerequisites hold and its consequence e does not hold), the attacker gains the new capability e with probability $p(\sigma)$.

Example 1. The attacker's behaviour in Fig. 1 contains four rule nodes, each of which is translated into a transition. For instance, the rule node $r2$ is translated to the transition $\langle \phi, \mathsf{remote\_DOS}, \mathcal{P}_U \rangle$ where:

$$\phi = p3 \wedge d4 \wedge p14 \wedge p15 \wedge \neg d1$$
$$\mathcal{P}_U(\{d1 \mapsto \top\}) = 0.74 \qquad \mathcal{P}_U(\emptyset) = 0.26.$$

This states that, if the attacker has capabilities $\{p3, d4, p14, p15\}$ but not $d1$, they can acquire $d1$ with a probability of 0.74, or fail with a probability of 0.26.

Defender Behaviour. The choices of each player depend on the moves of the other, i.e., their capabilities and privileges may change as a consequence of their opponent's moves. For example, if an attacker gains full control over a system through a ransomware attack, the defender will lose access to that system. Similarly, if the defender modifies configurations to block service access on a victim, the attacker may adjust its strategy accordingly.

Therefore, an attacker's decision to target a system should account for potential defensive countermeasures, and vice versa. We define two types of defence: *reactive defence* and *proactive defence*. Reactive defences are typically responses to an ongoing attack, whereas proactive defences are preventive actions taken to thwart potential future malicious activities. An example of reactive defence includes updating permissions to block an attacker's access to a system upon detection of malicious activity by an intrusion detection system. An example of proactive defences is regular vulnerability scans on critical systems to detect and rectify potential weaknesses, proactively patching applications, and monitoring critical security controls. Defences performed by the defender respond to the attacker gaining new capabilities, with the aim of either revoking those capabilities or preventing the attacker from acquiring specific capabilities in the future.

We define *defence-triggering capabilities* as a set of attacker capabilities V_{AD} that the defender can observe and against which it can apply countermeasures. Therefore, the defender's state variables include the defence-triggering state variables of the attacker in addition to its own internal variables. Furthermore, the actions of the attacker and the defender should be distinct.

Definition 3 (Defender Behaviour). *Let* $\mathrm{AT} = \langle V_A, \boldsymbol{\nu}_{A,0}, \Sigma_A, \Delta_A \rangle$ *be the behaviour of the attacker, and* $V_{AD} \subseteq V_A$ *be the set of defence-triggering capabilities of the attacker. The behaviour of the defender is defined as* $\mathrm{DE} = \langle V_D, \boldsymbol{\nu}_{D,0}, \Sigma_D, \Delta_D \rangle$ *where* $V_{AD} \subseteq V_D$, $\boldsymbol{\nu}_{D,0} \implies \boldsymbol{\nu}_{A,0}$, *and* $\Sigma_D \cap \Sigma_A = \emptyset$.

Example 2. A reactive defence to the capability of executing code with root privilege by the attacker on the system plycent02 is to patch the vulnerability cve-2018-7566 (the rule node r8 in Fig. 1). This defence is specified as a transition $\langle \phi, \mathsf{patch\_vul-2018-7566}, \mathcal{P}_U \rangle$ where:

$$\begin{aligned}
\phi &= \mathsf{has_root_exec_code_on_plycent02} \wedge \mathsf{vul_vul-2018-7566_exists_on_plycent02} \\
u &= \{\mathsf{has_root_exec_code_on_plycent02} \mapsto \bot; \\
&\qquad \mathsf{vul_vul-2018-7566_exists_on_plycent02} \mapsto \bot\} \\
\mathcal{P}_U(u) &= 0.85\ ,\ \mathcal{P}_U(\emptyset) = 0.15
\end{aligned}$$

This states that, if the attacker can execute code with root privileges on plycent02, exploiting the vulnerability patch_vul−2018−7566, this defence rule eliminates the vulnerability and revokes its root privileges with probability 0.85. We assume that such defence probabilities are determined by a domain expert.

Security Game. Given the behaviours of the attacker and defender, specified as SMDPs, and a scheduler sch, we construct a security game $\mathcal{G} = \langle \{A, D\}, V, S_A \cup S_D, s_0, \Sigma_D \cup \Sigma_A, \mathsf{sch}, \Delta \rangle$ according to Definition 2, where $\{A, D\}$ is the set of players, S_A is the set of states controlled by the attacker, and S_D is the set of states controlled by the defender. In each state of this security game, each action $\sigma \in \Sigma$ (where $\Sigma = \Sigma_A \cup \Sigma_D$) yields at most one probabilistic transition.

The security game can further be associated with reward structures that assign rewards or costs to the states or transitions.

We use the probabilistic model checker PRISM-games to analyse various classes of properties for a single player or for both players, e.g., the likelihood or costs associated with achieving specific capabilities or goals by the attacker. Our primary objective is to prevent the attacker from reaching its targets, which can include intermediate or final objectives such as gaining control of a specific system to access sensitive information on another victim. PRISM-games can also synthesize a strategy $\Gamma : S \rightarrow \Sigma$ that determines the optimal action to be taken in each state by the player controlling it. We use strategy synthesis to develop defence strategies aimed at enhancing system protection.

Game Assumptions. We make the following assumptions in our security games. The game consists of one attacker and one defender. The attacker's goal is to obtain as many capabilities as possible, and the defender's goal is to prevent the attacker from acquiring more capabilities and to revoke their existing ones. If an attacker obtains a capability, they will hold it until it gets revoked by the opponent. An attacker tries an action if it can result in gaining new capabilities. The defender has the ability to check and observe the consequences of (observable) attacks immediately, i.e. we rely on intrusion exploitation systems and intrusion detection systems to detect and report (some of) the attacks immediately.

4 One-Sided Partially-Observable Security Games

In a perfect stochastic game, each round involves one player independently choosing an action that is fully observable by the opponent, i.e. each player has complete knowledge of the opponent's capabilities. Most security games also assume perfect observation [13,14], meaning that players have full visibility of the game state and the opponent's actions. However, this assumption is not realistic in practice. Not all of the attacker's steps are observable by the defender, nor are all attacks easily detectable. Detecting some malicious activities and distinguishing them from normal operations can be very difficult or costly.

We instead assume that the attacker has full observation but the defender has partial observation, i.e., a *one-sided partially observable game* [11]. Note that if the defender wins in the one-sided setting, they will also win in a setting where the attacker has partial observation [10]. Similarly, if the attacker cannot win in this setting, they cannot win in a setting where the defender has full observation. We define a *partially observable stochastic two-player security game* as follows.

Definition 4 (One-Sided Partially-Observable Security Game). *Let* $P = \{A, D\}$*,* $i \in P$ *and* $\mathrm{M}_i = \langle V_i, \boldsymbol{\nu}_{i,0}, \Sigma_i, \delta_i \rangle$ *be two SMDPs representing the behaviour of the attacker and the defender. A (turn-based) stochastic two-player PO security game is a tuple* $\mathcal{G} = \langle P, V, S, \mathsf{Obs}, s_0, \Sigma, \mathsf{sch}, \Delta \rangle$ *where* V *is a vector defined over* $V_A \cup V_D \cup \{t\}$*,* $S \subseteq \mathcal{D}_V$ *is the set of states and* $\mathsf{Obs} : \mathcal{D}_V \rightarrow \mathcal{D}_{V_D}$ *is a function that defines the observation of the defender in a state. The initial state is* s_0 *such that* $s_0 \models \boldsymbol{\nu}_{A,0}$ *and* $\mathsf{Obs}(s_0) \models \boldsymbol{\nu}_{D,0}$*,*

$\Sigma = \Sigma_A \cup \Sigma_D$ *and* sch : $S \to P$ *is the scheduler. The transition* $\Delta : S \times \Sigma \to \mathbb{P}_U$ *is a (partial) transition function defined as follows, where* $\mathsf{up}(\mathsf{u}, \sigma)$ *is an update function:*

$$\Delta = \{\langle\langle s, \sigma\rangle, f(U, s, \sigma)\rangle | \exists\langle\phi, \sigma, \mathcal{P}_U\rangle \in \delta_A \wedge s \models \phi \vee \exists\langle\phi, \sigma, \mathcal{P}_U\rangle \in \delta_D \wedge \mathsf{Obs}(s) \models \phi\}$$

$$f(U, s, \sigma) = \begin{cases} \langle \mathsf{up}(u, \sigma)(s), p\rangle & u \in U, p = \mathcal{P}_U(u) \\ \text{undef} & \text{otherwise} \end{cases}$$

In this paper, we focus on a specific one-sided partially observable security game, defined as follows. We partition the actions of the attacker into two sets: *observable* and *unobservable* actions. The defender can observe only the observable actions of the attacker and their consequences. An attacker's action involves applying a rule to obtain a new derived capability; if the action is observable, the defender can also see the newly obtained capability. For instance, network traffic can be monitored to detect direct network access between hosts, whereas a DoS attack might go undetected if the host is not equipped with an appropriate IDS.

Therefore, we define the game state as $V = \langle v_{A,0}, \ldots, v_{A,n}, v_{D,0}, \ldots, v_{D,m}, t\rangle$, where $V_A = \langle v_{A,0}, \ldots, v_{A,n}\rangle$ represents the attacker's state, $V_D = \langle v_{D,0}, \ldots, v_{D,m}\rangle$ represents the defender's state, and t indicates the active player. The defender's observation in a game state $\boldsymbol{\nu}$ is defined as:

$$\mathsf{Obs}(\boldsymbol{\nu}) = \langle \boldsymbol{\nu}(v_{D,0}), \ldots, \boldsymbol{\nu}(v_{D,m}), t\rangle. \tag{1}$$

Note that V_{AD} is duplicated in V. Let $\overrightarrow{u}$ be a function that applies the updates of the variables in V_{AD} by u to the sub-states of both players. The function $\mathsf{up}(u, \sigma)$ applies the update of an unobservable action locally only to the attacker's sub-state. Otherwise, the updates should be applied to the both players' sub-states:

$$\mathsf{up}(u, \sigma) = \begin{cases} u & \sigma \notin \Sigma_O \cup \Sigma_D \\ \overrightarrow{u} & \text{otherwise} \end{cases} \tag{2}$$

where Σ_O gives the observable actions of the attacker.

Analyzing a Partially Observable Security Game. To analyze a partially observable (PO) security game, we transform it into a perfect security game and analyze the perfect game instead. If a derived capability is obtained through an observable action, it also becomes observable to the defender; otherwise, the update remains unobserved. If the defender knows the possible consequences of their observations, they can infer the attacker's next observable actions.

To achieve this, we need to identify the sets of observable prerequisites that can lead to an observable action being performed through a sequence of unobservable actions, ultimately resulting in the attacker achieving an observable derived capability. For instance, assume the defender cannot detect a memory tampering attack by the attacker (i.e., rule node r8 in Fig. 1 becomes unobservable). This means it will not be possible to detect whether the attacker can execute code with root privileges on `plycent02` (node d7). However, the defender knows that if the attacker holds the observable capabilities p9, p10 and p6, then it can ultimately perform the action in node r5 via performing r8 and then r5. Thus, the observable prerequisites of r5 become {p6,p9,p10}. There might be several sets of observable prerequisites that can lead to performing an observable action. For the algorithm to compute observable prerequisites, see [20].

We transform an attacker's behaviour into an abstract behaviour that hides the unobservable actions and only considers their impact on performing observable actions. Let $\mathsf{doPrequisites}(r)$ be a function that returns the set of all observable prerequisites of r. Each element dop of $\mathsf{doPrequisites}(r)$ represents the prerequisites of a specific path, and we associate a transition with each path. The guard of this transition is the conjunction of all observable capabilities in dop and the negation of r's consequence, i.e. this transition is triggered when all its observable prerequisites hold and r's consequence has not been achieved. This transition will set r's consequence with a probability that is the product of all the action probabilities along the path, i.e., this path can be taken if all the actions along it can be performed successfully.

Example 3. Let all the rule nodes in Fig. 1 be unobservable, except for r2. The observable behaviour of the attacker is translated into two symbolic transitions, corresponding to the paths {r11, r2} and {r8, r5, r2}. The transition associated to {r11, r2} is $\langle p_{14} \wedge p_{15} \wedge p_{12} \wedge p_{13} \wedge p_3 \wedge \neg d_1, \mathtt{path0}, \mathcal{P}_U \rangle$, where $U = \{\{d_1 \mapsto \top\}, \emptyset\}$, $\mathcal{P}_U(\{d_1 \mapsto \top\}) = 0.74 * 0.8 = 0.59$, and $\mathcal{P}_U(\emptyset) = 0.4$.

Definition 5 (Attacker's Observable Behaviour). *Let $\mathcal{R}$ be the set of the attacker actions, i.e., the set of rule nodes in the attack graph, and $\mathcal{C}$ and $\mathcal{H}$ be the set of observable primitive and derived capabilities, respectively. Let $\Sigma_O \subseteq \mathcal{R}$ be the set of observable actions and $p : \mathcal{R} \rightarrow [0, 1]$ be a function giving the probability of successfully applying action rules $r \in \mathcal{R}$. The observable behaviour of G is defined as $[\![\mathrm{AT}]\!] = \langle V_O, \boldsymbol{\nu}_{O,0}, \Sigma_O, \delta_O \rangle$, where V_O is a vector of variables defined on $\mathcal{C} \cup \mathcal{H}$. The initial conditions on the variables are given by: $\boldsymbol{\nu}_0 = \bigwedge_{\phi \in \mathcal{C}} \phi \wedge \bigwedge_{\phi \in \mathcal{H}} \neg\phi$. For each rule $r \in \Sigma_O$ and each of its distinct sets of observable prerequisites $\mathsf{dop} \in \mathsf{doPrequisites}(r)$, a transition $\langle \neg e \wedge \bigwedge_{d_i \in \mathsf{dop}} d_i, \mathsf{act}(\mathsf{dop}), \mathcal{P}_U \rangle \in \delta_O$ is defined, where $\mathsf{act}(\mathsf{dop})$ assigns an action label in Σ_O to dop, e corresponds to the successor derived node of r, $U = \{\emptyset, u\}$, $u = \{e \mapsto \top\}$, and:*

$$\mathcal{P}_U(u) = \prod_{r_i \in \mathsf{dop}} p(r_i), \ \mathcal{P}_U(\emptyset) = 1 - \mathcal{P}_U(u).$$

The reward structure for the attacker's actions is defined as $\xi'(r) = \sum_{r_i \in \mathsf{dop}} \xi(r_i)$.

We build and analyze a fully-observable security game, as given in Definition 5, instead of directly analyzing the partially observable security games constructed using the functions Obs and up defined in Eqs. 1 and 2. Let V'_{AD} be the attacker's copy of V_{AD} (i.e., the set of common variables between the attacker and the defender). The scheduler of the perfect game is defined as follows, where sch is the scheduler of the original PO security game:

$$\mathsf{sch}'(\boldsymbol{\nu}) = \mathsf{sch}(\boldsymbol{\nu}\downarrow_{(V_O \setminus V'_{AD}) \cup V_D \cup \{t\}}), \quad (3)$$

where the scheduler of a state $\boldsymbol{\nu}$ is the value returned by the original scheduler sch for the corresponding state in $\boldsymbol{\nu}$ in the original game, essentially projecting onto the state variables of the attacker, the defender, and the variable t.

Soundness. An *ODT (Observable Defence-Triggering) security game* is a PO security game in which all the defence-triggering capabilities of the attacker are observable, i.e., $V_{AD} \subseteq V_O$. We prove that the transformation of an ODT security game, using Definition 4 and the functions Obs and up defined in Eq. 1 and Eq. 2 to a perfect security game is sound for a subset of rPATL.

Definition 6. *A rPATL formula ϕ is an* observable step-unbounded defence objective, *if (i) it is defined over $V_O \cup V_D$ (i.e., it contains no unobservable variable), (ii) it contains no X or U^k operators, and (iii) in any sub-formula $\ll C \gg \mathsf{P}_{\bowtie\, p}[\psi]$, $C \subseteq \{D\}$.*

The results below state that an observable step-unbounded defence objective holds in an ODT security game defined in Definition 4, if and only if it is satisfied by a perfect game with the attacker behaviour obtained using Definition 5. Proofs of these results are in the extended version of this paper [20].

Theorem 1. *Let $\mathcal{G}$ be a one-sided partially observable security game and $[\mathcal{G}]$ be its transformation to a perfect game. For any observable step-unbounded defence objective ϕ, $\mathcal{G} \models \phi$ if and only if $[\mathcal{G}] \models \phi$.*

Theorem 2. *For an observable step-unbounded defence objective $\ll D \gg \mathsf{P}_{\bowtie q}[\psi]$ or $\ll D \gg \mathsf{R}_{\bowtie q}[\mathsf{F}\phi]$, PRISM-games synthesizes the same winning strategies for the defender in $\mathcal{G}$ and $[\mathcal{G}]$.*

5 Evaluation

Scenario. To evaluate our approach, we designed an attack scenario against a system shown in Fig. 2. Table 1 shows some of the services and software vulnerabilities present on each machine. In this scenario, the goal is to launch a DoS attack on the database server plycent02. The attacker is located on the internet and can access web pages served by the HTTP server hosted on plycent01. Dotted arrows show the sequence of service accesses made by the attacker to reach its final goal. The attack graph generated for this scenario using MulVAL comprises 50 nodes and 18 attack steps. We use the security metrics AGP provided by MulVAL, CVSS, and expert knowledge to determine the probability of attacker actions. The countermeasures considered in this attack scenario include stopping a service, limiting access to a service, or patching vulnerabilities.

We define two reward structures: (i) aCosts, which models the costs of an attack step for the attacker; and (ii) dCosts, which captures the cost of defence in addition to the damages an attacker can cause to the system by a successful attack step. To estimate the costs in aCosts, we considered several factors, including the time needed to perform the attack, ease of exploitation, and tools and requirements for performing the attack. To estimate the damage of an attack

Table 1. Services and Vulnerabilities

Machine	Software/ Service	Vulnerability	Consequence
plyrhel01	http	cve-2018-1000120	Remote Code Execution
plycent01	Linux kernel	cve-2017-13215	Privilege Escalation
plycent02	postgress		Improper Authentication
plycent03	ssh	cve-2018-7566	Memory Tampering, Authentication Bypass
	http	cve-2018-1273	Remote Code Execution

step (costs imposed on the defender), we use the impact score provided by the CVSS database, quantifying the outcome that an attacker can achieve as a result of exploiting the vulnerability, as well as business security preferences.

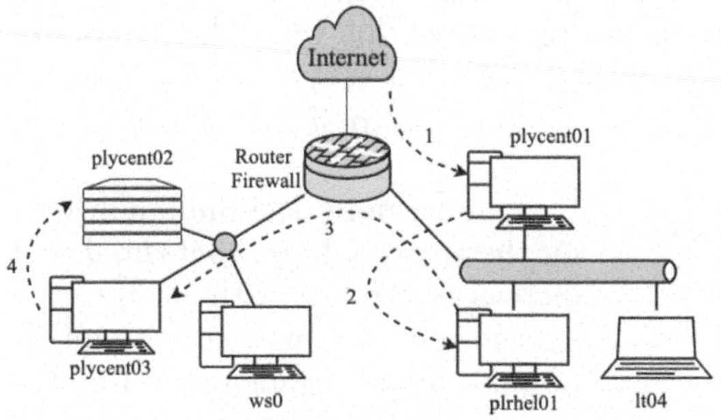

Fig. 2. The architecture and attack steps

We considered three cases of systems that can be developed with the architecture presented in Fig. 2: a tax system, an image hosting system, and a hotel booking system. Each has its own requirements and preferences in terms of service availability, confidentiality, and integrity of information. For the tax system, the integrity of information and the availability of the system during operation are of utmost importance, making the cost of taking any service down very high. Patching, on the other hand, is of minor importance. In the image hosting system, availability is important, but integrity and confidentiality are less important. In the hotel booking system, all three aspects-availability, confidentiality, and integrity-result in some loss of revenue and are therefore important. The cost of a defence varies from 0 to 500.

Results. We compute, with PRISM-games, the minimum or maximum probability of satisfying a property ψ that can be guaranteed by a coalition C ($\langle\langle C\rangle\rangle \mathsf{P}_{\mathsf{opt}}$ $[\psi]$, $\mathsf{opt} \in \{min, max\}$). The maximum or minimum reward can be computed similarly. We analyzed several properties for each game:

(1) The minimum cost (defence cost and damages caused by the attacker) to defend against the attack and block it: $\langle\langle \mathsf{def}\rangle\rangle \mathsf{R}^{\mathsf{dCosts}}_{\mathsf{min}=?}$ [F $\mathsf{attackerBlocked}$].
(2) The maximum cost for the attacker to launch a DoS attack against the web server plycent02: $\langle\langle \mathsf{def}\rangle\rangle \mathsf{R}^{\mathsf{aCosts}}_{\mathsf{max}=?}$ [F $\mathsf{DoS(plycent02)}$].
(3) The maximum probability with which the defender successfully blocks the attack: $\langle\langle \mathsf{def}\rangle\rangle \mathsf{P}_{\mathsf{max}=?}$ [F $\mathsf{attackerBlocked}$].
(4) The minimum probability which the attacker achieves its final goal: $\langle\langle \mathsf{att}\rangle\rangle \mathsf{P}_{\mathsf{min}=?}$ [F $\mathsf{DoS(plycent02)}$].

We carried out experiments with different schedulers. The attacker performs 14 different types of actions in total, and we considered three different schedulers that return control to the defender after an action of a specific type, e.g. when a suspicious log-in occurs or traffic is observed. Table 2 shows a partial analysis of the results. The first column shows the number of attacker action types after which control returns to the defender. For instance, a "2-actions" scheduler means that the attacker performs two actions, after which control is returned to the defender to apply a defense if necessary. The 'Model Size' column indicates the number of states and transitions of the security game for different systems.

The results show that, with an increase in the number of actions to which the defender can react, the size of model increases. This is expected, as more transitions from the defender will be included in the model and this will increase the state space. In addition, the minimum cost (both attacker damage and defence costs) imposed on the system decreases with an increase in the number of attacker actions to react to, e.g., the minimum cost to defend against the attack in the tax system changes from 732 units to 205 when the number of actions with a defence reaction changes from 2 to 6. This is because the defender has a better chance of applying an effective countermeasure if control is returned more often.

Table 2. Results for varying scenarios

Scheduler	Model size	Property	Case	Result
2-actions	17.6K/ 47K	(1)	Tax System	732
			Image Hosting	732
			Hotel Reservation	732
		(3)	-	0.31
4-actions	47K/ 121k	(1)	Tax System	277
			Image Hosting	266
			Hotel Reservation	318
		(3)	-	0.67
6-actions	97K/ 242K	(1)	Tax System	205
			Image Hosting	185
			Hotel Reservation	245
		(3)	-	0.68

Furthermore, the minimum cost for the attacker to reach its final goal increases slightly: with an increase in the defence actions, it might become more challenging for the attacker to succeed and it would need to try different scenarios. In a similar fashion, the probability that the defender succeeds in blocking the attack increases, e.g., from 0.31 with two action types to 0.68 for the case of 6 action types.

Performance Analysis. To evaluate the performance of our approach, we conducted experiments on a real-life network system comprising 16 hosts offering different services. We scanned the hosts and identified 155 types of software vulnerabilities, all reported to the CVSS database during the period of 2017-2018. All experiments were run on a machine with a 2.9 GHz Intel Core i7 CPU and 16 GB RAM, running macOS Catalina. We conducted experiments with different sets of observations, vulnerabilities, defence strategies, and objectives on a real-life case study. To test the implementation of our prototype, we ran approximately 1241 different experiments. Sample model files are available.[2]

The size of the game model depends on the size of the attack graph as well as the defences. *Defence strength* indicates the percentage of possible defences applied in the system. As the size of the attack graph and the defence strength increase, the number of states and transitions increase accordingly, as illustrated in Fig. 3(b). In this figure, colour represents the number of states, and the

[2] https://www.prismmodelchecker.org/files/sefm24/.

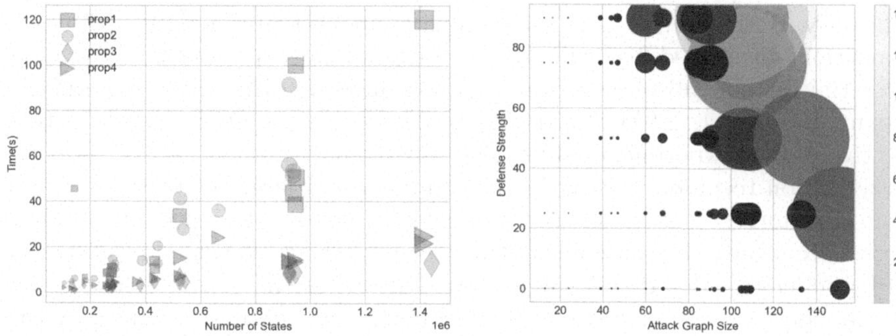

(a) (b)

Fig. 3. (a) Model checking time for varying game sizes. (b) Games size for varying defence strength and attack graph size (circle colour/size indicates the number of states/transitions, in the ranges $(0, 1.4 * 10^6)$ and $(0, 14.5 * 10^6)$, respectively).

marker size denotes the number of transitions at each point. For larger attack graphs with high defence strength, we encountered the state explosion problem. Figure 3(a) shows the model checking time for four different properties based on the number of model states. The marker size represents the number of transitions at each point. The model checking time ranged from a few milliseconds for smaller models to approximately 120 s for a model with around 1.4×10^6 states, and generally increases with the size of the model.

The number of transitions in a security game under perfect and partial observation for six different experiments is presented in Fig. 4. The x-axis shows the experiment ID, and the y-axis the sum of the number of transitions and states for different observations. In these experiments, the number of attacker action types ranged from 9–16. We ran each experiment under five different observation conditions, including full observation (Observable), and with n unobservable actions, for $1 \leq n \leq 4$. In this figure, $n-$Unobservable means that n actions of the attacker have become unobservable. Actions that are challenging to definitively associate with malicious activity are considered unobservable.

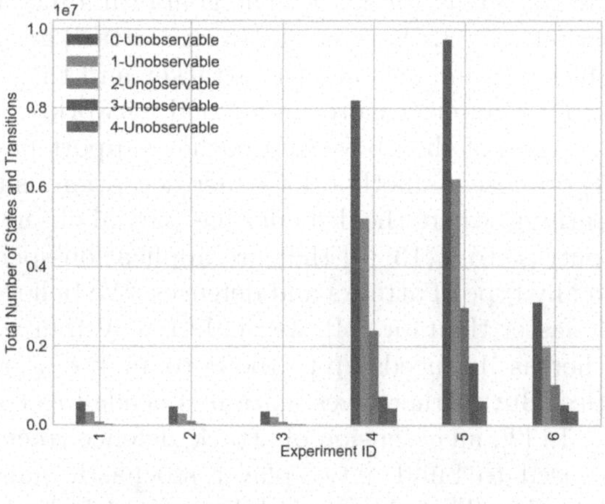

Fig. 4. Model Size vs Partial observation

In some experiments, while the number of state variables remained fixed (because the consequences of unobservable actions were partially observable, i.e., neither fully observable nor fully unobservable), the model size was reduced significantly. With an increase in the number of unobservable actions, the number of transitions decreased accordingly. For instance, in experiment 5, the model size for the case of full observation is approximately 9.7M, while it reduces to approximately 6.2M, 2.9M, 1.5M and 0.6M for 1 to 4 unobservable actions, respectively. Our experiments show that this transformation can be used as a state reduction technique to tackle the complexity of large-scale attack graphs. We can transform a perfect security game with a large state space into a smaller game, where some sub-scenarios that do not trigger any defence are abstracted away by being considered as a single step. This results in a more abstract game where the internal details of the attacker's behaviour are hidden, and only their interactions with the defender are taken into account.

6 Related Work

Games In Security. A recent survey by Hunt et al. [19] reviews research on attacker-defender games, but it focuses solely on protecting physical assets and does not address cybersecurity. The authors in [14] proposed a game-theoretic approach for a network hardening problem where the attacker plan is represented as an attack graph and the defender seeks an optimal solution to deploy honeypots into the network to deceive the attacker. A two-player strategic game based on an extension of attack trees was constructed in [4], where the defender wants to protect the system by buying countermeasures and the attacker tries to exploit the vulnerabilities and gain some profit. The game is solved by finding the Nash equilibria, with the goal of finding the most promising attack/defence actions. Chowdhary et al. [13] use attack graphs to build a zero-sum stochastic Markov game between the attacker and the defender to help the administrator apply countermeasures in a cloud network.

None of the above approaches support partial observations. The authors in [1] proposed a method for cyber-deception using game theory and reinforcement learning, where the defender has partial observations of the attacker's actions. In contrast to [1,13,14] that are application-specific, our approach can be applied to any type of attacks and defences. We believe the runtime for our method may be faster than for [14]: we analyze a system with 53 vulnerabilities in under 1 s, whereas [14] needs up to 1000 s to analyze a network with 8 types of vulnerabilities. But further investigation is needed to confirm this.

In [2], an extension of attack/defence trees with temporal ordering of actions is used to build a two-player stochastic game between the attacker and the defender. They use probabilistic model checking techniques to formally verify security properties of the attack-defence scenarios, and synthesize strategies for attackers or defenders using PRISM-games. A similar approach is taken in [15], but with some relaxed model assumptions and some additional optimizations. Gadyatskay et al. define a stochastic timed semantics for attack-defence trees in terms of a network of timed automata in [16]. They use the UPPAAL model checker to perform a quantitative analysis and find attacker parameters that minimize cost. In contrast to [2,15], we use attack graphs that can be generated fully automatically and we support partial observation, while automatic construction of attack trees is still a major challenge despite the recent efforts [33]. Our security game is boolean which makes it more scalable for analysis of realistic network systems, as confirmed by our experiments results.

Analysis under Partial Observation. Partially observable Markov decision processes (POMDPs) extend MDPs with partial observability and have many applications in fields such as AI, scheduling and planning. The formal verification community has studied POMDPs and presented both theoretical results, e.g. [9,10] and practical methods, e.g. [5,6,26], the latter being implemented in the popular model checkers PRISM [24] and Storm [17].

In [34], the problem of motion planning, that is often modeled as a POMDP, is reduced to a two-player stochastic game and solved using PRISM-games. The problem of controller synthesis for timed games under state-based partial observation has been studied in [8] and implemented in UPPAAL-TIGA [3]. Skandylas et al. [30] proposed an approach to synthesize countermeasures for component-based software systems, considering both the structure and the behaviour of the system. We can only reason about the system behaviour. However, in contrast to our work, they do not support partial observation.

7 Conclusions

In this paper, we propose a game-based approach for the analysis of attack graphs under partial observation. We construct a two-player security game from an attack graph and the defender's behaviour, and use PRISM-games to analyze the game and synthesize strategies for the players. To support defence under partial observation, we introduce one-sided partially observable security games and present an algorithm to transform them into perfect games, proving soundness for a subclass of security games and objectives. Our experiments show that the transformation algorithm is a promising state reduction technique to handle large-scale attack graphs. We plan to integrate our approach into a self-protection engine to support online defence, and also to extend our experiments to study the impact of different factors on the effectiveness of the defence.

Acknowledgements. This work was funded in part by the Swedish Knowledge Foundation (No. 20160186) and the UK Engineering and Physical Sciences Research Council (EP/X037274/1).

References

1. Anwar, A.H., Kamhoua, C.A., Leslie, N.O., Kiekintveld, C.: Honeypot allocation for cyber deception under uncertainty. IEEE Trans. Netw. Serv. Manag. **19**(3), 3438–3452 (2022)
2. Aslanyan, Z., Nielson, F., Parker, D.: Quantitative verification and synthesis of attack-defence scenarios. In: Proc. CSF'16, pp. 105–119 (2016)

3. Behrmann, G., Cougnard, A., David, A., Fleury, E., Larsen, K.G., Lime, D.: UPPAAL TIGA user-manual. Aalborg University (2007)
4. Bistarelli, S., Dall'Aglio, M., Peretti, P.: Strategic games on defense trees. In: Dimitrakos, T., Martinelli, F., Ryan, P.Y.A., Schneider, S. (eds.) FAST 2006. LNCS, vol. 4691, pp. 1–15. Springer, Heidelberg (2007). https://doi.org/10.1007/978-3-540-75227-1_1
5. Bork, A., Junges, S., Katoen, J.-P., Quatmann, T.: Verification of indefinite-horizon POMDPs. In: Hung, D.V., Sokolsky, O. (eds.) ATVA 2020. LNCS, vol. 12302, pp. 288–304. Springer, Cham (2020). https://doi.org/10.1007/978-3-030-59152-6_16
6. Bork, A., Katoen, J.-P., Quatmann, T.: Under-approximating expected total rewards in POMDPs. In: TACAS 2022. LNCS, vol. 13244, pp. 22–40. Springer, Cham (2022). https://doi.org/10.1007/978-3-030-99527-0_2
7. Carr, S., Jansen, N., Bharadwaj, S., Spaan, M.T., Topcu, U.: Safe policies for factored partially observable stochastic games. Science and System XVII, In Robotics (2021)
8. Cassez, F., David, A., Larsen, K.G., Lime, D., Raskin, J.: Timed control with observation based and stuttering invariant strategies. In: Proc. ATVA'07, pp. 192–206 (2007)
9. Chatterjee, K., Chmelik, M., Tracol, M.: What is decidable about partially observable Markov decision processes with omega-regular objectives. In: Proc. CSL'13, pp. 165–180 (2013)
10. Chatterjee, K., Doyen, L.: Partial-observation stochastic games: How to win when belief fails. ACM Trans. Comput. Log. **15**(2), 16:1–16:44 (2014)
11. Chatterjee, K., Doyen, L., Henzinger, T.A.: A survey of partial-observation stochastic parity games. Formal Methods Syst. Des. **43**(2), 268–284 (2013)
12. Chen, T., Forejt, V., Kwiatkowska, M., Parker, D., Simaitis, A.: Automatic verification of competitive stochastic systems. Formal Methods Syst. Des. **43**(1), 61–92 (2013)
13. Chowdhary, A., Sengupta, S., Alshamrani, A., Huang, D., Sabur, A.: Adaptive MTD security using Markov game modeling. In: International Conference on Computing, Networking and Communications, ICNC 2019, Honolulu, HI, USA, February 18-21, 2019, pp. 577–581 (2019)
14. Durkota, K., Lisý, V., Bosanský, B., Kiekintveld, C.: Optimal network security hardening using attack graph games. In: Proc. IJCAI'15, pp. 526–532 (2015)
15. Eisentraut, J., Křetínský, J.: Expected cost analysis of attack-defense trees. In: Parker, D., Wolf, V. (eds.) QEST 2019. LNCS, vol. 11785, pp. 203–221. Springer, Cham (2019). https://doi.org/10.1007/978-3-030-30281-8_12
16. Gadyatskaya, O., Hansen, R.R., Larsen, K.G., Legay, A., Olesen, M.C., Poulsen, D.B.: Modelling attack-defense trees using timed automata. In: Proc. FORMATS'16, pp. 35–50 (2016)
17. Hensel, C., Junges, S., Katoen, J., Quatmann, T., Volk, M.: The probabilistic model checker storm. Int. J. Softw. Tools Technol. Transf. **24**(4), 589–610 (2022)
18. Hong, J.B., Kim, D.S., Chung, C.-J., Huang, D.: A survey on the usability and practical applications of graphical security models. Comput. Sci. Rev. **26**, 1–16 (2017)
19. Hunt, K., Zhuang, J.: A review of attacker-defender games: Current state and paths forward. Eur. J. Oper. Res. **313**(2), 401–417 (2024)
20. Khakpour, N., Parker, D.: Partially-observable security games for attack-defence analysis in software systems. CoRR, abs/2211.01508 (2022)

21. Khakpour, N., Skandylas, C., Nariman, G.S., Weyns, D.: Towards secure architecture-based adaptations. In: Proceedings of the 14th International Symposium on Software Engineering for Adaptive and Self-Managing Systems, SEAMS@ICSE 2019, Montreal, QC, Canada, May 25-31, 2019, pp. 114–125, 2019
22. Kordy, B., Piètre-Cambacédès, L., Schweitzer, P.: DAG-based attack and defense modeling: Don't miss the forest for the attack trees. Comput. Sci. Rev. **13**, 03 (2013)
23. Kwiatkowska, M., Norman, G., Parker, D., Santos, G.: PRISM-games 3.0: stochastic game verification with concurrency, equilibria and time. In: Lahiri, S.K., Wang, C. (eds.) CAV 2020. LNCS, vol. 12225, pp. 475–487. Springer, Cham (2020). https://doi.org/10.1007/978-3-030-53291-8_25
24. Kwiatkowska, M., Norman, G., Parker, D.: PRISM 4.0: verification of probabilistic real-time systems. In: Gopalakrishnan, G., Qadeer, S. (eds.) CAV 2011. LNCS, vol. 6806, pp. 585–591. Springer, Heidelberg (2011). https://doi.org/10.1007/978-3-642-22110-1_47
25. Manshaei, M.H., Zhu, Q., Alpcan, T., Basar, T., Hubaux, J.: Game theory meets network security and privacy. ACM Comput. Surv. **45**(3):25:1–25:39 (2013)
26. Norman, G., Parker, D., Zou, X.: Verification and control of partially observable probabilistic systems. Real-Time Syst. **53**(3), 354–402 (2017)
27. Ou, X., Govindavajhala, S., Appel, A.W.: Mulval: A logic-based network security analyzer. In: Proceedings of the 14th Conference on USENIX Security Symposium - Volume 14, SSYM'05, p. 8, Berkeley, CA, USA, 2005. USENIX Association (2005)
28. Sheyner, O., Haines, J., Jha, S., Lippmann, R., Wing, J.M.: Automated generation and analysis of attack graphs. In: Proceedings 2002 IEEE Symposium on Security and Privacy, pp. 273–284. IEEE (2002)
29. Simaitis, A.: Automatic Verification of Competitive Stochastic Systems. PhD thesis, Department of Computer Science, University of Oxford (2014)
30. Skandylas, C., Khakpour, N., Cámara, J.: Security countermeasure selection for component-based software-intensive systems. In: 22nd IEEE International Conference on Software Quality, Reliability and Security, QRS 2022, Guangzhou, China, December 5-9, 2022, pp. 63–72. IEEE (2022)
31. Wang, L., Islam, T., Long, T., Singhal, A., Jajodia, S.: An attack graph-based probabilistic security metric. In: Data and Applications Security XXII, 22nd Annual IFIP WG 11.3 Working Conference on Data and Applications Security, London, UK, July 13-16, 2008, Proceedings, pp. 283–296 (2008)
32. Weiss, J.D.: A system security engineering process. In: Proceedings of the 14th National Computer Security Conference, vol. 249, pp. 572–581 (1991)
33. Wideł, W., Audinot, M., Fila, B., Pinchinat, S.: Beyond 2014: Formal methods for attack tree–based security modeling. ACM Comput. Surv. **52**(4), 75:1–75:36 (2019)
34. Winterer, L., et al.: Motion planning under partial observability using game-based abstraction. In: 56th IEEE Annual Conference on Decision and Control, CDC 2017, Melbourne, Australia, December 12-15, 2017, pp. 2201–2208 (2017)

Secure Smart Contracts with Isabelle/Solidity

Diego Marmsoler(✉), Asad Ahmed, and Achim D. Brucker

University of Exeter, Exeter EX4 4PY, UK
{d.marmsoler,a.ahmed6,a.brucker}@exeter.ac.uk

Abstract. Smart contracts are programs stored on the blockchain, often developed in a high-level programming language, the most popular of which is Solidity. Smart contracts are used to automate financial transactions and thus bugs can lead to large financial losses. With this paper, we address this problem by describing a verification environment for Solidity in Isabelle/HOL. The framework consists of a novel formalization of the Solidity storage model, a shallow embedding of Solidity expressions and statements, an implementation of Isabelle commands to support a user in specifying Solidity smart contracts, and a verification condition generator to support a user in the verification. Compliance of the semantics is tested by a set of unit tests and the approach is evaluated by means of three case studies. Our results show that the framework can be used to verify even complex contracts with reasonable effort. Moreover, they show that the shallow embedding significantly reduces the verification effort compared to an alternative approach based on a deep embedding.

Keywords: Program Verification · Smart Contracts · Isabelle · Solidity

1 Introduction

Blockchain [33] is a novel technology used to store data in a decentralized manner, thereby providing *transparency*, *security*, and *trust*. Although the technology was originally invented to enable cryptocurrencies, it quickly found applications in several other domains, such as *finance* [23], *healthcare* [4], *land management* [10], and *identity management* [46].

One important innovation which comes with blockchains are so-called *smart contracts*. These are digital contracts which are automatically executed once certain conditions are met and are typically used to automate transactions on the blockchain. For instance, a payment for an item might be released instantly once the buyer and seller meet all the specified parameters of a deal. Every day, hundreds of thousands of new contracts are deployed managing millions of dollars' worth of transactions [45].

Technically, a smart contract is code which is deployed to a blockchain, and which can be executed by sending special transactions to it. Smart contracts

A. Madeira and A. Knapp (Eds.): SEFM 2024, LNCS 15280, pp. 162–181, 2025.
https://doi.org/10.1007/978-3-031-77382-2_10

are usually developed in a high-level programming language, the most popular of which is *Solidity*. Solidity can be compiled to run on the Ethereum Virtual Machine (EVM), and thus, it works on all EVM-based smart contract platforms, such as Ethereum, Avalanche, Moonbeam, Polygon, BSC, and more. Currently, more than 90% of all smart contracts are developed using Solidity [27].

As with every computer program, *smart contracts may contain bugs which can be exploited*. However, since smart contracts are often used to automate financial transactions, such exploits may result in huge economic losses. For example, in 2016, a vulnerability in an Ethereum smart contract was exploited, resulting in a loss of approximately $60M [5]. More recently, hackers exploited a vulnerability in the DeFi-platform Poly Network to steal $600M [34]. Overall, it is estimated that since 2019, more than $5B have been stolen due to vulnerabilities in smart contracts [11].

The high impact of vulnerabilities in smart contracts, together with the fact that once deployed to the blockchain, they cannot be updated or removed easily, makes it important to "get them right" before they are deployed. To address this problem, we developed Isabelle/Solidity, a shallow embedding of Solidity in Isabelle/HOL. To this end, the major contributions of this paper are as follows:

1. *We provide a novel formalization of Solidity's storage model in Isabelle/HOL* (Sect. 3.1). The formalization provides definitions for all different stores used in Solidity as well as functions to manipulate data structures stored on them.
2. *We provide a shallow embedding of Solidity expressions and statements in Isabelle/HOL*. The embedding consists of a formalization of a state monad (Sect. 3.2) as well as definitions of a subset of expressions (Sect. 3.3) and statements (Sect. 3.4) in terms of the state monad.
3. *We implemented two new commands for Isabelle to support the specification and verification of Solidity smart contracts* (Sect. 3.5). The commands are implemented in Isabelle/ML and generate definitions, theorems, and proofs for a contract specification given by a user.
4. *We provide a formalization of a weakest precondition calculus and corresponding verification condition generator for our embedding* (Sect. 3.6). It can be used to reduce lemmas involving Solidity statements to HOL formulas which can then be discharged using standard Isabelle infrastructure.
5. *We provide a test suite to validate Solidity semantics* (Sect. 4.1). The test suite includes set of test cases to test the semantics of expressions and statements.
6. *We formalize and verify three smart contracts in Isabelle/Solidity* (Sect. 4.2). Each contract is specified using our framework, and then we verify a key invariant for each contract.

Our results suggest that the shallow embedding can significantly reduce the effort to verify concrete smart contracts. In particular, verifying the invariant of one of the case studies required 3250 lines of Isabelle/Isar code in a deep embedding. In our shallow embedding, the same invariant was verified in less than 100 lines (a reduction of 97%).

The formalization, implementation, and the case studies are available online[1]. We shall use to reference a certain term in the corresponding Isabelle source file. This will then be a clickable link which opens a theory file and highlights the corresponding formalization (for Example `skip_monad`). The paper's artefact contains a virtual machine with an Isabelle installation and a copy of the same source files. It is also available online at https://zenodo.org/records/12770521.

2 Solidity

To provide a first impression of the language, listing 1 shows a simple smart contract in Solidity which allows clients to deposit and withdraw funds. To this end, the contract keeps an internal record of funds transferred by its customers. This record is increased whenever a customer transfers additional funds via the `deposit` method. Once the customer calls the `withdraw` method, all its recorded funds are returned and its internal record reset to 0.

Listing 1: A simple banking contract in Solidity

```
1  contract Bank {
2      mapping(address => uint256) balances;
3      function deposit() public payable {
4       balances[msg.sender] = balances[msg.sender] + msg.value;
5      }
6      function withdraw() public {
7          uint256 bal = balances[msg.sender];
8          balances[msg.sender] = 0;
9          msg.sender.transfer(bal);
10     }
11 }
```

Although simple, the example already demonstrates several specialties of the Solidity programming language. In particular, every contract has access to an *internal* balance (not to confuse with mapping `balances` in line 2 which is simply a member variable of the contract). Funds can be transferred to and from this internal balance either explicitly (using function `transfer`) or implicitly (via an external method call). The address of the client (the one calling a contract's method) and the amount of funds transferred with a call can be accessed using keywords `msg.sender` and `msg.value`, respectively.

3 Isabelle/Solidity

Our semantics is based on the official documentation[2] of Solidity v0.8.25. It is formalized in higher-order logic (HOL) using inductive data types [7]. To this end, we use **bold** font for types and roman font for type constructors.

[1] https://github.com/dmarmsoler/isabelle-solidity-shallow.

[2] https://docs.soliditylang.org/en/v0.8.25/.

3.1 Storage Model

Solidity programs can make use of different types of stores for data: storage (for persistent data), memory (for volatile data), calldata (for volatile and read-only data), and stack. Our storage model is formalized in theory State.thy and consists of a formalization of all of these different types of stores.

Value Types. The basic data types stored in Solidity are called value types and defined as follows:

$$\textbf{valtype} \;::=\; \mathrm{Bool}(\textbf{bool}) \mid \mathrm{Sint}(\textbf{256 word}) \mid \mathrm{Address}(\textbf{address}) \mid \mathrm{Bytes}(\textbf{bytes}) \qquad (\texttt{valtype})$$

where **bool** is the type of boolean values, **256 word** the type of finite bit strings[3] of length 256, **address** the type of addresses, and **bytes** the type of bytes.

Storage. The persistent store can keep basic value types as well as complex types, such as arrays and hash-maps.

$$\textbf{sdata} \;::=\; \mathrm{Value}(\textbf{valtype}) \mid \mathrm{Array}(\textbf{sdata list}) \mid \mathrm{Map}(\textbf{valtype} \Rightarrow \textbf{sdata}) \qquad (\texttt{sdata})$$

where a **list** represents the type of lists over another type a.

Memory. The volatile store supports two types of data: basic value types and arrays.

$$\textbf{mdata} \;::=\; \mathrm{Value}(\textbf{valtype}) \mid \mathrm{Array}(\textbf{location list}) \qquad (\texttt{mdata})$$

where **location** represents memory locations which is just a synonym for the type of natural numbers.

Note that, unlike storage, memory arrays are organized as pointer structures.

Example 3.1 (Memory array). A simple array of 3 integers 5, 6, and 7, is represented as follows:

$$[\mathrm{Array}([1,2,3]), \mathrm{Value}(\mathrm{Sint}(5)), \mathrm{Value}(\mathrm{Sint}(6)), \mathrm{Value}(\mathrm{Sint}(7))]$$

Calldata. The read-only store can keep two types of data: basic value types and arrays.

$$\textbf{cdata} \;::=\; \mathrm{Value}(\textbf{valtype}) \mid \mathrm{Array}(\textbf{cdata list}) \qquad (\texttt{cdata})$$

[3] Bit strings are modelled using Isabelle's word library [14].

Stack. In Solidity, the stack can keep four different types of data: basic value types and pointers to storage, memory, or calldata, respectively.

$$\textbf{kdata} \quad ::= \quad \text{Value}(\textbf{valtype}) \mid \text{Storage}(\textbf{identifier}, \textbf{valtype list})$$
$$\mid \text{Memory}(\textbf{location}) \mid \text{Calldata}(\textbf{identifier}, \textbf{valtype list}) \qquad (\texttt{kdata})$$

Note that memory pointers are given in terms of memory locations while pointers to storage and calldata are given in terms of an identifier and a list of valtypes which represent the sequence of indices to reach the referenced element.

State. A state of a Solidity program consists of configurations of each of its stores. To define such a state, we first introduce the following type abbreviations:

$$\textbf{memory} ::= \textbf{mdata list} \qquad (\texttt{memory})$$
$$\textbf{stack} ::= \textbf{identifier} \rightharpoonup \textbf{kdata} \qquad (\texttt{stack})$$
$$\textbf{storage} ::= \textbf{address} \Rightarrow \textbf{identifier} \Rightarrow \textbf{sdata} \qquad (\texttt{storage})$$
$$\textbf{calldata} ::= \textbf{identifier} \Rightarrow \textbf{cdata} \qquad (\texttt{calldata})$$
$$\textbf{balances} ::= \textbf{address} \Rightarrow \textbf{nat} \qquad (\texttt{balances})$$

where $A \rightharpoonup B$ is the set of finite maps from A to B. Note that the formalization of storage assigns a private store to each contract (identified by its address which is known during execution).

A state is now defined as a record over the above types:

$$\textbf{state} \quad ::= \quad \textbf{memory} \times \textbf{calldata} \times \textbf{storage} \times \textbf{stack} \times \textbf{balances} \qquad (\texttt{state})$$

For a given state s, we denote with Memory(s), Calldata(s), Storage(s), *Stack*(s), *Balances*(s) its memory, calldata, storage, stack, and balances, respectively.

Auxiliary Definitions. Our model provides definitions for different functions to lookup and update data for each type of store. In addition, we provide definitions for functions to copy data from memory to storage (`copy_memory_storage`), memory to calldata (`copy_memory_calldata`), storage to memory (`copy_storage_memory`), calldata to memory (`copy_calldata_memory copy_calldata_memory`), and calldata to storage (`copy_calldata_storage`). These functions need to convert between the different representations of the data for each type of store.

3.2 State Monads

Statements and expressions are formalized using a state monad [12, 42] with exception and non-termination. State monads are formalized in State_Monad.thy. To this end, we first define a result type as follows:

$$\mathbf{result}(\mathbf{n}, \mathbf{e}) \quad ::= \quad \mathrm{Normal}(\mathbf{n}) \mid \mathrm{Exception}(\mathbf{e}) \mid \mathrm{NT} \qquad (\texttt{result})$$

The type **result** is defined over two type parameters, **n** and **e**, to denote the type of normal and exceptional return values, respectively. Normal(x) represents the result x of a normal execution, Exception(e) represents an exceptional return with exception e, and NT represents a non-terminating execution.

We can then define our state monad as follows:

$$\mathbf{state\_monad}(\mathbf{a}, \mathbf{e}, \mathbf{s}) \overset{\text{def}}{=} \mathbf{s} \Rightarrow \mathbf{result}(\mathbf{a} \times \mathbf{s}, \mathbf{e} \times \mathbf{s}) \qquad (\texttt{state\_monad})$$

The definition requires three type parameters: a type **a** for return values, a type **s** for states, and a type **e** for exceptions. The monad models an execution which starts in a certain state and either terminates in a new state with corresponding return value/exception, or does not terminate. We also define corresponding functions to create and execute monads, respectively (`create` , `execute`).

Monad Operations. To support the construction of monads, we defined several basic operations on monads. For example, the following constants denote normal and erroneous returns, respectively:

$$\mathrm{return}(a) \overset{\text{def}}{=} \lambda s.\ \mathrm{Normal}(a, s) \qquad (\texttt{return})$$

$$\mathrm{throw}(e) \overset{\text{def}}{=} \lambda s.\ \mathrm{Exception}(e, s) \qquad (\texttt{throw})$$

The bind operator $f \gg\!= g$ combines a monad $f\colon \mathbf{state\_monad}(\mathbf{a}, \mathbf{e}, \mathbf{s})$ with a function $g\colon \mathbf{a} \Rightarrow \mathbf{state\_monad}(\mathbf{b}, \mathbf{e}, \mathbf{s})$:

$$f \gg\!= g\ (s) \overset{\text{def}}{=} \begin{cases} g(a)(s') & \textit{if } f(s) = \mathrm{Normal}(a, s') \\ \mathrm{Exception}(e, s) & \textit{if } f(s) = \mathrm{Exception}(e, s) \\ \mathrm{NT} & \textit{if } f(s) = \mathrm{NT} \end{cases} \qquad (\texttt{bind})$$

To combine multiple monads we will often use the familiar do-notation. Then, denotes the monad given by return(1) $\gg\!=(\lambda a.\ \mathrm{return}(a))$.

Partial Functions. To model loops and recursive functions, we use Isabelle's partial function package [25]. This package resorts to domain theory to express general recursions over complete partial orders [44]. The package includes a setup for the option monad but can be extended to work with custom monads as well.

We implemented a new mode `sm` for the partial function package to work with our state monad. To this end, we provided a definition for a bottom element (`empty_result`), a corresponding ordering (`result_ord`), and a least upper bound (`result_lub`) for our state monad. Then, we needed to prove the following statement about admissible properties.

Lemma 3.1 (*`admissible_sm`*)*:* For each proposition P, the following proposition is admissible w.r.t. `result_ord` and `result_lub`:

$$\lambda f.\ \forall x, s, r.\ \text{effect}(f(x), s, r) \implies P(x, h, r)$$

where effect(m, s, r) defines that a state monad m, executed in state s either executes normally with result r or throws an exception r.

To support the partial function package in proving the existence of a unique least fixed-point, we also needed to prove monotonicity for some of our monads (`throw_monad_mono`, `return_monad_mono`, `bind_mono`, `option_monad_mono`).

3.3 Expressions

Solidity expressions and statements are formalized in terms of our state monad in Solidity.thy. To this end, we first define the result type of an expression as follows:

$$\textbf{rvalue} \ ::= \ \text{Storage}(\textbf{identifier}, \textbf{valtype list}) \mid \text{Memory}(\textbf{location})$$

$$\mid \text{Calldata}(\textbf{identifier}, \textbf{valtype list}) \mid \text{Value}(\textbf{valtype}) \mid \text{Empty} \qquad (\texttt{rvalue})$$

Thus, an expression can return a basic value type or a pointer to storage, memory, or calldata. In addition, an expression may also return nothing which is modelled by the constructor Empty. Now, we can define the expression monad as an instance of our state monad:

$$\textbf{expression\_monad} \ ::= \ \textbf{state\_monad}(\textbf{rvalue}, \textbf{ex}, \textbf{state})$$

where **ex** is a datatype for capturing the different types of errors.

Our formalization contains definitions for all the basic expressions in terms of the expression monad: basic constants (`bool_monad`, `sint_monad`, `address_monad`), arithmetic operators (`plus_monad`, `minus_monad`, `mult_monad`, `mod_monad`) as well as corresponding safe versions to check for overflows, comparison operators (`equals_monad`, `less_monad`), and boolean operators (`not_monad`, `and_monad`, `or_monad`).

In addition, we also provide definitions for Solidity specific operators, such as an operator to compute hash values (`keccak256_monad`), an operator to retrieve the address of the currently executing contract (`this_monad`), an operator to obtain the value which was sent by the sender (`value_monad`), and an operator to obtain the address of the message sender (`sender_monad`).

Finally, we provide monads to obtain the value of a storage or stack variable (`storeLookup` , `stackLookup`) and monads to compute the length of memory/storage arrays (`arrayLength` , `storeArrayLength`). Note that all the lookup functions take an optional list of expression monads to navigate complex data types such as arrays and hash-maps. In particular, the operators for stack variables need to check the location of the datatype (memory, storage, or calldata) and then navigate the structure in the corresponding store.

Example 3.2 (Stack lookup). Assuming st is a state with memory as defined in Example 3.1 and $Stack(st)(\text{"}x\text{"}) = \text{Memory}(0)$. Then

$$\text{stackLookup}(\text{"}x\text{"}, [\text{sint\_monad}(0)])(s) = \text{Normal}(\text{Value}(\text{Sint}(5)), s)$$

3.4 Statements

Again, we formalize all basic statements. Assignments, for example, are formalized by two monads to assign to stack (`assign_stack_monad`) or storage variables (`assign_storage_monad`). In Solidity, the behavior of assigning complex data types, such as arrays, depends on the location of the array. Table 1 summarizes the different cases which need to be considered. A complex data type can be located in any of the three types of stores: memory (M), storage (S), and calldata (C). In addition, we can have pointers to storage elements on the stack (P). Depending on whether we copy the complete array or just modify a pointer, we distinguish between deep copy (D) and shallow copies (S). For example, the first entry in Table 1 states that assigning a memory array to a memory array actually just assigns a pointer instead of copying the whole array.

Solidity also supports dynamic storage arrays which can be expanded at runtime. To this end, we provide also a monad to allocate new storage for an additional array element (`allocate`).

Conditionals and loops are formalized by two monads (`cond_monad` and `while_monad`). As mentioned in Sect. 3.2, loops are formalized using a partial recursive function. To this end, we first needed to verify some additional monotonicity results (`cond_mono` , `cond_K`) used by the partial function package to verify the existence of a corresponding fixed-point. The package then provides us with a fixed-point induction theorem which can be used to reason about loops.

Finally, we provide a formalization of the transfer statement which can be used to transfer funds to other

Table 1. Assignments for complex data types

LHS	RHS	Type
M	M	S
M	C	D
M	P	D
M	S	D
S	M	D
S	C	D
S	S	D
S	P	D
P	S	S
P	M	N/A
P	C	N/A
P	P	N/A
C	-	N/A

accounts (**transfer_monad**). Note that in Solidity, a transfer implicitly triggers the execution of a so-called fallback method and thus we postulate the existence of such a method for each contract address. In addition, we assume that such methods preserve invariants over the currently executing contract's storage and balance, given that we are able to show that a callback preserves invariants as well:

$$\frac{\forall s, r.\, P(s) \wedge \text{effect}(call, s, r) \Longrightarrow \text{inv}(r, P, E) \quad P(s)}{\forall a, r.\, \text{effect}(\text{fallback}(a), s, r) \Longrightarrow \text{inv}(r, P'(s), E'(s))} \quad (\texttt{fallback\_invariant})$$

where $\text{inv}(r, P, E)$ requires that predicate P holds for a successful termination r and E for an exceptional one. Moreover,

$$P'(s) = \lambda s'.Stack(s) = Stack(s') \wedge \text{Memory}(s) = \text{Memory}(s') \\ \wedge \text{Calldata}(s) = \text{Calldata}(s') \wedge P(s')$$

and E' is defined similarly as E.

3.5 Automation: Specification

To support a user in the specification and verification of a contract, we implemented a new definitional package for Isabelle using Isabelle/ML [43]. Our package is implemented in file Contract.thy.

Specification. To support a user with the specification of a contract, our package implements a new Isabelle command `contract`. This command requires a user to provide a *name* for the contract, followed by a list of declarations of storage variables. Then, the user can specify a constructor using keyword `constructor`, followed by an implementation of the constructor in terms of an expression monad. Finally, the user can specify a list of methods using the keyword `cmethod`. Each method can have an optional list of formal parameters followed by an implementation in terms of an expression monad.

Example 3.3 (Banking contract). The formalization of our example contract from listing 1 in Isabelle/Solidity looks as follows:

```
contract Bank
  for "STR ''balances''": "sdata.Map (mapping (sdata.Value sint))"

constructor where
  "skip_monad"

cmethod deposit where
  "assign_storage_monad (STR ''balances'') [sender_monad]
    (plus_monad_safe (storeLookup (STR ''balances'') [sender_monad]) (value_monad))" ,

cmethod withdraw where
  "do {
    decl (STR ''bal'') (storeLookup (STR ''balances'') [sender_monad]);
    assign_storage_monad (STR ''balances'') [sender_monad] (sint_monad 0);
    transfer_monad (sender_monad) (stackLookup (STR ''bal'') [])
  }"
```

Our package then generates definitions for the constructor and the contract's methods. To this end, we first initialize the contract's balance, storage variables, and stack. Then, we can just execute the monad provided by the user.

Example 3.4 (Constructor). Our package would generate the following definition for the constructor from the specification given in Example 3.3:

$$\text{bank\_constructor\_def} = \quad \textbf{do} \left[\begin{array}{l} \text{init\_balance} \\ \text{initStorage}(\text{“}\textit{balances}\text{”}, \text{Map}(\text{mapping}(\text{Value}(\text{Sint})))) \\ \text{emptyStack} \\ \text{skip\_monad} \end{array} \right.$$

The definition of the methods is a bit more elaborate since we want to allow for mutual recursive definitions. Again, we first initialize the balance and the stack, before we execute the monadic definition provided by the user. Note, however, that a method has a special parameter *call* which can be used in its definition. This is a construct which can be used to call internal or external methods. Note also that for each method we need to generate and prove a monotonicity lemma for the partial function package.

Example 3.5 (Methods). Our package would generate the following definition for the deposit method from the specification given in Example 3.3:

$$\text{deposit}(\textit{call}) = \quad \textbf{do} \left[\begin{array}{l} \text{init\_balance} \\ \text{emptyStack} \\ \text{assign\_storage\_monad}(\text{“}\textit{balances}\text{”}, [\text{sender\_monad}], \\ \text{plus\_safe}(\text{storeLookup}(\text{“}\textit{balances}\text{”}, [\text{sender\_monad}], \text{sender\_monad}))) \end{array} \right.$$

Our package would also generate a proof for the following lemma:

$$\text{sm.mono\_body}(\text{deposit}) \qquad (\texttt{deposit\_def\_mono})$$

where sm.mono_body(x) requires definition x to be monotonic w.r.t. the state monad ordering described in Sect. 3.2.

Finally, we generate a wrapper datatype for all methods of a contract and a corresponding definition for a function call over this data type. Since we allow for the specification of recursive methods, the definition of call uses the partial function package. The partial function package then provides us with a proof method to verify properties over (mutually recursive) functions using fixed-point induction (`call.raw_induct`).

Example 3.6 (Wrapper). Our package would generate the following wrapper for the specification given in Example 3.3.

$$\textbf{bank} ::= \text{Deposit\_m} \mid \text{Withdraw\_m} \qquad (\texttt{bank})$$

Moreover, the definition of call looks as follows:

$$\text{bank\_call}(m) = \begin{cases} \text{deposit}(\text{bank\_call}) & \text{for } m = \text{Deposit\_m} \\ \text{withdraw}(\text{bank\_call}) & \text{for } m = \text{Withdraw\_m} \end{cases}$$

Verification. To support a user with the verification of contract invariants, our package implements a new Isabelle command `invariant`. This command requires a user to provide the name of the contract, followed by a *name* for the invariant and two predicates formulated over the contracts private state and internal balance (one for normal executions and the other one for exceptional ones). The command then provides the user with a series of proof obligations which they need to discharge to verify the invariant.

Example 3.7 (Invariant). Assume that we want to verify that the sum of all registered deposits of our banking contract is always less or equal to the contract's internal balance:

$$\text{sum\_bal}(s, b) = b \geq \sum_{ad} (s(\text{“}balances\text{”})(ad)) \tag{1}$$

The corresponding specification in Isabelle/Solidity would then look as follows:

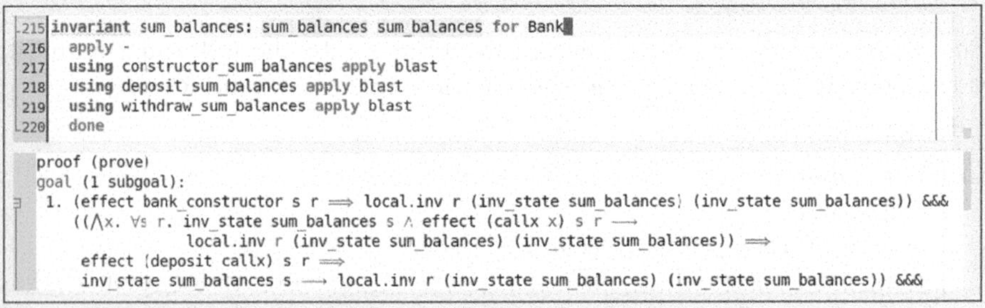

In the output window we can also see the proof obligations for the constructor and the deposit method which are then discharged by dedicated lemmas.

The invariant command requires the user to verify that the constructor establishes the invariant and that the methods preserve it. After discharging the proof obligations, our package then derives a general theorem which shows that the contract indeed preserves the invariant for all possible environments.

Example 3.8 (Proof obligations). The proof obligation for the deposit method generated from the specification provided in Example 3.7 looks as follows:

$$\text{effect}(\text{deposit}(\mathit{call}), s, s', r) \wedge \text{inv}(\text{sum\_bal}, s) \implies \text{inv}(\text{sum\_bal}, s')$$

Once the user discharges the proof obligations, our package then generates a proof for the following theorem:

Theorem 1 (bank.sum_bal).

$$\text{effect}(\text{call}(x'), s, s', r, e) \wedge \text{inv}(\text{sum\_bal}, s) \implies \text{inv}(\text{sum\_bal}, s')$$

The proof of the final theorem generated by our package uses the fixed-point induction theorem provided by the partial function package (`call.raw_induct`) and uses the lemmas provided by the user to discharge the different proof obligations required by the induction theorem.

3.6 Automation: Verification

To support a user in discharging the proof obligations generated by our package, we implemented a weakest precondition calculus [15] and corresponding verification condition generator for our monads in theory WP.thy.

The definition of the weakest precondition for our state monad is as follows:

$$\mathrm{wp}(f, P, E, s) = \begin{cases} P(r, s') & \text{if execute}(f, s) = \text{Normal}(r, s') \\ E(e, s') & \text{if execute}(f, s) = \text{Exception}(e, s') \\ \text{True} & \text{if execute}(f, s) = \text{NT} \end{cases} \qquad (\texttt{wp})$$

Note that we are only interested in partial correctness here (since smart contracts are always guaranteed to terminate). Thus, the weakest precondition of a non-terminating program is just True. We then prove corresponding lemmas for all our monads (in total ca. 100 lemmas).

We use Isabelle/Eisbach [32] to define the verification condition generator. Its purpose is to reduce the proof obligations to propositions in plain Isabelle/HOL which can then be proven using the proof methods available for Isabelle/HOL.

Example 3.9 (Verifying deposit). The proof for the deposit method (discussed in Example 3.8) using our VCG is shown below:

```
lemma deposit_sum_balances:
    fixes call:: "bank ⇒ (unit, ex, state) state_monad"
  assumes "effect (deposit call) s s' () e"
      and "inv_state sum_balances s"
    shows "inv_state sum_balances s'"
  using assms
  apply (erule_tac effect_wp)
  unfolding deposit_def inv_state_def
  by (vcg | auto simp add:1 | rule bal_msg_sender, assumption)+
```

We first unfold some definitions, and then we just combine the VCG with the standard method *auto* which is able to finish the proof.

4 Evaluation

4.1 Compliance and Unit Testing

An important problem in any formalization of a real-world (programming) language is to ensure that the formal semantics is a faithful representation of the real-world implementation, in our case, Solidity on the Etherum Blockchain. Furthermore, when developing the formal semantics further, for instance, adding new features, it is important to ensure that no unwanted changes are introduced.

We address this issue by translating, currently manually, the test cases from the reference test suite of Solidity [16] to our formalization (the test cases are implemented in file Unit_Tests.thy). Our semantics is executable for a finite address space. Thus, if we instantiate the generic address type (recall Sect. 3.1) with a finite address space (e.g., $1, \ldots, 100$), we can use Isabelle's code generator [18] to efficiently evaluate (ground) test cases. This allows us to explore the semantics using Isabelle's `value` statement as well as turn the test cases from [16] into formal lemmas.

Example 4.1 (Unit test). The following shows a simple unit test for the *assign_stack* monad.

```
lemma "is_Normal (execute (do {
        init (STR ''x'') (kdata.Value (Sint 0));
        init (STR ''y'') (kdata.Value (Sint 0));
        contract_assign_stack_monad (STR ''y'') [] (sint_monad 1);
        assert_monad (equals_monad (contract_stackLookup (STR ''x'') []) (sint_monad 0));
        assert_monad (equals_monad (contract_stackLookup (STR ''y'') []) (sint_monad 1))
      }) emptyState)"
  by (normalization, simp?)
```

All such "test case"-lemmas are proven by the `normalization` method, potentially followed by simplification. The `normalization` method uses a combination of simplification and code generation for a small, trusted subset of HOL [18]. We formalized over **50** test cases; their checking takes less than **30** seconds.

4.2 Case Studies

To evaluate the potential of the approach for verifying Solidity smart contracts we used it in three case studies.

Banking. For the first case study, we chose the banking contract shown in listing 1 since it is also verified in the deep embedding [28,30,31] and thus allows us to compare the two approaches. We specified the contract in our framework and then verified the invariant discussed in Example 3.7 (`sum_bal`).

The formalization is available in theory Token.thy and the effort of specifying and verifying the contract in Isabelle/Solidity is summarized in Fig. 1. The complete specification of the banking contract is just 11 lines of Isar code and consists of a specification of the constructor as well as the deposit and withdraw methods. It includes several basic features of Solidity, such as mappings and transfer statements. The verification of the invariant required to verify 70 lines of Isar code. One particular challenge in the verification was the fact that the invariant is a property formulated over the complete address space, which is a finite but arbitrarily large set.

Compared to previous verification attempts we can see a large reduction in effort. For example, the original verification of the very same invariant for the same contract was 3 000 lines of Isar [28,30]. Even using a weakest precondition calculus still required 700 lines of proof code [31].

Casino. For the second case study we chose the casino contract used in the previous "VerifyThis long-term verification challenge". The contract is available online[4]. The contract allows an operator to create a new game by placing a hidden secret in the form of a hash of a secret number inside the contract (using method `createGame`). A player can then place a bet (HEAD or TAIL) by transferring funds to the contract via the `placeBet` method. The operator can then invoke `decideBet` to start the game. To this end, the operator reveals the secret number to decide if HEAD (even) or TAIL (odd) wins. In the case the player wins, they get twice their bet back and the pot is deduced accordingly. In the case the player loses, their original bet is added to the pot. The operator can always increase the pot or deduce some amount (if no game is active).

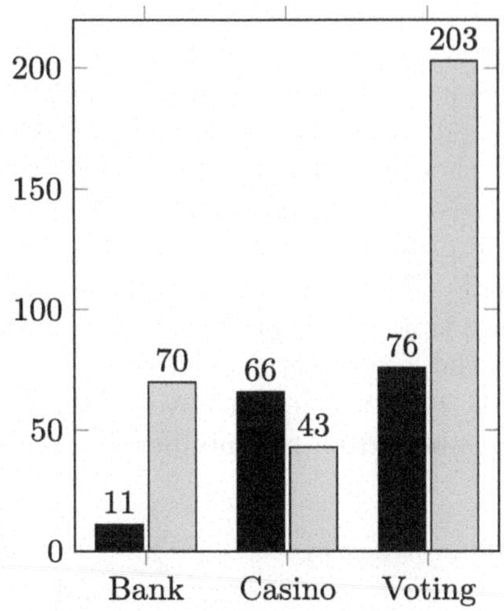

Fig. 1. Specification (black) and verification (grey) effort in terms of lines of proof code. (Color figure online)

One important property, from the player's perspective, is to ensure that the casino has always enough funds to cover the pot. Thus, for our case study, we verified the following invariant:

$$\text{pot\_balance}(s, b) = b \geq s(\text{“}pot\text{”}) \qquad (\text{pot\_balance})$$

The formalization of the casino contract is available in Casino.thy and the specification and verification effort is summarized in Fig. 1. Its specification in Isabelle/Solidity required 66 lines of code in total and consists of 7 member variables and 6 methods. It contains some advanced features of Solidity, such as enums, modifiers and hash functions.

The verification of the invariant was just 43 lines of code. The invariant is trivial for method `createGame`, since it does not modify the balance of the contract or the pot. However, all other methods modify either the balance or the value of the pot (or both), and thus require to show that the invariant is preserved.

Voting. For the third case study we chose a voting contract from the official Solidity documentation which states that "The following contract is quite complex, but showcases a lot of Solidity's features."

[4] https://verifythis.github.io/02casino/.

The contract is available online[5]. The idea is to create one contract per ballot, providing a short name for each option. Then the creator of the contract who serves as chairperson will give the right to vote to each address individually by calling the `giveRightToVote` method. The persons behind the addresses can then choose to either vote themselves or to delegate their vote to a person they trust. To vote themselves, they can invoke method `vote` by providing the number of the proposal. To delegate their vote, they can invoke method `delegate` and provide the address of the person they want to delegate to. At the end of the voting time, method `winningProposal` can be called to compute the proposal with the largest number of votes and declare it the winning proposal.

We then verified an invariant which guarantees that the number of votes is always bound by the number of eligible voters:

$$\text{sum\_votes}(s, b) = \sum_{i \leq \#s(\text{``}proposals\text{''})} (s(\text{``}proposals\text{''})[i].\text{``}voteCount\text{''}) \leq \sum_{ad \in \{ad | s(\text{``}voters\text{''})(ad).\text{``}voted\text{''}\}} (s(\text{``}voters\text{''})(ad).\text{``}weight\text{''}) \qquad (\texttt{sum\_votes})$$

The formalization is available in Voting.thy and the specification and verification effort is summarized in Fig. 1. Specification of the voting contract required 76 lines of Isabelle/Isar in total split across 5 methods. It showcases many advanced features of Solidity, such as hash maps, dynamic storage arrays, memory arrays, storage pointers and loops. Verifying the invariant required 200 lines of proof code. One particular challenge in the verification of this invariant was that the invariant was formulated over complex data structures which required advanced reasoning capabilities.

5 Related Work

The work presented in this paper is about the verification of Solidity smart contracts using Isabelle. Thus, related work can be found in two different areas: First, work related to the verification of Solidity and work related to general program verification using Isabelle. We discuss other works formalizing Solidity in Isabelle at the end of this section.

As outlined by Almakhour et al. [3] and Tolmach et al. [40], there is a growing amount of research about verification of smart contracts. Early work in this area was done by Bhargavan et al. [8] which describe an approach to map a Solidity contract to F* where it can then be verified. TinySol [6] and Featherweight Solidity [13], on the other hand, are two calculi formalizing some core features of Solidity. Ahrendt and Bubel describe SolidiKeY [2], a formalization of a subset of Solidity in the KeY tool [1] to verify data integrity for smart contracts. Hajdu and Jovanovic [19,20], provide a formalization of Solidity in terms of a simple SMT-based intermediate language and Tai et al. [35] provide an encoding of Solidity

[5] https://docs.soliditylang.org/en/v0.8.25/solidity-by-example.html#voting.

for Z3. Finally, and Jiao et al. [21,22], provide a formalization of Solidity in $\mathbb{K}$. All of these works use an axiomatic approach for defining the formal semantics of Solidity. In contrast, we use a conservative embedding into Isabelle/HOL, which ensures the consistency of our semantics "by construction".

Formalizing programming languages or specification languages in Isabelle is by no means a new technique. Over time, several languages and tools have been developed along this line, such as Isabelle/SIMPL [39], IMP [26,36] and the seL4 verification project [24]. Also, using a monadic representation of stateful computations is common. For example, the AutoCorres [9,17] (used in the seL4 verification project [24]) provides an abstraction of C code using monads, and also Clean [41], does use monads for modelling stateful computations. While work in this area provides support for many general features of program verification, they do not support specific features for Solidity.

To the best of our knowledge there are only two other formalizations of Solidity in Isabelle. Closely related is our own work on a deep embedding of Solidity in Isabelle [28]. In our deep embedding, Solidity statements are formalized as a dedicated datatype which allows to verify properties about the language itself. In general, it is also possible to use the deep embedding for the verification of concrete contracts. However, this requires quite some effort even for rather small contracts. This paper, on the other hand, provides a shallow embedding of Solidity in which statements are directly mapped to corresponding HOL definitions. This allows for better automation and can significantly reduce the effort to verify concrete contracts as shown in our first case study (recall Sect. 4.2). Thus, both approaches complement each other, and it depends on the concrete verification task which approach is better.

Ribeiro et al. [37]. adapt the Simpl language [38] to formalize a subset of Solidity in Isabelle/HOL. Compared to our work, SOLI is quite low-level and rather an intermediate language than a direct formalization of Solidity. Indeed, while it supports several features which are not provided by Solidity (Upd, Dyncom), it does not provide explicit support for Solidity-specific language features, such as different types of stores, a notion of Gas, fallback methods, external vs. internal functions, etc. Another difference to our work is that their semantics seems to be not executable and therefore difficult to evaluate. On the other hand, we considered it important to have an executable semantics that can be evaluated against the reference implementation.

6 Conclusion

With this paper, we present a verification environment for Solidity smart contracts based on Isabelle/HOL. The approach comes with a novel formalization of the Solidity storage model and a corresponding shallow embedding of Solidity expressions and statements. In addition, we implemented two new Isabelle commands to support the specification and verification of Solidity contracts in Isabelle. Finally, we formalized a weakest precondition calculus and implemented a corresponding verification condition generator to support a user in the verification. To validate our semantics, we implemented a test suite consisting of over 50 unit tests. Finally, we evaluated the approach by means of three case studies.

Our results show that the approach can be used to verify even complex contracts with reasonable effort. In addition, it significantly reduces the verification effort compared to a corresponding deep embedding. However, the case studies also revealed some limitations of the approach which lead to future work.

One limitation regards compliance of our semantics with the official Solidity documentation. Even though the unit tests provide some evidence that our semantics indeed matches the specification, we cannot guarantee full compliance. While it will never be possible to guarantee complete compliance, future work should provide further evidence in that regard. A promising approach would be to use semantic fuzzing as for example described in [29].

Another limitation concerns proof automation. Although the weakest precondition calculus and corresponding verification condition generator automate large parts of the proofs, there is still area for improvement. For example, some of our rules are rather general and split a goal into several subgoals where only some are indeed sensible for a given context. Thus, future work should focus on improving such rules by inspecting the context and apply more specialized rules for the given situation.

Acknowledgments. We thank the anonymous reviewers of SEFM 2024 for their careful reading and constructive comments to improve earlier versions of this paper. This work was supported by the Engineering and Physical Sciences Research Council [grant number EP/X027619/1].

References

1. Ahrendt, W., Beckert, B., Bubel, R., Hähnle, R., Schmitt, P.H., Ulbrich, M.: Deductive software verification–the KeY book, vol. LNCS 10001. Springer (2016). https://doi.org/10.1007/978-3-319-49812-6
2. Ahrendt, W., Bubel, R.: Functional verification of smart contracts via strong data integrity. In: Margaria, T., Steffen, B. (eds.) Leveraging Applications of Formal Methods, Verification and Validation: Applications: 9th International Symposium on Leveraging Applications of Formal Methods, ISoLA 2020, Rhodes, Greece, October 20–30, 2020, Proceedings, Part III, pp. 9–24. Springer International Publishing, Cham (2020). https://doi.org/10.1007/978-3-030-61467-6_2
3. Almakhour, M., Sliman, L., Samhat, A.E., Mellouk, A.: Verification of smart contracts: A survey. Pervasive Mob. Comput. **67**, 101227 (2020)
4. Azaria, A., Ekblaw, A., Vieira, T., Lippman, A.: MedRec: using blockchain for medical data access and permission management. In: 2016 2nd International Conference on Open and Big Data (OBD), pp. 25–30 (2016)

5. Bahrynovska, T.: History of Ethereum Security Vulnerabilities, Hacks and Their Fixes (2017)
6. Bartoletti, M., Galletta, L., Murgia, M.: A minimal core calculus for solidity contracts. In: Pérez-Solà, C., Navarro-Arribas, G., Biryukov, A., Garcia-Alfaro, J. (eds.) Data Privacy Management, Cryptocurrencies and Blockchain Technology: ESORICS 2019 International Workshops, DPM 2019 and CBT 2019, Luxembourg, September 26–27, 2019, Proceedings, pp. 233–243. Springer International Publishing, Cham (2019). https://doi.org/10.1007/978-3-030-31500-9_15
7. Berghofer, S., Wenzel, M.: Inductive datatypes in HOL — lessons learned in formal-logic engineering. In: Bertot, Y., Dowek, G., Théry, L., Hirschowitz, A., Paulin, C. (eds.) Theorem Proving in Higher Order Logics, pp. 19–36. Springer Berlin Heidelberg, Berlin, Heidelberg (1999). https://doi.org/10.1007/3-540-48256-3_3
8. Bhargavan, K., et al.: Formal verification of smart contracts: Short paper. In: Programming Languages and Analysis for Security, pp. 91–96. PLAS, ACM (2016)
9. Brecknell, M., et al.: Autocorres2. Archive of Formal Proofs (April 2024)
10. Chavez-Dreyfuss, G.: Sweden tests blockchain technology for land registry (2016)
11. CipherTrace: Cryptocurrency crime and anti-money laundering report. Tech. rep., Mastercard (2021)
12. Cock, D., Klein, G., Sewell, T.: Secure microkernels, state monads and scalable refinement. In: Mohamed, O.A., Muñoz, C., Tahar, S. (eds.) Theorem Proving in Higher Order Logics, pp. 167–182. Springer Berlin Heidelberg, Berlin, Heidelberg (2008). https://doi.org/10.1007/978-3-540-71067-7_16
13. Crafa, S., Di Pirro, M., Zucca, E.: Is solidity solid enough? In: Bracciali, A., Clark, J., Pintore, F., Rønne, P.B., Sala, M. (eds.) Financial Cryptography and Data Security: FC 2019 International Workshops, VOTING and WTSC, St. Kitts, St. Kitts and Nevis, February 18–22, 2019, Revised Selected Papers, pp. 138–153. Springer International Publishing, Cham (2020). https://doi.org/10.1007/978-3-030-43725-1_11
14. Dawson, J.: Isabelle theories for machine words. ENTCS **250**(1), 55–70 (2009), int. Workshop on Automated Verification of Critical Systems (AVoCS 2007)
15. Dijkstra, E.W.: Guarded commands, nondeterminacy and formal derivation of programs. Commun. ACM **18**(8), 453–457 (aug 1975)
16. Foundation, E.: Solidity semantic reference test suite (version 0.8.25). https://github.com/ethereum/solidity/tree/v0.8.25/test/libsolidity/semanticTests (2023)
17. Greenaway, D., Andronick, J., Klein, G.: Bridging the gap: automatic verified abstraction of C. In: Beringer, L., Felty, A. (eds.) Interactive Theorem Proving, pp. 99–115. Springer Berlin Heidelberg, Berlin, Heidelberg (2012). https://doi.org/10.1007/978-3-642-32347-8_8
18. Haftmann, F., Bulwahn, L.: Code generation from Isabelle/HOL theories (2023). http://isabelle.in.tum.de/doc/codegen.pdf
19. Hajdu, Á., Jovanović, D.: solc-verify: a modular verifier for solidity smart contracts. In: Chakraborty, S., Navas, J.A. (eds.) Verified Software. Theories, Tools, and Experiments: 11th International Conference, VSTTE 2019, New York City, NY, USA, July 13–14, 2019, Revised Selected Papers, pp. 161–179. Springer International Publishing, Cham (2020). https://doi.org/10.1007/978-3-030-41600-3_11
20. Hajdu, Á., Jovanović, D.: SMT-friendly formalization of the solidity memory model. In: ESOP 2020. LNCS, vol. 12075, pp. 224–250. Springer, Cham (2020). https://doi.org/10.1007/978-3-030-44914-8_9
21. Jiao, J., Kan, S., Lin, S.W., Sanan, D., Liu, Y., Sun, J.: Semantic understanding of smart contracts: executable operational semantics of Solidity. In: SP, pp. 1695–1712. IEEE (2020)

22. Jiao, J., Lin, S.-W., Sun, J.: A generalized formal semantic framework for smart contracts. In: Wehrheim, H., Cabot, J. (eds.) Fundamental Approaches to Software Engineering: 23rd International Conference, FASE 2020, Held as Part of the European Joint Conferences on Theory and Practice of Software, ETAPS 2020, Dublin, Ireland, April 25–30, 2020, Proceedings, pp. 75–96. Springer International Publishing, Cham (2020). https://doi.org/10.1007/978-3-030-45234-6_4
23. Kelly, J.: Banks adopting blockchain 'dramatically faster' than expected: IBM (2016)
24. Klein, G., et al.: seL4: formal verification of an operating-system kernel. Commun. ACM **53**(6), 107–115 (2010)
25. Krauss, A.: Recursive definitions of monadic functions. ENTCS **43**, 1–13 (2010)
26. Lammich, P., Wimmer, S.: IMP2 – simple program verification in Isabelle/HOL. Archive of Formal Proofs (2019)
27. Llama, D.: TVL breakdown by smart contract language (2024). https://defillama.com/languages
28. Marmsoler, D., Brucker, A.D.: A denotational semantics of Solidity in Isabelle/HOL. In: Calinescu, R., Pasareanu, C. (eds.) SEFM. LNCS 13085, Springer (2021). https://doi.org/10.1007/978-3-030-92124-8_23
29. Marmsoler, D., Brucker, A.D.: Conformance testing of formal semantics using grammar-based fuzzing. In: Kovacs, L., Meinke, K. (eds.) Tests And Proofs. LNCS 13361, Springer-Verlag (2022)
30. Marmsoler, D., Brucker, A.D.: Isabelle/Solidity: a deep embedding of solidity in Isabelle/HOL. Archive of Formal Proofs (July 2022)
31. Marmsoler, D., Thornton, B.: SSCalc: a calculus for solidity smart contracts. In: Ferreira, C., Willemse, T.A.C. (eds.) Software Engineering and Formal Methods, pp. 184–204. Springer, Cham (2023)
32. Matichuk, D., Murray, T., Wenzel, M.: Eisbach: a proof method language for isabelle. J. Autom. Reason. **56**, 261–282 (2016)
33. Nakamoto, S.: Bitcoin: A Peer-to-Peer Electronic Cash System (2008)
34. BBC News: Hackers steal $600m in major cryptocurrency heist (2021)
35. Nguyen, T.D., Pham, L.H., Sun, J., Le, Q.L.: An idealist's approach for smart contract correctness. In: Li, Y., Tahar, S. (eds.) Formal Methods and Software Engineering. pp. 11–28. Springer (2023). https://doi.org/10.1007/978-981-99-7584-6_2
36. Nipkow, T.: Winskel is (almost) right: Towards a mechanized semantics textbook. Formal Aspects Comput. **10**(2), 171–186 (1998)
37. Ribeiro, M., Adão, P., Mateus, P.: Formal verification of ethereum smart contracts using Isabelle/HOL. In: Nigam, V., Ban Kirigin, T., Talcott, C., Guttman, J., Kuznetsov, S., Thau Loo, B., Okada, M. (eds.) Logic, Language, and Security. LNCS, vol. 12300, pp. 71–97. Springer, Cham (2020). https://doi.org/10.1007/978-3-030-62077-6_7
38. Schirmer, N.: Verification of Sequential Imperative Programs in Isabelle/HOL. Ph.D. thesis, Technische Universität München (2006)
39. Schirmer, N.: A sequential imperative programming language syntax, semantics, hoare logics and verification environment. Archive of Formal Proofs (Feb 2008)
40. Tolmach, P., Li, Y., Lin, S.W., Liu, Y., Li, Z.: A survey of smart contract formal specification and verification. ACM Comput. Surv. **54**(7) (2021)
41. Tuong, F., Wolff, B.: Clean – an abstract imperative programming language and its theory. Archive of Formal Proofs (Oct 2019)

42. Wadler, P.: Monads for functional programming. In: Broy, M. (ed.) Program Design Calculi, pp. 233–264. Springer (1993). https://doi.org/10.1007/978-3-662-02880-3_8
43. Wenzel, M.: The Isabelle/Isar implementation (2013)
44. Winskel, G.: The formal semantics of programming languages: an introduction. MIT press (1993)
45. YCharts.com: Ethereum transactions per day (2024)
46. Yurcan, B.: How blockchain fits into the future of digital identity (2016)

Deductive Verification of SYCL in VerCors

Ellen Wittingen, Marieke Huisman, and Ömer Şakar(✉)

University of Twente, Enschede, The Netherlands
ellenwittingen@protonmail.com, {m.huisman,o.f.o.sakar}@utwente.nl

Abstract. SYCL is a C++ programming model for the development of heterogeneous programs. It uses the concept of kernels, where multiple instances of a computation are executed concurrently on a computing unit. This concurrency entails that the set of possible program behaviours can be of considerable size, which makes these programs error-prone. Formal verification could be used to ensure the correctness of all these possible program behaviours. However, there exist no formal verification tools for SYCL.

In this paper, SYCL support is added to VerCors, a formal verification tool for concurrent software, by encoding SYCL constructs into VerCors' internal language COL. To the extent of our knowledge, this is the first deductive verification tool for SYCL. We show how SYCL's basic- and ND-range kernels are encoded, along with the encoding and challenges related to scheduling kernels and the execution order of those kernels. In addition, we discuss how SYCL's buffers and data accessors are encoded, focusing on the challenges related to it, in particular enabling memory transfer between host and device. The usability of the added SYCL support and how it was evaluated are discussed as well.

Keywords: VerCors · SYCL · Formal verification · Heterogeneous computing

1 Introduction

SYCL [18] is a C++ programming model for developing heterogeneous programs, where code is executed on multiple, possibly different, computing units. It allows such programs to be declared on a high level and code for all computing units to be declared inside the main body of a program, instead of separately. This has a smaller learning curve for programmers new to heterogeneous programming than, for example, OpenCL [17]. Moreover, it supports computing units from multiple vendors, unlike, for instance, CUDA [24]. It uses the concept of kernels, where multiple instances of a computation are executed in parallel on a computing unit. The number of possible program behaviours increases exponentially with the size of the parallel parts of a program and the number of threads that execute it [6]. This means that the concurrency of SYCL's kernels results

This work is supported by NWO TTW grant 17249 for the ChEOPS project.

A. Madeira and A. Knapp (Eds.): SEFM 2024, LNCS 15280, pp. 182–199, 2025.
https://doi.org/10.1007/978-3-031-77382-2_11

in many possible program behaviours. This has the problem that bugs which only occur in a few possible program behaviours are easily overlooked. To solve this, formal verification can be used to reason about the correctness of all possible behaviours of a program. There exist various formal verification tools for heterogeneous programs, e.g. GPUVerify [5], PUG [22], CIVL [32], the tool by Xing et al. [30], and VerCors [6]. However, none of these verify SYCL programs.

In this paper, we present the deductive verification of SYCL programs in VerCors. To the extent of our knowledge, this is the first deductive verification tool for SYCL. VerCors is a formal verification tool targeted at concurrent programs in various languages and frameworks, including subsets of the heterogeneous computing frameworks OpenCL, CUDA, and OpenMP. It aims to be language-independent, such that support for new languages can be added without redesigning the entire toolset. For every supported language, it has an encoding into a program in its internal language COL, which is then verified against specifications provided by the user.

To enable SYCL developers to formally verify their programs, support was added for SYCL to VerCors, by encoding several SYCL constructs into COL, keeping to SYCL's execution semantics as close as possible.
Concretely, the contributions of this paper are as follows:

- The encodings and the encountered challenges of the following SYCL constructs and behaviours are explained and illustrated with examples:
  - Basic- and ND-range kernel executions and the ability to explicitly wait on their termination (Sect. 3).
  - The construction and destruction of buffers (Sect. 4).
  - The construction of data accessors and how they interact with elements of their buffers (Sect. 5).
  - The execution ordering of kernels (Sect. 6).
- An evaluation of the implementation and usability of the supported subset of SYCL (Sect. 7).

The support for SYCL partially builds on top of the current support for OpenCL and CUDA. The common encoding of kernels between SYCL, OpenCL and CUDA was used as a basis on top of which SYCL-specific behaviour is encoded. The challenge was mainly in the encoding of new concepts, namely 1) the scheduling of (SYCL) kernels, where SYCL kernels can also be executed out of order and 2) memory transfer between the host and device through SYCL's buffers and data accessors, resulting in the list of contributions above.

These contributions only cover the most relevant SYCL constructs and behaviours. For more details on the entire subset of supported SYCL constructs and their encodings, we refer to the related Master's thesis [29].

2 Background

2.1 VerCors

Verification Process. VerCors [6] uses separation logic to prove partial correctness of concurrent programs. Figure 1 shows an overview of how VerCors achieves

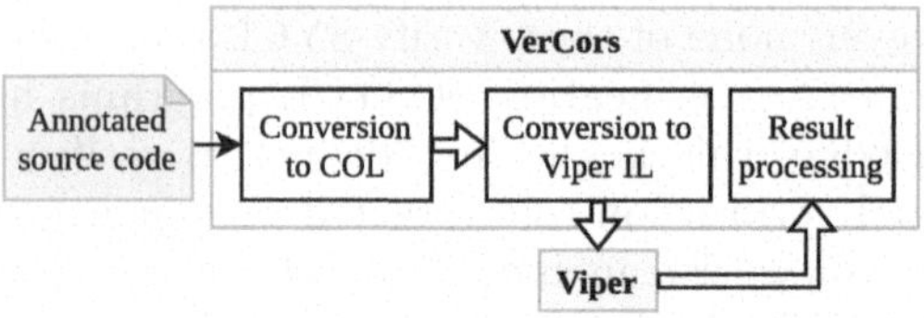

Fig. 1. Overview of Vercors verification process.

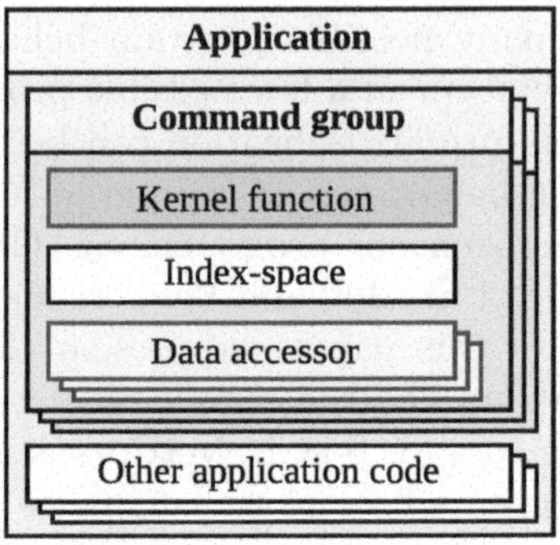

Fig. 2. Overview of SYCL's application structure.

this. It takes source code annotated with specifications and encodes this into its internal language COL, a Java-like language with specific constructs to express concurrency. A running example of such an encoding is the method `someMethod` in Listing 3 (covered in detail in Sect. 3). It is encoded into a similarly named COL method on lines 18–25 in Listing 4. This COL encoding is then converted in several steps to Viper's [23] intermediate verification language. VerCors then passes this off to Viper, which verifies it using Z3 [14]. The results from Viper's verification are processed in VerCors. If the verification fails, VerCors shows an error message along with the location of the error in the original SYCL program.

Specifications. In VerCors, specifications are written in an annotation language similar to JML [21]. In this annotation language, `requires expr` represents a pre-condition and `ensures expr` represents a post-condition. Inside these specifications, `(\forall decls; cond; expr)` denotes that `expr` must hold for all possible values for the variables declared in `decls` that meet the conditions described in `cond`. Moreover, statements regarding permission-based separation logic (PBSL) [2,9], which allows users to reason about what data on the heap is accessible when and by which threads, are also included in this specification language. By default, it is assumed that a thread does not access any heap data. However, access to an element `x` can be modelled using the notation `Perm(x, p)`, where `p` represents the kind of permission. The permissions relevant to this paper are `read` and `write`, which represent, respectively, read-only and read-write permission. Internally, permissions are fractions, where `write` represents 1 and `read` a fraction $[0, 1)$. An example of a specification in VerCors can be seen on line 1 in Listing 3, where a thread requires read-write permission to some global variable `x` to execute `someMethod`.

Listing 3: SYCL program where a basic kernel is submitted to a queue, and then, after some arbitrary host code, the submitted kernel's termination is awaited.

```
1  //@ requires Perm(x, write);
2  void someMethod(sycl::queue queueObject) {
3    sycl::event ev = queueObject.submit(
4      [&](sycl::handler& commandGroupHandler){
5        commandGroupHandler.parallel_for(sycl::range<2>(6,4),
6          //@ requires kernel pre-conditions;
7          //@ ensures kernel post-conditions;
8          [=] (sycl::item<2> it){ kernel body });
9      });
10   arbitrary host code
11   ev.wait();
12 }
```

2.2 SYCL

Programming Model. SYCL [18] is a C++ programming model that enables different types of computing units to be used in tandem in a single application, where a computing unit is a physical component in a system that can perform calculations. Examples of computing units are CPUs, GPUs, and FPGAs [25,27,31]. To enable this, a SYCL application consists of *host code* and *kernels*. Host code consists of code that is executed on the main computing unit (the *host*) of the system. Code inside kernels can be executed many times in parallel on a computing unit of choice, concurrently with host code.

Kernels. There are two main types of SYCL kernels: *basic kernels* and *ND-range (N-dimensional range) kernels*. These kernels are invoked with a specific index-space, where for every point an instance of the kernel is executed by a *work-item*. Work-items are organized based on the type of kernel and the index-space.

Both basic and ND-range kernels have a one-, two-, or three-dimensional index-space. In addition to this, the work-items of an *ND-range kernel* are organised into *work-groups*. A work-group is a collection of work-items that can synchronize using barriers.

In SYCL, a kernel and its properties, such as its index-space and data accessors (discussed in Sect. 5), are declared inside a *command group*, as illustrated in the overview of SYCL's application structure in Fig. 2. An example of a command group can be seen on lines 4–9 in Listing 3, where an invocation of the `parallel_for` method inside the command group is used to declare the kernel's index-space and body. The index-space is represented by a `range` object for a basic kernel or an `nd_range` object for an ND-range kernel. The index-space described on line 5 in Listing 3 states that the work-items are organized in two dimensions, 6 by 4 work-items, and those will execute the body of the basic kernel declared inside the lambda method on line 8.

3 Encoding of SYCL's Kernels

Listing 3 shows a basic SYCL kernel submission to a queue, the waiting for the termination of that kernel, and arbitrary host code in between. Listing 4 shows the COL encoding of this program. The encoding of ND-range kernels is similar to basic kernels, unless indicated otherwise.

Listing 4: The encoding of the SYCL program in Listing 3. *Constructs with the same highlighting as in Listing 3 are the encoding of that specific construct. α represents the event-class, β the kernel-runner, γ the kernel-parblock, and ϵ the host code.* `context` *expr; is shorthand for* `requires` *expr;* `ensures` *expr;*.

```
α       class SYCL_EVENT_CLASS {
α         int dim0;  int dim1;
α
α β       context Perm(this.dim0, read) ** this.dim0 >= 0;
α β       context Perm(this.dim1, read) ** this.dim1 >= 0;
α β       requires (\forall* int ID_0, int ID_1; 0 <= ID_0 && 0 <= ID_1 &&
α β       ↪ ID_0 < this.dim0 && ID_1 < this.dim1 ; kernel pre-conditions );
α β       ensures (\forall* int ID_0, int ID_1; 0 <= ID_0 && 0 <= ID_1 &&
α β       ↪ ID_0 < this.dim0 && ID_1 < this.dim1 ; kernel post-conditions );
α β       run {
α β γ       par SYCL_BASIC_KERNEL(
α β γ         int ID_0 = 0 .. this.dim0 ,  int ID_1 = 0 .. this.dim1
α β γ       ) context Perm(this.dim0, read) ** this.dim0 >= 0;
α β γ         context Perm(this.dim1, read) ** this.dim1 >= 0;
α β γ         requires kernel pre-conditions ;
α β γ         ensures kernel post-conditions ;  {  kernel body  } } }

ϵ       requires Perm(x, write);
ϵ       void someMethod(ref queueObject) {
ϵ         SYCL_EVENT_CLASS sycl_event_ref;
ϵ         sycl_event_ref = new SYCL_EVENT_CLASS(6,4);
ϵ         fork sycl_event_ref;
ϵ         arbitrary host code
ϵ         join sycl_event_ref;
ϵ       }
```

3.1 Kernel Submissions

SYCL's Behaviour. A SYCL kernel is *submitted to a queue* in the host code. The queue then schedules the execution of the kernel, whilst the host continues with executing the statements that come after the kernel submission. Currently, only one of SYCL's kernel submission patterns is supported. This pattern is used in various SYCL teaching materials [10–12, 15], and appears to be the simplest way to declare a kernel. However, adding support for the other submission patterns would not be difficult, as the COL encoding could be the same since they contain the same key elements, albeit using different syntax. In the supported pattern, the `submit` method of the `queue` class is invoked with a command group as argument. An example of a kernel submission can be seen on lines 3–9 in Listing 3. To enable users to reason about SYCL kernels in VerCors, work-item-level specifications, referred to as *user-kernel-specifications*, can be added as a contract to the lambda expression in which a kernel's body is declared, as can be seen on lines 6–7 in Listing 3.

Encoding. For each submission of a kernel, a new COL class, referred to as the *event-class*, is created in the encoding, as can be seen on lines 1–16 in Listing 4. On lines 20–21 an instance of that class is created in the encoding of the host code by calling its constructor[1] with the dimension sizes of the kernel's index-space as arguments. The constructor then sets the fields of the *event-class*, shown on line 2, to those dimension sizes. This allows the sizes of the dimensions, which do not have to be a constant, to be used inside the *event-class*. A run-method, referred to as the *kernel-runner*, is added to the *event-class*, which can be seen on lines 4–16. This *kernel-runner* is executed in parallel with the *host code* when the instance of the *event-class* is forked on line 22. This models the behaviour that the host continues executing when a kernel is submitted to a queue.

The kernel's body is encoded similarly to how CUDA kernel declarations are encoded into COL [26]: they are encoded as a single nested parblock for basic kernels, or a double nested parblock for ND-range kernels. Parblocks are denoted by `par NAME(work_items) specs { body }`, where `body` is executed in parallel by the work-items declared in `work_items`. The work-item-level specifications denoted by `specs` are a pre-/post style contract which should hold right before and after the execution of `body` respectively.

The encoding of the parallel execution of the kernel body from Listing 3 can be seen on lines 11–16 in Listing 4, where the kernel body is put inside a parblock in the *kernel-runner* on line 16, referred to as the *kernel-parblock*, which has `dim0` by `dim1` work-items with each work-item being assigned identifiers `ID_0` and `ID_1` on line 12.

To enable the kernel body in the *kernel-parblock* to use the *event-class*'s dimension fields, specifications are added to the contracts of the *kernel-runner* and *kernel-parblock*, which check for read access to those fields and that they are not negative. The *user-kernel-specifications* are inserted into those contracts as well. The contract of the *kernel-parblock* is on the same work-item-level as the *user-kernel-specifications*, so the *user-kernel-specifications* are simply inserted, as can be seen on lines 15–16 in Listing 4. In the *kernel-runner*'s contract, the *user-kernel-specifications* are quantified over a range with the same number of work-items as the kernel's index-space, as can be seen on lines 6–9. Furthermore, all the permissions a *kernel-runner* is supposed to have are already included in its contract by the encoding (such as permissions to data accessors, described in Sect. 5), so the *user-kernel-specifications* cannot be blindly inserted into its contract. If they were, permissions to an element `x` could end up being declared twice, which makes the encoding unsound. Therefore, all statements regarding permissions in the user-kernel-specifications are filtered out, such that they are not added to the kernel-runner's contract.

[1] Definition has been omitted from this paper for brevity.

Listing 5: Construction and destruction of a two-dimensional buffer in SYCL.

```
1 {
2   sycl::buffer<T,2> buff =
3          ↪ sycl::buffer(hostData, sycl::range<2>(dim0, dim1));
4   ...
5 } // the buffer is destroyed here
```

3.2 Explicitly Waiting on a Kernel's Termination

Calling `wait()` on an `event` returned by the submission of a kernel forces the host to wait for that kernel to terminate. For instance, on line 11 in Listing 3 the host waits on the kernel submitted on lines 3–9. In the encoding, the instance of the *event-class* belonging to the kernel is joined, as shown on line 24 in Listing 4, which assumes the *kernel-runner*'s post-conditions to hold at that point.

4 Encoding of SYCL's Buffers

4.1 Buffer Constructions

A SYCL buffer can be seen as a copy of a piece of data on the host. It allows this data to be accessed in kernels through data accessors (see Sect. 5). Buffers are typically declared in the host code, and can be constructed with a pointer to data, called the `hostData`, together with a one-, two-, or three-dimensional `range` object, which describes how the buffer's copy will appear to be structured to the user. An example of such a buffer construction can be seen on lines 2–3 in Listing 5, where a buffer is constructed with `hostData` as its data and a `dim0` by `dim1` two-dimensional structure. The encoding of creating a copy of the `hostData` when a buffer is constructed is shown on lines 1–2 in Listing 6. As can be seen, a new COL array is created, referred to as a *buffer-array*, and the part of `hostData` within the provided range is copied to that array using the generated method `copy_hostdata_to_buffer` (See Footnote 1). It was decided to always generate a one-dimensional *buffer-array* as specifications about one-dimensional arrays are easier to verify than specifications about multi-dimensional arrays.

The SYCL specification [18] (page 128) states that when a buffer is constructed with `hostData`, the buffer acquires exclusive access to `hostData`, such that `hostData`'s contents are unspecified during the buffer's lifetime. However, the extent of this exclusive access is not stated, so the assumption was made that only the part within the bounds of the buffer's range parameter will be unspecified. The buffer's exclusive access to that part of `hostData` is encoded by the generated predicate `exclusive_hostdata_access` (see Footnote 1) on line 3. This predicate is *folded*, i.e. the contents of the predicate is exchanged for an instance of the predicate. Folding the predicate has the effect that it hides read-write permission to the part of `hostData` within the buffer's range from the host. This means that from that point onwards, it will be verified that the host does not access it. This encoding does have as a result that read-write permission to `hostData` is required to construct a buffer, even if the buffer remains unused.

Listing 6: The encoding of the buffer construction and destruction in Listing 5. *Constructs with the same highlighting as a construct in Listing 5 are the encoding of that specific construct.*

```
1 T[] buff;
2 buff = copy_hostdata_to_buffer(hostData,dim0 * dim1);
3 fold exclusive_hostdata_access(hostData,dim0 * dim1);
4 ...
5 waiting on kernel terminations
6 copy_buffer_to_hostdata(hostData, buff);
7 unfold exclusive_hostdata_access(hostData,dim0 * dim1);
```

If the buffer does later turn out to claim the entirety of its `hostData`, the predicate should cover the entire size of the `hostData` pointer instead.

4.2 Buffer Destructions

When a buffer variable goes out of scope, such as on line 5 in Listing 5, it is destroyed. When it is destroyed, the host first waits for the termination of all submitted kernels for which it is required that the buffer's contents are copied back to the host. The assumption was made that this covers all kernels with *read-write* access to the buffer, as those can alter the state of the buffer, and thus the state of the `hostData` on the host. Then, if necessary, the contents of the buffer are copied to the `hostData` to make sure its values match the buffer's latest contents. After the buffer's destruction, the entire contents of `hostData` can be used again without undefined behaviour. On lines 5–7 in Listing 6 the encoding of the buffer destruction in Listing 5 is shown. First, all running kernels with *read-write* access to the buffer are explicitly waited upon, using the same encoding as for invocations of the `event::wait()` method (described in Sect. 3.2). After that, the buffer's contents are copied to `hostData` using the generated method `copy_buffer_to_hostdata` (See Footnote 1). This copy is always executed, to avoid having to evaluate whether it is necessary. Last of all, the predicate `exclusive_hostdata_access` is unfolded to make read-write permission to access `hostData` available to the host again.

5 Encoding of SYCL's Data Accessors

In this section, SYCL's data accessors and its encoding are explained, which together with SYCL's buffers define SYCL's memory transfer between host and device. The encoding of SYCL's buffers and data accessors is new in VerCors.

Listing 7: Construction of a two-dimensional data accessor in SYCL.

```
void someMethod(sycl::queue q, sycl::buffer<T,2> buff) {
  q.submit([&](sycl::handler& cgh) {
    sycl::accessor<T,2> acc = sycl::accessor(buff,cgh,mode);
    cgh.parallel_for(...); });
}
```

5.1 Data Accessor Constructions

SYCL's Behaviour. Data accessors allow memory objects on the host, such as buffers, to be accessed inside kernels. A data accessor can be constructed inside a command group with a buffer object, the command group's handler object and an access mode. The access mode determines how the accessor's buffer can be accessed. The access modes chosen to be supported in VerCors are *read-only* and *read-write*, as they could directly be translated to COL permissions. An example of a data accessor construction can be found on line 3 in Listing 7, where a data accessor is constructed with `mode` access to the two-dimensional buffer `buff`.

Some of the unsupported access modes are used in SYCL teaching materials [10,12,15]. However, in those materials they could be replaced by supported ones whilst maintaining a similar, but slightly less efficient behaviour. The unsupported access mode *no-init-read-write* is similar to the *read-write* access mode, except that the previous contents of the buffer are discarded, so it is possible to add support for it. Adding support for SYCL *write-only* and *no-init-write-only* access modes would be more complicated, as there is no direct way to express write permission without read permission in PBSL.

Encoding. The encoding of the data accessor construction in Listing 7 is shown in Listing 8. Because a data accessor allows a buffer to be used inside the kernel's body, the encoding of that buffer needs to be accessible inside the encoding of the kernel's body, i.e. the body of the *kernel-parblock*. Furthermore, changes made to the buffer in the encoding of the kernel's body need to be accessible to the encoding of the host code, where the encoding of the buffer resides. These challenging requirements could only be satisfied by adding a field to the *event-class* with the same contents as the buffer's *buffer-array*, referred to as the *buffer-field*. Furthermore, to share the size of each dimension of the data accessor's buffer, a field is added for each dimension, referred to as *buffer-range-fields*. These two kinds of fields can be seen on line 2 in Listing 8. To pass the contents of the *buffer-array* and its dimension sizes from the *host code* to these fields, the constructor of the *event-class* is extended to take them as parameters and to use them to set those fields.

To access these fields in the body of the *kernel-parblock*, specifications are added to the contracts of the *kernel-runner* and the *kernel-parblock*, as can be seen on lines 4–8 and 11 in Listing 8. They state that all the fields are read-only. Furthermore, to verify that subscripts to the data accessor are within the *buffer-field*'s bounds, the length of the *buffer-field* is specified to be equal to the length of the *buffer-array*, by stating it is the product of all the *buffer-range-fields*. On line 8, the body of the *kernel-runner* is additionally given read-write permission to all elements of the *buffer-field* if the accessor's access mode is *read-write*, or read-only permission if the accessor's access mode is *read-only*. To let the user decide what work-items have access to what parts of the buffer, this last specification is not added to the *kernel-parblock*. These described specifications are positioned before the encoding of the *user-kernel-specifications*, such that users have enough permission to use the data accessors in their kernel specifications.

Listing 8: Additions to the *event-class* for the encoding of the data accessor construction in Listing 7. *The notation* `\array(name, size)` *denotes that array* `name` *is not null and has size* `size`. *For the ternary operator inside the bordered frame only the result is inserted. Constructs with the same highlighting as in Listing 7 are the encoding of that specific construct. The kernel dimension fields and related specifications have been omitted.*

```
1  class SYCL_EVENT_CLASS {
2    T[] acc; int acc_dim0; int acc_dim1;
3
4    context Perm(this.acc_dim0, read);
5    context Perm(this.acc_dim1, read);
6    context Perm(this.acc, read);
7    context \array(this.acc, this.acc_dim0 * this.acc_dim1);
8    context Perm(this.acc[*],
       ↪ [ mode == read_write ? write : read ] );
9    run {
10     par SYCL_BASIC_KERNEL(dimensions in index-space)
11     same as lines 4-7
12     { ... }
13   } }
```

Data Accessors with Same Buffer. The possibility in SYCL to declare multiple data accessors for the same buffer object for the same kernel added a challenge to the encoding. It affects the kernel's access to a buffer: it will equal the most permissive access mode of the data accessors for that buffer [18] (page 26–27). To give an example, a kernel with a *read-write* and a *read-only* data accessor to the same buffer will be given *read-write* access to that buffer. Another challenge was that changes written to one data accessor must be present in all other data accessors for that buffer as well. In the encoding this is solved by only creating a single *buffer-field* and a single set of *buffer-range-fields* for each buffer the kernel has one or more data accessors for. All data accessor usages for a buffer are encoded to use those fields, and the permission given in the contract of the *kernel-runner* to the elements of the *buffer-field* is the permission that corresponds with the combined access mode. One downside to this approach is that if a kernel contains a *read-write* and a *read-only* data accessor for the same buffer, the user is allowed to write to the *read-only* data accessor in the kernel body, because the kernel body has read-write access to the *buffer-field* in the encoding due to the access mode combination. However, the state of the buffer is not affected by which data accessor is used, so the encoding is sound.

Listing 9: Subscripting a two-dimensional data accessor in a kernel in SYCL.

```
//@ context idx0 < acc.get_range().get(0);
//@ context idx1 < acc.get_range().get(1);
//@ context Perm(acc[idx0][idx1], write);
[=] (sycl::item<2> it) { acc[idx0][idx1] = value; }
```

5.2 Interacting with Elements of a Data Accessors' Buffer

The elements of an accessor's buffer can be accessed in kernels and their contracts in the same way as C++ arrays are accessed: with subscripts on the data accessor object, where the number of required subscripts equals the number of dimensions of the data accessor's buffer. To give an example, the data accessor `acc`, declared on line 3 in Listing 7, which provides access to a two-dimensional buffer, would be accessed with two subscripts, as can be seen on line 4 in Listing 9. These data accessor subscripts are encoded as a one-dimensional subscript on the data accessor's *buffer-field*, by means of linearization with the buffer's dimension sizes.

Required User Specifications. To interact with a data accessor, the user needs to specify in the contract of the kernel what elements of the buffer each work-item is allowed to access, as that contract is merged with the contract of the *kernel-parblock*. An example of such a specification can be seen on line 3 in Listing 9. VerCors checks whether subscripts on an array are within the array's bounds. However, VerCors can often not infer this by itself for data accessors due to the complexity of the encoding. In such cases, the user needs to specify in the kernel's contract that the subscripts are within the bounds of the dimensions they index. To give an example, in Listing 9 the user needs to specify on lines 1–2 that the subscripts are smaller than the bounds of the data accessor.

Updating the Buffer. In SYCL, when a user updates an element of a buffer through a data accessor, the data accessor writes this update to the buffer. In the encoding, all updates are written to the data accessor's *buffer-field* instead. This means that changes made to the *buffer-field* need to be manually copied to the *buffer-array* in the *host code*. This needs to happen before another kernel attempts to read the buffer, otherwise it might read old values. This problem was solved by, for all data accessors with *read-write* access, assigning a data accessor's *buffer-field* to the *buffer-array* in the *host code* right after the kernel terminates, i.e. right after it is joined. At that point in time no further updates will be made to the *buffer-field*, and other kernels cannot access the buffer yet, as they need to wait till the kernel has finished terminating.

6 Encoding of SYCL's Kernel Execution Order

As mentioned in Sect. 3.1, the queue schedules the execution of submitted kernels. In the encoding, the execution order is determined by the rules below, where data accessors for the same buffer are considered equivalent. The support for scheduling kernels is new in VerCors.

When a new kernel is submitted and it is...

- ... **independent** from the currently running kernels: it has either an independent set of data accessors or an intersection, where all data accessors in the intersection provide *read-only* access, it is immediately started.

- ... **dependent** on one or more of the currently running kernels: it has an intersection of data accessors, where one or more data accessors in the intersection provide *read-write* access, then the host halts to wait for all the running kernels with those data accessors to terminate (by joining their *event-classes*, as described in Sect. 3.2) before starting the new kernel.

Out-of-Order Scheduling. The SYCL specification states that kernels are executed *in an **out-of-order** fashion based on dependency information*, but that kernels dependent of each other are executed in order of submission to the queue [18] (page 22–23). This implies that submitted kernels that are independent of each other could be re-ordered at run-time.

To give an example of a possible out-of-order execution, suppose we have three kernels CG_{ind}, CG_a and CG_b where CG_{ind} is independent of CG_a and CG_b and suppose CG_a and CG_b are already submitted to the queue in that order. If CG_{ind} is submitted, it might be that CG_b is waiting for CG_a if CG_b depends on CG_a. In that case, CG_{ind} can be scheduled before CG_b due to the independences of the kernels.

In the encoding the *host code* halts when a submitted kernel CG_w needs to wait, so any kernel submissions declared after CG_w will not be submitted till it starts executing. This means that kernels are always executed *in-order* in the encoding. Notice that this is a sound encoding, because SYCL can only reorder kernels independent of each other, and their independence means that their results are the same regardless of their execution order.

Halting Host Code. In SYCL, host code does not halt when a submitted kernel CG_k is waiting on other kernels to terminate before executing, which allows host code *hc* declared directly after a submission of a waiting kernel to be executed before CG_k is started. This behaviour is different in the encoding, where, as mentioned previously, host code halts at the point where CG_k is scheduling till CG_k can start executing.

The only heap-data that kernels and host code share are buffers, which host code can neither read nor write to. A kernel could be submitted in *hc*, which uses a buffer that CG_k uses as well. However, that kernel is either independent of CG_k (they both require *read-only* access), in which case the ordering does not influence the results (see the previous paragraph), or dependent on CG_k, in which case it has to wait on CG_k to execute and terminate, in both SYCL and the encoding. The host code could also interact with a destroyed buffer's `hostData`. However, if CG_k requires *read-write* access to it, the destruction of the buffer has to wait on CG_k to execute and terminate in the encoding as well as in SYCL. If CG_k requires *read-only* access to it, *hc* writing to it does not affect CG_k, because CG_k will read from the buffer's version of `hostData`. From this, we conclude that the encoding remains sound, since the difference between the encoding and the SYCL specification does not influence the program's results.

Listing 10: Test program that reads from a part of `a` that is currently claimed by `aBuffer`. `\pointer(a, 10, write)` *denotes that pointer* `a` *is not null, and that* `a` *to* `a+9` *are valid locations with read-write permission to them.*

```
#include <sycl/sycl.hpp>
//@ requires \pointer(a, 10, write);
void test(bool* a) {
  sycl::buffer<bool, 1> aBuffer =
                        ↪ sycl::buffer(a, sycl::range<1>(10));
  bool x = a[5]; // Not allowed
}
```

7 Evaluation

7.1 Correctness of the Implementation

The implementation of the encoding of SYCL into COL was purely additive: code was added to VerCors' source code [28] that performs the encoding of SYCL, but the already existing implementations of encodings of other languages and frameworks were not altered, nor how the resulting encodings are verified.

The encoding of SYCL into COL was developed in such a way that if the COL program is proven correct, then the SYCL program is proven correct. This was not formally proven. The implementation of the encoding was tested on a large number of examples: examples that are expected to verify and examples that are expected to fail. VerCors already had a framework for this, which takes programs and their expected results, which can be a successful verification or a certain error being thrown and presented back to the user in the original source language. An example of an integration test is the test program in Listing 10, of which the verification is expected to fail because the program reads a part of data claimed by a buffer, which returns undefined results (see Subsect. 4.1). For every supported SYCL concept, it was tested whether the implementation matches the described encoding. Furthermore, integration tests were added to test the occurrence of specific errors in specific cases. The number of tests per SYCL construct can be seen in Table 1.

Table 1. Number of tests per construct.

Construct	Tests
Kernels	15
Item methods[a]	12
Buffers	16
Data accessors	23
Local accessors[a]	12

[a]Not covered in this paper.

Table 2. Profiling of the usability programs.

Phase	Time (s) for Program 1	Time (s) for Program 2
Parsing	80,1	129,7
Name Resolution	1,1	1,7
Transformation	13,5	21,3
Verification	39,8	154,9
Total	144,4	314,7

All these tests pass and were run using the ScalaTest [4] test runner in IntelliJ [16]. Averaged over 5 runs, executing all tests takes 9 min and 30 s in total.[2] This paper is accompanied with an artifact to run and evaluate the SYCL examples, which can be found in [33].

7.2 Usability of the Supported Subset of SYCL

To show that the supported subset of SYCL is extensive enough to verify statements about SYCL programs performing full tasks, two annotated, real-life SYCL programs were created, which can be successfully verified by VerCors[3].

Program 1 (Listing 13) has a method `vector_add` which performs vector addition: adding the elements of arrays `a` and `b` of size `n` and storing the results in array `c`. Vector addition was chosen because most SYCL teaching materials [10,12,15] use vector addition as an example program. This means that SYCL developers, most likely, know how vector addition is performed, and can now see how they could verify such a SYCL program.

Program 2 is a more complex, real-life SYCL program. It has been developed as a typical program that SYCL developers would write. In addition, it showcases all the different supported SYCL features. The program contains a method which applies a function to each element of a two-dimensional matrix and then transposes the results. For the interested reader, the program is listed in Appendix A.2 in the related Master's thesis [29].

VerCors occasionally fails to establish the pre-conditions of one of the kernels in the method, even though they are sound. Normally, non-deterministic results should be impossible for formal verifiers. However, for quantified expressions without triggers, which indicate when a quantification should be instantiated, Z3 uses heuristics and randomisation to instantiate them. Triggers are not included in the encoding of SYCL programs, because they need to be inserted in such a way that quantifications are instantiated in all necessary cases, which can be complicated to determine. Therefore, it is most likely that the incidental verification failures are caused by a failure to instantiate one of the triggerless quantified expressions in the encoding.

Profiling. The profiling of the two programs for the different phases in VerCors is shown in Table 2. For both programs, an average from five successful verifications was taken for each of VerCors' phases (see Footnote 5) [4]. As can be seen, verification of *Program 1* took 2 min and 24 s, and verification of *Program 2* took 5 min and 14 s. From the table, we read that a significant portion of the total time is spent in the parsing phase, so a large portion of the recorded time is spent on parsing rather than verifying the encoding of these programs. This

[2] Run in Fedora 38 on a laptop with an Intel Core i7-1165G7 CPU (4 cores, 2 threads per core, avg. 2.8 GHz, max. 4.7 GHz) and 16 GB RAM (DDR4, max. 3200 MT/s).

[3] The VerCors version used for running the examples is commit `acdfe83` [28].

[4] The flag `--no-infer-heap-context-into-frame`, which disables an optimization step, needs to be enabled to verify these SYCL programs..

is most likely caused by the fact that VerCors uses the C++ ANTLR grammar provided by ANTLR, into which VerCors-related grammar-rules were inserted. Some initial investigation has shown that the grammar was written inefficiently, but it requires further investigation to pinpoint the precise issue.

Listing 13: A SYCL program that performs vector addition of two arrays.

```
#include <sycl/sycl.hpp>

//@ context n >= 0;
//@ context \pointer(a, n, write);
//@ context \pointer(b, n, write);
//@ context \pointer(c, n, write);
//@ ensures (\forall int i; 0 <= i && i < n; c[i] == a[i] + b[i]);
void vector_add(int n, int* a, int* b, int* c) {
  sycl::queue q;
  sycl::buffer<int,1> a_buf = sycl::buffer(a,sycl::range(n));
  sycl::buffer<int,1> b_buf = sycl::buffer(b,sycl::range(n));
  sycl::buffer<int,1> c_buf = sycl::buffer(c,sycl::range(n));

  q.submit([&](sycl::handler& cgh) {
    sycl::accessor<int, 1, sycl::access_mode::read> a_acc =
                  ↪ sycl::accessor(a_buf, cgh, sycl::read_only);
    sycl::accessor<int, 1, sycl::access_mode::read> b_acc =
                  ↪ sycl::accessor(b_buf, cgh, sycl::read_only);
    sycl::accessor<int, 1> c_acc =
                 ↪ sycl::accessor(c_buf, cgh, sycl::read_write);

    cgh.parallel_for(sycl::range(n),
      //@ context it.get_id(0) < a_acc.get_range().get(0);
      //@ context Perm(a_acc[it.get_id(0)], read);
      //@ context it.get_id(0) < b_acc.get_range().get(0);
      //@ context Perm(b_acc[it.get_id(0)], read);
      //@ context it.get_id(0) < c_acc.get_range().get(0);
      //@ context Perm(c_acc[it.get_id(0)], write);
      //@ ensures c_acc[it.get_id(0)] ==
                   ↪ a_acc[it.get_id(0)] + b_acc[it.get_id(0)];
      [=](sycl::item<1> it) {
        c_acc[it.get_id(0)] =
                   ↪ a_acc[it.get_id(0)] + b_acc[it.get_id(0)];
      } ); }); }
```

8 Related Works

Our work is the first to offer formal verification for SYCL programs. In terms of informal verification, there do not seem to exist any SYCL-specific testing frameworks, but there does exist a performance benchmark tool called SYCL-Bench [19,20], and a runtime debugger based on GDB [1]. The support added to VerCors for SYCL is built upon on the encodings of GPGPU languages similar to SYCL into languages similar to COL, described by Blom et al. [7] and Darabi

[13] for a subset of OpenMP, and described by Safari & Huisman [26] for a subset of CUDA. Inspiration was also taken from the approaches to verifying GPGPU kernels and their incorporation into VerCors described by Amighi et al. [3], Blom et al. [8], and Darabi [13]. There also exist other formal verification tools for GPGPU programs, which might be able to extend their support to SYCL as well, such as GPUVerify by Betts et al. [5] for OpenCL and CUDA, PUG by Li & Gopalakrishnan [22] for CUDA, the tool by Xing et al. [30] for CUDA, and CIVL by Zheng et al. [32] for kernels from different languages.

9 Conclusion

This paper described how a core subset of SYCL constructs are encoded into VerCors' internal language COL to support verification of SYCL programs. More precisely, the encodings of the following SYCL constructs were discussed and illustrated with examples: submissions of basic- and ND-range kernels, explicitly waiting on their termination, constructions and destructions of buffers, constructions of data accessors, and interactions with elements of their buffers. Furthermore, the encoding of SYCL's kernel ordering and its soundness were discussed. To evaluate the added support, integration testing was used. The usability of the supported subset of SYCL was also shown. Vector addition, used as an example in most SYCL teaching materials, can be verified with VerCors. Function applications to a matrix and transposing the results using a combination of all of the supported SYCL features can be verified as well, may it be with the occasional false negatives due to the lack of triggers in the encoding. All in all, our work makes VerCors the first tool to formally verify (a subset of) SYCL programs.

10 Future Work

To solve the issue of VerCors occasionally giving false negatives, we plan to investigate how to insert triggers in the right places in the encoding of SYCL programs. We would also like to add support to VerCors for more SYCL constructs that could be useful to developers. SYCL's group barriers and memory fences can be used to control the reordering of memory loads and stores in a kernel and allow work-items to synchronise with each other. To add support for these constructs we could take inspiration from the encoding of their OpenCL and CUDA counterparts. SYCL has a virtual generic address space that overlaps its global, local, and private address spaces (which are already supported in VerCors). It can be used in cases where it is not known in advance, or irrelevant, in what address space data is stored. There exists no VerCors support for any similar constructs at the time of writing, making it also interesting to investigate. As always, we plan to do more complex case-studies to both test our SYCL support and find the limits of the current support. Last of all, we would like improve the usability of VerCors for SYCL programmers, by, for instance, including the often required user specifications about the bounds of the subscripts on data accessors in the encoding, such that they will no longer need to specify them.

References

1. Aktemur, B., Metzger, M., Saiapova, N., Strasuns, M.: Debugging SYCL programs on heterogeneous Intel® architectures. In: Proceedings of the International Workshop on OpenCL, pp. 1–10 (2020)
2. Amighi, A., Haack, C., Huisman, M., Hurlin, C.: Permission-based separation logic for multi-threaded Java programs. Logic. Methods Comput. Sci. **11**(1), 2 (2015). https://doi.org/10.2168/LMCS-11(1:2)2015
3. Amighi, A., Darabi, S., Blom, S., Huisman, M.: Specification and verification of atomic operations in GPGPU programs. In: Calinescu, R., Rumpe, B. (eds.) SEFM 2015. LNCS, vol. 9276, pp. 69–83. Springer, Cham (2015). https://doi.org/10.1007/978-3-319-22969-0_5
4. Artima. ScalaTest support in the IntelliJ Scala plugin. https://www.scalatest.org/user_guide/using_scalatest_with_intellij. Accessed 15 Apr 2024
5. Betts, A., Chong, N., Donaldson, A., Qadeer, S., Thomson, P.: GPUVerify: a verifier for GPU kernels. In: Proceedings of the ACM International Conference on Object Oriented Programming Systems Languages and Applications (OOPSLA 2012), pp. 113–132. Association for Computing Machinery (2012). https://doi.org/10.1145/2384616.2384625
6. Blom, S., Darabi, S., Huisman, M., Oortwijn, W.: The VerCors tool set: verification of parallel and concurrent software. In: Polikarpova, N., Schneider, S. (eds.) IFM 2017. LNCS, vol. 10510, pp. 102–110. Springer, Cham (2017). https://doi.org/10.1007/978-3-319-66845-1_7
7. Blom, S., Darabi, S., Huisman, M., Safari, M.: Correct program parallelisations. Int. J. Softw. Tools Technol. Transfer **23**(5), 741–763 (2021). https://doi.org/10.1007/s10009-020-00601-z
8. Blom, S., Huisman, M., Mihelil, M.: Specification and verification of GPGPU programs. Sci. Comput. Program. **95**, 376–388 (2014). Special Section: ACM SAC-SVT 2013 + Bytecode 2013
9. Bornat, R., Calcagno, C., O'Hearn, P.W., Parkinson, M.: Permission accounting in separation logic. In: Proceedings of the 32nd ACM SIGPLAN-SIGACT Symposium on Principles of Programming Languages, pp. 259–270 (2005). https://doi.org/10.1145/1040305.1040327
10. Codeplay Software Ltd. Introduction to SYCL. https://tech.io/playgrounds/48226/introduction-to-sycl/hello-world. Accessed 15 Apr 2024
11. Codeplay Software Ltd. SYCL Guide. https://developer.codeplay.com/products/computecpp/ce/2.11.0/guides/sycl-guide. Accessed 15 Apr 2024
12. Codeplay Software Ltd. SYCL Academy on GitHub (2024). https://github.com/codeplaysoftware/syclacademy
13. Darabi, S.: Verification of program parallelization. Ph.D. thesis, University of Twente (2018). iPA Dissertation Series No. 2018-02 IDS PhD. Thesis Series No. 18-458
14. De Moura, L., Bjørner, N.: Z3: an efficient SMT solver. In: Tools and Algorithms for the Construction and Analysis of Systems: 14th International Conference, TACAS, 29 March–6 April 2008, Proceedings 14. pp. 337–340. Springer, Heidelberg (2008)
15. Intel. Explore SYCL with Samples from Intel (2023). https://www.intel.com/content/www/us/en/docs/oneapi/code-samples-dpcpp/2023-1/overview.html
16. JetBrains s.r.o. IntelliJ IDEA the Leading Java and Kotlin IDE. https://www.jetbrains.com/idea/. Accessed 15 Apr 2024

17. Khronos® OpenCL Working Group. OpenCL™ Specification (2024). https://registry.khronos.org/OpenCL/specs/3.0-unified/pdf/OpenCL_API.pdf
18. Khronos® SYCL™ Working Group. SYCL™ 2020 Specification (revision 7) (2023). https://registry.khronos.org/SYCL/specs/sycl-2020/pdf/sycl-2020.pdf. Compiled from https://github.com/KhronosGroup/SYCL-Docs/tree/SYCL-2020/final-rev7
19. Lal, S., et al.: SYCL-Bench: a versatile cross-platform benchmark suite for heterogeneous computing. In: Malawski, M., Rzadca, K. (eds.) Euro-Par 2020. LNCS, vol. 12247, pp. 629–644. Springer, Cham (2020). https://doi.org/10.1007/978-3-030-57675-2_39
20. Lal, S., et al.: SYCL-Bench: a versatile single-source benchmark suite for heterogeneous computing. In: Proceedings of the International Workshop on OpenCL (IWOCL 20). Association for Computing Machinery (2020). https://doi.org/10.1145/3388333.3388669
21. Leavens, G.T., et al.: JML reference manual, DRAFT, Rev. 2344. http://www.jmlspecs.org/refman/jmlrefman.pdf
22. Li, G., Gopalakrishnan, G.: Scalable SMT-based verification of GPU kernel functions. In: Proceedings of the Eighteenth ACM SIGSOFT International Symposium on Foundations of Software Engineering, pp. 187–196 (2010)
23. Müller, P., Schwerhoff, M., Summers, A.J.: Viper: a verification infrastructure for permission-based reasoning. In: Jobstmann, B., Leino, K.R.M. (eds.) VMCAI 2016. LNCS, vol. 9583, pp. 41–62. Springer, Heidelberg (2016). https://doi.org/10.1007/978-3-662-49122-5_2
24. NVIDIA. CUDA Toolkit Documentation 12.1 (2024). https://docs.nvidia.com/cuda/index.html
25. Reinders, J., Ashbaugh, B., Brodman, J., Kinsner, M., Pennycook, J., Tian, X.: Data Parallel C++. Apress (2021). https://doi.org/10.1007/978-1-4842-5574-2
26. Safari, M., Huisman, M.: Formal verification of parallel prefix sum and stream compaction algorithms in CUDA. Theor. Comput. Sci. **912**, 81–98 (2022). https://doi.org/10.1016/j.tcs.2022.02.027
27. Siegel, H.J., Antonio, J.K., Metzger, R.C., Tan, M., Li, Y.A.: Heterogeneous Computing. ECE Technical Reports, p. 206 (1994)
28. UTwente FMT Group. VerCors' Source Code on GitHub (2024). https://github.com/utwente-fmt/vercors
29. Wittingen, E.: Deductive verification for SYCL. Master's thesis (2024). http://essay.utwente.nl/97976/
30. Xing, Y., Huang, B., Gupta, A., Malik, S.: A formal instruction-level GPU model for scalable verification. In: 2018 IEEE/ACM International Conference on Computer-Aided Design, ICCAD 2018 - Digest of Technical Papers. Institute of Electrical and Electronics Engineers Inc. (2018). https://doi.org/10.1145/3240765.3240771
31. Zahran, M.: Heterogeneous computing: here to stay: hardware and software perspectives. Queue **14**(6), 31–42 (2016). https://doi.org/10.1145/3028687.3038873
32. Zheng, M., Rogers, M.S., Luo, Z., Dwyer, M.B., Siegel, S.F.: CIVL: formal verification of parallel programs. In: 2015 30th IEEE/ACM International Conference on Automated Software Engineering (ASE), pp. 830–835 (2015). https://doi.org/10.1109/ASE.2015.99
33. Sakar, Ö., Wittingen, E., Huisman, M.: Artifact for paper (Deductive verification of SYCL in VerCors) (2024). https://doi.org/10.4121/45d37292-cce5-4fb7-8d4e-a1b32cfa3028

Minuska: Towards a Formally Verified Programming Language Framework

Jan Tušil(✉) and Jan Obdržálek

Masaryk University, Brno, Czech Republic
jan.tusil@mail.muni.cz, obdrzalek@fi.muni.cz

Abstract. Programming language frameworks allow us to generate language tools (e.g., interpreters) just from a formal description of the syntax and semantics of a programming language. As these frameworks tend to be quite complex, an issue arises whether we can trust the generated tools. To address this issue, we introduce a practical formal programming language framework called Minuska, which always generates a *provably correct* interpreter given a valid language definition. This is achieved by (1) defining a language MinusLang for expressing programming language definitions and giving it formal semantics and (2) using the Coq proof assistant to implement an interpreter parametric in a MinusLang definition and to prove it correct. Minuska provides strong correctness guarantees and can support non-trivial languages while performing well.

1 Introduction

To rigorously reason about software that controls computer systems – e.g., to guarantee their security, reliability, or safety – one must be able to assign precise meaning to programs. This can be rigorously done by providing *formal semantics* to programming languages. It has been argued, e.g., in [11], that encoding a language's semantics *in a mechanized formal language* can yield both theoretical and practical benefits. Using a practical *semantic framework* such as PLT-Redex [11] or $\mathbb{K}$ [16], one can take a formal description of a programming language and derive from it a parser, an interpreter [10,11], or a deductive verifier [18].

In another line of research, recent years have witnessed the emergence of formally verified programming language tools. For example, CompCert [3] is a compiler for the C programming language, formally verified in Coq, and CakeML [12] is a compiler for a variant of ML, verified using HOL4.

In [4], the authors have presented, within the auspices of the $\mathbb{K}$ semantics framework, their vision of combining the best of the two worlds: A semantics framework which, given some formal syntax and semantics of a programming language, can produce the tools above together with guarantees of their correctness. These guarantees are mathematical proofs, which can be mechanically machine-checked by a trustworthy proof checker.

A. Madeira and A. Knapp (Eds.): SEFM 2024, LNCS 15280, pp. 200–214, 2025.
https://doi.org/10.1007/978-3-031-77382-2_12

The paper [4] also contains the first step to achieving this vision. The authors formalize program execution as mathematical proof and create a tool that generates a *certifying interpreter* (given a formal description of a programming language). This interpreter is given a program and its input and produces the result of running the program on the input and a *certificate* in the form of a complete execution trace, more precisely, its associated proof object. A simple Metamath [14]-based proof checker can subsequently check this proof object. This way, one can detect if the interpreter does not behave correctly (the execution trace does not conform to the formal semantics of the language) on a given program input.

In this work, we advance further. Instead of having an interpreter that would provide us with machine-checkable certificate (proof) that the execution was correct, we want to produce an interpreter which is *provably correct*. This way we not only get stronger guarantees, but also do not have to spend computational resources on checking the generated certificates. Thus, there are at least two motivations for having such a verified semantics framework: *correctness*, and *performance*.

1.1 Our Approach

In our work, we have built a new semantics framework, called Minuska, instead of working within the $\mathbb{K}$ framework. There are several reasons for this. First, while being human-readable, the $\mathbb{K}$ input language is not suitable for formal verification since it does not have formal semantics. Therefore, [4] works with the intermediate Kore language, to which the $\mathbb{K}$ framework translates its input language. While Kore is much simpler to handle, it does not have formal semantics either – tools from the $\mathbb{K}$ framework handle its various features (such as subsorting and attributes) in an ad-hoc way. In [4], the authors, therefore, target only its strict subset, which is then given formal semantics by translating it into a logic named "matching logic" [6]. While this fragment of Kore is expressive enough to encode simple rewriting systems like the one used as a running example in [4] or the ones included therein for performance evaluation, it is not expressive enough to fully handle even the simple IMP programming language definition, which serves as a motivating example of the paper: according to [4], their system supports neither the use of built-in collection datatypes nor evaluation order attributes, both of which IMP relies on.

A second reason we have decided to go with creating a new framework (and a new input language) is that the fragment of Kore supported in [4] allows for language definitions that are internally inconsistent – due to the presence of function symbols. Indeed, one can have a user-defined function symbol s and axiomatize it to be equal to the integer value 3 and the integer value 4 simultaneously, and the $\mathbb{K}$ framework will happily accept such a definition. With such a contradiction, we could generate "proofs" which do not guarantee anything.

We designed the input language of Minuska to avoid the issues above. It has a simple but formal semantics, and its interpreter is written in the Coq proof assistant [19] and formally proven correct. The input language of Minuska is strong enough to express the motivating example of [4], which the 𝕂-based certifying interpreter of [4] could not handle, but our verified interpreter can. Moreover, our formally verified interpreter outperforms the certifying interpreter of [4], which was said to show "promising performance", by a factor of at least 20.

1.2 Contributions

Our main technical contributions are:

1. *MinusLang* – a language embedded in Coq, with formal semantics, for specifying operational semantics of programming languages, with no room to introduce logical inconsistency to the language definition;
2. an *interpreter* for any programming language that has a well-formed MinusLang semantics;
3. a mechanized *proof of the soundness and completeness* of that interpreter.

On the conceptual level, the main takeaways of our paper are the following:

1. One can have a programming language framework that is practical, formally verified, and inexpensive to develop. (It took about 4 person-months to develop the framework with the verified interpreter).
2. The use of foundational formal verification can result in a significantly more performant tool than retrofitting after-the-task certificate generation and checking to a professionally developed but unverified tool, even without clever optimizations on the side of the verified tool.

The rest of the paper is organized as follows: We start by giving a short overview of semantic frameworks in Sect. 2. The following presents Minuska – in Sect. 3.1 we present the term rewriting system on which MinusLang is based and Sect. 3.3 is devoted to the treatment of built-in types (which are one of the important aspects of Minuska). The universal interpreter is described in Sect. 3.4 and finally Sect. 3.5 discusses the usage of Minuska and its inherent trust base. We follow by examing the performance of Minuska, both with respect to [4] and on its own, in Sect. 4, which also discusses Minuska's limitations and future work. The formal syntax and semantics of MinusLang, as well as the full definition of semantics for a simple imperative language, can be found in the extended version [22] of this paper. Minuska is available at: https://github.com/h0nzZik/minuska/tree/v0.3.0 and on Zenodo [20].

2 Semantic Frameworks and Their Correctness

A *programming language semantic framework* is a software tool in which formal semantics of various programming languages can be encoded and that derives other artefacts from the semantics. Among the most widely known semantic frameworks, there is Ott [17] that generates parsers, LaTeX code, and theorem prover (Coq, HOL, and Isabelle/HOL) definitions from a definition of a language's syntax and semantics; 𝕂 [5] that generates parsers, interpreters, and

```
@frames: [simple(X): c[X, STATE]];
@value(X):
    (bool.or(z.is(X), bool.or(bool.is(X),
     term.same_symbol(X, [unitValue[]])))) ;
@strictness:
    [plus of_arity 2 in [0,1], ite of_arity 3 in [0]];
@rule/simple [aexpr.plus]:
    plus[X,Y] => z.plus(X, Y) where bool.and(z.is(X), z.is(Y)) ;
@rule/simple [stmt.ite.true]:
    ite[B, X, Y] => X where bool.eq(B, bool.true()) ;
@rule/simple [stmt.ite.false]:
    ite[B, X, Y] => Y where bool.eq(B, bool.false()) ;
@rule/simple [while.unfold]:
    while[B, S] => ite[B, seq[S, while[B, S]], unitValue[]]
    where bool.true() ;
```

Fig. 1. A fragment of the formal semantics of a simple imperative language, written in the sugared concrete syntax of Minuska.

deductive verifiers; and PLT-Redex [11] that generates parsers, interpreters, and LaTeX code. To the best of our knowledge, none of these tools has been formally verified. As mentioned earlier, Minuska is directly inspired by $\mathbb{K}$ framework.

Figure 1, which serves as our running example, shows how a simplified fragment of formal definition of language semantics for a simple imperative language can look like. (The syntax is explained in Sect. 3.2, and the full definition of the IMP language semantics can be found in [22]).

2.1 Interpreters as Testing Tools

In the context of semantic frameworks, interpreters enable language designers to test that a formally defined language semantics behaves as intended. One has just to generate an interpreter and test, whether its exhibited behaviour corresponds to designers' intentions. This has already been observed in the literature around the $\mathbb{K}$ framework, e.g. in [7]. However, for this testing to be effective, the generated interpreter needs to *faithfully capture* the language semantics[1]. Thus, an automatically generated interpreter formally verified with respect to the semantics would also increase the trustworthiness of the whole framework, including the languages modelled in it.

3 Minuska

This section describes Minuska—a formally verified semantic framework that generates interpreters from formal programming language definitions. The framework is implemented in the Coq proof assistant and consists of three main parts:

[1] Automated testing of a verified compiler for a fixed language is discussed, e.g., in [15].

1. the language *MinusS* for static reasoning about program configurations,
2. the language *MinusLang* for describing computational steps, and
3. a formally verified generator of interpreters.

While Minuska is directly inspired by the 𝕂 framework and uses similar concepts, it is based on a different foundational theory – *first-order term rewriting over built-in types.* This design decision has been crucial for us to be able to formally verify Minuska.

The 𝕂 framework uses a complex logic ("matching logic") with quantifiers and other connectives to formally capture reasoning about program configurations and their relations with semantic rules. If one wanted to formally verify 𝕂's reasoning in a proof assistant such as Coq, one would have to formalize not only the matching logic itself but also many important idioms that 𝕂 uses on top of matching logic. Similarly, one would need to define a matching logic theory of built-in data types implemented in the 𝕂 framework, such as integers, lists, and maps. Neither is considered in the existing work on the mechanization of matching logic in proof assistants, such as [21]. We also note that the built-in data types of 𝕂 are not implemented in the Metamath-based formalization of matching logic in [4].

Since Minuska is based on first-order term rewriting *over built-in types*, we do not have to axiomatize these types and their behavior – we borrow them directly from Coq. The result is much simpler than what would be needed to formalize 𝕂, and avoids the abovementioned soundness holes.

We do not formally describe the syntax and semantics of MinusLang here and refer the reader to [22]. Instead, in the following section, we informally describe the term rewriting system of Minuska.

3.1 Term Rewriting System

Configurations. In Minuska, we represent program configurations as *ground terms* - first-order terms without variables but possibly with special constants representing (potentially infinitely many) *built-in values.* These values inhabit one of the *built-in types.* For example, a configuration of a simple imperative program may look like

```
c[ (y := x + y; z := y - 1;), (x |-> 3, y |-> 4) ]
```

where `c` is a symbol, `y := x + y; z := y - 1;` is the program to be executed and `x |-> 3, y |-> 4` is a built-in value of a dictionary type, (representing the execution environment) that maps the program variable `x` to value 3 and the program variable `y` to value 4. (Both 3 and 4 are values of the built-in integer type.)

Rewriting Rules. At runtime, programs evolve by applying rewriting rules of the form α `=>` β to configurations. (A set Γ of rewriting rules is called a *rewriting theory.* Such a theory therefore encodes semantics of a given programming language.) Both α and β are terms with variables that can *match* program configurations in a given *valuation* (mapping variables to ground terms). In Minuska, rewriting rules are conditional, and the *right-hand sides* and side conditions can use operations defined for our built-in types. (One can think of the built-in types with their associated operations as forming the *static model* of Minuska.)

For example, take the following rule `aexpr.plus`, for binary addition, from the IMP definition in Fig. 1

```
plus[X,Y] => z.plus(X, Y) where bool.and(z.is(X), z.is(Y))
```

Its left-hand side matches any term where the "plus" symbol is the top level operator, applied to two operands; the side condition introduced by the `where` keyword states that both operands have to be integers; and the right-hand side adds the two operands using the built-in function for integer addition.

3.2 Sugared Syntax for MinusLang

However, the rule above is not directly applicable to configurations like the one in the previous section, which contains both a sequence of statements and an environment. Even for simpler configurations of the form `c[`*expression*, *state* `]` we want to pattern-match only on the ***expression*** part of the configuration. This is achieved by the "`@rule/simple [aexpr.plus]:`" declaration, which states that the `aexpr.plus` rule uses the `simple(CODE): c[CODE, STATE]` *frame*. In such a frame, only the part corresponding to the meta-variable `CODE` is used for pattern matching and subsequent evaluation (cf. the `@frames:` declaration in the first line of Fig. 1). Additionally, `@strictness` declarations like

```
plus of_arity 2 in [0,1]
```

of Fig. 1 are used to generate rules that ensure that both arguments of `plus` are evaluated to values. A term is considered a value according to the predicate defined by the keyword `@value`. Finally, `@context` plays a role similar to that of `@frames` for the strictness declarations.

This sugared syntax makes the MinusLang definitions more concise and readable. For example, using this syntax, a complete definition of IMP programming language semantics takes less than one page – see [22]. The translation from the sugared syntax to pure MinusLang is defined in frontend.v and default_everything.v.

3.3 Static Model

In the $\mathbb{K}$ framework, the user can describe the desired model by using axioms in matching logic, which can lead to inconsistencies or underspecification, with no way to detect these. In Minuska, one has to provide the model directly, which avoids these problems. The question is then how to describe such a model. Since Minuska is built inside Coq, one can use the full power of calculus of inductive construction - the logic of Coq that has been proven to be sound with respect to set theory. While it is true that Coq allows its users to assume some axioms without proving them, this can be easily detected by Coq-provided tools (or a simple `grep`). Moreover, such axioms would not live inside a language definition but in the metalevel, so a semantic engineer working inside Minuska has no way of accidentally assuming them.

Default Static Model. Minuska comes with a default static model. In the model, built-in values are defined as if by the following snippet:

```
Inductive BuiltInValue :=
| bv_error
| bv_bool (b : bool)
| bv_Z (z : Z)
| bv_sym (s : symbol)
| bv_str (s : string)
| bv_list (m : list GroundTerm)
| bv_finite_dict (m : finite_dict GroundTerm GroundTerm).
```

That is, a built-in value is either an error value, a boolean, an integer, a symbol (that is used to build terms), a string, a list of ground terms, or a finite dictionary from ground terms to ground terms. Technically, to satisfy Coq's positivity checker, the last case is implemented as a finite dictionary from positive natural numbers to ground terms (we used the `pmap` type that in the Coq stdpp library implements the extensional trie of [2]), together with the countability property of ground terms and built-in values.

The provided built-in functions are standard; these include some arithmetic operations on integers (based on the `ZArith` module of the Coq standard library), boolean operations (based on the `Bool` module of the Coq standard library), and operations for manipulating dictionaries (based on the `pmap` module of stdpp).

3.4 Interpreter

In the context of Minuska, we consider a *one-step interpreter* to be a partial function that takes a current configuration (described by a ground term) and performs one computational step within the current rewriting theory (if possible), returning the next configuration. As we mentioned previously, our interpreter is implemented wholly within Coq.

Instead of defining a new interpreter for each language, in Minuska we have defined a simple universal interpreter STEP. This interpreter is *universal* in that it takes as an input not only an input configuration but also a rewriting theory Γ (encoding the semantics of a programming language). The interpreter works by simply pattern-matching the left-hand side of a rule, evaluating the side condition in the resulting valuation, and interpreting the right-hand side using that valuation. The process of rule selection is currently somewhat *naive*, based on linear search in the list of rules representing the rewriting theory Γ.

Algorithm 1 Interpreter Step

```
function NAIVESELECT(rewriting theory Γ, ground term g)
    for (l ⇒ r if c) ∈ Γ do
        if TRYMATCH(l, g) is ρ ∈ Val then
            if EVALUTECONDITION(ρ, c) then
                return ((l ⇒ r if c), ρ)
    return None

function STEP(rewriting theory Γ, ground term g)
    if NAIVESELECT(Γ, g) is ((l ⇒ r if c), ρ) then
        return EVALUATE(ρ, r)
    else
        return None
```

The significant benefit of Minuska is that we can prove that our interpreters are always correct in the following sense: We say that an interpreter is *sound* with respect to a rewriting theory iff for every input ground term, if the interpreter returns a ground term, then the two are related by the semantics of the rewriting theory. Conversely, we say that an interpreter is *complete* iff for every input ground term, the interpreter returns some ground term unless the input ground term is stuck - i.e., has no successor in the semantics. Observe that with such a definition, an interpreter is allowed to resolve non-determinism arbitrarily.

Theorem 1. *Function* STEP *(when applied to a well-formed theory* Γ*) is a sound and complete interpreter (with respect to* Γ*).*

The theorem follows directly from the correctness of its components. The function TRYMATCH returns a valuation in which the rule's left-hand side is satisfied the current program configuration (if there is some); the function EVALUATE-CONDITION checks whether the rule's side condition is satisfied in the given valuation; and the function EVALUATE returns a concrete program configuration that satisfies the rule's right-hand side in the given valuation. A more detailed proof scatch is in [22].

The implementation of the universal interpreter is around 150LoC long, and the proof of correctness takes about 3kLoC (both excluding supporting infrastructure). What made our proofs simpler is that in the implementation, we abstracted away the details about built-in values: the interpreter only assumes that built-in values are equipped with a decidable equality. The decision procedure for the supported built-in values is non-trivial (~1500LoC); however, because of the abstraction, its details do not complicate the proof of the interpreter's correctness.

3.5 Usage and Trust Base

The size of trust base of Minuska depends on the way Minuska is used. With Minuska, one can

1. put the language definition into a `*.m` file and invoke the `minuska compile` command to check the language definition for well-formedness and generate an executable interpreter; or

2. put the language definition into a `*.m` file and use the `minuska def2coq` command to generate a Coq (`*.v`) file containing the language definition and the associated interpreter, then load the generated file into Coq and use it from within Coq; or
3. write the language definition directly in Coq.

In the first situation one needs to trust the hand-written OCaml code that implements the `minuska` executable, as well as Coq's extraction mechanism and OCaml compiler; in the second case, the trust base consists of the `minuska` executable and Coq's kernel; in the last case, only the kernel of Coq needs to be trusted. In principle, the trust base of the first case could be reduced by using a formally verified extraction mechanism (to OCaml [9] or C [1]) and a formally verified compiler (such as CompCert [3]).

3.6 Concrete Syntax and Parsing

While Minuska internally operates on the abstract syntax of the given program, and also the semantic rules of a programming language are written with respect to the language's abstract syntax, Minuska provides an interface to connect a user-provided parser for the target language.

4 Evaluation

We evaluate Minuska from two perspectives, *expressivity* and *performance*, with respect to the $\mathbb{K}$-framework implementation of [4], as well as on its own. For performance evaluation with respect to [4], we have to choose benchmarks supported by both Minuska and $\mathbb{K}$. In [4], the authors choose two sets of benchmarks: a rewriting system (named "two-counters") implementing summation from 1 to n of unary-encoded natural numbers, executed with various inputs, and a selection of benchmarks from the rewriting engines competition (REC [8]), with reduced inputs, adapted to $\mathbb{K}$. However, the adapted REC benchmarks use user-defined function symbols, which (as discussed in Sect. 1) allows for a logical inconsistency in a $\mathbb{K}$-based language definition. Moreover, the REC benchmarks were designed for benchmarking rewriting engines, and not semantic frameworks, and thus exercise neither the idioms used in developments of language definitions using $\mathbb{K}$ (such as *strictness* for specifying evaluation order) nor the supporting infrastructure for these as implemented in both $\mathbb{K}$ (*strictness attributes*) and Minuska (*strictness declaration*).

On the other hand, the "two-counters" benchmark is too simple for our purposes (Fig. 2). Therefore, to compare Minuska with respect to $\mathbb{K}$, we crafted two new benchmarks that are simple enough to be handled by $\mathbb{K}$ and simultaneously idiomatic enough in the sense that they use strictness idioms. As mentioned in [4], their tool does not support the native strictness attribute of $\mathbb{K}$. Therefore, in the $\mathbb{K}$ version of the benchmarks, we emulated this feature manually in the same style as done in the version of the benchmarks for Minuska. Since $\mathbb{K}$ does

```
@rule [step]:
state[M, N] => state[z.minus(M, [(@builtin-int 1)]), z.plus(N, M)]
where z.lt([(@builtin-int 0)],M);
```

count-to	Native compute time [s]
1'000	0.01
10'000	0.06
100'000	0.45
1'000'000	4.39

count-to	Compute time [s]	coqc time [s]
10	0.028	0.75
100	0.044	0.78
1'000	0.213	0.92
10'000	1.871	2.58

Fig. 2. "two-counters": the running example of [4] in Minuska. "Native compute time" means wall-clock time of the system executed in an extracted and compiled standalone interpreter. "Compute time" is the time needed to evaluate the benchmark using Coq's `Compute` command, and "coqc time" is time needed to evaluate a Coq (`*.v`) file containing the command.

not support generating proofs for (its) builtin integers, we also restrain from using builtin values, with the exception of builtin booleans which are used in the side conditions of rules both in $\mathbb{K}$ and in Minuska. The two new benchmarks are: computing the n-th member of the Fibonacci sequence, and computing the factorial of n, both done in the iterative manner over unary-encoded natural numbers.

name	$\mathbb{K}$ parameters [s]	$\mathbb{K}$ cert-gen [s]	$\mathbb{K}$ cert-check [s]	M compute [s]	M coqc [s]
tc 10	38.01	1.40	2.71	0.03	0.75
tc 20	79.14	2.41	2.97	0.03	0.75
tc 50	192.64	6.92	2.84	0.04	0.76
tc 100	377.83	14.44	2.81	0.04	0.78
fib 5	95.28	4.92	2.83	0.20	0.89
fact 3	247.50	19.71	3.35	0.48	1.40

Fig. 3. Running times of shared $\mathbb{K}$/Minuska benchmarks. The meaning of the columns is as follows. For $\mathbb{K}$, "$\mathbb{K}$ parameters" is the time required to generate proof parameters for a single execution, including time required argument parsing; "$\mathbb{K}$ cert-gen" is the time of certificate generation from those parameters; and "$\mathbb{K}$ cert-check" is the time required for checking those certificates. For Minuska, "M compute" is the time to evaluate the benchmark using Coq's Compute mechanism, measured inside Coq using its Time command; and "M coqc" is the time required for Coq to process a file with the benchmark, as measured by the GNU `time` utility.

4.1 Performance of Minuska vs $\mathbb{K}$

To benchmark $\mathbb{K}$, we use the infrastructure of [4], which we modified so as to measure also the time to execute a given program on a given input while generating so-called "proof parameters". We measure the performance on Intel Core I7 10th Gen (model name Intel(R) Core(TM) i7-10510U CPU @ 1.80GHz) in a virtual machine limited to 12 GiB of RAM, running Ubuntu 20.04 (for which the available artifact is intended). To benchmark Minuska, we use the same hardware running virtualized Ubuntu 23.10, with the same memory limit. We use a newer OS for Minuska because it depends on Coq 8.19, which was not available in Ubuntu 20.04.

Our benchmarking results are in Fig. 3; the "two-counters" benchmark is abbreviated as "tc". We argue that the most interesting measure of $\mathbb{K}$'s interpreter is the *sum* of all three measured times: to ensure that one gets a valid result, one needs to first run the interpreter while generating proof parameters, then to generate a certificate, and finally to check it. Unfortunately, the times required for generating proof parameters are so high because of the rather naive approach applied: the $\mathbb{K}$ tool is called repeatedly as many times as there are computational steps needed for the execution. We note that the "$\mathbb{K}$ parameters" column is not reported in [4].

Regarding Minuska, the difference between the 'Compute' time and the 'coqc' time is almost constant, over 0.6 seconds; we interpret this difference as the time required to load Coq and the Minuska library. Minuska's certified (but naive) interpreter outperforms $\mathbb{K}$'s certifying interpreter by a large margin. Perhaps surprisingly, it is faster to start Coq and perform a verified computation inside than to verify the proof certificate generated by $\mathbb{K}$ for an equivalent computation.

Discussion. In our opinion, one reason why Minuska's verified but naive interpreter outperforms $\mathbb{K}$'s certifying interpreter is the size of the generated proof objects. This is likely due to the choice of *matching logic* as the logic of the proof certificates: matching logic is rather low-level and its Hilbert-style proof system makes it hard to come up with compact proofs without resorting to metalevel reasoning. Even a very fast proof checker can hardly compensate for the size of $\mathbb{K}$'s proof certificates, which is often in hundreds of megabytes of text data.

4.2 IMP Semantics in Minuska

In addition, we use the full definition of a simple imperative language IMP, adapted from [4], to demonstrate that Minuska can do more than the version of $\mathbb{K}$ of [4]: to interpret a program in a programming language, and to do so with a reasonable performance. According to Fig. 4, one iteration of the main loop of `imp-count-to` takes about half a second when interpreted by Coq, and about 10 milliseconds when executing natively. The example uses built-in integers, as well as built-in maps; the source code is available in imp.m and in [22].

4.3 Other Benchmarks

To get a fuller understanding of Minuska's performance, we have used an additional set of benchmarks based on computing Fibonacci numbers and factorials.

```
/* imp-count-to-n */
n := $arg ;
sum := 0 ;
while (1 <= n) {
    sum := sum + n ;
    n := n + (-1) ;
};
sum
```

$arg	Compute [s]	coqc [s]	native
1	0.66	1.49	0.02
2	1.15	1.86	0.02
3	1.57	2.28	0.03
4	2.03	2.78	0.04
5	2.45	3.13	0.04
6	2.95	3.62	0.05
7	3.41	4.16	0.06

Fig. 4. Running times of a program for computing $\Sigma_{i=i}^{n} i$ in a simple imperative language IMP with semantics defined in Minuska. 'Compute' means the time of the 'Compute' command within Coq, 'coqc' means the total time of the 'coqc' command on a file containing the Compute command, and 'native' means the time of the native code generated by the OCaml compiler for the interpreter extracted from Coq into OCaml.

The results are in Fig. 5. Here "unary-fib" is the same Fibonacci system as in Fig. 3, and "unary-fact" is the same code for computing factorials, both measured with growing input parameter. The "unary" prefix means that a naive unary encoding of natural numbers is used, with addition of two numbers being computed in a linear number of steps in the value of the first addend. Also, in both cases a naive recursive algorithm is used. The "native-fib" collection of benchmarks exercise a different implementation of the Fibonacci sequence: the code is more imperative in style, always remembering the last two values of the sequence instead of recursing to compute them; moreover, it uses Minuska's built-in integers implemented using Coq's binary integers.

benchmark	Compute [s]	coqc [s]
native-fib 1	0.026	0.74
native-fib 11	0.042	0.80
native-fib 21	0.058	0.79
native-fib 31	0.068	0.78
native-fib 41	0.079	0.79
native-fib 51	0.110	0.79
native-fib 61	0.125	0.81
native-fib 71	0.141	0.82
native-fib 81	0.152	0.82
native-fib 91	0.161	0.84
native-fib 101	0.172	0.86

benchmark	Compute [s]	coqc [s]
unary-fib 1	0.094	0.77
unary-fib 2	0.102	0.78
unary-fib 3	0.120	0.80
unary-fib 4	0.151	0.84
unary-fib 5	0.199	0.89
unary-fib 6	0.285	0.98
unary-fib 7	0.428	1.21
unary-fib 8	0.818	1.53
unary-fib 9	1.233	2.02
unary-fib 10	2.171	2.91
unary-fib 11	3.313	4.04
unary-fact 1	0.159	0.90
unary-fact 2	0.222	0.95
unary-fact 3	0.476	1.40
unary-fact 4	1.107	1.85
unary-fact 5	3.108	3.86
unary-fact 6	12.785	13.60

Fig. 5. Other benchmarks of Minuska

4.4 Development Effort

The part of Minuska reported in this paper cost about 4 person-months to develop and consists of approximately 16kLOC of Coq code, only approximately 700LOC of which are specifications (of MinusLang etc.), the rest being implementation and proofs.

5 Conclusion

We have introduced Minuska: a formally-verified programming language framework capable of generating interpreters from language definitions. The generated interpreters, while using a naive pattern matching algorithm, have better performance than the certifying interpreters of [4], while also having the advantage of being formally verified to behave correctly with respect to the given language definition. However, more future work remains.

Future Developments. When it comes to semantic frameworks, having a verified semantic-based interpreter is a good start, but one can go further.

1. As has been demonstrated by [18], semantic frameworks can implement symbolic execution and deductive verification facilities.
2. Although our pattern-matching-based interpreter is more performant than the certifying competition, it is still rather slow. We believe we could reuse some existing work for performant pattern matching that has been done in the context of compilers - for example, [13]. The $\mathbb{K}$ tool already has an unverified implementation of some of these ideas.
3. In both Minuska and $\mathbb{K}$, the constructs for *evaluation contexts*, *strictness*, and *order of evaluation* of subexpression have no formal semantics, but are implemented only as a syntactic sugar on top of ordinary rewriting rules. It would be better if these had a formal semantics, since it would make reasoning about a language semantics more high-level.
4. It would also be interesting to model some of the larger languages defined in $\mathbb{K}$ in Minuska as well.

Acknowledgement. We are grateful to Traian Florin Șerbănuță for his input to discussions around Minuska, and to anonymous reviewers for their feedback on a previous version of this paper.

References

1. Anand, A., et al.: CertiCoq: a verified compiler for Coq. In: CoqPL workshop (2016). https://api.semanticscholar.org/CorpusID:9607775
2. Appel, A.W., Leroy, X.: Efficient extensional binary tries. J. Autom. Reason. **67**(1), 8 (2023). https://doi.org/10.1007/S10817-022-09655-X

3. Boldo, S., Jourdan, J., Leroy, X., Melquiond, G.: A formally-verified C compiler supporting floating-point arithmetic. In: Nannarelli, A., Seidel, P., Tang, P.T.P. (eds.) 21st IEEE Symposium on Computer Arithmetic, ARITH 2013, Austin, TX, USA, April 7-10, 2013, pp. 107–115. IEEE Computer Society (2013). https://doi.org/10.1109/ARITH.2013.30
4. Chen, X., Lin, Z., Trinh, M.-T., Roşu, G.: Towards a trustworthy semantics-based language framework via proof generation. In: Silva, A., Leino, K.R.M. (eds.) CAV 2021. LNCS, vol. 12760, pp. 477–499. Springer, Cham (2021). https://doi.org/10.1007/978-3-030-81688-9_23
5. Chen, X., Roşu, G.: A language-independent program verification framework. In: Margaria, T., Steffen, B. (eds.) ISoLA 2018. LNCS, vol. 11245, pp. 92–102. Springer, Cham (2018). https://doi.org/10.1007/978-3-030-03421-4_7
6. Chen, X., Roşu, G.: Matching μ-logic. In: 34th Annual ACM/IEEE Symposium on Logic in Computer Science, LICS 2019, Vancouver, BC, Canada, June 24-27, 2019, pp. 1–13. IEEE (2019). https://doi.org/10.1109/LICS.2019.8785675
7. Dasgupta, S., Park, D., Kasampalis, T., Adve, V.S., Roşu, G.: A complete formal semantics of x86-64 user-level instruction set architecture. In: McKinley, K.S., Fisher, K. (eds.) Proceedings of the 40th ACM SIGPLAN Conference on Programming Language Design and Implementation, PLDI 2019, Phoenix, AZ, USA, June 22-26, 2019, pp. 1133–1148. ACM (2019). https://doi.org/10.1145/3314221.3314601
8. Durán, F., Garavel, H.: The rewrite engines competitions: a rectrospective. In: Beyer, D., Huisman, M., Kordon, F., Steffen, B. (eds.) Tools and Algorithms for the Construction and Analysis of Systems, pp. 93–100. Springer, Cham (2019)
9. Forster, Y., Sozeau, M., Tabareau, N.: Verified extraction from coq to ocaml. Proc. ACM Program. Lang. **8**(PLDI) (2024) https://doi.org/10.1145/3656379
10. Hills, M., Serbănuţă, T., Roşu, G.: A rewrite framework for language definitions and for generation of efficient interpreters. In: Denker, G., Talcott, C.L. (eds.) Proceedings of the 6th International Workshop on Rewriting Logic and its Applications, WRLA 2006, Vienna, Austria, April 1-2, 2006. Electronic Notes in Theoretical Computer Science, vol. 176, pp. 215–231. Elsevier (2006). https://doi.org/10.1016/J.ENTCS.2007.06.017
11. Klein, C., Clements, J., et al.: Run your research: on the effectiveness of lightweight mechanization. In: Field, J., Hicks, M. (eds.) Proceedings of the 39th ACM SIGPLAN-SIGACT Symposium on Principles of Programming Languages, POPL 2012, Philadelphia, Pennsylvania, USA, January 22-28, 2012, pp. 285–296. ACM (2012). https://doi.org/10.1145/2103656.2103691
12. Kumar, R., Myreen, M.O., Norrish, M., Owens, S.: CakeML: a verified implementation of ML. In: Jagannathan, S., Sewell, P. (eds.) The 41st Annual ACM SIGPLAN-SIGACT Symposium on Principles of Programming Languages, POPL '14, San Diego, CA, USA, January 20-21, 2014. pp. 179–192. ACM (2014). https://doi.org/10.1145/2535838.2535841
13. Maranget, L.: Compiling pattern matching to good decision trees. In: Proceedings of the 2008 ACM SIGPLAN Workshop on ML, ML '08, , pp. 35–46. Association for Computing Machinery, New York (2008). https://doi.org/10.1145/1411304.1411311
14. Megill, N.D., Wheeler, D.A.: Metamath: a Computer Language for Mathematical Proofs. Lulu Press, Morrisville, North Carolina (2019). http://us.metamath.org/downloads/metamath.pdf

15. Monniaux, D., Gourdin, L., Boulmé, S., Lebeltel, O.: Testing a formally verified compiler. In: Prevosto, V., Seceleanu, C. (eds.) Tests and Proofs - 17th International Conference, TAP 2023, Leicester, UK, July 18-19, 2023, Proceedings. Lecture Notes in Computer Science, vol. 14066, pp. 40–48. Springer (2023). https://doi.org/10.1007/978-3-031-38828-6_3
16. Roşu, G., Serbănută, T.: An overview of the K semantic framework. J. Log. Algebraic Methods Program. **79**(6), 397–434 (2010). https://doi.org/10.1016/J.JLAP.2010.03.012
17. Sewell, P., et al.: Ott: effective tool support for the working semanticist. J. Funct. Program. **20**(1), 71–122 (2010). https://doi.org/10.1017/S0956796809990293
18. Stefănescu, A., Park, D., Yuwen, S., Li, Y., Roşu, G.: Semantics-based program verifiers for all languages. In: Visser, E., Smaragdakis, Y. (eds.) Proceedings of the 2016 ACM SIGPLAN International Conference on Object-Oriented Programming, Systems, Languages, and Applications, OOPSLA 2016, part of SPLASH 2016, Amsterdam, The Netherlands, October 30 - November 4, 2016, pp. 74–91. ACM (2016). https://doi.org/10.1145/2983990.2984027
19. The Coq Development Team: The Coq proof assistant (2023). https://doi.org/10.5281/zenodo.8161141
20. Tušil, J.: Minuska: Towards a Formally Verified Programming Language Framework, June 2024. https://doi.org/10.5281/zenodo.12599432
21. Tušil, J., Bereczky, P., Horpácsi, D.: Interactive matching logic proofs in Coq. In: Ábrahám, E., Dubslaff, C., Tarifa, S.L.T. (eds.) Theoretical Aspects of Computing - ICTAC 2023 - 20th International Colloquium, Lima, Peru, December 4-8, 2023, Proceedings. Lecture Notes in Computer Science, vol. 14446, pp. 139–157. Springer (2023). https://doi.org/10.1007/978-3-031-47963-2_10
22. Tušil, J., Obdržálek, J.: Minuska: towards a formally verified programming language framework (2024). https://arxiv.org/abs/2409.11530

Hierarchical Learning of Generative Automaton Models from Sequential Data

Benjamin von Berg[1(✉)], Bernhard K. Aichernig[1], Maximilian Rindler[1], Darko Štern[3], and Martin Tappler[2]

[1] Institute of Software Technology, Graz University of Technology, Graz, Austria
{benjamin.vonberg,aichernig}@ist.tugraz.at,
maximilian.rindler@student.tugraz.at
[2] TU Wien, Vienna, Austria
martin.tappler@tuwien.ac.at
[3] AVL List GmbH, Graz, Austria
darko.stern@avl.com

Abstract. Passive automata learning is a method for inferring automaton models from a given collection of observations of system behavior (traces). It has been applied to reactive systems with probabilistic behavior. In particular, IOAlergia is a well known algorithm for inferring models in the form of deterministically labeled Markov decision processes from system traces. The quality of the resulting model depends heavily on the provided data set and suffers if data is scarce. However, in many cases additional knowledge about the system is available. This work aims to incorporate knowledge about system modes into the learning process in order to improve model quality for low-data scenarios. This is done by splitting the traces according to system modes, learning individual models for each mode and combining those models into one model with sub-regions corresponding to individual system modes. In our evaluation on artificial models, our method outperforms the baseline in at least 90 % of cases for all considered metrics. This method was developed to learn generative models of human driving behavior. Data from recorded test drives on highways was used to learn a hierarchical stochastic model of typical acceleration behavior of human drivers. In the automotive industry, such models make the simulations of driving emissions more realistic.

Keywords: generative models · model inference · Markov decision processes · passive automata learning · real driving emissions

1 Introduction

The inference of generative models from a collection of samples is a topic that has become increasingly popular in recent years, with a main application being the generation of new data via sampling. The inferred models encode data distributions. This is also the case for probabilistic reactive systems, which can

A. Madeira and A. Knapp (Eds.): SEFM 2024, LNCS 15280, pp. 215–233, 2025.
https://doi.org/10.1007/978-3-031-77382-2_13

be modeled as Markov decision processes (MDPs). For these systems, the samples are traces describing system behavior, where each trace is an alternating sequence of inputs and outputs. A benefit of MDPs is that they aid explainability by virtue of providing explicit models, which can be used for model checking [6]. One method for inferring MDP models is IOAlergia [19], an algorithm from the domain of passive automata learning, which is capable of inferring instances from the class of deterministically labeled MDPs in the limit. However, the quality of the models suffers significantly when data is scarce. This is a result of shortcomings of the original Alergia algorithm [33], that also apply to IOAlergia. Often, however, additional information about the system under learning (SUL) is available. Unfortunately, IOAlergia and (to the best of our knowledge) other passive automata learning algorithms have no mechanisms to utilize this information.

To address this, we propose a novel method called Hierarchical Automata Learning (HAL) for incorporating domain knowledge and heuristics into the learning process. In particular, we consider information about system modes. We assume, that the system behavior can be split into groups of behavior patterns corresponding to system modes and that a method for identifying modes from system observations is known. In our method HAL, we use this knowledge as a segmentation criterion to split each of the provided traces according to the system modes. We then learn a model for each system mode and recombine them into a model of the whole system. While HAL is motivated by issues related to IOAlergia, the method is agnostic with respect to the automata learning algorithm used for learning sub-models and could even be applied to learning algorithms for other automaton models such as Moore machines with minor modifications. An implementation is provided online.[1]

We evaluated HAL on randomly generated systems, which showed favorable results on all considered metrics. We use this approach to tackle a problem from the automotive domain. More specifically, we apply HAL to learn probabilistic models of human driver behavior that can be used to generate artificial velocity profiles that mimic human driving on highways in response to a sequence of road features such as the speed limit and curvature.

The structure of the paper is as follows. Section 2 gives a motivating example. In Sect. 3, we discuss the necessary background. In Sect. 4, we present our novel method for enhancing passive learning of automaton models, which is the main contribution of this work. We evaluate our approach on artificial models and the motivating example in Sect. 5. This is followed by a brief discussion of related work in Sect. 6. Finally, Sect. 7 concludes our work with a discussion of our findings and future work.

2 Motivating Example

Real driving emissions (RDE) is a topic from the automotive domain that is concerned with estimating emissions for a specific vehicle for some route under realistic driving conditions. This is commonly achieved using simulation tools.

[1] https://github.com/benjaminvonberg/hierarchical-automata-learning.

However, such simulations heavily depend on the behavior of the driver. This motivates learning a driver model that can be used in simulation to produce realistic instances of driver behavior – in particular velocity profiles – for arbitrary routes from a limited number of test drives.

The data is given as a number of time series obtained from test drives. Each data point in a time series consists of a fixed set of measured and derived quantities. This includes static road features (e.g. curvature, traffic signs) and dynamic behavior of the test vehicle/driver such as velocity. Those time series have local dependencies between data points. Take for example an overtaking maneuver, which is made up of an acceleration phase followed by a deceleration phase. To account for such dependencies, a behavioral (stateful) model is required.

The provided data lacks important information, such as the specific situation on the road (behavior of other traffic participants, state of traffic lights) and the state of the driver (alert, tired, stressed, etc.). Probabilistic models can be used to deal with this uncertainty without modeling the unknowns explicitly. While this does not allow to reason about what exactly triggered the driver to choose one possible way of driving along a specific section of a road, we can still model the frequency with which different options are taken, resulting in a generative model. This suggests the perspective of modeling the driver as a probabilistic reactive system acting on known environment stimuli. Driving combines discrete actions – such as the decision to overtake the car ahead – and continuous adjustment to the environment, for example when driving along a curvy road. This twofold nature can be represented using a Markov decision process (MDP). An issue here is that the available learning algorithms support only discrete MDPs with finite sets of inputs and outputs. For this reason, we need to introduce some form of discretization/abstraction for both input and output data.

As recording test drives is expensive, only limited data is available. This is in conflict with the fact that common model inference algorithms require good coverage of system states. While it might not be possible to give a perfect description of operating modes for human drivers, we can still use heuristics that capture high-level properties of human driving to aid learning algorithms.

3 Preliminaries

The terminology introduced here follows the conventions of Tappler et al. [28]. We denote the set of partial functions mapping from set A to another set B as $A \rightharpoonup B$ and we write $\mathit{Distr}(A)$ for the set of probability distributions over A. We denote sequences using angled brackets and the concatenation of two sequences s_1 and s_2 as $s_1 \cdot s_2$. For example $\langle x_1, x_2\rangle \cdot \langle x_3\rangle = \langle x_1, x_2, x_3\rangle$. We lift concatenation to sets of sequences and atoms by letting the concatenation of two sets be the set containing the concatenation of any ordered pair of sequences or atoms drawn from the two sets. For example $\{x_1, \langle x_1, x_2\rangle\} \cdot \{x_3\} = \{\langle x_1, x_3\rangle, \langle x_1, x_2, x_3\rangle\}$. We denote the set of finite sequences comprised of elements of X as X^*, which can be obtained by repeated concatenation.

3.1 Markov Decision Processes

In essence, a Markov decision process (MDP) is an automaton with a finite number of states, where input symbols (or actions) trigger probabilistic state changes. We use labeled MDPs, where each state emits an output symbol (or observation) when active.

Definition 1. *A Markov decision process is a tuple* $M = (Q, q_0, I, O, L, \delta)$ *where*

- Q *is a finite set of states*
- $q_0 \in Q$ *is the initial state*
- I *is a finite set of input symbols*
- O *is a finite set of output symbols*
- $L : Q \rightarrow O$ *is an output function assigning each state a specific output symbol*
- $\delta : Q \times I \rightharpoonup Distr(Q)$ *is a probabilistic transition function.*

An MDP is *input enabled* iff δ is a total function. For input-enabled MDPs, any combination of states and inputs has a non-empty set of possible successors. An MDP is *deterministically labeled* iff – for each combination of state and input symbol – the observed output uniquely identifies the resulting state:

$$\forall q, q_1, q_2 \in Q, i \in I : \delta(q,i)(q_1) = 0 \vee \delta(q,i)(q_2) = 0 \vee q_1 = q_2 \vee L(q_1) \neq L(q_2)$$

Since this work is restricted to deterministically labeled MDPs, the term MDP will henceforth refer to deterministically labeled MDPs unless explicitly noted.

An IO trace is a sequence that alternates between symbols from a set of inputs I and a set of observations O, starting and ending with an output symbol. The set of IO traces over an input alphabet I and output alphabet O is defined as $\mathcal{TR}_{I,O} = O \cdot (I \cdot O)^*$. We omit the subscript if I and O are clear from the context. We write IO traces as sequences of outputs joined by arrows superscripted by the inputs: $o_0 \xrightarrow{i_1} o_1 \xrightarrow{i_2} o_2 \xrightarrow{i_3} o_3$

In passive automata learning, the goal is to infer an automaton model of a system from a limited number of observations (i.e. IO traces). A popular algorithm for inferring MDPs is IOAlergia [19]. This algorithm is a typical state-merging algorithm, which first organizes the given data in the form of a prefix tree. Then, pairs of states of the tree are merged based on a statistical compatibility test, starting from the root. The construction of the tree assumes deterministic labeling, which is preserved by the merging procedure, which results in deterministically labeled MDPs. A common problem with IOAlergia is that it merges too aggressively [28]. In the context of the similar Alergia method for stochastic regular grammars [10], Young-Lai and Tompa observed that the statistical compatibility test becomes unreliable when one of the merge candidates has not been observed often enough [33], which is usually the case for nodes closer to the leaves. This issue is exacerbated when using IOAlergia, where the (commonly) large number of possible input-output combinations leads to sparse prefix trees where the amount of data per node thins out quickly.

3.2 Similarity Metrics

To assess the quality of the resulting models, we use metrics covered in the overview paper on similarity metrics for MDPs by Garcia et al. [14]. While the focus of their paper is on reinforcement learning with rewards, it also features metrics that translate well to our setting.

In the case where an MDP representation of the ground truth is available, the work of Ferns et al. [13] can be applied [28]. They defined a family of *bisimilarity distances* for MDPs where each member d follows a fixed point definition via some functional $F(d)$. More specifically we use

$$F^{\lambda}(d)(q_1, q_2) = \begin{cases} 1 & \text{if } L(q_1) \neq L(q_2) \\ \lambda \underset{i \in I}{\Phi} W_d(\delta(q_1, i), \delta(q_2, i)) & \text{otherwise} \end{cases}$$

where $\lambda \in [0, 1]$ is a discounting factor, $W_d(p_1, p_2)$ denotes the Wasserstein distance of two distributions p_1 and p_2 under the metric d and $\Phi_{i \in I}$ denotes either the maximum or average over $i \in I$. The discounting factor determines the importance of future behavior. The operator Φ can be seen as a method for aggregating the contributions of the individual inputs $i \in I$ and is commonly chosen as the maximum over all actions. This establishes a relation to a simple real-valued modal logic, in particular, to the formula that results in the greatest difference when evaluated on the two MDPs [12]. Stemming from a verification setting, this approach is pessimistic, since actions are chosen in a way that maximizes differences in behavior.

In the case where no MDP model of the ground truth is available, we have to resort to sampling-based metrics. We use *compliance*, which measures the average probability of an MDP M_1 generating experience tuples from a collection of samples stemming from a second MDP M_2 [14]. An experience tuple $\langle s, i, s' \rangle$ denotes that the state s' was observed after applying an input i in state s. Given an IO trace, experience tuples can be generated by replaying the trace on the MDP M_1. For a collection of IO traces $T \subset \mathcal{TR}$ sampled from M_2 we can then define compliance as the average step probability resulting from replaying the traces in T on M_1.

4 Methodology

We provide a method called Hierarchical Automata Learning (HAL) of incorporating knowledge about system modes into the learning algorithm to alleviate previously mentioned issues related to low-data scenarios. The general idea is to split the learning task into smaller sub-tasks that can be learned individually in a way that allows recombining the resulting models into a model of the whole system. This corresponds to learning hierarchical automata, where the individual sub-models are superstates corresponding to individual system modes. To achieve this, we assume knowledge of sensible system modes and how to identify them in the data or – in more technical terms – a method for segmenting IO traces and labeling the resulting segments.

We expect this to aid the learning process in two ways. When applying HAL, the internal learning algorithm does not have to infer the concept of the different system modes, but only their behavior. A less obvious benefit related to IOAlergia specifically is that by splitting the IO traces according to system modes, we effectively trade trace length for quantity. As a result, we get prefix trees that are less deep but more densely populated, which makes statistical compatibility testing more reliable.

Given a multiset of IO traces T and a segmentation function f_{seg}, a brief outline of HAL is given as follows:

1. Segment each IO trace and assign labels to all segments using f_{seg}
2. Learn a model for each label using a passive learning algorithm for MDPs
3. Compose the individual models into an MDP $M = (Q, q_0, I, O, L, \delta)$

In the following, we discuss these three phases of HAL in more detail.

4.1 Segmentation and Labeling

The first step is to segment and label the provided IO traces $T \subseteq \mathcal{TR}$ using the segmentation function f_{seg}. The set of labels is given as X.

A *segmentation function* $f_{seg} : \mathcal{TR} \to (X \times \mathcal{TR})^*$ maps an IO trace t to a sequence of labeled segments, which are pairs of sub-traces and their labels. Segmentation functions have to retain the structure of any IO trace t, which is to say that the sequence obtained from joining all sub-traces from $f_{seg}(t)$ by overlapping the first and last elements in consecutive sub-traces has to be equal to the original IO trace t. Applying f_{seg} to each IO trace in the multiset T results in a new multiset T_s of segmented IO traces.

Example 1. Consider a set of outputs $O = \{o_1, o_2, o_3\}$ such that $o_1 < o_2 < o_3$ and a segmentation function f_{seg} that splits IO traces into sequences of rising and falling values, using the labels r and f accordingly. An example where this function is applied to an IO trace t is given below.

$$t = o_1 \xrightarrow{i_1} o_2 \xrightarrow{i_2} o_3 \xrightarrow{i_1} o_2 \xrightarrow{i_2} o_1 \xrightarrow{i_2} o_2$$

$$f_{seg}(t) = \langle \langle r, o_1 \xrightarrow{i_1} o_2 \xrightarrow{i_2} o_3 \rangle, \langle f, o_3 \xrightarrow{i_1} o_2 \xrightarrow{i_2} o_1 \rangle, \langle r, o_1 \xrightarrow{i_2} o_2 \rangle \rangle$$

4.2 Learning

Next, we use the segmented IO traces to learn an MDP model for each label $x \in X$ using only those segmented IO traces that are labeled with x. Since the segmentation function allows for arbitrary splits, we might end up with IO traces that have no common initial output symbol. This is a problem when learning MDPs since they require a unique initial state. This is solved by prepending each labeled segment with a common initial symbol *init* and a special input that corresponds to the first output.

To facilitate the composition of the individual models, we let the segments overlap by one output and include the label of the next segment. This is omitted for the last segment in each sequence of labeled segments since it has no successor. Other options implying differences in how the models are composed and the structure of the resulting model are conceivable, but were not explored in this work.

Together, this leads to IO traces of the following form:

$$init \xrightarrow{out} \left(out \xrightarrow{in}\right)^* (\langle out,\ next\rangle \mid out)$$

Example 2. Consider the following segmented IO trace:

$$t_s = \langle\langle r, o_1 \xrightarrow{i_1} o_2 \xrightarrow{i_2} o_3\rangle, \langle f, o_3 \xrightarrow{i_1} o_2 \xrightarrow{i_2} o_1\rangle\rangle$$

From t_s we extract two IO traces, one for each of the labels r and f, which are given below as t_r and t_f respectively.

$$t_r = init \xrightarrow{o_1} o_1 \xrightarrow{i_1} o_2 \xrightarrow{i_2} \langle o_3, f\rangle$$

$$t_f = init \xrightarrow{o_3} o_3 \xrightarrow{i_1} o_2 \xrightarrow{i_2} o_1$$

The last output of t_r signifies that the last input prompted the system to enter the mode corresponding to f.

For each system mode and corresponding label $x \in X$, we use the multiset of all IO traces with the same label T_x to learn a model $M_x = (Q_x, q_{0,x}, I_x, O \cup O \times X \cup \{init\}, L_x, \delta_x)$ using IOAlergia or another passive automata learning algorithm for MDPs. The input alphabet $I_x = I \cup O$ includes the initial outputs of the segments in T_x. Similarly, the output set is extended as discussed above.

Due to how we handle the inexistence of a unique initial observation, the initial state of each of the resulting models is a placeholder, that will be removed when the models are composed. We call the direct successors of the placeholder $q_{0,x}$ *entry states*, because they serve as entry points for the respective system mode, given some initial state corresponding to their respective output. For a given output o, we denote the corresponding entry state of a sub-model M_x as $\alpha_{o,x}$ and the set of all such states as A_x.

We use the term *exit state* for states that produce not only an output symbol but also a label that determines the next mode. As a result of how the training data for the individual sub-models is structured, none of those states have successors. Given a model M_x, we denote the set of exit states as Ω_x.

Example 3. Fig. 1 depicts a learned sub-model M_r corresponding to label r. Rounded rectangles depict states and their respective outputs and edges represent transitions between states. For brevity, we omit input symbols and transition probabilities. Regarding entry and exit states, we have $\alpha_{o_2,r} = q_{1,r}$, $\alpha_{o_1,r} = q_{2,r}$ and $\Omega_r = \{q_{5,r}\}$.

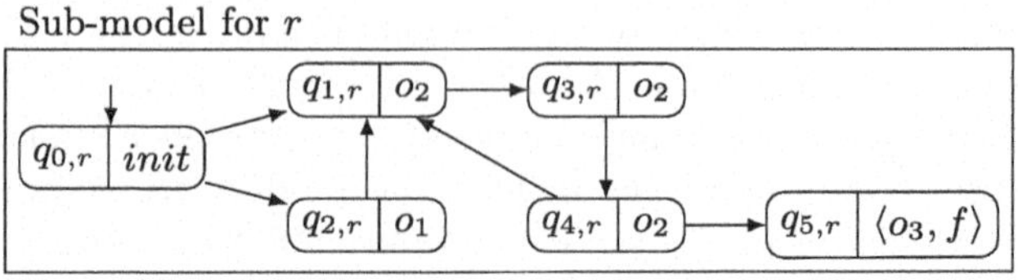

Fig. 1. A learned sub-model without input symbols and transition probabilities

4.3 Composition

As a final step, we compose the individual models M_x, resulting in an MDP $M = (Q, q_0, I, O, L, \delta)$. Apart from a few exceptions, Q, L and δ can be carried over from the individual sub-models. There are two main questions when composing the models: (1) How to handle transitions between sub-models? (2) How to create an initial state? Those questions need to be answered such that the resulting MDP is consistent with the input data. That is, when replaying the input data on M, each transition should be taken according to its probability. Before giving a formal definition of the composition process, we want to give an intuition for it using an example.

Example 4. Figure 2 illustrates the composition process using a system with two modes r and f. The initial output of the system is o_2. For the sake of simplicity, we omit input symbols and transition probabilities. The learned sub-models for r and f are shown in Fig. 2a. First, we remove the initial states of the sub-models ($q_{0,r}$ and $q_{0,f}$) as shown in Fig. 2b. The arrows with no source pointing to $q_{1,r}$ and $q_{1,f}$ indicate that they are initial states of the overall system. Furthermore, the dashed lines show which entry and exit states need to be merged. This information is specified in the output of each exit state. For example, the output of $q_{5,r}$ is $\langle o_3, f\rangle$, which corresponds to $q_{2,r}$, the entry state in sub-model f with output o_3. Then, we merge those states. The result is shown in Fig. 2c. Finally, the global initial state q_0 is added in Fig. 2d. Since the initial output of the entire system is o_2, its initial state q_0 should exhibit behavior similar to the two entry states with the same output ($q_{1,r}$ and $q_{1,f}$). Consequently, q_0 has transitions to $q_{3,r}$ and $q_{3,f}$, which are the successor states of those states. Note that the state $q_{1,f}$ is now unreachable and can be pruned. This is because no sub-model transitions to f on output o_2.

Transitions Between Sub-models. The individual models are recombined by merging exit states with entry states. The initial states are removed since they only serve as placeholders to facilitate learning MDPs with several initial states. Given a exit state ω, we determine which entry state to merge with by considering the exit state's output $\langle o, x\rangle$, where o is the state's output symbol and x the label corresponding to the system mode that is entered next. Together, those two values determine a unique entry state $\alpha_{o,x}$ that is compatible with ω. This is also the state with which ω is merged, which is done by asserting their equality (i.e. $\alpha_{o,x} = \omega$). Note that the information about outgoing transitions of

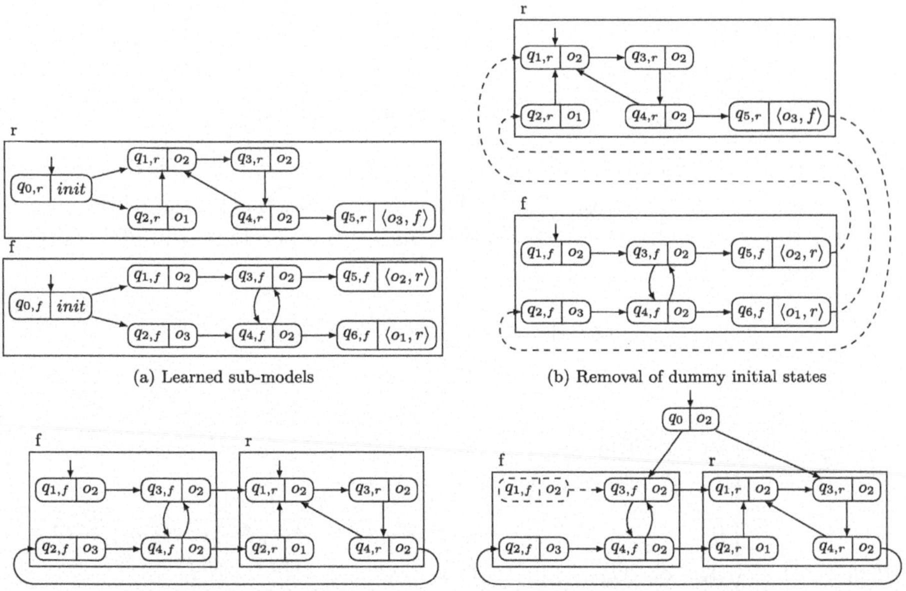

(a) Learned sub-models (b) Removal of dummy initial states

(c) Merged terminal and entry states (d) Final composed model with initial state

Fig. 2. Example of automata composition

ω and its output is encoded in δ_x and L_x respectively. We obtain this information from the transition and labeling functions of the sub-model where ω is an entry state. Consequently, δ_x and L_x are used to define $\delta(\omega, i)$ and $L(\omega)$. For all other states, the transition and output information can be directly obtained from the respective sub-models as well. This means that for each state q other than the initial state of M, the transition and output information can be taken from the unique sub-model M_x in which q is a non-exit state, or in other words $L_x(q) \in O$. This and how exit and entry states are merged is expressed in the following formula:

$$\begin{aligned} &\forall x, x' \in X, q \in Q_x, o \in O: \\ &\quad (L_x(q) = \langle o, x' \rangle \implies q = \alpha_{o,x'}) \wedge \\ &\quad (L_x(q) = o \implies L(q) = o \wedge \forall i \in I : \delta(q, i) = \delta_x(q, i)) \end{aligned}$$

Initial State. From the initial state, we transition to each sub-model according to the probability p_x of the corresponding label x being the first in a sequence of labeled segments. More specifically, we transition to $\alpha_{o_0,x}$, which is the entry point of the sub-model that outputs the initial observation o_0 of the overall system. Since an MDP needs to have a unique initial state, we introduce a new initial state q_0 not present in any of the learned sub-models, that mimics the behavior of the states $\alpha_{o_0,x}$ according to the probability p_x of the sub-model with label x being the first sub-model in a segmented IO trace. This gives the following properties of q_0:

$$L(q_0) = o_0$$

$$\delta(q_0, i)(q') = \begin{cases} 0 & \text{if } q' = q_0 \\ p_x * \delta_x(\alpha_{o_0,x}, i)(q') & \text{for } x such that q' \in Q_x \end{cases}$$

Definition of *M*. By asserting the equality of entry and exit states, we avoid explicitly merging those states. This allows us to define each case of the output and transition functions of M by considering only a single sub-model. Given a set of sub-models $\{M_x | x \in X\}$, we have

$$Q = \{q_0\} \cup \bigcup_{x \in X} Q_x \setminus \{q_{0,x}\}$$

$$L(q) = \begin{cases} o_0 & \text{if } q = q_0 \\ L_x(q) & \text{for } x \text{ such that } q \in Q_x \setminus \Omega_x \end{cases}$$

$$\delta(q, i)(q') = \begin{cases} 0 & \text{if } q' = q_0 \vee (q \neq q_0 \wedge \nexists y : \{q, q'\} \subseteq Q_y) \\ p_x * \delta_x(\alpha_{o_0,x}, i)(q') & \text{if } q = q_0 \\ \delta_x(q, i)(q') & \text{if } q \in Q_x \end{cases}$$
$$\text{where } x \text{ is chosen such that } q' \in Q_x$$

4.4 Properties of the Algorithm

The algorithm inherits many properties of the internally used learning algorithm $\mathcal{A}$. For example, the resulting model M is input enabled if all of the non-exit states of its sub-models are input enabled. If the models produced by $\mathcal{A}$ are not input enabled, it is possible to replay all IO traces that were used to learn it by construction if this is a property of $\mathcal{A}$. However, the resulting model can be non-deterministically labeled even if its sub-models are not. This is due to the construction of the initial state and the removal of the information about system modes – which is encoded in the outputs of the sub-models – during composition. An example of this can be seen in Fig. 2d, where the states q_0 and $q_{3,f}$ feature non-deterministic labeling. Non-deterministic labelling cannot occur when mode changes can be inferred from a single transition. If the segmentation function splits traces based on data after the split point, the resulting segmented traces already can contain nondeterminism, which inevitably leads to a non-deterministically labelled MDP. In between those two extreme cases, both behavior is possible. In this case – while not explored in this work – determinism could be enforced by adapting the internally used learning algorithm.

Note that the segmentation function prescribes a certain automaton structure since each sub-model has at most one entry state per output. This implies that, when switching between sub-models, the future behavior is independent of previous behavior except for the last output. Further, entry states become unreachable in the resulting model M if their behavior is relevant only at the start of system executions as shown in Fig. 2d.

5 Evaluation

The method was evaluated on randomly generated MDPs and an industrial case study. We learned models using IOAlergia with and without HAL and compared the resulting models based on different metrics. When the ground truth is a known MDP M, the similarity to a learned model $\hat{M}$ with respect to a bisimilarity distance d can be expressed as $1 - d(q_0, \hat{q}_0)$, where q_0 and $\hat{q}_0$ are the respective initial states. We use bisimilarity distances with a discounting factor of 0.95 and the pessimistic standard interpretation (i.e. maximum). However, in a generative setting, the interest is not in bounding worst case behavior, but in capturing a wide range of system behaviors. This is better captured by taking the average distance over all actions, which we report as a second similarity measure. We also use the compliance of a learned model with respect to a validation sample from the ground truth. Note that these metrics range from zero to one, where larger values correspond to higher similarity.

5.1 Artificial Systems

The generation of random MDPs is based on several parameters. To construct an individual MDP M, we first fix the sizes of the input and output alphabets ($|I|$ and $|O|$) and define according alphabets. Next, we create a set of N_M deterministically labeled MDPs $M_i = \langle Q_i, q_{0,i}, I, O, L_i, \delta \rangle$ with a fixed number of states N_Q. Those MDPs correspond to the different modes of the overall system M. To connect them, we choose a set of N_e entry states $Q_{e,i} \subseteq Q_i$ with distinct outputs for each sub model M_i. We then replace the target state of some of the transitions in each sub model M_i with entry states of other sub models, which results in a new transition function δ_i'. Modes are connected according to one of three topologies: A one-way ring where each M_i can transition to M_{i+1} or M_1 in the case of $i = N_M$, a two-way ring where each mode can also transition to its predecessor and a fully connected topology where every mode can transition into any other. We fix the number of transitions per pair of connected modes as N_c. We choose the initial state of the first sub model $q_{0,1}$ as initial of M. This lets us define $M = \langle \bigcup_{i=1}^{N_M} Q_i, q_{0,1}, I, O, L, \delta \rangle$ where L and δ denote the functions obtained from joining L_i and δ_i' over their (disjoint) domains. During random generation, we ensure that mode changes can be detected from a single observation. This limits the complexity of the required segmentation function such that constructing it does not require knowledge about the exact structure of the system which would heavily favor HAL.

We sample a multiset T of N_T traces t_i from M from which we learn approximations $\hat{M}_{IOA}$ and $\hat{M}_{HAL}$ of M using IOAlergia without and with HAL. When using our method, the traces are segmented based on the mode from which the individual data points stem. In particular, we use $|I| \in \{2, 5, 10\}$, $|O| \in \{2, 5, 10\}$, $N_M \in \{2, 3, 4, 5\}$, $N_Q \in \{5, 15, 30\}$ and $N_c \in \{1, 5, 10\}$ for MDP generation. For the generation of traces we use $N_T \in \{100, 300, 900\}$ traces with a fixed length in $\{100, 300\}$. Together with the three topologies, this results in 3888 configurations

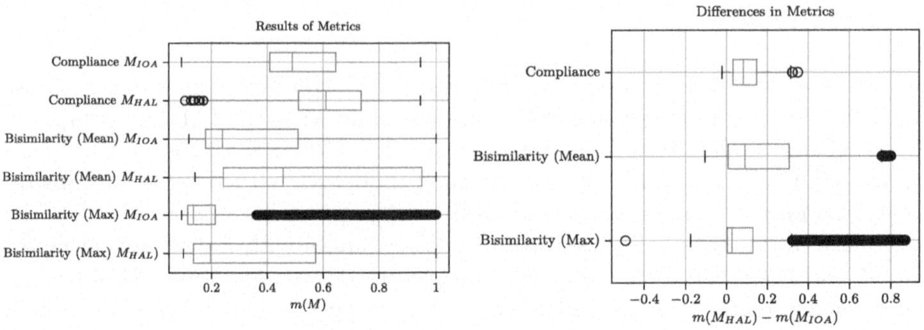

(a) Direct comparison of metrics

(b) Improvement/Deterioration

Fig. 3. Comparison of the quality of the learned models with different metrics over all tested configurations

after excluding invalid and redundant configurations. Compliance was evaluated using 1000 traces of length 100 sampled randomly from the ground truth model.

Figure 3a shows the results. From these boxplots we can already see that our method *HAL* significantly improves performance on all considered metrics. This is beneficial especially when the focus is on the generative aspect of the learned models. Considering verification, the most relevant metric is maximum-based bisimilarity. From the results for this metric it is apparent that while our method outperforms the baseline, it is not a silver bullet for verification in low-data scenarios. Intuitively, this becomes obvious when we consider the extreme case in which the training data does not even contain data from all states of the ground truth. For each similarity metric $m(\hat{M})$, Fig. 3b shows boxplots of $m(\hat{M}_{HAL}) - m(\hat{M}_{IOA})$, which corresponds to the improvement (or degradation) of our method. HAL does not only improve average performance but does so rather consistently. The percentage of cases where HAL performs worse, the average deterioration in this case and the average improvement are shown in Table 1. For all metrics, the number of deteriorating cases is below ten percent. The evaluation code is part of the online repository[2].

Table 1. Statistics over all configurations

Metric	Worse Cases [%]	Avg. Improvement	Avg. Deterioration
Bisimilarity (Max)	9.36	0.1394	−0.0177
Bisimilarity (Mean)	6.46	0.1927	−0.0129
Compliance	0.77	0.0943	−0.0023

[2] https://github.com/benjaminvonberg/hierarchical-automata-learning.

5.2 Industrial Case Study

The approach was evaluated on a data set from the domain of real driving emissions (RDE) with the aim of generating a model of human driver behavior that can be used to generate realistic velocity profiles for highway routes.

Data Description and Preprocessing. The data was provided by AVL List GmbH and consists of several measurement sequences describing driver behavior, which were recorded during real-world test drives and augmented with information about static road features. The data is comprised of 21 test drives from three different routes covering environments such as urban and highway driving. The majority (17) of the test drives corresponds to the same route. The individual measurements are sampled with a uniform spatial step of 5 m and encompass continuous (e.g. velocity, curvature) and discrete features (e.g. traffic signs). From this, we extracted 314 IO traces based on the criterion that the speed limit is greater than 80 km/h. The total length of those sequences is 1150 km with an average length of 3656 m or 731 samples, ranging from 200 m to 32.5 km. During feature selection, we reduced the feature space to four features: past speed limit, future speed limit, road curvature and road category (highway, freeway, etc.). We discretized the velocity (uniform 2.5 km/h steps) and curvature values (logarithmic scaling) since the employed methodology requires discrete data. This leaves us with six discrete values for the curvature and five values for past and future speed limits as well as the road category.

Learning. We use a segmentation function that splits traces into segments with rising and falling velocity. This choice encodes the assumption that the behavior during acceleration and deceleration phases does not depend on the history prior to the start of the phase. While this assumption is not realistic, the differences in behavior caused by the influence of prior history is small enough to be outweighed by the benefit of exploiting the common structure in acceleration and deceleration phases. The chosen segmentation function is similar to Example 1. However, we adapt the segmentation to let the last output in each segmented trace be the first output that contradicts the label of the trace and fix the first mode to be rising. This makes mode changes detectable via a single transition which ensures deterministic models. For learning the individual sub-models, we used the IOAlergia implementation of the AALpy automata learning library [21].

Sequence Generation. To generate a velocity profile for a new route given as a series of road features, we first apply similar pre-processing as before. This results in a sequence of inputs that can be used to sample output sequences from the model. However, the learned model is not input enabled. This is to be expected since our training data contains about 230 000 data points while even the simplest input-enabled model based on our discretization has at least $|I| \cdot |O| \approx 45000$ transitions. Sampling from non-input-enabled models is problematic since we might end up in a state where the provided input is not enabled, resulting in undefined behavior. This can be remedied by modeling the new route as an automaton and using a process similar to the composition of interface automata [3]. The latter can be thought of as turning the two automata into a closed-loop system by letting the output of the route model act as input for the driver model and vice versa. The result of this composition is a Markov chain that describes all valid paths through the learned model for the specified route. To account for pruning invalid paths, we need to normalize the transition probabilities.

Evaluation. Since no ground truth model is available, we only use the compliance metric. We use leave-one-out cross validation in order to maximize the number of data during learning and weigh the individual contributions according to the length of the trace used for validation. The models learned using plain IOAlergia and with HAL obtain scores of 0.2390 and 0.2734 respectively, which corresponds to an improvement of about 14.48%. An evaluation by domain experts at AVL concluded that the traces generated by the model show behavior sufficiently similar to human driving behavior for use in RDE computations. Figure 4 shows five samples drawn from two models for the same route, which covers a stretch of highway starting with an acceleration lane. The curves in light green show 17 real-world recordings for this route. Dotted lines show environment features (speed limit and curvature). Solid curves in other colors show the generated velocity profiles, which were created by smoothing the heavily discretized outputs of the learned model. The plot on the left shows velocity profiles generated using a model that was learned using standard IOAlergia serving as a baseline. The plot on the right shows curves generated using our method as outlined above. Those examples show that HAL is able to consistently capture features that are poorly covered by the baseline. Take for example the acceleration at the beginning of the route, where the baseline accelerates to about 100 km/h with high probability, whereas the original data and HAL show a wider distribution of velocities. HAL also better captures behavior patterns with short duration and high dynamics.

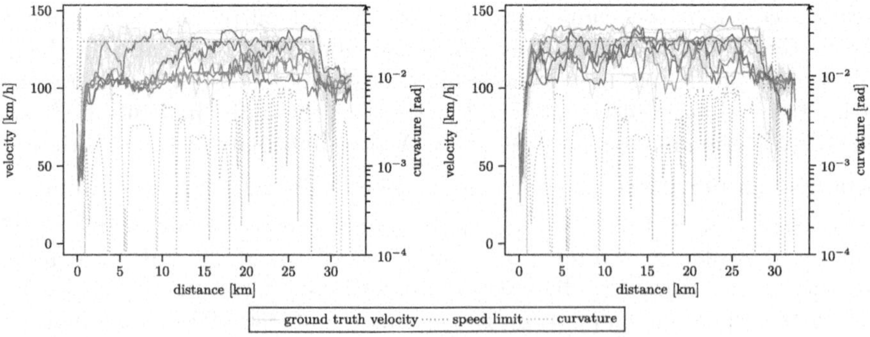

Fig. 4. Samples drawn from models generated using IOAlergia (left) and our method of Hierarchical Automata Learning (right).

6 Related Work

The IOAlergia algorithm is closely related to Alergia [10] for learning probabilistic deterministic finite-state automata (PDFAs). An overview of adaptations of Alergia aiming to address its shortcomings is given by Verwer and Hammerschmidt [29,30]. An approach based on genetic algorithms was given by Wang et al. [32]. In the field of specification mining, the popular k-Tails algorithm [9] was also adapted to PDFAs in the sk-strings algorithm [26]. A different approach based on parameter estimation for a given automaton structure is the Baum-Welch algorithm [25]. A more recent algorithm proposed by Bazille et al. [8] guarantees that the learned model behaves similarly to the original system with respect to a wide range of temporal properties. An approach by Wang et al. [31] uses predicate abstraction and counterexample-guided abstraction refinement to learn models at the right level of abstraction. Those algorithms and their adaptations do not apply directly to our problem since they handle PDFAs or Markov chains. The Baum-Welch algorithm has been adapted for MDPs [11], but requires knowledge of the MDP's structure or a method for estimating it. An algorithm by Akram and de la Higuera [2] learns probabilistic subsequent transducers. However, this class of automata behaves deterministically on a given input sequence, making it inapplicable for our use case. There are three major frameworks for learning automaton models that implement formalisms for passively learning probabilistic automata: FlexFringe [30], AALpy [21] and Jajapy [27].

The work of Tappler et al. [22,28] and Bacci et al. [5] is concerned with active learning of MDPs based on Angluin's L* algorithm [4] and Baum-Welch respectively. In this setting, the system to be modeled can be queried, which is different from our work where a fixed set of observations is available. Work by Abel and Reineke [1] considers active learning for serial compositions of Mealy machines, aided by knowledge of a component of the system. Labbaf et al. [18] provide an algorithm based on the assumption that the underlying system is made up of several components under a parallel interleaving composition.

The idea of segmenting traces has been used before. This is the case for a recent paper by Gurung et al. [16] in which they learn hybrid systems. They use change-point detection for segmenting IO traces, cluster the resulting segments into modes and – for each mode – learn a system of differential equations instead of an MDP. Bartocci et al. [7] abstract away from system modes and learn a deterministic finite automaton directly from the sequence of labels. For each label, they fit a curve segment to the set of corresponding segments. They use linear segments, which allows for automatic segmentation and results in a language describing piecewise linear functions. Neither of those methods produce probabilistic automata. In the context of active learning for use case testing, Meinke and Khosrowjerdi [20] used segmentation based on criteria specific to the use case to facilitate learning with constraints on the input.

The neural network community has contributed several generative approaches for sequential data, including variational autoencoders [15] and generative adversarial networks [23]. Methods based on neural networks are inherently data driven and – to the best of our knowledge – no methods for using domain knowledge about system modes exist. In contrast to automaton models, neural networks usually model the data distribution implicitly [24] and are consequently less interpretable and do not lend themselves to model checking as easily.

7 Conclusion

We presented a method to aid learning algorithms for MDPs using domain knowledge and heuristics. Our algorithm exploits knowledge about system modes. This is achieved by splitting IO traces according to system modes, learning a model for each mode and recombining the individual sub-models. This results in a hierarchic MDP where sub-regions correspond to system modes, which also aids explainability. We evaluated our method on artificial systems showing strong results, outperforming the baseline in over 90 % of cases for all considered metrics. A second evaluation was done on an industrial case study, where we learned a generative model of human driver behavior on highways that can be used to generate velocity profiles for new routes. Our method led to an improvement by over 14 %, even when using heuristics instead of exact knowledge.

In low-data scenarios, the IOAlergia algorithm produces low-quality models. This is in part due to the inherent difficulty to learn correct models from little data. However, the problem is amplified by the statistical compatibility test used. Our method can help alleviate both of those problems when domain knowledge about system modes is available or heuristics are applicable.

From this paper, several opportunities for future work arise. The method can be further evaluated to determine for which types of systems the approach works well, the influence of data coverage and segmentation criteria or – for heuristic criteria – potential inaccuracies thereof. We also want to extend the algorithm to allow for different input abstractions for each system mode. Further, we aim to add more aspects of hierarchic modeling such as multi-level hierarchies and transitions on the level of super-states, similar to statecharts [17].

Acknowledgments. This work is funded by the AIDOaRt project (grant agreement No 101007350) from the ECSEL Joint Undertaking (JU). The JU receives support from the European Union's Horizon 2020 research and innovation programme and Sweden, Austria, Czech Republic, Finland, France, Italy, and Spain.

References

1. Abel, A., Reineke, J.: Gray-box learning of serial compositions of mealy machines. In: Rayadurgam, S., Tkachuk, O. (eds.) NFM 2016. LNCS, vol. 9690, pp. 272–287. Springer, Cham (2016). https://doi.org/10.1007/978-3-319-40648-0_21
2. Akram, H.I., de la Higuera, C.: Learning probabilistic subsequential transducers from positive data. In: ICAART 2013 - Proceedings of the 5th International Conference on Agents and Artificial Intelligence. pp. 479–486. SciTePress (2013). https://doi.org/10.5220/0004359904790486

3. de Alfaro, L., Henzinger, T.A.: Interface automata. In: Proceedings of the 8th European Software Engineering Conference, pp. 109–120. ACM (2001). https://doi.org/10.1145/503209.503226
4. Angluin, D.: Learning regular sets from queries and counterexamples. Inf. Comput. **75**(2), 87–106 (1987). https://doi.org/10.1016/0890-5401(87)90052-6
5. Bacci, G., Ingólfsdóttir, A., Larsen, K.G., Reynouard, R.: Active learning of Markov decision processes using Baum-Welch algorithm. In: 20th IEEE International Conference on Machine Learning and Applications, ICMLA 2021, pp. 1203–1208. IEEE (2021). https://doi.org/10.1109/ICMLA52953.2021.00195
6. Baier, C., Katoen, J.: Principles of model checking. MIT Press (2008). https://doi.org/10.1093/comjnl/bxp025
7. Bartocci, E., Deshmukh, J., Mateis, C., Nesterini, E., Ničković, D., Qin, X.: Mining shape expressions with ShapeIt. In: Calinescu, R., Păsăreanu, C.S. (eds.) SEFM 2021. LNCS, vol. 13085, pp. 110–117. Springer, Cham (2021). https://doi.org/10.1007/978-3-030-92124-8_7
8. Bazille, H., Genest, B., Jegourel, C., Sun, J.: Global PAC bounds for learning discrete time markov chains. In: Lahiri, S.K., Wang, C. (eds.) CAV 2020. LNCS, vol. 12225, pp. 304–326. Springer, Cham (2020). https://doi.org/10.1007/978-3-030-53291-8_17
9. Biermann, A.W., Feldman, J.A.: On the synthesis of finite-state machines from samples of their behavior. IEEE Trans. Comput. **21**(6), 592–597 (1972). https://doi.org/10.1109/TC.1972.5009015
10. Carrasco, R.C., Oncina, J.: Learning stochastic regular grammars by means of a state merging method. In: Carrasco, R.C., Oncina, J. (eds.) ICGI 1994. LNCS, vol. 862, pp. 139–152. Springer, Heidelberg (1994). https://doi.org/10.1007/3-540-58473-0_144
11. Chrisman, L.: Reinforcement learning with perceptual aliasing: the perceptual distinctions approach. In: Proceedings of the 10th National Conference on Artificial Intelligence, pp. 183–188. AAAI Press / The MIT Press (1992)
12. Desharnais, J., Jagadeesan, R., Gupta, V., Panangaden, P.: The metric analogue of weak bisimulation for probabilistic processes. In: 17th IEEE Symposium on Logic in Computer Science (LICS 2002), 22-25 July 2002, Copenhagen, Denmark, Proceedings, pp. 413–422. IEEE Computer Society (2002). https://doi.org/10.1109/LICS.2002.1029849
13. Ferns, N., Panangaden, P., Precup, D.: Metrics for finite markov decision processes. In: UAI 2004, Proceedings of the 20th Conference in Uncertainty in Artificial Intelligence, Banff, Canada, 7-11 July 2004, pp. 162–169. AUAI Press (2004)
14. García, J., Visús, Á., Fernández, F.: A taxonomy for similarity metrics between markov decision processes. Mach. Learn. **111**(11), 4217–4247 (2022). https://doi.org/10.1007/S10994-022-06242-4
15. Girin, L., Leglaive, S., Bie, X., Diard, J., Hueber, T., Alameda-Pineda, X.: Dynamical variational autoencoders: a comprehensive review. Foundat. Trends Mach. Learn. **15**(1–2), 1–175 (2021). https://doi.org/10.1561/2200000089
16. Gurung, A., Waga, M., Suenaga, K.: Learning nonlinear hybrid automata from input-output time-series data. In: Automated Technology for Verification and Analysis - 21st International Symposium, ATVA 2023. vol. 14215, pp. 33–52. Springer (2023). https://doi.org/10.1007/978-3-031-45329-8_2
17. Harel, D.: Statecharts: a visual formalism for complex systems. Sci. Comput. Program. **8**(3), 231–274 (1987). https://doi.org/10.1016/0167-6423(87)90035-9

18. Labbaf, F., Groote, J.F., Hojjat, H., Mousavi, M.R.: Compositional learning for interleaving parallel automata. In: Foundations of Software Science and Computation Structures - 26th International Conference, FoSSaCS 2023, vol. 13992, pp. 413–435. Springer (2023). https://doi.org/10.1007/978-3-031-30829-1_20
19. Mao, H., Chen, Y., Jaeger, M., Nielsen, T.D., Larsen, K.G., Nielsen, B.: Learning deterministic probabilistic automata from a model checking perspective. Mach. Learn. **105**(2), 255–299 (2016). https://doi.org/10.1007/s10994-016-5565-9
20. Meinke, K., Khosrowjerdi, H.: Use case testing: a constrained active machine learning approach. In: Loulergue, F., Wotawa, F. (eds.) TAP 2021. LNCS, vol. 12740, pp. 3–21. Springer, Cham (2021). https://doi.org/10.1007/978-3-030-79379-1_1
21. Muskardin, E., Aichernig, B.K., Pill, I., Pferscher, A., Tappler, M.: AALpy: an active automata learning library. Innovations Syst. Softw. Eng. **18**(3), 417–426 (2022). https://doi.org/10.1007/S11334-022-00449-3
22. Muskardin, E., Tappler, M., Aichernig, B.K., Pill, I.: Active model learning of stochastic reactive systems (extended version). Softw. Syst. Model. **23**(2), 503–524 (2024). https://doi.org/10.1007/S10270-024-01158-0
23. Pei, H., Ren, K., Yang, Y., Liu, C., Qin, T., Li, D.: Towards generating real-world time series data. In: IEEE International Conference on Data Mining, ICDM 2021, pp. 469–478. IEEE (2021). https://doi.org/10.1109/ICDM51629.2021.00058
24. Piatkowski, N., Posch, P.N., Krause, M.: How to trust generative probabilistic models for time-series data? In: Simos, D.E., Pardalos, P.M., Kotsireas, I.S. (eds.) LION 2021. LNCS, vol. 12931, pp. 283–298. Springer, Cham (2021). https://doi.org/10.1007/978-3-030-92121-7_23
25. Rabiner, L.R.: A tutorial on hidden Markov models and selected applications in speech recognition. Proc. IEEE **77**(2), 257–286 (1989). https://doi.org/10.1109/5.18626
26. Raman, A.V., Patrick, J.D., North, P.: The sk-strings method for inferring PFSA. In: Proceedings of the workshop on automata induction, grammatical inference and language acquisition at the 14th ICML (1997)
27. Reynouard, R., Ingólfsdóttir, A., Bacci, G.: Jajapy: a learning library for stochastic models. In: Quantitative Evaluation of Systems - 20th International Conference, QEST 2023, vol. 14287, pp. 30–46. Springer (2023). https://doi.org/10.1007/978-3-031-43835-6_3
28. Tappler, M., Aichernig, B.K., Bacci, G., Eichlseder, M., Larsen, K.G.: L^*-based learning of Markov decision processes (extended version). Formal Aspects Comput. **33**(4–5), 575–615 (2021). https://doi.org/10.1007/S00165-021-00536-5
29. Verwer, S., Hammerschmidt, C.A.: FlexFringe: a passive automaton learning package. In: 2017 IEEE International Conference on Software Maintenance and Evolution, ICSME 2017, pp. 638–642. IEEE Computer Society (2017). https://doi.org/10.1109/ICSME.2017.58
30. Verwer, S., Hammerschmidt, C.A.: FlexFringe: Modeling software behavior by learning probabilistic automata. CoRR arXiv: abs/2203.16331 (2022)
31. Wang, J., Sun, J., Qin, S., Jégourel, C.: Automatically "verifying" discrete-time complex systems through learning, abstraction and refinement. IEEE Trans. Software Eng. **47**(1), 189–203 (2021). https://doi.org/10.1109/TSE.2018.2886898

32. Wang, J., Sun, J., Yuan, Q., Pang, J.: Learning probabilistic models for model checking: An evolutionary approach and an empirical study. Int. J. Softw. Tools Technol. Transfer **20**(6), 689–704 (2018). https://doi.org/10.1007/S10009-018-0492-7
33. Young-Lai, M., Tompa, F.W.: Stochastic grammatical inference of text database structure. Mach. Learn. **40**(2), 111–137 (2000). https://doi.org/10.1023/A:1007653929870

Composing Run-Time Variability Models

Salman Farhat[1], Simon Bliudze[1](✉), Laurence Duchien[1], and Olga Kouchnarenko[2]

[1] Univ. Lille, Inria, CNRS, Centrale Lille, UMR 9189 CRIStAL, 59000 Lille, France
{Salman.Farhat,Simon.Bliudze,Laurence.Duchien}@inria.fr

[2] Université de Franche-Comté, CNRS, Institut FEMTO-ST, 25000 Besançon, France
Olga.Kouchnarenko@femto-st.fr

Abstract. The sheer complexity of modern systems requires compositional approaches to variability modelling. To manage the variability of large systems' architecture, feature models are widely used at design-time, with several operators defined to allow their composition. However, complex systems' architectures may evolve at run-time by acquiring new features and functionalities while respecting new constraints. To address this challenge, this paper defines composition operators for component-based run-time variability models that not only encode these feature model composition operators, but also ensure safe run-time reconfiguration. To prove the correctness and compositionality properties, we propose a novel *multi-step $\mathcal{UP}$-bisimulation* equivalence and use it to show that the component-based run-time variability models preserve the semantics of the composed feature models. In addition, reachability results permit safe reconfiguration.

Keywords: System Architecture Evolution · Component-based Systems · Variability Models · Composition Operators · Multi-step Bisimulation

1 Introduction

Software evolution [10] is the continual development of system software to extend its own functionality over time by integrating new functionalities not originally modeled. Systems are expected to evolve over time, new functionalities can be introduced to the system that expands the configuration space that was previously modeled. To enable modeling a system as it evolves, there must be a means to integrate sub-models encapsulating new functionality to the original model. To support such an evolution, component models are expected to be composable in such a way as to be able to merge two separate models into one model that encapsulates the modified configuration space. For instance, consider a component-based model that represents the services of the Heroku Cloud platform [17]. Cloud platforms are dynamic and evolve over time [19], driven

S. Bliudze—Partially supported by the ANR grant ANR-23-CE25-0012 (SmartCloud).
O. Kouchnarenko—Partially supported by the ANR-23-CE25-0004 grant (ADAPT) and the ANR-17-EURE-0002 grant (EIPHI Graduate School) during her research leave at Inria Lille.

A. Madeira and A. Knapp (Eds.): SEFM 2024, LNCS 15280, pp. 234–252, 2025.
https://doi.org/10.1007/978-3-031-77382-2_14

not only by enhancements from its core development team but also through contributions from its user community. Clients of Heroku Cloud, for instance, can develop and introduce new services, such as advanced monitoring tools or supplementary management features, and subsequently offer these services on the Heroku marketplace. Then it becomes necessary to integrate these newly modeled services with the existing Heroku Cloud model, as the new services modify the configuration space of what was originally modeled. This integration ensures that the evolving Heroku Cloud is effectively modeled and adapted to accommodate the newly introduced services.

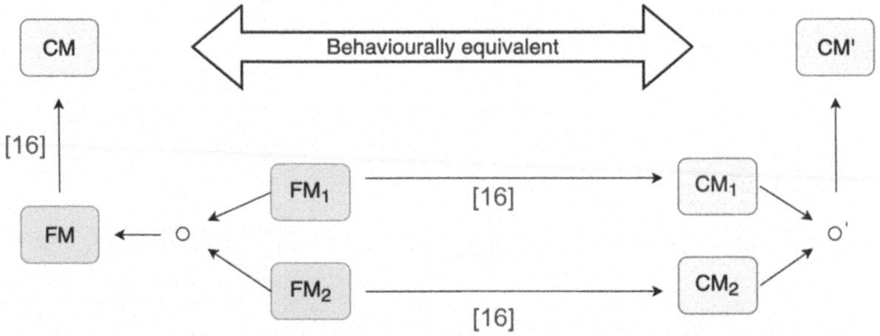

Fig. 1. Overview of Feature and JavaBIP models composition

In software product line engineering domain, the composition of static variability models [11,22] like feature models (FMs) [7,18] is an active research area [20]. Various composition operators to compose FMs [1–4,9] have been proposed, and featured transition systems [12] are well-established models used for verification and validation purpose in different application domains. As highlighted in [12], it is challenging for these static models to support CPS or AI-intensive systems development. In the domain of component-based models, a recent survey [13] emphasizes the need for a suitable methodology to ensure the correctness of reconfigurations in component-based systems.

In this context, an automated model transformation approach has been developed for enforcing safe reconfiguration of software products by constructing, from feature models, executable component-based run-time variability models (CBRTVMs) [16]. These CBRTVMs, generated and executed in the JavaBIP framework [8], ensure that whenever a user requests the selection of a feature, all the required dependencies are selected at the same time (and similarly for feature deselection). If this is not possible, the operation is postponed without blocking other requests.

In this paper, we build upon that work, focusing on the compositionality of the approach (cf. Figure 1, where CM stand for component-based models, and FM for feature models). We consider three FM composition operators $\circ$ from [4] and define corresponding operators $\circ'$ over JavaBIP models. We introduce a novel notion of *multi-step $\mathcal{UP}$-bisimulation* to show that the composition of two CBRTVMs is behaviourally equivalent to the CBRTVM obtained from the composition of the corresponding FMs (Fig. 1, at the top). Thus, we render the approach compositional while preserving the safety of dynamic reconfiguration.

Contributions and Outline. This paper introduces composition operators for JavaBIP CBRTVMs, enabling an automated construction of component-based systems in a modular fashion while providing reusability, flexibility, and adaptability. In this context, the paper aims to address the following research question (RQ):

RQ1: How to encode Feature Model composition on CBRTVMs?
RQ2: How to define a behavioural equivalence to prove the correctness and compositionality of such an encoding?

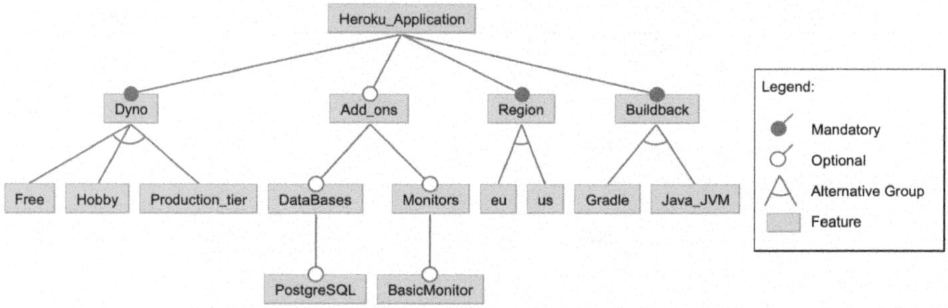

Fig. 2. Part of the Heroku Cloud feature model.

The paper is organised as follows. Section 2 provides a motivating example. Background material is presented in Sect. 3. In Sect. 4, we address RQ1 by defining three composition operators on JavaBIP models and study their properties. In Sect. 5, we address RQ2 by defining the notion of a multi-step $\mathcal{UP}$-bisimulation and proving the correctness and compositionality of the encoding. Section 6, provides an experimental validation of our results. Section 7 discusses related work. Section 8 concludes the paper.

2 Motivating Example

Heroku Cloud is a platform-as-a-service provider, that offers a range of API-controlled services such as Dyno types, add-ons, and Regions [17]. Add-ons are supplementary functionalities encompassing services such as databases, monitoring, and messaging. We use a feature model representing a sub-set of Heroku services shown in Fig. 2.

Suppose a new monitoring service, CloudWatch [24], is implemented and provided by Heroku. CloudWatch is an add-on service designed to monitor the performance of the computing units within the system. Its key functionality includes conducting comprehensive metric analyses, specifically focusing on CPU and memory usage metrics. This new service can be modelled in a separate feature model as presented in Fig. 3.

To incorporate this service, the Heroku *FM* and the CloudWatch *FM* must be composed into one model that includes these new functionalities. Composition techniques, as outlined by Acher et al. [1], facilitate this process for static feature models. This allows independent development of sub-feature models by different stakeholders and enables the reuse of existing models. In [16], the transformation process encodes static feature models in terms of component-based runtime variability models allowing safe reconfiguration at runtime. To allow a modular construction and composability of CBRTVMs, this paper defines composition operators for CBRTVMs that correctly encode the composition operators of feature models with the advantage of supporting configuration evolution at runtime.

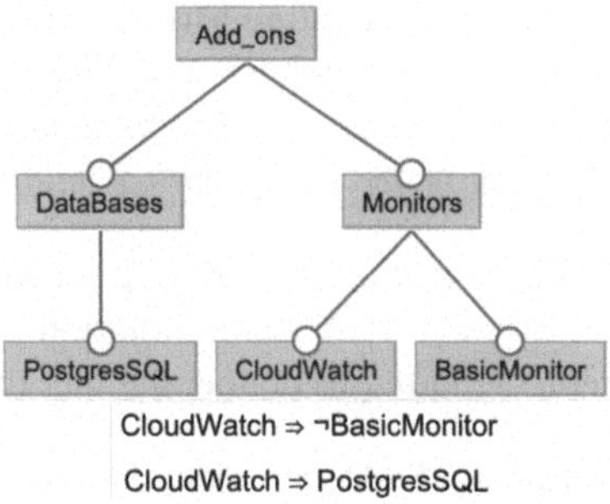

Fig. 3. CloudWatch FM

3 Background

This section describes the preliminary notions related to feature models and their composition on the one hand, and to the JavaBIP component-based framework, on the other hand.

3.1 Feature Models

Introduced for product lines, feature models are used for representing the commonality and variability of features and of relationships among them [7]. A feature could be a software artifact such as a part of code, a component, or a requirement (cf. Figures 2 and 3). To express the variability of the system, feature models provide 1) a decomposition in sub-features, where a sub-feature may be mandatory (*black circle*), or optional (*unfilled circle*), 2) XOR-group or an OR-group. In a XOR-group, exactly one feature is selected, while in an OR-group, one or more features are selected, whenever the parent feature is selected. In addition, the combination of the optional and mandatory features is seen as an AND-group. In the main hierarchy, cross-tree constraints can be used to describe dependencies between arbitrary features, e.g. selecting a feature *requires* the selection of another one, or that two features mutually *exclude* each other.

We recall the formalisation of feature models that we have used in [16].

Definition 1 (Feature Diagram). *A feature diagram is a tree-like structure conforming to the following grammar:*

$$\begin{aligned} \mathit{Node} ::= {} & \mathtt{OR}(\mathit{Node}_1, \ldots, \mathit{Node}_k) \mid \mathtt{XOR}(\mathit{Node}_1, \ldots, \mathit{Node}_k) \\ & \mid \mathtt{AND}([\mathbf{mand}]\mathit{Node}_1, \ldots, [\mathbf{mand}]\mathit{Node}_k) \mid \mathit{leaf} \end{aligned}$$

We denote by $\pi \subseteq \mathit{Node} \times \mathit{Node}$ *the* parent *relation, i.e. a node* n *is a child of* n' *iff* $\pi(n) = n'$. *Let* $\mu \subseteq \mathit{Node} \times \mathit{Node}$ *be the reflexive and transitive closure of* π^{-1}, *i.e.* $\mu(n)$ *is the set of all descendants of* $n \in \mathit{Node}$, *including itself.*

Definition 2 (Feature Model). *A feature model over a set of features F is a tuple $FM = (root, \phi, \rho, \chi)$, where $root \in Node$ is a feature diagram, $\phi : \mu(root) \rightarrow F$ is a bijective function associating features to nodes, and $\rho, \chi \subseteq F \times F$ are the* requires *and* excludes *relations, respectively, with χ being symmetric.*[1]

For a feature $f \in F$ in the FM, we denote $n_f \stackrel{\text{def}}{=} \phi^{-1}(f)$, i.e. n_f is the node, such that $\phi(n_f) = f$. Abusing notation, we also write $\pi(f) = f'$ iff $\pi(n_f) = n_{f'}$. We use the predicate *mand* to denote the fact that a given node represents a mandatory feature.

Definition 3 (Dependency Graph). *Given an FM $(root, \phi, \rho, \chi)$ over F, its* dependency graph *is a directed graph $G = (F, E)$, where F is the set of features, and $E \subseteq F \times F$ is the set of directed edges representing the parent, mandatory and requires relations:*

$$E \stackrel{\text{def}}{=} \{(f_1, f_2) \,|\, \pi(f_1) = f_2\} \cup \{(f_1, f_2) \,|\, \pi(f_2) = f_1 \wedge mand(f_2)\} \cup \rho\,.$$

Definition 4 (Configuration Semantics). *Let $FM = (root, \phi, \rho, \chi)$ be a feature model over a set of features F and let (F, E) be its dependency graph. A* configuration *is a set of features $\Phi \subseteq F$. We say that Φ is*

1. free from internal conflict *if, for any $f_1, f_2 \in \Phi$, holds $(f_1, f_2) \notin \chi$;*
2. saturated *if, for any $f \in \Phi$, holds $E(f) \subseteq \Phi$;*
3. valid *if it is saturated, free from internal conflict and respects structural constraints of* `XOR` *and* `OR` *nodes: exactly one (*`XOR`*) or at least one (*`OR`*) child feature selected, respectively (saturation implies that* `AND`*-node constraints are respected);*
4. partial-valid *if there exists a valid configuration $\Phi' \supseteq \Phi$.*

The FM semantics is the set of its valid configurations, denoted $[[FM]]$ [23].

Assumption 1. *We follow [16] in assuming that all considered feature models are such that any configuration free from internal conflict is partial-valid.*

3.2 Composition of Feature Models

In this paper, we adopt a denotational logic-based methodology for the composition of feature models, as outlined in [4]. This methodology encompasses the following steps:

1. The input feature models FM_1 and FM_2 are encoded as propositional formulae ϕ_{FM_1} and ϕ_{FM_2} respectively.
2. The composition operator is translated into a Boolean logic formula ϕ_c representing the composed feature model FM.
3. The feature diagram is then synthesized from ϕ_c.

[1] We write $f_1 \Rightarrow f_2$ iff $\rho(f_1, f_2)$ and $f_1 \Rightarrow \neg f_2$ (equivalently $f_2 \Rightarrow \neg f_1$) iff $\chi(f_1, f_2)$.

We focus on three composition operators inspired by the ones in [4] and defined by the following Boolean formulae:

Intersection ($\cap$):	$\phi = \phi_{FM_1} \wedge \phi_{FM_2}$
Strict Intersection ($\dot{\cap}$):	$\phi = (\phi_{FM_1} \wedge not(F_2 \setminus F_1)) \wedge (\phi_{FM_2} \wedge not(F_1 \setminus F_2))$
Union ($\cup$):	$\phi = \phi_{FM_1} \vee \phi_{FM_2}$

where the set of features of the composed feature model is $F = F_1 \cup F_2$, and, for a given set of features $F' \subseteq F$, we define $not(F') \stackrel{\text{def}}{=} \bigwedge_{f \in F'} \neg f$.

Thus, a configuration $\Phi \subset F_1 \cup F_2$ is valid in $FM_1 \cap FM_2$ iff $\Phi \cap F_i$ is valid in FM_i for both $i = 1, 2$. It is valid in $FM_1 \dot{\cap} FM_2$, iff Φ is valid in FM_1 *and* FM_2. Finally, Φ is valid in $FM_1 \cup FM_2$ if the constraints for each feature in Φ are satisfied in either FM_1 or FM_2, i.e. holds $[[FM_1]] \cup [[FM_2]] \subseteq [[FM]]$ but not necessarily $[[FM_1]] \cup [[FM_2]] = [[FM]]$.

When synthesizing feature diagrams from Boolean formulas, it is important to note that a single Boolean formula corresponds to multiple possible feature model structures. Despite potential differences in dependency graphs, these varying structures encode the same set of valid configurations. In our work, we do not restrict the structure of the diagram for a given Boolean formula. Any algorithm can be used for synthesizing composed feature models, as long as the diagram is equivalent to the original formula.

3.3 JavaBIP Component-Based Approach

A component is a software object that encapsulates certain behaviours of a software element. The concept of components is broad and may be used for component-based software systems, microservices, service-oriented applications, and so on. For the coordination of concurrent components, we make use of JavaBIP [8], which is an open-source Java implementation of the BIP (Behaviour-Interaction-Priority) framework [6].

In this context, the component behaviour is defined by a finite state machine (FSM) $(Q, P, \rightarrow)$, whose states (Q) are linked by transitions labelled by involved ports (P). JavaBIP allows two types of ports: *enforceable* and *spontaneous*. Enforceable ports represent actions controlled by the JavaBIP engine. They can be *synchronised*, i.e. executed together atomically. Spontaneous ports represent notifications that components receive about events that happen in their environment. They cannot be synchronised with other ports. An *interaction* is a set of ports—either one or several enforceable ports, or exactly one spontaneous port. To define allowed interactions, JavaBIP provides *requires* and *accepts* macros associated with enforceable ports and representing causal and acceptance constraints, respectively [8]. This allows JavaBIP to provide a coordination layer that is powerful enough to model—naturally and compositionally—the constraints expressed in the feature model. Intuitively, the requires macro specifies ports required for synchronization with the given port. For example, "$C1.p$ **Requires** $(C2.q; C3.r), C4.s$"[2] means that port p of component C1 must be synchronized with at least one of the two ports q and r of components C2 and C3, respectively, and with the s of component C4. The accepts macro lists all ports that are

[2] We use a notation that is slightly different from that in [8] without change of meaning.

allowed to synchronize with the given port, thus allowing *optional* ports. For example, "$C1.p$ **Accepts** $C2.q, C3.r, C4.s, C5.t$" means that in addition to the ports listed by the requires macro, the port t of component C5 is *also* allowed to synchronize with p despite not being required by it. Graphically, allowed interactions are defined by *connectors*. The behaviour specification of each component along with the set of requires and accepts macros are provided to the *JavaBIP engine*. The engine orchestrates the overall execution of the whole component-based system by deciding which component transitions must be executed at each cycle.

Let $JB = (\mathsf{C}, \rho, \alpha)$ be a JavaBIP model[3], where: C is the set of components, ρ is the set of the requires macros, and α is the set of the accepts macros. For a set of ports $a \subset \bigcup_{B \in \mathsf{C}} P_B$, we write $a \models \rho, \alpha$ to denote that a satifies the conjunction of all the constraints in ρ and α seen as Boolean formulae (see [8] for detailed presentation). Note that, in particular, this implies the transitivity of the requires constraints.

The operational semantics of JB is defined by the labelled transition system (LTS) $L_{JB} = (Q, P, \rightarrow)$, where:

- $Q \stackrel{\text{def}}{=} \prod_{B \in \mathsf{C}} Q_B$ is the Cartesian product of the sets of component states,
- $P \stackrel{\text{def}}{=} \bigcup_{B \in \mathsf{C}} P_B$ is the set of all the enforceable and spontaneous ports in the system,
- $\rightarrow \subseteq Q \times 2^P \times Q$ is the set of transitions $q \xrightarrow{a} q'$, such that
  - either $a = \{p\}$ with $p \in P_B$ a spontaneous port of some component $B \in C$, (q_B, p, q'_B) a transition in B and $q_{B'} = q'_{B'}$, for all $B' \neq B$,
  - or all ports in a are enforceable, $a \models \rho, \alpha$, and, for any component $B \in C$, either $(q_B, a \cap P_B, q'_B)$ is a transition in B, or $a \cap P_B = \emptyset$ and $q_B = q'_B$.

A state q' is *reachable* from a state q if there exists a sequence of interactions $e_1, e_2, \ldots, e_n$ such that $(q, e_1, q_1), (q_1, e_2, q_2), \ldots, (q_{n-1}, e_n, q') \in \rightarrow$.

4 CBRTVMs and Their Composition

Throughout the paper, we use the term *Component-Based Run-Time Variability Model* (CBRTVM) to highlight the following facts: 1) the model in question is executable and can be *used at run time* to enforce the variability constraints, and 2) the set of valid configurations is never computed explicitly but is derived from components representing individual features. Thus, a JavaBIP implementation of a CBRTVM is a JavaBIP model with 1) one component per feature, encoding the feature life-cycle, and 2) a set of synchronisation macros encoding the dependencies among features. We build on such an implementation proposed in our previous paper [16].

[3] Throughout this paper, we use JB to denote arbitrary JavaBIP models, as opposed to CM, which is used to denote CBRTVMs, i.e. JavaBIP models generated from FMs.

4.1 Feature Model Encoding

For each feature f in a feature model FM, we define the corresponding component $enc(n_f)$ as shown in Fig. 4. Each state represents either the presence or the absence of the corresponding feature in the configuration. The states S_f and SR_f represent the feature (de)activation having been requested but not yet realised. Transitions labeled by enforceable ports are shown as solid black arrows, whereas those labeled by spontaneous ports are shown as dashed green arrows. Below, ns_f, a_f, s_f, d_f denote, respectively, $not\_selected_f$, $activate_f$, $selected_f$ and $deactivate_f$. Let $L = (Q, P, \rightarrow)$ be the LTS of a JavaBIP model CM generated from FM. We define a mapping $\psi : Q \rightarrow 2^F$ that associates each state of the LTS to the configuration of the FM by putting $\psi(q) \stackrel{\text{def}}{=} \{f \in F \mid q_f \in \{f, SR\_f\}\}$.

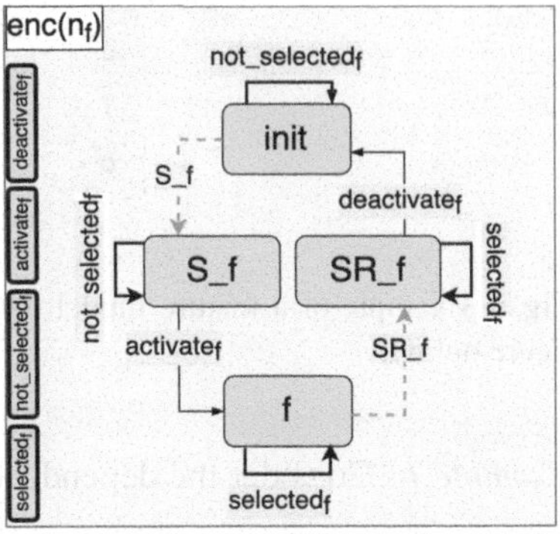

Fig. 4. FSM for a feature

Denote by SCC_f the strongly connected component of the dependency graph G_{FM} containing the feature f. For the feature f to be activated, 1) all features in SCC_f must be activated at the same time, 2) all *other* features that f depends on must either be activated at the same time or already selected, and 3) all features in conflict with f must not be selected. Thus, the synchronisation macros for the port a_f are defined by

$$
\begin{aligned}
&a_f \textbf{ Requires } (a_{f'})_{f' \in SCC_f \setminus \{f\}},\ (s_{f'}; a_{f'})_{f' \in E(f) \setminus SCC_f},\ (ns_{f'})_{f' \in \chi(f)}, \\
&a_f \textbf{ Accepts } (a_{f'})_{f' \in SCC_f \setminus \{f\}},\ (a_{f'})_{f' \in E^*(f) \setminus SCC_f},\ (s_{f'})_{f' \in E^*(f) \setminus SCC_f},\ (ns_{f'})_{f' \in \chi(f)},
\end{aligned}
\tag{1}
$$

where E^* is the transitive closure of E. Notice that, due to cascading dependencies, there are more accepted ports than required ports.

Similarly, for the feature f to be deactivated, 1) all features in SCC_f must be deactivated at the same time and 2) all features that depend on f must either be deactivated at the same time or not yet selected. Thus, the synchronisation macros for the port d_f are defined by

$$
\begin{aligned}
&d_f \textbf{ Requires } (d_{f'})_{f' \in SCC_f \setminus \{f\}},\ (ns_{f'}; d_{f'})_{f' \in E^{-1}(f) \setminus SCC_f}, \\
&d_f \textbf{ Accepts } (d_{f'})_{f' \in SCC_f \setminus \{f\}},\ (d_{f'})_{f' \in \overline{(E^{-1})^*(f)} \setminus SCC_f}.
\end{aligned}
\tag{2}
$$

Finally, the ports s_f and ns_f accept but do not require synchronisation with any other ports, i.e. their **Requires** macros are empty while their **Accepts** macros contain all enforceable ports in the system.

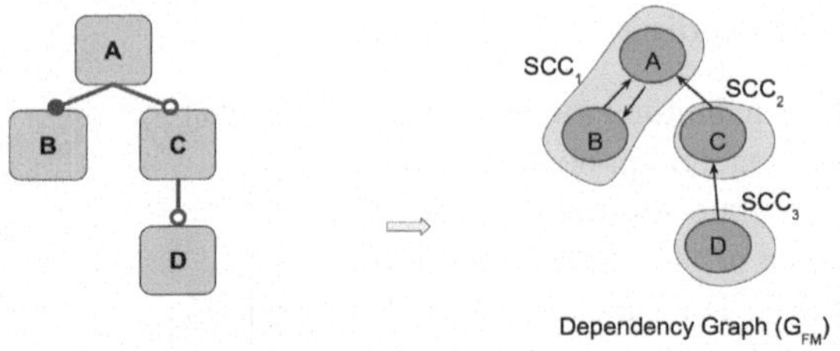

Fig. 5. Example of a feature model with its dependency graph (SCCs shown in yellow) (Color figure online)

Example 1. Consider the dependency graph in Fig. 5. For feature C, we have

$$a_C \textbf{ Requires } a_A; s_A \qquad \text{and} \qquad a_C \textbf{ Accepts } a_A, s_A, a_B, s_B\,,$$

meaning that the port a_c can be synchronized with both a_A and a_B (allowing SCC_2 to be activated together with SCC_1), or with s_A and s_B (allowing SCC_2 to be activated after SCC_1). It is easy to see that, for instance, a_A and s_B cannot be enabled at the same time since activation of B would have required that of A.

Note. The encoding presented above is different from the one in [16]. Component behaviour in Fig. 4 has additional looping transitions $\texttt{not\_selected}_f$ and $\texttt{selected}_f$ on states S_f and SR_f, respectively. Synchronisation macros (1) and (2) allow (de)activation of features at the same time as features in other SCCs, which we did not allow in [16]. However, these differences do not impact the theoretical results presented there. Specifically, any reachable state in the generated JavaBIP model corresponds to a saturated partial-valid configuration of the feature model. Conversely, if there exists a valid configuration in the feature model, it is guaranteed to be reachable in the JavaBIP model.

4.2 Composition Operators on Macros

Our approach is structural. Let CM_1 and CM_2 be two JavaBIP CBRTVMs. To compose them into CM' based on a composition operator $\circ'$, we take the union of their component sets, and compose the sets of their coordination macros. This section explains how these macros are composed for each of the composition operators presented in Sect. 3.2.

Composing Requires Macros. Let us consider two sets of Requires macros, denoted ρ_1 and ρ_2. A new set ρ of Requires macros will be obtained in relation with operator $\circ' \in \{\cup, \cap, \dot{\cap}\}$.

Definition 5 (Composition Operators). *Let ρ_1 and ρ_2 be two sets of Requires macros. We define the following composition operators:*

– ***Intersection ($\cap$):***

$$\rho_1 \cap \rho_2 \stackrel{\text{def}}{=} \{x \textbf{ Requires } L_1\,,\ L_2 \mid (x \textbf{ Requires } L_1) \in \rho_1 \textit{ and } (x \textbf{ Requires } L_2) \in \rho_2\} \cup \{(x \textbf{ Requires } L) \in \rho_1 \mid x \in P_1 \setminus P_2\} \cup \{(x \textbf{ Requires } L) \in \rho_2 \mid x \in P_2 \setminus P_1\}$$

– ***Strict Intersection*** *($\dot{\cap}$):* $\rho_1 \dot{\cap} \rho_2 \stackrel{\text{def}}{=} \overline{\rho_1} \cap \overline{\rho_2}$, *where, for* $i \in 1, 2$,

$$\overline{\rho_i} \stackrel{\text{def}}{=} \rho_i \cup \{x \textbf{ Requires } false \mid x \in P_{3-i} \setminus P_i\}.$$

(A port that requires false will never be executed.)

– ***Union*** *($\cup$):*

$$\rho_1 \cup \rho_2 \stackrel{\text{def}}{=} \{x \textbf{ Requires } L_1 \ ; \ L_2 \mid (x \textbf{ Requires } L_1) \in \rho_1 \ and \ (x \textbf{ Requires } L_2) \in \rho_2\} \cup \{x \textbf{ Requires } true \mid x \in P_1 \setminus P_2\} \cup \{x \textbf{ Requires } true \mid x \in P_2 \setminus P_1\}$$

*(A port that has a "**Requires** true" constraint can be executed as a singleton.)*

Saturation Process for Accepts Macros. The composition of Accepts macros is independent of the composition operator used. For two sets of macros α_1 and α_2, it is defined as the saturation of the set:

$$\{x \textbf{ Accepts } L_1 \ , \ L_2 \mid (x \textbf{ Accepts } L_1) \in \alpha_1 \ and \ (x \textbf{ Accepts } L_2) \in \alpha_2\} \cup \{x \textbf{ Accepts } L_1 \mid x \in \mathrm{P}_1 \setminus \mathrm{P}_2\} \cup \{x \textbf{ Accepts } L_2 \mid x \in \mathrm{P}_2 \setminus \mathrm{P}_1\}.$$

Notice that, without saturation, ports required for interaction may be excluded from the Accepts macros. For instance, consider a scenario where port x requires port y (i.e. x **Requires** y), and port y requires port z (i.e. y **Requires** z). If the Accept macro for x only contains y (i.e. x **Accepts** y) after composition, then port z will be excluded (cf. Section 3.3). However, based on the Requires macros, x transitively requires z since y **Requires** z. To address this, saturation expands the right-hand side of each Accepts macro to include all ports required for interaction. In the example, it would add z to the Accepts macro for x, ensuring x accepts all necessary ports.

Let $\alpha = \{a_1, a_2, ..., a_n\}$ represent the set of Accepts macros, where each macro is denoted as $a_i : x_i$ **Accepts** L_i. We perform a saturation on α, which systematically iterates over each Accepts macro $a_i \in \alpha$, initializing the right-hand side rhs_i with L_i. It then expands rhs_i by conjoining additional ports from other Accepts macros that can interact with ports currently in rhs_i. This iteration continues until rhs_i stabilizes.

The resulting set α contains saturated Accepts macros, where the right-hand side of each macro encompasses all ports across composed interactions. This ensures the Accepts macros handle all relevant ports involved in potential interactions.

4.3 Composition Operators on JavaBIP Models

Definition 6 (Composition). *Let* $CM_1 = (C_1, \rho_1, \alpha_1)$ *and* $CM_2 = (C_2, \rho_2, \alpha_2)$ *be JavaBIP models as defined in Sect. 3.3. Their composition by* $\circ' \in \{\cup, \cap, \dot{\cap}\}$ *is the JavaBIP model* $CM' = (C', \rho', \alpha')$ *where:*

– $C' = C_1 \cup C_2$ *is the union of their components,*
– ρ' *is the composed require macros such that* $\rho' = \rho_1 \circ' \rho_2$ *as defined in Sect. 4.2,*
– α' *is the saturated accept macros as defined in Sect. 4.2.*

Note that, when these composition operators are applied to CBRTVMs, the resulting models can be optimised. In the process of synthesizing a feature diagram from a Boolean formula in feature modelling [4], dead features can be identified and removed as they cannot be part of any valid configuration of FM. This goes beyond the scope of this paper, it is worth noting that the composed CBRTVM can be similarly optimised when a (sub)set of dead features is known. When composing the JavaBIP models $CM' = CM_1 \circ' CM_2$, the component set is defined as the union $C' = C_1 \cup C_2$ (see Sect. 4.3). Consequently, C' may contain components corresponding to dead features that may be excluded when synthesizing the composed feature model FM. To that end, CM' can also be modified by removing all such components corresponding to dead features. In addition, macros should be refined by removing ports associated with components corresponding to dead features. Ports that are on the left-hand side of a macro, e.g. p_f **Requires** L_1, should be removed. For ports that appear on the right-hand side of a macro, e.g. $p_{f'}$ **Requires** L_1 with $a_f \in L_1$, the list L_1 can be replaced by *false*, since at least one of the ports required to fire p'_f (the one corresponding to the dead feature) will never be enabled. For *accept* macros, ports linked to dead features are simply removed.

5 A Bisimulation for Correctness and Compositionality Results

Bisimulation is a binary relation commonly used in Concurrency Theory (e.g. [21]) to establish the behavioural equivalence between two transition systems: whenever one system can execute an action, the same action can be executed by the other from any equivalent state, and vice versa. Bisimilarity ensures that, not only the states reachable within the two systems are equivalent but so are the execution options at every moment. In this section, we propose the notion of multi-step $\mathcal{UP}$-bisimulation, which extends the concept of bisimulation by allowing transitions to match over multiple steps. The multi-step $\mathcal{UP}$-bisimulation is then used to show that the composed CBRTVMs preserve the semantics of the composed feature models (correctness of the encoding), and the equivalence is the congruence for the defined composition operators (compositionality of the encoding).

In the context of FMs, various structures can be synthesized from the same Boolean formula, leading to differing saturated partial-valid configurations. However, the set of valid configurations is the same. On their side, two CBRTVMs generated from a FM have the same set of valid configurations reachable from the initial configuration, but they may have different paths and intermediate states to reach the valid configuration. To deal with such a situation, we consider paths in the LTSs, rather than single transitions.

Definition 7 ($\mathcal{P}$-Path). *Let $L = (Q, P, \rightarrow)$, with $\rightarrow \subseteq Q \times 2^P \times Q$, be an LTS. Let $\mathcal{P}$ be a predicate on Q. A* $\mathcal{P}$-path *in L is a sequence of transitions $q_1 \xrightarrow{l_1} q_2 \xrightarrow{l_2} \ldots \xrightarrow{l_k} q_{k+1}$, such that both $\mathcal{P}(q_1)$ and $\mathcal{P}(q_{k+1})$ hold. We write $q_1 \underset{\mathcal{P}}{\overset{u}{\Rightarrow}} q_{k+1}$, with $u = \bigcup_{i=1}^{k} l_i$.*

Note that $\mathcal{P}$ may hold on some intermediate states of a $\mathcal{P}$-path. We now introduce the notion of the multi-step $\mathcal{UP}$-bisimulation. This allows us to compare behaviors of two LTSs w.r.t. states that satisfy a given predicate along the $\mathcal{P}$-paths where the sets of observable actions coincide. This way the multi-step $\mathcal{UP}$-bisimulation tolerates non-atomicity of interactions.

Definition 8 (Multi-step $\mathcal{UP}$-Bisimulation). *Let $L_i = (Q_i, P_i, \to_i)$, with $i = 1, 2$ and $\to_i \subseteq Q_i \times 2^P \times Q_i$ be two LTSs. Let $\mathcal{P}$ be a predicate on $Q_1 \cup Q_2$. Let $\mathcal{U} \subseteq P_1 \cup P_2$ be a set of unobservable ports, such that $P_1 \setminus \mathcal{U} = P_2 \setminus \mathcal{U}$. A relation $R \subseteq Q_1 \times Q_2$ is a* multi-step $\mathcal{UP}$-bisimulation *if, for all $(q_1, q_2) \in R$, hold the following two conditions:*

- *for any $q_1 \overset{u_1}{\underset{\mathcal{P}}{\Rightarrow}} q_1'$, there exists $q_2 \overset{u_2}{\underset{\mathcal{P}}{\Rightarrow}} q_2'$, such that $(q_1', q_2') \in R$ and $u_1 \setminus \mathcal{U} = u_2 \setminus \mathcal{U}$,*
- *and symmetrically for any $q_2 \overset{u_2}{\underset{\mathcal{P}}{\Rightarrow}} q_2'$ in L_2.*

Notice that, in the classical setting, when transition labels are singleton, i.e. $\to \subseteq Q \times \{\{p\} \mid p \in P\} \times Q$ and $P_1 = P_2$, multi-step $\mathcal{UP}$-bisimulation reduces to the classical bisimulation by taking $\mathcal{P} = true$ and $\mathcal{U} = \emptyset$.

Definition 9 (Multi-step $\mathcal{UP}$-Bisimilarity). *Given two JavaBIP models JB_1 and JB_2, a predicate $\mathcal{P}$ on their states and a set of unobservable ports $\mathcal{U}$, we say that they are* multi-step $\mathcal{UP}$-bisimilar, *denoted $JB_1 \simeq_{\mathcal{UP}} JB_2$, if there exists a multi-step $\mathcal{UP}$-bisimilation relating the initial states of their semantic LTSs.*

Multi-step $\mathcal{UP}$-bisimilarity allows us to speak of the equivalence of JavaBIP models in general and of CBRTVMs in particular.

Let FM_1 and FM_2 be two feature models, $\circ \in \{\cup, \cap, \dot{\cap}\}$, CM and CM' be the CBRTVMs derived as in Fig. 1 with F and F' their respective sets of features. We are interested in comparing the configurations reached by the two models. Thus, we want to observe what features are (de)activated following given (de)activation requests.

Notice that, while $F \subseteq F' = F_1 \cup F_2$ by construction, it is possible that $F \subsetneq F'$, since dead features may be eliminated in $FM_1 \circ FM_2$.

In this context, we define the set of unobservable ports (cf. Figure 4) to be

$$\mathcal{U} \overset{\text{def}}{=} \{\texttt{selected}_f, \texttt{not\_selected}_f \mid f \in F'\} \cup \{\mathtt{S}_f, \mathtt{SR}_f \mid f \in F' \setminus F\}.$$

Since the notion of a "saturated partial-valid configuration" is specific to any given feature model, to establish equivalence of two CBRTVMs, we have to limit our consideration to valid configurations only. Thus we take $\mathcal{P}$ to be the predicate, such that $\mathcal{P}(q)$ evaluates to *true* exactly when either $q_f = \texttt{init}$, for all $f \in F$ or $\psi(q)$ is a valid configuration of the composed feature model $FM_1 \circ FM_2$ (cf. Figure 1).

To prove the correctness of the composition operators' encodings, we have to show that, for any FM_1 and FM_2, holds $CM \simeq_{\mathcal{UP}} CM'$. Under Assumption 1, we can prove the following propositions:

Proposition 1. *Let FM_1 and FM_2 be two feature models. Let $L = (Q, P, \to)$ and $L' = (Q', P', \to)$ be the semantic LTSs of the corresponding CBRTVMs CM and CM' as in Fig. 1. Then $CM \simeq_{\mathcal{UP}} CM'$ with $\mathcal{P}$ and $\mathcal{U}$ defined as above.*

Sketch of the Proof. The relation $R \subseteq Q \times Q'$, such that $(q, q') \in R$ iff $q_f = q_f'$, for all $f \in F$, and $q_f' \in \{\texttt{init}, \texttt{S\_f}\}$, for all $f \in F' \setminus F$, is a multi-step $\mathcal{UP}$-bisimulation relating the initial states $(\texttt{init})_{f \in F}$ and $(\texttt{init})_{f \in F'}$ of L and L', respectively.

Multi-step $\mathcal{UP}$-bisimulation is not a congruence on JavaBIP models since it allows the breaking of interaction atomicity. However, it is a congruence on the sub-algebra of models generated from CBRTVMs by the composition operators defined in Sect. 4.

Table 1. Feature inclusion in configurations Φ_1, Φ_2, and Φ_3

Configuration \ Features	**Heroku_Application**	**Dyno**	**Free**	**Hobby**	**Production_tier**	**Add_ons**	**DataBases**	**PostgreSQL**	**Monitors**	**BasicMonitor**	**CloudWatch**	**Region**	**eu**	**us**	**BuildPack**	**Gradle**	**Java_JVM**	**Intersection**	**Strict Intersection**	**Union**
Φ_1	✓	✓			✓	✓	✓	✓	✓	✓	✓	✓	✓		✓	✓		*Invalid*	*Invalid*	*Valid*
Φ_2	✓	✓			✓	✓	✓	✓	✓		✓	✓	✓		✓	✓		*Valid*	*Invalid*	*Valid*
Φ_3	✓	✓			✓	✓	✓	✓	✓	✓		✓	✓		✓	✓		*Valid*	*Valid*	*Valid*

Proposition 2. *Let CM_1, CM_2, and CM_3 be composed from CBRTVMs. Let $\mathcal{P}$ be a predicate on the states of CM_1 and CM_2 and $\mathcal{U}$ a set of unobservable ports, such that $CM_1 \simeq_{\mathcal{UP}} CM_2$. For any $\circ' \in \{\cup, \cap, \dot{\cap}\}$, holds $CM_1 \circ' CM_3 \simeq_{\mathcal{U'P'}} CM_2 \circ' CM_3$, with*

- *$\mathcal{P}'(q) = true$ iff $P(q_{12}) = true$ and $\psi(q_3)$ is a valid configuration in CM_3, with q_{12} and q_3 the projections of q on the union of state spaces of CM_1 and CM_2, and on the state space of CM_3, respectively,*
- *$\mathcal{U}' \stackrel{\text{def}}{=} \mathcal{U} \cup \{\texttt{selected}_f, \texttt{not\_selected}_f \mid f \in F_3\}$, where F_3 is the set of features in CM_3.*

Sketch of the Proof. The key observation is that any $\mathcal{P}$-path can be extended to a longer one in the semantic LTS of the same CBRTVM by firing unobservable (`not_`)`selected` ports after the firing of the corresponding (`de`)`activate` ports. □

These new results with the multi-step $\mathcal{UP}$-bisimulation used guarantee that for a given composition operator, a reachable state in the composed CBRTVM corresponds to a saturated partial-valid configuration in the composed feature model.

6 Experimental Validation

Integration of CloudWatch Service. For evaluation purposes, we use the Heroku Cloud FM (Fig. 2) as FM_1. As FM_2, we take the CloudWatch FM (Fig. 3) extended with all mandatory features from the Heroku Cloud FM alongside the first option within these mandatory features, excluding *Dyno*, to which *Production_tier* is specifically appended. This setup allows us to better illustrate and experimentally validate the three composition operators studied in the paper.

Feature models (FMs) are taken as input and transformed into CBRTVMs. They are executable and can be *used at run time* to enforce the variability constraints. As explained in Sect. 4, the set of valid configurations is never computed explicitly but is derived from components representing individual features. Thus, CBRTVMs include

JavaBIP component specifications along with synchronisation macros for coordination. We have developed a Java-based composer dealing with the macros that support three composition operators: union, intersection, and strict intersection. The component specifications sets of CBRTVMs to compose and a resulting macro file for a chosen composition operator are then packaged to create a composed CBRTVM.

Table 1 shows the configurations Φ_1, Φ_2, and Φ_3, and their validity in the composed FM across three distinct operators. We carried out our experiment by starting from an empty initial configuration and initiating spontaneous activation requests to the composed CBRTVM for all the features in configuration Φ_1 in random order. We repeated this process 50 times to observe the reached configurations for each case.

Figure 6 sums up the reachability outcomes across the operators used for the composition. As anticipated, the CBRTVM model aligned with theoretical results across all cases, transitioning to valid configurations while preventing invalid ones from being reached. Specifically, in the intersection case depicted in Fig. 6, Φ_1 was never reached due to the exclusion constraint between *CloudWatch* and *BasicMonitor*. On the contrary, both Φ_2 or Φ_3 are reached depending on the activation sequence of *BasicMonitor* and *CloudWatch*, explaining the outcomes in Fig. 6. In the strict intersection scenario, Φ_3 was the only valid configuration and was consistently reached, as Φ_1 and Φ_2 were never attained since they are not valid (cf. Table 1). Finally, in the union case, all configurations are reachable from the initial configuration, making Φ_1 attainable upon activating all features within it, as shown in Table 1. Φ_2 and Φ_3 in the union case are valid configurations however they are never reached (zero on the plot) since the activation of all features in Φ_1 is requested, and one has $\Phi_2 \subset \Phi_1$ and $\Phi_3 \subset \Phi_1$. However, if the activation of all features in only Φ_2 or Φ_3 were requested instead, then those configurations would be reached.

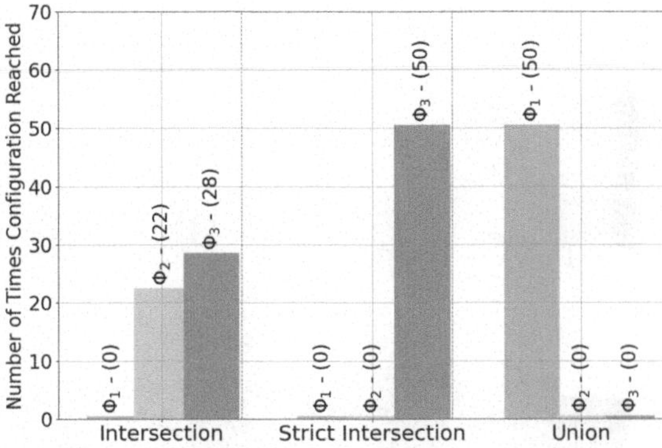

Fig. 6. Observed configurations.

Illustration of $\mathcal{P}$-Path Equivalence. Let us illustrate the multi-step transition matching, where a sequence of transitions in one model corresponds either to a single transition or to a sequence of transitions in the other model. Consider the feature models *FM1* and *FM2* shown in Fig. 7a and 7b. Following the process in Fig. 1, we have automatically generated the CBRTVMs for these two feature models. We then used the macros composer for the intersection operator to generate the model CM'.

The behaviour of CM' must be compared with that of a CBRTVM CM generated for a feature model representing *FM1* $\cap$ *FM2*. However, as described in [4], several feature models can be used to represent *FM1* $\cap$ *FM2*, among which, in particular, any

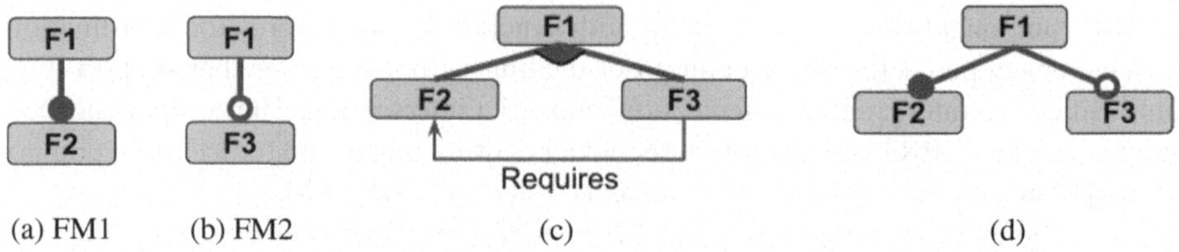

Fig. 7. Two feature models (a,b) and two options for their intersection (c,d)

of the two FMs shown in Fig. 7c and 7d. It is easy to see that these resulting feature models have the same set of valid configurations despite their different structures.

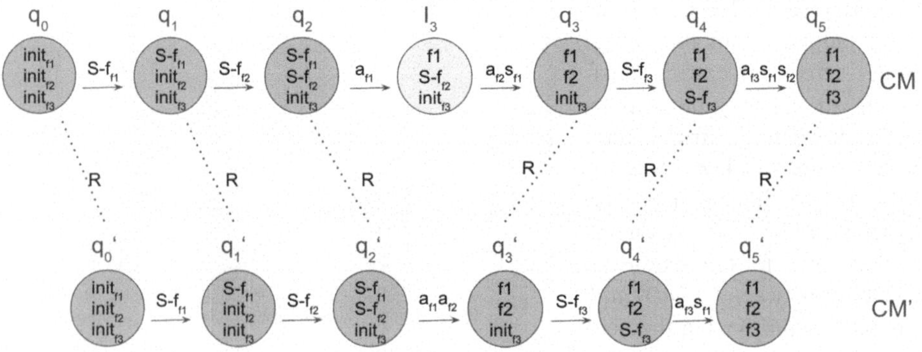

Fig. 8. Execution traces of CM and CM', with CM generated from the FM in Fig. 7c.

The CBRTVM generated for the FM in Fig. 7d behaves exactly as CM'. Since our goal, here, is to illustrate the equivalence of different paths, we focus on the FM in Fig. 7c. Let CM be the generated CBRTVM corresponding to this FM.

Consider the execution traces associated with a specific sequence of reconfiguration requests: activation of the feature $F1$, followed by $F2$, then $F3$. Figure 8 shows how both models respond to this sequence of requests starting from the initial states q_0 and q'_0 of CM and CM' that are related by R as defined in Sect. 5. The sets of ports used as labels for the two paths in Fig. 8 coincide up to the unobservable ports s_{f1} and s_{f2}.

From their initial states q_0 and q'_0, upon reception of the activation request for $F1$ (through the spontaneous port $S\text{-}f_{f_1}$), both CM and CM' transition to states q_1 and q'_1, respectively. These target states are linked by the relation R. Then, when the activation request for $F2$ is received, both models transition to q_2 and q'_2, where $(q_2, q'_2) \in R$. Afterwards, CM moves to the state I_3 (in yellow in Fig. 8), which corresponds to a saturated partial-valid configuration that is not a valid one. Hence, $\mathcal{P}(I_3) = false$, meaning that a $\mathcal{P}$-path cannot terminate in I_3. Hence, according to Definition 8, this state does not need to be related to any state in CM'. However, the next transition in CM leads to the state q_3, which corresponds to a valid configuration. On its side, from q'_2 CM' performs the transition $a_{f1}a_{f2}$. Finally, following the reception of the request for the activation of

$F3$, the two $\mathcal{P}$-paths in Fig. 8 reach their terminal states $(q_5, q'_5) \in R$. Notice that the last transition in the top trace involves two unobservable ports, s_{f1} and s_{f2}, as opposed to the one in the bottom trace, which only involves s_{f1}. This reflects the fact that $F3$ has an explicit dependency on both features $F1$ and $F2$ in the FM of Fig. 7c, but only on $F1$ in $FM2$.

7 Related Work

In the context of static variability models based on feature models [1,3,9], the techniques for composing FMs using predefined operators such as union and intersection have been studied. To respect the semantics of these operators, specific rules for merging common features during composition were defined. In addition, the work in [2,4] introduced more advanced techniques to enable composing FMs under arbitrary user-defined operators. The approach encodes input FMs as Boolean formulas and translates the composition operator into a Boolean formula over encoded models to obtain the composed model formula. The resulting feature model diagram can then be synthesized from the boolean formula. Another approach relates features through constraints in a separate view model aggregated with inputs. In line with this research (cf. Figure 1), we contribute with composition operators designed for composing run-time component models. While existing feature model composition focuses on static variability models, our framework provides automated support for dealing with configuration evolution in a modular and a compositional fashion.

A comparison of variability modeling and decision modeling approaches can be found in [14]. Both approaches focus on variability modeling but from different points of view, and both provide model derivation support. Our composition approach is FM-oriented as hierarchy, (de)composition, as well as configuration constraints, are essential in FM. Furthermore, our framework provides automated support for dealing with configuration workflows, which is essential in decision modelling approaches.

In Featured Transitions Systems (FTS) [12], each transition is annotated with a combination of features to determine the variants that can execute it. As they were initially thought in the static setting where all the features and their relationships could be specified in advance and not allowed to change, FTS do not support run-time adaptation, e.g., of CPS or AI-intensive systems with new features, constraints and functionalities. In [15], the composition of features is tackled by both superimposition and parallel composition, which are the most used in variability-intensive systems engineering. The authors introduce compositional feature-oriented systems (CFOSs) as a unified formal way for programs in a guarded command language. Unlike FTS-based verification and validation, our compositional approach allows mixing design-time and run-time techniques, and thus by some means they support operations over FTS such as FTS merge.

An early description of the distinction between positive and negative variability can be found in [25], where authors combine model-driven and aspect-oriented software development to support both variability types. In [25], features are separated in models and composed by aspect-oriented composition techniques on model level. Aspect-oriented techniques enable the explicit expression and modularization of variability on model, code, and template level. Differently from [25], our approach is only model-driven when supporting composition and reconfiguration to allow both variability types.

In the domain of component-based models, a recent survey [13] emphasizes that a suitable methodology to ensure the correctness of reconfigurations in component-based systems is still needed. We believe that the present work contributes to this active research topic, at both development and management stages (cf. [13], Fig. 1).

Component-based models are compositional by their intrinsic nature. Nevertheless, adding composition operators for building complex component-based systems is of interest, both theoretical and practical, namely because of safety properties to ensure or to preserve by construction. In this domain, Attie et al. [5] propose a formal framework for compositional construction of software architectures by introducing an associative, commutative intersection composition operator for architectures. If architectures A_1 and A_2 enforce safety properties ϕ_1 and ϕ_2 respectively, [5] shows that their intersection composition $A_1 \cap A_2$ enforces the conjunction $\phi_1 \wedge \phi_2$. Our approach to CBMs composition also aims to facilitate incremental software system construction. However, in our approach the composition is directly performed on the syntactic representation of coordination constraints rather than by encoding interaction models into Boolean formulas. In addition, we introduce new composition operators beyond intersection.

8 Conclusion and Future Work

This paper introduces composition operators for CBRTVMs, enabling automated construction of component-based systems. It provides reusability by allowing CBRTVM models to be reused across systems and instances through composition, flexibility by enabling models to be composed according to specific user needs through various operators, and adaptability by facilitating the incremental addition of functionalities.

In a broader software engineering perspective, we have automatically related the composition of feature models, which are well-established variability models for software evolution, with the composition of component-based models. We have also provided new composition operators for the CBRTVMs, that preserve the FM semantics. These contributions push FM variability and their composition, which are available at the design and development stages, into safe runtime reconfiguration that is automatically ensured at the management stage.

In future work, we plan to develop a more generalized composition approach that goes beyond the predefined operators currently examined. By allowing for user-defined composition, we intend to provide greater flexibility in constructing CBRTVMs.

To prove the correctness and compositionality of our approach, we have introduced a novel multi-step $\mathcal{UP}$-bisimulation relation. We have shown that it is a congruence on the sub-algebra of JavaBIP models generated by CBRTVMs but not on JavaBIP models in general. In future work, we are planning to study and characterise the maximal sub-algebra of models for which multi-step $\mathcal{UP}$-bisimulation is a congruence.

Acknowledgements. The authors are very grateful to the SEFM 2024 PC chairs and to the anonymous reviewers for the excellent organisation of the selection process and for the very constructive reviews contributing to the final version of this paper.

Disclosure of Interests. The authors have no competing interests to declare that are relevant to the content of this article.

References

1. Acher, M., Collet, P., Lahire, P., France, R.: Composing feature models. In: van den Brand, M., Gašević, D., Gray, J. (eds.) SLE 2009. LNCS, vol. 5969, pp. 62–81. Springer, Heidelberg (2010). https://doi.org/10.1007/978-3-642-12107-4_6
2. Acher, M., Collet, P., Lahire, P., France, R.: Comparing approaches to implement feature model composition. In: Kühne, T., Selic, B., Gervais, M.-P., Terrier, F. (eds.) ECMFA 2010. LNCS, vol. 6138, pp. 3–19. Springer, Heidelberg (2010). https://doi.org/10.1007/978-3-642-13595-8_3
3. Acher, M., Collet, P., Lahire, P., France, R.: Managing variability in workflow with feature model composition operators. In: Baudry, B., Wohlstadter, E. (eds.) SC 2010. LNCS, vol. 6144, pp. 17–33. Springer, Heidelberg (2010). https://doi.org/10.1007/978-3-642-14046-4_2
4. Acher, M., Combemale, B., Collet, P., Barais, O., Lahire, P., France, R.B.: Composing your compositions of variability models. In: Moreira, A., Schätz, B., Gray, J., Vallecillo, A., Clarke, P. (eds.) MODELS 2013. LNCS, vol. 8107, pp. 352–369. Springer, Heidelberg (2013). https://doi.org/10.1007/978-3-642-41533-3_22
5. Attie, P., Baranov, E., Bliudze, S., Jaber, M., Sifakis, J.: A general framework for architecture composability. Formal Aspects Comput. **28**(2), 207–231 (2016)
6. Basu, A., et al.: Rigorous component-based system design using the BIP framework. IEEE Softw. **28**(3), 41–48 (2011)
7. Berger, T., et al.: A survey of variability modeling in industrial practice. In: Proceedings of the 7th Seventh International Workshop on Variability Modelling of Software-intensive Systems, pp. 1–8 (2013)
8. Bliudze, S., Mavridou, A., Szymanek, R., Zolotukhina, A.: Exogenous coordination of concurrent software components with JavaBIP. Softw. Pract. Exper. **47**(11), 1801–1836 (2017)
9. Carbonnel, J., Huchard, M., Miralles, A., Nebut, C.: Feature model composition assisted by formal concept analysis. In: International Conference on Evaluation of Novel Approaches to Software Engineering, vol. 2, pp. 27–37. SciTePress (2017)
10. Chapin, N., Hale, J.E., Khan, K.M., Ramil, J.F., Tan, W.G.: Types of software evolution and software maintenance. J. Softw. Maint. Evol. Res. Pract. **13**(1), 3–30 (2001)
11. Chen, L., Babar, M.A.: A systematic review of evaluation of variability management approaches in software product lines. Inf. Softw. Technol. **53**(4), 344–362 (2011). https://doi.org/10.1016/J.INFSOF.2010.12.006
12. Cordy, M., et al.: A decade of featured transition systems. In: ter Beek, M.H., Fantechi, A., Semini, L. (eds.) From Software Engineering to Formal Methods and Tools, and Back. LNCS, vol. 11865, pp. 285–312. Springer, Cham (2019). https://doi.org/10.1007/978-3-030-30985-5_18
13. Coullon, H., Henrio, L., Loulergue, F., Robillard, S.: Component-based distributed software reconfiguration: a verification-oriented survey. ACM Comput. Surv. **56**(1), 2:1–2:37 (2024). https://doi.org/10.1145/3595376
14. Czarnecki, K., Grünbacher, P., Rabiser, R., Schmid, K., Wasowski, A.: Cool features and tough decisions: a comparison of variability modeling approaches. In: Eisenecker, U.W., Apel, S., Gnesi, S. (eds.) Proceedings of 6th International Workshop on Variability Modelling of Software-Intensive Systems, Germany, 2012, pp. 173–182. ACM (2012). https://doi.org/10.1145/2110147.2110167
15. Dubslaff, C.: Compositional feature-oriented systems. In: Ölveczky, P.C., Salaün, G. (eds.) SEFM 2019. LNCS, vol. 11724, pp. 162–180. Springer, Cham (2019). https://doi.org/10.1007/978-3-030-30446-1_9

16. Farhat, S., Bliudze, S., Duchien, L., Kouchnarenko, O.: Toward run-time coordination of reconfiguration requests in cloud computing systems. In: Jongmans, S., Lopes, A. (eds.) COORDINATION 2023. LNCS, vol. 13908, pp. 271–291. Springer, Cham (2023). https://doi.org/10.1007/978-3-031-35361-1_15
17. Heroku cloud application platform. https://www.heroku.com, Accessed 22 Feb 2024
18. Kang, K.C., Cohen, S.G., Hess, J.A., Novak, W.E., Peterson, A.S.: Feature-oriented domain analysis (FODA) feasibility study. Carnegie-Mellon Univ Pittsburgh, Pa, Software Engineering Inst, Tech. rep. (1990)
19. Kratzke, N.: A brief history of cloud application architectures. Appl. Sci. **8**(8), 1368 (2018)
20. Nešić, D., Krüger, J., Stănciulescu, u., Berger, T.: Principles of feature modeling. In: Proceedings of the 2019 27th ACM Joint Meeting on European Software Engineering Conference and Symposium on the Foundations of Software Engineering, ESEC/FSE 2019, pp. 62-73. Association for Computing Machinery, New York (2019). https://doi.org/10.1145/3338906.3338974
21. Sangiorgi, D.: Introduction to bisimulation and coinduction. Cambridge University Press (2011)
22. Schmid, K., Rabiser, R., Grünbacher, P.: A comparison of decision modeling approaches in product lines. In: Proceedings of the 5th International Workshop on Variability Modeling of Software-Intensive Systems, pp. 119–126 (2011)
23. Schobbens, P., Heymans, P., Trigaux, J.: Feature diagrams: a survey and a formal semantics. In: 14th IEEE International Conference on RE 2006, pp. 136–145. IEEE Computer Society (2006)
24. Stephen, A., Benedict, S., Kumar, R.A.: Monitoring IaaS using various cloud monitors. Clust. Comput. **22**(Suppl. 5), 12459–12471 (2019)
25. Voelter, M., Groher, I.: Product line implementation using aspect-oriented and model-driven software development. In: 11th International Conference on SPLC 2007, pp. 233–242. IEEE Computer Society (2007). https://doi.org/10.1109/SPLINE.2007.23

Model-Checking the Implementation of Consent

Raúl Pardo[1](✉) and Daniel Le Métayer[2]

[1] IT University of Copenhagen, Copenhagen, Denmark
raup@itu.dk
[2] Univ Lyon, Inria, INSA Lyon, CITI, 69621 Villeurbanne, France

Abstract. Privacy policies define the terms under which personal data may be collected and processed by data controllers. The General Data Protection Regulation (GDPR) imposes requirements on these policies that are often difficult to implement. Difficulties arise in particular due to the heterogeneity of existing systems (e.g., the Internet of Things (IoT), web technology, etc.). In this paper, we propose a method to refine high level GDPR privacy requirements for informed consent into low-level computational models. The method is aimed at software developers implementing systems that require consent management. We mechanize our models in TLA$^+$ and use model-checking to prove that the low-level computational models implement the high-level privacy requirements; TLA$^+$ has been used by software engineers in companies such as Microsoft or Amazon. We demonstrate our method in two real world scenarios: an implementation of cookie banners and a IoT system communicating via Bluetooth low energy.

1 Introduction

The EU General Data Protection Regulation [9] (GDPR) adopted in May 2016 has been welcomed by many experts as a step forward for privacy protection. The GDPR grants new rights to individuals and imposes new obligations on controllers (hereafter, respectively, data subjects, or DSs, and data controllers, or DCs, following the GDPR terminology)—with significant penalties that could act as a deterrent even for large companies. However, its actual impact will depend to a large extent on its interpretation and monitoring, but also on the existence of technical tools to implement its provisions. In this respect, the implementation of consent, which is one of the most widely used legal bases for data processing, raises specific challenges. For example, Recital 32 of the GDPR states that "consent should be given by a clear affirmative act establishing a freely given, specific, informed and unambiguous indication of the data subject's agreement to the processing of personal data relating to him or her, such as by a written statement, including by electronic means, or an oral statement."

In practice, internet users generally have to consent on the fly, when they want to use a service, which leads them to accept mechanically the conditions of the

A. Madeira and A. Knapp (Eds.): SEFM 2024, LNCS 15280, pp. 253–271, 2025.
https://doi.org/10.1007/978-3-031-77382-2_15

provider (e.g., [14]). Evidently, this does not meet the above GDPR requirements to provide informed consent. This situation will become even worse with the advent of the internet of things ("IoT"), which has the potential to extend to the "real world" the tracking already in place on the internet.

A common way to tackle this problem is to design privacy languages where users can define their privacy preferences [22]. First, privacy policy languages appeared as a way for users to express and enforce privacy preferences (e.g. [3,5,8,19,27]). For example, users may define who can collect their data or whether data can be transferred to 3rd parties. After the GDPR appeared, some of these languages became partly outdated, as the GDPR introduced new requirements that were not previously foreseen. This has produced a wave of new languages focused on enforcement and verification of GDPR requirements, e.g., [15,28]. To enforce GDPR requirements, these languages impose certain architectural constraints in the system implementation; for instance, on the way different parties communicate. However, in practice, not all systems use the same architecture. There are systems where devices do not support "direct" communication with each other, and "indirect" means of communication (e.g., via policy repository) are required.

This raises the following question: *How can we design and verify that implementations of consent management mechanisms ensure GDPR requirements?* In this paper, we propose a method to verify that different implementations of consent management systems satisfy GDPR requirements. We build on the PILOT privacy policy language [27]—whose syntax was designed to capture the information that users and service providers must provide to satisfy GDPR requirements. Our method uses program graphs (extended state machines) as design language. Then, we use a mechanization of PILOT semantics and program graphs in TLA$^+$ [17] to formally verify whether a given implementation refines PILOT semantics. We show how to prove (via model-checking) that PILOT semantics satisfy requirements for informed consent, and that an implementation refines PILOT semantics (which implies that it satisfies the same informed consent requirements). The proposed method is aimed at software engineers, which is the reason why we selected TLA$^+$ as verification tool and extended state machines as design language. TLA$^+$ has been used in industrial applications (e.g. [10,23]), and state machines is a basic model familiar to most software engineers.

In summary, our contributions are: i) a formal semantics for PILOT; ii) a framework for software engineers to design implementations of consent management systems using extended state machines known as *program graphs*; iii) two case studies modeling real world consent management scenarios: web cookie banners and an IoT system communicating via Bluetooth low energy; and iv) a mechanization in TLA$^+$ of PILOT semantics and the program graphs in the case studies. We use the formalization to verify (via the TLA$^+$ model-checker) that the PILOT semantics satisfies privacy requirements for informed consent, and that our case study implementations refine PILOT semantics (and, consequently, satisfy the same requirements for informed consent). The TLA$^+$ mechanization is available in the accompanying artifact [26] and repository [20].

2 Privacy Policy Language

Basic Definitions. We start with a set $\mathcal{D}$ of *devices* that can store, process and communicate data—e.g., smartphones, laptops or servers. Let $\mathcal{E}$ denote the set of *entities* such as Google or Alphabet and $\leq_{\mathcal{E}}$ the associated partial order—e.g., since Google belongs to Alphabet we have *Google* $\leq_{\mathcal{E}}$ *Alphabet*. Entities include DCs and DSs. Every device is associated with an entity. However, entities may have many devices associated with them. The function $\texttt{entity} : \mathcal{D} \rightarrow \mathcal{E}$ defines the entity associated with a given device. Let $\mathcal{I}$ be a set of *data items* corresponding to the pieces of information that devices communicate. Let $\mathcal{T}$ be a set of datatypes and $\leq_{\mathcal{T}}$ the associated partial order. The function $\texttt{type} : \mathcal{I} \rightarrow \mathcal{T}$ associates a datatype to each data item. Examples of datatypes are: age, address, city and clinical records. Since *city* is one of the elements that the datatype *address* may be composed of, we have *city* $\leq_{\mathcal{T}}$ *address*. We use datatype to refer to the semantic meaning of data items. We use $\mathcal{V}$ to the denote the set of all values of data items, $\mathcal{V} = (\bigcup_{t \in \mathcal{T}} \mathcal{V}_t)$ where $\mathcal{V}_t$ is the set of values for data items of type t. A special element $\bot \in \mathcal{V}$ denotes the undefined value. The device where a data item is created (its source) is called the *owner* device of the data item. The function $\texttt{owner}: \mathcal{I} \rightarrow \mathcal{D}$ associates an owner device to each data item. We denote by $\mathcal{P}$ the set of *purposes* and $\leq_{\mathcal{P}}$ the associated partial order. For instance, if newsletter is considered as a specific type of advertisement, then we have *newsletter* $\leq_{\mathcal{P}}$ *advertisement*. PILOT privacy policies are contextual: they may depend on *conditions* regarding information stored in the devices where they are evaluated. An example of condition is: *"Only data from adults may be collected."* We use a simple logical language to express conditions. Let $\mathcal{F}$ denote a set of functions, and *terms* t be defined as: $t ::= i \mid c \mid f(\vec{t})$ where $i \in \mathcal{I}$ is data item, $c \in \mathcal{V}$ is a constant value, $f \in \mathcal{F}$ is a function, and $\vec{t}$ is a list of terms matching the arity of f. The syntax of the logical language is $\phi ::= t_1 * t_2 \mid \neg\phi \mid \phi_1 \wedge \phi_2 \mid tt \mid ff$ where $*$ is an arbitrary binary predicate, t_1, t_2 are terms; tt and ff represent respectively true and false. For instance, the condition above is modeled as $age \geq 18$. We denote the set of well-formed conditions as $\mathcal{C}$.

Abstract Syntax of PILOT Privacy Policies. PILOT policies express the conditions under which data can be communicated. We consider two types of data communication: *data collection* and *data transfer*. Data collection corresponds to DCs collecting DS information. A transfer is the event of sending previously collected data to third-party DCs.

Definition 1 (PILOT **Privacy Policies Syntax).** *Given entity* $\in \mathcal{E}$, *Purposes* $\in 2^{\mathcal{P}}$, *condition* $\in \mathcal{C}$, *retention_time* $\in \mathbb{N}$, *and datatype* $\in \mathcal{T}$, *the syntax of* PILOT *policies is defined as follows:*

$$\begin{aligned}
\textit{Pilot Privacy Policy} &::= (\textit{datatype}, \textit{dcr}, \textit{TR}) \\
\textit{Data Communication Rule}\,(\textit{dcr}) &::= \langle \textit{condition}, \textit{entity}, \textit{dur} \rangle \\
\textit{Data Usage Rule}\,(\textit{dur}) &::= \langle \textit{Purposes}, \textit{retention_time} \rangle \\
\textit{Transfer Rules}(\textit{TR}) &::= \{\textit{dcr}_1, \textit{dcr}_2, \ldots\}
\end{aligned}$$

We use $\mathcal{DUR}$, $\mathcal{DCR}$, $\mathcal{PP}$ to denote the sets of data usage rules, data communication rules and Pilot privacy policies, respectively. The set of transfer rules is defined as the set of sets of data communication rules, $TR \in 2^{\mathcal{DCR}}$.

The purpose of *data usage rules* is to define the operations that may be performed on the data. *Purposes* is the set of allowed purposes and *retention_time* is the deadline for erasing the data. For example, consider the data usage rule $dur_1 = \langle\{research\}, 19/04/2024\rangle$; tacitly mapping dates to $\mathbb{N}$. This rule states that data may be used only for the purpose of research until *19/04/2024*.

Data communication rules define the conditions under which data must be collected by or communicated to an entity. The outer layer of data communication rules—i.e., the condition and entity—should be checked by the sender whereas the data usage rule is to be enforced by the receiver. The first element, *condition*, imposes constraints on the data item and the context (state of the DS device); *entity* indicates the entity allowed to receive the data; *dur* is a data usage rule stating how *entity* may use the data. For example, $\langle age > 18, AdsCom, dur_1\rangle$ states that data may be communicated to the entity AdsCom which may use it according to dur_1 (defined above). It also requires that *age* is greater than 18; *age* may be the data item to be sent or contextual information stored in the device.

Transfer rules form a set of data communication rules specifying the entities to which the data may be transferred.

DSs and DCs use Pilot *privacy policies* to describe how data may be used, collected and transferred. The element *datatype* indicates the type of data the policy applies to, *dcr* defines the collection conditions, and *TR* the transfer rules. Several Pilot policies may be necessary to capture the privacy choices for a datatype. For instance, a DS may allow only her employer to collect her data when she is at work, and, when being in a museum, only the museum. To this end, the DS must define two policies, one for each location. A *subsumption* relation $p_1 \sqsubseteq p_2$ indicates that p_1 is more restrictive than (or subsumes) p_2. Intuitively, a policy is less restrictive than another if it allows for data items to be used for a larger set of purposes, for a longer period of time or sent/transferred to a larger set of entities. The subsumption relation of Pilot is formally defined in [27].

Running Example: Cookie Banners. Cookie banners are HTML forms that websites use to let users express their choices regarding the use of cookies. Typically, they include: the entities allowed to collect the data, the purposes for which they may use it, the retention period and the allowed transfers to third parties.

Figure 1 shows an example where DSs can select the check boxes in the top bar to agree on having the DC using their data for the specified purposes. The cookie banner provides detailed information about the types of cookies that the DC may choose.

Fig. 1. Example Cookie Banner

Table 1. PILOT policies for cookie banner.

	PILOT Policy	Textual form for end user GUI
1.	$\perp$	Collected data may be used only for necessary purposes.
2.	$(cookie, \langle tt, flights.com, \langle\{special\_offers\}, 21/12/2024\rangle\rangle, \emptyset)$	Data of type *cookie* can be collected by *flights.com* and used for *special_offers* purposes until *21/12/2024*.
3.	$(cookie, \langle tt, flights.com, \langle\{special\_offers\}, 21/12/2024\rangle\rangle, \{\langle tt, hotels.com, \langle\{hotel\_ads\}, 19/04/2024\rangle\rangle\})$	Data of type *cookie* can be collected by *flights.com* and used for *special_offers* purposes until *21/12/2024*. This data may be transferred by *flights.com* to *hotels.com* which may use it for *hotel_ads* purpose until *19/04/2024*.
4.	$(cookie, \langle tt, flights.com, \langle\emptyset, 0\rangle\rangle, \{\langle tt, hotels.com, \langle\{hotel\_ads\}, 19/04/2024\rangle\rangle\})$	Data of type *cookie* can be collected by *flights.com* and transferred to *hotels.com* which may use it for *hotel_ads* purposes until *19/04/2024*.

Figure 1 shows information related to advertisement cookies—DSs may click on left tabs to visualize the information related to other cookies. The main panel indicates the cookie name, provider (DC), a description of the purpose for data collection, expiration time, and required communication protocol. Note that sometimes a DC may set cookies (called third-party cookies) for a different DC.

When the GDPR came into force, many DCs had to adapt their cookie banners to be compliant with the new regulation. This is all the more important in the view that, according to Recital 42 of the GDPR, *"where processing is based on the data subject's consent, the controller should be able to demonstrate that the DS has given consent to the processing."* Many websites include unique identifiers in cookies. These identifiers may be used for different purposes such as integrity of online sessions, security, statistics or personalized advertisement. Since users can be uniquely identified using these cookies, according to GDPR, they are *personal data*. Therefore, DCs can use them only as necessary for the delivery of their services unless they have obtained a valid consent of the DSs for additional purposes. For instance, in the list above, using cookies for integrity of online sessions or communication security does not require explicit consent of the DS because it is necessary for the correct functioning of the website. However, statistics or advertising are additional purposes for which the consent of the DSs is required. In what follows, we show how to use PILOT to encode the information in cookie banners and its advantages as opposed to current cookie banner technology.

Consider the DC, *flights.com*, operating a flight search engine website. The website *flights.com* uses cookies to track users and show special offers. Furthermore, *flights.com* transfers data to a partner company *hotels.com*. The website *hotels.com* is a hotel search engine that may use data received from *flights.com* to show advertisements, e.g., hotels in users' flight destinations. Legally speaking, *flights.com* must obtain the explicit consent of the users to transfer their data to *hotels.com* for this purpose. To this end, *flights.com* allows users to choose among four options. They are shown on left column in Table 1.

The options correspond to the different configurations shown in Fig. 1, i.e., selecting: 1) only "Necessary"; 2) "Necessary" and "Special offers"; 3) "Necessary", "Special offers" and "Advertisement"; 4) "Necessary" and "Advertisement". The policy $\perp$ (option 1) corresponds to an *empty policy*, which does not allow *flights.com* to use cookies for purposes other than the necessary ones. The condition (tt) means absence of specific conditions for the cookies to be collected (options 2, 3, 4) or transferred to *hotels.com* (options 3 and 4). The data usage rule $\langle \emptyset, 0 \rangle$ in Option 4 means that *flights.com* is not allowed to use cookies for any other purpose than required to deliver its service. In Option 4, it is only allowed to share information with *hotels.com* which can use it to provide hotel advertisements. This scenario corresponds to the common third-party advertisement business model. PILOT policies can be mapped to natural language for their use in GUIs [27]. We show the natural language version on the right column of Table 1.

To obtain DS consent, *flights.com* must provide the above PILOT policy options the first time that the DS interacts with the website. A possibility is to attach an XML version of the PILOT policies for each option in the HTML form—see [21] for an encoding of PILOT policies in an IoT system, and not allow DSs to use the website until they make a choice. Then, the selected policy is sent together with the cookie to inform the DC of the DS choice. Alternatively, DSs may define their own PILOT policy before visiting the website. Consider a *flights.com* user, Alice, who likes to benefit from special offers. Alice is a security aware person, and she only agrees to have cookies collected if they are communicated via HTTPS. Cookies contain the attribute *Secure*, which can be enabled to indicate that they must be transmitted via HTTPS. To this end, Alice sets the following PILOT policy: $(cookie, \langle cookie.Secure = tt, flights.com, \langle \{special\_offers\}, 21/12/2024 \rangle\rangle, \emptyset)$ In practice, Alice would express her policy in its natural language version [27]: *flights.com may collect data of type cookie if the attribute cookie.Secure is active and use it for special_offers purposes until 21/12/2024* . The condition $cookie.Secure = tt$ means that the PILOT policy can be used only if the secure cookie attribute of the cookie used by *flights.com* is enabled. When Alice visits *flights.com*, only two options can be selected from the four proposed by *flights.com*. If *flights.com* does not use secure cookies, then Alice's policy is not enabled and the first option ($\bot$) must be chosen. If *flights.com* enables secure cookies, then option 2 can also be selected. By using a language like PILOT, this process can be carried out automatically.

Though implementing cookie banners seems an easy task, it has been shown that many implementations failed to comply with GDPR requirements [18]. Thus, a remaining question is: How can we assist software engineers in designing and implementing cookie banners that enforce GDPR requirements? The following sections use this example to describe a method to tackle this problem.

3 Abstract Operational Semantics

The *abstract* operational semantics of PILOT defines the conditions under which devices may exchange policies and data. This semantics does not describe *how* communication or checks are implemented. Implementation details are specified using lower level models (cf. Sect. 4). We build on the system state introduced in [27].

Systems are composed of devices that communicate data and use PILOT policies to express DSs and DCs privacy requirements. Every device has a set of associated policies. A policy is associated with a device if it was defined in the device or the device received it. DS devices have a set of data associated with them. This models the data stored in the device, e.g., the device MAC address or the user's email. We keep track of the data collected by DC devices together with their corresponding PILOT policies. The system state is formally defined as follows.

Definition 2 (System state). *The system state is a triple* $\langle \nu, \pi, \rho \rangle$ *where: i)* $\nu : \mathcal{D} \times \mathcal{I} \rightharpoonup \mathcal{V}$ *is a mapping from the data items of a device to their corresponding value in that device. ii)* $\pi : \mathcal{D} \rightarrow 2^{\mathcal{D} \times \mathcal{PP}}$ *is a function denoting the* policy base *of a device. The policy base contains the policies created by the owner of the device and the policies sent by other devices in order to state their collection requirements. A pair* (d, p) *means that* PILOT *policy* p *belongs to device* d*. We write* π_d *to denote* $\pi(d)$*. iii)* $\rho : \mathcal{D} \rightarrow 2^{\mathcal{D} \times \mathcal{I} \times \mathcal{PP}}$ *returns a set of triples* (s, i, p) *indicating the data items and* PILOT *policies that a controller has received. If* $(d', i, p) \in \rho(d)$*, we say that device* d *has received or collected data item* i *from device* d' *and policy* p *describes how the data item must be used. We write* ρ_d *to denote* $\rho(d)$*. We denote the universe of all possible states as* $\mathcal{S}$*.* □

In Definition 2, ν returns the local value of a data item in the specified device. When the value of a data item in a device is undefined, ν returns $\perp$. The policy base of a device d, π_d, contains received PILOT policies or policies that have been defined locally. If $(d, p) \in \pi_d$, the policy p corresponds to a policy that d has defined in the device itself. If $(e, p) \in \pi_d$ where $d \neq e$, p is a policy sent from device e. Policies stored in the policy base are used to compare the privacy policies of two devices before the data is communicated. The information that a device has received is recorded in ρ. Also, ρ contains the PILOT policy describing how data must be used. The difference between policies in π and ρ is that policies in π are used to determine whether data can be communicated, and policies in ρ are used to describe how a data item must be used by the receiver.

Example 1. Figure 2 shows a state composed of two devices: Alice's web browser, and *flights.com*'s server. The figure depicts the situation after Alice's browser has loaded *flights.com* and she has chosen an option in the cookie banner.

The database in Alice's state (ν_{Alice}) contains a data item of type cookie, $cookie_{Alice}$, with value c. The policy base in Alice's browser (π_{Alice}) contains two policies: ($Alice, p_{Alice}$) representing a policy that Alice defined, and (*flights.com*, $p_{flights.com}$) which represents a policy $p_{flights.com}$ sent by *flights.com*. We assume that p_{Alice} and $p_{flights.com}$ are the policies applying to data items of type cookie.

The state of *flights.com* contains one more element than Alice's state, namely, the set of received data ($\rho_{flights.com}$). This set contains the item $cookie_{Alice}$ collected from Alice, and the policy $p_{flights.com}$ that describing how to handle the data. Note that $p_{flights.com}$ was the PILOT policy originally defined by *flights.com*. To satisfy Alice's privacy preferences, $p_{flights.com}$ must be more restrictive than Alice's policy p_{Alice}, which is denoted by $p_{flights.com} \sqsubseteq p_{Alice}$. This condition can easily be enforced by comparing the policies before data is collected. The first element in ($Alice$, $cookie_{Alice}$, $p_{flights.com}$) indicates that the data comes from

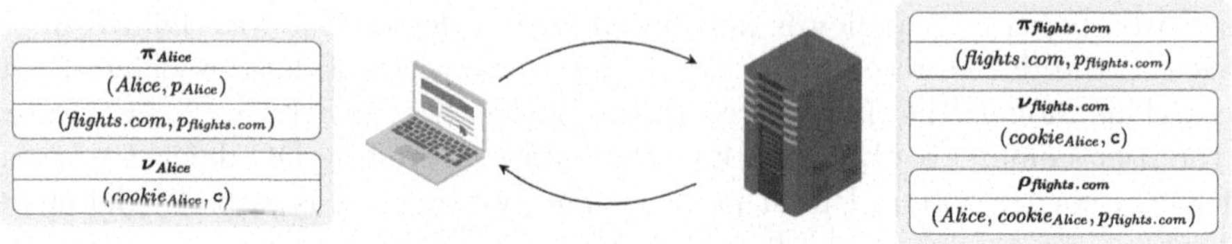

Fig. 2. Cookie Banner System State Example

Table 2. Small Step Operational Semantics of Events.

REQUEST

$$\text{R1}\ \frac{(sndr,p) \in \pi_{sndr} \qquad \forall (sndr,q) \in \pi_{rcv} \cdot p \not\sqsubseteq\!\!\not\sqsupseteq q}{\langle \nu, \pi, \rho\rangle \xrightarrow{request(sndr,rcv,t,p=(t,\_,\_))} \langle \nu, \pi', \rho\rangle}\ \textit{with}\ \pi'_{rcv} = \pi_{rcv} \cup \{(sndr,p)\}$$

$$\text{R2}\ \frac{(sndr,p) \in \pi_{sndr} \qquad (sndr,q) \in \pi_{rcv} \qquad p \sqsubseteq\!\!\sqsupseteq q}{\langle \nu, \pi, \rho\rangle \xrightarrow{request(sndr,rcv,t,p=(t,\_,\_))} \langle \nu, \pi', \rho\rangle}\ \textit{with}\ \pi'_{rcv} = (\pi_{rcv} \setminus q) \cup \{(sndr,p)\}$$

SEND

$$\frac{\begin{array}{ll}(rcv, p_{rcv}) \in \pi_{sndr} & \texttt{activePolicy}(p_{rcv}, send(sndr,rcv,i), st) \\ (sndr, p_{sndr}) \in \pi_{sndr} & \texttt{activePolicy}(p_{sndr}, send(sndr,rcv,i), st) \\ p_{rcv} \sqsubseteq p_{sndr} & \nu(sndr,i) \neq \bot\end{array}}{st = \langle \nu, \pi, \rho\rangle \xrightarrow{send(sndr,rcv,i)} \langle \nu', \pi, \rho'\rangle}\ \textit{with} \begin{cases}\rho'_{rcv} = \rho_{rcv} \cup \{(sndr, i, p_{rcv})\} \\ \nu'(rcv,i) = \nu(sndr,i)\end{cases}$$

TRANSFER

$$\frac{\begin{array}{c}(\_, i, p) \in \rho_{sndr} \qquad tr \in p.TR \\ \texttt{activeTransfer}(tr, p, transfer(sndr,rcv,i), st) \\ (rcv, p_{rcv}) \in \pi_{sndr} \qquad \texttt{activePolicy}(p_{rcv}, transfer(sndr,rcv,i), st) \\ p_{rcv} \sqsubseteq (p.t, tr, p.TR) \qquad \nu(sndr,i) \neq \bot\end{array}}{st = \langle \nu, \pi, \rho\rangle \xrightarrow{transfer(sndr,rcv,i)} \langle \nu', \pi, \rho'\rangle}\ \textit{with} \begin{cases}\rho'_{rcv} = \rho_{rcv} \cup \{(sndr, i, p_{rcv})\} \\ \nu'(rcv,i) = \nu(sndr,i)\end{cases}$$

Alice's device. Finally, *flights.com*'s policy base has one policy: its own policy $p_{flights.com}$, which was communicated to Alice for data collection.

System Events. We define the abstract semantics of the events in [27] focused on exchange of data items and PILOT policies. The set of events, denoted as E, includes: *request*, *send*, and *transfer*. *Traces* are sequences of state-event pairs (s_1, e_1), (s_2, e_2), (s_3, e_3), ... where $s_i \in \mathcal{S}$ is a system state and $e_i \in E$ is an event. A state s_{i+1} is the result of executing e_i on state s_i. We write $s \xrightarrow{e} s'$ to denote that s' is reached by executing e on state s. Every event is tagged with a timestamp indicating when the event occurs. We use a function $\texttt{time} : E \to \mathbb{N}$ to assign the timestamp—represented as a natural number.

Table 2 shows the definition of the events using small step operational semantics rules. The conditions of the rules are written as premises and the state updates are written on the right hand side. The functions `activePolicy` and `activeTransfer` determine whether a policy is active upon sending/transferring a data item. Intuitively, a policy is active if it applies to the data item to be sent, to the receiving entity, the retention time has not yet been reached, and its condition holds. The same must hold for active transfers (but for the transfer rule), and also the retention time for the sender (i.e., the retention time in the policy) must not have been reached. See [27] for the formal definition of these functions. We use $p.t$, $p.TR$ and $p.dcr.e$ to refer to the datatype associated to p, its set of transfer rules and the entity specified in the communication rule, respectively.

The event $request(sndr, rcv, t, p)$ models a data request from a DC to a DS or another DC. Thus, $sndr$ is always a DC device, and rcv may be a DC or DS device. A request includes the type t of the requested data and a PILOT policy p. The policy is required to refer to the datatype that is requested, i.e., $p = (t, \_, \_)$. After executing *request*, the pair $(sndr, p)$ is added to π_{rcv} (R1). If rcv already received a comparable policy from $sndr$ ($p \overset{\sqsubseteq}{\underset{\sqsupseteq}{}} q \triangleq p \sqsubseteq q \vee q \sqsubseteq p$), then q is replaced with p (R2); as new DCs policies may be more or less restrictive. Thus, rcv is informed about the updated terms for data handling.

The event $send(sndr, rcv, i)$ models collection of data item i from DS $sndr$ by DC rcv. Devices can only send i if defined in the state, $\nu(sndr, i) \neq \bot$. To execute *send*, it must hold that π_{sndr} contains: i) an active policy defined by $sndr$, p_{sndr}, indicating how $sndr$ allows DCs to use her data, and ii) an active policy sent by rcv, p_{rcv}, indicating how it commits to use the data. Data is sent if p_{rcv} is more restrictive than p_{sndr} (i.e., $p_{rcv} \sqsubseteq p_{sndr}$). We record the exchange in ρ_{rcv} indicating: the sender, the data item and rcv's PILOT policy, $(sndr, i, p_{rcv})$. We update rcv's database with the value of i in $sndr$'s state, $\nu(rcv, i) = \nu(sndr, i)$.

The event $transfer(sndr, rcv, i)$ models a DC ($sndr$) transferring a data item i to another DC (rcv)—if defined in the state, $\nu(sndr, i) \neq \bot$. First, it must hold that π_{sndr} contains an active policy from rcv, p_{rcv}. Let p denote the policy sent by the data owner along with i. There must exist an active transfer rule (tr) in the set of transfers rules of p. As before, the policy sent by rcv must be more restrictive than those sent by data owners, i.e., $p_{rcv} \sqsubseteq p_{tr}$ where p_{tr} is a policy with the active transfer tr in the place of the data communication rule and with the same set of transfers as p. Data items can be transferred more than once to the entities in the set of transfers as long as the retention time has not been reached. This is not an issue in terms of privacy as data items are constant values. We update ρ_{rcv} with the sender, the data item and rcv's PILOT policy, $(sndr, i, p_{rcv})$. Note that the owner of the data item is not $sndr$ since transfers always correspond to exchanges of previously collected data, $\texttt{owner}(i) \neq sndr$. The database of rcv is updated with the current value of i in ν_{sndr}.

4 Refinement Into Operational Models

A *refinement* is an operational model that can be directly implemented—i.e., it can easily be translated to source code. Refinements provide information about the *communications* between devices and the *locality of the computations*; these details are omitted in the abstract semantics. A refinement must include operational models for each device in the system. We model refinements using a symbolic representation of labeled transition systems called *program graphs* (PGs) [2]. These models can be seen as extended state machines—and should be familiar to most software engineers, as they are part of their basic education. For each PG, we consider a (finite) set of variables Var. Each variable $x \in Var$ belongs to a domain D_x, we use $D = \bigcup_{x \in Var} D_x$ to denote the set of all domains. Functions $\eta\colon Var \to D$ map variables to a value in their corresponding domain, and we use $Eval(Var)$ to denote the set of all η functions. We use $Cond(Var)$ to denote a set of conditions on variables. Program graphs are defined as follows:

Definition 3 (Program Graph [2]). *A* program graph *PG over a set of variables Var is a tuple* $(Loc, Act, \mathit{Effect}, \rightarrow, Loc_0, g_0)$ *where Loc is a set of locations and Act is a set of actions; Effect*: $Act \times Eval(Var) \rightarrow Eval(Var)$ *is an effect function;* $\rightarrow_{PG} \subseteq Loc \times Act \times Cond(Var) \times Loc$ *is a conditional transition relation;* $Loc_0 \subseteq Loc$ *is a set of initial locations; and* $g_0 \in Cond(Var)$ *is the initial condition.*

When no confusion may arise, we omit the subscript in $\rightarrow_{PG}$. By convention the shape of the actions in Act is $a(\vec{x})$ where $\vec{x} = x_1, x_2, \ldots$ is a finite vector of variables, called the *parameters* of the action. We write $q \xrightarrow{a(\vec{x})/\phi} q'$ to denote that there exists a transition from q to q' in the PG labeled by $a(\vec{x})/\phi$, i.e., $(q, a(\vec{x}), \phi, q') \in \rightarrow_{PG}$. For simplicity, when $\phi = \top$ we write $q \xrightarrow{a(\vec{x})} q'$.

In the following we define the synchronous composition of PGs. To this end, we use *synchronization actions*. For any synchronization action $a(\vec{x})$, there are corresponding sending $(a^{\uparrow}(\vec{x}))$, and receiving $(a^{\downarrow}(\vec{x}))$ actions. Two devices communicate via $a(\vec{x})$ by each of them executing one of the corresponding sending and receiving action. We use $\eta[\vec{x}_{a^{\downarrow}} \mapsto \eta(\vec{x}_{a^{\uparrow}})]$ to denote that the variables in the receiving action are bind with the values of the sending action in η. We use synchronization actions to formally define the synchronous composition of PGs.

Definition 4 (Synchronous Composition). *Given two PGs* PG_1 *and* PG_2*, such that* $PG_i = (Loc_i, Act_i, \mathit{Effect}_i, \rightarrow_i, Loc_{0_i}, g_{0_i})$*, the* synchronous composition *over the actions* $H = \{a(\vec{x}) \mid a^{\uparrow}(\vec{x}) \in Act_j \wedge a^{\downarrow}(\vec{x}) \in Act_k$ *for* $j, k \in \{1, 2\}$ *and* $j \neq k\}$ *is defined as,* $PG_1 ||_H PG_2 \triangleq (Loc_1 \times Loc_2, Act_1 \cup Act_2 \cup H, \mathit{Effect}, \rightarrow, Loc_{0_1} \times Loc_{0_2}, g_{0_1} \wedge g_{0_2})$ *and the transition relation* $\rightarrow$ *is defined as*

$$\frac{q_i \xrightarrow{a(\vec{x})/\phi_i}_i q_i' \qquad a(\vec{x}) \notin H}{(q_1, q_2) \xrightarrow{a(\vec{x})/\phi_1} (q_1', q_2)} \text{ with } i \in \{1,2\} \qquad \frac{q_1 \xrightarrow{a^{\uparrow}(\vec{x})/\phi_1}_1 q_1' \qquad q_2 \xrightarrow{a^{\downarrow}(\vec{x})/\phi_2}_2 q_2' \qquad a(\vec{x}) \in H}{(q_1, q_2) \xrightarrow{a(\vec{x})/\phi_1 \wedge \phi_2} (q_1', q_2')}$$

$$\textit{and, } \mathit{Effect}(a(\vec{x}), \eta) = \begin{cases} \mathit{Effect}_i(a(\vec{x}), \eta) & \textit{if } a(\vec{x}) \notin H \textit{ and } a(\vec{x}) \in Act_i \textit{ with } i \in \{1,2\} \\ \eta[\vec{x}_{a^{\downarrow}} \mapsto \eta(\vec{x}_{a^{\uparrow}})] & \textit{if } a(\vec{x}) \in H \end{cases}$$

In what follows, we use PGs to model implementations of different system architectures. We model devices that can communicate directly and indirectly. We consider, w.l.o.g., policies and transfers that are always active; note that this check can always be added as a prerequisite before sending data. We prove that the implementations refine the abstract semantics of Pilot in Sect. 5.

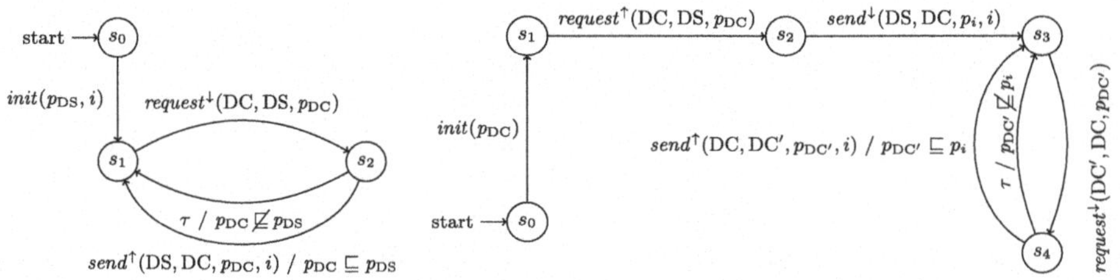

(a) Data Subject Gateway. (b) Data Controller Gateway.

Fig. 3. Direct Communication Program Graphs.

Direct Communication: Cookie Banners. We return to our cookie banner example. We define two PGs for the two devices in the example: Alice's laptop (DS device) and the server hosting *flights.com* (DC device). These PGs precisely describe the program that Alice and the server must execute in their devices, and the communication between them. We model a system where the DS defines a policy *a priori* and data collection is allowed if the DC policy complies with the DS policy. Note that this differs from the usual interaction where the DS is presented with several DC policies, and she must select one (cf. Figure 1).

Data Subject Gateway (DS Program). This program allows data collection only if the DC policy respects (subsumes) Alice's policy. Figure 3a shows the data subject gateway PG. This PG runs on Alice's browser (DS device). It contains the following variables: p_{DS} corresponding to $\pi(\mathrm{DS}, \mathrm{DS})$ in the abstract semantics, p_{DC} corresponding to $\pi(\mathrm{DS}, dc)$, and the current state σ of the PG (not in abstract semantics). We define *Effect* as: $\mathit{Effect}(\mathit{init}(i, p_{\mathrm{DS}}), \eta) = \eta[p_{\mathrm{DS}} \mapsto \texttt{policy\_init()}, i \mapsto \texttt{data\_init()}]$ and $\mathit{Effect}(\tau, \eta) = \eta$. The functions `policy_init()` and `data_init()` model machine-level functions that retrieve: the policy from the user (e.g., via a browser extension or settings form), and the data item (e.g., when entered by the user or automatically retrieved by the browser), respectively. For each data item, an instance of the data subject gateway is executed. Internal actions τ model transitions with no effect on PG variables. The synchronization events *request* and *send* are defined as in Definition 4; they synchronize with the corresponding events in the DC program described below.

Intuitively, the PG in Fig. 3a starts with an initialization action, $\mathit{init}(p_{\mathrm{DS}}, i)$, where Alice's inputs her policy (p_{DS}) and the data item (i). Then, the data subject gateway waits for data collection requests, $\mathit{request}^{\downarrow}(\mathrm{DC}, \mathrm{DS}, p_{\mathrm{DC}})$. A request includes the sender DC, the receiver DS, and the policy of the DC. Upon receiving a request, the data subject gateway checks whether the DC policy complies with that of the DS, $p_{\mathrm{DC}} \sqsubseteq p_{\mathrm{DS}}$. If so, it sends the item (i) along with the policy (p_{DC}) that must be enforced when processing i, $\mathit{send}^{\uparrow}(\mathrm{DS}, \mathrm{DC}, p_{\mathrm{DC}}, i)$. Otherwise, data collection does not take place, and the PG goes back to wait for further requests.

Data Controller Gateway (DC Program). This program can request data from DSs, process it according to its privacy policy, and transfer it (if requested by another DC and allowed by the policy). Figure 3b shows the controller gateway PG. This PG runs on the server hosting *flights.com*. It consist of the following variables: p_i and i correspond to the policy and data item sent by the DS: $(i, \mathrm{DS}, p_i) \in \rho(\mathrm{DC})$ in the abstract semantics, $p_{\mathrm{DC}} = \pi(\mathrm{DC}, \mathrm{DC})$, $p_{\mathrm{DC}'} = \pi(\mathrm{DC}, \mathrm{DC}')$, and current state σ of the PG (not in abstract semantics). The *Effect* function is defined as: $\mathit{Effect}(\mathit{init}(p_{\mathrm{DC}}), \eta) = \eta[p_{\mathrm{DC}} \mapsto \texttt{policy\_init()}]$ and $\mathit{Effect}(\tau, \eta) = \eta$. In this case, `policy_init()` retrieves the DC policy.

The PG in Fig. 3b starts by initializing the DC policy, p_{DC}. Then, it sends a request to collect data of the type specified in p_{DC}. This occurs, for instance, when a client visits *flights.com*. At this point, the data controller gateway waits to receive the data from the DS. Upon receiving the data, it can transfer the data to another data controller DC′. This corresponds to the edges between s_3 and s_4. This interaction is identical to that of the data subject gateway (cf. Fig. 3a). The only difference is that the policy used to determine the compliance with the DS preferences is p_i, i.e., the policy sent by the DS during data collection. Note that this ensures that DS preferences are enforced even if data items are transferred—this property is formally proved in Sect. 5.

This implementation is applicable to systems with support for direct communication. For example, a system where users upload data from a smartwatch to fitness social networks such as Strava or Fitbit. However, this implementation cannot be applied to systems that automatically broadcast data—e.g., Bluetooth protocols—where receivers can record DS data as soon as DS devices enter the collection range. Below we describe an alternative refinement for these systems.

Indirect Communication: Bluetooth Low Energy. Many wireless communication protocols, such as *Bluetooth low energy* (BLE), require broadcasting identifying information such as MAC addresses to operate. Unfortunately, this information is becoming a common way to track DSs in public places [4,7,21,24]. This type of data collection is especially dangerous as it occurs without DSs being aware or notified; data is collected as soon as DSs enter the range of the collecting device. This is known as *passive* data collection. The GDPR imposes restrictions on (passive) data collection; namely it can only be carried out if DSs provide explicit consent. We describe a refinement for passive data collection, which makes it possible for DSs to provide (or not) explicit consent.

Consider a Bluetooth tracking system installed in a shopping mall. The system is composed by data collection devices (DC devices) that automatically record the Bluetooth MAC address of DS devices within their range—e.g., smartphones, smartwatches, wireless headsets, etc. Direct communication cannot be applied here. DC devices can *only* collect data broadcast by DS devices, and DC devices cannot communicate the DC policy prior to collecting the data. Nevertheless, DS devices can communicate data items and policies via Bluetooth. We exploit this feature to make it possible for the DSs to provide consent.

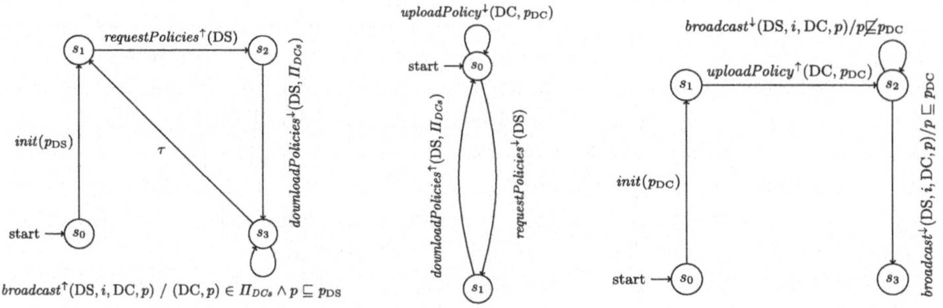

(a) Data Subject Gateway. (b) Repository. (c) Data Controller Gateway.

Fig. 4. Indirect Communication Program Graphs.

Policy Repository. DCs can upload their policies to a *public repository.* These repositories store and send policies, but do not modify them. The repository could be hosted by the DC or governmental entities such as Data Protection Agencies. DS devices download DC policies from repositories *before* entering the operation range of the DC device. Otherwise, DCs cannot store the DS data (see details below). Figure 4b shows the policy repository PG. The variable p_{DC} corresponds to $\pi(\mathrm{DC}, \mathrm{DC})$. The database of all received policies is denoted as Π_{DCs}. This is a temporary variable to support indirect exchange of policies between DCs and DSs; not part of the abstract semantics. The PG includes the current state σ (not in abstract semantics). The *Effect* function is defined by synchronization actions; except for the action $\mathit{uploadPolicy}^{\downarrow}(\mathrm{DC}, p_{\mathrm{DC}})$ that additionally updates the repository database with p_{DC}, $\Pi_{\mathrm{DCs}} \cup \{(\mathrm{DC}, p_{\mathrm{DC}})\}$. The repository can either receive DC policies, $\mathit{uploadPolicy}^{\downarrow}(\mathrm{DC}, p_{\mathrm{DC}})$, or send policies to DSs, $\mathit{downloadPolicies}^{\uparrow}(\mathrm{DS}, \Pi_{DCs})$, upon receiving a request $\mathit{requestPolicies}^{\downarrow}(\mathrm{DS})$.

Data Subject Gateway (DS Program). This program broadcasts a data item and DS policy together. Figure 4a shows the PG. The DS policy p_{DS} corresponds to $\pi(\mathrm{DS}, \mathrm{DS})$. Π_{DCs} represents the repository database, and σ the PG current state (none in the abstract semantics). *Effect* is defined as $\mathit{Effect}(\mathit{init}(p_{\mathrm{DS}}, i), \eta) = \eta[p_{\mathrm{DS}} \mapsto \texttt{policy\_init()}, i \mapsto \texttt{data\_init()}]$, and $\mathit{Effect}(\tau, \eta) = \eta$.

The PG starts with an initialization action, $\mathit{init}(p_{\mathrm{DS}})$, where the DS defines her policy and data item i is recorded. The function `policy_init()` retrieves the policy from the DS, and, `data_init()` initializes i to the Bluetooth MAC address of the device. Then, it requests from the policy repository the database of DC policies, $\mathit{requestPolicies}^{\uparrow}(\mathrm{DS})$. Upon receiving them, $\mathit{downloadPolicies}^{\downarrow}(\mathrm{DS}, \Pi_{DCs})$, the data subject gateway starts to broadcast the data item i, receiver DC, and policy p—this might be implemented as in [21]. This step iterates over all policies in Π_{DCs} that comply with the p_{DS}. Non-deterministically (or, alternatively, triggered by the DS), the data subject gateway can update its policy database—action τ in the PG.

Data Controller Gateway (DC Program). This program can upload the DC policy to the policy repository, and collect and process DS data according to their policy. We omit transfers as they are identical to that in Fig. 3b; it simply requires adding s_4 and the connecting edges. Figure 4c shows the PG. Variables p and i correspond to the policy and data item sent by the DS: $(i, \mathrm{DS}, p) \in \rho(\mathrm{DC})$ in the abstract semantics. As in previous PGs, there is a current state variable σ (not in the abstract semantics). The *Effect* function is defined by synchronization actions and a policy initialization machine-level function.

The PG starts by initializing the DC policy, p_{DC}. In order for DSs to access p_{DC}, the PG uploads it to the policy repository, $uploadPolicy^{\uparrow}(\mathrm{DC}, p_{\mathrm{DC}})$. Then, the data controller gateway starts collecting MAC addresses and corresponding policies from DS devices within its range of operation. When the received policy does not conform p_{DC} (loop in s_2), the data item and policy are discarded, and the PG continues collecting data. Note that the DC device may receive policies for other DCs, in such a case the policy will fail to subsume that of the DC. We remark that, in our setting, policies are not secret, e.g., there is no problem in Amazon learning the policy that Alice defined for Google.

5 Verification of Legal Privacy Requirements

We use model-checking to verify that: i) the abstract semantics complies with privacy requirements inspired by the GDPR; and ii) the PGs in Sect. 4 refine the abstract semantics—thus, satisfying the same privacy requirements. We mechanize the abstract semantics and PGs in TLA$^+$ [17], and use the TLA$^+$ Toolbox [16] to automatically verify privacy requirements and refinements. The TLA$^+$ code is available in [20, 26].

TLA$^+$ *Mechanization.* The abstract semantics is directly encoded as defined in Table 2—TLA$^+$ includes set theoretic operations as well as the next state operator *prime* ($'$). As for PGs, the only challenge is encoding synchronization actions (see Definition 4). To this end, we use a variable, *msgs*, modeling the set of messages in transit. Actions $a^{\uparrow}(\vec{x})$ and $a^{\downarrow}(\vec{x})$ add and remove an element $\langle a, \vec{x} \rangle$ in *msgs*, respectively. Note that this type of asynchronous communication differs from the synchronous composition in Definition 4. Consequently, the PGs in Sect. 4 are designed so that, if the PG is in a state waiting receive data (i.e., a state with an outgoing transition labeled with a receiving action), then the PG cannot make progress unless the corresponding message is sent. Hence, they exhibit the same synchronization behavior as specified in Definition 4.

This formalization serves as a guideline for software engineers to verify privacy requirements and refinements. TLA$^+$ has been used in real case studies by engineers in large companies such as Amazon [23]. We demonstrate the use of the model-checker in the TLA$^+$ Toolbox to verify privacy requirements and refinements on a model comprising: a DS, a data item (owned by the DS), two DCs, three Pilot policies p_1, p_2, p_3 (randomly selected by devices in their initialization steps) with $p_1 \sqsubseteq p_2$. As before, these policies are always active. This corresponds to worse-case analysis (as required in security and privacy applications) as it permits data communication for all data collection and transfer rules. We chose this model as it is the smallest model triggering all events (which are explored non-deterministically by the model-checker). To improve the performance of model-checking, we abstracted the syntax of PILOT policies. The relation $\sqsubseteq$ is explicitly encoded as a partial order in the model. Model-checking privacy requirements and refinements on these models takes less than 10 s on a 1×1.7GHz virtual machine with 4G of RAM. Unfortunately, verifying models including more entities, data items or policies introduces a scalability problem due to state explosion. However, we conjecture that these additions will not change the results. Note that: i) consent properties concern each data item separately (i.e., the handling of consent for one item does not affect another); ii) we consider (non-deterministically) independent and dependent (in terms of $\sqsubseteq$) policies for each item; and iii) all communication events are (non-deterministically) triggered. Our future work includes mechanizing a formal proof of this conjecture.

Legal Privacy Requirements. We verify that: i) the abstract semantics do not allow DCs to violate DS policies; and ii) one of the necessary conditions for informed consent according to the GDPR.

Privacy Requirement 1 (DS Policy Compliance). *DCs always follow a policy p_i for processing a data item i that complies with the policy defined by the DS, $p_{DS} \sqsubseteq p_i$.*

This requirement ensures that DCs cannot bypass the constraints imposed by DSs in processing their data. Formally, given device d, data controller dc, and data subject ds,

$$\text{if } (d, i, p_i) \in \rho_{dc} \text{ and } p_{\mathrm{DS}} = \pi(ds, ds) \text{ then } p_i \sqsubseteq p_{\mathrm{DS}}$$

with $\mathtt{type}(i) \leq_{\mathcal{T}} p_{\mathrm{DS}}.t$. The requirement is formalized and successfully verified [26]. This requirement is of utmost importance as it ensures that DSs choices are never violated, and confirms the correctness of the design of our semantics.

The GDPR states that consent must be *informed*. Intuitively, this requirement means that *before* data is collected the DS must be informed about how data will processed and whether it will be transferred. This requirement is of special interest, as there exist implementations of cookie banners that failed to comply with informed consent [18]. Below we state two necessary privacy requirements to enforce informed consent.

Privacy Requirement 2 (Informed Consent for Data Collection). *Before a DC receives data item i, the owner of i must have received a* PILOT *policy from the DC.*

Formally, given a DS $sndr$, DC rcv, and data item i,

$$\begin{aligned} &\text{if } (sndr, i, \_) \in \rho_{rcv} \text{ and } \mathtt{owner}(i) = sndr \\ &\qquad\qquad \text{then } (rcv, p) \in \pi_{\mathtt{owner}(i)} \text{ and } \mathtt{type}(i) \leq_{\mathcal{T}} p.t. \end{aligned}$$

This property states that a DS has provided informed consent for data collection iff every time that a DC collects data from a DS, the DS has received a policy for the collected item from the DC. This privacy requirement concerning informed consent is successfully verified (see [26]).

We have verified that PILOT abstract semantics enforces two privacy properties which are required by the GDPR. This result shows that software engineers (such as cookie banner developers) could use PILOT abstract semantics as a high-level design for their implementations. Furthermore, as we describe below, they can use our formalization to verify that their implementations satisfy our abstract semantics; thus satisfying the privacy requirements discussed here.

Refinements. In TLA$^+$, refinement (or implementation) amounts to logical implication; the so called *refinement mappings* [1]. Formally, a specification I implements an abstract specification S iff $I \implies S$. This proof technique requires mapping state variables in the specification to state variables in the implementation. We described this mapping for all the PGs in Sect. 4—see our TLA$^+$ mechanization for details [26].

Let *AbstSem* denote the abstract semantics specification (Table 2), *DirectRef* the specification of direct communication (PGs in Fig. 3), and *IndirectRef* the specification of indirect communication (PGs in Fig. 4). We successfully verify that i) $\mathit{DirectRef} \Longrightarrow \mathit{AbstSem}$; and ii) $\mathit{IndirectRef} \Longrightarrow \mathit{AbstSem}$ (see [26]).

The most important consequence of this result is that both refinements are guaranteed (proven) to enforce the privacy requirements above. Furthermore, new privacy requirements proven on the abstract semantics will also hold in the refinements. This is useful in practice as formal reasoning on the abstract semantics is much easier; the abstract semantics omit implementation details unnecessary for reasoning about privacy.

6 Related Work and Concluding Remarks

Related Work. Several languages have been proposed to formally define privacy policies e.g., S4P, CI, PrivacyAPI, PrivacyLFP and PILOT [3,5,8,19,27]. Generally, these works focus on reasoning about system behavior with respect to privacy policies and regulations. However, none of them address the gap between formal definition and implementation. Our refinement method (Sect. 4) contributes to bridging this gap, and demonstrates it for the PILOT language—although our method can be applied to any privacy policy language whose policies and system behavior can be formally defined. In [27], the authors used the SPIN model-checker [12] to answer privacy risk queries. However, the model used for verification was based on an informal description of system events. Here we formalize the abstract semantics in TLA$^+$, we formalize two GDPR requirements for the implementation of consent, and introduce a method to specify and verify refinements.

Different enforcement implementations for the P3P privacy policy language [6] have been studied via refinements [25]. Papanikolaou et al. translate P3P policies into CSP [11] and refinement is interpreted as a comparison between policies [25]. Instead, we use a system level notion of refinement. We verify that the behavior of the implementation is equivalent to that of an abstract semantics satisfying GDPR requirements for informed consent.

Some programming languages are designed to embed the enforcement of privacy requirements [15,28]. In [28], the authors propose a programming language that includes consent management. However, it does not include notions of data transfer and DC policy. Therefore, it cannot be used to address the GDPR requirements in this paper. DPL [15] covers more GDPR requirements than our work, but its operational semantics is higher level than PGs. The system configuration operates on objects but it does not specify how different devices execute each program—as we did for our PGs. Our refinement method could be used to refine DPL semantics to lower level implementations.

Hublet et al. introduced an enforcement of GDPR requirements for web applications [13]. The authors present an enforceable GDPR specification for web applications written in Metric First-Order Temporal logic. Their work covers more GDPR requirements than the work presented here, but it is limited to web applications. Our method does not impose constraints on architecture. For instance, we showed a refinement of a Bluetooth-based communication system in Sect. 4.

Conclusion. We proposed a method to implement and verify legal requirements for consent management. The method aims to assist software engineers in designing and verifying systems that require consent management. The design/implementation language is program graphs—extended state machines that are common in the education of software engineers. We use a verification toolbox [16] that has been used by software engineers in industry [10,23]. We provided a formal abstract semantics for the Pilot language, and verified that it satisfies GDPR requirements for informed consent. We introduced a notion of refinement as operational models to design the implementation of the devices in the system. We demonstrated the use of refinements to implement direct and indirect communication systems. We verified that the implementations refine Pilot abstract semantics, i.e., they ensure the same GDPR requirements for informed consent. We mechanized the abstract semantics, refinements and privacy requirements in TLA^+, and used model-checking for verification.

References

1. Abadi, M., Lamport, L.: The existence of refinement mappings. Theor. Comput. Sci. **82**(2), 253–284 (1991)
2. Baier, C., Katoen, J.: Principles of model checking. MIT Press (2008)
3. Barth, A., Datta, A., Mitchell, J.C., Nissenbaum, H.: Privacy and contextual integrity: framework and applications. In: Proceedings of the 27th IEEE Symposium on Security and Privacy, S&P 2006, pp. 184–198 (2006)
4. Becker, J.K., Li, D., Starobinski, D.: Tracking anonymized bluetooth devices. Proc. Priv. Enhancing Technol. **2019**(3), 50–65 (2019)
5. Becker, M., Malkis, A., Bussard, L.: S4P: A generic language for specifying privacy preferences and policies. Tech. rep. (2010)

6. Cranor, L.F., Egelman, S., Sheng, S., McDonald, A.M., Chowdhury, A.: P3P deployment on websites. J. Electr. Commerce Res. Appli. **7**(3), 274–293 (2008)
7. Danis, F.S., Cemgil, A.T.: Model-based localization and tracking using Bluetooth low-energy beacons. Sensors **17**(11), 2484 (2017)
8. DeYoung, H., Garg, D., Jia, L., Kaynar, D.K., Datta, A.: Experiences in the logical specification of the HIPAA and GLBA privacy laws. In: Proceedings of the 9th ACM Workshop on Privacy in the Electronic Society, WPES 2010, pp. 73–82. ACM (2010)
9. European Union: Regulation 2016/679 of the European Parliament and of the council of 27 april 2016 on the protection of natural persons with regard to the processing of personal data and on the free movement of such data, and repeating directive 95/46/ec (General Data Protection Regulation) (May 2016). https://eur-lex.europa.eu/legal-content/EN/TXT/?uri=uriserv:OJ.L_.2016.119.01.0001.01.ENG&toc=OJ:L:2016:119:TOC
10. Hackett, A.F., Rowe, J., Kuppe, M.A.: Understanding inconsistency in Azure Cosmos DB with TLA+. In: 45th IEEE/ACM International Conference on Software Engineering: Software Engineering in Practice, SEIP@ICSE 2023, pp. 1–12. IEEE (2023)
11. Hoare, C.A.R.: Communicating sequential processes. Commun. ACM **21**(8), 666–677 (1978)
12. Holzmann, G.J.: The SPIN Model Checker - Primer and Reference Manual. Addison-Wesley (2004)
13. Hublet, F., Basin, D.A., Krstic, S.: Enforcing the GDPR. In: Computer Security - ESORICS 2023 - 28th European Symposium on Research in Computer Security. LNCS, vol. 14345, pp. 400–422. Springer (2023). https://doi.org/10.1007/978-3-031-51476-0_2
14. Jensen, C., Potts, C.: Privacy policies as decision-making tools: an evaluation of online privacy notices. In: Proceedings of the 2004 Conference on Human Factors in Computing Systems, CHI 2004, pp. 471–478. ACM (2004)
15. Karami, F., Basin, D.A., Johnsen, E.B.: DPL: a language for GDPR enforcement. In: 35th IEEE Computer Security Foundations Symposium, CSF 2022, pp. 112–129. IEEE (2022)
16. Kuppe, M.A., Lamport, L., Ricketts, D.: The TLA+ toolbox. In: Proceedings of Fifth Workshop on Formal Integrated Development Environment, F-IDE@FM 2019. EPTCS, vol. 310, pp. 50–62 (2019)
17. Lamport, L.: Specifying Systems. Addison-Wesley, The TLA+ Language and Tools for Hardware and Software Engineers (2002)
18. Matte, C., Bielova, N., Santos, C.: Do cookie banners respect my choice? : measuring legal compliance of banners from IAB europe's transparency and consent framework. In: Proceedings of 41st IEEE Symposium on Security and Privacy, S&P 2020, pp. 791–809. IEEE (2020)
19. May, M.J., Gunter, C.A., Lee, I.: Privacy APIs: Access control techniques to analyze and verify legal privacy policies. In: Proceedings of the 19th IEEE Computer Security Foundations Workshop, CSFW 2006, pp. 85–97. IEEE Computer Society (2006)
20. TLA^+ mechanization of abstract semantics, program graphs, and privacy requirements, https://github.com/raulpardo/pilot-tla/
21. Morel, V., Cunche, M., Le Métayer, D.: A generic information and consent framework for the iot. In: Proceedings of 18th IEEE International Conference On Trust, Security And Privacy In Computing And Communications, TrustCom 2019, pp. 366–373. IEEE (2019)

22. Morel, V., Pardo, R.: Sok: three facets of privacy policies. In: Proceedings of the 19th Workshop on Privacy in the Electronic Society, WPES 2020, pp. 41–56. ACM (2020)
23. Newcombe, C., Rath, T., Zhang, F., Munteanu, B., Brooker, M., Deardeuff, M.: How amazon web services uses formal methods. Commun. ACM **58**(4), 66–73 (2015)
24. Oosterlinck, D., Benoit, D.F., Baecke, P., Van de Weghe, N.: Bluetooth tracking of humans in an indoor environment: An application to shopping mall visits. Appl. Geogr. **78**, 55–65 (2017)
25. Papanikolaou, N., Creese, S., Goldsmith, M.: Refinement checking for privacy policies. Sci. Comput. Program. **77**(10–11), 1198–1209 (2012)
26. Pardo, R., Le Métayer, D.: Model-Checking the Implementation of Consent (Accompanying Artifact). https://doi.org/10.5281/zenodo.12550375
27. Pardo, R., Le Métayer, D.: Analysis of privacy policies to enhance informed consent. In: Foley, S.N. (ed.) DBSec 2019. LNCS, vol. 11559, pp. 177–198. Springer, Cham (2019). https://doi.org/10.1007/978-3-030-22479-0_10
28. Tokas, S., Owe, O.: A formal framework for consent management. In: Gotsman, A., Sokolova, A. (eds.) FORTE 2020. LNCS, vol. 12136, pp. 169–186. Springer, Cham (2020). https://doi.org/10.1007/978-3-030-50086-3_10

GrammarForge: Learning Program Input Grammars for Fuzz Testing

Hannes Sochor(✉), Flavio Ferrarotti, and Robert Wille

Software Competence Center, Hagenberg i. M., Upper Austria, Austria
{hannes.sochor,flavio.ferrarotti,robert.wille}@scch.at

Abstract. Providing good methods for testing properties of software is critical. Such methods often depend on a formal description of the program input language, in particular, when they are based on grammar-based fuzzing. Unfortunately, it cannot be ensured that such a formal description is always available. To tackle this problem, we propose a new method that automates grammar learning for the input language of the software under test, combining classical language membership queries with light weight source code analysis tools such as control flow graphs and program instrumentation. We present a prototype implementation (*GrammarForge*) of our method, which works following a process of automated conservative substitution of place holders by terminals, starting from an initial grammar structure extracted from the source code. It targets arbitrary parses implemented using recursive descent techniques. We perform extensive experimentation, which shows that *GrammarForge* outperforms alternative tools with respect to accuracy of the learned grammar. Moreover, and different to all other state of the art methods, our learning process does not need seed inputs from the target language.

1 Introduction

Software quality in general is becoming more and more critical. High quality software production requires that bugs and security weaknesses are detected early on. Even after the software is deployed, it is still necessary to continuously search for potential weaknesses. One of the most successful and widely adopted techniques to achieve this goal is fuzzing [15]. As software solutions constantly evolve and their complexity increases, the methods used to test and search for potential flaws need to adapt. Thus, over the years, fuzz testing has evolved from simply executing randomly generated test data to more sophisticated approaches, such as those implemented by state of the art tools AFL [26] and SAGE [9].

In this context, grammar-based fuzzing is fundamental to efficiently test deep program paths. As such, it significantly increases the chances of discovering relevant bugs and weaknesses. This field has gained importance with ever more

This work is supported by BMK, BMDW, and the Province of Upper Austria in the frame of the COMET–Competence Centers for Excellent Technologies Programme and the COMET Module DEPS managed by FFG.

A. Madeira and A. Knapp (Eds.): SEFM 2024, LNCS 15280, pp. 272–289, 2025.
https://doi.org/10.1007/978-3-031-77382-2_16

sophisticated approaches [1,7,17,21], especially for testing parser and compilers. In general, a grammar is provided and is then subsequently used to efficiently generate random inputs that are well formed for the software under test, i.e. inputs that are not discarded in the initial parsing phase of the target program. This enables the detection of bugs hidden deeper in the program logic of the given application. However, such an approach can only be applied if a suitable grammar is readily available. In practice that is unfortunately not always the case, rather the contrary.

The lack of suitable grammars for fuzzing can be addressed by applying grammar learning techniques. Grammar learning (aka. grammar inference) aims to find automated methods to extract grammars that capture as faithfully as possible the input language of the target program (or software under test). Usually, grammar inference is performed prior to the actual fuzzing process and is treated as a separate entity. We follow a radically different approach by integrating both processes. That is, in our approach we use the information gained during fuzzing for grammar learning, and, at the same time, we incrementally improve fuzzing in each step of the learning process. Based on this idea, we developed a new algorithm for grammar learning as well as a prototype implementation (*GrammarForge*), which integrates grammar inference into the fuzzing process. In this sense, we can see *GrammarForge* as a tool for grammar-based fuzzing that interactively builds its own grammar from scratch, and that is able to explore and penetrate the software under test more efficiently with each step.

In order to learn suitable grammars, known techniques [5,10,13,20] rely on deep program analysis, plus a set of initial seed inputs from the target language (inputs that should somehow be representative enough). In previous works we have been able to obtain good results and at the same time reduce the reliance on sophisticated program analysis down to Abstract Syntax Tree (AST) analysis and basic program instrumentation [24,25]. In addition, we have shown that a minimal set of inputs is sufficient to learn good quality input grammars.

In this work we make a rather radical change by directly exploiting in the approach implemented by *GrammarForge* the core strength of fuzzing itself, efficiently generating a large set of inputs from scratch. Thus, *GrammarForge* does not need seed inputs to learn the target program input grammar. Instead, it makes use of control flow analysis to identify sub-elements of the program input language that enables incremental learning using fuzzing. Then it applies an iterative approach that continuously searches for minimal incremental additions to the grammar, extending it until its language approaches closely the target program input language. Furthermore, we show through extensive experimental evaluation that *GrammarForge* outperforms state of the art grammar inference tools w.r.t. accuracy of the inferred grammar. Last but not least, *GrammarForge* only relies on well-known widely available program analysis techniques, which makes it more broadly applicable than other known methods.

The paper is organized as follows. We discuss in Sect. 2 related work in the field of grammar-based fuzzing as well as grammar inference. In Sect. 3 we fix the notation and required background. We describe the grammar learning method implemented by *GrammarForge* in detail in Sect. 4. This is followed by a thorough evaluation of it performance in Sect. 5. Before the conclusion in Sect. 7, we discuss in Sect. 6 the current limitations of *GrammarForge*.

2 Related Work

There are several works in the field of grammar-based fuzzing that try to adapt to the target program while fuzzing. We can divide them in two main approaches. The first consists on using a given grammar to guide input generation into promising execution paths, applying diverse methods to increase the probability of finding a faulty program behaviour [7,18]. The second generative approach, starts without prior knowledge and aims to collect information needed to generate a suitable model or grammar from scratch. Our work falls into this category. In particular, we are concerned with related work that focus on grammar inference, i.e., in learning a program input grammar by observing the behaviour of the program under test for different inputs.

The field of grammar inference has been largely defined by the impossibility to exactly identify any language in the Chomsky hierarchy in the limit by just providing positive words, i.e. words that are in the language itself [8]. However, it is possible to identify regular as well as context-free languages given a good enough teacher that can answer queries as well as provide counterexamples, i.e. words that are not in the language [4]. As such, state of the art methods try to provide a good enough teacher or similar information for identifying context-free languages nonetheless.

Broadly speaking, grammar learning can be done by either applying black- or white-box approaches. The former type solely relies on heuristic methods that use membership queries to approximate the target language. In this case, one needs to provide a good enough set of seed inputs and then incrementally generalize the language as in [5]. In the context of domain-specific languages, this approach has shown promising results using genetic programming based inference couple with positive and negative samples of expressions [6,14]. A related "grey" box approach proposed in [23] uses limited additional information from an static source code analysis to enhance its otherwise black-box learning approach, and thus easy its reliance on a good set of seed inputs.

On the other hand, white-box approaches try to extract knowledge from the source code to guide the algorithm during the learning process. This can come in various forms. If good seed inputs that are representative of the target language are available, then grammar inference methods based on sophisticated dynamic tainting [13] and dynamic control flow [10] can produce high quality results. Via the use of additional semantic information, the proposals in [20] and [16] are able to improve the quality of the learned grammars of the previous methods. Machine learning algorithms to infer regular languages are used in [24,25]. This is then combined with control flow information gained through program instrumentation in order to learn targeted context free grammars. The work in [22] proposes to translate the source code of the parser to an intermediate representation, which can then be used as a machine that accepts the target language. Finally, the authors of [11] propose a fuzzer that automatically learns an input grammar from command-line invocations. The target in this case it to efficiently generate inputs for command-line fuzzing.

3 Preliminaries

In this section we introduce the notation used in this paper. We assume the reader is familiar with basic concepts of language theory. An excellent reference for that is the classical book by Hopcroft and Ullman [12].

Let Σ be an *alphabet*, i.e., a finite set of symbols. A finite sequence of symbols taken from Σ is called a *word* or *string* over Σ. The free monoid of Σ, i.e., the set of all (finite) strings over Σ plus the empty string λ, is denoted as Σ^* and known as the *Kleene star* of Σ. If $v, w \in \Sigma^*$, then $vw \in \Sigma^*$ is the *concatenation* of v and w and $|vw| = |v| + |w|$ is its length. If $u = vw$, then v is a *prefix* of u and w is a *suffix*. A *language* is any subset of Σ^*.

A *grammar* is formally defined as a 4-tuple $G = (N, \Sigma, P, S)$, where N and Σ are finite disjoint sets of *nonterminal* and *terminal symbols* respectively, $S \in N$ is the *start symbol* and P is a finite set of *production rules*, each of the form:

$$(\Sigma \cup N)^* N (\Sigma \cup N)^* \rightarrow (\Sigma \cup N)^*.$$

We say G *derives* (or equivalently *produces*) a string y from a string x in one step, denoted $x \Rightarrow y$, iff there are $u, v, p, q \in (\Sigma \cup N)^*$ such that $x = upv$, $p \rightarrow q \in P$ and $y = uqv$. We write $x \Rightarrow^* y$ if y can be derived in zero or more steps from x, i.e., $\Rightarrow^*$ denotes the reflexive and transitive closure of the relation $\Rightarrow$.

The language of G, denoted as $\mathcal{L}(G)$, is the set of all strings in Σ^* that can be derived in a finite number of steps from the start symbol S. In symbols,

$$\mathcal{L}(G) = \{w \in \Sigma^* \mid S \Rightarrow^* w\}$$

In this work, Σ always denotes the "input" alphabet (e.g., the set of ASCII characters) of a given executable (binary) program p. The set of *valid inputs of* p is defined as the subset of Σ^* formed by all well formed inputs for p. In symbols:

$$\mathit{validInputs}(p) = \{w \in \Sigma^* \mid w \text{ is a well formed input for } p\}$$

The definition of a well formed input for a given program p depends on the application at hand. In our setting we only need to assume that it is possible to determine whether a given input string w is well formed or not for a program p by simply running p with input w.

As usual, we assume that $\mathit{validInputs}(p)$ is a context-free language. Consequently, there is a context-free grammar G_p such that $\mathcal{L}(G_p) = \mathit{validInputs}(p)$. Recall that a grammar is context-free if its production rules are of the form $A \rightarrow \alpha$ with A a single nonterminal symbol and α a possibly empty string of terminals and/or nonterminals.

In this paper we propose a novel algorithm that takes as input a program p and infers a grammar G_p such that $\mathcal{L}(G_p)$ approximates *validInputs*(p). We say "approximates" since it is *not* decidable in our setting (see [8]) whether $\mathcal{L}(G_p) =$ *validInputs*(p). To evaluate how well $\mathcal{L}(G_p)$ approximates *validInputs*(p), we measure the precision and recall of $\mathcal{L}(G_p)$ w.r.t. *validInputs*(p) as in [5], among others.

In our setting we first fix a procedure to calculate the probability distribution of a language, starting from its corresponding grammar. Following [5] we use random sampling of strings. Let $G = (N, \Sigma, P, S)$ be a context-free grammar. As a first step, G is converted to a *probabilistic context-free grammar* by assigning a *discrete distribution* $\mathcal{D}_A$ to each nonterminal $A \in N$. As usual, $\mathcal{D}_A$ is of size $|P_A|$, where P_A is the subset of productions in P of the form $A \to \alpha$. Here, we assume that $\mathcal{D}_A$ is *uniform*. We can then *randomly sample a string* x *from the language* $\mathcal{L}(G, A) = \{w_i \in \Sigma \mid A \Rightarrow^* w_i\}$, denoted $x \sim \mathcal{P}_{\mathcal{L}(G,A)}$, as follows:

- Using $\mathcal{D}_A$ to select randomly a production $A \to A_1 \cdots A_k \in P_A$.
- For $i = 1, \ldots, k$, recursively sample $x_i \sim \mathcal{P}_{\mathcal{L}(G,A_i)}$ if $A_i \in N$; otherwise let $x_i = A_i$.
- Return $x = x_1 \cdots x_k$.

The *probability distribution* $\mathcal{P}_{\mathcal{L}(G)}$ *of the language* $\mathcal{L}(G)$ is simply defined as the probability $\mathcal{P}_{\mathcal{L}(G,S)}$ induced by sampling strings in the probabilistic version of G defined above.

We can now measure the quality of a learned (or inferred) language $\mathcal{L}'$ with respect to the target language $\mathcal{L}$ in terms of precision and recall.

- The *precision* of $\mathcal{L}'$ w.r.t. $\mathcal{L}$, denoted *precision*$(\mathcal{L}', \mathcal{L})$, is defined as the probability that a randomly sampled string $w \sim \mathcal{P}_{\mathcal{L}'}$ belongs to $\mathcal{L}$. In symbols, $\Pr_{w \sim \mathcal{P}_{\mathcal{L}'}}[w \in \mathcal{L}]$.
- Conversely, the *recall* of $\mathcal{L}'$ w.r.t. $\mathcal{L}$, denoted *recall*$(\mathcal{L}', \mathcal{L})$, is defined as $\Pr_{w \sim \mathcal{P}_{\mathcal{L}}}[w \in \mathcal{L}']$.

We say that $\mathcal{L}'$ is a good approximation to $\mathcal{L}$ if it has both, high precision and high recall. Note that, a language $\mathcal{L}' = \{w\}$, where $w \in \mathcal{L}$, has perfect precision, but most likely has also very low recall. On the other hand, $\mathcal{L}' = \Sigma^*$ has perfect recall, but probably low precision.

4 Algorithm

Given a program p, we define G_p to be a context-free grammar such that its language $\mathcal{L}(\tilde{G}_p)$ has high precision and high recall w.r.t. *validInputs*(p). Subsequently, our goal is to infer G_p given the program p. As usual, we assume that we know the input alphabet Σ of p and that the learning algorithm can freely ask (and get the correct answer to) membership queries of the form $w \in$ *validInputs*(p)? for arbitrary inputs $w \in \Sigma^*$. Since we use a white-box approach, we naturally assume access to the source code of the subroutine of p that does the parsing of the input, i.e., decides $w \in$ *validInputs*(p)?.

We propose a method that combines techniques from grammar based fuzzing, with membership queries, program analysis and instrumentation to learn such a grammar $\tilde{G}_p$ for the input language *validInputs*(p) of the program p. Our method has the following two major steps, which are explained in detail below:

1. Extraction of a core grammar structure.
2. Resolution of place holders.

For illustration of the method we use a small running example, assuming a program p with input alphabet $\{+, -, (,), *, /, 1, 2, 3\}$, $\mathit{validInputs}(p) = \mathcal{L}(G_p)$ and grammar[1] G_p with the following production rules:

$$\begin{aligned} \texttt{Expr} &\rightarrow \texttt{Term}\ [\ (+|-)\ \texttt{Term}\ ] \\ \texttt{Term} &\rightarrow \texttt{Factor}\ [\ (*|/)\ \texttt{Factor}\ ] \\ \texttt{Factor} &\rightarrow 1 \mid 2 \mid 3 \mid (\ \texttt{Expr}\ ) \end{aligned}$$

4.1 Extraction of a Core Grammar Structure

This step consists on extracting a *core grammar structure* (CGS) starting from the *control flow graphs* (CtrlFGs) of the program p. A CGS is simply a grammar where instead of terminal symbols, we use place holders. Place holders are denoted as $\bigcirc_i$ with $i \in \mathbb{N}$. Thus, the language of a CGS is always a subset of $\{\bigcirc_1, \ldots, \bigcirc_n\}^*$ for some $n \geq 0$. The special case of $n = 0$ means that there do not exist any terminals in our grammar and such the language we want to learn has to be empty.

In the following, $G(p.a)$ stands for the CtrlFG of procedure a in program p. CtrlFGs were introduced in 1970 by Allen [2] and are very well known in the program analysis community. In this work, we use the eknows tool [19] to extract such CtrlFGs from source code. Intuitively, a CtrlFG represents all paths that might be traversed through a procedure of a program during its execution. More concretely, a ctrlFG is a digraph where each of its nodes represents a basic code block, i.e., a "straight-line" piece of code without any jumps or jump targets; jump targets start a block, and jumps end a block. An initial CtrlFG extracted from our running example for the procedure `Expr` is shown in Fig. 1a. We use the classical convention that each CtrlFG has a unique entry block and a unique exit block. Whenever a directed edge in a CtrlFG from a code block S_i to a code block S_j is the result of a call to a function f with optional parameters $\bar{x}$, we add the label $f(\bar{x})$ to this edge (S_i, S_j). The remaining directed edges with empty labels are the result of jumps due to control flow statements such as e.g. `if` or `while`.

The process for extraction of a CGS G_{struc} from p is based in that described in Sect. 5.2 in [25]. In this work however, we use new heuristic refinements that increase, as confirmed by our experiments, the quality of the resulting CGS.

We start by refining the edge labels of the CtrlFGs by inserting place holders $\bigcirc_i$ (for terminal symbols). We identify each node S_j that has two or more

[1] We use the well-known Backus-Naur form (BNF) notation for our grammars.

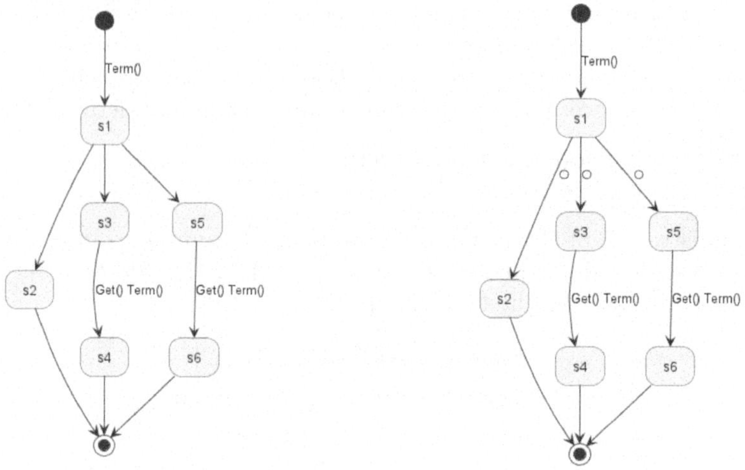

(a) Control Flow of CoCo/R parser

(b) Refined Control Flow

Fig. 1. Control Flow Graph Refinement of Method *Expr*

outgoing edges. As the control flow splits here, we assume that this is due to a potentially consumed terminal. Consequently, we add $\bigcirc_i$ to the start of each outgoing edge of S_j. Furthermore, we make sure that we do not miss consumed terminals that are provided to a function $f(\bar{x})$ that checks if the given terminal is present at the current position. To do so, we simply treat each function $f(\bar{x})$ as a potentially consumed terminal and replace each $f(\bar{x})$ in $minimal(p.a)$ with $\bigcirc_i$. The result of this operation is shown in Fig. 1b

The resulting CGS G_{struc} has as start symbol S_{struc} the name of the main procedure of p. In our running example this is `Parse`. The set of non-terminals N_{struc} is formed by all procedure/function names that appear in the edge labels in the refined CtrlFGs of p, while the set of terminals Σ_{struc} is formed by the place holder symbols $\bigcirc_i$ that appear in those labels. Finally, the set of production rules P_{struc} are extracted from the refined CtrlFGs as follows. Let $R(p.A)$ be the refined CtrlFG of procedure A. We add for every path in $R(p.A)$ from the unique entry block node to the unique exit block node a rule of the form $A \rightarrow L_0 \ldots L_n$, where $L_0 \ldots L_n$ are the concatenation of the labels of the directed edges along this path. In addition, whenever we find two or more consecutive $\bigcirc_i \cdots \bigcirc_j$ we summarize them to one single $\bigcirc_i$. Finally, this results in the case of our running example in the following CGS G_{struc}:

$$
\begin{aligned}
\texttt{Parse} &\rightarrow \texttt{Expr}\ \bigcirc_0 \\
\texttt{Expr} &\rightarrow \texttt{Term}\ (\ \bigcirc_1\ \texttt{Get Term} \mid \bigcirc_2\ ) \\
\texttt{Term} &\rightarrow \texttt{Factor}\ (\ \bigcirc_3\ \texttt{Get Factor} \mid \bigcirc_4\ ) \\
\texttt{Factor} &\rightarrow \bigcirc_5\ \texttt{Get} \mid (\ \bigcirc_6\ \texttt{Get} \mid (\ \bigcirc_7\ \texttt{Get} \mid (\ \bigcirc_8\ (\ \bigcirc_9 \mid \bigcirc_{10}\ \texttt{Get Expr}\ \bigcirc_{11}\ )\ )\ )\ ) \\
\texttt{Get} &\rightarrow \bigcirc_{12} \mid \bigcirc_{13}\ \texttt{Get}
\end{aligned}
$$

4.2 Resolution of Place Holders

Now we need to transform the obtained CGS G_{struc} into a proper grammar G_p for the input language of program p. That is, we have to replace every placeholder $\bigcirc_i$ in G_{struc} by an appropriate terminal symbol t_j taken from the alphabet Σ of p, so that the language $\mathcal{L}(G_p)$ of the resulting grammar G_p approximates *validInputs*(p) with good precision and recall.

In broad terms, the idea is to repeatedly apply the following steps until all place holders in P_{struc} have been replaced by terminals in Σ. The resulting grammar is denoted as G_p.

1. Generate a $w \in \mathcal{L}(G_{struc})$ using a random walk though the productions of G_{struc}.
2. Collect in a set T_w all the different place holders for terminals that appear in w.
3. For each $\bigcirc_i \in T_w$, choose a terminal $t_i \in \Sigma$.
4. Replace every place holder $\bigcirc_i$ that appears in w by its corresponding terminal t_i (as selected in the previous step), obtaining $w' \in \Sigma^*$.
5. If $w' \notin$ *validInputs*(p), return to step (3) above, choosing a different combination of terminal symbols.
6. For every rule in P_{struc}, replace every place holder $\bigcirc_i \in T_w$ by its corresponding terminal t_i

Of course, we cannot directly apply this broad strategy to learn G_p, as it would require in the worst case to examine $\mathcal{O}(|\Sigma|^{|\Sigma_{struc}|})$ possible combinations. In order to make this approach tractable, we refine step (1) above as follows:

1.1 Fix a threshold x, and set $n = 0$ and $w = \epsilon$.
1.2 Generate a word $u \in \mathcal{L}(G_{struc})$ using a random walk through the productions of G_{struc}.
1.3 If $|T_u| < |T_w|$ or $T_w = \emptyset$, then assign u to w.
1.4 If $|T_w| > 2$ and $n < x$, then add 1 to n and go to (1.2).

This modification means that we start by resolving a minimal number of place holders and then incrementally solve the remaining ones. If the iteration threshold is chosen right (in our experiments x was set to 1000), then the possible combinations of terminals that one needs to examine is of order quadratic on $|\Sigma|$.

Need for Solution Classes. In the strategy described above, different choices for place holders in step (3) frequently lead to the extraction of different sets of derivation rules from the grammar structure G_{struct}. While individually, each of these sets of rules defines grammars that can only derive words that belong to *validInputs*(p), it is not necessarily the case that all of them are good candidates for inference of the target language. Let us illustrate this point with a simple example. Assume the target grammar, i.e., the one used by the parser, is the one in Fig. 2a. Let the CGS obtained from the parser be as in Fig. 2b.

(a) Target Grammar	(b) Core Grammar Structure
S → A	S → $\bigcirc_0$ A
A → B | (B)	A → $\bigcirc_4$ B | $\bigcirc_1$ B $\bigcirc_2$
B → 1 | 2	B → $\bigcirc_3$

Fig. 2. CGS with Conflicting Place Holders Resolutions

Assume we want to find a solution for the word $\bigcirc_0\ \bigcirc_1\ \bigcirc_3\bigcirc_2$ produced by the CGS. Clearly, we could choose to replace the place holders in following two different ways, where both replacements give grammar rules that produce the word "(1)" belonging to the language of the target grammar.

i. $\bigcirc_0 = (, \bigcirc_1 = \epsilon, \bigcirc_3 = 1, \bigcirc_2 =)$
ii. $\bigcirc_0 = \epsilon, \bigcirc_1 = (, \bigcirc_3 = 1, \bigcirc_2 =)$

Moreover, these two alternative sets of rules will give us grammar with prefect precision 1. However, following (i), we would get a refined CGS with the following rules: S → (A, A → $\bigcirc_4$ B | B) and B → 1. This CGS can now produce "($\bigcirc_4$1", which cannot be refined to a proper grammar since any replacement of $\bigcirc_4$1 leads to a word that is not in the target language. Therefore, we would need in principle to explore all these possible alternative resolutions for the place holders via a trial and error approach. This however can quickly lead to an explosion of cases and make the problem unfeasible in practice.

In order to mitigate this explosion of cases, we follow a heuristic approach consisting on grouping the partial grammars obtained by different potential resolution of a list of place holders, into classes formed by those that have similar properties. Then we only take a representative grammar for each resulting class, effectively reducing the number of cases that need to be explored into a tractable size. Two different grammars G_1 and G_2 (or CGS depending on whether there are remaining place holders in the rules or not) obtained after replacing a given list of place holders by different terminals are consider to belong to a same class if, and only if, the precision of their union is 1. That is, the grammar obtained by taking the union of G_1 and G_2 only produces words that are recognized by the parser.

Forking the Search Process. The previous process gives a series of grammar classes after each iteration in which new placeholders are resolved. Let us say $C_0, \ldots, C_n$. From each of these classes C_i we choose (arbitrarily) a representative grammar G_i. We insert these grammars into a queue, where the grammar structures are ordered according to the number of place holders in their respective rules, being that with the least number of place holders the first in this queue. At this point we can use parallel processes (forks) to resolve the place holders in every remaining grammar structure. Each parallel process will apply the same procedure as explained before, but now to a different grammar G_i taken from the queue. The forked process with input G_i will either (a) discard G_i, (b) produce one or more classes $C_{i0}, \ldots, C_{im}$ of candidate grammar structures, or (c) produce one or more final candidate grammars without place holders in their rules. The first case arises when a substitution of (some) remaining place holders results in a grammar that produces words that are not recognized by the parser. If case (a) is not verified, then there are one or more possible substitutions of place holders, each leading to grammars that only produce words accepted by the parser (case (c)), or to grammar structures that have this same property (case (b)). If case (b) is verified, then a representative grammar G_{ij} is chosen from each class C_{ij} and inserted (in the order determined by the number of place holders in the rules) into the queue. The process continues until a case c has either recall 1 or the queue is emptied. At this point, the candidate grammar with the highest recall is selected as result.

Need for Instrumentation. We apply instrumentation to check whether the derivation trees (produced by the successive refined grammars) of words accepted by p match the actual paths the program takes in its call tree while parsing these inputs. Assume that we have the word “1*1”. We can produce this by taking two potentially ambiguous paths while expanding our core grammar structure:

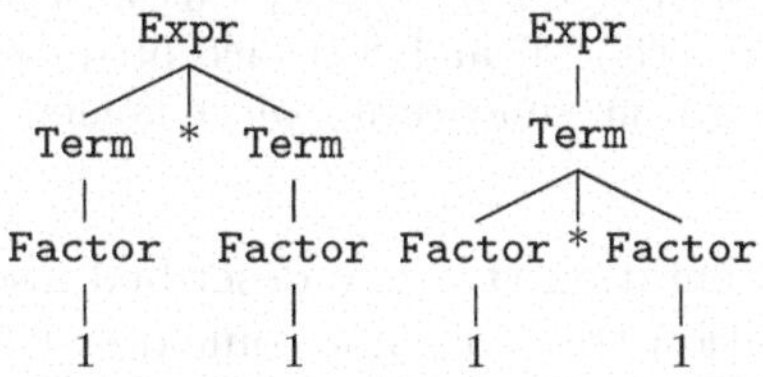

If we do not check which of these derivation trees actually match the call tree of p and take both as valid, then we would end up with the following productions.

$$
\begin{aligned}
\texttt{Expr} &\rightarrow \texttt{Term}\ [\ (+|-|*)\ \texttt{Term}\ ] \\
\texttt{Term} &\rightarrow \texttt{Factor}\ [\ (*|/)\ \texttt{Factor}\ ] \\
\texttt{Factor} &\rightarrow 1 \mid 2 \mid 3 \mid (\ \texttt{Expr}\ )
\end{aligned}
$$

Thus, we could produce words such as "1*1*1" which do not belong to the input language of p. As the search process will be forked when encountering such ambiguous paths, we will eventually discard the faulty branch. However, using instrumentation enables us to discard such incorrect branches early on which decreases significantly the total number of paths that need to be explored.

Example. Let G_{struc} be the CGS extracted from the ExprParser example in Sect. 4.1. Assume that the random walk from step (1) described in the beginning produces the word: $w = \bigcirc_5\ \bigcirc_{12}\ \bigcirc_4\ \bigcirc_1\ \bigcirc_{12}\ \bigcirc_5\ \bigcirc_{12}\ \bigcirc_3\ \bigcirc_{12}\ \bigcirc_5\ \bigcirc_{12}\bigcirc_0$. We thus obtain $T_u = \{\bigcirc_0\bigcirc_1, \bigcirc_3, \bigcirc_4\ \bigcirc_5\ \bigcirc_{12}\}$. Since $|T_u| > 2$, we proceed to generate the next word. We repeat this until we find that the shortest word we are able to produce is $w = \bigcirc_5\ \bigcirc_{12}\ \bigcirc_4\ \bigcirc_2\ \bigcirc_0$ (recall the refined steps (1.1–1.4) of step (1) explained earlier). Via random testing of different terminal symbols substitutions for the place holders, the algorithm discovers that many of the different alternative substitutions result in derivation rules that produce words accepted by the parser. Figure 3 shows the syntax tree of w as well as resulting parse trees obtained by substitution of place holders by symbols that result in different words w_0 = "1", w_1 = "2", w_2 = "3" and w_3 = "(2)" accepted by the parser.

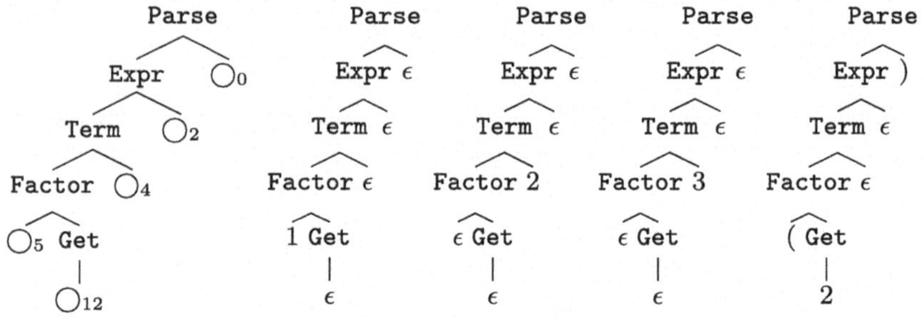

Fig. 3. Derivation tree of word "$\bigcirc_5\ \bigcirc_{12}\ \bigcirc_4\ \bigcirc_2\ \bigcirc_0$" using G_{struc} and corresponding derivation trees of words "1", "2", "3" and "(2)" accepted by the parser (and obtained from the grammars resulting from substituting place holders in G_{struc}).

Applying the instrumentation strategy described above, our algorithm discards w_3, since its derivation tree does not coincide with the call tree resulting from an instrumented execution of the parser. As the trees for w_0, w_1 and w_2 all pass this step, we now apply the strategy to divide them in disjoint classes. Let G_{w_0}, G_{w_1} and G_{w_2} be the grammars corresponding to the substitution of place $\bigcirc_5\ \bigcirc_{12}\ \bigcirc_4\ \bigcirc_2\ \bigcirc_0$ in the rules of G_{struc} by the corresponding symbols in the derivation tress of w_0, w_1 and w_2 shown in Fig. 3, respectively. We can easily see that G_{w_1} and G_{w_2} belong to a same class, while G_{w_0} belongs to a different class. Indeed, the union of G_{w_0} with G_{w_1} results in a grammar that can derive the word "12" which is not accepted by the parser. Likewise, the union of G_{w_0} with G_{w_2} can derive the word "13" which is again not accepted by the parser.

```
Parse → Expr ϵ
  Expr → Term ( ○1 Get Term | ϵ )
  Term → Factor ( ○3 Get Factor | ϵ )
Factor → 1 Get | ( ○6 Get | ( ○7 Get | ( ○8 ( ○9 | ○10 Get Expr ○11 ) ) ) )
   Get → ϵ | ○13 Get

 Parse → Expr ϵ
  Expr → Term ( ○1 Get Term | ϵ )
  Term → Factor ( ○3 Get Factor | 2 )
Factor → ϵ Get | ( ○6 Get | ( ○7 Get | ( ○8 ( ○9 | ○10 Get Expr ○11 ) ) ) )
   Get → ϵ | ○13 Get
```

Fig. 4. Rules of the intermediate grammar structures G_{w_0} and G_{w_1}, respectively.

As a result, the algorithm produces a fork in the search process, and explores further independent resolutions of the remaining place holders in the grammars G_{w_0} and G_{w_1} (assuming w.l.o.g. that they are the chosen representative grammars of their respective classes). The rules of these two grammar structures are shown in Fig. 4. After a number of further iterations, our algorithm will be able to refine G_{w_0} into a correct grammar for the target language. It will also find out that further refinement of G_{w_1} do not lead to good candidate grammars.

5 Experiments and Evaluation

To evaluate *GrammarForge* we have carried on series of experiments. These experiments start from a given context-free language in the form of a context-free grammar, so that we can then precisely evaluate the performance of our approach. For each grammar, a different parser (program) is generated using existing automated tools, namely ANTLR and COCO/R. The obtained parsers, plus their source code, are then the starting point for testing *GrammarForge* performance. Note that no further information, e.g. in the form of seed inputs, is provided. Then *GrammarForge* tries to infer the target grammar using as only input the source and executable code of the parser. The grammars as well as the corresponding generated parsers used in our experiments are accessible online[2].

During the experiments, we calculate precision and recall via random sampling of 1 000 words for each instance. The graph in Fig. 5 show the obtained values of recall for diverse target grammars. Note that we do not need to show precision as this is always one, since our method starts from a CGS with recall = 0 and precision = 1, recall is increased periodically during the learning process, and intermediate grammar structures which bring precision below 1 are directly discarded as possible solutions. The curves in Fig. 5 correspond to the evolving (class representative) grammars in the branch that led to the best solution

[2] https://github.com/software-competence-center-hagenberg/fbgl/.

in each case. Recall that the learning process can produce many different forks depending on the possible grammar classes determined by the algorithm. Figure 6 provides a visualization in the form of a tree of the different forks produced by the algorithm while learning the grammar of the JSON language. The root node of the tree depicts the grammar resulting from the CFG analysis described in Sect. 4.1. Each subsequent node depicts a grammar (structure) resulting from the search process described in Sect. 4.2. Yellow leaves denote branches that have been discarded due to low precision (i.e., where no suitable substitution for the remaining place holders was found). The green leaf denotes the grammar learned by the algorithm, which in this case has both recall and precision equal to 1.

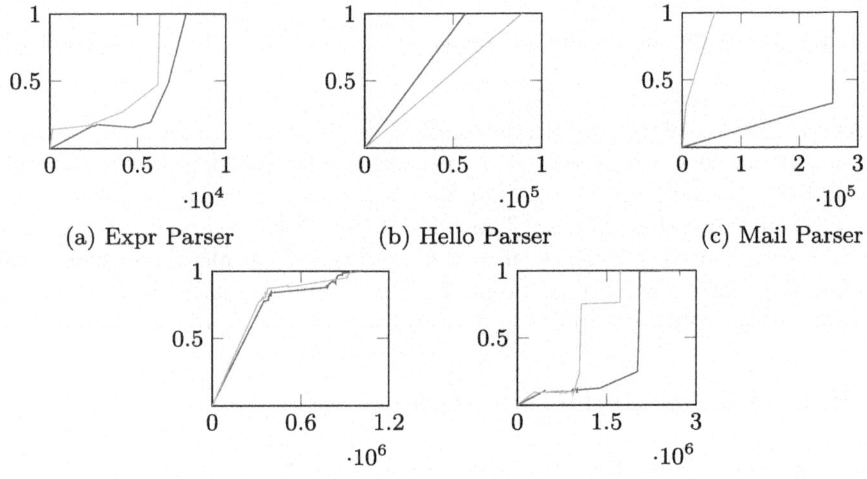

(a) Expr Parser (b) Hello Parser (c) Mail Parser

(d) Json Parser (e) URL Parser

Fig. 5. Evolution of recall along the learning process (Red = CoCo/R, Green = ANTLR). The x-axis shows the amount of queries while the y-axis shows recall.

Table 1. Experiment Results in comparison to related work.

Language	Autogram [13]			Mimid [10]			FbGL [25]			GrammarForge		
	f1	queries	seeds	f1	queries	seeds	f1	queries	seeds	f1	queries	seeds
MathExpr	1.0	n/a	n	0.0	n/a	n	1.0	15 361	1	1.0	7 760	0
Json	0.0	n/a	n	0.95	n/a	n	1.0	841 514	1	1.0	1 011 157	0
URL	1.0	n/a	n	0.98	n/a	n	1.0	1 270 165	3	1.0	2 719 994	0

Whenever possible we compare the results obtained by *GrammarForge* w.r.t. other state of the art methods, namely Autogram [13], Mimid [10] and FbGL [25].

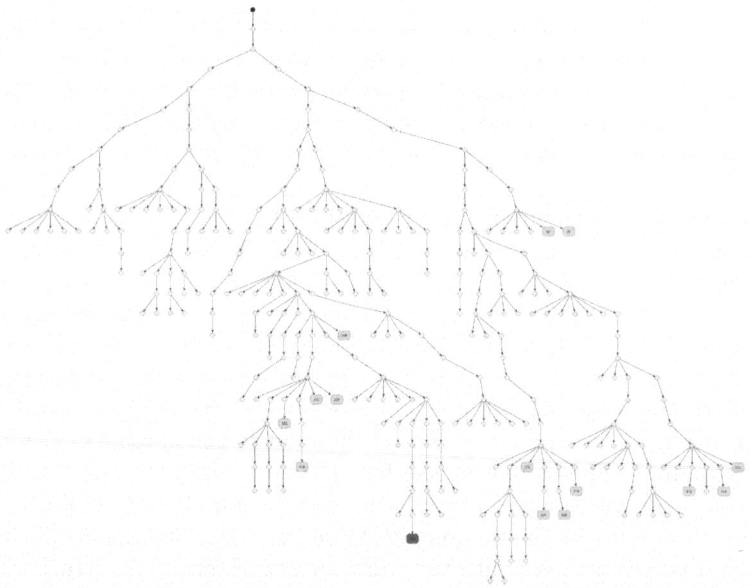

Fig. 6. Visualisation of all forked branches while learning JSON from a CoCo/R generated parser. Each node depicts a new grammar that has been identified during the learning process where the root node is the grammar returned from the CFG analysis. (Color figure online)

Given a set of seed inputs S, Autogram as well as Mimid infer for each input $s \in S$ a corresponding grammar that accepts exactly s. To infer these grammars, they use dynamic tainting and dynamic control flow, respectively. Then the obtained grammars are combined into one, which constitutes the final inferred grammar. Instead FbGL extracts a core grammar structure, similar to the one we use in this work. The difference is that FbGL uses a machine-learning based approach to fill in the gaps (place holders) in the core grammar structure, applying a modified version of the well known L* algorithm [3] for inferring regular languages. Table 1 shows that *GrammarForge* obtains top values for f1-scores of both precision and recall (i.e., in terms of their respective harmonic means). The next column shows the number of queries needed to infer the grammar from a CoCo/R parser by a single run. We see that our method needs a few more queries than other related methods (where such numbers are provided). This however does not affect its effectiveness for the purpose of inferring a grammar for fuzzing. Regarding seed inputs, we would like to note that Autogram and Mimid both require a large number n of seed inputs. Depending on the targeted language, as well as the quality of the given seed inputs, n may vary greatly. To be able to infer a grammar, the n given seed inputs must cover every distinct path in the targeted parser. This number has however already been drastically decreased by our previous fuzzing-based Grammar Inference approach in [25]. In this work however, we have been able to completely remove this dependency.

Thus, our evaluation underlines our main contribution. We have completely removed the dependence on any seed input as opposed to related work. The trade-off is an increase in required number of membership queries, which nevertheless does not have a negative impact for our targeted application. On the contrary, it removes any need for a priori knowledge of the language recognized by the target parser.

Finally, we discuss the languages recognized by the different parsers used in our experiments in relation to the obtained results: **Expr** is the language of simple aritmetic expressions described in Sect. 4. The recall curve in Fig. 5a shows an steady improvement of recall in each successive step (of the shown branch). This is due to the fact that in this case the algorithm mostly ends up learning the required terminal symbols one at a time. **Hello** is the language corresponding to all possible combinations of upper and lower case letters of the word "hello". As shown in Fig. 5b we are able to correctly identify the language with the first returned grammar. This is due to the fact that our algorithm have to consider many possible substitutions of place holders by terminals until it finds one corresponding to a word in this language. After that, the algorithm quickly finds outs all possible alternatives with the same subset of terminals. **Mail** is the language of email address such as "example@xyz.com". The first step in Fig. 5c is due to the algorithm finding an initial correct word. This already accounts for a big portion of the language. This first word enables us to identify all characters accepted by the parser in the body of the address as well as that the mail address is separated by "@" and ".". The second step that leads to recall 1 finds that the country tag may has an additional character instead of the two that have been used initially. **Json** is well known and widely used[3]. The initially fast increase in recall shown in Fig. 5d occurs while the algorithm learns the basic structure of Json objects. At this point, they consist mainly out of simple structures such as characters and numbers. For instance, the first word in the language learned by the algorithm is "true". Periodically, the algorithm embeds these words in more complex structures, e.g., arrays. First it identifies structures such as the empty array"[]". It then proceeds to learn the rules for producing non-empty arrays, e.g., "[true, true]". Since at this point the algorithm already knows that "true" belongs to the language, only needs to identify that the values in an array are separated by commas. It takes a larger number of queries to learn the more complex object structures later on in the process. **Url** is again a well known language[4]. The initial rise in recall in Fig. 5e is due to steadily learning gopher and http addresses that mostly consist out of alphanumeric symbols that can be discovered incrementally. However, at this point, the algorithm has not discovered substitutions of place holders corresponding to telnet and ftp addresses. Therefore, the recall remains low despite correctly identifying integer or string structures. Once it finds out that there are also telnet and ftp addresses, a sudden spike in recall happens. Then, most of the remaining correct substitutions for place holders are quickly discovered by the algorithm.

---

[3] https://www.json.org/json-en.html.

[4] https://www.ietf.org/rfc/rfc1738.txt.

6 Discussion

Before we give our conclusions on the proposed method and the *GrammarForge* prototype, let us analyse its possible limitations. *GrammarForge* relies on three main prerequisites: (1) Access to the source code of the program, (2) a good set of tokens and literals as input alphabet and (3) a robust method for control flow analysis. Access to the source code of the program under test, being for static analysis or instrumentation, is quite common in the field of fuzzing. This also applies for the input alphabet. An incomplete alphabet will lower the quality of achieved results. On the other hand, an alphabet that includes additional symbols to those actually used by the target language, will only degrade the running time performance of *GrammarForge*. Finally, the requirement for a good method for control flow analysis has proven to be critical for the success of our grammar learning approach when applied to the parsers used in our evaluation.

Finding correct words to learn a program input grammar is hard in practice. Ultimately, it comes down to the total number of queries required to identify all critical words of each given length n that belong to the target language. The search space is given by Σ^n, and thus it is exponential in n. Moreover, the target language might include very few words for certain lengths n, or none at all. Our algorithm deals with this problem by first inspecting words of the shortest possible length that are produced by the core grammar structure, and then incrementally inspecting words of greater length by only considering the remaining place holders for terminals. Assuming that the shortest word in our language has length m. The number of place holders that we need to resolve will be $n \leq m$ (as the shortest word may include a same terminal more than once). Indeed, the largest value of n that we came across in our experiment was 3 for the cases of Json or URL parsers. We can then conclude that there are two main prerequisites for applying *GrammarForge* to successfully learn a grammar for the input language of a given program p: (a) The parsing subroutine of p should be clearly identifiable; and (b) it should apply a recursive descending parsing technique. In practice, a parser will be most likely embedded in more complex software. At this point, we have not considered automatically identifying and/or isolating the actual parsing subroutine, which justifies requirement (a). Requirement (b) is due to the techniques we use for core grammar extraction as well as for tracking, using instrumentation, the paths in the call tree followed by the parser subroutine for different inputs.

7 Conclusion

In this work we have discussed the importance of grammar inference as a good starting point for further testing software. The main goal of this work was to provide a robust method to infer context-free program input grammars for arbitrary recursive descending parser. As such, we have proposed *GrammarForge*: A novel approach for grammar inference that (1) is able to infer grammars from arbitrary recursive descending parser that perfectly match the language accepted by those parser and (2) we have shown that it is feasible to infer such a grammar without providing any additional information like seed input. In our experiments we have demonstrated that *GrammarForge* works in practice, outperforms related work and provides a significant improvement by removing the dependence on a set of seed inputs. Our experiments show that we have been able to remove the dependence on prior knowledge about the target language with only a small increase in program runs needed to identify the target language. As future work we plan to (1) improve our source code analysis approach by making it more robust and more widely applicable as well as (2) work on methods that will help identifying the actual input parsing subroutines of more complex software solutions. Furthermore, our long-term goal is to remove the dependence on recursive descending parser.

References

1. Al Salem, H., Song, J.: A review on grammar-based fuzzing techniques. Inter. J. Comput. Sci. Sec. (IJCSS) **13**(3), 114–123 (2019)
2. Allen, F.E.: Control flow analysis. In: Northcote, R.S. (ed.) Proceedings of a Symposium on Compiler Optimization, Urbana-Champaign, Illinois, USA, 27-28 July 1970, pp. 1–19. ACM (1970). https://doi.org/10.1145/800028.808479
3. Angluin, D.: Learning regular sets from queries and counterexamples. Inf. Comput. **75**(2), 87–106 (1987)
4. Angluin, D.: Queries and concept learning. Mach. Learn. **2**(4), 319–342 (1987)
5. Bastani, O., Sharma, R., Aiken, A., Liang, P.: Synthesizing program input grammars. In: PLDI, pp. 95–110. ACM (2017)
6. Crepinsek, M., Mernik, M., Bryant, B.R., Javed, F., Sprague, A.P.: Inferring context-free grammars for domain-specific languages. In: Boyland, J., Hedin, G. (eds.) Proceedings of the Fifth Workshop on Language Descriptions, Tools, and Applications, LDTA@ETAPS 2005, Edinburgh, UK, 3 April 2005. ENTCS, vol. 141, pp. 99–116. Elsevier (2005). https://doi.org/10.1016/j.entcs.2005.02.055
7. Eberlein, M., Noller, Y., Vogel, T., Grunske, L.: Evolutionary grammar-based fuzzing. In: Aleti, A., Panichella, A. (eds.) SSBSE 2020. LNCS, vol. 12420, pp. 105–120. Springer, Cham (2020). https://doi.org/10.1007/978-3-030-59762-7_8
8. Gold, E.: Language identification in the limit. Inf. Control **10**(5), 447–474 (1967)
9. Godefroid, P., Levin, M.Y., Molnar, D.: Sage: Whitebox fuzzing for security testing. Commun. ACM **55**(3), 40-44 (2012). https://doi.org/10.1145/2093548.2093564
10. Gopinath, R., Mathis, B., Zeller, A.: Inferring input grammars from dynamic control flow. CoRR arXiv: abs/1912.05937 (2019)
11. Gupta, A., Gopinath, R., Zeller, A.: Clifuzzer: mining grammars for command-line invocations. In: Proceedings of the 30th ACM Joint European Software Engineering Conference and Symposium on the Foundations of Software Engineering, pp. 1667-1671. ESEC/FSE 2022. Association for Computing Machinery, New York (2022)
12. Hopcroft, J.E., Ullman, J.D.: Introduction to Automata Theory. Addison-Wesley, Languages and Computation (1979)
13. Höschele, M., Zeller, A.: Mining input grammars with AUTOGRAM. In: ICSE (Companion Volume), pp. 31–34. IEEE Computer Society (2017)

14. Javed, F., Mernik, M., Sprague, A.P., Bryant, B.R.: Incrementally inferring context-free grammars for domain-specific languages. In: Zhang, K., Spanoudakis, G., Visaggio, G. (eds.) Proceedings of the Eighteenth International Conference on Software Engineering & Knowledge Engineering (SEKE 2006), San Francisco, CA, USA, 5-7 July 2006, pp. 363–368 (2006)
15. Klees, G., Ruef, A., Cooper, B., Wei, S., Hicks, M.: Evaluating fuzz testing. In: Proceedings of the 2018 ACM SIGSAC Conference on Computer and Communications Security, CCS 2018, pp. 2123-2138. Association for Computing Machinery, New York (2018). https://doi.org/10.1145/3243734.3243804
16. Kovačević, Z., Mernik, M., Ravber, M., Črepinšek, M.: From grammar inference to semantic inference-an evolutionary approach. Mathematics **8**(5) (2020)
17. Le, X.B.D., Pasareanu, C., Padhye, R., Lo, D., Visser, W., Sen, K.: Saffron: adaptive grammar-based fuzzing for worst-case analysis. SIGSOFT Softw. Eng. Notes **44**(4), 14 (2019)
18. Le, X.B.D., Pasareanu, C., Padhye, R., Lo, D., Visser, W., Sen, K.: Saffron: adaptive grammar-based fuzzing for worst-case analysis. SIGSOFT Softw. Eng. Notes **44**(4), 14 (2019). https://doi.org/10.1145/3364452.3364455
19. Moser, M., Pichler, J.: eknows: platform for multi-language reverse engineering and documentation generation. In: 2021 IEEE International Conference on Software Maintenance and Evolution (ICSME), pp. 559–568 (2021)
20. Pointner, A.: Mining attributed input grammars and their applications in fuzzing. In: 2023 IEEE Conference on Software Testing, Verification and Validation (ICST), pp. 493–495 (2023)
21. Sargsyan, S., et al.: Advanced grammar-based fuzzing. In: 2022 Ivannikov Memorial Workshop (IVMEM), pp. 61–64 (2022)
22. Schröder, M., Cito, J.: Grammars for free: toward grammar inference for ad hoc parsers. In: Proceedings of the ACM/IEEE 44th International Conference on Software Engineering: New Ideas and Emerging Results, pp. 41–45 (2022)
23. Sochor, H., Ferrarotti, F.: A refinement based algorithm for learning program input grammars. In: Bowles, J., Broccia, G., Pellungrini, R. (eds.) From Data to Models and Back. DataMod 2021. LNCS, vol. 13268, pp. 138–156. Springer, Cham (2021). https://doi.org/10.1007/978-3-031-16011-0_10
24. Sochor, H., Ferrarotti, F., Kaufmann, D.: Fuzzing-based grammar inference. In: Fournier-Viger, P., Yousef, A.H., Bellatreche, L. (eds.) Model and Data Engineering. MEDI 2022. LNCS, vol. 13761, pp. 72–86. Springer, Cham (2022). https://doi.org/10.1007/978-3-031-21595-7_6
25. Sochor, H., Ferrarotti, F., Kaufmann, D.: Fuzzing-based grammar learning from a minimal set of seed inputs. J. Comput. Lang. **78**, 101252 (2024). https://doi.org/10.1016/j.cola.2023.101252
26. Zalewski, M.: Technical "whitepaper" for afl-fuzz. Technical report. https://lcamtuf.coredump.cx/afl/technical_details.txt

Verified Configuration and Deployment of Layered Attestation Managers

Adam Petz, Will Thomas(✉), Anna Fritz, T. J. Barclay, Logan Schmalz, and Perry Alexander

Institute for Information Sciences, The University of Kansas, Lawrence, KS 66045, USA
{ampetz,30wthomas,arfritzz,tjbarclay,loganschmalz,palexand}@ku.edu

Abstract. Effective layered attestation systems require a trusted mechanism for their implementation, configuration, and deployment. Core to these systems are a distributed collection of Attestation Manager (AM) components that orchestrate primitive services and bundle evidence. Despite the trust placed in AMs, their configuration and deployment remain tedious and error prone, even for relatively simple attestation topologies. Beginning with a semantically sound layered attestation protocol language, we develop a verified toolchain for configuring attestation components and decidable algorithms for evaluating protocol executability and constrained evidence disclosure. The toolchain operates on configuration artifacts for AMs called Manifests that denote local attestation resources and facilitate coordination amongst remote AMs. The Manifest Generator and Manifest Compiler tools jointly synthesize collections of Manifests from attestation protocol terms and specialize Manifests resulting in executable AMs. The resulting workflow automatically generates infrastructure for attestation protocol execution.

Keywords: Remote Attestation · Verification · Formal Techniques

1 Introduction

In high assurance contexts, it is not enough to develop ostensibly secure software and deploy it in a trusted system context – experience shows that a sufficiently powerful adversary may compromise even the best designed software and systems over time [16]. To establish trust in a component or system, the best one can do is provide sound *evidence* of its integrity and execution context, such that the adversary's task of compromising a component without detection becomes

This work is funded in part by the NSA Science of Security initiative contracts #H98230-18-D-0009 and #H98230-23-C-0277 and Honeywell FMT Purchase Order #N000422909. The views and conclusions contained in this document are those of the authors and should not be interpreted as representing the official policies, either expressed or implied, of the U.S. Government.

A. Madeira and A. Knapp (Eds.): SEFM 2024, LNCS 15280, pp. 290–308, 2025.
https://doi.org/10.1007/978-3-031-77382-2_17

increasingly difficult. The process of gathering evidence and producing a verifiable report that can be utilized to establish trust is called *attestation*.

In the simplest form of attestation, a *relying party* makes an attestation request of a *target* specifying desired *measurements* and adding a nonce for freshness. The target responds with evidence consisting of measurement values and the nonce, bundled and signed by the target. Finally, an *appraiser* assesses the evidence bundle and provides a result to the relying party. Ultimately, the relying party uses the appraisal result to establish trust in the target.

To make this process more concrete, consider the attestation scenario depicted in Fig. 1: A collection of servers S that process sensitive information, and a collection of client machines C that initiate transactions of sensitive information with the servers on behalf of end users. In this scenario, the relying party is a client machine $c_i \in C$, the target is a server $s_j \in S$, and the desired measurements are of the server's software and configuration. A third-party appraisal server A consumes evidence from any server $s_j \in S$ and produces a certificate consumable by any client $c_i \in C$. The goal of this certificate is to convince the client of the server's integrity and its ability to protect sensitive information. Each client may have its own standards when assessing the integrity of a given server. Likewise, each server may decide to disclose only certain evidence to certain clients. A high–level depiction of the interaction amongst multiple such clients, servers, and an appraisal server A appears on the left in Fig. 1.

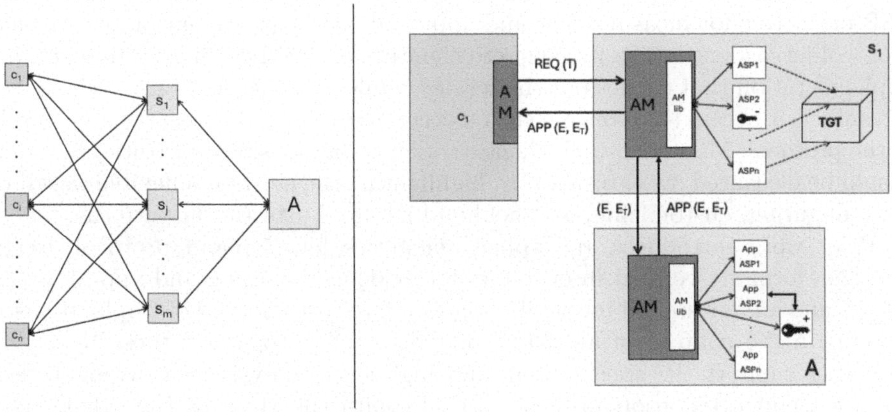

Fig. 1. Example Attestation Architectures

A more detailed view of an interaction between an individual client, server, and appraiser appears on the right in Fig. 1. The client initiates an attestation request $\mathsf{REQ(T)}$ that includes the attestation protocol T to run on the server. The server executes that protocol to produce an evidence bundle E that reflects the integrity of a collection of target components TGT. The server then constructs an appraisal request consisting of the raw evidence bundle E along with an

Evidence Type specification $\mathsf{E_T}$ indicating the structure of the raw evidence. The subscript T here indicates that the Evidence Type is computed based on the protocol term T. Finally, the appraisal server unbundles E according to $\mathsf{E_T}$ and returns an appraisal result $\mathsf{APP(E, E_T)}$.

Layered remote attestation [4,24,28] is a technique developed to perform attestation on distributed, heterogeneous systems like that of Fig. 1. In a layered attestation architecture, a target performs attestation by a combination of direct measurements and attestation dispatch requests to its sub-components and peers. These components may in turn request attestations of other components resulting in a tree of evidence referred to as an *evidence bundle*. Layered attestation systems rely on one or more pre-programmed *attestation managers* (AMs) to orchestrate primitive work units called *attestation service providers* (ASPs) that collect and bundle evidence. Because each appraiser may have unique standards for evidence curation, an *attestation protocol* specifies fine-grained composition of ASPs and interaction amongst AMs [4]. The architecture of Fig. 1 requires that each client, server, and appraisal component be configured with AMs and ASPs sufficient to carry out execution *and appraisal* of attestation protocol T.

There are a number of subtleties that arise when configuring, deploying, executing, and maintaining systems that support layered attestation scenarios. Minimally, the attestation mechanisms deployed at each place must have a means to interpret primitives delegated to them. In particular, each place must know how to contact its peer in the protocol— c_i to s_j, s_j to A —and instantiate its ASP primitives for measurement and appraisal. Each refinement of an abstract, protocol-level identifier to its concrete counterpart involves linking to a specific implementation that carries out the service, while also ensuring each such service has sufficient access to resources such as cryptographic data to carry out its role in the protocol. Moreover, each client $c \in C$ may have its own priorities for what should be measured on a given $s \in S$, highlighting the need for a flexible workflow for configuring, customizing, and fielding high-level attestation patterns.

Prior work introduces an explicit semantics for Copland protocol execution [24], formally-verified interpreters for evidence bundling and appraisal [14, 19,22], and an automated model finding tool for trust analysis of Copland-based systems in the context of an active adversary [27]. Together, these tools and semantics support the specification and high-level analysis of a diverse collection of useful attestation patterns [11]. Despite the rigor of these languages and tools, architectures and execution contexts for layered attestation systems remain largely implicit or configured in a manual, *ad hoc* manner. To support a more principled treatment of run-time attestation system configuration and deployment our work makes the following contributions:

- Formal definitions and semantics for configuration artifacts: Manifests, Attestation Manager Libraries, and Attestation Manager Configurations (Sect. 2)
- Formally verified Manifest Generator that synthesizes a collection of Manifests that together reliably execute a collection of arbitrary Copland protocols and appraise its evidence results (Sects. 3.1 and 4.1)

- Formally verified Manifest Compiler that compiles Manifests to Attestation Manager Configurations – explicit runtime contexts for Copland execution (Sects. 3.2 and 4.2)
- An attestation build system – linking together the above tools to automatically synthesize collections of Attestation Manager executables (Sect. 2.2)

2 Attestation Managers and Manifests

While a relying party may care only about the integrity of specific components on a target system, the soundness of trust decisions depends critically and often implicitly on underlying components and the attestation mechanisms themselves [4]. A critical element of this attestation mechanism is the Attestation Manager—a privileged thread responsible for carrying out system measurements, bundling evidence, enforcing attestation policy, and interacting with other Attestation Managers. Here we consider Attestation Managers that execute attestation protocols specified in Copland, a domain specific language for layered, remote attestation protocols [6]. Copland's formal language definition, verified execution semantics, and automated analysis capabilities appear in prior work [19,24,27]. A stylized version of the Copland language grammar targeted by tools in this paper appears in Fig. 2.

2.1 Copland DSL for Attestation

Copland atomic actions A specify primitive measurement and cryptographic services, along with evidence bundling operations. The ASP primitive produces evidence by invoking a pre-configured service indicated by ASP identifier i. The remaining parameters to ASP indicate the target of measurement (r), the target's place (P), and how evidence should be passed in to the service (sp) and bundled afterwards (bd). Cryptographic primitives C include SIG, HSH, and ENC that transform evidence by signing, hashing, and encrypting evidence bundles. The encryption primitive (ENC P) is unique among these due to its parameterization over P, the consuming place of the encrypted bundle.

$$\begin{aligned}
T &::= A \mid *P,n : T \mid @P[T] \mid (T \to T) \mid (T\ sp{<}sp\ T) \mid (T\ sp{\sim}sp\ T) \\
A &::= C \mid (\mathsf{ASP}\ sp\ bd\ i\ P\ r) \\
C &::= \mathsf{SIG} \mid \mathsf{HSH} \mid \mathsf{ENC}\ P \mid \cdots \\
sp &::= + \mid - \\
bd &::= \mathsf{COMP} \mid \mathsf{EXTD} \mid \mathsf{ENCR} \mid \cdots
\end{aligned}$$

Fig. 2. Copland grammar, where occurences of P are strings utilized as place identifiers.

The dispatch operation, specified by $@P[T]$, requests that the Attestation Manager at place P perform protocol T. Dispatch is how Copland Attestation

Managers distribute work and how protocols define architectures. While flexible, dispatch hides details of remote work necessitating layered configuration of Attestation Managers. Remaining terms specify measurement composition, ordering, and evidence dataflow. $T_1 \rightarrow T_2$ represents sequential execution where evidence from T_1 is made available to T_2. $T_1\ sp\!<\!sp\ T_2$ and $T_1\ sp\!\sim\!sp\ T_2$ specify sequential and parallel branching where evidence collected by T_1 and T_2 remain disjoint, and sp indicates whether or not input evidence is routed to a branch.

Based on the layered attestation scenario of Fig. 1 we have created a corresponding Copland phrase in Fig. 3. In the example protocol, n represents a nonce, our top-level client is represented by some place $c_i \in C$, our sensitive information server targeted for measurement by some place $s_j \in S$, and place A represents the appraisal server. The `attest` primitive measures server components and configurations, then bundles evidence results. Dually, `appraise` unbundles evidence and performs piecewise appraisal over primitive measurement values. Finally, `certificate` collapses the appraisal result into a summary of server integrity in a form easily verified by top-level clients.

```
*c_i, n : @ s_j [ (attest s_j sys) ->
                  @ A [(appraise s_j sys) -> (certificate s_j sys)] ]
```

Fig. 3. Example Copland Protocol

2.2 AM Core

While Copland's flexibility depends on its parameterization over attestation domains and measurement services, core portions of the Copland semantics depend on fixed behavior and predictability to ensure attestation integrity. During attestation, specific measurement services must be invoked in a precise order, and their individual evidence results must be composed into a predictably-shaped evidence bundle [26,28]. Dually, a Copland appraisal procedure must reliably unbundle evidence, invoke primitive appraisal services, and return a summary of the appraised evidence. Petz and Alexander [19] introduces the Copland Virtual Machine (CVM) and its dual appraisal procedure for orchestrating and appraising arbitrary Copland-based attestations. These components are purely functional, and thus verified first-class in Coq with respect to a denotational reference semantics guaranteeing measurement ordering. The CVM provides a guarantee that if required ASPs are available to the Attestation Manager, the measurements made with those ASPs will be invoked in the correct order, with the correct parameters, and will produce evidence bundles of a predictable shape.

2.3 Copland Manifests

```
Record Manifest := {
  my_plc          : Plc ;
  asps            : list ASP_ID ;
  appraisal_asps  : list (Plc * ASP_ID) ;
  uuidPlcs        : list Plc ;
  pubKeyPlcs      : list Plc ;
  targetPlcs      : list Plc ;
  policy          : PolicyT ;
}.
```

Fig. 4. Manifest definition in Coq.

A defining characteristic of Copland is its parametric nature, where primitive measurements (the i parameter of ASP) and attestation domains (the P parameter of @, ASP, and ENC terms) remain abstract. While this enables a wide variety of useful attestation patterns [11], it leaves many aspects of Attestation Manager configuration underspecified. As a first step in reasoning about Copland-based Attestation Manager configuration, Fritz and Alexander [9] introduced the idea of a *Manifest* as an analysis artifact in the context of Copland protocol negotiation. We extend the Manifest to capture the configuration of an Attestation Manager and its external dependencies abstractly, while maintaining properties necessary for negotiation and analysis. Specifically, we include a place name, lists of available ASPs for attestation and appraisal, known external Attestation Manager place names, cryptographic items, and policy for measurement selection and disclosure. These abstract representations are useful for reasoning about Attestation Manager behavior prior to committing to an implementation. Figure 4 shows the Manifest definition as a record datatype in Coq.

3 Deploying Layered Attestation Managers

To help deploy Attestation Managers we developed the verified workflow shown in Fig. 5. The workflow begins with a collection of Copland protocols specifying measurements, work dispatch, and bundling operations. A *Manifest Generator* creates Manifests for a set of Attestation Managers that will run the protocols. Each Manifest is then compiled with the *Manifest Compiler* to generate a corresponding *Attestation Manager Configuration.* An *Attestation Manager Library* is included during compilation to provide mappings from abstract Copland operations to concrete implementations for specific Attestation Manager Configurations. Finally, the *AM Build System* combines the verified Attestation Manager Core with the *AM Configuration* to yield executable Attestation Managers. Each of these tools is verified to ensure the fielded attestation managers will correctly execute the input Copland protocols.

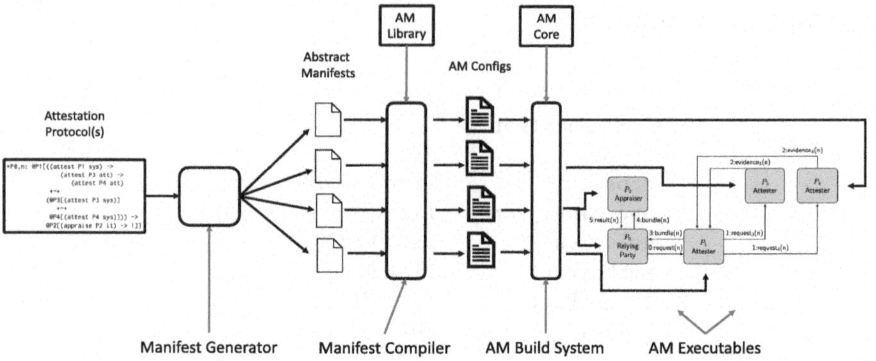

Fig. 5. Manifest Tools Workflow where (AM = Attestation Manager)

3.1 Manifest Generator

Manually crafting Manifests to support specific attestation protocols is tedious and error-prone, particularly for systems that support a large number of Copland protocols. A Manifest must support multiple attestation protocols and evidence appraisals in multiple contexts. Additionally, executing a single protocol often requires coordinated configuration of multiple Attestation Managers, each with their own roles, resources, and distributed services. Thus, the successful execution of an attestion protocol relies on the totality of Manifests for all Attestation Managers involved in the protocol to be configured correctly.

To reduce the burden of configuring multiple, interacting Attestation Managers to carry out broad attestation scenarios, we introduce the *Manifest Generator*. The core of the generator inputs a collection of Copland protocols and generates a collection of Manifests that support distributed execution of all input protocols. The output of generation is a mapping of all Copland places mentioned in the protocols to their corresponding Manifests. We refer to this collection of Manifests as a *Manifest Environment*, or simply *Environment*.

When the generator encounters a Copland ASP term within the protocol, it minimally adds the ASP ID to the list of supported ASPs in the Manifest. In addition to ASP IDs, Manifests are updated with configuration items like static measurement targets and cryptographic dependencies like public keys that provide valuable metadata for use in both protocol executability analysis and concrete evidence appraisal.

Example: Returning to our example attestation scenario from the introduction, an example output from the Manifest Generator is shown in Fig. 6. This output was created when the Manifest Generator was given as input the example Copland phrase from Fig. 3, top-level place c_i, and an empty initial Environment: Here we see a Manifest Environment that contains a Manifest for all places mentioned in the example Copland phrase. The top-level client place c_i must know how to contact s_j with the initial attestation request, as well as how to *appraise* the certificate evidence generated during protocol execution. This

```
{ my_plc := c_i;
  asps := [];
  appraisal_asps:=
   [(A, cert_id)];
  uuidPlcs:=[c_i, s_j]
  ... }
```

```
{
  my_plc := s_j;
  asp :=[attest_id];
  appraisal_asps:=[]
  uuidPlcs:=[s_j, A]
  ... }
```

```
{ my_plc := A;
  asps:=[cert_id,
    appraise_id];
  appraisal_asps:=
    [(s_j, attest_id)]
  uuidPlcs := [A];
  ... }
```

Fig. 6. Example Manifests generated for places c_i, s_j, A.

appraisal configuration is populated by a dual appraisal Manifest Generator that takes as input arbitrary Copland evidence bundles. Place s_j's Manifest declares that it should support execution of the attest ASP and know how to contact the Attestation Manager at place A. Finally, place A must support the appraise and cert ASPs, as well as an appraisal asp for the attest that occured on the server. However, since A is at the tail-end of the protocol it does not need to contact any additional places. This includes s_j and c_i surprisingly, as A only needs to contact s_j as a response to an incoming request. Upon receiving a request to attest or appraise a Copland protocol, the requester is cached by the Attestation Manager to determine where to return the results, thus not restricting the place that can make requests to those in uuidPlcs. We instead use Mandatory Access Control policy to restrict such requests.

3.2 Manifest Compiler

A generated Manifest represents the abstract functionality an Attestation Manager must provide. In contrast, an *Attestation Manager Configuration* defines specific run-time capabilities that configure an Attestation Manager during protocol execution and appraisal. These concrete representations specialize the common verified Attestation Manager Core (Sect. 2.2) with ASP implementations, known places, public keys for known places, and attestation targets (collectively referred to as AM Components). Access to these components may be specified directly as local callback routines or delegated to external servers with known addresses. The formal definition of an Attestation Manager Configuration appears in Fig. 7 as AM_Config.

The Manifest Compiler takes a Manifest and an *Attestation Manager Library* and returns an Attestation Manager Configuration. Attestation Manager Libraries operate similarly to a C/C++ library, providing concrete and reusable implementations for abstractly referenced items. In the case of attestation, this is a collection of available ASPs, places, public keys and server addresses. Library functionality is implemented using callback functions that provide concrete interfaces for the Attestation Manager to invoke. While minor differences may occur in callback construction for different AM Components, the general procedure is to filter the relevant components out of the AM Library and construct a

```
Record AM_Config : Type := {
  absMan        : Manifest ;
  am_clone_addr : UUID ;
  aspCb         : (ASPCallback DispatcherErrors) ;
  app_aspCb     : (ASPCallback DispatcherErrors) ;
  pubKeyCb      : PubKeyCallback ;
  uuidCb        : UUIDCallback ;
}.
```

Fig. 7. Attestation Manager Configuration

miniaturized library with the exact functionality that the Attestation Manager needs. We ensure the required AM Components are included in callbacks for each Attestation Manager as specified by its Manifest. This ensures the availability of components called during attestation or appraisal, thus supporting guarantees about executablilty of protocols, while excluding spurious components.

A secondary function of the Attestation Manager Library is providing a means for sharing common attestation and appraisal functionality between multiple Attestation Managers. Rather than implementing each Attestation Manager with an implementation of signing, hashing, encrypting, and other basic functions, a single implementation is included in the Attestation Manager Library. This ensures that each Attestation Manager compiled with that Attestation Manager Library will utilize a specific ASP implementation, and that the implementations will be compatible with all other Attestation Managers compiled with the same library. We foresee this being a beneficial feature in large attestations where configuring and assuring each Attestation Manager uses common, verified functionality leaves room for many errors. The Attestation Manager Library and Manifest Compiler together ensure that all Attestation Managers compiled with the same Attestation Manager Library share functionality as specified in common Manifest fields.

Example: Utilizing the same running example Copland protocol, we now generate the Manifest Compiler output for our protocol utilizing the Manifests generated in Sect. 3.1 and a sufficient Attestation Manager Library is provided. An abridged version of the output highlighting Attestation Manager Configurations is provided in Fig. 8.

Since place s_j must execute the attestation ASP and A the appraisal and certificate ASPs, these are populated in their respective aspCbs, with stub functions $\mathsf{f}, \mathsf{f}', \mathsf{g}, \mathsf{h}$ shown in place of their full implementations for brevity. s_j's UUID callback also encodes how to contact A's Attestation Manager. Note that we have only included output for s_j and A for brevity, but the output for the top-level client c_i is also produced by the compiler.

3.3 Attestation Manager Build System

The Attestation Manager (AM) Build System takes Attestation Manager Configurations resulting from compilation, a common Attestation Manager Core,

```
{
  absMan      := (* sj Manifest *) ;
  aspCb       :=
    fun aspid ⇒ lookup aspid
      [( attest_id → f)] ;
  uuidCb          :=
    fun plc ⇒ lookup plc
      [( sj → ("localhost::5001")),
      (A → ("localhost::5002"))]
  ...
}
```

```
{ absMan      := (* A Manifest *) ;
  aspCb       :=
   fun aspid ⇒ lookup aspid
     [( appraise_id → g) ;
      (cert_id → h)] ;
  app_aspCb       :=
   fun (plc, id) ⇒ lookup (plc,id)
     [(( sj, attest_id) → f')];
  uuidCb          :=
   fun plc ⇒ lookup plc
     [( A → ("localhost::5002"))]
  ... }
```

Fig. 8. Abridged Attestation Manager Configurations for Example places s_j and A

and Attestation Manager Libraries and composes them into a running Attestation Manager. The AM Core is a common component specified and verified in Coq and automatically synthesized to CakeML. This implementation path ensures the generated Attestation Manager is semantically correct.

While our primary goal is ensuring Copland protocols are correct and executable, individual Attestation Managers must also protect themselves with policies that restrict access to services and evidence. This highlights the inherent conflict between appraisers that desire comprehensive information and their target's need to constrain disclosure of critical information [4].

Attestation managers are implemented on the Copland Virtual Machine (CVM) [19,20] where the Attestation Manager implements mandatory access control (MAC) policy enforcement. MAC policy is specified in a Manifest as a *disallow list* and enforcement occurs at the level of CVM invocation of CakeML callback functions. This policy survives compilation in the Attestation Manager Configuration, thus the Manifest Compiler compiles the policy field of a Manifest to a corresponding concrete policy. With the policy specification available in the Attestation Manager Configuration, the policy is checked during AM execution directly in the CVM interpreter and occurs before each remote request.

The original CVM semantics operated over option and State monads combined into one, causing error handling to be very coarse-grained. We generalize the CVM monad to be parameterizable over an error type E, then instantiate E with an inductive datatype that distinguishes between two different types of errors that may arise during protocol execution: Unavailable and Runtime. The first Error Unavailable is raised when the CVM asks its configuration for a resource or service that it cannot provide. The second type of Error is Runtime to indicate errors that occur in services external to the CVM, and are unfalsifiable by the CVM itself.

Example: Considering our running example, if you refer to the Attestation Manager Configurations generated by the Manifest Compiler in Fig. 8 we can consider how the two types of CVM Errors may occur: An Unavailable error would occur if the Attestation Manager for s_j needed to utilize the public key for place A, but the key is not available in the Attestation Manager Configuration. A Runtime error would occur if the Attestation Manager for s_j is executing the attest_id function f, and f attempts to read a file over the network, but the network is down. In both cases, the CVM monad will return an error result to the caller, which can then be handled by the caller as needed.

Overall, the Build System can take an AM Configuration and the verified AM Core skeleton, and produce Attestation Manager executables. These executables are guaranteed to provide all functionality specified in the AM Configuration, and enforce MAC policy during execution, as well as leverage formally verified primitives to distinguish between failure modes that may arise during protocol design, execution, and appraisal.

4 Formal Verification

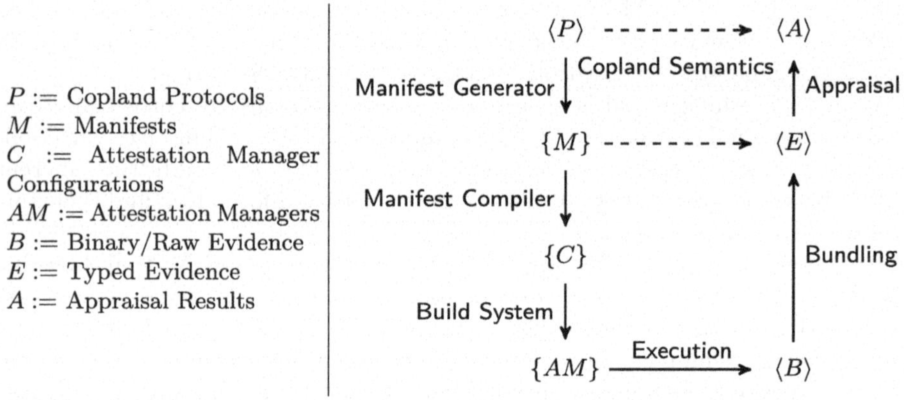

Fig. 9. Verification flow

We verify the correctness of the Manifest Tools Workflow in Fig. 5 by showing the collection of synthesized Attestation Managers correctly executes the protocols used to produce them. The verification workflow we followed is shown in Fig. 9. A relying party can request any protocol $p_k \in \langle P \rangle$ be executed on $\{AM\}$ and receive some appraisal result $a_k \in \langle A \rangle$. In a correct system, that appraisal result will satisfy $[\![p_k]\!] = a_k$, where $[\![p_k]\!]$ is Copland's denotational semantics [24]. Our workflow is correct if we can verify the set of Attestation Managers $\{AM\}$ will execute each protocol $p_k \in \langle P \rangle$ resulting in $a_k \in \langle A \rangle$. To achieve this end we verify the following:

1. Manifest Generator—$\langle P \rangle$ will run on the set of Manifests $\{M\}$ generated by the Manifest Generator and produce evidence $\langle E \rangle$ that appraises to $\langle A \rangle$ as defined by the Copland execution semantics.

2. Manifest Compiler and Build System—$\langle P \rangle$ will execute in the environment $\{AM\}$ synthesized by the Manifest Compiler and build system resulting in raw evidence $\langle B \rangle$ such that bundling $b_k \in \langle B \rangle$ results in the same evidence type $e_k \in \langle E \rangle$ as predicted by the semantics of p_k and $\{M\}$.
3. Protocol Execution—each Attestation Manager in $\{AM\}$ correctly implements execution of Copland phrases as defined by the Copland semantics.

Prior work has verified that the base Attestation Manager we build from correctly implements the Copland semantics [19], giving us an AM Core that correctly executes protocols. What remains is verifying correctness of the Manifest Generator and the Manifest Compiler/Build System combination.

4.1 Manifest Generator Verification

```
Theorem man_gen_always_supports : forall (t : Term) t' tp p env (man : Manifest),
    map_get (manifest_generator' tp t env) p = Some man →
    In p (places tp t) →
    In t' (place_terms t tp p) →
    manifest_support_term man t'.
```

Fig. 10. All manifests output by the Manifest Generator supports execution of their respective terms.

The verification goal for the Manifest Generator specifies that the output of the Manifest Generator preserves protocol executability. Specifically, every protocol input to the generator will run on the output Manifests. The primary theorem for this goal is man_gen_always_supports shown in Fig. 10. The conclusion of this proof is for any Copland protocol t and top level Place tp, running the Manifest Generator on the given protocol will yield a collection of Manifests for which every term corresponding with a place p mentioned in the top level protocol will be **supported**. The meaning of **supported** in this context is that any Attestation Manager properly fulfilling the Manifests specification of functionality will allow the execution of the **supported** term. This is combined with proofs showing that an Attestation Manager with a manifest M that **supports** a term t will faithfully execute the term t with respect to Copland denotational semantics.

4.2 Manifest Compiler Verification

For verification goal (2) we show the Attestation Manager built and configured via our Manifest Generator and Compiler toolchain will guarantee the execution of the Copland protocol used as input. We prove that for any abstract Manifest output from the Manifest Generator, if that Manifest is compiled by the Manifest Compiler with a sufficiently supporting AM Library, the resulting AM

Configuration will **support** the execution of all terms and places mentioned in the Copland Protocol given the semantics of the Copland Virtual Machine.

We define **support** in this case to mean that the running of any Copland Virtual Machine configured with the output AM Configuration with any term corresponding to a place in the Copland Protocol will always either successfully execute with a result or fail with an unfalsifiable Runtime Error.

4.3 Soundness Proof Corollaries

Having verified goals (1) and (2), we know that a Copland protocol will successfully execute on an Attestation Manager built using the Manifest Generator, Compiler, Build System toolchain. However, no statement regarding the correctness of this execution was immediately shown. In previous work Petz and Alexander [18] proved that if an Attestation Manager is properly configured, it will faithfully and correctly execute Copland protocols to their corresponding evidence and appraisals.

The key feature our work provides is the verified toolchain to satisfy the "properly configured" hypothesis of this existing proof. With this toolchain in hand, an overall proof now for Copland Attestation Manager's becomes: "forall protocols P, creating Attestation Managers through the use of the toolchain in Fig. 5 and running the protocol through the output Attestation Managers will yield a guaranteed to execute correct Attestation Evidence and Appraisal Result." With this result, we complete verification goal (3) and the complete connection is made in our verification workflow. Utilizing the toolchain and its accompanying proofs, we have demonstrated that the verified configuration and deployment of Attestation Managers that execute arbitrary Copland protocols can be automated, yet guaranteed to execute with correct results.

4.4 Soundness of Evidence Disclosure Policy Enforcement

Earlier we introduced the notion of constrained evidence disclosure, access control policy, and how disclosure policies are integrated into Attestation Manager execution. Here we summarize the verification results that justify the soundness of the translation in the Manifest Compiler from declarative policies to policy enforcement mechanisms in the AM. First, recall from the Copland grammar of Fig. 2 that evidence may be split (or dropped) either at explicit branching points ($<$ or $\sim$) or before being passed as input to primitive ASPs. The signatures of Copland request and reply events indicate the precise structure (and presumed contents) of the evidence bundles shared amongst the places involved in the remote attestation session. Because the Copland execution semantics is *evidence-cumulative* by default, care must be taken to only forward evidence to authorized parties when sensitive evidence is generated during a protocol.

The Copland Virtual Machine [19] is a formally verified Copland interpreter that emits attestation events that are consistent with the denotational Copland reference semantics [24]. Here we augment this CVM with a disclosure policy checking mechanism and leverage the semantics of Copland and the CVM to justify its soundness. The main soundness result appears in Fig. 11 as the Coq theorem: cvm_respects_term_disclosure. This theorem states that if an (*Evidence*∗ *Plc*) pair (et, r) is not disclosed according to term_discloses, it is also not disclosed by any event emitted in a concrete CVM execution trace.

```
(* Main Disclosure Soundness Theorem *)
Theorem cvm_respects_term_disclosure:
    forall t p e r bits bits' p' e' cvm_tr ac ac' et,
        ~ (term_discloses t p e (et, r)) →
        (build_cvmP t
            (mk_st (evc bits e) [] p _ ac)
            (resultC tt)
            (mk_st (evc bits' e') cvm_tr p' _ ac')) →
        ~ (cvm_trace_discloses cvm_tr (et, r)).
```

Fig. 11. Disclosure Soundness Theorem

The predicate term_discloses intentionally resembles a policy checking function. It is defined recursively over a Copland term, place and initial evidence type. Critically, a term will be considered to disclose evidence et to a remote target r in either of the three cases: (i) et is sent directly to r; (ii) the current place is r and received a bundle of evidence from another place that resolves to et; or (iii) a subterm of the current term discloses et to r. The predicate cvm_trace_discloses captures when at least one event in a CVM trace is a communication event that discloses evidence. Because the formal result in Fig. 11 is generic over the type of evidence disclosed, additional predicates are required to capture more fine grained assurances such as: "evidence is always encrypted for place P while in transit". While we leave such evidence policy predicates as future work, we believe this approach can support more flexible and relaxed disclosure policies while still maintaining soundness by leveraging the core CVM disclosure properties verified in this work.

5 Implementation and Evaluation

Our formal specifications of the Manifest Generator, Manifest Compiler, and Attestation Manager Core are implemented in Coq; where proving our critical properties of guaranteed executability, availability, and integrity of a collection of layered attestation protocols was possible. The proofs of the critical properties were completed and verified in Coq in a time-consuming, yet standard approach of defining semantics and proving each step, followed by connecting all the corresponding theorems as described in Sect. 4.

Despite the many benefits Coq provided, it is not a practical language for a running implementation of an Attestation Manager. For this reason, we chose to synthesize our Attestation Manager to CakeML [15] taking advantage of its verified compiler. Virtually all the implementation is extracted from Coq with a bespoke CakeML extraction functionality [2] creating a verified chain from Coq specification to assembly language. The extraction mechanism generates shims for any function signature that is admitted without definition. The shims are clearly marked and cause the CakeML compiler to throw an error if not given an implementation post synthesis. These shims help keep implementation details of networking stack and crypto algorithms that are too difficult to recreate in Coq abstract until they are concretized when the Attestation Manager is built. Shims also allow for the previously mentioned implementation capabilities to be referenced from an abstract Attestation Manager which is then concretized by the Build System post-extraction.

Helble et al. [11] define several idioms that attestation systems should implement known colloquially as *the flexible mechanisms*. These attestation idioms were expanded and implemented as Copland phrases that we utilized to test our workflow. We evaluated our implementation by ensuring that each of the flexible mechanisms Copland protocols builds and runs successfully on our toolchain. Each protocol is extracted and input to the verified Manifest Generator – Manifest Compiler toolchain creating a collection of AM Configurations, one for each Attestation Manager required by the Copland phrases. These configurations are then provided to the AM Build System, yielding custom-built Attestation Managers that collectively run the specified protocols.

Example: In the case of our client, server, appraisal server example (Fig. 3), we take the Copland protocol encoded in Coq, extract it to CakeML, and input the extracted phrase to our Manifest Generator. For each output Manifest we input them into the Manifest Compiler to yield three AM Configurations (one for c_i, s_j, A) We then distribute these AM Configurations to the systems for the attestation to be run, where they will be built by the AM Build System and run on their respective systems.

6 Related Work

Haldar et al. [10] provides the first definition of semantic remote attestation using language-based security and virtual machines. Our work is based on a definition of attestation that extends Haldar et al. [10] to layered systems by Coker et al. [4]. The Remote ATtestation procedureS (RATS) working group provides a complimentary working definition of layered attestation [13] under the auspices of IETF.

A number of researchers examine attestation of distributed systems that are not layered. Rabbani et al. [23], Carpent et al. [3] present *swarm attestation* techniques that address attestation of interconnected devices that are not layered. Shi et al. [30], Yang et al. [31], Conti et al. [5] similarly provide attestation for general distributed systems. None of these works formalize their approaches, but each provides useful perspectives on attestation approaches and implementation.

In the vein of formalized attestation approaches, HYbrid Design for Remote Attestation (HYDRA) [7] uses a hybrid hardware/software architecture composing formally verified components to achieve design goals from Francillon et al. [8]. Further, Verifiable Remote Attestation for Simple Embedded Devices (VRASED) [17] extends ideas from HYDRA to a concrete architecture where they verify attestation soundness properties using linear temporal logic. The result is a fully-verified remote attestation implementation for a specific system architecture. The verified Attestation Manager we build upon in this work was developed by Petz and Alexander [19], and utilizes a Coq specification to define the behavior and semantics of a generic class of Attestation Managers for layered architectures.

Similar to our Attestation Manager workflow, Viaduct [1] and Pirouette [12] provide capabilities for compiling distributed systems with predictable properties. Pirouette compiles programs to distributed, interacting systems with guaranteed properties by utilizing its type system. Viaduct similarly compiles distributed systems with the additional feature of guaranteed security properties. Pirouette and Viaduct are both closer to general purpose tools while this work is domain specific, making verification simpler and more focused.

7 Conclusion

Remote attestation is a technique for producing a verifiable report of evidence suitable for appraisal to determine the status of a target system. Layered attestation is a realization of remote attestation that uses a collection of Attestation Managers to gather run-time evidence from arbitrarily complex distributed systems. If appraisal results are to be trusted the appraiser must in turn trust the attestation mechanism that provides evidence. Formally deriving Attestation Managers from protocols they are expected to run provides this trust in appraisal results. Specifically, knowing that properly configured, verified Attestation Managers gathered evidence leads to trust that evidence faithfully describes the target system.

We leverage the Copland formal semantics and a verified Attestation Manager implementation in synthesizing layered attestation systems configurations. A Manifest Generator synthesizes Manifests describing Attestation Manager Configurations that implement an execution environment for required protocols. A Manifest Compiler in turn transforms those Manifests into concrete Attestation Manager implementations. The tool chain from protocols to Attestation Managers is verified to ensure correctness of the resulting attestation system proving a trusted mechanism as defined by Coker et al. [4].

A major objective of the Manifest Compiler workflow is reducing the burden of developing correct attestation systems. With this work users may write protocols and automatically generate an attestation environment with guaranteed executability, availability, and integrity for the given input protocols. We are assured the right measurements are invoked in the right order, but determining whether those measurements produce useful evidence is an open question. Significant work remains to relate attestation results to systems including measurement semantics, ASP verification, and protocol evaluation.

Additionally, our work allows for the given attestation protocols to be run on the synthesized Attestation Managers, but cannot provide any protection should the given protocol be flawed. We are working on techniques for comparing attestation protocols to determine a "best" protocol for a given attestation scenario. Specifically, we plan to look at sets of attacks allowed by protocols [25,29] and compare those attacks to order protocols based on which constrains the set of possible attacks most. This ordering is the basis for a negotiation framework for selecting protocols [9].

Our implementation of the toolchain outlined in this paper, as well as corresponding formal specification and verification results, is available online [21].

References

1. Acay, C., Recto, R., Gancher, J., Myers, A.C., Shi, E.: Viaduct: an extensible, optimizing compiler for secure distributed programs. In: Proceedings of the 42nd ACM SIGPLAN International Conference on Programming Language Design and Implementation, pp. 740–755 (2021)
2. Barclay, T., Thomas, W.: A fork of coq for cakeml extraction. https://github.com/ku-sldg/coq (2024)
3. Carpent, X., ElDefrawy, K., Rattanavipanon, N., Tsudik, G.: Lightweight swarm attestation: a tale of two lisa-s. In: Proceedings of the 2017 ACM on Asia Conference on Computer and Communications Security, pp. 86–100 (2017)
4. Coker, G., et al.: Principles of remote attestation. Int. J. Inf. Secur. **10**(2), 63–81 (2011)
5. Conti, M., Dushku, E., Mancini, L.: Radis: Remote attestation of distributed iot services. In: 2019 6th International Conference on Software Defined Systems, SDS 2019. pp, 25–32. IEEE, United States (Jun 2019), Conference date: 10-06-2019 Through 13-06-2019
6. Copland Consortium: The copland framework website (2019). https://copland-lang.org
7. Eldefrawy, K., Rattanavipanon, N., Tsudik, G.: Hydra: hybrid design for remote attestation (using a formally verified microkernel). In: Proceedings of the 10th ACM Conference on Security and Privacy in wireless and Mobile Networks, pp. 99–110 (2017)
8. Francillon, A., Nguyen, Q., Rasmussen, K.B., Tsudik, G.: A minimalist approach to remote attestation. In: 2014 Design, Automation & Test in Europe Conference & Exhibition (DATE), pp. 1–6. IEEE (2014)
9. Fritz, A., Alexander, P.: A framework for policy based negotiation. In: NASA Formal Methods Symposium. pp. 207–223. Springer (2023). https://doi.org/10.1007/978-3-031-33170-1_13

10. Haldar, V., Chandra, D., Franz, M.: Semantic remote attestation – a virtual machine directed approach to trusted computing. In: Proceedings of the Third Virtual Machine Research and Technology Symposium. San Jose, CA (May 2004)
11. Helble, S.C., Kretz, I.D., Loscocco, P.A., Ramsdell, J.D., Rowe, P.D., Alexander, P.: Flexible mechanisms for remote attestation. ACM Trans. Privacy Sec. (TOPS) **24**(4), 1–23 (2021)
12. Hirsch, A.K., Garg, D.: Pirouette: higher-order typed functional choreographies. Proc. ACM Programming Lang. **6**(POPL), 1–27 (2022)
13. IETF RATS Working Group: Remote ATtestation ProcedureS (RATS) (2023). https://datatracker.ietf.org/wg/rats/about/
14. Jurgensen, G., et al.: A copland attestation manager (am) in cakeml (2021). https://github.com/ku-sldg/am-cakeml
15. Kumar, R., Myreen, M.O., Norrish, M., Owens, S.: Cakeml: a verified implementation of ml. In: Proceedings of the 41st ACM SIGPLAN-SIGACT Symposium on Principles of Programming Languages, POPL 2014, pp. 179–191. ACM, New York (2014). http://doi.acm.org/10.1145/2535838.2535841
16. Loscocco, P.A., Smalley, S.D., Muckelbauer, P.A., Taylor, R.C., Turner, S.J., Farrell, J.F.: The inevitability of failure: the flawed assumption of security in modern computing environments. In: In Proceedings of the 21st National Information Systems Security Conference, pp. 303–314 (1998)
17. Nunes, I.D.O., Eldefrawy, K., Rattanavipanon, N., Steiner, M., Tsudik, G.: Vrased: a verified hardware/software co-design for remote attestation. In: 28th USENIX Security Symposium (USENIX Security 19), pp. 1429–1446 (2019)
18. Petz, A., Alexander, P.: A copland attestation manager. In: Hot Topics in Science of Security (HoTSoS 2019), 8-11 April, Nashville, TN (2019)
19. Petz, A., Alexander, P.: An infrastructure for faithful execution of remote attestation protocols. Innovat. Syst. Softw. Eng. (2022)
20. Petz, A., Jurgensen, G., Alexander, P.: Design and formal verification of a copland-based attestation protocol. In: Proceedings of the 19th ACM-IEEE International Conference on Formal Methods and Models for System Design, MEMOCODE 2021, pp. 111–117. Association for Computing Machinery, New York (2021). https://doi.org/10.1145/3487212.3487340
21. Petz, A., Thomas, W., Fritz, A., Barclay, T., Schmalz, L., Alexander, P.: Verified configuration and deployment of layered attestation managers. zenodo (2024). https://doi.org/10.5281/zenodo.12734609
22. Petz, A., et al.: copland-avm (2020). https://github.com/ku-sldg/copland-avm
23. Rabbani, M.M., Vliegen, J., Winderickx, J., Conti, M., Mentens, N.: Shela: scalable heterogeneous layered attestation. IEEE Internet Things J. **6**(6), 10240–10250 (2019)
24. Ramsdell, J., et al.: Orchestrating layered attestations. In: Principles of Security and Trust (POST 2019), 8-11 April, Prague, Czech Republic (2019)
25. Ramsdell, J.: Chase: A model finder for finitary geometric logic (2020). https://github.com/ramsdell/chase
26. Rowe, P.D.: Confining adversary actions via measurement. In: Third International Workshop on Graphical Models for Security, pp. 150–166 (2016)
27. Rowe, P., Ramsdell, J., Kretz, I.: Automated trust analysis of copland specifications for layered attestations. In: Principles and Practice of Declarative Programming (PPDP 2021) (Sep 2021)
28. Rowe, P.D.: Bundling evidence for layered attestation. In: Franz, M., Papadimitratos, P. (eds.) Trust 2016. LNCS, vol. 9824, pp. 119–139. Springer, Cham (2016). https://doi.org/10.1007/978-3-319-45572-3_7

29. Rowe, P.D.: On orderings in security models. In: Protocols, Strands, and Logic: Essays Dedicated to Joshua Guttman on the Occasion of his 66.66 th Birthday, pp. 370–393. Springer (2021)
30. Shi, E., Perrig, A., Van Doorn, L.: Bind: a fine-grained attestation service for secure distributed systems. In: 2005 IEEE Symposium on Security and Privacy, pp. 154–168. IEEE (2005)
31. Yang, Y., Wang, X., Zhu, S., Cao, G.: Distributed software-based attestation for node compromise detection in sensor networks. In: 2007 26th IEEE International Symposium on Reliable Distributed Systems (SRDS 2007), pp. 219–230. IEEE (2007)

Right or Wrong – Understanding How Users Write Software Models in Alloy

Ana Jovanovic and Allison Sullivan(✉)

The University of Texas at Arlington, Arlington, TX, USA
{ana.jovanovic,allison.sullivan}@uta.edu

Abstract. Writing declarative models has numerous benefits, ranging from automated reasoning and correction of design-level properties before systems are built, to automated testing and debugging of their implementations after they are built. Alloy is a declarative modeling language that is well-suited for verifying system designs. A key strength of Alloy is its scenario-finding toolset, the Analyzer, which allows users to explore all valid scenarios that adhere to the model's constraints up to a user-provided scope. However, even with visualized scenarios, it is difficult to write correct Alloy models. This paper presents an empirical study of over 93,000 models written mainly by users trying to learn Alloy to form a comprehensive series of observations to guide the growing body of debugging and educational efforts for Alloy model development.

1 Introduction

In today's society, we are becoming increasingly dependent on software systems. However, we also constantly witness the negative impacts of buggy software. One way to help develop better software systems is to leverage software models. Alloy [17] is a relational modeling language. A key strength of Alloy is the ability to develop models in the Analyzer [2], an automatic analysis engine based on off-the-shelf SAT solvers, which the Analyzer uses to generate scenarios that highlight how the modeled properties either hold or are refuted, as desired. The user is able to iterate over these scenarios one by one, inspecting them for correctness. Alloy has been used to verify software system designs [6,11,34,36], and to perform various forms of analyses over the corresponding implementation, including deep static checking [14,18], systematic testing [24], data structure repair [35], automated debugging [15] and to generate security attacks [1,25,29].

However, to gain the many benefits that come from utilizing software models, the model itself needs to be correct. For Alloy models, there are two types of errors that can appear: (1) *underconstrained* errors in which the model allows scenarios it should prevent, and (2) *overconstrained* errors in which the model prevents scenarios it should allow. To detect an underconstrained error, during scenario enumeration, the user needs to observe a scenario that they did not expect to see. Unfortunately, even if the user notices something is wrong with a scenario, according to a recent user study, both novice and expert Alloy modelers

A. Madeira and A. Knapp (Eds.): SEFM 2024, LNCS 15280, pp. 309–327, 2025.
https://doi.org/10.1007/978-3-031-77382-2_18

struggle to refine a faulty formula given an incorrectly produced scenario [23]. To detect an overconstrained error, after enumeration, the user needs to realize that an expected scenario was never present. Since Alloy commands can produce hundreds of scenarios, this places a high burden on the user.

Given these difficulties, there is a growing body of work looking at how to debug faulty Alloy models. AUnit is a unit testing framework [27,28], which enables users to check if a specific scenario is allowed or prevented. AUnit has been used for mutation testing [20,31], fault localization [32], and automated repair [16,30]. Since then, fault localization and repair of Alloy models has become an active research area [9,10,38,39]. As this field grows, we believe it is important to understand what mistakes developers actually make when writing models so that these techniques can be effective for the majority of mistakes made.

In addition, Alloy has a reputation for being a user friendly formal method, mainly due to its IDE the Analyzer. As a result, over the years, there have been several efforts to build introductory formal methods courses centered around Alloy and the Analyzer [5,8,21,22,26]. Unfortunately, these studies have revealed that even with the Analyzer, new users still feel overwhelmed trying to learn the language. Therefore, to improve debugging and educational efforts for Alloy, this paper presents an empirical study that explores 93,283 submissions made by students learning Alloy to Alloy4Fun, an online educational website for Alloy. In this paper, we make the following contributions:

Empirical Study: We present a systematic study of models written by Alloy users with revision histories that capture back-to-back incremental changes. We explore questions spanning correct and incorrect models, including: how hard is it for users to make a model that compiles, how do user's correct answers differ from expert oracles, what common mistakes do users make, and how often are users actually close to a correct formula.

Practical Impacts: We distill our observations into practical guidelines for future work in debugging models and building educational material.

Benchmarks for Alloy: We reorganize the dataset into two benchmarks: (1) a collection of faulty models broken down by type of fault and (2) a collection of models that tracks incremental changes, which can be used to evaluate and improve incremental analysis techniques for Alloy [7,19,33,37].

Open Source: We release our benchmarks and analysis at: https://github.com/AlloyUserStudy/Alloy4FunDataAnalysis.

2 Background

In this section, we describe the key concepts of Alloy and Alloy4Fun.

```
var sig File { var link : lone File }
var sig Trash in File {}
var sig Protected in File {}
//protected file is never sent to trash
pred prop9 { no Protected & Trash }
//SECRET
pred prop9o { always no Protected & Trash }
check prop9Ok { (prop9 and not prop9o)
   implies (prop9o iff prop9) }
```

(a)

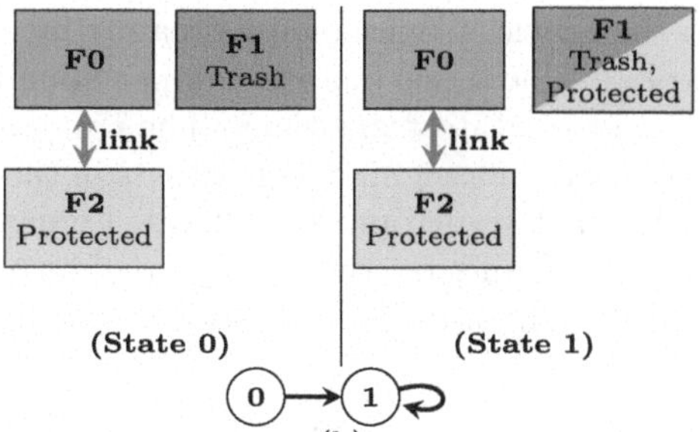

(b)

Fig. 1. Faulty Submission of an Alloy Model of a File System Trash Can

2.1 Alloy

Figure 1 (a) displays a faulty temporal model of a file system trash can from the Alloy4Fun dataset [4]. Signature paragraphs introduce named sets and can define relations, which outline relationships between elements of sets. Line 1 introduces a named set `File` and establishes that each `File` atom connects to zero or one (`lone`) `File` atoms through the `link` relation. Lines 2 and 3 introduce the named sets `Trash` and `Protected` as subsets (`in`) of `File`. Signatures and relations can be declared mutable (`var`), which means that the elements of these sets can vary across different states in the same scenario. In our example, all 3 signatures and the one relation are mutable.

Predicates introduce named formulas that can be invoked elsewhere. The predicate `prop9` on line 5 uses empty set (‘`no`’) and set intersection (‘`&`’) to incorrectly attempt to establish that a protected file is never sent to the trash. However, since the signatures are mutable, the incorrect version is true as long as no protected files are in the trash for the *first* state but does not require the constraint to be true in *every* state. To correct this, the linear temporal operator `always` can be appended to the start.

2.2 Alloy4Fun Exercises

Alloy4Fun is an educational platform for Alloy where users can write and compile Alloy models through an online interface. Alloy4Fun contains several starter models in which the signature paragraphs are given. Each starter model contains a varying number of empty predicates with a corresponding English description of the property that the user can attempt to encode into formal logic. To check their answer for a given predicate, Alloy4Fun will compare if their written submission is equivalent to a hidden oracle. If their submission is not equivalent to the oracle, the user will be presented with a counterexample: a scenario that depicts a situation where the user's formula behaves differently than the oracle. The user can then continue to iterate on their formula until it is correct.

To illustrate, in Fig. 1 (a), every line after the `SECRET` comment is hidden from the user. The check command (lines 8–9) compares if a submission is equivalent to the oracle. Commands indicate which formulas to invoke and what scope to explore. The scope places an upper bound on the size of all signature sets and the number of state transitions. The command on line 8 instructs the Analyzer to search for an assignment to all sets in the model using up to 3 `File` atoms and up to 10 state transitions by default. Figure 1 (b) displays the first counterexample scenario found by the Analyzer, which informs the user that their model is incorrect: in state 1, `F1` is both in the trash and protected.

3 Experiment SetUp

In this paper, we will use the following terminology. A *submission* consists of the base model, the user's current attempt for a specific exercise, and any helper predicates invoked. An *edit path* is the series of submissions a user makes starting with the starter model and ending with their last submission. Edit paths can contain submissions across multiple different exercises but are all within the same base model. An *attempt* is the series of submissions within an edit path that the user makes for a specific exercise.

3.1 Experimental Data

In our study, we use the publicly released Alloy4Fun dataset, which contains real-world models obtained from master's students submissions from the University of Minho (UM) and the University of Porto (UP) in the academic period from Fall 2019 to Spring 2023 [4]. In total, there are 97,755 submissions that span 17 different Alloy models and 183 predicates to be filled in (exercises). Of these, we filtered out 2,024 submissions that change the model's structure or are only changes to the theme settings for visualization. In addition, we filtered 2,448 submissions that are empty. Empty submissions are underconstrained faults. However, since empty submissions do not fundamentally illustrate any effort by the user, we removed them to avoid skewing the conclusions. As a result, we end up with 93,283 submissions, all of which have tangible user content.

Table 1 gives an overview of the complexity of the models used in our study in terms of the universe of discourse each model creates. Column **#Sig** is the total number of signatures in the model, **#Abs** is the number of abstract signatures, **#Ext** is the number of signatures that extend another signature, **#Rel** is the number of relations, **Arity** is the average arity of all relations in the model (2 indicates a binary relation), **#Exe** is the number of exercises and **#AST** is the average number of abstract syntax tree (AST) nodes in the oracle solutions for all exercises of that model. Models with an underscore in their name represent models that have multiple versions in the dataset. Between versions, the number of exercises, instructional text, and/or the type of logic can change.

For the 183 exercises, we classify them into one of the following categories: relational logic (RL), predicate logic (PL), first-order logic (FOL), and linear temporal logic (LTL). PL and LTL contain their traditional operators as supported within Alloy's grammar [3]. RL operators contain all set theory operators, comparison operators, and multiplicity operators from Alloy's grammar. FOL contains both quantifier operators and comprehension operators. Exercises were classified based on the highest operator present in the oracle solution according to the partial order of RL → PL → FOL → LTL. In total, 51 are RL exercises, 1 is a PL exercise, 95 are FOL exercises and 36 are LTL exercises.

Table 1. Complexity of Base Models

	#Sig	#Abs	#Ext	#Rel	Arity	#Exe	#AST
classroom_fol	5	0	2	3	2.33	15	10.00
classroom_rl	5	0	2	3	2.33	15	10.13
courses_v1	6	0	2	5	2.2	15	16.87
courses_v2	6	0	2	5	2.2	15	16.87
cv_v1	5	1	2	4	2	4	19.75
cv_v2	5	1	2	4	2	4	21.75
graphs	1	0	0	1	2	8	7.63
lts	3	0	1	1	3	6	19.71
productionLine_v1	5	0	2	3	2	4	14.25
productionLine_v2	10	1	7	4	2	10	14.90
productionLine_v3	10	1	7	4	2	10	14.90
socialMedia	5	0	2	5	2	8	15.75
trainstation_fol	7	0	5	2	2	10	13.40
trainstation_ltl	6	0	4	3	2	17	23.44
trash_rl	3	0	2	1	2	10	4.80
trash_ltl	3	0	2	1	2	20	8.55
trash_fol	3	0	2	1	2	10	4.80
AVG	**5.18**	**0.24**	**2.71**	**2.94**	**2.12**	**10.65**	**13.97**

3.2 Classification of Submissions

Within our dataset, a submission falls into one of the following categories: correct, overconstrained (over), underconstrained (under), both over- and underconstrained (both), type error (type), and syntax error (syntax). Correct submissions are semantically equivalent to the oracle, overconstrained submissions prevent valid scenarios from being generated, underconstrained submissions allow invalid scenarios to be generated, both submissions allow a combination of over- and underconstrained behaviors, type errors are formulas that fail to typecheck, and syntax errors are formulas that fail to adhere to the grammar rules. To determine which category a submission falls under, we use Alloy4Fun's hidden oracle check command for correctness. If not correct, we use the following command templates to determine the type of fault:

```
under: check {prop9 and !prop9o}
over: check {!prop9 and prop9o}
```

In addition, if the model fails to compile, we use the generated error message to determine if there was a type or a syntax error.

3.3 Recreating Submission Revision Histories

When a student checks an exercise, Alloy4Fun logs the student submission with a unique id key and a "derivationOf" parameter that contains the unique id of the parent entry that is either the original Alloy4Fun example model or a previous submission. We use this information to re-build edit paths that capture the series of edits a user makes. As an example, the following is the edit path for our example in Fig. 1 where U means underconstrained and C means correct:

```
inv9 U: no Protected & Trash
inv9 C: always no Protected & Trash
```

For edit paths, we do include empty submissions. While empty submissions do not hold much value as individual submissions, in the middle of an edit path, an empty submission can convey when users reset their attempt on an exercise.

3.4 Methodology

We first explore general trends across all submissions (RQ1-RQ2) before exploring how users write invalid submissions (RQ3), correct submissions (RQ4), and incorrect submissions (RQ5-RQ6). Finally, we consider how users incrementally problem solve (RQ7).

For RQ1 and RQ2, we analyze submissions based on their classification. For RQ2, we additionally separate submissions into unique versus duplicate buckets. We consider two forms of equivalence: syntactic and semantic. Syntactical duplicates covey the rate at which users literally write the same exact formula, while semantic duplicates allow us to explore the rate at which users express the same underlying concept. To determine if two submissions are syntactically equivalent, we used a PrettyStringVisitor to reprint formulas in a consistent format that removes trivial differences in formatting, such as white spaces. For semantically equivalent, we used the Analyzer to check for logical equivalence.

For RQ3, we investigate attempts that have invalid (syntax and type errors) submissions. We also pull out back to back edits in attempts in which the user repeatedly makes 5 or more invalid submissions in a row, in order to manually inspect these edits to determine what aspects of the Analyzer's error reports may be preventing users from correcting the structure of their formula.

For RQ4, we consider only correct submissions. We rank correct submissions from most repeated submission to least per exercise. From there, we then manually analyze attributes of the top submitted formulas' structure and compare different AST properties to explore how user submissions differ from the oracle formula. Similarly, for RQ5, we focus on "hot hit" submissions in which the same syntactic faulty submission is made at least 10 times. As with correct submissions, we manually investigated each "hot hit" and label it with core tenants of the mistake. In addition, for all faulty submissions, we also we use MuAlloy, a mutation testing tool [20], to generate all first-order mutants. We then check if any of the mutated models are equivalent to the oracle submission. If so, we classify the submission as "one mistake away" and explore different attributes of these fixable models in RQ6.

Finally, for RQ7, we analyze the changes in classifications that happen within back to back edits for each edit path.

4 Empirical Evaluation

4.1 RQ1: What Classification of Submissions Do Users Make?

To get a general overview of the submissions made, Fig. 2 shows pie charts depicting the breakdown in the classification of submissions, ranging from all submissions to a breakdown per type of logic. Submissions were sorted into different types of logic based on the logic in the user's submission.

As the pie charts indicate, users are the most effective at writing relational logic properties, which users express correctly 37.05% of the time. In contrast, users struggle more with FOL and LTL properties, in which less than a fourth of the submissions are correct: 23.62% and 24.13% respectively. This decrease in accuracy for FOL and LTL exercises is expected, as the introduction of quantified formulas and temporal constraints is non-trivial.

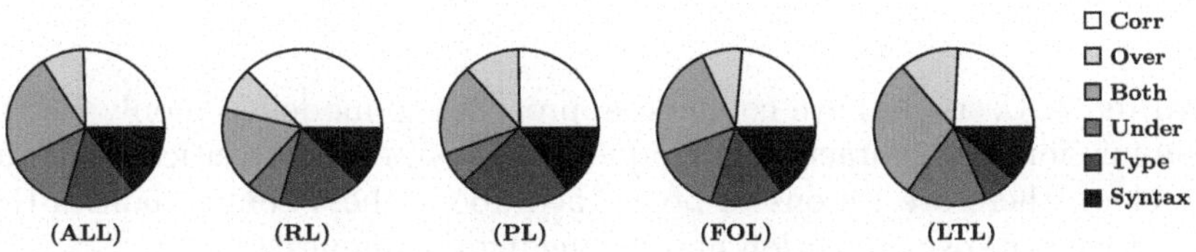

Fig. 2. Breakdown of Submission Results

While correct submissions are the largest individual chunk at 25.4%, faulty submissions (both, over and under) combine to account for 45.3% of all submissions. Faults that are both over- and underconstrained account for the largest portion of mistakes at 23.28% of all submissions. As RQ6 will highlight, this implies that faulty models are not likely to have small, simple corrections. In addition, as the complexity of the formula structure increases (FOL and LTL), users are also more likely to write properties that are accidentally too permissive. Notably, most Alloy fault localization and repair techniques struggle to perform when the issue is that constraints are missing [9,30].

Invalid submissions combine to account for 29.28% of all submissions and are almost evenly split between syntax errors (14.64%) and type errors (14.65%). While the rate of syntax errors is relatively consistent across types of logic, LTL formulas do have notably less type errors.

Finding 1: For LTL formulas, only some of the signatures and relations are mutable, which narrows down for the user which elements should appear in temporal constraints. This could be the reason for LTL formula's reduction in type errors. FOL formulas could benefit from this, as educators can emphasize that the domain of the quantified formula also limits the types that should be reasoned over. In addition, if a quantified formulas trivially reasons over sets with different types than the domain, debugging efforts should focus on modifying these sets to match the type of the domain.

4.2 RQ2: How Often Do Users Make the Same Submission?

If users often repeat the same submission, then this represents underlying common approaches that users take to modeling. Therefore, we investigate how often new users make duplicate submissions. Table 2 show the rate at which submissions are syntactically and semantically unique broken down by classification (**Clx**) and additionally type of logic for syntactic. Column **#Sub** is the total number of submissions, column **#Uni** is the number of submissions that are unique syntactically or semantically, **%Uni** is the percentage of total submissions that are unique. Syntax and Type submissions do not have semantically equivalent values since they do not compile.

Finding 2: Users do have common approaches to modeling – only 55.55% of submissions are syntactically unique and 16.55% are semantically unique. Therefore, there are lessons to be learned about these commonalities that can inturn improve education and debugging techniques.

There are two trends that impact this. First, there is high redundancy in correct submissions, which is expected as semantically, all correct submissions are equivalent. Second, there is notably less redundancy in type and syntax errors, meaning that users make a broader range of mistakes when incorrectly structuring a formula compared to writing a formula that is wrong.

Table 2. Rate of Syntactically Unique Submissions

RL					
Cx	#Sub	Syntatic #Uni	Syntatic %Uni	Semantic #Uni	Semantic %Uni
Correct	4418	397	15.70	51	0.56
Both	2029	1139	62.32	1061	37.29
Over	1091	558	51.52	293	18.16
Under	880	434	65.89	212	17.01
Syntax	1503	1150	84.88		
Type	2004	1460	77.07		
SUM/AVG	11925	5138	43.09	1617	19.21

PL					
Cx	#Sub	Syntatic #Uni	Syntatic %Uni	Semantic #Uni	Semantic %Uni
Correct	390	60	13.93	1	0.36
Both	294	208	72.49	103	44.98
Over	177	100	44.00	22	22.00
Under	105	77	80.85	9	19.15
Syntax	227	199	78.63		
Type	356	279	83.64		
SUM/AVG	1549	923	59.59	135	13.98

FOL					
Cx	#Sub	Syntatic #Uni	Syntatic %Uni	Semantic #Uni	Semantic %Uni
Correct	17373	3800	21.85	94	0.73
Both	17561	11592	65.47	5946	35.33
Over	6081	3672	61.61	1135	20.07
Under	10459	5422	50.06	857	8.45
Syntax	11188	9361	82.50		
Type	10878	8596	78.33		
SUM/AVG	73540	42443	57.71	8032	15.60

LTL					
Cx	#Sub	Syntatic #Uni	Syntatic %Uni	Semantic #Uni	Semantic %Uni
Correct	1513	205	12.58	30	2.06
Both	1831	1191	64.70	744	41.10
Over	748	420	53.64	209	28.67
Under	1015	522	50.68	147	14.33
Syntax	736	643	87.03		
Type	426	330	76.64		
SUM/AVG	6269	3311	52.82	1130	22.13

4.3 RQ3: How Effective Is the Analyzer's Compilation Error Reports?

Nearly a third of the time, a user will create a submission that fails to compile. Therefore, we investigate the effectiveness of Alloy's current compiler-based error reporting, by looking at the rate at which users fix these errors.

This is summarized in Table 3. For each model, column 2 reports the percentage of attempts that have at least one invalid submission, and column 3 presents the percentage of attempts that never turned into valid formulas. The remaining three columns quantify how a user goes from an invalid submission to a valid submission. We first collected all invalid subpaths, which are the portions of attempts that consist of only type or syntax error edits. Then, we report the average length, the percentage of subpaths that have a length of 5 or more, and the max length. Compilation errors are prevalent - over 40% of attempts have them, but error reports do help users correct an error within 2 attempts on average.

Table 3. Details for Invalid Attempts

Model	% w/ Invalid	% Nvr Valid	Subpath Len. Avg	$\% \geq 5$	Max
classroom_fol	30.44	2.75	1.93	7.50	11
classroom_rl	38.68	4.44	2.04	8.63	15
courses_v1	48.89	1.79	2.10	8.89	22
courses_v2	50.28	2.71	1.81	4.57	20
cv_v1	41.90	5.93	1.81	2.91	18
cv_v2	43.48	0.00	1.87	5.66	9
graphs	26.18	2.09	1.76	4.29	9
lts	40.95	8.62	2.34	10.11	17
productionLine_v1	32.91	1.28	2.10	8.77	15
productionLive_v2	41.43	1.00	1.84	5.15	37
productionLine_v3	36.38	1.54	1.84	4.65	11
socialMedia	48.27	4.19	2.06	8.56	23
trainStation_fol	50.25	0.98	1.91	6.20	11
trianStation_ltl	37.73	4.09	1.98	6.85	12
trash_fol	26.40	4.40	1.96	8.67	11
trash_ltl	32.35	0.67	1.91	7.71	9
trash_rl	28.81	3.17	2.10	8.67	15
SUM/AVG	**42.06**	**2.88**	**1.99**	**7.48**	**37**

Mishandling Primitive Type Errors. While our results highlight that users are often able to work through compilation mistakes, there is still the 7.88% of attempts that fall into long edit chains to try and make the model compile and the 2.88% of attempts in which the users give up. Looking into these attempts, we discovered that the Analyzer's current error reporting does not handle primitive type errors well. A primitive type error occurs when the user creates a formula that produces a set when a boolean is expected, or vice versa. To demonstrate, consider the following chain of edits for `courses_v1 inv12`:

```
inv12 T: all s:Student | s.enrolled.grades
inv12 T: all s:Student | s.enrolled.grades.s
inv12 T: all s:Student | s.(s.enrolled.grades)
```

With each edit, the user is informed that the highlighted text must "*be a formula expression.*," There is no definition of a "formula expression" and no mention of the expectation that this formula needs to evaluate to a boolean. As a result, this user keeps trying to edit the highlighted formula as if the type error is within the highlight. However, the highlighted formulas typecheck individually. In the end, the user never realizes that the issue is that the quantified formula encompassing the highlighted formulas expects a boolean not a set subformula.

Finding 3: The fact that Alloy formulas inherently produce a set or a boolean result is a subtle feature of the language that is not well highlighted in Alloy's own compiler-based error reports. Since users are able to better resolve other syntax and type errors, updating error reports to directly call out the primitive type error could help prevent the long error chains, especially if the highlighted formula ambiguously compiles in isolation.

4.4 RQ4: How Do Users' Correct Answers Differ from the Oracle?

Table 4. Location of Oracle

Type	Top 1	Top 5	Top 10	Nil
RL	22	44	49	3
PL	1	1	1	0
FOL	25	58	65	24
LTL	12	21	22	9
SUM	**60**	**156**	**169**	**36**

The oracle solution often represents one of several ways in which the property could be expressed. Therefore, we wanted to explore the ways novice users' thinking may differ from the expert-written oracles. Table 4 displays the location of the oracle submission derived by ranking all syntactically unique correct submissions in decreasing order from most to least duplicate submissions. Column **Type** displays the type of exercises under consideration based on the oracle. The remaining columns show the number of exercises for that type in which the oracle is in the **Top 1** location, **Top 5**, **Top 10**, or never submitted (**Nil**).

For RL exercises, the oracle is frequently submitted by users. RL exercise use the smallest subset of operators, and this seems to translate to less diversity in how a property can be correctly expressed. This is further supported by Table 2, in which only 15.7% of correct RL submissions are syntactically unique. However, there is a notable dropoff in users creating the oracle solution for FOL and LTL exercises. By location 10, the oracle is only present in 68.42% and 61.11% of these exercises respectively. Moreover, a forth of the time, the oracle is never submitted for these exercises.

Finding 4: In conjunction with Table 2, it is clear that correct FOL exercises simply have a lot of syntactic diversity. The structure of a FOL formula introduces a lot of opportunities for user's to make design choices, such as selecting the quantifier and selecting the domain, leading to wide variability and loweing the oracle's presence. However, correct LTL submissions lack diversity but also fail to utilize the structure of the oracle.

Top Submission Differences With Oracle. To build a better understanding of why LTL exercises often do not contain the oracle submission, and to further investigate the differences users make compared to the oracle, we manually investigated the differences between the top 1 correct solution and the oracle. Table 5 displays for each identified difference the number of top 1 correct submissions that have this difference (column # **Occ**) and the percentage that this accounts for out of all top 1 submissions (column **Rate**).

Table 5. Differences - Oracle and Top 1

Difference	# Occ	Rate
Upscaled quantification	55	29.25
Downscaled quantification	21	11.17
Different quantification domains	11	5.85
Sim, Different order of operands	12	6.38
Sim, Formed different sets	7	3.72
Sim, Different operator	19	10.11
Sim, Additional trivial operator	1	0.53
Expanded out formula	2	1.06
No Change	60	31.91

35 submissions are similar (sim) but involve minor differences, such swapping the order of operands. Many of these submissions are LTL exercises in which the location of the temporal operator `always` varies. In addition, the three of the four "additional trivial operator" are LTL exercises in which the user appends an unnecessary leading `always` operator. Together, these similar submissions highlight common modeling preferences that result in the oracle being less present for LTL exercises.

Finding 5: Users prefer leading with temporal operators, while the oracle solutions insert them close to the subformula of interest. For instance, a user will write "`always all a: A | F`" while the oracle will use "`all a : A | always F`." However, this preference does not always create equivalent formulas. Debugging techniques should consider patch steps that relocate temporal operators closer to the subformula of interest.

Size of Correct Solutions. Overall, the most prevalent difference in Table 5 is that users increase the degree of quantification in the formula, which is seen in 55 of the top 1 solutions. For instance, consider the following for `inv1` from the `productionLine_v2`. Only 21 correct submissions match the oracle (o) (8.71%) while 101 correct submissions (41.91%) use the quantified formula (s).

```
o: Worker = Human + Robot //  Workers are either human or robots
s: all w: Worker | w in Human or w in Robot
```

To quantify this impact, Table 6 displays the Abstract Syntax Tree (AST) difference between the oracle solution and all of the correct submissions. Column $\mathbf{Dif}_{Tot}$ displays the average difference in total number of AST nodes between the oracle and all correct submissions. The next four columns display the average difference in total number of AST nodes of each type of logic. For these columns, a negative number means the oracle had less AST nodes. To give context to how significant the difference in nodes is, column $\mathbf{Dif}_{Mag}$ displays average magnitude in difference between the oracle and correct submissions.

RL and PL exercises see the largest increase in size, with the oracle being on average a 0.38× smaller formula. This is not surprising, as users writing FOL versions instead would naturally increase the size. However, even FOL exercises, which already have a quantified formula, also see a large increase in the number of AST nodes. Therefore, even when quantification is expected, users add more nested quantification than the oracle formulation.

Finding 6: Users are not likely to rely on condensed relational logic to express properties, and will often write verbose formulas that apply first order logic more than is actually needed to express the constraint. Since this can impede execution runtime, it is worthwhile investing in discovering refactoring strategies to reduce quantification.

Table 6. AST Differences Between Oracle and Corr. Subs

Type	**Dif$_{Tot}$**	**Dif$_{RL}$**	**Dif$_{PL}$**	**Dif$_{FOL}$**	**Dif$_{LTL}$**	**Dif$_{Mag}$**
RL	−11.53	−2.49	−0.69	−1.16	−0.02	0.38
PL	−10.74	−1.79	−0.03	−1.26	0.00	0.38
FOL	−8.17	−1.87	−0.82	−0.52	0.00	0.81
LTL	−3.70	−0.89	−0.43	−0.24	−0.07	0.77
AVG	**−9.08**	**−2.03**	**−0.76**	**−0.72**	**−0.01**	**0.66**

4.5 RQ5: What Mistakes Do Users Make When Writing Formulas?

As indicated by Table 2, users often repeat the same mistake. To learn what these mistakes are, we manually investigate and label each "hot hit" faulty submission with the main aspects of the mistake. Correspondingly, Table 7 displays the common mistakes made broken down by classification of submission and type of logic. Column **#Occ** represent the number of unique "hot hit" submissions of that mistake and column **#Sub** represents the total number of submissions with duplicates included. In green, we highlight the top 4 mistakes.

Across all logic types, the single most common mistake is the incorrect use of an operator. Our dataset includes a detailed breakdown of which operators are incorrectly applied and at what rates. Expectedly, several of these mistakes involve users making the wrong choice between two similar operators, i.e. transitive closure ('^') instead of reflexive transitive closure ('*'). However, there were also several mistakes that reflect users picking operators that are not within the same grammar division, but are used to capture two different but similar ideas. To illustrate, consider the following submission (s) to `inv6` from `productionLine_v2` that 20 users submitted and the closest correct solution (c):

```
// Components built of dangerous parts are also dangerous
s: all c: Component | c.parts in Dangerous => c in Dangerous
c: all c: Component | some c.parts & Dangerous => c in Dangerous
```

As shown, several users choose to encode this by checking some set intersection instead of a subset check. For their formulas, these two operators behave the

Table 7. Common Mistakes Made by Users (subs with at least 10 repeats)

Difference	RL		FOL		LTL		Total	
	#Occ	#Sub	#Occ	#Sub	#Occ	#Sub	#Occ	#Sub
More complex quant. domain	0	0	4	64	0	0	4	64
Narrowed quant. domain	0	0	70	1338	0	0	70	1338
Different quant. domain	0	0	6	183	0	0	6	183
Upscaled quant. level trying to state relationships	0	0	101	1990	8	159	109	2149
Incorrect order of nested quant.	0	0	4	78	0	0	4	78
Nested quant. disjoint mistake	0	0	17	413	0	0	17	413
Downscaled quant. level leading to incorr. expr range	23	378	15	264	2	34	40	676
Tried to inverted concept	2	37	6	144	2	38	10	219
Trying to explictly outline steps	0	0	0	0	2	24	2	24
Incorrect use of operator	14	238	130	2438	12	208	156	2884
Operator not commumtative	1	14	16	294	3	71	20	379
Missing operator	1	10	7	175	8	146	16	331
Incorrectly scoped expr, missing parentheses	0	0	1	23	0	0	1	23
Incorrect application of extension signature	3	46	65	1181	1	23	69	1250
Subportion of total concept	5	128	23	492	3	46	31	666
Wrong understanding of exercise	4	61	3	55	3	53	10	169
Total	53	912	468	9132	44	802	565	10846

same except for when the left-hand side of the operator is empty. In this case, if `c.parts` is empty, then `c.parts in Dangerous` evaluates to `true`, which prevents scenarios from being generated in which there are no dangerous components.

> **Finding 7:** While users make the wrong choice between two closely related operators, it is also clear that users make mistakes by encoding incorrect but closely related *concepts*. Both of these modeling mistakes often show up as a subtle bug in which only a few scenarios, usually involving corner cases like an empty set, differentiate the formulas. Users should explore corner case scenarios to ensure the proper boundary behavior of their constraints.

FOL submissions are prevalent in Table 7, accounting for 468 of the 565 hot hit submissions. In addition, half of the frequently repeated classification of mistakes (column **Mistakes**) involve errors related to quantification. Therefore, there are fundamental misunderstandings users have about how and when to use quantification. The most common quantifier mistake is that users try to upscale the level of quantification in an attempt to explicitly outline relationships, where upscale means the submission inserted more quantifiers than the oracle.

As an example, consider the following submission for `classroom_rl inv5`:

```
s: all t:Teacher| some t.Teaches
c: some Teacher.Teaches //There are classes assigned to teachers.
```

that accounts for 30 (35.29%) of the both over- and underconstrained submissions. In this case, the subformula is correct, but the quantifier is wrong. While there are often ways to express a RL formula with an equivalent FOL formula, the increase in complexity of the formula structure introduces more opportunities for users to make a mistake. Hand in hand with upscaling, downscaling the level of quantification is also a common mistake that often results in a constraint being satisfied incorrectly if at least one element of the set satisfies it.

Finding 8: Debugging techniques should consider transformations that change the degree of quantification, knowing that users frequently pick the wrong quantification level. Moreover, educators should emphasize when the use of quantification is appropriate to express the relationship per *atom* versus when not to use quantification to express the relationship per *type*.

Users also make mistakes picking the right domain to reason over, often by making the domain of a quantified formula too narrow. A narrower quantification domain almost always occurred on models that had extension signatures and the user used an extension signature for the domain in place of the base signature. As an example, consider the following submission for `inv3` for model `courses_v2` which accounts for 65 (40.37%) of the underconstrained submissions:

```
s: all c : Course | some p : Professor | c in p.teaches
c: all c : Course | some p : Person | c in p.teaches // Courses must have teachers.
```

Finding 9: Users can write the right subformula but use the wrong domain in quantified formulas. Debugging techniques should explore changes to the domain, with a focus on making the domain more restrictive.

4.6 RQ6: How Often Are Users "One" Mistake Away?

Our results in RQ5 indicate that users often make mistakes by encoding a similar but different concepts. However, similar concepts can be represented with notably different logic. Therefore, we wanted to explore how often users are actually close to the correct solution using MuAlloy to find submissions that are "one mistake away." Table 8 depicts the frequency at which mutants fix submissions broken down by the type of logic present in the submission and the classification of the submission. Column **#Fixes** displays the total number of mutants that fixed a submission, column **# Sub**$_f$ shows the number of submissions that were fixed and column **% Sub**$_f$ shows what percentage of submissions **# Sub**$_f$ is. The number of fixes is more than the number of submissions fixed because some submissions could be fixed by multiple different mutations.

Table 8. Frequency of Mutant Corrections

Clx/Type	# Fixes	# Sub$_f$	% Sub$_f$
Both	1089	882	6.24
Over	1456	871	18.34
Under	1527	999	15.48
RL	247	192	5.61
PL	47	29	11.69
FOL	3092	2120	10.83
LTL	686	411	19.74
SUM	**4072**	**2752**	**10.86**

Overall, only 10.86% of submissions can be corrected by the current mutant operators. The rate is notably lowest for RL submissions, but is nearly quadrupled for LTL submissions. One reason for this is that mutant operators not do tend to create fundamentally new constraints, even when insertion operators are applied. While LTL submissions can often be fixed with inserting or deleting temporal operators, RL submissions often need to fundamentally change the sets being formed. Case in point, only 6.24% of both over- and underconstrained faults can be fixed with mutants. This is expected as these formulas are sometimes too permissive and sometimes too restrictive, which is likely to lead to multi-step edits not captured by first-order mutants.

Finding 10: The overall low fix rate is in line with observations from RQ5 in which users often make small encoding mistakes, but the difference in logic is often multiple edit steps away, not one. For instance, there is no first order mutation operator that transforms "`a in b`," into "`some a & b`." While blanket generation of second-order mutants would have scalability issues, the results from RQ5 should be utilized to produce a select subset of higher order mutants that reflects common mistakes.

Table 9. Breakdown of Mutant Operators That Fixed Subs

Mutant Op	# Fixes	Percent
Unary Operator Insertion	1269	31.16
Unary Operator Deletion	160	3.93
Unary Operator Replacement	340	8.35
Binary Operator Deletion	272	6.68
Binary Operator Replacement	810	19.89
Binary Operator Exchange	167	4.10
List Operator Deletion	221	5.43
List Operator Replacement	53	1.30
Quantifier Operator Replacement	724	17.78
Prime Operator Insertion	55	1.35

Although the fix rate is low, we still want to learn about the mutant operators that do correct models. Table 9 displays the rate at which individual mutant operators fixed submissions. Column **#Fixes** is the number of faulty submissions fixed and **Percentage** is what percentage of fixed submissions the preceding **#Fixes** represents. A majority of the fixes come from replacement (47.32%) and insertions (32.51%). The high rate of replacement fixes is supported by observations from our common mistakes (RQ5), where we found that the most frequent mistake is that users incorrectly select between similar but different operators. For insertions, Unary Operator Insertion (UOI) fixes are dominant. UOI fixes for LTL formulas almost always involve inserting temporal operators later in a formula, which is not unexpected as RQ4 highlights that users tend to push temporal operators to the front of formulas.

Finding 11: Mutant operators that aligned with common mistakes are correlated with the ability to fix more faulty submissions. Therefore, it is worth investing in refining existing and creating new mutant operators based the patterns in RQ5.

4.7 RQ7: How Do Users Respond to Their Mistakes?

As users incrementally work towards a correct solution, users make changes that may move their submission from one classification to the next. Table 10 displays the classification change, or lack thereof, produced by back to back edits. The letter `E` represents empty submissions. Row **# Edit '?'** represents the number of edits that start as one classification and move to a new one based on the corresponding column, while Row **% Edit '?'** represents what percentage this number is out of the total edits that start as classification '?'. For instance, there are 4,133 edits in which the user starts with an overconstrained formula and produces an overconstrained formula (`O-O`).

Table 10. Details of Back-to-Back Edits

Change	O-O	O-U	O-B	O-S	O-T	O-C	O-E
# Edits O	4133	526	1484	762	877	2339	84
% Edits O	40.50	5.15	14.54	7.47	8.59	22.92	0.82
Change	U-O	U-U	U-B	U-S	U-T	U-C	U-E
# Edits U	548	9472	2884	1464	1248	2603	110
% Edits U	2.99	51.68	15.73	7.99	6.81	14.20	0.60
Change	B-O	B-U	B-B	B-S	B-T	B-C	B-E
# Edits B	1918	3952	19261	2871	2545	2855	178
% Edits B	5.71	11.77	57.36	8.55	7.58	8.50	0.53
Change	S-O	S-U	S-B	S-S	S-T	S-C	S-E
# Edits S	1214	2116	3731	8371	2239	2814	203
% Edits S	5.87	10.23	18.03	40.46	10.82	13.60	0.98
Change	T-O	T-U	T-B	T-S	T-T	T-C	T-E
# Edits T	1116	1647	3233	1720	10528	2402	184
% Edits T	5.36	7.91	15.52	8.26	50.54	11.53	0.88
Change	C-O	C-U	C-B	C-S	C-T	C-C	C-E
# Edits C	692	752	676	526	659	11395	51
% Edits C	4.69	5.10	4.58	3.57	4.47	77.25	0.35
Change	E-O	E-U	E-B	E-S	E-T	E-C	E-E
# Edits E	111	181	225	261	202	344	581
% Edits E	5.83	9.50	11.81	13.70	10.60	18.06	30.50

Based on Table 10, a user is significantly more likely to make an edit that does not change the classification, which implies that users often make small edits. In addition, users do frequently go from an overconstrained to a correct formula (22.92%), which is in line with our "one step away" results in which overconstrained formulas were often close to a correct model. In contrast, syntax errors, type errors and both submissions are the most likely to lead to a student resetting their attempt by erasing down to an empty submission, which indicates for these categories users are more likely to feel as if they ended up far off from the solution. Interestingly, users do go from a correct submission to all the other classifications. There are two main reasons for this. First, some of the exercises ask for an answer using a specific type of logic, but Alloy4Fun does not restrict the available operators. Therefore, users will create a correct submission and attempt to re-write it into the required logic. Second, users refine their submission, often trying to create a more condense formula.

Finding 12: Given the active research around automated repair, repair techniques should consider that users are not likely to buy into a large change to their formula. However, given RQ6 results, repair patches are likely to need to make multiple changes. Therefore, repair tools should focus on providing users with supporting evidence of the validity of larger patches, such as counterexamples with explanation templates.

5 Threats to Validity

There exist several threats to the validity of our results. First, the dataset we use does not contain any information related to what users were thinking. Therefore, we are limited in some of the conclusions we can form. Second, the users are all master's students from the University of Minho (UM) and the University of Porto (UP) between 2019 and 2023. While there is breadth to the date range of the study, we do not know the details of the educational performance and background of the master's students, which may lack diversity. Third, MuAlloy, and the Analyzer itself, do not support higher-order quantification. In theory, a higher order formula could be correct. However, since the current tools cannot evaluate them, we do not factor them into our one step away calculations. Lastly, students could have collaborated together, resulting in higher duplication rates.

6 Related Work

Alloy4Fun. The creators of the Alloy4Fun dataset have published an experience paper outlining the first semester that they used Alloy4Fun in their classroom [22]. This paper focuses largely on lessons learned utilizing Alloy4Fun in the classroom but does contain some preliminary analysis of the data collected, such as the rate of correct versus incorrect submissions and commonly reported error messages. This data is from an early benchmark and consists of 9 models and only 5000 executions. Our analysis is more in-depth and spans the significantly larger version of the dataset.

User Studies and Empirical Studies Over Alloy. There have been a few user studies exploring how developers work with Alloy [12,13,23]. The most recent study explored the debugging behavior of novice and expert users and discovered that users struggle to refine Alloy predicates using only the visual representation of scenarios [23]. Another recent study found that if users are shown a small collection of valid and invalid scenarios before writing a predicate, then users better understand what behavior the user should be trying to codify into a constraint [13]. In addition, there was a user study that explored how users interact with different enumeration strategies [12]. While our efforts focus on how to better teach and debug constraints, these user studies highlight best practices for how to present and guide users through the output of these constraints.

Tangent to our work, there is a static profile of 1,652 publicly available Alloy models pulled from GitHub that investigates how often users engage with different parts of Alloy's grammar and explores the average size and complexity of Alloy models. This study is not concerned with the accuracy of the constraints, but does give suggestions for education based on frequently used and underutilized features. These recommendations are complementary to our recommendations.

7 Conclusion

Given Alloy's popularity and well supported toolset, there is a growing body of work to debug faulty models and to use the Alloy in an educational setting. To help guide future research directions for both of these avenues, this paper explores a dataset of over 93,000 submissions made by new users. We highlight several key findings, including common patterns in correct and incorrect submissions and the realistic effectiveness of existing mutant operators.

References

1. Akhawe, D., Barth, A., Lam, P.E., Mitchell, J., Song, D.: Towards a formal foundation of web security. In: 2010 23rd IEEE Computer Security Foundations Symposium, pp. 290–304 (2010)
2. Alloy analyzer Website (2019). http://alloytools.org
3. Alloy Grammar Reference (2024). https://alloytools.org/spec.html
4. Alloy4Fun Benchmark (2022). https://zenodo.org/record/4676413
5. Askarpour, M., Bersani, M.M.: Teaching formal methods: an experience report. In: Bruel, J.-M., Capozucca, A., Mazzara, M., Meyer, B., Naumchev, A., Sadovykh, A. (eds.) FISEE 2019. LNCS, vol. 12271, pp. 3–18. Springer, Cham (2020). https://doi.org/10.1007/978-3-030-57663-9_1
6. Bagheri, H., Kang, E., Malek, S., Jackson, D.: A formal approach for detection of security flaws in the Android permission system. Formal Asp. Comput. (2018)
7. Bagheri, H., Malek, S.: Titanium: efficient analysis of evolving alloy specifications. In: Proceedings of the 2016 24th ACM SIGSOFT Symposium on the Foundations of Software Engineering (FSE), pp. 27–38 (2016)
8. Boyatt, R., Sinclair, J.: Experiences of teaching a lightweight formal method (2008)
9. Brida, S.G., et al.: Bounded exhaustive search of alloy specification repairs. In: ICSE (2021)
10. Cerqueira, J., Cunha, A., Macedo, N.: Timely specification repair for alloy 6. In: Schlingloff, B.H., Chai, M. (eds.) SEFM 2022. LNCS, vol. 13550, pp. 288–303. Springer, Cham (2022). https://doi.org/10.1007/978-3-031-17108-6_18
11. Chong, N., Sorensen, T., Wickerson, J.: The semantics of transactions and weak memory in x86, Power, ARM, and C++. SIGPLAN Not. **53**(4), 211–225 (2018)
12. Danas, N., Nelson, T., Harrison, L., Krishnamurthi, S., Dougherty, D.J.: User studies of principled model finder output. In: Cimatti, A., Sirjani, M. (eds.) SEFM 2017. LNCS, vol. 10469, pp. 168–184. Springer, Cham (2017). https://doi.org/10.1007/978-3-319-66197-1_11
13. Dyer, T., Nelson, T., Fisler, K., Krishnamurthi, S.: Applying cognitive principles to model-finding output: the positive value of negative information. Proc. ACM Program. Lang. **6**(OOPSLA1), 1–29 (2022)
14. Galeotti, J.P., Rosner, N., Pombo, C.G.L., Frias, M.F.: TACO: efficient SAT-based bounded verification using symmetry breaking and tight bounds. TSE (2013)
15. Gopinath, D., Malik, M.Z., Khurshid, S.: Specification-based program repair using SAT. In: Abdulla, P.A., Leino, K.R.M. (eds.) TACAS 2011. LNCS, vol. 6605, pp. 173–188. Springer, Heidelberg (2011). https://doi.org/10.1007/978-3-642-19835-9_15
16. Gutiérrez Brida, S., et al.: ICEBAR: feedback-driven iterative repair of alloy specifications. Association for Computing Machinery, New York, NY, USA (2023)
17. Jackson, D.: Software Abstractions: Logic, Language, and Analysis. The MIT Press (2006)
18. Jackson, D., Vaziri, M.: Finding bugs with a constraint solver. In: ISSTA, August 2000
19. Jovanovic, A., Sullivan, A.: Reach: refining alloy scenarios by size (tools and artifact track). In: 2022 IEEE 33rd International Symposium on Software Reliability Engineering (ISSRE), pp. 229–238 (2022)
20. Jovanovic, A., Sullivan, A.: Mutation testing for temporal alloy models. In: 26th ACM/IEEE International Conference on Model Driven Engineering Languages and Systems, MODELS, pp. 228–238 (2023)

21. Krishnamurthi, S., Nelson, T.: The human in formal methods. In: ter Beek, M.H., McIver, A., Oliveira, J.N. (eds.) FM 2019. LNCS, vol. 11800, pp. 3–10. Springer, Cham (2019). https://doi.org/10.1007/978-3-030-30942-8_1
22. Macedo, N., et al.: Experiences on teaching alloy with an automated assessment platform. In: Raschke, A., Méry, D., Houdek, F. (eds.) ABZ 2020. LNCS, vol. 12071, pp. 61–77. Springer, Cham (2020). https://doi.org/10.1007/978-3-030-48077-6_5
23. Mansoor, N., Bagheri, H., Kang, E., Sharif., B.: An empirical study assessing software modeling in alloy. In: International Conference on Formal Methods in Software Engineering, pp. 44–54 (2023)
24. Marinov, D., Khurshid, S.: TestEra: a novel framework for automated testing of Java programs. In: ASE (2001)
25. Nelson, T., Barratt, C., Dougherty, D.J., Fisler, K., Krishnamurthi, S.: The Margrave tool for firewall analysis. In: LISA (2010)
26. Simonot, M.: Teaching abstraction in mathematics and computer science - a computer-supported approach with alloy (2012)
27. Sullivan, A., Wang, K., Zaeem, R.N., Khurshid, S.: Automated test generation and mutation testing for alloy. In: ICST (2017)
28. Sullivan, A., Zaeem, R.N., Khurshid, S., Marinov, D.: Towards a test automation framework for alloy. In: Proceedings of the 2014 SPIN Workshop on Software Model Checking, pp. 113–116 (2014). http://doi.acm.org.ncat.idm.oclc.org/10.1145/2632362.2632369
29. Trippel, C., Lustig, D., Martonosi, M.: Security verification via automatic hardware-aware exploit synthesis: The CheckMate Approach. IEEE Micro (2019)
30. Wang, K., Sullivan, A., Khurshid, S.: Automated model repair for Alloy. In: ASE (2018)
31. Wang, K., Sullivan, A., Khurshid, S.: MuAlloy: a mutation testing framework for alloy. In: Proceedings of the 40th International Conference on Software Engineering (ICSE) Demo Track, pp. 29–32 (2018). https://doi.org/10.1145/3183440.3183488
32. Wang, K., Sullivan, A., Khurshid, S.: Fault localization for declarative models in Alloy. In: ISSRE (2020)
33. Wang, W., Wang, K., Gligoric, M., Khurshid, S.: Incremental analysis of evolving alloy models. In: Vojnar, T., Zhang, L. (eds.) TACAS 2019. LNCS, vol. 11427, pp. 174–191. Springer, Cham (2019). https://doi.org/10.1007/978-3-030-17462-0_10
34. Wickerson, J., Batty, M., Sorensen, T., Constantinides, G.A.: Automatically comparing memory consistency models. In: POPL (2017)
35. Nokhbeh Zaeem, R., Khurshid, S.: Contract-based data structure repair using Alloy. In: D'Hondt, T. (ed.) ECOOP 2010. LNCS, vol. 6183, pp. 577–598. Springer, Heidelberg (2010). https://doi.org/10.1007/978-3-642-14107-2_27
36. Zave, P.: How to make Chord correct (using a stable base). CoRR abs/1502.06461 (2015)
37. Zheng, G., Bagheri, H., Rothermel, G., Wang, J.: Platinum: reusing constraint solutions in bounded analysis of relational logic. In: International Conference on Fundamental Approaches to Software Engineering (2020)
38. Zheng, G., et al.: ATR: template-based repair for alloy specifications. In: Proceedings of the 31st ACM SIGSOFT International Symposium on Software Testing and Analysis, ISSTA 2022. pp. 666–677 (2022)
39. Zheng, G., et al.: Flack: counterexample-guided fault localization for alloy models. In: 2021 IEEE/ACM 43rd International Conference on Software Engineering (ICSE), pp. 637–648 (2021)

An Operational Semantics for Yul

Vasileios Koutavas[1,3], Yu-Yang Lin[1], and Nikos Tzevelekos[2](✉)

[1] Trinity College Dublin, Dublin, Ireland
{Vasileios.Koutavas,linhouy}@tcd.ie
[2] Queen Mary University of London, London, UK
nikos.tzevelekos@qmul.ac.uk
[3] Lero - Science Foundation Ireland Research Centre for Software, Limerick, Ireland

Abstract. We present a big-step and small-step operational semantics for Yul—the intermediate language used by the Solidity compiler to produce EVM bytecode—in a mathematical notation that is congruous with the literature of programming languages, lends itself to language proofs, and can serve as a precise, widely accessible specification for the language. Our two semantics stay faithful to the original, informal specification of the language but also clarify under-specified cases such as void function calls. Our presentation allows us to prove the equivalence between the two semantics. We also implement the small-step semantics in an interpreter for Yul which avails of optimisations that are provably correct. We have tested the interpreter using tests from the Solidity compiler and our own. We envisage that this work will enable the development of verification and symbolic execution technology directly in Yul, contributing to the Ethereum security ecosystem, as well as aid the development of a provably sound future type system.

Keywords: Yul · Ethereum · Operational semantics · Programming languages · Formal methods

1 Introduction

Smart contracts are programs stored on a blockchain, executed within transactions, which read and write data on said blockchain. They form an underpinning technology for decentralised finance applications by enabling the programming of autonomous services offering lending, auction, new cryptocurrency creation, and virtually any type of transactional facilities. On Ethereum—the largest blockchain with the ability to execute them—smart contracts are typically written in a high-level programming language, predominantly Solidity, and then compiled down to Ethereum Virtual Machine (EVM) instructions. Smart contracts already control significant amounts of cryptocurrency[1], making them security-critical software. Numerous documented exploits and bugs have resulted

[1] As of 24 June 2024, DefiLlama (https://defillama.com/chain/Ethereum) lists a Total Value Locked (TVL) of USD 59.937bn, equal to ETH 17.31 m, on Ethereum.

A. Madeira and A. Knapp (Eds.): SEFM 2024, LNCS 15280, pp. 328–346, 2025.
https://doi.org/10.1007/978-3-031-77382-2_19

in the loss of billions of dollars worth of cryptocurrency for users [1,15,37], making smart contract correctness and security a problem of critical importance, especially since smart contracts are immutable once deployed on the blockchain.

The Solidity compiler team recently introduced Yul, an intermediate representation (IR) language sitting between Solidity and EVM bytecode, with one of its stated goals being to help with the implementation of formal verification and optimisation techniques [38]. Although such tools for Ethereum smart contracts exist, they either work with Solidity (e.g. SOLHINT [9], SLITHER [8, 19], ECHIDNA [5,22], GAMBIT [6]) or EVM bytecode (e.g. MYTHRIL [7,36], OYENTE [2,30], MANTICORE [4,33]), making them hard to develop and maintain because of the feature-rich, often evolving syntax of the former, or the low-level stack- and jump-based design of the latter. Thus, Yul is designed on a small number of high-level constructs—loops, functions, conditional/switch and local variables—avoiding stack and jump complexity, and includes flexible, dialect-specific built-ins and data types.[2] All modern Solidity code can be compiled to Yul through the Solidity compiler, and almost all existing EVM bytecode can be decompiled to it [21].

In order for Yul to serve its intended purpose, it needs to have precise formal semantics on which formal verification techniques can be developed and optimisations can be proven correct. The official documentation of Yul [38][3] only provides an informal description of the language, its grammar, scoping rules, and its operational semantics in terms of an evaluation function written in pseudocode. Although sufficient to understand the intent of the language constructs, the documentation is not a rigorous enough specification of Yul on which to base formal proofs. As an example, the operational semantics in the documentation does not explicitly handle the case for calling functions with no return variables, which must be treated as statements rather than expressions (cf. Sect. 3.5 and Remark 10).

A number of mechanisations of the intended semantics of Yul in formal tools have appeared online. These include a shallow embedding of Yul into Dafny [11,12], and deep embeddings into the K-framework [18], Isabelle/HOL [3], Lean [34], and ACL2 [25]. Although these contribute significantly towards the goal of giving a solid mathematical footing for the semantics of Yul, they have inherent shortcomings. Besides not being peer-reviewed, their main drawback is that in order to understand these mechanisations, one is required to have working knowledge of the formal tools used, something that, although increasingly more common, is not universal among those who have received training in programming languages. Moreover, the tools used lend themselves more readily to mechanically formalising the details of various semantics rather than communicating them to experts. For example, the mechanisations of Yul contain explicit implementation of mathematical details that are conceptually straightforward (e.g. pattern-matching and manipulation of low-level dependencies such as sets, map-

[2] Although currently Yul is used only with EVM primitives, it is designed to be parametric to a *dialect* specifying the data types and machine instructions.

[3] Current latest version and the one accessed is v0.8.26 of the Solidity compiler.

pings, lists, etc.), making them too lengthy and complex to serve as a high-level model of the language. Moreover, formalisation tools often incur engineering considerations that arise from their specific framework or underlying theories, which may require reshaping the presentation into a less standard form. Finally, to even write a mechanisation of the Yul semantics one must first have a conceptual mathematical model of the language, which to our knowledge does not yet publicly exist. All this makes the existing Yul mechanisations hard to understand or trust as being equivalent to each other, which limits their suitability as definitive presentations of the semantics of Yul. For these reasons, we believe that the development of a diverse tool ecosystem for Yul would benefit from a more abstract, widely understandable standard mathematical model thereof.

In this paper we contribute to this direction by providing two mathematical semantics of the language in textbook notation that, staying faithful to the intent of the original informal specification, can serve as a useful, widely understood, precise reference document. We hope our work will aid future formal verification research and implementations for Yul, contribute to the evolution of the language—such as when the community decides to introduce a type system and prove its soundness—and assist in validating existing mechanisations by providing a more abstract model to compare them to.

We present here an abstract syntax of Yul (Sect. 2), together with both a big-step and small-step operational semantics (Sect. 3), and prove their correspondence (Sect. 4). We choose to present both styles of semantics because a big-step semantics is typically more intuitive and human-readable, and more readily relates to the informal specification of Yul, while a small-step semantics is easier to implement, especially in interpreters and symbolic execution tools. Note that we present only the semantics for Yul, which is given separately from the semantics of EVM bytecode and dialect-specific notation such as objects. As mentioned earlier, this is because Yul is intended to be parametric to the specific dialect implemented. We also present a modular implementation of the semantics of Yul in the form of an interpreter that is parametric on a given dialect and avails of optimisations that are provably correct (Sect. 5). At the moment, this interpreter includes a subset of the semantics of the Shanghai upgrade of EVM as its only dialect, which is sufficient to evaluate the correctness of our semantics experimentally. As such, our prototype interpreter only executes *closed* programs that make use of a subset of the instructions available to the EVM. We evaluate our implementation with sample implementations of standard algorithms and tests from the Solidity compiler. Finally, we discuss related work (Sect. 6) and conclusions (Sect. 7). Our work has been motivated by our ongoing efforts to implement a complete symbolic execution engine of EVM-dialect Yul, which would not have been possible without the semantics presented herein.

2 Yul Syntax

Yul is designed to be a highly readable language with simple syntax and semantics that is as direct to transform into bytecode as possible. Yul achieves these

$$\begin{array}{ll}\textsf{Stmt:} & S ::= \{S^*\} \mid \textsf{function}\, x\,(\vec{x}) \!\rightarrow\! \vec{x}\{S^*\} \mid \textsf{let}\ \vec{x}\!:=\!M \mid \vec{x}\!:=\!M \mid M \mid \textsf{if}\, M\{S^*\} \\ & \quad \mid \textsf{switch}\, M(\textsf{case}\, v\{S^*\})^*\textsf{default}\{S^*\} \mid \textsf{for}\{S^*\}M\{S^*\}\{S^*\} \\ & \quad \mid \textsf{break} \mid \textsf{continue} \mid \textsf{leave} \\ \textsf{Exp:} & M ::= x(\vec{M}) \mid \mathit{op}\,(\vec{M}) \mid x \mid v \qquad \textsf{Val:}\ u, v, c \qquad \textsf{Var:}\ x, y, z, f\end{array}$$

Fig. 1. Yul source-level syntax.

goals by providing high-level syntax that replaces EVM's (the primary target of the language) low-level jumps for control flow, and explicit stack operations for variable management.

We define the *source-level* abstract syntax of Yul; that is, the syntax of Yul programs, in Fig. 1. The grammar in this figure ranges over (dialect-specific) values or constants with u, v, c, variables/identifiers with x, y, z, statements with S and expressions with M, and variants thereof. We use vector syntax (e.g. $\vec{x}$) to mean a comma-separated, consecutively-indexed list of syntax $(x_1, x_2, \ldots, x_n)$, and the Kleene star (e.g. S^*) to mean consecutively-indexed juxtaposition of syntax without commas $(S_1 S_2 \ldots S_m)$. We next explain the syntactical constructs and their intention.

- **Block statement:** $\{S^*\}$. These are sequences of statements that are to be executed one after the other unless a halting statement is encountered.
- **Function definition:** $\textsf{function}\, x\,(\vec{x}_a) \!\rightarrow\! \vec{x}_r\{S^*\}$.

These contain the function name x, vectors of argument, $\vec{x}_a$, and return, $\vec{x}_r$, variables, and a function body block $\{S^*\}$. Functions can return zero (hereafter referred to as void functions), one, or a tuple of values (multi-value functions). Blocks are leveraged to define the scope of variables in a function call. Actual arguments are assigned to $\vec{x}_a$ when entering, and return values are those assigned to $\vec{x}_r$ when exiting, the function block. Nested function declarations are allowed by Yul's specification [38].

- **Variable declaration/assignment:** $\textsf{let}\ \vec{x}\!:=\!M$ / $\vec{x}\!:=\!M$. Their behaviour is identical except for the conditions involved: $\vec{x}$ cannot be in scope if declared with a let-statement and must be in scope for standard assignment. The syntax allows for multi-value assignment, with M being an expression which must match the arity of $\vec{x}$. As tuples are not part of the source-level syntax, they can only occur as a result of calling a multi-value function. Tuples do not appear in Fig. 1 but will be introduced in the runtime syntax in Sect. 3. The Yul specification [38] allows for uninitialised declarations. For simplicity we consider these to be syntactic sugar for function calls returning the correct arity of zeros.
- **Conditional statement:** $\textsf{if}\, M\{S^*\}$. M must evaluate to a constant that represents either $\textsf{tt}$ or $\textsf{ff}$, and $\{S^*\}$ is a block for scoping reasons; there are no else-branches in conditionals.
- **Switch statement:** $\textsf{switch}\, M(\textsf{case}\, v\{S^*\})^*\textsf{default}\{S^*_d\}$. If M evaluates to constant v_i then block $\{S^*_i\}$ executes, otherwise $\{S^*_d\}$ does.

- **Loop:** $\texttt{for}\{S_i^*\}M\{S_p^*\}\{S_b^*\}$. Loops comprise an initialisation block $\{S_i^*\}$, a conditional expression M which evaluates to tt or ff at each iteration, a post-iteration block $\{S_p^*\}$ for updating loop variables, and a loop body $\{S_b^*\}$.
- **Halting statement:** break, continue, leave. These are control-flow statements; break and continue may only occur in the body of the innermost loop that contains them, and outside of any function defined in that loop body. They are used to exit (break) said loop or skip the rest of the loop body and continue to the post-iteration block (continue). Statement leave only occurs inside function bodies and exits the current function.
- **Function call expression:** $x(\vec{M})$. A function call is normally a part of an expression and returns a single value. However there are two special cases of note: (1) a function call can appear as the expression of a multi-value declaration/assignment and must return a tuple of values of the correct arity; (2) a void function call that appears at the place of a statement, in which case it must return regular (i.e. similar to void or unit values in other languages—see Sect. 3); this is the only allowed expression that can appear at the place of a statement. Arguments are evaluated *right-to-left*.
- **Opcode execution expression:** $op(\vec{M})$. These are calls to dialect-specific instructions external to Yul. Like function calls, arguments are evaluated right-to-left and return zero, one, or multiple values. Unlike function calls, opcodes may return exceptional values which form part of the dialect, not named by the Yul specification. We will treat them as abnormal program exit values in our small-step semantics in the following section.

Example 1. To illustrate the source-level language, consider a naive recursive implementation of a Fibonacci term generator. Note that in Yul double forward slashes are comments.

```
{ // Function that computes Fibonacci via naive recursion
  function fibonacci_rec(n) -> result {
    if lt(n,3) {
        result := 1
    }
    if gt(n,2) {
        result := add(fibonacci_rec(sub(n,1)),fibonacci_rec(sub(n,2)))
    }
  } // Call Fibonacci with 10
  let fib_10 := fibonacci_rec(10)
  mstore(0x00, fib_10)
}
```

In the program above, the function `fibonacci_rec` computes the n-th Fibonacci number, where `lt`/`gt`, `add`/`sub` and `mstore` are comparison, arithmetic and memory instructions respectively. These are opcodes in the EVM dialect of Yul. Functions do not require a return statement. Instead, the defined output variable `result` is assigned and its value returned at the end. Nesting function calls within opcode/function calls is allowed, and is only constrained by the stack limit of the underlying dialect (the EVM stack limit is 1024 words). The program computes the 10th Fibonacci term and stores it at position `0x00` in EVM memory. ■

Remark 2 (Typing). Although simple checks are in place in the Solidity compiler, such as for the arity of function arguments/returns, Yul at the moment provides no formal specification for a type system. Its default dialect involves only EVM bytecode operations with a single value type of 256-bit unsigned integers (U256). While the Yul source language involves literals of various kinds (such as hex literals), there is an implicit assumption that these are appropriately translated into values of the underlying dialect—e.g. U256 for the EVM dialect.

Remark 3 (Dialects). As mentioned in the Introduction, because Yul is meant to be target-independent, it is designed to be modular with regards to multiple so-called dialects. Each dialect in Yul would in principle be defined in relation to the specific back-end bytecode that it is meant to compile into. For this purpose, dialects amount to a collection of machine opcodes that remain after excluding those associated with control flow and variable management, and the respective value types used by said opcodes. Thus, while we use tt and ff values in our semantics, these do not necessarily represent boolean values; instead they are placeholders for whichever values are considered true and false in a given dialect. For instance, in the EVM dialect, zero represents ff while non-zero values are considered tt. This is a conceptually simple mapping that entails a variety of subtle behaviours one has to be careful about in the EVM (e.g. negating a "true" value does not make it a "false" one, as negation is bit-wise and could produce another non-zero value).

3 Yul Semantics

In this section we present big- and small-step semantics for Yul. We present them together, grouped thematically under rules for blocks, variable manipulation, branching statements, loops, and expressions. For small-step semantics specifically, we additionally define top-level rules that carry around the evaluation contexts and handle external opcode instructions. We prove the correspondence of the two semantics in Sect. 4. For both semantics, we shall use configurations of the form:

$$\langle S \mid G ; L ; \mathcal{N} \rangle$$

with the following components:

- **Statement** S (or *term*) being evaluated. Statements are drawn from an extended *operational syntax* defined in Fig. 2 (top), and discussed further below.
- **Global environment** G that is external to the semantics of Yul itself, and in the context of smart contracts is meant to contain the state of the blockchain, the data of external calls to a smart contract, etc.; G will be passed as state by the semantics of Yul and may change only by calls to dialect opcodes.
- **Local state** L of all variables. This is a dictionary $L : x \mapsto v$. All variables in scope for the term being evaluated will be in L.
- **Namespace** $\mathcal{N}$ of all functions visible to the term being evaluated. This is like a function repository $\mathcal{N} : x \mapsto (\vec{x}_a, \vec{x}_r, S_b)$ for all the functions in scope.

$$\begin{array}{rl} \textsf{Stmt:} & S ::= \ldots \mid \textsf{regular} \mid \mathcal{M} \mid \{\vec{S}\}^{\mathcal{N}}_{L} \mid [\![S]\!]_{\textsf{brk}} \mid [\![S]\!]_{\textsf{cnt}} \mid (\!|S|\!)^{\vec{x}}_{L} \\ \textsf{Exp:} & M ::= \ldots \mid <\vec{v}> \\ \textsf{Mode:} & \mathbb{M} ::= \textsf{break} \mid \textsf{continue} \mid \textsf{leave} \mid \textsf{regular} \mid \mathcal{M} \\ \textsf{ExMode:} & \mathcal{M} \end{array}$$

$$\begin{array}{rl} \textsf{SCxt:} & E ::= [\cdot] \mid \{E, \vec{S}\}^{\mathcal{N}}_{L} \mid \textsf{let}\ \vec{x}\texttt{:=}E \mid \vec{x}\texttt{:=}E \mid E_{\textsf{Exp}} \mid [\![E]\!]_{\textsf{cnt}} \mid [\![E]\!]_{\textsf{brk}} \mid \textsf{if}\ E_{\textsf{Exp}}\{S^*\} \\ & \quad \mid \textsf{switch}\ E_{\textsf{Exp}}(\textsf{case}\ v\{S^*\})^*\textsf{default}\{S^*\} \\ \textsf{ECxt:} & E_{\textsf{Exp}} ::= [\cdot] \mid x(\vec{M}, E_{\textsf{Exp}}, \vec{v}) \mid op\,(\vec{M}, E_{\textsf{Exp}}, \vec{v}) \mid (\!|E|\!)^{\vec{x}}_{L} \end{array}$$

Fig. 2. Yul operational syntax (omitting constructs shown in Fig. 1).

Next, we describe the extended syntax for statements which adds regular, representing the successful completion of a statement, and the following statements that arise from certain small-step reductions (cf. Definition 6):

- **Block scoping:** $\{\vec{S}\}^{\mathcal{N}}_{L}$. This is used to implement the scoping rules for blocks and are distinct from source-level blocks $\{S^*\}$. Here $\mathcal{N}$ records functions and L variables in scope before entering a block, needed when reinstating this scope after exiting the block.
- **Break/continue catching:** $[\![S]\!]_{\textsf{brk}}$ / $[\![S]\!]_{\textsf{cnt}}$. These catch break and continue statements respectively within loop body blocks.
- **Function call framing:** $(\!|S|\!)^{\vec{x}}_{L}$. These encode function call frames by remembering the L at call site and the return variables $\vec{x}$. At return, L is used to restrict the domain and ensure correct scoping (similar to blocks) and $\vec{x}$ is used to retrieve the function return values. Function calls do not need to reinstate $\mathcal{N}$; this is done indirectly via the block of the function body (see Sect. 3.5 and Example 9).

We also extend expressions M with tuples $<\vec{v}>$, needed for multi-value assignments and function returns, which are defined when $|\vec{v}| > 1$. Finally, we introduce *modes* $\mathbb{M}$, as in the Yul specification, which can signal regular termination (regular), e.g. of a void function call, break/continue modes for for-loops, and leave mode for returning early from functions. Modes also include *external irregular modes* $\mathcal{M}$ that may be returned by opcode evaluation. These are parametric to the Yul semantics and depend on the specific dialect implemented.

In Fig. 2 (bottom) we define statement (SCxt) and expression (ECxt) evaluation contexts for our small-step semantics. Most evaluation contexts are derived in a standard way from the syntax of the language and implement correct evaluation order in small-step semantics. For example block statements are evaluated left-to-right, whereas function and opcode call arguments are evaluated right-to-left. The inclusion of function call contexts $(\!|E|\!)^{\vec{x}}_{L}$ encodes a call stack in our small-step semantics. As functions have a fresh variable scope when they are called, the surrounding scope L of the caller must be recorded and reinstated at function return. The return variables must also be recorded to be returned to the caller.

In the following subsections we present the rules of the big- and small-step semantics of Yul, grouped by the kind of term they handle. These rules precisely define the predicates of the next two definitions.

Definition 4 (Big-step semantics). *We define a big-step semantics on successful executions of statements that do not result in external irregular modes:*

$$\langle S \mid G\,; L\,; \mathcal{N} \rangle \Downarrow \langle \mathbb{M} \mid G'\,; L'\,; \mathcal{N}' \rangle$$

We additionally define variants thereof for the evaluation of:

- *sequences of statements within blocks,* $\langle \vec{S} \mid G\,; L\,; \mathcal{N} \rangle \Downarrow_{\mathsf{seq}} \langle \mathbb{M} \mid G'\,; L'\,; \mathcal{N}' \rangle$
- *expressions,* $\langle M \mid G\,; L\,; \mathcal{N} \rangle \Downarrow_{\mathsf{exp}} \langle S' \mid G'\,; L'\,; \mathcal{N}' \rangle$*, where* $S' \in \{v, <\vec{v}>, \mathsf{regular}\}$

The above are concretely defined by the top rules in Fig. 3 to Fig. 7. We also assume a dialect-specific reduction relation for opcodes denoted by $\Downarrow_{\mathsf{opc}}$*.*

Remark 5. Although it would have been possible to define big-step rules to deal with propagation of external irregular modes, we follow standard practice and define $\Downarrow$ only on successful computation, excluding irregular modes. We do handle these modes in the small-step semantics, which more closely specifies an interpreter for the language.

Definition 6 (Small-step semantics). *We write*

$$\langle S \mid G; L\,; \mathcal{N} \rangle \rightarrow \langle S' \mid G'; L'\,; \mathcal{N}' \rangle$$

for a small-step transition in our small-step semantics. When a transition does not change G (as only opcode execution does) we omit G from the configurations. The reduction rules are shown in the bottom part of Fig. 3 to Fig. 7, with the additional top-level rules:

(1) $\langle E[S] \mid G; L\,; \mathcal{N} \rangle \rightarrow \langle E[S'] \mid G'; L'\,; \mathcal{N}' \rangle$ *if* $\langle S \mid G; L\,; \mathcal{N} \rangle \rightarrow \langle S' \mid G'; L'\,; \mathcal{N}' \rangle$
(2) $\langle E[\mathcal{M}] \mid G; L\,; \mathcal{N} \rangle \rightarrow \langle \mathcal{M} \mid G; L\,; \mathcal{N} \rangle$

The top-level rules decompose the term to an evaluation context with an inner statement in its hole that can either: (1) perform a Yul reduction, or (2) is an irregular return mode that terminates the program. We next present the rules for small- and big-step semantics for each type of term.

3.1 Block Statements

The first rules are those for blocks, shown in Fig. 3. Blocks sequentially execute statements and define a local namespace for variables and functions. The big-step semantics handles function scoping in the BLOCK rule, where the existing function namespace $\mathcal{N}$ is extended by the functions defined in the block (given by $\mathcal{N}_1 = \mathsf{funs}(\{S_1..S_n\})$), and block statements are evaluated under $\mathcal{N} \uplus \mathcal{N}_1$.

$$\frac{\mathcal{N}_1 = \mathsf{funs}(\{S_1..S_n\}) \qquad \langle S_1, .., S_n \mid G ; L ; \mathcal{N} \uplus \mathcal{N}_1\rangle \Downarrow_{\mathsf{seq}} \langle \mathbb{M} \mid G_1 ; L_1 ; \mathcal{N} \uplus \mathcal{N}_1\rangle}{\langle \{S_1..S_n\} \mid G ; L ; \mathcal{N}\rangle \Downarrow \langle \mathbb{M} \mid G_1 ; L_1 \restriction L ; \mathcal{N}\rangle} \textsc{Block}$$

$$\frac{}{\langle \varepsilon \mid G ; L ; \mathcal{N}\rangle \Downarrow_{\mathsf{seq}} \langle \mathsf{regular} \mid G ; L ; \mathcal{N}\rangle} \textsc{SeqEmpty}$$

$$\frac{\langle S_1 \mid G ; L ; \mathcal{N}\rangle \Downarrow \langle \mathsf{regular} \mid G_1 ; L_1 ; \mathcal{N}\rangle \quad \langle \vec{S} \mid G_1 ; L_1 ; \mathcal{N}\rangle \Downarrow_{\mathsf{seq}} \langle \mathbb{M} \mid G_2 ; L_2 ; \mathcal{N}\rangle}{\langle S_1, \vec{S} \mid G ; L ; \mathcal{N}\rangle \Downarrow_{\mathsf{seq}} \langle \mathbb{M} \mid G_2 ; L_2 ; \mathcal{N}\rangle} \textsc{SeqR}$$

$$\frac{\langle S_1 \mid G ; L ; \mathcal{N}\rangle \Downarrow \langle \mathbb{M} \mid G_1 ; L_1 ; \mathcal{N}\rangle \qquad \mathbb{M} \in \{\mathsf{break}, \mathsf{continue}, \mathsf{leave}\}}{\langle S_1, \vec{S} \mid G ; L ; \mathcal{N}\rangle \Downarrow_{\mathsf{seq}} \langle \mathbb{M} \mid G_1 ; L_1 ; \mathcal{N}\rangle} \textsc{SeqI}$$

$$\frac{}{\langle \mathsf{function}\, x\,(\vec{y}) \to \vec{z}\, S \mid G ; L ; \mathcal{N}\rangle \Downarrow \langle \mathsf{regular} \mid G ; L ; \mathcal{N}\rangle} \textsc{FunDecl}$$

BStart : $\langle \{S_1..S_n\} \mid L ; \mathcal{N}\rangle \to \langle \{S_1, .., S_n\}^{\mathcal{N}}_{L} \mid L ; \mathcal{N} \uplus \mathcal{N}_1\rangle$ if $\mathcal{N}_1 = \mathsf{funs}(\{S_1..S_n\}), n > 0$

BEmpty : $\langle \{\} \mid L ; \mathcal{N}\rangle \to \langle \mathsf{regular} \mid L ; \mathcal{N}\rangle$

SCnt : $\langle \{\mathsf{regular}, \vec{S}\}^{\mathcal{N}}_{L} \mid L_1 ; \mathcal{N}_1\rangle \to \langle \{\vec{S}\}^{\mathcal{N}}_{L} \mid L_1 ; \mathcal{N}_1\rangle$ if $\vec{S} \neq \epsilon$

SReg : $\langle \{\mathsf{regular}\}^{\mathcal{N}}_{L} \mid L_1 ; \mathcal{N}_1\rangle \to \langle \mathsf{regular} \mid L_1 \restriction L ; \mathcal{N}\rangle$

SIrreg : $\langle \{\mathbb{M}, \vec{S}\}^{\mathcal{N}}_{L} \mid L_1 ; \mathcal{N}_1\rangle \to \langle \mathbb{M} \mid L_1 \restriction L ; \mathcal{N}\rangle$ if $\mathbb{M} \in \{\mathsf{break}, \mathsf{continue}, \mathsf{leave}\}$

FDef : $\langle \mathsf{function}\, x\,(\vec{y})\, \vec{z}\, S \mid L ; \mathcal{N}\rangle \to \langle \mathsf{regular} \mid L ; \mathcal{N}\rangle$

Fig. 3. Big-step (top) and small-step (bottom) block semantics. Note that G is omitted in small-step rules that leave it unchanged (cf. Definition 6).

Moreover, any new variables defined within the scope (discussed in the following subsection), are pruned in the resulting configuration of the rule by $L_1 \restriction L$, which restricts the variable environment L_1 to only the variables in L. Rules SeqEmpty, SeqR (regular case) and SeqI (irregular case) handle the sequencing of statement execution with the last one skipping all remaining statements in a sequence if a Yul mode other than regular is encountered, which causes early exit from a loop iteration, an entire loop, or a function body. Function declarations are ignored by rule FunDecl, as these are put in scope by the Block rule.

On the small-step side, we make use of a context $\{\ldots\}^{\mathcal{N}}_{L}$ that remembers the variable and function namespaces to handle scoping. This context is introduced when a block is entered and removed (with the appropriate scope restriction) when exiting the block. Note that, in this semantics and the Yul specification, functions do not need to be declared before being called, as long as they are in the same, or surrounding, block of the call.

Remark 7 (Block optimisation). It is sound to simplify any $\{\ldots\{\{\cdot\}^{\mathcal{N}}_{L_1}\}^{\mathcal{N}}_{L_2}\ldots\}^{\mathcal{N}}_{L_n}$ to $\{\cdot\}^{\mathcal{N}}_{L}$, provided $\mathsf{dom}(L_1) = \ldots = \mathsf{dom}(L_n)$, avoiding redundant block-exit reductions. However, this may not provide a performance gain as calculating equality of domains can be costlier than the additional reductions.

$$\frac{\langle M \mid G\,;L\,;\mathcal{N}\rangle \Downarrow_{\mathsf{exp}} \langle v \mid G_1\,;L_1\,;\mathcal{N}\rangle \qquad x \notin \mathsf{dom}(L)}{\langle \mathsf{let}\; x\mathtt{:=}M \mid G\,;L\,;\mathcal{N}\rangle \Downarrow \langle \mathsf{regular} \mid G_1\,;L_1[x \mapsto v]\,;\mathcal{N}\rangle}\ \textsc{VarDecl}$$

$$\frac{\langle M \mid G\,;L\,;\mathcal{N}\rangle \Downarrow_{\mathsf{exp}} \langle \mathtt{<}\vec{v}\mathtt{>} \mid G_1\,;L_1\,;\mathcal{N}\rangle \qquad \vec{x} \notin \mathsf{dom}(L)}{\langle \mathsf{let}\; \vec{x}\mathtt{:=}M \mid G\,;L\,;\mathcal{N}\rangle \Downarrow \langle \mathsf{regular} \mid G_1\,;L_1[\vec{x} \mapsto \vec{v}]\,;\mathcal{N}\rangle}\ \textsc{TupleDecl}$$

$$\textsc{TDecl} : \langle \mathsf{let}\; \vec{x}\mathtt{:=<}\vec{v}\mathtt{>} \mid L\,;\mathcal{N}\rangle \to \langle \mathsf{regular} \mid L[\vec{x} \mapsto \vec{v}]\,;\mathcal{N}\rangle \text{ if } \vec{x} \notin \mathsf{dom}(L)$$

$$\textsc{VDecl} : \langle \mathsf{let}\; x\mathtt{:=}v \mid L\,;\mathcal{N}\rangle \to \langle \mathsf{regular} \mid L[x \mapsto v]\,;\mathcal{N}\rangle \quad \text{ if } x \notin \mathsf{dom}(L)$$

Fig. 4. Big-step (top) and small-step (bottom) declaration semantics. Similar rules for assignments (e.g. $\vec{x}\mathtt{:=<}\vec{v}\mathtt{>}$, with $\vec{x} \in \mathsf{dom}(L)$) omitted for economy.

$$\frac{\langle M \mid G\,;L\,;\mathcal{N}\rangle \Downarrow_{\mathsf{exp}} \langle \mathsf{ff} \mid G_0\,;L_0\,;\mathcal{N}\rangle}{\langle \mathsf{if}\; MS \mid G\,;L\,;\mathcal{N}\rangle \Downarrow \langle \mathsf{regular} \mid G_0\,;L_0\,;\mathcal{N}\rangle}\ \textsc{IfFalse}$$

$$\frac{\langle M \mid G\,;L\,;\mathcal{N}\rangle \Downarrow_{\mathsf{exp}} \langle \mathsf{tt} \mid G_0\,;L_0\,;\mathcal{N}\rangle \qquad \langle S \mid G_0\,;L_0\,;\mathcal{N}\rangle \Downarrow \langle \mathbb{M} \mid G_1\,;L_1\,;\mathcal{N}\rangle}{\langle \mathsf{if}\; MS \mid G\,;L\,;\mathcal{N}\rangle \Downarrow \langle \mathbb{M} \mid G_1\,;L_1\,;\mathcal{N}\rangle}\ \textsc{IfTrue}$$

$$\frac{\langle M \mid G\,;L\,;\mathcal{N}\rangle \Downarrow_{\mathsf{exp}} \langle v \mid G_0\,;L_0\,;\mathcal{N}\rangle \qquad \langle S_d \mid G_0\,;L_0\,;\mathcal{N}\rangle \Downarrow \langle \mathbb{M} \mid G_1\,;L_1\,;\mathcal{N}\rangle}{\langle \mathsf{switch}\; MC_1..C_n\mathsf{default}S_d \mid G\,;L\,;\mathcal{N}\rangle \Downarrow \langle \mathbb{M} \mid G_1\,;L_1\,;\mathcal{N}\rangle}\ \textsc{SwD}$$

$$\frac{\langle M \mid G\,;L\,;\mathcal{N}\rangle \Downarrow_{\mathsf{exp}} \langle c_{n+1} \mid G_0\,;L_0\,;\mathcal{N}\rangle \qquad \langle S_{n+1} \mid G_0\,;L_0\,;\mathcal{N}\rangle \Downarrow \langle \mathbb{M} \mid G_1\,;L_1\,;\mathcal{N}\rangle}{\langle \mathsf{switch}\; MC_1..C_{n+1}..\mathsf{default}S_d \mid G\,;L\,;\mathcal{N}\rangle \Downarrow \langle \mathbb{M} \mid G_1\,;L_1\,;\mathcal{N}\rangle}\ \textsc{SwC}$$

$$\textsc{IfFalse} : \langle \mathsf{if}\; \mathsf{ff}\; S \mid L\,;\mathcal{N}\rangle \to \langle \mathsf{regular} \mid L\,;\mathcal{N}\rangle \qquad \textsc{IfTrue} : \langle \mathsf{if}\; \mathsf{tt}\; S \mid L\,;\mathcal{N}\rangle \to \langle S \mid L\,;\mathcal{N}\rangle$$

$$\textsc{SwDeflt} : \langle \mathsf{switch}\; v\, C_1..C_n\mathsf{default}\; S_d \mid L\,;\mathcal{N}\rangle \to \langle S_d \mid L\,;\mathcal{N}\rangle$$

$$\textsc{SwCase} : \langle \mathsf{switch}\; c_{n+1}\, C_1..C_{n+1}..\mathsf{default}\; S_d \mid L\,;\mathcal{N}\rangle \to \langle S_{n+1} \mid L\,;\mathcal{N}\rangle$$

Fig. 5. Big-step (top) and small-step (bottom) branching semantics. For switch rules we assume side conditions: $C_i = \mathsf{case}\, c_i S_i$ and $v, c_{n+1} \notin \{c_1, .., c_n\}$.

3.2 Variable Manipulation Statements

Single- and multi-value variable declaration are handled by the rules in Fig. 4. Assignment rules are similar, with the only differences being that the statement is missing the let-keyword, and the side condition in all rules requires $x \in \mathsf{dom}(L)$ (or $\vec{x} \in \mathsf{dom}(L)$) instead of $x \notin \mathsf{dom}(L)$ (resp., $\vec{x} \notin \mathsf{dom}(L)$). These rules behave as expected: they add or update L bindings. Unlike functions, variables must be declared before use. Only function and opcode calls may return multiple values. Although unrestricted in the rules, $\Downarrow_{\mathsf{exp}}$ does not change L.

3.3 Branching Statements

Control branching in Yul is done by conditional and switch statements. Conditionals make use of tt and ff, which are not necessarily boolean values (as Yul is parametric in the dialect types) but, instead, placeholders for values that are to be interpreted correspondingly. We assume a dialect comes equipped with predicates that let us identify which values are tt and ff.

$$\frac{\langle \{S_1..S_n\ \mathsf{for}\{\}MS_pS_b\} \mid G_1\,;L_1\,;\mathcal{N}\rangle \Downarrow \langle \mathbb{M} \mid G_2\,;L_2\,;\mathcal{N}\rangle \qquad n>0}{\langle \mathsf{for}\{S_1..S_n\}MS_pS_b \mid G_1\,;L_1\,;\mathcal{N}\rangle \Downarrow \langle \mathbb{M} \mid G_2\,;L_2\,;\mathcal{N}\rangle}\ \textsc{ForInit}$$

$$\frac{\langle M \mid G\,;L\,;\mathcal{N}\rangle \Downarrow_{\mathsf{exp}} \langle \mathsf{ff} \mid G_1\,;L_1\,;\mathcal{N}\rangle}{\langle \mathsf{for}\{\}MS_pS_b \mid G\,;L\,;\mathcal{N}\rangle \Downarrow \langle \mathsf{regular} \mid G_1\,;L_1\,;\mathcal{N}\rangle}\ \textsc{ForFalse}$$

$$\frac{\langle M \mid G\,;L\,;\mathcal{N}\rangle \Downarrow_{\mathsf{exp}} \langle \mathsf{tt} \mid G_1\,;L_1\,;\mathcal{N}\rangle \quad \langle S_b \mid G_1\,;L_1\,;\mathcal{N}\rangle \Downarrow \langle \mathbb{M}_{lb} \mid G_2\,;L_2\,;\mathcal{N}\rangle}{\langle \mathsf{for}\{\}MS_pS_b \mid G\,;L\,;\mathcal{N}\rangle \Downarrow \langle \mathbb{M}'_{lb} \mid G_2\,;L_2\,;\mathcal{N}\rangle}\ \textsc{Halt1}$$

$$\frac{\begin{array}{c}\langle M \mid G\,;L\,;\mathcal{N}\rangle \Downarrow_{\mathsf{exp}} \langle \mathsf{tt} \mid G_1\,;L_1\,;\mathcal{N}\rangle\\ \langle S_b \mid G_1\,;L_1\,;\mathcal{N}\rangle \Downarrow \langle \mathbb{M}_{\neq lb} \mid G_2\,;L_2\,;\mathcal{N}\rangle \quad \langle S_p \mid G_2\,;L_2\,;\mathcal{N}\rangle \Downarrow \langle \mathsf{leave} \mid G_3\,;L_3\,;\mathcal{N}\rangle\end{array}}{\langle \mathsf{for}\{\}MS_pS_b \mid G\,;L\,;\mathcal{N}\rangle \Downarrow \langle \mathsf{leave} \mid G_3\,;L_3\,;\mathcal{N}\rangle}\ \textsc{Halt2}$$

$$\frac{\begin{array}{c}\langle M \mid G\,;L\,;\mathcal{N}\rangle \Downarrow_{\mathsf{exp}} \langle \mathsf{tt} \mid G_1\,;L_1\,;\mathcal{N}\rangle \qquad \langle S_b \mid G_1\,;L_1\,;\mathcal{N}\rangle \Downarrow \langle \mathbb{M}_{\neq lb} \mid G_2\,;L_2\,;\mathcal{N}\rangle\\ \langle S_p \mid G_2;L_2;\mathcal{N}\rangle \Downarrow \langle \mathsf{regular} \mid G_3;L_3;\mathcal{N}\rangle \quad \langle \mathsf{for}\{\}MS_pS_b \mid G_3;L_3;\mathcal{N}\rangle \Downarrow \langle \mathbb{M} \mid G_4;L_4;\mathcal{N}\rangle\end{array}}{\langle \mathsf{for}\{\}MS_pS_b \mid G\,;L\,;\mathcal{N}\rangle \Downarrow \langle \mathbb{M} \mid G_4\,;L_4\,;\mathcal{N}\rangle}\ \textsc{Loop}$$

$$\begin{array}{ll}
\textsc{FInit}: \langle \mathsf{for}\{S_1..S_n\}MS_pS_b \mid L\,;\mathcal{N}\rangle \to \langle \{S_1..S_n\ \mathsf{for}\{\}MS_pS_b\} \mid L\,;\mathcal{N}\rangle & \text{if } n>0\\
\textsc{FIf}: \langle \mathsf{for}\{\}MS_pS_b \mid L\,;\mathcal{N}\rangle \to \langle [\![\mathsf{if}\ M\{[\![S_b]\!]_{\mathsf{cnt}}S_p\mathsf{for}\{\}MS_pS_b\}]\!]_{\mathsf{brk}} \mid L\,;\mathcal{N}\rangle & \\
\textsc{FCnt1}: \langle [\![\mathbb{M}]\!]_{\mathsf{cnt}} \mid L\,;\mathcal{N}\rangle \to \langle \mathbb{M} \mid L\,;\mathcal{N}\rangle & \text{if } \mathbb{M} \in \{\mathsf{regular}, \mathsf{break}, \mathsf{leave}\}\\
\textsc{FCnt2}: \langle [\![\mathsf{continue}]\!]_{\mathsf{cnt}} \mid L\,;\mathcal{N}\rangle \to \langle \mathsf{regular} \mid L\,;\mathcal{N}\rangle & \\
\textsc{FBrk1}: \langle [\![\mathbb{M}]\!]_{\mathsf{brk}} \mid L\,;\mathcal{N}\rangle \to \langle \mathbb{M} \mid L\,;\mathcal{N}\rangle & \text{if } \mathbb{M} \in \{\mathsf{regular}, \mathsf{leave}\}\\
\textsc{FBrk2}: \langle [\![\mathsf{break}]\!]_{\mathsf{brk}} \mid L\,;\mathcal{N}\rangle \to \langle \mathsf{regular} \mid L\,;\mathcal{N}\rangle &
\end{array}$$

Fig. 6. Big-step (top) and small-step (bottom) loop semantics. Side conditions: $(\mathbb{M}_{lb}, \mathbb{M}'_{lb}) \in \{(\mathsf{leave}, \mathsf{leave}), (\mathsf{break}, \mathsf{regular})\}$, whereas $\mathbb{M}_{\neq lb} \in \{\mathsf{regular}, \mathsf{continue}\}$.

The rules for these statements are given in Fig. 5. On the big-step side, we have standard IfFalse and IfTrue rules for conditionals. Switch statements evaluate expression M to a value v; if v matches c_i from the listed cases, the statement of that case is evaluated (SwC), otherwise the default case statement is (SwD). The same behaviour is captured by standard small-step rules. Source-level syntax requires inner statements in conditional and switch statements be blocks.

3.4 Loop Statements

Loops in Yul consist of four parts: an initialisation block, a condition, a post-iteration block, and a loop-body block. In well-formed Yul programs break and continue may appear only in a loop body. On the other hand, leave may appear in any part of a loop, so long as the loop itself occurs inside a function. The semantics for loops is given in Fig. 6.

Here we once again make use of the semantics of blocks, this time to handle the sequencing of loops. ForInit refactors the initialisation block out of the loop and places the whole loop in a new block that prefixes the initialisation

$$\frac{}{\langle x \mid G\,; L\,; \mathcal{N}\rangle \Downarrow_{\mathsf{exp}} \langle L(x) \mid G\,; L\,; \mathcal{N}\rangle}\ \textsc{Id} \qquad \frac{\langle M \mid G\,; L\,; \mathcal{N}\rangle \Downarrow_{\mathsf{exp}} \langle \mathsf{regular} \mid G'\,; L'\,; \mathcal{N}'\rangle}{\langle M \mid G\,; L\,; \mathcal{N}\rangle \Downarrow \langle \mathsf{regular} \mid G'\,; L'\,; \mathcal{N}'\rangle}\ \textsc{Exp}$$

$$\frac{\begin{array}{c}\langle M_n \,|\, G; L; \mathcal{N}\rangle \Downarrow_{\mathsf{exp}} \langle v_n \,|\, G_1; L_1; \mathcal{N}\rangle \ldots \langle M_1 \,|\, G_{n-1}; L_{n-1}; \mathcal{N}\rangle \Downarrow_{\mathsf{exp}} \langle v_1 \,|\, G_n; L_n; \mathcal{N}\rangle \\ \langle S_b \mid G_n\,; L_f\,; \mathcal{N}\rangle \Downarrow \langle \mathbb{M} \mid G''\,; L'\,; \mathcal{N}\rangle \qquad \mathbb{M} \in \{\mathsf{regular}, \mathsf{leave}\}\end{array}}{\langle f\,(M_1, .., M_n) \mid G\,; L\,; \mathcal{N}\rangle \Downarrow_{\mathsf{exp}} \langle <L'(z_1), .., L'(z_m)> \mid G''\,; L_n\,; \mathcal{N}\rangle}\ \textsc{Fun}$$

$$\frac{\begin{array}{c}\langle M_n \,|\, G; L; \mathcal{N}\rangle \Downarrow_{\mathsf{exp}} \langle v_n \,|\, G_1; L_1; \mathcal{N}\rangle \ldots \langle M_1 \,|\, G_{n-1}; L_{n-1}; \mathcal{N}\rangle \Downarrow_{\mathsf{exp}} \langle v_1 \,|\, G_n; L_n; \mathcal{N}\rangle \\ \langle op\,(v_1, .., v_n) \mid G_n\rangle \Downarrow_{\mathsf{opc}} \langle v_1', .., v_m' \mid G''\rangle\end{array}}{\langle op\,(M_1, .., M_n) \mid G\,; L\,; \mathcal{N}\rangle \Downarrow_{\mathsf{exp}} \langle <v_1', .., v_m'> \mid G''\,; L_n\,; \mathcal{N}\rangle}\ \textsc{Opc}$$

$\textsc{Ident} : \langle x \mid L\,; \mathcal{N}\rangle \rightarrow \langle L(x) \mid L\,; \mathcal{N}\rangle$ if $x \in L$

$\textsc{FCall} : \langle f\,(\vec{v}) \mid L\,; \mathcal{N}\rangle \rightarrow \langle (\!|S_b|\!)^{\vec{z}}_{L} \mid L_f\,; \mathcal{N}\rangle$

$\textsc{FRet} : \langle (\!|\mathbb{M}|\!)^{z_1,..,z_m}_{L} \,|\, L'\,; \mathcal{N}\rangle \rightarrow \langle <L'(z_1), .., L'(z_m)> \,|\, L\,; \mathcal{N}\rangle$ if $\mathbb{M} \in \{\mathsf{leave}, \mathsf{regular}\}$

$\textsc{OpCall} : \langle op\,(\vec{v}) \mid G; L; \mathcal{N}\rangle \rightarrow \langle S' \mid G'; L; \mathcal{N}\rangle$ if $\langle op\,(\vec{v}) \,|\, G\rangle \Downarrow_{\mathsf{opc}} \langle S' \,|\, G'\rangle$ and $S' \in \{<\vec{v}>, \mathcal{M}\}$

Fig. 7. Big-step (top) and small-step (bottom) expression semantics. Side-conditions: $\mathcal{N}(f) = ((y_1, .., y_n), (z_1, .., z_m), S_b)$, $L_f = \{(y_1, .., y_n) \mapsto (v_1, .., v_n)\} \uplus \{\{z_1, .., z_m\} \mapsto 0\}$. For uniformity, we slightly abuse tuple notation to write $<v> = v$ and $<> = \mathsf{regular}$.

statements—the small-step rule mirrors this exactly. Halt1 handles break and leave statements within the loop body, while Halt2 handles leave statements within the post-iteration. Note that continue is handled implicitly by the big-step rules; we piggyback off SeqI in Fig. 3 to exit out of the loop body if continue– i.e. an irregular mode—is encountered. The small-step side handles irregular modes more explicitly: special evaluation contexts $[\![\ldots]\!]_{\mathsf{brk}}$ and $[\![\ldots]\!]_{\mathsf{cnt}}$ are used to encode the frames that check for break and continue respectively. Lastly, note that while Loop directly executes the loop body and otherwise breaks with ForFalse, the small-step equivalent further leverages the semantics of conditional statements to encode this behaviour.

Remark 8 (Break optimisation). Multiple small-step unrollings of a for-loop result in statements containing the pattern $[\![\{[\![\{[\![\ldots\{[\![\cdot]\!]_{\mathsf{brk}}\}^{\mathcal{N}}_{L_n}\cdots]\!]_{\mathsf{brk}}\}^{\mathcal{N}}_{L_2}]\!]_{\mathsf{brk}}\}^{\mathcal{N}}_{L_1}]\!]_{\mathsf{brk}}$ with $\mathsf{dom}(L_1) = \ldots = \mathsf{dom}(L_n)$. Using our semantics we prove that such statements can be simplified by dropping the inner break and block contexts. This has brought significant speedup in the implementation of our interpreter. That is, for any E that contains only interleavings of $[\![\cdot]\!]_{\mathsf{brk}}$ and empty $\{\,\cdot\,\}^{\mathcal{N}}_{L_j}$ contexts with the same $\mathcal{N}$ and domain in all L_j's:

$$\langle [\![E[[\![S']\!]_{\mathsf{brk}}]]\!]_{\mathsf{brk}} \,|\, L'; \mathcal{N}'\rangle \rightarrow^* \langle \mathbb{M} \,|\, L''; \mathcal{N}''\rangle \text{ iff } \langle [\![E[S']]\!]_{\mathsf{brk}} \,|\, L'; \mathcal{N}'\rangle \rightarrow^* \langle \mathbb{M} \,|\, L''; \mathcal{N}''\rangle$$

$$\langle \{E[\{S'\}^{\mathcal{N}}_{L_2}]\}^{\mathcal{N}}_{L_1} \,|\, L'; \mathcal{N}'\rangle \rightarrow^* \langle \mathbb{M} \,|\, L''; \mathcal{N}''\rangle \text{ iff } \langle \{E[S']\}^{\mathcal{N}}_{L_1} \,|\, L'; \mathcal{N}'\rangle \rightarrow^* \langle \mathbb{M} \,|\, L''; \mathcal{N}''\rangle$$

3.5 Expressions

Finally, we define the semantics of expressions, handling variable look-up, function calls and opcode calls. Because of this, they either return values, regular, or an external irregular mode $\mathcal{M}$ if handled. The rules are given in Fig. 7.

ID and its small-step counterpart behave as expected; they look up the value of x within L. Function calls (FUN) on the other hand are less standard. Instead of substitution for function application, calls assign in L the correct value for every argument and then leverage the semantics of blocks to set up the namespace. Similarly, for returns, instead of a return statement, functions assign to the return variables and look up their values in the local L, again leveraging block semantics to clean up the namespace. Note that in FUN, functions may return either a sequence of values if there are return variables, or regular if the function is not expected to return anything (analogous to void functions in C-like languages). As in Sect. 3.2, FUN leaves this unrestricted but argument evaluation does not change L. Opcode calls (OPC) mirror function calls. Note that we do not handle external modes in the big-step semantics. For the small-step transitions involving function calls we introduce a special context $(\!|\ldots|\!)^{\vec{z}}_{L}$. Much like with other special contexts introduced in the small-step semantics, its purpose is to encode within the evaluation context all the frames that form the call stack, including the local state L to reinstate and the return variables $\vec{z}$. Rule EXP allows void function calls to be evaluated as statements. Example 9 illustrates call scoping.

Example 9. Let $\mathcal{N} = f \mapsto ((a,b), r, \{r\,\texttt{:=add}\,(a,b)\,\texttt{function}\,g\,\texttt{()}\,\{\}\})$, $L' = \{a \mapsto 5, b \mapsto 6, r \mapsto 0\}$, $\mathcal{N}' = \mathcal{N} \uplus \{g \mapsto (\varepsilon, \varepsilon, \{\})\}$, and let there be some L.

$$\langle f\,(5,6) \mid L\,;\mathcal{N}\rangle \rightarrow \langle (\!|\{r\,\texttt{:=add}\,(a,b)\,\texttt{function}\,g\,\texttt{()}\,\{\}\}|\!)^{r}_{L} \mid L'\,;\mathcal{N}\rangle$$
$$\rightarrow \langle (\!|\{r\,\texttt{:=add}\,(a,b)\,\texttt{function}\,g\,\texttt{()}\,\{\}\}^{\mathcal{N}}_{L'}|\!)^{r}_{L} \mid L'\,;\mathcal{N}'\rangle$$
$$\rightarrow^{*} \langle (\!|\{\texttt{regular}\}^{\mathcal{N}}_{L'}|\!)^{r}_{L} \mid L'[r \mapsto 11];\mathcal{N}'\rangle \rightarrow \langle (\!|\texttt{regular}|\!)^{r}_{L} \mid L'[r \mapsto 11];\mathcal{N}\rangle \rightarrow \langle 11 \mid L;\mathcal{N}\rangle$$

■

Remark 10 (Undefined void return and modes). The evaluation function provided in the Yul specification [38] is undefined for void function calls. This introduces ambiguity in the intended details of the Yul semantics. We decided to resolve this in a consistent manner to [38], making modes a subset of statements, produced by evaluation, and for regular to be returned by void functions. Since such functions are called in block statements, it was necessary that they return regular in order for the evaluation of subsequent block statements to occur.

4 Semantic Equivalence

Here we show that the big-step and small-step semantics are equivalent. A necessary result is compatibility of the small-step semantics with respect to evaluation contexts.

Lemma 11 (Small-step Compatibility). *Given a context E and reduction $\langle S \mid G\,;L\,;\mathcal{N}\rangle \rightarrow^{*} \langle S' \mid G'\,;L'\,;\mathcal{N}'\rangle$ then $\langle E[S] \mid G; L; \mathcal{N}\rangle \rightarrow^{*} \langle E[S'] \mid G'; L'; \mathcal{N}'\rangle$.*

Proof. This follows by induction on the length of the reduction. □

Theorem 12 (Semantics Equivalence). *Given statement S in source syntax, statement sequence $\vec{S}$, expression M, global environment G, local state L, and function namespace $\mathcal{N}$, then:*

1. $\langle S \,|\, G\,;L\,;\mathcal{N}\rangle \Downarrow \langle \mathbb{M} \,|\, G'\,;L'\,;\mathcal{N}'\rangle$ *iff* $\langle S \,|\, G\,;L\,;\mathcal{N}\rangle \rightarrow^* \langle \mathbb{M} \,|\, G'\,;L'\,;\mathcal{N}'\rangle$
2. $\langle \vec{S} \,|\, G\,;L\,;\mathcal{N}\rangle \Downarrow_{\mathsf{seq}} \langle \mathbb{M} \mid G'\,;L'\,;\mathcal{N}'\rangle$ *iff* $\langle \vec{S} \,|\, G\,;L\,;\mathcal{N}\rangle \rightarrow^* \langle \mathbb{M} \mid G'\,;L'\,;\mathcal{N}'\rangle$
3. $\langle M \mid G\,;L\,;\mathcal{N}\rangle \Downarrow_{\mathsf{exp}} \langle S' \mid G'\,;L'\,;\mathcal{N}'\rangle$ *iff* $\langle M \mid G\,;L\,;\mathcal{N}\rangle \rightarrow^* \langle S' \mid G'\,;L'\,;\mathcal{N}'\rangle$

where $S' \in \{v, <\vec{v}>, \mathsf{regular}\}$.

Proof. We prove the three statements simultaneously in each direction. For the forward direction we proceed by induction on the size of the big-step derivation trees, and for the reverse direction we proceed by induction on the length of the reduction sequences. Here we show the case of function application where $S = f\,(M_1, .., M_n)$ and $\mathcal{N}(f) = (\vec{y}, \vec{z}, S_b)$. We refer to Lemma 11 by SC and the inductive hypothesis by IH.
Forward Direction. We assume the big-step derivation from rule FUN in Fig. 7:

$$\langle f\,(M_1, .., M_n) \mid G\,;L\,;\mathcal{N}\rangle \Downarrow_{\mathsf{exp}} \langle S_{ret} \mid G'\,;L_n\,;\mathcal{N}\rangle$$

with $L_f = \{\vec{y} \mapsto \vec{v}\} \uplus \{\{\vec{z}\} \mapsto 0\}$ and S_{ret} being: $L'(z_1)$ if $|\vec{z}| = 1$; $<L'(z_1), .., L'(z_m)>$ if $|\vec{z}| > 1$; $\mathsf{regular}$ if $|\vec{z}| = 0$. We then obtain the corresponding reduction as follows:

$$\begin{array}{ll}
\langle f\,(M_1, .., M_n) \mid G\,;L\,;\mathcal{N}\rangle & \\
\;\rightarrow^* \langle f\,(M_1, ..M_{n-1}, v_n) \mid G_1\,;L_1\,;\mathcal{N}\rangle & \text{by SC and IH}\langle M_n \mid G\,;L\,;\mathcal{N}\rangle \\
\;\ldots & \\
\;\rightarrow^* \langle f\,(v_1, .., v_n) \mid G_n\,;L_n\,;\mathcal{N}\rangle & \text{by SC and IH}\langle M_1 \mid G_{n-1}\,;L_{n-1}\,;\mathcal{N}\rangle \\
\;\rightarrow \langle (\!|S_b|\!)^{\vec{z}}_{L} \mid G_n\,;L_f\,;\mathcal{N}\rangle & \text{where } \mathcal{N}(f), L_f \text{ as above} \\
\;\rightarrow^* \langle (\!|\mathbb{M}|\!)^{\vec{z}}_{L_n} \mid G'\,;L'\,;\mathcal{N}\rangle & \text{by SC and IH}\langle S_b \mid G_n\,;L_f\,;\mathcal{N}\rangle \\
\;\rightarrow \langle S_{ret} \mid G'\,;L_n\,;\mathcal{N}\rangle &
\end{array}$$

Reverse Direction. For a term $S = f\,(M_1, .., M_n)$, a reduction to S_{ret} requires the intermediate reductions:

$$\begin{array}{l}
\langle f\,(M_1, .., M_n) \mid G_0\,;L_0\,;\mathcal{N}\rangle \rightarrow^* \langle f\,(v_1, .., v_n) \mid G_n\,;L_n\,;\mathcal{N}\rangle \\
\;\rightarrow^* \langle (\!|S_b|\!)^{\vec{z}}_{L_n} \mid G_n\,;L_f\,;\mathcal{N}\rangle \rightarrow^* \langle (\!|\mathbb{M}|\!)^{\vec{z}}_{L_n} \mid G'\,;L''\,;\mathcal{N}\rangle \rightarrow^* \langle S_{ret} \mid G'\,;L_n\,;\mathcal{N}\rangle
\end{array}$$

with $\mathcal{N}(f), L_f, S_{ret}$ as in the forward direction above, and intermediate steps:

$$\langle M_i \mid G_{n-i}\,;L_{n-i}\,;\mathcal{N}\rangle \rightarrow^* \langle v_i \mid G_{n-i+1}\,;L_{n-i+1}\,;\mathcal{N}\rangle \qquad (\mathrm{A}_i)$$

$$\langle S_b \mid G_n\,;L_f\,;\mathcal{N}\rangle \rightarrow^* \langle \mathbb{M} \mid G'\,;L'\,;\mathcal{N}\rangle \qquad (\mathrm{B})$$

To obtain (1), by IH on (A_i): $\langle M_i \mid G_{n-i}\,;L_{n-i}\,;\mathcal{N}\rangle \Downarrow \langle v_i \mid G_{n-i+1}\,;L_{n-i+1}\,;\mathcal{N}\rangle$. Next, by IH on (B): $\langle S_b \mid G_n\,;L_f\,;\mathcal{N}\rangle \Downarrow \langle \mathbb{M} \mid G'\,;L'\,;\mathcal{N}\rangle$. We therefore obtain by FUN: $\langle f\,(M_1, .., M_n) \mid G_0\,;L_0\,;\mathcal{N}\rangle \Downarrow_{\mathsf{exp}} \langle S_{ret} \mid G'\,;L_n\,;\mathcal{N}\rangle$. □

5 Implementation

We implemented YulTracer [27,28], a prototype interpreter based on our operational semantics for Yul that is parametric on dialect implementations. Currently, a partial implementation of the Shanghai upgrade (Solidity 0.8.20 to 0.8.23) of the EVM execution specifications [16] is provided as its sole dialect. We provide opcodes for the following categories: Arithmetic, Bitwise, Comparison, Control-flow, Memory, Stack, and Storage. We omit the implementation of opcodes that are not listed in the official documentation for Yul [38] under version 0.8.23, but otherwise adapt the Python specification to our use as faithfully as possible. YulTracer implements our small-step semantics in the style of CEK machines [20] and is written using OCaml. Modularity for dialects is achieved using functors: a module signature is provided for dialects to satisfy, which are then used to instantiate any concrete implementation of the interpreter.

We evaluate our interpreter using custom tests—1263 Lines of Code (LoC)—and a subset of tests found in the Solidity compiler repository [17]—269 LoC. From the 50 files found under test/libyul/yulInterpreterTests in the Solidity repository (commit 2b2c76c), we kept 19 files that do not make use of unimplemented EVM instructions: opcodes for inter-contract communication in the System category; those in the Block, Environment or Log categories; the opcode for Keccak, which is implemented but unused as it uses a model that requires symbolic execution; or opcodes implemented in the Cancun upgrade (i.e. Solidity 0.8.24) such as those for transient memory or mcopy. From the 19 remaining tests, we mark and omit 3 tests that do not behave according to the official specifications of the EVM; these are: access_large_memory_offsets.yul, which under standard operation would exceed the gas limit when trying to access large offsets but does not; expr_nesting_depth_exceeded.yul, which imposes a nesting limit on expressions that is not specified in the Yul documentation; and hex_literals.yul, which uses underscores _ in hexadecimal strings, not allowed by the official Yul grammar. For our own custom examples, we implemented two categories of programs: sequence generators (426 LoC) and sorting algorithms (837 LoC). For the former, we have generators for Catalan numbers, the Heighway dragon curve, Fibonacci numbers, Pell numbers, Prime numbers, and the Thue-Morse sequence. For the latter we have implementations of bubble, heap, insertion, quick and shell sort on arrays of 6, 300 and 1000 items. These were chosen as non-trivial algorithms with standard implementations that we can compare to for reference that also make use of a range of Yul features and EVM opcodes while testing YulTracer's performance.

All examples executed correctly on a laptop featuring an 8-core Intel Core i7-8665U CPU with 32 GiB of RAM running Ubuntu 23.04. The interpreter was compiled with the OCaml 4.10.0 compiler using the Dune build system. We measure for each batch of examples a three-trial average total execution time of 0.478 s for all 8 sequence generator files, 31.960 s for all 12 sorting algorithm files, and 2.932 s for all 16 of the Solidity tests (including an infinite loop set to time out at 2 s). YulTracer produced the expected output for all programs.

6 Related Work

As discussed in the Introduction, the body of work on formalising Yul involves mechanisations in e.g. Dafny [11,12], the K-framework [18], Isabelle/HOL [3], Lean [34], and ACL2 [25]. To our knowledge, there is no peer-reviewed tool-independent presentation of a formal semantics for Yul. Closely related is the area of formalising Solidity, for which a more substantial body of work exists: e.g. [32] mathematically presents a calculus to reason about Solidity smart contracts and then implements and mechanically verifies its soundness in Isabelle/HOL; [10] presents a shallow embedding of Solidity in F*; [14] presents an operational semantics for a subset of Solidity and presents an abstract model for memory; [40] formalises another subset of Solidity by presenting a big-step semantics; [24] presents a semantics for the memory model of Solidity by mapping a fragment of Solidity to SMT-based constructs; [31] implements a denotational semantics for a subset of Solidity in 1500 lines of Isabelle. Also relevant are specifications for the EVM, which are necessary to implement the EVM dialect for Yul, such as: the Ethereum execution specification in Python [16]; other formalisation work such as [23], which presents the first complete small-step semantics of EVM bytecode and formalises it in F*; and [13], which presents a complete and formal specification in Dafny. Lastly, formalisations efforts are also common practice outside smart contracts, such as with the Glasgow Haskell Compiler (GHC) intermediate language Core which implements System FC [39] and features a maintained formal specification [35].

7 Conclusions

In this paper, we have presented an operational semantics for Yul. We first defined a source-level abstract syntax constructed by inspecting the grammar specified in [38] (Sect. 2), which we subsequently extended with constructs necessary for evaluation (Sect. 3). We then presented big- and small-step semantics, constructed by carefully inspecting the pseudocode evaluation function provided in [38], and supplied a proof of semantic equivalence between them (Theorem 12). Lastly, we presented YulTracer, an interpreter that implements our small-step semantics for a subset of the EVM dialect based on the Shanghai upgrade [16]. We evaluated our implementation against tests from the Solidity repository [17] and our own ones based on standard sequence generators and sorting algorithms.

We believe our work offers multiple advantages. Being in standard mathematical notation, and free of implementation or formalisation considerations, our semantics can serve to unify various extant tool-specific formalisations and verify any current and future implementations, while it can also be directly used in mathematical proofs, especially those involving the development and verification of language properties. Moreover, we provide an exhaustive specification for statements that irons out issues with ambiguity arising from under-specification of the semantics; e.g. function returns with no return variables. Lastly, we anticipate that a semantics such as ours will aid the development of future theories for Yul. We shall discuss this last point in more detail next.

This document focuses only the semantics of Yul statements. As such, we leave a detailed discussion of the EVM dialect and object semantics for future work. In particular, the EVM semantics includes behaviours which may be of technical interest, such as instructions related to transactions and interaction with the blockchain, as well as inter-contract communication. YulTracer and our semantics work towards the development of symbolic execution tools and theories developed directly in Yul, avoiding low-level complexities of EVM bytecode and the feature-rich, evolving syntax of Solidity; in particular those which combine symbolic execution with game semantics (e.g. [26,29]) to model higher-order interactions of smart contracts relevant to reentrancy exploits. Lastly, our semantics could lead to soundness proofs for a future Yul type system.

Acknowledgements. This work was supported in part by: Science Foundation Ireland under grant number 13/RC/2094_2; the Cisco University Research Program Fund, a corporate advised fund of Silicon Valley Community Foundation; and Ethereum Foundation grant FY23-1127.

References

1. Smart Contract Vulnerabilities (SCV) list. https://github.com/sirhashalot/SCV-List. Accessed 6 June 2024
2. Oyente, March 2017. https://github.com/enzymefinance/oyente/releases/tag/0.2.7
3. Yul-Isabelle: Executable formal semantics of Yul (2021). https://github.com/mmalvarez/Yul-Isabelle/tree/master. Accessed 24 June 2024
4. Manticore, February 2022. https://github.com/trailofbits/manticore/releases/tag/0.3.7
5. Echidna, March 2024. https://github.com/crytic/echidna/releases/tag/v2.2.3
6. Gambit: Mutant generation for Solidity, May 2024. https://github.com/Certora/gambit/releases/tag/v1.0.5
7. Mythril, March 2024. https://github.com/Consensys/mythril/releases/tag/v0.24.8
8. Slither, June 2024. https://github.com/crytic/slither/releases/tag/0.10.3
9. Solhint, May 2024. https://github.com/protofire/solhint/releases/tag/v5.0.1
10. Bhargavan, K., et al.: Formal verification of smart contracts: short paper. In: Proceedings of the 2016 ACM Workshop on Programming Languages and Analysis for Security, PLAS 2016, pp. 91–96. Association for Computing Machinery, New York, NY, USA (2016). https://doi.org/10.1145/2993600.2993611
11. Cassez, F.: Formal and executable semantics of Yul in Dafny, October 2023. https://hackmd.io/@FranckC/BJz02K4Za. Accessed 24 June 2024
12. Cassez, F.: yul-dafny, October 2023. https://github.com/franck44/yul-dafny. Accessed 24 June 2024
13. Cassez, F., Fuller, J., Ghale, M.K., Pearce, D.J., Quiles, H.M.A.: Formal and executable semantics of the Ethereum virtual machine in Dafny. In: Chechik, M., Katoen, J.P., Leucker, M. (eds.) FM 2023. LNCS, vol. 14000, pp. 571–583. Springer, Cham (2023). https://doi.org/10.1007/978-3-031-27481-7_32
14. Crosara, M., Centurino, G., Arceri, V.: Towards an operational semantics for Solidity (2019). https://api.semanticscholar.org/CorpusID:249983842

15. Crystal Intelligence: Adolescent anarchy: Thirteen years of crypto crimes unveiled. https://crystalintelligence.com/rohirov/2024/06/Crystal-Intelligence-Thirteen-Years-of-Crypto-Crimes-Unveiled.pdf. Accessed 25 June 2024
16. ethereum.org: Ethereum execution client specifications. https://github.com/ethereum/execution-specs.git. Accessed 14 June 2024
17. ethereum.org: The Solidity contract-oriented programming language. https://github.com/ethereum/solidity.git. Accessed 13 June 2024
18. ethereum.org: Yul-K (2019). https://github.com/ethereum/Yul-K. Accessed 24 June 2024
19. Feist, J., Greico, G., Groce, A.: Slither: a static analysis framework for smart contracts (2019). https://doi.org/10.1109/WETSEB.2019.00008
20. Felleisen, M., Friedman, D.P.: Control operators, the SECD-machine, and the λ-calculus. In: Wirsing, M. (ed.) Formal Description of Programming Concepts - III: Proceedings of the IFIP TC 2/WG 2.2 Working Conference on Formal Description of Programming Concepts - III, Ebberup, Denmark, 25–28 August 1986, pp. 193–222. North-Holland (1987)
21. Grech, N., Lagouvardos, S., Tsatiris, I., Smaragdakis, Y.: Elipmoc: advanced decompilation of Ethereum smart contracts. Proc. ACM Program. Lang. **6**(OOPSLA1) (2022). https://doi.org/10.1145/3527321
22. Grieco, G., Song, W., Cygan, A., Feist, J., Groce, A.: Echidna: effective, usable, and fast fuzzing for smart contracts, pp. 557–560 (2020). https://doi.org/10.1145/3395363.3404366
23. Grishchenko, I., Maffei, M., Schneidewind, C.: A semantic framework for the security analysis of Ethereum smart contracts. In: Bauer, L., Küsters, R. (eds.) POST 2018. LNCS, vol. 10804, pp. 243–269. Springer, Cham (2018). https://doi.org/10.1007/978-3-319-89722-6_10
24. Hajdu, Á., Jovanović, D.: SMT-friendly formalization of the Solidity memory model. In: ESOP 2020. LNCS, vol. 12075, pp. 224–250. Springer, Cham (2020). https://doi.org/10.1007/978-3-030-44914-8_9
25. Kestrel Institute: Yul directory, Kestrel Books in ACL2 repository (2023). https://github.com/acl2/acl2/tree/master/books/kestrel/yul. Accessed 24 June 2024
26. Koutavas, V., Lin, Y.-Y., Tzevelekos, N.: From bounded checking to verification of equivalence via symbolic up-to techniques. In: TACAS 2022. LNCS, vol. 13244, pp. 178–195. Springer, Cham (2022). https://doi.org/10.1007/978-3-030-99527-0_10
27. Lin, Y.Y.: LaifsV1/YulTracer: alpha 0.1.1: parametric parser and main, June 2024. https://doi.org/10.5281/zenodo.12511493
28. Lin, Y.Y.: Yultracer: Alpha 0.1.1 (artefact), June 2024. https://doi.org/10.5281/zenodo.12588076
29. Lin, Y., Tzevelekos, N.: Symbolic execution game semantics. In: FSCD. Schloss Dagstuhl - Leibniz-Zentrum für Informatik (2020)
30. Luu, L., Chu, D., Olickel, H., Saxena, P., Hobor, A.: Making smart contracts smarter. In: Weippl, E.R., Katzenbeisser, S., Kruegel, C., Myers, A.C., Halevi, S. (eds.) Proceedings of the 2016 ACM SIGSAC Conference on Computer and Communications Security, Vienna, Austria, 24–28 October 2016, pp. 254–269. ACM (2016). https://doi.org/10.1145/2976749.2978309
31. Marmsoler, D., Brucker, A.D.: A denotational semantics of Solidity in Isabelle/HOL. In: Calinescu, R., Păsăreanu, C.S. (eds.) SEFM 2021. LNCS, vol. 13085, pp. 403–422. Springer, Cham (2021). https://doi.org/10.1007/978-3-030-92124-8_23

32. Marmsoler, D., Thornton, B.: SSCalc: a calculus for Solidity smart contracts. In: Ferreira, C., Willemse, T.A.C. (eds.) SEFM 2023. LNCS, vol. 14323, pp. 184–204. Springer, Cham (2023). https://doi.org/10.1007/978-3-031-47115-5_11
33. Mossberg, M., et al.: Manticore: a user-friendly symbolic execution framework for binaries and smart contracts, pp. 1186–1189 (2019). https://doi.org/10.1109/ASE.2019.00133
34. NethermindEth: Yul IR specification in Lean (2021). https://github.com/NethermindEth/Yul-Specification. Accessed 24 June 2024
35. Peyton Jones, S.: System FC, as implemented in GHC (May). https://gitlab.haskell.org/ghc/ghc/-/blob/master/docs/core-spec/core-spec.pdf. Accessed 27 June 2024
36. Sharma, N., Sharma, S.: A survey of Mythril, a smart contract security analysis tool for EVM bytecode **13**, 51003–51010 (2022)
37. Solidity Team: List of known bugs - Solidity 0.8.27 documentation. https://docs.soliditylang.org/en/develop/bugs.html. Accessed 6 June 2024
38. Solidity Team: Yul - Solidity 0.8.27 documentation. https://docs.soliditylang.org/en/latest/yul.html. Accessed 6 June 2024
39. Sulzmann, M., Chakravarty, M., Peyton Jones, S., Donnelly, K.: System F with type equality coercions. In: ACM SIGPLAN International Workshop on Types in Language Design and Implementation (TLDI 2007), pp. 53–66. ACM, January 2007. https://www.microsoft.com/en-us/research/publication/system-f-with-type-equality-coercions/
40. Zakrzewski, J.: Towards verification of Ethereum smart contracts: a formalization of core of Solidity. In: Piskac, R., Rümmer, P. (eds.) VSTTE 2018. LNCS, vol. 11294, pp. 229–247. Springer, Cham (2018). https://doi.org/10.1007/978-3-030-03592-1_13

Execution-Time Opacity Control for Timed Automata

Étienne André[1,2(✉)], Marie Duflot[3(✉)], Laetitia Laversa[1,4(✉)], and Engel Lefaucheux[3(✉)]

[1] Université Sorbonne Paris Nord, LIPN, CNRS UMR 7030, Villetaneuse, France
ea.ndre13@lipn13.fr
[2] Institut universitaire de France (IUF), Paris, France
[3] Université de Lorraine, CNRS, Inria, LORIA, 54000 Nancy, France
marie.duflot-kremer@loria.fr, engel.lefaucheux@inria.fr
[4] Université Paris Cité, IRIF, CNRS UMR 8243, Paris, France
laetitia.laversa@irif.fr
https://lipn.univ-paris13.fr/~andre/, https://members.loria.fr/MDuflot/,
https://l-laversa.github.io/, https://elefauch.github.io/

Abstract. Timing leaks in timed automata (TA) can occur whenever an attacker is able to deduce a secret by observing some timed behavior. In execution-time opacity, the attacker aims at deducing whether a private location was visited, by observing only the execution time. It can be decided whether a TA is opaque in this setting. In this work, we tackle control, and show that we are able to decide whether a TA can be controlled at runtime to ensure opacity. Our method is constructive, in the sense that we can exhibit such a controller. We also address the case when the attacker cannot have an infinite precision in its observations.

Keywords: timed automata · opacity · side-channel attacks · timed control

1 Introduction

In order to infer sensitive information, side-channels attacks [28] exploit various observable aspects of a system rather than directly exploiting its computational processes, such as power consumption, electromagnetic emissions, or time. In particular, by observing subtle differences in timing, attackers can infer valuable information about the internal state of the system. For example, in [22], a timing attack vulnerability is identified in the Chinese public key cryptography standard; the authors show how the most significant zero-bit leakage obtained from the execution time allows to extract the secret key.

Timed automata (TAs) [1] are a powerful formalism to reason about real-time systems mixing timing constraints and concurrency. Timing leaks can occur whenever an attacker is able to deduce a secret by observing some behavior of a TA.

This work is partially supported by ANR-NRF ProMiS (ANR-19-CE25-0015 / 2019 ANR NRF 0092) and by ANR BisoUS (ANR-22-CE48-0012).

A. Madeira and A. Knapp (Eds.): SEFM 2024, LNCS 15280, pp. 347–365, 2025.
https://doi.org/10.1007/978-3-031-77382-2_20

Related Works. Franck Cassez proposed in [21] a first definition of *timed* opacity for TAs: the system is opaque when an attacker can never deduce whether some secret sequence of actions (possibly with timestamps) was performed, by only observing a given set of observable actions together with their timestamp. It is then proved in [21] that it is undecidable whether a TA is opaque. This notably relates to the undecidability of timed language inclusion for TAs [1]. The undecidability holds even for the restricted class of *event-recording automata* [2] (a subclass of TAs), for which language inclusion is known to be decidable. The aforementioned negative result leaves hope only if the definition or the setting is changed, which was done in four main lines of works.

First, in [30,31], the input model is simplified to *real-time automata* [24], a restricted formalism compared to TAs considering a single clock, reset at each transition. [27] works on constant-time labeled automata, a subclass of real-time automata where events occur at constant values. In this setting, initial-state and current-state opacity become decidable. In [32], Zhang studies labeled real-timed automata (a subclass of labeled TAs); in this setting, state-based (at the initial time, the current time, etc.) opacity is proven to be decidable by extending the observer (that is, the classical powerset construction) from finite automata to labeled real-timed automata.

Second, in [5,8], the opacity was studied in the setting of Cassez' definition, but with restrictions in the model: one-clock automata, one-action automata, or over discrete time. Similarly, in [26], discrete-timed automata with several clocks are considered and transformed into tick automata in order to verify the current-state opacity.

Third, in [4], the authors consider a time-bounded notion of the opacity of [21], where the attacker has to disclose the secret before an upper bound, using a partial observability. Deciding opacity in this setting is shown to be decidable for TAs.

Fourth, in [10], an alternative definition to Cassez' opacity is proposed, by studying execution-time opacity (ET-opacity): the attacker has only access to the *execution time* of the system, as opposed to Cassez' partial observations where some events (with their timestamps) are observable. In that case, most problems for TAs become decidable.

Several works address non-interference for TAs. Different notions of equivalence (e.g., bisimulation) can be considered for this property. Several papers [9,14,15] present some decidability results, while control is considered in [16]. General security problems for TAs are surveyed in [12].

Note that a preliminary version of control is considered in [6] for ET-opacity, but only untimed, i.e., the actions could only be enabled or disabled once and for all, thus severely diminishing the possibilities to render the system ET-opaque. Finally note that [10] considers also *parametric* versions of the opacity problems, in which timing parameters [3] can be used in order to make the system ETopaque. Our notion of control is orthogonal to parameter synthesis, as another way to ensure the system becomes ET-opaque.

Controller synthesis can be described and solved thanks to game theory; finding a strategy for a controller can be equivalent to computing a winning strategy in a corresponding game. Several game models have been considered, as timed games that can be used to solve synthesis problem on timed automata. In this context, [13] aims to restrict the transition relation in order to satisfy certain properties, while [25] completes this result, minimizing the execution time, and [18] studies the reachability with robust strategies only.

Contributions. In this work, we aim at tuning a system to make it ET-opaque, by *controlling* it at runtime.

Our attacker model is as follows: the attacker has a knowledge of the system model, but can only observe the execution time. This can correspond to an attacker observing the energy consumption of a device, clearly denoting the execution time of a program or process; or to an attacker observing communications over a shared network, with an observable message acknowledging the end of execution.

As usual, we consider that the system actions are partitioned between controllable and uncontrollable. Our controller relies on the following notion of strategy: at each timestamp, the strategy enables only a subset of the controllable actions. Our technique relies on a novel *ad-hoc* construction inspired by the region automaton for TAs. We show that the existence of a controller to make the system ET-opaque is decidable, and our approach is constructive. We also address the case when the attacker cannot have an infinite precision in its observations.

Outline. Section 2 recalls the necessary material. Section 3 defines the control problem for ET-opacity. Sections 4 and 5 define the core of our approach. Section 6 extends our method when the attacker cannot have an infinite precision in observing the execution time. Section 7 highlights future works.

2 Preliminaries

Clocks are real-valued variables that all evolve over time at the same rate. Throughout this paper, we assume a set $\mathbb{X} = \{x_1, \dots, x_H\}$ of *clocks*. A *clock valuation* is a function $\mu : \mathbb{X} \rightarrow \mathbb{R}^H_{\geq 0}$. Given $R \subseteq \mathbb{X}$, we define the reset of a valuation μ with respect to R, denoted by $[\mu]_R$, as follows: $[\mu]_R(x) = 0$ if $x \in R$, and $[\mu]_R(x) = \mu(x)$ otherwise. We write $\mathbf{0}$ for the clock valuation assigning 0 to all clocks. Given a constant $d \in \mathbb{R}_{\geq 0}$, $\mu + d$ denotes the valuation s.t. $(\mu + d)(x) = \mu(x) + d$, for all $x \in \mathbb{X}$. We assume $\bowtie \in \{<, \leq, =, \geq, >\}$. A *constraint* C is a conjunction of inequalities over $\mathbb{X}$ of the form $x \bowtie d$, with $d \in \mathbb{Z}$.

We define timed automata as in [1], with an extra private location, which encodes the secret that shall not be leaked.

Definition 1 (Timed automaton). *A* timed automaton *(TA) $\mathcal{A}$ is a tuple $\mathcal{A} = (\Sigma, L, \ell_0, \ell_{priv}, F, \mathbb{X}, I, E)$ where: 1) Σ is a finite set of actions, 2) L is a finite set of locations, 3) $\ell_0 \in L$ is the initial location, 4) $\ell_{priv} \in L$ is the private* *location, 5) $F \subseteq L \setminus \{\ell_{priv}\}$ is the set of final locations, 6) $\mathbb{X} = \{x_1, \dots, x_H\}$ is a finite set of clocks, 7) I is the invariant, assigning to every $\ell \in L$ a constraint $I(\ell)$, 8) E is a finite set of edges $\mathsf{e} = (\ell, g, a, R, \ell')$ where $\ell, \ell' \in L$ are the source and target locations, $a \in \Sigma \cup \{\varepsilon\}$, where ε denotes the silent action, $R \subseteq \mathbb{X}$ is a set of clocks to be reset, and g is a constraint over $\mathbb{X}$ (called* guard*).*

Example 1. Figure 1a depicts a TA $\mathcal{A}_1$ with a single clock x, where $\Sigma = \{a, b, u\}$. The edge e_1 between ℓ_0 and the private location ℓ_{priv} is available only when the valuation of x is equal to 0. The edge e_6 between ℓ_0 and ℓ_2 resets x.

Since we are only interested in the (first) arrival time in a final location, the following assumption does not restrict our framework, but simplifies the subsequent definitions and results.

Assumption 1. *We consider every final location as* urgent *(where time cannot elapse): formally, there exists $x \in \mathbb{X}$ such that, for all $(\ell, g, a, R, \ell') \in E, \ell' \in F$, we have $x \in R$ and "$x = 0$" $\in I(\ell')$. Moreover, final locations cannot have outgoing transitions: formally, there is no $(\ell, g, a, R, \ell') \in E$ s.t. $\ell \in F$.*

Definition 2 (Semantics of a TA). *Let $\mathcal{A} = (\Sigma, L, \ell_0, \ell_{priv}, F, \mathbb{X}, I, E)$ be a TA, the semantics of $\mathcal{A}$ is given by the timed transition system $TTS_{\mathcal{A}} = (S, s_0, \Sigma \cup \mathbb{R}_{\geq 0}, \delta)$, with 1) $S = \{(\ell, \mu) \in L \times \mathbb{R}^H_{\geq 0} \mid \mu \models I(\ell)\}$, 2) $s_0 = (\ell_0, \mathbf{0})$, 3) δ consists of the discrete and (continuous) delay transition relations: i) discrete transitions: $(\ell, \mu) \overset{\mathsf{e}}{\mapsto} (\ell', \mu')$, if $(\ell, \mu), (\ell', \mu') \in S$, and there exists $\mathsf{e} = (\ell, g, a, R, \ell') \in E$, such that $\mu' = [\mu]_R$, and $\mu \models g$. ii) delay transitions: $(\ell, \mu) \overset{d}{\mapsto} (\ell, \mu + d)$, with $d \in \mathbb{R}_{\geq 0}$, if $\forall d' \in [0, d], (\ell, \mu + d') \in S$.*

We write $(\ell, \mu) \xrightarrow{d,\mathsf{e}} (\ell', \mu')$ for a combination of a delay and a discrete transitions when $\exists \mu'' : (\ell, \mu) \overset{d}{\mapsto} (\ell, \mu'') \overset{\mathsf{e}}{\mapsto} (\ell', \mu')$.

Given a TA $\mathcal{A}$ with semantics $(S, s_0, \Sigma \cup \mathbb{R}_{\geq 0}, \delta)$, a *run* of $\mathcal{A}$ is a finite alternating sequence of states of $TTS_{\mathcal{A}}$ and pairs of delays and edges starting from s_0 of the form $s_0, (d_0, \mathsf{e}_0), s_1, \dots, s_n$ where for all $i < n, \mathsf{e}_i \in E, d_i \in \mathbb{R}_{\geq 0}$ and $s_i \xrightarrow{d_i, \mathsf{e}_i} s_{i+1}$. The duration of a run $\rho = s_0, (d_0, \mathsf{e}_0), s_1, \dots, (d_{n-1}, \mathsf{e}_{n-1}), s_n$ is $dur(\rho) = \sum_{0 \leq i \leq n-1} d_i$. We define $last(\rho) = s_n$.

Extra Clock. We will need an extra clock z that will help us later to keep track of the elapsed absolute time. This clock is reset exactly every 1 time unit, and therefore each reset corresponds to a "tick" of the absolute time. (Note that its actual value remains in $[0, 1]$ and therefore always matches the fractional part of the absolute time.) In all subsequent region constructions, we assume the existence of $z \in \mathbb{X}$. For each location ℓ, we add the constraint "$z \leq 1$" to $I(\ell)$, and we add a self-loop edge $(\ell, z = 1, \varepsilon, \{z\}, \ell)$.

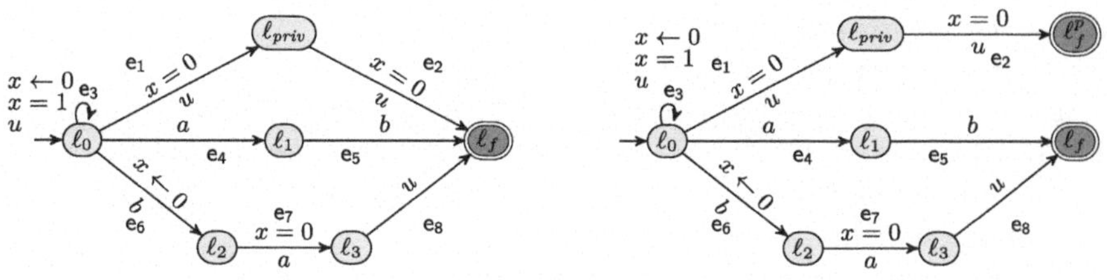

(a) TA $\mathcal{A}_1$ (b) Duplicated version of $\mathcal{A}_1$

Fig. 1. A TA and its duplicated version (introduced in Sect. 4)

2.1 Regions

Given a TA $\mathcal{A}$, for a clock x_i, we denote by c_i the largest constant to which x_i is compared within the guards and invariants of $\mathcal{A}$: formally, $c_i = \max_j\{d_j \mid x_i \bowtie d_j$ appears in a guard or invariant of $\mathcal{A}\}$. Given a clock valuation μ and a clock x_i, $\lfloor \mu(x_i) \rfloor$ (resp. $\mathrm{fr}(\mu(x_i))$) denotes the integral (resp. fractional) part of $\mu(x_i)$.

Definition 3 (Equivalence relation [1]**).** *Two clocks valuations μ, μ' are* equivalent, *denoted by $\mu \approx \mu'$, when the following three conditions hold for any clocks $x_i, x_j \in \mathbb{X}$:*

1. $\lfloor \mu(x_i) \rfloor = \lfloor \mu'(x_i) \rfloor$ *or* $\mu(x_i) > c_i$ *and* $\mu'(x_i) > c_i$;
2. *if* $\mu(x_i) \leq c_i$ *and* $\mu(x_j) \leq c_j$: $\mathrm{fr}(\mu(x_i)) \leq \mathrm{fr}(\mu(x_j))$ *iff* $\mathrm{fr}(\mu'(x_i)) \leq \mathrm{fr}(\mu'(x_j))$;
3. *if* $\mu(x_i) \leq c_i$: $\mathrm{fr}(\mu(x_i)) = 0$ *iff* $\mathrm{fr}(\mu'(x_i)) = 0$.

The equivalence relation $\approx$ is extended to the states of $TTS_{\mathcal{A}}$: given two states $s = (\ell, \mu), s' = (\ell', \mu')$ of $TTS_{\mathcal{A}}$, we write $s \approx s'$ iff $\ell = \ell'$ and $\mu \approx \mu'$. We denote by $[s]$ and call *region* the equivalence class of a state s for $\approx$. The set of all regions of $\mathcal{A}$ is denoted $\mathsf{R}_{\mathcal{A}}$. A region $r = [(\ell, \mu)]$ is *final* whenever $\ell \in F$. The set of final regions is denoted by $\mathsf{R}^F_{\mathcal{A}}$. A region r is *reachable* when there exists a run ρ such that $last(\rho) \in r$.

Region Automaton. We now define a region automaton based on [20, Proposition 5.3] with two-component labels on the transitions: the first component indicates how the fractional part of z evolved, with symbol "0" corresponding to an absence of change, symbol "0^+" corresponding to a change remaining in $(0, 1)$ and symbol "1" corresponding to a change where the fractionnal part either starts or ends at 0. The second component is either ε if the transition represents time elapsing in the TA, or provides the action that labels the corresponding discrete transition in the TA.

Given a state $s = (\ell, \mu)$, and $d \in \mathbb{R}_{\geq 0}$, we write $s + d$ to denote $(\ell, \mu + d)$. We write $r \cup r'$ for $\{s \mid s \in r \text{ or } s \in r'\}$.

Definition 4 (Labeled Region Automaton). *For a given TA $\mathcal{A}$, the region automaton $\mathcal{R}_{\mathcal{A}}$ is given by the tuple $(\mathsf{R}_{\mathcal{A}}, \Sigma^{\mathsf{R}}, \delta^{\mathsf{R}})$ where:*

1. $\mathsf{R}_{\mathcal{A}}$ *is the set of states,*
2. $\Sigma^{\mathsf{R}} = \{0, 0^+, 1\} \times (\Sigma \cup \{\varepsilon\})$,
3. *given two regions* $r, r' \in \mathsf{R}_{\mathcal{A}}$ *and* $\zeta \in \Sigma^{\mathsf{R}}$, *we have* $(r, \zeta, r') \in \delta^{\mathsf{R}}$ *if there exist* $s = (\ell, \mu) \in r, s' = (\ell', \mu') \in r'$ *such that one of the following holds:*
   (a) $\zeta = (0, a)$ *and* $(\ell, \mu) \overset{\mathsf{e}}{\mapsto} (\ell', \mu') \in \delta$ *in* $TTS_{\mathcal{A}}$ *with* $\mathsf{e} = (\ell, g, a, R, \ell')$ *for some* g *and* R*;*
   (b) $\zeta = (0^+, \varepsilon)$ *and* $\exists d \in \mathbb{R}_{>0}$ *such that 1)* $s \overset{d}{\mapsto} s'$, *2)* $\forall 0 < d' < d$, $s + d' \in r \cup r'$ *and 3)* $\mathrm{fr}(\mu(z)) \neq 0$ *and* $\mathrm{fr}(\mu'(z)) \neq 0$*;*[1]
   (c) $\zeta = (1, \varepsilon)$ *and* $\exists d \in \mathbb{R}_{>0}$ *such that 1)* $s \overset{d}{\mapsto} s'$, *2)* $\forall 0 < d' < d$, $s+d' \in r \cup r'$, *and 3)* $\mathrm{fr}(\mu'(z)) = 0$ *iff* $\mathrm{fr}(\mu(z)) \neq 0$.

We write $r \xrightarrow{\zeta}_{\mathsf{R}} r'$ for $(r, \zeta, r') \in \delta^{\mathsf{R}}$.

2.2 Execution-Time Opacity of a TA

Let us now recall from [10] the notions of private and public runs. Given a TA $\mathcal{A}$ and a run ρ, we say that ℓ_{priv} is *visited on the way to a final location in* ρ when ρ is of the form $(\ell_0, \mu_0), (d_0, \mathsf{e}_0), (\ell_1, \mu_1), \ldots, (\ell_m, \mu_m), (d_m, \mathsf{e}_m), \ldots, (\ell_n, \mu_n)$ for some $m, n \in \mathbb{N}$ such that $\ell_m = \ell_{priv}$ and $\ell_n \in F$. We denote by $\mathit{Visit}^{priv}(\mathcal{A})$ the set of those runs, and refer to them as *private* runs. We denote by $D\mathit{Visit}^{priv}(\mathcal{A})$ the set of all the durations of these runs.

Conversely, we say that ℓ_{priv} is *avoided on the way to a final location in* ρ when ρ is of the form $(\ell_0, \mu_0), (d_0, \mathsf{e}_0), (\ell_1, \mu_1), \ldots, (\ell_n, \mu_n)$ with $\ell_n \in F$ and $\forall 0 \leq i < n, \ell_i \notin \{\ell_{priv}\}$. We denote the set of those runs by $\overline{\mathit{Visit}^{priv}}(\mathcal{A})$, referring to them as *public* runs, and by $D\overline{\mathit{Visit}^{priv}}(\mathcal{A})$ the set of all the durations of these public runs.

These concepts can be seen as the set of execution times from the initial location ℓ_0 to a final location while visiting (resp. not visiting) ℓ_{priv}.

Example 2. Consider the following two runs of the TA $\mathcal{A}_1$ in Fig. 1a. Note that we use (ℓ_0, v) as a shortcut for (ℓ_0, μ) such that $\mu(x) = v$.

$$\rho_1 = (\ell_0, 0), (1, \mathsf{e}_3), (\ell_0, 0), (0, \mathsf{e}_1), (\ell_{priv}, 0), (0, \mathsf{e}_2), (\ell_f, 0)$$
$$\rho_2 = (\ell_0, 0), (0.1, \mathsf{e}_6), (\ell_2, 0), (0, \mathsf{e}_7), (\ell_3, 0), (0.8, \mathsf{e}_8), (\ell_f, 0.8)$$

Run $\rho_1 \in \mathit{Visit}^{priv}(\mathcal{A}_1)$ is a private run, and $dur(\rho_1) = 1 \in D\mathit{Visit}^{priv}(\mathcal{A}_1)$. Run $\rho_2 \in \overline{\mathit{Visit}^{priv}}(\mathcal{A}_1)$ is a public run with $dur(\rho_2) = 0.8 \in D\overline{\mathit{Visit}^{priv}}(\mathcal{A}_1)$.

Definition 5 (Full ET-opacity). *A TA* $\mathcal{A}$ *is* fully ET-opaque *when* $D\mathit{Visit}^{priv}(\mathcal{A}) = D\overline{\mathit{Visit}^{priv}}(\mathcal{A})$.

[1] Condition 2) ensures that we only move from one region to the "next" one (no intermediate region), and condition 3) adds that we stay in the same region for z (changing the region for z is handled in item (c)).

That is, if for any run of duration d reaching a final location after visiting ℓ_{priv}, there exists another run of the same duration reaching a final location but not visiting ℓ_{priv}, and vice versa, then the TA is fully ET-opaque.

Example 3. Consider again $\mathcal{A}_1$ in Fig. 1a. Each time x is equal to 1, we can reset it via e_3, and take edges e_1 and e_2 instantaneously. It results that $DVisit^{priv}(\mathcal{A}_1) = \mathbb{N}$. We have seen that $0.8 \in DVisit^{\overline{priv}}(\mathcal{A}_1)$ in Example 2. So $DVisit^{priv}(\mathcal{A}_1) \neq DVisit^{\overline{priv}}(\mathcal{A}_1)$ and $\mathcal{A}_1$ is not fully ET-opaque.

3 Problem: Controlling TA to Achieve ET-Opacity

We assume $\Sigma = \Sigma_c \uplus \Sigma_u$ where Σ_c (resp. Σ_u) denotes controllable (resp. uncontrollable) actions. The uncontrollable actions are always available, whereas the controllable actions can be enabled and disabled at runtime.

The controller has a *strategy*, i.e., a function $\sigma : \mathbb{R}_{\geq 0} \to 2^{\Sigma_c}$ which associates to each time a subset of Σ_c, these actions are enabled, while others are disabled.

Definition 6 (Semantics of a controlled TA). *Given a TA* $\mathcal{A} = (\Sigma, L, \ell_0, \ell_{priv}, F, \mathbb{X}, I, E)$ *and a strategy* $\sigma : \mathbb{R}_{\geq 0} \to 2^{\Sigma_c}$*, the semantics of the controlled TA* $\mathcal{A}^\sigma$ *is given by* $TTS_{\mathcal{A}^\sigma} = (S, s_0, \Sigma \cup \mathbb{R}_{\geq 0}, \delta^\sigma)$ *with*

1. $S = \{(\ell, \mu, t) \in L \times \mathbb{R}^H_{\geq 0} \times \mathbb{R}_{\geq 0} \mid \mu \models I(\ell)\}$, $s_0 = (\ell_0, \mathbf{0}, 0)$,
2. δ^σ *consists of the discrete and (continuous) delay transition relation:*
   (a) *discrete transitions:* $(\ell, \mu, t) \overset{\mathsf{e}}{\mapsto}_\sigma (\ell', \mu', t)$, *if* $(\ell, \mu, t), (\ell', \mu', t) \in S$ *and there exists* $\mathsf{e} = (\ell, g, a, R, \ell') \in E$ *such that* $\mu' = [\mu]_R$, $\mu \models g$, *and* $a \in \sigma(t) \cup \Sigma_u$ *(a is enabled by the strategy at time t, or uncontrollable);*
   (b) *delay transitions:* $(\ell, \mu, t) \overset{d}{\mapsto}_\sigma (\ell, \mu + d, t + d)$, *with* $d \in \mathbb{R}_{\geq 0}$, *if* $\forall d' \in \mathbb{R}_{>0}$ *such that* $d' < d$, $(\ell, \mu + d', t + d') \in S$.

We write $(\ell, \mu, t) \xrightarrow{d,\mathsf{e}}_\sigma (\ell', \mu', t')$ for a combination of a delay and discrete transitions when $\exists \mu''$ such that $(\ell, \mu, t) \overset{d}{\mapsto}_\sigma (\ell, \mu'', t') \overset{\mathsf{e}}{\mapsto}_\sigma (\ell', \mu', t')$.

A run $\rho = (\ell_0, \mu_0), (d_0, \mathsf{e}_0), \ldots, (\ell_n, \mu_n)$ is *σ-compatible* when, $\forall 0 \leq i < n$, it holds that $(\ell_i, \mu_i, \sum_{j<i} d_j) \xrightarrow{d_i,\mathsf{e}_i}_\sigma (\ell_{i+1}, \mu_{i+1}, \sum_{j\leq i} d_j)$. We let

- $Visit^{priv}_\sigma(\mathcal{A}) = \{\rho \mid \rho$ is private and σ-compatible$\}$,
- $Visit^{\overline{priv}}_\sigma(\mathcal{A}) = \{\rho \mid \rho$ is public and σ-compatible$\}$,
- $DVisit^{priv}_\sigma(\mathcal{A}) = \{dur(\rho) \mid \rho$ is private and σ-compatible$\}$,
- $DVisit^{\overline{priv}}_\sigma(\mathcal{A}) = \{dur(\rho) \mid \rho$ is public and σ-compatible$\}$.

Definition 7 (Full ET-opacity with strategy). *For a strategy* σ*, a TA* $\mathcal{A}$ *is* fully ET-opaque with σ *when* $DVisit^{priv}_\sigma(\mathcal{A}) = DVisit^{\overline{priv}}_\sigma(\mathcal{A})$.

Finitely-Varying Strategies. To be able to manage strategies in the following constructions, we expect them to behave in a "reasonable" way. We only consider *finitely-varying strategies* where the number of changes are finite for any closed time interval. Indeed, we can assume that a controller cannot change infinitely frequently its strategy in a finite time: it is unrealistic to consider, in a bounded interval, neither a system that can perform an infinite number of actions, nor a controller that can make an infinite number of choices. Finitely-varying strategies are reminiscent of non-Zeno behaviors, in the sense that finitely-varying strategies have a finite number of strategy changes in every bounded interval.

More formally, a strategy σ is *finitely-varying* when, for any closed time interval I, there is a finite partition $p_1, \dots, p_n$ of I such that each p_i is an interval within which σ makes the same choice (i.e., for all $\tau_1, \tau_2 \in p_i$, $1 \leq i \leq n$, $\sigma(\tau_1) = \sigma(\tau_2)$). See [7] for an example of non-finitely-varying strategy.

In this paper, we are interested in several ET-opacity control problems i.e., related to a strategy σ making the TA $\mathcal{A}^\sigma$ ET-opaque. Those problems differ on whether we want to prove the existence of a finitely-varying strategy enforcing the ET-opacity or synthesize this strategy.

Full ET-opacity finitely-varying controller emptiness problem:
INPUT: A TA $\mathcal{A}$
PROBLEM: Decide whether the set of finitely-varying strategies σ such that $\mathcal{A}^\sigma$ is fully ET-opaque is empty.

Full ET-opacity finitely-varying controller synthesis problem:
INPUT: A TA $\mathcal{A}$
PROBLEM: Synthesize a finitely-varying strategy σ such that $\mathcal{A}^\sigma$ is fully ET-opaque.

Example 4 (Non-ET-opaque TA). There is no strategy such that TA $\mathcal{A}_1$ in Fig. 1a is fully ET-opaque. Indeed, as $\Sigma_u = \{u\}$ and $\Sigma_c = \{a, b\}$, the transitions e_1 and e_2 are uncontrollable, so we can reach ℓ_f at any integer time along a run visiting ℓ_{priv}. However, even if we can allow transitions a and b at integer times too, the last transition e_8 is uncontrollable and can be taken at any time. Then, location ℓ_f can be reached at any time along a run not visiting ℓ_{priv}.

4 The Belief Automaton

In this section, we build an automaton called the "belief automaton", that will allow us to determine in which regions the system can be after a given execution time. This automaton considers a duplicated TA instead of the original TA in order to distinguish the final state reached by a private or a public run.[2]

[2] This could equally have been encoded using a Boolean variable remembering whether ℓ_{priv} was visited, as in [11].

4.1 Separating Private and Public Runs

We define a duplicated version of a TA $\mathcal{A}$, denoted by $\mathcal{A}^{dup}$, making it possible to decide if a given run avoids ℓ_{priv} or not just looking at the final reached location. Note that any run of $\mathcal{A}$ has an equivalent one in $\mathcal{A}^{dup}$ where each location is replaced by its duplicated version if a previous visited location is ℓ_{priv}. In particular, $DVisit^{\overline{priv}}(\mathcal{A}) = DVisit^{\overline{priv}}(\mathcal{A}^{dup})$ and $DVisit^{priv}(\mathcal{A}) = DVisit^{priv}(\mathcal{A}^{dup})$.

Definition 8 (Duplicated TA). *Let* $\mathcal{A} = (\Sigma, L, \ell_0, \ell_{priv}, F, \mathbb{X}, I, E)$ *be a TA. The associated* duplicated TA *is* $\mathcal{A}^{dup} = (\Sigma', L', \ell'_0, \ell'_{priv}, F', \mathbb{X}', I', E')$ *where: 1)* $\Sigma' = \Sigma$*, 2)* $L' = L_{pub} \uplus L_{priv}$ *with* $L_{pub} = L \setminus \ell_{priv}$ *and* $L_{priv} = \{\ell^p \mid \ell \in L\} \cup \{\ell_{priv}\}$*, 3)* $\ell'_0 = \ell_0$*, 4)* $\ell'_{priv} = \ell_{priv}$*, 5)* $F' = \{\ell^p_f \mid \ell_f \in F\} \cup F$*, 6)* $\mathbb{X}' = \mathbb{X}$*,*
7) I' *is the invariant such that* $\forall \ell \in L, I'(\ell) = I'(\ell^p) = I(\ell)$*,*
8) $E' = \{(\ell_1, g, a, R, \ell_2) \mid (\ell_1, g, a, R, \ell_2) \in E \text{ and } \ell_1 \neq \ell_{priv}\} \cup \{(\ell^p_1, g, a, R, \ell^p_2) \mid (\ell_1, g, a, R, \ell_2) \in E\} \cup \{(\ell_{priv}, g, a, R, \ell^p) \mid (\ell_{priv}, g, a, R, \ell) \in E\}$

Example 5. Figure 1b depicts $\mathcal{A}_1^{dup}$, the duplicated version of $\mathcal{A}_1$ in Fig. 1a. We do not depict unreachable locations. Observe that each run avoiding ℓ_{priv} ends in ℓ_f, and that the only outgoing transition of ℓ_{priv} is modified to go to ℓ^p_f.

4.2 Beliefs

A *belief*[3], denoted by $\mathfrak{b}$, represents the set of regions in which the attacker *believes* to be, according to their observations: elapsed time and enabled actions.

We write $\mathfrak{C} \subseteq \Sigma_c$ for a set of enabled actions, and define as follows the belief automaton, constructing the belief the attacker has, according to elapsed time and enabled actions.

Definition 9 (Belief automaton). *For* $\mathcal{A}$ *a TA with* $\Sigma = \Sigma_c \uplus \Sigma_u$*, we define the* belief automaton *as the tuple* $\mathcal{B}_\mathcal{A} = (\mathfrak{S}^{\mathcal{B}_\mathcal{A}}, \mathfrak{A}^{\mathcal{B}_\mathcal{A}}, \bot, \mathfrak{d}^{\mathcal{B}_\mathcal{A}})$ *where:*

1. $\mathfrak{S}^{\mathcal{B}_\mathcal{A}} = 2^{\mathsf{R}_{\mathcal{A}^{dup}}} \cup \{\bot\}$ *is the set of states,*
2. $\mathfrak{A}^{\mathcal{B}_\mathcal{A}} = \{0, 0^+, 1\} \times 2^{\Sigma_c}$,
3. $\bot$ *is the initial state,*
4. $\mathfrak{d}^{\mathcal{B}_\mathcal{A}} \subseteq (\mathfrak{S}^{\mathcal{B}_\mathcal{A}} \times \mathfrak{A}^{\mathcal{B}_\mathcal{A}} \times \mathfrak{S}^{\mathcal{B}_\mathcal{A}})$ *and*
   (a) $(\bot, (0, \mathfrak{C}), \mathfrak{b}) \in \mathfrak{d}^{\mathcal{B}_\mathcal{A}}$ *iff* $\mathfrak{b}$ *is the largest set such that* $\forall r \in \mathfrak{b}$, $\exists n \geq 0$, $[s_0] \xrightarrow{(0,a_1)}_{\mathsf{R}} \cdots \xrightarrow{(0,a_n)}_{\mathsf{R}} r$ *in* $\mathcal{R}_{\mathcal{A}^{dup}}$ *with* $\forall 1 \leq i \leq n$, $a_i \in (\mathfrak{C} \cup \Sigma_u)$,
   (b) $(\mathfrak{b}, (\dagger_1, \mathfrak{C}), \mathfrak{b}') \in \mathfrak{d}^{\mathcal{B}_\mathcal{A}}$ *iff* $\mathfrak{b} \neq \bot$, $\mathfrak{b}'$ *is the largest set such that* $\forall r' \in \mathfrak{b}'$, $\exists r \in \mathfrak{b}$, $\exists n \geq 1$, $r \xrightarrow{(\dagger_1, \varepsilon)}_{\mathsf{R}} \cdots \xrightarrow{(\dagger_n, a_n)}_{\mathsf{R}} r'$ *in* $\mathcal{R}_{\mathcal{A}^{dup}}$ *with* $\forall 1 < i \leq n, a_i \in (\mathfrak{C} \cup \Sigma_u \cup \{\varepsilon\})$ *and* $\dagger_1 \in \{0^+, 1\}$ *and* $\forall 1 < i \leq n, \dagger_i \in \{0, 0^+\}$.

We first consider transitions from the initial belief $\bot$: time cannot elapse here; one can do a sequence of actions allowed at time 0 (condition 4a). Then, from the other beliefs, a transition is made of a sequence of transitions from the region automaton, the first one of which lets time elapse, and all the following actions need to be allowed at that time (condition 4b).

[3] We follow the vocabulary from, e.g., [17]. This is also close to the concept of *estimator* (e.g., [26]).

Example 6. In this example and the following ones, we associate each belief either to an open interval or to an integer, and, by abuse of notation, since the automaton has only one clock, we write $(\ell, (\tau, \tau'))$ for the region containing the state $(\ell, \mu(x_1))$ with $\mu(x_1) \in (\tau, \tau'), \tau \in \mathbb{N}, \tau' = +\infty$ if $\tau = c_1$, $\tau' = \tau + 1$ otherwise. Similarly, we write (ℓ, τ) for the region containing the state $(\ell, \mu(x_1))$, $\mu(x_1) = \tau \in \mathbb{N}$.

Let $\mathcal{A}_2$ be the TA in Fig. 2a. With the global invariant $x \leq 1$, we have the following beliefs. Here, the value of clock z is not given as, in this example, it is equivalent to the value of x. The corresponding belief automaton is depicted in Fig. 2b.

$$\mathfrak{b}'_0 = \{(\ell_0, 0), (\ell_{priv}, 0), (\ell^p_f, 0)\} \qquad \mathfrak{b}_0 = \mathfrak{b}'_0 \cup \{(\ell_f, 0)\}$$
$$\mathfrak{b}'_{(0,1)} = \{(\ell_0, (0,1)), (\ell_{priv}, (0,1))\} \qquad \mathfrak{b}_{(0,1)} = \mathfrak{b}'_{(0,1)} \cup \{(\ell_f, (0,1))\}$$
$$\mathfrak{b}'_1 = \{(\ell_0, 1), (\ell_0, 0), (\ell_{priv}, 0), (\ell^p_f, 0)\} \qquad \mathfrak{b}_1 = \mathfrak{b}'_1 \cup \{(\ell_f, 0)\}$$

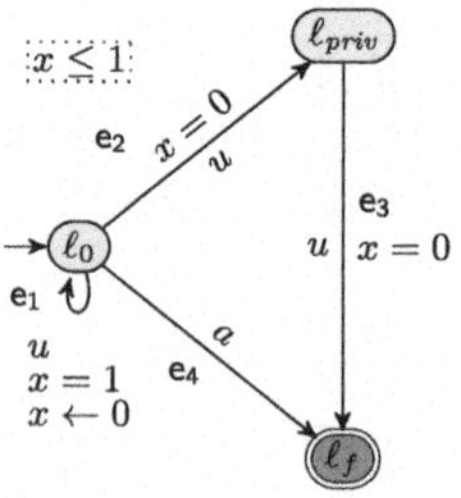

(a) TA $\mathcal{A}_2$

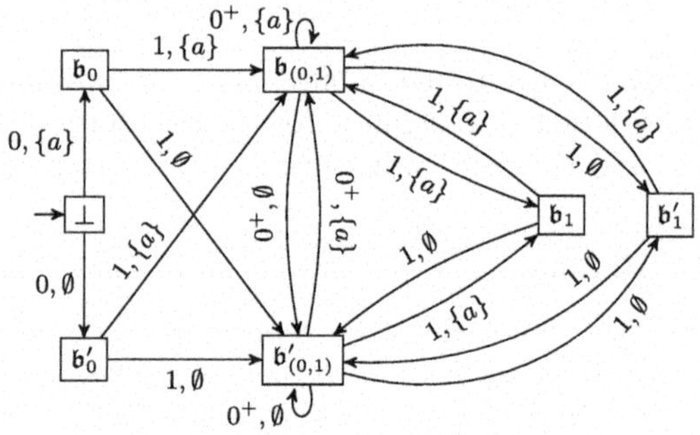

(b) Belief automaton $\mathcal{B}_{\mathcal{A}_2}$

Fig. 2. $\mathcal{A}_2$ and the corresponding belief automaton

Bad Beliefs. Intuitively, a bad belief allows to discriminate private and public runs. For a given TA $\mathcal{A}$, we denote $\mathsf{Secret}_{\mathcal{A}} = \{[(\ell, \mu)] \mid \ell \in L_{priv}, \mu \in \mathbb{R}^H_{\geq 0}\}$ the set of regions reachable on a run visiting ℓ_{priv} in $\mathcal{A}^{dup}$, and $\overline{\mathsf{Secret}_{\mathcal{A}}} = \{[(\ell, \mu)] \mid \ell \in L_{pub}, \mu \in \mathbb{R}^H_{\geq 0}\}$ the set of regions reachable on a run not visiting ℓ_{priv} in $\mathcal{A}^{dup}$.

For a given TA $\mathcal{A}$, a belief $\mathfrak{b}$ is said to be *bad for full ET-opacity* when exactly one of the following two conditions is satisfied: 1) $(\mathfrak{b} \cap \mathsf{R}^F_{\mathcal{A}} \cap \mathsf{Secret}_{\mathcal{A}} \neq \emptyset)$, or 2) $(\mathfrak{b} \cap \mathsf{R}^F_{\mathcal{A}} \cap \overline{\mathsf{Secret}_{\mathcal{A}}} \neq \emptyset)$. This means that finishing in this belief leaks an information to the attacker: only one final state is possible (private or public, but not both).

Beliefs and Strategy. For a TA $\mathcal{A}$ and a strategy σ, we denote by $\mathfrak{b}^\sigma_t$ the set of regions in which we can be after a time t while following a strategy σ in $\mathcal{A}$, i.e., $r \in \mathfrak{b}^\sigma_t$ when there exists ρ in $\mathcal{A}^{dup}$ such that ρ is σ-compatible, $last(\rho) \in r, r \in \mathsf{R}_{\mathcal{A}^{dup}}$ and $dur(\rho) = t$.

We define $\mathbb{B}^{\sigma}_{\mathcal{A}}$ as the set of beliefs reachable by a strategy σ. Formally, for a given strategy σ: $\mathbb{B}^{\sigma}_{\mathcal{A}} = \{\mathfrak{b}^{\sigma}_{t} \mid t \in \mathbb{R}_{\geq 0}\}$.

We can first characterize the ET-opacity of a controlled TA with beliefs. The proof of all results can be found in [7].

Lemma 1 (Beliefs characterization for full ET-opacity). *A TA $\mathcal{A}$ is fully ET-opaque with a strategy σ iff, for all $\mathfrak{b} \in \mathbb{B}^{\sigma}_{\mathcal{A}}$, $\mathfrak{b}$ is not bad for full ET-opacity.*

A strategy for a belief automaton, called a $\mathfrak{b}$-*strategy*, is a function which associates to a sequence of actions the next available action. Formally, a $\mathfrak{b}$-strategy is a function $\alpha : (\mathfrak{A}^{\mathcal{B}_{\mathcal{A}}})^* \rightarrow \mathfrak{A}^{\mathcal{B}_{\mathcal{A}}}$. A *state* in a belief automaton controlled by a $\mathfrak{b}$-strategy is made of the sequence of actions performed until that state is reached, and the current belief.

Definition 10 (Controlled belief automaton). *For a belief automaton $\mathcal{B}_{\mathcal{A}}$ and a $\mathfrak{b}$-strategy α, we define $\mathcal{B}^{\alpha}_{\mathcal{A}} = (\mathfrak{S}^{\mathcal{B}^{\alpha}_{\mathcal{A}}}, \mathfrak{A}^{\mathcal{B}^{\alpha}_{\mathcal{A}}}, (\varepsilon, \bot), \mathfrak{d}^{\mathcal{B}^{\alpha}_{\mathcal{A}}})$ the belief automaton controlled by α as follows:*

1. *$\mathfrak{S}^{\mathcal{B}^{\alpha}_{\mathcal{A}}} = (\mathfrak{A}^{\mathcal{B}_{\mathcal{A}}})^* \times \mathfrak{S}^{\mathcal{B}_{\mathcal{A}}}$ is the set of states,*
2. *$\mathfrak{A}^{\mathcal{B}^{\alpha}_{\mathcal{A}}} = \mathfrak{A}^{\mathcal{B}_{\mathcal{A}}} = \{0, 0^+, 1\} \times 2^{\Sigma_c}$ is the alphabet,*
3. *$(\varepsilon, \bot)$ is the initial state,*
4. *$\mathfrak{d}^{\mathcal{B}^{\alpha}_{\mathcal{A}}} \subseteq (\mathfrak{S}^{\mathcal{B}^{\alpha}_{\mathcal{A}}} \times \mathfrak{A}^{\mathcal{B}^{\alpha}_{\mathcal{A}}} \times \mathfrak{S}^{\mathcal{B}^{\alpha}_{\mathcal{A}}})$ and $((v, \mathfrak{b}), (\dagger, \mathfrak{C}), (v \cdot (\dagger, \mathfrak{C}), \mathfrak{b}')) \in \mathfrak{d}^{\mathcal{B}^{\alpha}_{\mathcal{A}}}$ if $(\mathfrak{b}, (\dagger, \mathfrak{C}), \mathfrak{b}') \in \mathfrak{d}^{\mathcal{B}_{\mathcal{A}}}$, and $\alpha(v) = (\dagger, \mathfrak{C})$ with $\dagger \in \{0, 0^+, 1\}$.*

We define a *finitely-varying* $\mathfrak{b}$-*strategy* α in such a way that it corresponds to a finitely-varying strategy for a TA: for all $k \in \mathbb{N}$ such that $\alpha^{(k)}(\varepsilon) = (0^+, \mathfrak{C})$ for some $\mathfrak{C}$, there exists a $k' > k \in \mathbb{N}$ such that $\alpha^{(k')}(\varepsilon) = (1, \mathfrak{C}')$ for some $\mathfrak{C}'$, with $\alpha^{(i)}(\varepsilon) = \alpha(\dots(\alpha(\varepsilon)))$ where α is applied i times.

In order to define the correspondence between a strategy for a TA and a $\mathfrak{b}$-strategy for the corresponding belief automaton, we need to associate an interval of time $t(v)$ to a sequence of transitions $v = (\dagger_1, \mathfrak{C}_1) \cdots (\dagger_n, \mathfrak{C}_n)$, knowing that two transitions of the form $(1, \mathfrak{C})$ are necessary to go from an integer time to another one. Let $\#_{\dagger}(v)$ be the number of indices $i, 0 < i \leq n$, such that $\dagger_i = 1$; then

$$t(v) = \begin{cases} \{\#_{\dagger}(v)/2\} & \text{if } \#_{\dagger}(v) \equiv 0 \pmod 2 \\ (\lfloor \#_{\dagger}(v)/2 \rfloor, \lfloor \#_{\dagger}(v)/2 \rfloor + 1) & \text{otherwise.} \end{cases}$$

Example 7. Let $v_1 = (0, \mathfrak{C}_0) \cdot (1, \mathfrak{C}_1) \cdot (0^+, \mathfrak{C}_2) \cdot (1, \mathfrak{C}_3) \cdot (1, \mathfrak{C}_4)$ and $v_2 = v_1 \cdot (1, \mathfrak{C}_5)$. By definition, $t(v_1) = (1, 2)$ and $t(v_2) = \{2\}$. This means that for all runs ρ_1 and ρ_2 corresponding respectively to v_1 and v_2, we have $dur(\rho_1) \in (1, 2)$ and $dur(\rho_2) = 2$.

Definition 11 (Strategy correspondence). *Let $\mathcal{A}$ be a TA. We say that σ, a finitely-varying strategy of $\mathcal{A}$,* corresponds *to α, a finitely-varying $\mathfrak{b}$-strategy of $\mathcal{B}_{\mathcal{A}}$, denoted by $\sigma \vdash\!\dashv \alpha$, when:*

1. *$\alpha(\varepsilon) = (0, \sigma(0))$,*
2. *for $v \in (\mathfrak{A}^{\mathcal{B}_{\mathcal{A}}})^+$,*

- *if* $v = v' \cdot (1, \mathfrak{C}_0) \cdot (0^+, \mathfrak{C}_1) \cdot \ldots \cdot (0^+, \mathfrak{C}_n)$, $n \geq 0$, *and there exist* $\tau_0 < \ldots < \tau_{n+1}$ *such that for all* $0 \leq i \leq n+1$, $\tau_i \in t(v)$, $\sigma(\tau_i) = \mathfrak{C}_i$, *for all* $0 \leq i \leq n$, $\mathfrak{C}_i \neq \mathfrak{C}_{i+1}$ *and there is no* τ_i', $\tau_i < \tau_i' < \tau_{i+1}$, *such that* $\sigma(\tau_i) \neq \sigma(\tau_i') \neq \sigma(\tau_{i+1})$, *then* $\alpha(v) = (0^+, \mathfrak{C}_{n+1})$,
- *otherwise,* $\alpha(v) = (1, \mathfrak{C})$ *for* $\tau \in t(v \cdot (1, \mathfrak{C}))$, $\sigma(\tau) = \mathfrak{C}$ *and there is no* $\tau' < \tau$ *such that* $\tau' \in t(v \cdot (1, \mathfrak{C}))$ *and* $\sigma(\tau') \neq \sigma(\tau)$.

In other words, within a time interval of the form $(t, t+1)$ with $t \in \mathbb{N}$, the $\mathfrak{b}$-strategy α does not keep track of the precise timestamps of strategy changes in σ but makes the same changes in the same order. A belief $\mathfrak{b}$ is *reachable in* $\mathcal{B}_{\mathcal{A}}^{\alpha}$ when there exists a word $v \in (\mathfrak{A}^{\mathcal{B}_{\mathcal{A}}})^*$ such that the state $(v, \mathfrak{b})$ is reachable.

We prove in the following that a strategy in the TA matches a $\mathfrak{b}$-strategy in the belief automaton as do the runs and sequences of actions in belief automaton.

Lemma 2 (Strategy correspondence). *Let* $\mathcal{A}$ *be a TA. Given a finitely-varying strategy* σ *of* $\mathcal{A}$, *there is a finitely-varying* $\mathfrak{b}$*-strategy* α *of* $\mathcal{B}_{\mathcal{A}}$ *such that* $\sigma \vdash\!\dashv \alpha$. *Reciprocally, given a finitely-varying* $\mathfrak{b}$*-strategy* α *of* $\mathcal{B}_{\mathcal{A}}$, *there is a finitely-varying strategy* σ *of* $\mathcal{A}$ *such that* $\sigma \vdash\!\dashv \alpha$.

Proof. Let σ be a finitely-varying strategy for $\mathcal{A}$. For any interval $[i, i+1)$, $i \in \mathbb{N}$, let $p_{i_0}, p_{i_1}, \ldots, p_{i_{n_i}}$ be the smallest finite partition into intervals such that $p_{i_0} = \{i\}$ and σ makes the same choice within each p_{i_j}. We build the $\mathfrak{b}$-strategy α:

- $\alpha(\varepsilon) = (0, \sigma(0))$,
- for all $v \in (\mathfrak{A}^{\mathcal{B}_{\mathcal{A}}})^+$, with $|v|$ denoting the length of the word v,
  - if $t(v) = \{\iota\}, \iota \in \mathbb{N}$, is a singleton then by assumption, $p_{\iota_0} = t(v)$ and we set $\alpha(v) = (1, \sigma(\tau))$ for some $\tau \in p_{\iota_1}$,
  - otherwise, $v = v' \cdot (1, \mathfrak{C}_1) \cdot v''$ such that $v'' = (0^+, \mathfrak{C}_2) \cdot \ldots \cdot (0^+, \mathfrak{C}_k)$ and as σ is finitely-varying, there exist ι, n_ι such that $\bigcup_{j=1}^{n_\iota} p_{\iota_j} = t(v)$ and, as we took the smallest partition, we know that for all $1 \leq j < n$, for any $\tau \in p_{\iota_j}$, $\tau' \in p_{\iota_{j+1}}$, $\sigma(\tau) \neq \sigma(\tau')$. Then,

$$\alpha(v) = \begin{cases} (0^+, \sigma(\tau)), \text{ for some } \tau \in p_{\iota_{2+|v''|}} & \text{if } |v''| < n_\iota - 1 \\ (1, \sigma(\tau)), \text{ for some } \tau \in p_{\iota'_0}, \iota' = \iota + 1 & \text{otherwise.} \end{cases}$$

By construction, α is finitely-varying and $\sigma \vdash\!\dashv \alpha$.

Conversely, let α be a finitely-varying $\mathfrak{b}$-strategy, let us build σ such that $\sigma \vdash\!\dashv \alpha$. Let $\tau \in \mathbb{R}_{\geq 0}$ be a time instant and $v = (\dagger_0, \mathfrak{C}_0) \cdot \ldots \cdot (\dagger_k, \mathfrak{C}_k) = (\alpha)^{(1)}(\varepsilon) \cdot \ldots \cdot (\alpha)^{(k)}(\varepsilon)$ be the smallest sequence such that $t(v) = \{\iota\}$ is a singleton and $\iota \geq \tau$. As the strategy is finitely-varying this sequence is finite, and we have $\dagger_k = 1$, then:

- either τ is an integer, then we fix $\sigma(\tau) = \mathfrak{C}_k$;
- otherwise, let $j < k$ be the greatest integer such that $\dagger_j = 1$. Consider then the sequence $(\alpha)^{(j)}(\varepsilon) \cdot \ldots \cdot (\alpha)^{(k)}(\varepsilon) = (1, \mathfrak{C}_j) \cdot (0^+, \mathfrak{C}_{j+1}) \cdot \ldots \cdot (0^+, \mathfrak{C}_{k-1}) \cdot (1, \mathfrak{C}_k)$ and denote $m = k - j$, we define $\sigma(\tau) = \mathfrak{C}_i$ where $i = j + \lfloor \mathrm{fr}(\tau) * m \rfloor$.

By construction, σ is finitely-varying and $\sigma \vdash\!\dashv \alpha$. ☐

We define a run that follows a $\mathfrak{b}$-strategy as follows.

Definition 12 (Feasible run). *Let $\mathcal{A}$ be a TA, ρ be a run of $\mathcal{A}^{dup}$ and $v \in (\mathfrak{A}^{\mathcal{B}_\mathcal{A}})^*$. We say that ρ* admits *v, denoted by $\rho \models v$, when one of the following holds:*

1. $\rho = (\ell_0, \mathbf{0})$ *and* $v = (0, \mathfrak{C}_0)$ *with* $\mathfrak{C}_0 \subseteq \Sigma_c$,
2. $\rho = \rho', (d_{n-1}, \mathsf{e}_{n-1}), (\ell_n, \mu_n)$ *with* $\mathsf{e}_{n-1} = (\ell_{n-1}, g, a, R, \ell_n)$ *and one of the following holds:*
   (a) $d_{n-1} = 0$, $\rho' \models v$, $v = v' \cdot (\dagger, \mathfrak{C})$ *and* $a \in \mathfrak{C} \cup \Sigma_u \cup \{\varepsilon\}$,
   (b) $0 < d_{n-1} < 1$, $v = v' \cdot (1, \mathfrak{C}_0) \cdot (0^+, \mathfrak{C}_1) \cdots (0^+, \mathfrak{C}_{m-1})(\dagger, \mathfrak{C}_m)$, $a \in \mathfrak{C}_m \cup \Sigma_u \cup \{\varepsilon\}$, *there exists* $i, 0 \leq i \leq m$, $\rho' \models v' \cdot (1, \mathfrak{C}_0) \cdot (0^+, \mathfrak{C}_1) \cdots (\dagger', \mathfrak{C}_i)$, $\dagger' = 0^+$ *if* $i < m$ *and* $\dagger' = \dagger$ *otherwise, and either*
      - $\mathrm{fr}(\mu_{n-1}(z)) \neq 0$, $\mathrm{fr}(\mu_n(z)) \neq 0$, *and* $\dagger = 0^+$, *or*
      - $\mathrm{fr}(\mu_{n-1}(z)) = 0$ *or* $\mathrm{fr}(\mu_n(z)) = 0$ *and* $\dagger = 1$,
   (c) $d_{n-1} = 1$, $a \in \mathfrak{C} \cup \Sigma_u \cup \{\varepsilon\}$, $v = v' \cdot (1, \mathfrak{C}_0) \cdot (0^+, \mathfrak{C}_1) \cdots (0^+, \mathfrak{C}_m) \cdot (1, \mathfrak{C})$ *with* $0 \leq m$ *and such that* $\rho' \models v'$.

Given a $\mathfrak{b}$-strategy α, ρ is feasible in $\mathcal{B}^\alpha_\mathcal{A}$ when there exist $v \in (\mathfrak{A}^{\mathcal{B}_\mathcal{A}})^*$ and a belief $\mathfrak{b} \in \mathfrak{S}^{\mathcal{B}_\mathcal{A}}$ such that $\rho \models v$ and $(v, \mathfrak{b})$ is reachable in $\mathcal{B}^\alpha_\mathcal{A}$.

Example 8. Let $\mathcal{A}_2$ be the TA in Fig. 2. Let σ be a strategy such that $\mathcal{A}_2$ is fully ET-opaque defined as follows:

$$\sigma(\tau) = \begin{cases} \{a\} & \text{if } \tau \in \mathbb{N} \\ \emptyset & \text{otherwise} \end{cases}$$

Let α be a $\mathfrak{b}$-strategy for $\mathcal{B}_{\mathcal{A}_2}$ such that $\sigma \vdash\!\dashv \alpha$:

$$\alpha(v) = \begin{cases} (0, \{a\}) & \text{if } v = \varepsilon \\ (1, \emptyset) & \text{if } v \in (0, \{a\}) \cdot ((1, \emptyset) \cdot (1, \{a\}))^* \\ (1, \{a\}) & \text{if } v \in (0, \{a\}) \cdot (1, \emptyset) \cdot ((1, \{a\}) \cdot (1, \emptyset))^* \end{cases}$$

Then, the first states of the automaton $\mathcal{B}^\alpha_{\mathcal{A}_2}$ are depicted in Fig. 3.

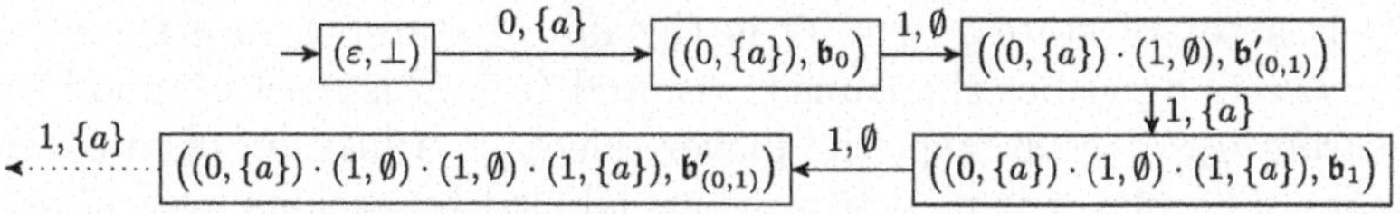

Fig. 3. $\mathcal{B}^\alpha_{\mathcal{A}_2}$: First states of the controlled belief automaton for TA $\mathcal{A}_2$ and $\mathfrak{b}$-strategy α

Runs ρ_1 and ρ_2 are feasible in $\mathcal{B}^\alpha_{\mathcal{A}_2}$:

$$\rho_1 = (\ell_0, 0), (1, \mathsf{e}_1), (\ell_0, 0), (0, \mathsf{e}_2), (\ell_{priv}, 0), (0, \mathsf{e}_3), (\ell^p_f, 0)$$

$$\rho_2 = (\ell_0, 0), (1, \mathsf{e}_1), (\ell_0, 0), (0, \mathsf{e}_4), (\ell_f, 0)$$

For $v = (0, \{a\}) \cdot (1, \emptyset) \cdot (1, \{a\})$ a sequence of actions in the automaton $\mathcal{B}^\alpha_{\mathcal{A}_2}$, we have $\rho_1 \models v$ and $\rho_2 \models v$.

We can now link a strategy and a $\mathfrak{b}$-strategy, from the point of view of runs. The proof of the following lemma can be found in [7].

Lemma 3 (Strategies and runs acceptance). *Let $\mathcal{A}$ be a TA, ρ a run of $\mathcal{A}^{dup}$, σ a finitely-varying strategy and α a finitely-varying $\mathfrak{b}$-strategy such that $\sigma \vdash\!\dashv \alpha$. We have: ρ is σ-compatible iff ρ is feasible in $\mathcal{B}^{\alpha}_{\mathcal{A}}$.*

5 Solving ET-Opacity Problems Through the belief automaton

Finally, we can prove that reasoning on the TA is equivalent to reasoning on the belief automaton.

Theorem 1. *Let $\mathcal{A}$ be a TA. There exists a finitely-varying strategy σ such that $\mathcal{A}$ is fully ET-opaque with σ iff there exists a finitely-varying $\mathfrak{b}$-strategy α such that $\sigma \vdash\!\dashv \alpha$ and there is no reachable belief in $\mathcal{B}^{\alpha}_{\mathcal{A}}$ that is bad for full ET-opacity.*

Proof. Let $\mathcal{A}$ be a TA and σ a finitely-varying strategy such that $\mathcal{A}$ is fully ET-opaque with σ. By Lemma 2, the existence of the finitely-varying strategy σ is equivalent to the existence of α a finitely-varying $\mathfrak{b}$-strategy with $\sigma \vdash\!\dashv \alpha$. By Lemma 3, we know that it is equivalent for a run ρ to be σ-compatible or feasible in $\mathcal{B}^{\alpha}_{\mathcal{A}}$. By Definition 12, this means that there is a sequence v of actions of $\mathcal{B}^{\alpha}_{\mathcal{A}}$ such that $\rho \models v$ and there is a belief $\mathfrak{b} = \mathfrak{b}^{\sigma}_{dur(\rho)} \in \mathbb{B}^{\sigma}_{\mathcal{A}}$ such that $(v \cdot \mathfrak{b})$ is reachable in $\mathcal{B}^{\alpha}_{\mathcal{A}}$. This results that the set of reachable beliefs in $\mathcal{B}^{\alpha}_{\mathcal{A}}$ is equal to the set $\mathbb{B}^{\sigma}_{\mathcal{A}}$. Finally, by Lemma 1, there is no belief bad for full ET-opacity reachable in $\mathbb{B}^{\sigma}_{\mathcal{A}}$, and therefore, as the two sets are equal, neither in $\mathcal{B}^{\alpha}_{\mathcal{A}}$. □

Intuitively, finding a $\mathfrak{b}$-strategy which avoids bad beliefs within $\mathcal{B}_{\mathcal{A}}$ amounts to solving a one-player safety game on a finite arena where the bad beliefs are the states to avoid. However, this approach would not necessarily produce a finitely-varying strategy. We will therefore rely on one-player Büchi games instead. More precisely, a one-player Büchi game can be defined by a tuple $\mathcal{G} = (Q, q_0, \Sigma, \delta^{\mathcal{G}}, G)$ where Q is a set of states, $q_0 \in Q$ is the initial state, Σ is a set of actions, $\delta^{\mathcal{G}} \subseteq Q \times \Sigma \times Q$ describes the transitions, and $G \subseteq \Sigma$ is a set of "good" actions. Starting from q_0, at each step, the player selects a transition from $\delta^{\mathcal{G}}$ to reach a new state. The player wins if transitions labeled by actions from G are taken infinitely often (note that Büchi games usually require that a set of "good" *states* is visited infinitely often instead of actions, but both frameworks are trivially equivalent).

Lemma 4 ([29])**.** *Deciding the existence of a winning strategy in a one-player Büchi game can be done in* NLOGSPACE. *Moreover this strategy, if it exists, can be constructed in polynomial time.*

As shown in [10], the full ET-opacity problem for timed automata (without control) is decidable in NEXPTIME. The ability to control the system slightly increases the complexity:

Theorem 2. *The full ET-opacity finitely-varying controller emptiness problem is decidable in* EXPSPACE*; and the full ET-opacity finitely-varying controller synthesis problem is solvable in* 2-EXPTIME.

6 Extension: Robust Definitions of ET-Opacity

So far, the attacker needed to measure the execution time with an infinite precision—this is often unrealistic in practice [19,23]. We therefore consider variants of opacity where intervals of non-opaque execution times can be considered acceptable as long as they are of size 0, i.e., reduced to a point (note that there can be an infinite number of them).

In order to formally define these two new notions, we introduce new notations: given a set S, then let $[\![S]\!]$ denote the *closure* of S (i.e., the smallest closed set containing S) and let $(\!|S|\!)$ denote the *interior* of S (i.e., the largest open set contained in S). Let $\oplus$ denotes the exclusive OR operator such that, for two sets A and B, $A \oplus B = \{v \mid v \in (A \cup B) \setminus (A \cap B)\}$.

Let us first define *almost full ET-opacity*, where every punctual opacity violation is ignored. That is, a TA is almost fully ET-opaque whenever all non-opaque durations are isolated from each other; that is, since these non-opaque durations must be punctual, then the interior of intervals of non-opaque durations must be empty.

Definition 13 (Almost full ET-opacity). *A TA $\mathcal{A}$ is almost fully ET-opaque when $(\!|DVisit^{priv}(\mathcal{A}) \oplus DVisit^{\overline{priv}}(\mathcal{A})|\!) = \emptyset$.*

Let us now define *closed full ET-opacity*, where a punctual violation is ignored only if it is followed or preceded by an opaque interval. That is, we say a TA is closed fully ET-opaque when the closure of the private durations equals the closure of the public durations.

Definition 14 (Closed full ET-opacity). *A TA $\mathcal{A}$ is closed fully ET-opaque when $[\![DVisit^{priv}(\mathcal{A})]\!] = [\![DVisit^{\overline{priv}}(\mathcal{A})]\!]$.*

A difference between both definitions is, for example, whenever a non-opaque duration is such that the immediately neighboring durations do not correspond to any accepting run (neither public nor private). In that case, this non-opaque duration will be left out by almost full ET-opacity, but will still be considered non-opaque by closed full ET-opacity.

Example 9. Let $\mathcal{A}_3$ be a TA such that $DVisit^{priv}(\mathcal{A}_3) = (0,1) \cup \{2\}$ and $DVisit^{\overline{priv}}(\mathcal{A}_3) = (0,1)$. $\mathcal{A}_3$ is not fully ET-opaque. $(\!|DVisit^{priv}(\mathcal{A}_3) \oplus DVisit^{\overline{priv}}(\mathcal{A}_3)|\!) = \emptyset$ so $\mathcal{A}_3$ is almost fully ET-opaque. $[\![DVisit^{priv}(\mathcal{A}_3)]\!] = [0,1] \cup \{2\} \neq [\![DVisit^{\overline{priv}}(\mathcal{A}_3)]\!] = [0,1]$ so $\mathcal{A}_3$ is not closed fully ET-opaque (Fig. 4).

We are interested in the same problems as before. In particular, our aim is to build a controller to make a TA closed ET-opaque with a finitely-varying strategy.

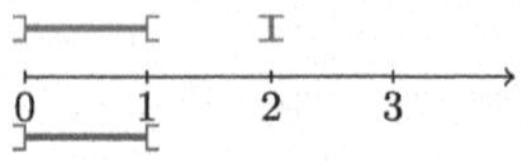

Fig. 4. Representation of private (above in red) and public (below in blue) durations in $\mathcal{A}_3$(Color figure online)

Characterization. A single belief is not sufficient to characterize a TA that is not almost ET-opaque (resp. closed). Indeed, suppose a time t such that $\mathfrak{b}_t$ is bad for full ET-opacity. This means that a punctual violation of opacity exists. This kind of violation can be allowed in the context of almost and closed full ET-opacity. It is problematic if the times around it are also a violation of opacity.

More specifically, a violation to almost full ET-opacity corresponds to a succession of bad beliefs, i.e., every punctual violation is ignored. On the other hand, a violation to closed full ET-opacity corresponds either to a succession of bad beliefs, or to a unique bad belief surrounded by beliefs that do not contain any final region. Intuitively, a punctual violation is ignored if it belongs to an interval where private and public final states can be reached.

The formal definitions of bad belief for almost ET-opacity and closed ETopacity can be found in [7].

Theorem 3. *The closed full ET-opacity finitely-varying controller emptiness problem is decidable; the closed full ET-opacity finitely-varying controller synthesis problem is solvable.*

As for full ET-opacity, this result is due to the equivalence between finding a strategy for a TA and finding a strategy in the corresponding belief automaton, and to the fact that such a strategy corresponds to a winning strategy in a one-player safety game. Similar reasoning and results are presented for almost full ET-opacity in [7].

7 Conclusion

We addressed here the control of a system modeled by a TA to make it fully ET-opaque. We showed that the controller synthesis problem can be effectively solvable for these two definitions. We also addressed two extensions (closed full ET-opacity and almost full ET-opacity) which can relate to a *robust* setting where the attacker cannot have an infinite precision.

Future Works. A natural next step will be to introduce timing parameters *à la* [10], and address control in that setting.

Addressing the control for the definition of opacity (based on languages) as in [21] would be interesting in two settings: 1) the general setting, where the controller synthesis will be undecidable but may terminate for some semi-algorithms, and 2) decidable subclasses that remain to be exhibited, presumably one-clock TAs.

Finally, the implementation of this work is on our agenda. While implementing the beliefs directly would be straightforward, it would probably result in an unnecessary blowup, and therefore an adaptation with structures such as zones (which does not seem immediate) should be designed.

References

1. Alur, R., Dill, D.L.: A theory of timed automata. TCS **126**(2), 183–235 (1994). https://doi.org/10.1016/0304-3975(94)90010-8
2. Alur, R., Fix, L., Henzinger, T.A.: Event-clock automata: a determinizable class of timed automata. TCS **211**(1–2), 253–273 (1999). https://doi.org/10.1016/S0304-3975(97)00173-4
3. Alur, R., Henzinger, T.A., Vardi, M.Y.: Parametric real-time reasoning. In: STOC, pp. 592–601. ACM (1993). https://doi.org/10.1145/167088.167242
4. Ammar, I., El Touati, Y., Yeddes, M., Mullins, J.: Bounded opacity for timed systems. J. Inf. Secur. Appl. **61**, 1–13 (2021). https://doi.org/10.1016/j.jisa.2021.102926
5. An, J., Gao, Q., Wang, L., Zhan, N., Hasuo, I.: The opacity of timed automata. In: Platzer, A., Rozier, K.Y., Pradella, M., Rossi, M. (eds.) FM. LNCS, vol. 14933, pp. 620–637. Springer, Cham (2024). https://doi.org/10.1007/978-3-031-71162-6_32
6. André, É., Bolat, S., Lefaucheux, E., Marinho, D.: strategFTO: untimed control for timed opacity. In: FTSCS, pp. 27–33. ACM (2022). https://doi.org/10.1145/3563822.3568013
7. André, É., Duflot, M., Laversa, L., Lefaucheux, E.: Execution-time opacity control for timed automata. Technical, report, abs/2409.10336, arXiv (2024). http://arxiv.org/abs/2409.10336
8. André, É., Dépernet, S., Lefaucheux, E.: The bright side of timed opacity. In: Ogata, K., Sun, M., Méry, D. (eds.) ICFEM (2024, to appear)
9. André, É., Kryukov, A.: Parametric non-interference in timed automata. In: ICECCS, pp. 37–42 (2020). https://doi.org/10.1109/ICECCS51672.2020.00012
10. André, É., Lefaucheux, E., Lime, D., Marinho, D., Sun, J.: Configuring timing parameters to ensure execution-time opacity in timed automata. In: TiCSA. Electronic Proceedings in Theoretical Computer Science, vol. 392, pp. 1–26 (2023). https://doi.org/10.4204/EPTCS.392.1. Invited paper
11. André, É., Lime, D., Marinho, D., Sun, J.: Guaranteeing timed opacity using parametric timed model checking. ACM Trans. Softw. Eng. Methodol. **31**(4), 1–36 (2022). https://doi.org/10.1145/3502851
12. Arcile, J., André, É.: Timed automata as a formalism for expressing security: a survey on theory and practice. ACM Comput. Surv. **55**(6), 1–36 (2023). https://doi.org/10.1145/3534967
13. Asarin, E., Maler, O., Pnueli, A., Sifakis, J.: Controller synthesis for timed automata. IFAC Proc. Vol. **31**(18), 447–452 (1998). https://doi.org/10.1016/S1474-6670(17)42032-5. Proceedings of the 5th IFAC Conference on System Structure and Control (SSC 1998)

14. Barbuti, R., Francesco, N.D., Santone, A., Tesei, L.: A notion of non-interference for timed automata. FI **51**(1-2), 1–11 (2002)
15. Barbuti, R., Tesei, L.: A decidable notion of timed non-interference. FI **54**(2-3), 137–150 (2003)
16. Benattar, G., Cassez, F., Lime, D., Roux, O.H.: Control and synthesis of non-interferent timed systems. Int. J. Control **88**(2), 217–236 (2015). https://doi.org/10.1080/00207179.2014.944356
17. Bertrand, N., Fabre, É., Haar, S., Haddad, S., Hélouët, L.: Active diagnosis for probabilistic systems. In: Muscholl, A. (ed.) FoSSaCS 2014. LNCS, vol. 8412, pp. 29–42. Springer, Heidelberg (2014). https://doi.org/10.1007/978-3-642-54830-7_2
18. Bouyer, P., Fang, E., Markey, N.: Permissive strategies in timed automata and games. Electron. Commun. Eur. Assoc. Softw. Sci. Technolo. **72** (2015). https://doi.org/10.14279/tuj.eceasst.72.1015
19. Bouyer, P., Markey, N., Sankur, O.: Robustness in timed automata. In: Abdulla, P.A., Potapov, I. (eds.) RP 2013. LNCS, vol. 8169, pp. 1–18. Springer, Heidelberg (2013). https://doi.org/10.1007/978-3-642-41036-9_1
20. Bruyère, V., Dall'Olio, E., Raskin, J.F.: Durations and parametric model-checking in timed automata. ACM Trans. Comput. Logic **9**(2), 12:1–12:23 (2008). https://doi.org/10.1145/1342991.1342996
21. Cassez, F.: The dark side of timed opacity. In: Park, J.H., Chen, H.-H., Atiquzzaman, M., Lee, C., Kim, T., Yeo, S.-S. (eds.) ISA 2009. LNCS, vol. 5576, pp. 21–30. Springer, Heidelberg (2009). https://doi.org/10.1007/978-3-642-02617-1_3
22. Chen, A., Hong, C., Shang, X., Jing, H., Xu, S.: Timing leakage to break SM2 signature algorithm. J. Inf. Secur. Appl. **67**, 103210 (2022). https://doi.org/10.1016/J.JISA.2022.103210
23. De Wulf, M., Doyen, L., Markey, N., Raskin, J.-F.: Robustness and implementability of timed automata. In: Lakhnech, Y., Yovine, S. (eds.) FORMATS/FTRTFT -2004. LNCS, vol. 3253, pp. 118–133. Springer, Heidelberg (2004). https://doi.org/10.1007/978-3-540-30206-3_10
24. Dima, C.: Real-time automata. J. Autom. Lang. Comb. **6**(1), 3–23 (2001). https://doi.org/10.25596/jalc-2001-003
25. Jurdziński, M., Trivedi, A.: Reachability-time games on timed automata. In: Arge, L., Cachin, C., Jurdziński, T., Tarlecki, A. (eds.) ICALP 2007. LNCS, vol. 4596, pp. 838–849. Springer, Heidelberg (2007). https://doi.org/10.1007/978-3-540-73420-8_72
26. Klein, J., Kogel, P., Glesner, S.: Verifying opacity of discrete-timed automata. In: FormaliSE, pp. 55–65. ACM (2024). https://doi.org/10.1145/3644033.3644376
27. Li, J., Lefebvre, D., Hadjicostis, C.N., Li, Z.: Observers for a class of timed automata based on elapsed time graphs. IEEE Trans. Autom. Control **67**(2), 767–779 (2022). https://doi.org/10.1109/TAC.2021.3064542
28. Standaert, F.: Introduction to side-channel attacks. In: Verbauwhede, I. (ed.) Secure Integrated Circuits and Systems. Integrated Circuits and Systems, pp. 27–42. Springer, Boston (2010). https://doi.org/10.1007/978-0-387-71829-3_2
29. Vardi, M.Y., Wolper, P.: Reasoning about infinite computations. Inf. Comput. **115**(1), 1–37 (1994). https://doi.org/10.1006/INCO.1994.1092
30. Wang, L., Zhan, N.: Decidability of the initial-state opacity of real-time automata. In: Jones, C., Wang, J., Zhan, N. (eds.) Symposium on Real-Time and Hybrid Systems. LNCS, vol. 11180, pp. 44–60. Springer, Cham (2018). https://doi.org/10.1007/978-3-030-01461-2_3

31. Wang, L., Zhan, N., An, J.: The opacity of real-time automata. IEEE Trans. Comput. Aided Des. Integr. Circuits Syst. **37**(11), 2845–2856 (2018). https://doi.org/10.1109/TCAD.2018.2857363
32. Zhang, K.: State-based opacity of labeled real-time automata. TCS **987**, 114373 (2024). https://doi.org/10.1016/J.TCS.2023.114373

Unlocking the Power of Environment Assumptions for Unit Proofs

Siddharth Priya[1(✉)], Temesghen Kahsai[2], and Arie Gurfinkel[1]

[1] University of Waterloo, Waterloo, Canada
siddharth.priya@uwaterloo.ca, arie.gurfinkel@uwaterloo.ca
[2] Amazon, Seattle, USA

Abstract. Clearly articulating the assumptions of the execution environment is crucial for the successful application of code-level formal verification. The process of specifying a model for the environment can be both laborious and error-prone, often requiring domain experts. In contrast, when engineers write unit tests, they frequently employ mocks (tMocks) to define the expected behavior of the environment in which the function under test operates. These tMocks describe how the environment behaves, e.g., the return types of an external API call (stateless behaviour) or the correct sequence of function calls (stateful behaviour). Mocking frameworks have proven to be highly effective tools for crafting unit tests. In our work, we draw inspiration from tMocks and introduce their counterpart in the realm of formal verification, which we term *vMocks*. vMocks offer an intuitive framework for specifying a *plausible* environment when conducting code-level formal verification. We implement a vMock library for the verification of C programs called SeaMock. We investigate the practicality of vMocks by, first, comparing specifications styles in the communication layer of the Android Trusty Trusted Execution Environment (TEE) open source project, and second, in the verification of mbedTLS, a widely used open source C library that provides secure communication protocols and cryptography primitives for embedded systems. Based on our experience, we conclude that vMocks complement other forms of environment models. We believe that vMocks ease adoption of code-level formal verification among developers already familiar with tMocks.

1 Introduction

Formal verification can provide stronger guarantees for software than testing. To scale and efficiently perform code-level formal verification, it is imperative to establish the boundary of a verification task. This delineation defines what falls within the purview of the verification and what lies beyond, essentially giving rise to two core components: the System Under Verification (SUT[1]) and the assumptions governing the SUT's operating environment.

[1] We use the more familiar SUT as an acronym instead of the more accurate SUV.

A. Madeira and A. Knapp (Eds.): SEFM 2024, LNCS 15280, pp. 366–384, 2025.
https://doi.org/10.1007/978-3-031-77382-2_21

Code-level formal verification in industry is typically lead by verification experts and takes months to become reliable. Even with expertise, effective environment models can take months to years to fine-tune in the context of complex industrial codebases [5,22]. The difficulty of designing environments is specially pronounced in new development projects where a reference implementation of the environment may be unavailable.

Contrarily, in test driven development (TDD), developers use testing mocking frameworks (a.k.a., tMocks) to implement environments for SUTs. tMock environments do not specify a complete environment. Instead, they are plausible only for a single function (the SUT) in a unit test. This methodology circumvents the problem of defining a complete test environment operationally (which may be complex to get right and may change over time) by instead describing how it *behaves* (e.g., how many times an environment function may be invoked or the sequence of environment function calls).

Inspired by the success of tMocks, we introduce vMocks – a mocking framework for code-level formal verification. Developers can use vMocks to clearly and efficiently model the environment for the SUT when performing code-level verification. We believe that vMocks will be transformative in enabling the adoption of code-level formal verification early in the software development cycle.

The practice of mocking rests on an effective Domain Specific Language (DSL) for describing externally visible *actions* taken by a mock. It is important to have the right DSL design and implementation. First, the DSL must be *concise* since each unit test has its own environment and a verbose language may result in developer fatigue and introduce specification errors. Second, the DSL must be *embedded* in the host programming language to avoid complexity of translating between the DSL semantics and the SUT. Finally, the specification (mock) must be *executable* with the chosen testing framework.

Existing tMock frameworks satisfy these characteristic with their intended usage scenario. For example, frameworks like cMocka [12] and GoogleMock [24] for C and C++ respectively offer concise DSLs for concrete execution, are embedded in the programming language, and are executable with unit testing frameworks. However, they do not fit well with verification tools. Such tools employ symbolic execution environments. Here, a single unit proof[2] may explore multiple concrete executions and thus the DSL must express non-determinism in the mock environment. Additionally, valid design choices for concrete execution contexts can become very expensive in symbolic executions. For example, cMocka uses a runtime map of function names to mock actions that is queried on each function call to the mock environment. GoogleMock uses dynamic dispatch to wire virtual calls to corresponding mock implementation. Therefore, using existing frameworks has considerable friction.

To address these problems, we have developed, to our knowledge, the first, compile-time mocking framework, called SEAMOCK. Its GoogleMock-inspired DSL uses C++ meta-programming to provide actions (including non–

[2] A *unit proof* is a symbolic unit test used in code-level verification.

determinism) to describe vMock behaviour. However, unlike GoogleMock, all function calls are resolved at compile time. Thus, no cost is incurred at runtime.

Our empirical evaluation is on benchmarks in C thus the choice of C++ to write mocks may seem un-intuitive. However, C++ metaprogramming is the best possible solution in our opinion. First, C++ enables a compile time DSL that is similar to GoogleMock but constructs a mock function at compile-time. This cannot be accomplished using C macros alone to the best of our knowledge. An alternative would be a custom processor for the DSL. However, this would be complex since it would need to parse C code that may be contained in a DSL program. Second, Using a DSL that allows dropping down to C++ enables full use of C/C++ expressiveness when needed, without the user learning new a language to be productive. Third, though SEAMOCK uses advanced metaprogramming, the user needs only a basic understanding of template metaprogramming. The complexity is hidden behind an object oriented DSL.

SEAMOCK, released as an open source library[3], is well suited for code-level verification tools that piggyback on a modern compilation strategy like LLVM [23]. In our evaluation, we use SEAHORN [29], but expect SEAMOCK to work with other verification tools such as SMACK [31], KLEE [9], or Crux [1]. SEAMOCK is intended to be used in verification contexts but is not necessarily limited to it and we think it may be useful in unit testing as well.

To test the efficacy of SEAMOCK, we use it to verify memory safety properties, which are important properties for security and reliability. First, we evaluate how mocks differ from existing environment specification styles by writing different environments for the same unit proof that verifies a message handling function in the Android Trusty Trusted Execution Environment (TEE) [14]. Second, we verify 31 public functions of the SSL messaging component of the mbedTLS [13] library. This component has around 6 000 lines of code. We compare the unit proof development in mbedTLS with similar industrial verification projects [10,17] and find that, *prima facie*, utilizing vMocks makes unit proof development at least three times faster.

In summary, the paper makes the following contributions: (1) introduces the idea of using mocking (vMocks) in the context of code-level formal verification, (2) a novel implementation of vMocks optimized for symbolic environments – SEAMOCK, and, (3) illustration of efficacy of the vMock philosophy and the SEAMOCK implementation through evaluation on an open source project.

The rest of the paper is organized as follows: In Sect. 2, we motivate vMocks by comparing its advantages to other environment styles in the Android Trusty project. In Sect. 3, we present the design and implementation of SEAMOCK library. In Sect. 4, we describe an extensive evaluation of vMocks on verification of memory safety of mbedTLS. We discuss usability issues in Sect. 5, related work in Sect. 6, and conclude in Sect. 7.

[3] https://github.com/seahorn/seamock.

2 Motivation

To motivate the utility of mocks, we use our experience from verifying the Android Trusty Trusted Execution Environment (TEE) [14] that provides a framework to build secure applications. These applications must communicate with unsecure applications running outside the TEE. The communication happens through an `ipc` layer. Figure 1a is a simplified representation of a core function `do_handle_msg` in the `ipc` layer. It reads an incoming message from the TEE kernel and calls an appropriate application function. We want to verify that `do_handle_msg` has no out-of-bounds memory accesses and that it does not modify the message bytes before they are passed to the application. These expectations are encoded in the unit proof in Fig. 1b. The environment consists of the following functions provided by the TEE. Functions `create_channel` and `wait_for_msg` create a collection of channels and choose a channel non-deterministically, respectively. The `get_msg` function returns the length of the incoming message. The `read_msg` function copies the message contents into a provided buffer. The `put_msg` function retires the message indicating that it is not accessed further by the application. We use the SeaHorn BMC engine for verifying `do_handle_msg`. Before looking at various styles for specifying the environment, we provide some background on the verification tool itself.

SeaHorn. The SeaHorn BMC engine [29] is a bit precise bounded model checker for LLVM programs. It uses `Clang` to compile C programs to LLVM bitcode. It provides a number of builtins to enable writing specifications in the style of C functions. **`sassert`** and **`assume`** codify verification assertions and assumptions respectively. Undefined but declared functions starting with `nd_` return non deterministic values of the declared return type. The `is_deref` builtin checks if a memory access is within allocated bounds. The SeaHorn pipeline automatically adds an `is_deref` check before every memory access. The `is_modified` builtin checks if an allocation was modified since `reset_modified` was called on that allocation. The `memhavoc` builtin havocs a newly created memory allocation.

Unit Proof. A verification task needs a harness to setup the environment and start the SUT with valid arguments passed to the chosen entry point. A methodology for designing function specific harnesses is discussed in [10]. In [30], this harness specification is called a unit proof, after unit tests. Figure 1b shows a typical unit proof. The unit proof is packaged as a C `main` function. Note that the specification language for pre-and-post conditions is C, the same language as the function under verification. This is for ease of developers already familiar with the target language. A detailed rationale is found in [30], which calls it Code-As-Specification (CaS). The setup involves creating two channels. One of the channels is chosen using `wait_for_msg` at line 9. Finally the `do_handle_msg` is called, passing in a message handler and the chosen channel. In production, `do_handle_msg` passes the incoming message to the application using a passed-in message handler. For the unit proof, the message handler is defined in `test_msg_handler`. Line 3 checks that the given `msg` arg has not been modified since being reset. The reset is part of the environment and hence not part of Fig. 1b. The `test_msg_handler` is free to return an `error` (< 0) or `ok` ($>= 0$) code. Thus, we can return any non deterministic integer at line 4 using `nd_int`.

Environment Specification Styles. A unit proof requires an environment to function correctly. The environment, operationally, is a sequence of function calls that supply valid data to the SUT. When it comes to modeling the environment, there are several design choices at hand. The environment can either be stateless, where it provides fresh, non–deterministic values with each function call, or stateful, in which case it holds a more comprehensive specification of the environment required for the SUT to function correctly. In the case of a stateless environment, each function call can be represented using a function summary, which is a declarative specification assuming a simple stateless environment. However, if the environment requires state, it can be modeled using a construct referred to as a *fake*. We explore these ways of specifying the environment next.

```
1 extern int get_msg(int, size_t *);
2 extern int read_msg(int, char *);
3 extern int put_msg(int);
4
5 #define MAX_SIZE 4096
6 typedef int (*msg_handler_t)(char* msg,
7                               size_t msg_size);
8 #define FREE_AND_RET(msg, rc) \
9   do { free(msg); return rc; } while(0)
10 #define ERROR -1
11 int do_handle_msg(
12     msg_handler_t msg_handler,
13     int chan) {
14   char *msg = (char *)malloc(MAX_SIZE);
15   size_t msg_len;
16   int rc = get_msg(chan, &msg_len);
17   if (rc < 0) FREE_AND_RET(msg, ERROR);
18   rc = read_msg(chan, msg);
19   put_msg(chan);
20   if (rc < 0) FREE_AND_RET(msg, ERROR);
21   if (((size_t) rc) < msg_len)
22     FREE_AND_RET(msg, ERROR);
23   rc = msg_handler(msg, msg_len);
24   FREE_AND_RET(msg, rc);
25 }
```

(a) C function under verification.

```
1 static int test_msg_handler(
2     char *msg, size_t msg_size) {
3   sassert(!sea_is_modified((char *)msg));
4   return nd_int(); }
5 int main(void) {
6   // create 2 channels
7   create_channel();
8   create_channel();
9   int chan = wait_for_msg();
10  do_handle_msg(
11      test_msg_handler, chan);
12  return 0;
13 }
```

(b) Unit proof for `do_handle_msg`.

Fig. 1. An SUT and its unit proof from Android Trusty TEE.

Option1: Faking the Environment. The most general approach to modelling the environment is by creating a fake – a replica of the original environment with simpler internals. A fake environment for `do_handle_msg` is defined in Fig. 2a. This environment fakes incoming messages by providing an array of messages indexed by a channel.

To simulate multiple clients connecting to the TEE, the function `create_channel` creates a channel with a pending message and adds it to a global queue of messages `msgs`. Line 20 chooses a non–deterministic length for the message. The `memhavoc` builtin at line 22 marks the message buffer as containing non–deterministic sequence of bytes. `memhavoc` ensures that `do_handle_msg` does

Table 1. vMock expectation DSL.

Expectation (method)	Meaning
`times(Predicate<N>())`	Predicate ($<, >, =$) applied to number of mock calls and N is satisfied.
`returnFn(f)`	Mock function returns output of function f.
`captureArgAndInvoke<N>(f)`	Mock function captures Nth positional argument, applies function f on it.
`invokeFn(f)`	Mock function invokes function f with all arguments.

not depend on a specific byte sequence, especially, if we want to check that a message is never altered by the function. The function `wait_for_msg` chooses from channels available currently. Thus, when `create_channel` function is called from the unit proof in Fig. 1b, it choose from one of two channels.

The `get_msg` function may return an error so the return value is non–deterministic at line 37. The subsequent **`sassert`** statement checks that the function pre-conditions are met.

The `read_msg` function checks pre-conditions and copies the (non–deterministic) message from the internal message buffer to the one passed in, i.e. `msg`. It also invokes a builtin `sea_reset_modified` to mark `msg` as being sensitive to modification. Henceforth, any store to `msg` will taint the memory and cause the corresponding `sea_is_modified` builtin to return true.

Finally, the function `put_msg` retires the message. In our simple fake, we only want a channel to provide a single message so we mark the channel as processed using a counter `g_already_processed_channel`.

Though a fake faithfully represents the actual environment, there are two problems that arise in using them in verification. First, the fake may require complicated internal data structures that are expensive to symbolically execute (in a BMC tool). In this example, the choice of the array data structure is important since it is efficient. A simple associative array data structure suffices because a channel is really an opaque type `handle_t`. Since it is opaque, we are free to map it to **`int`** and use an array instead of a more expensive data structure. Second, fakes themselves may become complex enough to require their own verification. This adds to the verification burden of the project. To circumvent the problems posed by fakes, we next look at how a minimum environment can be modelled using function summaries.

Option 2: Function Summaries. A stateful environment is complex. A stateless environment is easier to model. Figure 2b defines the summaries for our running example. We use function summaries to (1) declare the preconditions for each function in the environment and, (2) to declare valid values that the function can output through output arguments and return statements. Notice that we don't need to provide any summary for `create_channel` and `wait_for_msg` since these functions are never called from `do_handle_msg`. Unfortunately, this summary specification is not strong enough to guarantee correctness of `do_handle_msg`. The summary of `read_msg` chooses a non–deterministic integer for `len` in line 16. The length maybe greater than the size of `msg` buffer. This condition is not handled in `do_handle_msg`. It also leads to undefined behaviour in `memcpy`. Thus, we discover that a correctly functioning environment has a stronger specification – that the length returned by `get_msg` is less–than–or–equal to that used in `read_msg`.

Towards Mock Environments. We have learned a valuable lesson from the exercise so far. On the one hand, a fake environment works in practice but is expensive to construct. On the other hand, using function summaries enables us to create an inexpensive partial environment but it may need minimum state to satisfy client requirements. Thus, we want a partial environment that is just right – with function summaries that encourage non–determinism and minimum state for the correct functioning of the program function.

For our example, Fig. 2c shows a partial environment that records the length when `get_msg` is called and recalls it for `read_msg` at line 18. It is similar to Fig. 2c in other respects. This satisfies our immediate goals. However, on closer examination, we see that we have really designed the new environment in response to how it is to *behave* with `do_handle_msg`. In particular, it implicitly assumes that `get_msg` is called before `read_msg` so that message length (`g_msg_size`) is set before it is read. In concrete testing, such behavorial specifications are codified using tMocks. We thus want their counterpart in verification i.e., vMocks. We also note a key difference between a fake and a mock.

Discussion. We summarise our experience in going from a fake to a mock. Developing a fake required the following steps: (1) understanding the `ipc` layer, corresponding environment interface and implicit contracts between the SUT and environment, (2) implementing a fake that is faithful to external contracts but internally simple for verification, and, (3) developing unit proofs for the fake, finding and fixing bugs. Thus, developing a fake became its own project with the usual develop-debug-fix cycle. In contrast, we developed a vMock environment just for `do_handle_msg`. Thus, it was simple enough to not require verification. Additionally, with SeaMock, the implementation was auto-generated, removing the opportunity for trivial errors. To make vMocks practical, we require a DSL that satisfies two criteria. First, it must be similar to how mocks are specified in concrete tests. This would make it attractive to developers who already have experience with mocks. Second, it must be inexpensive to execute symbolically (e.g., in a BMC tool). Thus, whatever language constructs it provides, must produce minimum overhead during verification. To satisfy these requirements, we describe the SeaMock framework for creating user friendly and efficient vMocks in the next section.

3 The SeaMock Framework

Requirements Analysis. tMock frameworks are designed to be executed in concrete environments. The same design choices may not be ideal for symbolic environments. For example, in gMock, calls to mock functions are resolved using dynamic dispatch. Resolving such calls dynamically in a symbolic environment is, in general, hard. Another framework, cMocka [12] for C programs aims to have

```c
#define MAX_CHANNELS 10

// The next channel number to initialize
// Incremented on every create_channel call
static int g_next_available_channel;
// The first yet unprocessed channel
// Incremented on every put_msg call
static int g_already_processed_channel;

typedef struct msg {
  char* buf;
  size_t len;
} MSG;

static MSG msgs[MAX_CHANNELS];

int create_channel() {
  sassert(g_next_available_channel <
    MAX_CHANNELS);
  size_t len = nd_size_t();
  char *msg = (char *)malloc(len);
  memhavoc(msg, len);
  int chan = g_next_available_channel++;
  msgs[chan].buf = msg;
  msgs[chan].len = len;
  return chan;}
int wait_for_msg() {
  int channel = nd_int();
  assume(
    channel > g_already_processed_channel &&
    channel < g_next_available_channel);
  return channel;}

int get_msg(int chan, size_t *len) {
  int err_code = nd_int();
  if (err_code < 0) return err_code;
  sassert(chan > 0 &&
      chan < MAX_CHANNELS &&
      len != NULL);
 *len = msgs[chan].len;
  return 0; }

int read_msg(int chan, char *msg) {
  sassert(chan > 0 &&
      chan < g_next_available_channel &&
      msg != NULL);
  memcpy(msg, msgs[chan].buf, msgs[chan].len);
  sea_reset_modified(msg);
  return 0;}

int put_msg(int chan) {
  sassert(chan > 0 && chan <
      g_next_available_channel);
  int err_code = nd_int();
  if (err_code < 0) return err_code;
  free(msgs[chan].buf);
  g_already_processed_channel++;
  return 0;}
```

(a) A fake environment.

```c
#define MAX_SIZE 4096

int create_channel() {/* NOP */ return nd_int(); }
int wait_for_msg() {/* NOP */ return nd_int(); }

int get_msg(int chan, size_t *len) {
  sassert(chan > 0 && len != NULL);
  *len = nd_size_t();
  return nd_int(); // error_code
}

int read_msg(int chan, char *msg) {
  sassert(chan > 0 && msg != NULL);
  char buf[MAX_SIZE];
  memhavoc(&buf);
  size_t len = nd_size_t();
  assume(len < MAX_SIZE);
  memcpy(msg, buf, len);
  sea_reset_modified(msg);
  return nd_bool() ? -1 : len; }

int put_msg(int chan) {
  sassert(chan > 0);
  return nd_int(); }
```

(b) Function summaries for environment.

```c
#define MAX_SIZE 4096

int create_channel() {/* NOP */ return nd_int(); }
int wait_for_msg() {/* NOP */ return nd_int(); }

static size_t g_msg_size;

int get_msg(int chan, size_t *len) {
  sassert(chan > 0 && len != NULL);
  g_msg_size = nd_size_t();
  return nd_int(); }

int read_msg(int chan, char *msg) {
  sassert(chan > 0 && msg != NULL);
  char buf[MAX_SIZE];
  memhavoc(&buf);
  size_t len = nd_size_t();
  assume(len <= g_msg_size);
  memcpy(msg, buf, len);
  sea_reset_modified(msg);
  return len; }

int put_msg(int chan) {
  sassert(chan > 0);
  return nd_int(); }
```

(c) A mock environment.

Fig. 2. Different environment specification styles for `do_handle_msg`.

minimal dependencies on libraries or latest compiler features for wide applicability. It uses a runtime map keyed by function names to store expected behaviours. This runtime map is similarly expensive to use in a symbolic environment.

In some cases, it may be possible to adapt symbolic environments to work well with existing mock frameworks. However, we take a novel approach of creating a gMock inspired framework and DSL where function calls are resolved at compile time while retaining the familiar call-chain syntax. This is done using modern C++ template meta-programming[4]. We use C++ meta-programming instead of a custom preprocessor because the template mechanism is supported by industrial C++ compilers is widely available and avoids dependencies on tools that may not be available on a particular platform.

It is important to note that SeaMock does not aim to be a general purpose mocking framework. It may be useful to adapt it to unit testing, however the current implementation depends on a compiler with modern C++ features and has been tested on the `Clang` compiler toolchain only. We do expect SeaMock to work with other verification tools such as SMACK [31], KLEE [9], or Crux [1] that use LLVM.

Usage. The SeaMock DSL is embedded in C++. It is in the spirit of gMock which in-turn is inspired by jMock [11] and EasyMock [16]. jMock and gMock use a declarative scheme to build expectations on a mock object using a call chain syntax (builder pattern) [19]. The declarative scheme to specify tMock behavior is well established in industry and thus familiar to developers. Therefore SeaMock DSL also uses a declarative builder scheme as shown in Table 1. An `ExpectationBuilder` constructs an expectation object using methods to setup expectations before calling `build()`. For example, the method call `times(Eq<3>())` creates an expectation that a mock function must be called `3` times in all execution paths. A built expectation can be attached to a mock function using `MOCK_FUNCTION(name, expectation, return_type, (argument_type, ...))` where `name` is the function name, `expectation` is the user expectation, `return_type` is the return type of the function, and `(argument_type, ...)` a tuple of arguments for the function. To constraint order of execution, the macro `MOCK_FUNCTION_W_ORDER(..., (MAKE_PRED_FN SET(predecessor_fn)), ...)` is used.

In Fig. 3, line 29 shows how the mock `get_msg` function is specified. The expectation is built above in line 16 to line 20. The `ReturnFn` for `get_msg` is set in line 18. It returns a non-deterministic **`size_t`** value. We would like to capture the pointer `len` and set it to a non-deterministic value. This is the first (starting from zero) argument for `get_msg`. This is setup in two steps. First, the effect of the capture is defined using a lambda at line 3. Second, the lambda is wired to the correct positional argument using a setter at line 19. SeaMock provides built-in logic like call cardinality and sequencing that have to be hand-coded otherwise

In the spirit of need driven development [18], the user only has to specify the absolute minimum required. If a particular expectation is unspecified then a mock function is assembled with defaults. For example, we do not specify the order constraint in Fig. 3, line 29 since we don't expect any other mock function

[4] SeaMock is built against C++17.

```
1 static size_t g_msg_size;
2 // *** Begin: Mock arg capture ***
3 static constexpr auto set_ptr_fn_get_msg = [](size_t *len) {
4   *len = nd_size_t();
5   g_msg_size = *len;
6 };
7 static constexpr auto set_ptr_fn_read_msg = [](char *msg) {
8   char *blob = (char *)malloc(g_msg_size);
9   memhavoc(blob, g_msg_size);
10  sassert(msg);
11  memcpy((size_t *)msg, (size_t *)blob, g_msg_size);
12  sea_reset_modified(msg);
13 };
14 // *** End: Mock arg capture ***
15 // *** Begin: mock expect definition ***
16 constexpr auto get_msg_expectations = ExpectationBuilder()
17                                         .times(Eq<1>())
18                                         .returnFn(nd_int)
19                                         .captureArgAndInvoke<1>(set_ptr_fn_get_msg)
20                                         .build();
21
22 constexpr auto read_msg_expectations = ExpectationBuilder()
23                                         .times(Lt<2>())
24                                         .returnFn(MOCK_UTIL_WRAP_VAL(g_msg_size))
25                                         .captureArgAndInvoke<1>(set_ptr_fn_read_msg)
26                                         .build();
27 // *** End: mock expect definition ***
28 extern "C" {
29 MOCK_FUNCTION(get_msg, get_msg_expectations, int, (int, size_t *))
30 MOCK_FUNCTION_W_ORDER(read_msg, read_msg_expectations, MAKE_PRED_FN_SET(get_msg), int, (int, char *))
31 LAZY_MOCK_FUNCTION(put_msg, int, (int))
32 SETUP_POST_CHECKS((get_msg, read_msg, put_msg))}
```

Fig. 3. vMock example using SEAMOCK.

to be called before `get_msg`. The default (no expectation) is assumed when a particular constraint is unspecified. We do specify an order for the `read_msg` mock in line 30 because we expect that if it is called in an execution, then it is always after `get_msg`. Last, if we just want to specify a function summary – that just returns non–deterministic values then a mock can be declared lazy using `LAZY_MOCK_FUNCTION` with no expectations specified as in line 31.

Implementation. SEAMOCK is implemented using C++ metaprogramming. The metaprogram constructs mock functions from the expectations setup through the DSL. It is developed using the Boost Hana library [15], which provides a functional programming layer over the base metaprogramming environment. Before explaining the details particular to C++, we discuss the high level design of the library. Each mock function requires a mapping of an expectation to an action. For example, a return function expectation results in returning the value of a particular function application on mock function exit. This mapping, called the expectation map, is setup by the user using the SEAMOCK DSL. The map is a compile-time entity and thus after the C++ template pre-processor executes, a mock function is wired with values gotten from its expectation map and the map ceases to exist. Specifically, there is no lookup at run-time.

We present an example of how a return function expectation is setup internally in the framework in Fig. 4 using a compile-time expectation map (E). Basic types available to the compile time metaprogram are constant naturals (C_n), constant string (C_s) and a function object (C_f). These collectively represent

$$insert(M, k, v) \triangleq M \cup (k, v),\ where\ M : C_v \rightarrow C_v, k : C_v, v : C_v$$
$$atkey(M, k) \triangleq v \text{ if } (k, v) \in M,\ where\ M : C_v \rightarrow C_v, k : C_v, v : C_v$$
$$putReturnFn(E, retfn) \triangleq insert(M, ReturnFn, retfn),\ where\ E : C_s \rightarrow C_v, ReturnFn : C_s, retfn : C_f$$
$$getReturnFn(E) \triangleq atkey(E, ReturnFn),\ where\ E : C_s \rightarrow C_v, ReturnFn : C_s$$
$$skeletal(E) \triangleq getReturnFn(E)()$$

Fig. 4. Expectation map (M) definition and mechanism for wiring a return function.

$$putCaptureMap(E, capmap) \triangleq insert(E, CaptureMap, capmap),\ where\ E : C_s \rightarrow C_v,\ CaptureMap : C_s, capmap : C_n \rightarrow C_f$$
$$getCaptureMap(E) \triangleq atkey(E, CaptureMap),\ where\ E : C_s \rightarrow C_v, CaptureMap : C_s$$
$$args \triangleq \langle arg_1, arg_2, ..., \text{arg}_n \rangle$$
$$invokeWithCapturedArg(args, E) \triangleq \{f_j(args[i_j]) \mid (i_j, f_j) \in getCaptureMap(E)\}$$

Fig. 5. High-level mechanism for `captureArgAndInvoke`.

constant value types (C_v). The expectation map stores an action (data) keyed by an expectation, which is of type C_s. The *putReturnFn* function inserts a value (a 0–arity function object) for the *ReturnFn* key. The *getReturnFn* function extracts an inserted function object for the *ReturnFn* key. The *getReturnFn* function is applied in a *skeletal* function, that is the core of a mock function.

In Fig. 5, the mechanism of `captureArgAndInvoke<N>` is defined. Through the DSL, the user provides a mapping (*CaptureMap*) from function argument positions to invoked functions. The framework constructs a tuple (*args*) from the given function arguments. The *skeletal* uses *CaptureMap* and *args* to match functions to arguments and apply the functions left-to-right.

The Boost Hana functional C++ metaprogramming library is used instead of the bare-bones template metaprogramming environment to improve programmer efficiency and correctness since C++ metaprogramming can get tedious and error-prone to work with in advanced use cases. Note that all Hana abstractions are compiled away and thus incur no runtime cost. Hana requires C++14 or beyond. SeaMock uses C++17 to allow the use of `constexpr` lambdas, which are not necessarily used currently but maybe useful in future. Only the mock environment needs a C++ compiler. Once this unit is compiled to LLVM IR, it can be linked to the SUT written in C/C++ that has also been compiled to LLVM IR. Thus, the choice of implementing SeaMock in C++ generally does not limit the SUT source language and C may be used. An exception to this rule is when a C header file contains a function definition that may be accepted by the C compiler but not the C++ compiler. We found this case during evaluation and discuss it in Sect. 4.

A simplified low-level implementation of the SeaMock internals is shown in Fig. 6a. The core of the SeaMock implementation is the `skeletal` lambda function at line 29. The `skeletal` function creates a mock function with desired actions at compile time based on the expectations setup by the user. The user sets up expectations using the `MOCK_FUNCTION` macro. For simplicity, only a return

```
1 constexpr auto ReturnFn = [](auto ret_fn_val, auto expectations_map) {
2   auto tmp = hana::erase_key(expectations_map, RETURN_FN);
3   return hana::insert(tmp, hana::make_pair(RETURN_FN, ret_fn_val));
4 };
5 // Use: idx=i, type=T1 -> T1 argi
6 #define CREATE_PARAM(r, data, idx, type) (type BOOST_PP_CAT(arg, idx))
7 // Use: (int, float, char) ->
8 // int arg0, float arg1, char arg2
9 #define UNPACK_TRANSFORM_TUPLE(func, tuple) \
10   BOOST_PP_TUPLE_ENUM(BOOST_PP_SEQ_TO_TUPLE( \
11   BOOST_PP_SEQ_FOR_EACH_I(func, DONT_CARE, \
12       BOOST_PP_TUPLE_TO_SEQ(tuple))))
13 // Expectation map key
14 #define RETURN_FN BOOST_HANA_STRING("return_fn")
15 static constexpr auto Defaults = hana::make_map();
16 #define CREATE_ND_FUNC_NAME(name, type) \
17     BOOST_PP_CAT(nd_, \
18     BOOST_PP_CAT(name, BOOST_PP_CAT(type, _fn)))
19
20 #define MOCK_FUNCTION(name, \
21     expect_map, ret_type, args_tuple) \
22     ret_type name( \
23     UNPACK_TRANSFORM_TUPLE(CREATE_PARAM, \
24         args_tuple)) {\
25     return hana::apply(skeletal, expect_map,\
26         hana::make_tuple( \
27         UNPACK_TRANSFORM_TUPLE(CREATE_ARG, args_tuple))); \
28   }
29 static auto skeletal = [](auto &&expectations_map,
30     auto &&args_tuple) {
31   auto ret_fn = hana::at_key(expectations_map,
32       RETURN_FN);
33   return ret_fn();
34 };
```

(a) Wiring of Simplified MOCK_FUNCTION implementation.

```
template
<typename MapType=decltype(DefaultExpectationsMap)>
s ExpectationBuilder {
ate:
MapType expectationsMap;
ic:
// Constructor to initialize with an existing map
constexpr ExpectationBuilder(
    const MapType& map) : expectationsMap(map) {}

// Default constructor
constexpr ExpectationBuilder() :
    expectationsMap(DefaultExpectationsMap) {}

template<typename ReturnFnType>
constexpr auto returnFn(ReturnFnType i) const {
  auto updatedMap = ReturnFn(i, expectationsMap);
  return ExpectationBuilder<
      decltype(updatedMap)>(updatedMap);
}

// Finalize build
constexpr auto build() const {
    return expectationsMap;
}
```

(b) Expectation Builder.

Fig. 6. Seamock implementation. User interacts using the Builder interface (Fig. 6b).

function expectation is setup. A mock function is constructed in the following way at compile time. (1) A return function is added to the expectation map at Sect. 3 through the user DSL. (2) A mock function definition is created at line 24. (3) The definition applies the `skeletal` function to the expectation map and the arguments passed to the mock function at line 25. This application creates a specialized `skeletal` lambda for the given mock function.

Developers use tMocks through a fluent interface (builder like pattern). To enable easy adoption of vMocks, we encapsulate the metaprogramming in the same pattern. Specifically SeaMock uses a compile-time builder pattern (available in C++11 and beyond). A simplified version is shown in Fig. 6b. Each call to a setter method adds a key,value pair to the expectations map. The fully constructed expectation maps is returned using the `build` method. In summary, SeaMock provides a familiar interface to developers and they need not know advanced C++ metaprogramming or the Boost Hana framework to be productive. In the next section, we describe our experience in using SeaMock to verify an open source industrial project, mbedTLS.

4 Evaluation

To evaluate vMocks, we verified a core component of the mbedTLS open source project using SeaMock and SeaHorn. The mbedTLS project is a C library that implements cryptographic primitives, SSL/TLS and DTLS protocols. Its

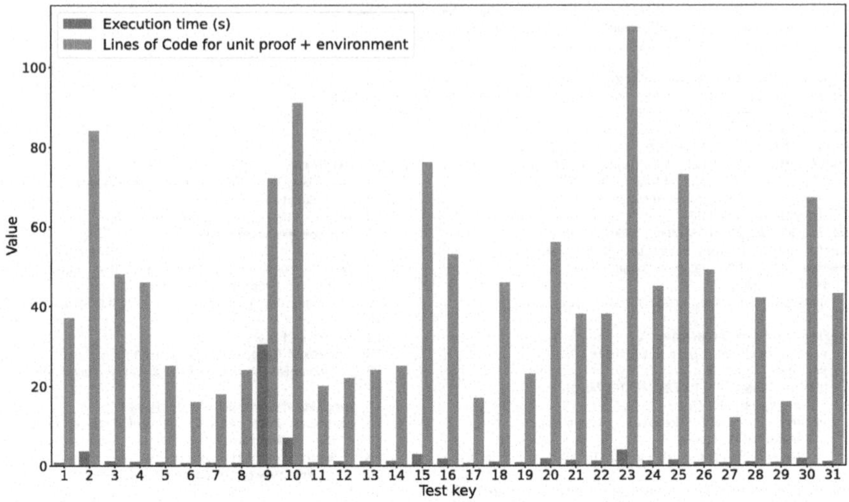

Fig. 7. Performance and size of unit proofs. Key to test name map in the extended version [28].

small code footprint and multiple configuration options makes it suitable for embedded systems. The choice of mbedTLS was guided by our industrial partners, who use the library extensively in their codebases.

In mbedTLS, we undertook the exercise of verifying functions dealing with SSL messages. These functions are present in the `ssl_msg.c` source file which is 6 000 lines of code including comments. The goal of this exercise was to understand the tradeoffs provided by vMocks in formal verification. Thus, our aim was *not* to find bugs in the implementation or prove their absence. Our goals were to study the following: (1) The practicality of developing unit proofs for a *legacy* codebase (without unit tests), (2) the flexibility of using SEAMOCK to develop environments, and, (3) a qualitative understanding of how code structure affects development of unit proofs.

The `ssl_msg.c` compilation unit contains 44 public (non-static) functions. For our evaluation, we decided to verify low level properties, specially memory safety for these public functions. We developed unit proofs for 31 functions. Of the remaining 13 public functions, 9 functions are trivial – getters, setters and simple boolean checks. The remaining 4 either were specifications themselves or did not have memory accesses. Seethe extended version [28] for details. We were able to develop unit proofs utilizing vMocks for all functions of interest. Almost all unit proofs used the SEAMOCK DSL, the remaining few had to be hand coded in C because their environments needed a header file (`ssl_misc.h`) that compiled under a C compiler but not under a C++ compiler. SEAMOCK can be used for all functions once this problem is corrected at source in the mbedTLS project. The experiments were conducted on an Intel(R) Xeon(R) CPU E5-2680 running at 2.70 GHz with 64 GiB of main memory. Total build time for all unit proofs was 5 s.

The results are given in Fig. 7. All execution times are single seconds except `mbedtls_ssl_read` (key = 9) where the unit proof checks that all bytes are copied from one buffer to another. This is a more involved proof and takes closer to a half a minute to run. Of particular interest is the source code complexity for the unit proof and the environment. The average unit proof (harness) size is 24 lines of code and the average environment size is 47 lines of code. Both excluding comments. This is an indication that developing a single unit proof does not involve a lot of coding. The artifacts from the study are open sourced [27]. We discuss our findings next.

Process. Here we describe our process of verifying the SSL message component of the mbedTLS library. First, useful pre-and-post conditions were intuited by breaking the overall verification goal into unit proofs aimed at verifying individual functions. Next, using a list of callees of the function, we decided on functions to mock – we sometimes mocked only a subset of callees to verify more of the production code. Lastly, a decision was made on how *lazy* a mock function should be. Implementations written using `LAZY_MOCK_FUNCTION` did not add any expectations on the mock function. For verifying memory safety, if the production function accessed passed-in buffers, then the mock function checked that such buffers were large enough to accommodate all accesses.

```
static size_t nb_bytes;

constexpr auto invoke_fn_mbedtls_ssl_recv_t = []
(void *ctx, unsigned char *buf, size_t len) {
  if (buf != NULL) {
    sassert(sea_is_deref(buf, len));
  }
  int ret = nd_int();
  assume(ret <= 0 || ret >= (int)nb_bytes);
  return ret;
};
extern "C" {
void set_min_recv_bytes(size_t num_bytes) { nb_bytes = num_bytes; }
constexpr auto expectations_mbedtls_ssl_recv_t =
    seamock::ExpectationBuilder()
        .times(seamock::Lt<2>())
        .invokeFn(invoke_fn_mbedtls_ssl_recv_t)
        .build();
MOCK_FUNCTION(ssl_recv_fn, expectations_mbedtls_ssl_recv_t, int,
    (void * /* ctx */, unsigned char * /* buf */, size_t /* len */))
SETUP_POST_CHECKS((ssl_recv_fn))}
```

Fig. 8. `ssl_recv_fn` mock used in the unit proof for `ssl_msg_fetch_input`.

Table 2. Comparison of engineer efficiency across verification projects.

Project	Unit Proofs(U)	Weeks(W)	Persons(P)	$Rate = U/(W \times P)$
mbedTLS (vMocks)	31	5	1	6.2
aws-c-common	171	24	3	2.4
firecracker-vmm	27	30	2	0.5

The vMock Language. We found that in verifying a legacy codebase (without unit tests) written by a third party was challenging because the pre-and-post conditions were not made explicit and the verification engineer could not explicate what these invariants could be. Thus we found that coming up with the declarative behaviour of an environment was complex. Instead, it was practical to use the `InvokeFn` action to invoke a simple function stub. Thus, most environments were written as such rather than using more behaviorial actions like `After` and `ReturnFn`. We posit that in a new software project, a rich set of actions in the mocking DSL is more useful since the environment is yet unspecified and behaviors are easier to model

A typical example of a mock function is shown in Fig. 8. Here we see the use of `InvokeFn` to invoke a function at line 3. The function checks that the passed-in `buf` can be dereferenced upto `len` bytes. We also want to provide at least as many bytes as requested by the unit proof. To wire this logic in, the unit proof calls the `set_min_recv_bytes` function before calling the SUT. Now when `ssl_recv_fn` is called, we make sure that atleast that many bytes are returned.

Outcome and Learning. A single verification engineer with no previous familiarity with the codebase was able to verify 31 functions is the SSL message component of mbedTLS in five weeks. To put this into perspective, we looked at similar projects using the unit proof methodology of code-level verification for BMC but does not use a DSL based mocking methodology – the aws-c-common verification project from AWS [10] in C and the Firecracker Virtual Machine Monitor verification project [17] in Rust, again from AWS. The comparative rate of developing unit proofs is given in Table 2. The properties under verification and the complexity of the codebase vary across projects. Thus it is hard to make an apples-to-apples comparison. These numbers are only indicative that vMocks may be useful, especially bootstrapping a verification project.

With mbedTLS, it was challenging to determine pre-and-post conditions for functions since most of the considered functions did not specify them in comments or employ unit tests. In essence, verifying legacy code using unit proof faces similar problems as faced by developers retrofitting unit tests into such codebases. The next section discusses the use case for vMocks based on industrial experience with tMocks.

5 Usability of Mocks

tMocks and TDD. tMocks are an essential tool for test driven development (TDD). TDD is a methodology where unit tests are written before the SUT function. The test initially fails since the function is not implemented. The function and tests are then refined in lockstep until all the unit tests pass. tMocks play a vital role in this refinement process since they specify how the function interacts with the environment. There has been continued discussion on the efficacy of TDD over the last twenty years [6,25,32]. TDD is not a silver bullet to improve software quality. However, used judiciously, it has shown to improve software quality outcomes [26]. Moreover, it is a promoted methodology of code development in industry [33].

In TDD, tMocks inform the design of object interfaces. As [18] states, "By testing an object in isolation, the programmer is forced to consider an object's interactions with its collaborators in the abstract, possibly before those collaborators exist. TDD with Mock Objects guides interface design by the services that an object requires, not just those it provides." Thus, tMocks compel the SUT to evolve into a form that is robust and well tested. In contrast, current approaches to formal verification assume the SUT has already reached a robust design, having undergone sufficient testing. It is in this context that formal verification is applied to software, often by a team of verification specialists who are different from the original developers [9,10,20].

Using the lessons of TDD, this work present vMocks, to lower the startup costs of formal verification such that developers themselves use formal verification early on in software projects. With mocking, the program under verification and the environment need not be fully fleshed out to gain confidence in design and implementation. SUT functions can be verified in isolation as they are developed, i.e., using verification driven development (VDD).

Lifecycle of Mocks. We know from industrial experience that tMocks become difficult to maintain once the project reaches maturity and environment interfaces are fully fleshed out[5]. At this point, investing time and effort in fakes is better for the long term. We imagine that vMocks will have a similar lifecycle. They will be invaluable early on in a project when developers are designing a system incrementally or refactoring a legacy codebase. However, once a SUT is fully fleshed out with the aid of mocking, using fake environments will be natural and serve the project better in the long run. We see VDD supplementing TDD since the startup cost of TDD will be lower. Where VDD will find its utility relative to TDD is unexplored. This paper contributes a methodology and tooling to conduct research in this area.

5 https://abseil.io/resources/swe-book/html/ch13.html#prefer_realism_over_isolation.

6 Related Work

This work stands on both research in formal verification and the practice of test driven development. Designing abstract environments is an integral part of any code-level formal verification effort. Environments were described using function summaries in the static driver verification project (SDV) [5] from Microsoft Research. As another design example, a fake filesystem was implemented by the KLEE authors for verifying coreutils [9]. Angelic verification [22] from MSR, is a methodology to auto generate environments. It was a response to the long lead times in delivering software environments in the SDV project. However, automatic generation of environments is a program synthesis problem and is inherently hard for complex environments.

In test driven development, the need to test with an environment before it can be defined led naturally to tMocks [18]. Their applicability with respect to test driven development has been studied over the last two decades [6,25,32]. More interestingly, tMocks have been widely promoted in industry. There is a large body of advice of how to use them, including caveats [33]. In this vein, the reader may find various ToTT [2] blog posts (e.g., [3,4]) from Google interesting. It is hard to maintain parity between a tMock and the real environment as a project evolves. To mitigate the effort required to maintain tMocks, there has been interest in academia [8] and industry (e.g., [7,21]) on automatically generating tMocks. Similar techniques may be useful in generating vMocks.

Software verification, including modeling environments for verification, remains a specialized endeavour as highlighted in a recent case study by AWS [10]. To our knowledge, there has been no published work on adapting testing mocks (tMocks) for verification (vMocks). This presentation takes the first step towards remedying the situation.

7 Conclusion

This work takes inspiration from mocks in testing (tMocks) and introduces their counterpart in verification (vMocks). Like tMocks, vMocks define environments behaviorally. We hope that vMocks catalyze formal methods in software development. The presented case study uses vMocks for writing proofs using vMocks for public functions of the SSL messaging layer of the mbedTLS project with low engineering effort. For the case study, we developed SeaMock, an open-source vMock DSL library embedded in C++ for the SeaHorn BMC tool. A future direction would be to adapt static analysis of tools like SeaHorn to reason about runtime polymorphism efficiently enabling the use of tMock frameworks like gMock in symbolic execution. Alternatively, the use of SeaMock could be extended to concrete testing.

References

1. Crux (2023). https://crux.galois.com/
2. Authors, T.: Introducing “Testing on the Toilet” (2007). https://testing.googleblog.com/2007/01/introducing-testing-on-toilet.html
3. Authors, T.: Tott: partial mocks using forwarding objects (2009). https://testing.googleblog.com/2009/02/tott-partial-mocks-using-forwarding_19.html
4. Authors, T.: Testing on the toilet: Don’t mock types you don’t own (2020). https://testing.googleblog.com/2020/07/testing-on-toilet-dont-mock-types-you.html
5. Ball, T., et al.: Thorough static analysis of device drivers. In: Berbers, Y., Zwaenepoel, W. (eds.) 2006 EuroSys Conference, Leuven, Belgium, April 18-21, 2006, Proceedings, pp. 73–85. ACM (2006). https://doi.org/10.1145/1217935.1217943
6. Beck, K.: Test-driven development: by example. Addison-Wesley Professional (2003)
7. Boeira, M.: Using sourcery to automatically generate mocks (2019). https://medium.com/@mdboeira/using-sourcery-to-automatically-generate-mocks-73ced75b2863
8. Bragg, N.F.F., Foster, J.S., Roux, C., Solar-Lezama, A.: Program sketching by automatically generating mocks from tests. In: Silva, A., Leino, K.R.M. (eds.) CAV 2021. LNCS, vol. 12759, pp. 808–831. Springer, Cham (2021). https://doi.org/10.1007/978-3-030-81685-8_38
9. Cadar, C., Dunbar, D., Engler, D.R.: KLEE: unassisted and automatic generation of high-coverage tests for complex systems programs. In: Draves, R., van Renesse, R. (eds.) 8th USENIX Symposium, OSDI 2008, December 8-10, 2008, San Diego, California, USA, Proceedings, pp. 209–224. USENIX Association (2008). https://dl.acm.org/doi/10.5555/1855741.1855756
10. Chong, N., Cook, B., Eidelman, J., Kallas, K., Khazem, K., Monteiro, F.R., Schwartz-Narbonne, D., Tasiran, S., Tautschnig, M., Tuttle, M.R.: Code-level model checking in the software development workflow at amazon web services. Softw. Pract. Exp. **51**(4), 772–797 (2021). https://doi.org/10.1002/spe.2949
11. jMock Developers: jmock (2019). http://jmock.org/
12. cmocka Developers.: cmocka website (2023). https://cmocka.org/
13. mbedTLS Developers: mbedtls project (2023). https://github.com/Mbed-TLS/mbedtls
14. Developers, A.: Trusty tee (2023), https://source.android.com/docs/security/features/trusty
15. Developers, B.H.: Boost.hana (2023). https://boostorg.github.io/hana/index.html
16. Developers, E.: Easymock (2022). https://easymock.org/
17. Developers., K.: Using kani to validate security boundaries in aws firecracker (2024). https://model-checking.github.io/kani-verifier-blog/2023/08/31/using-kani-to-validate-security-boundaries-in-aws-firecracker.html
18. Freeman, S., Mackinnon, T., Pryce, N., Walnes, J.: Mock roles, objects. In: Vlissides, J.M., Schmidt, D.C. (eds.) OOPSLA 2004, Vancouver, BC, Canada, pp. 236–246. ACM (2004). https://doi.org/10.1145/1028664.1028765
19. Freeman, S., Pryce, N.: Evolving an embedded domain-specific language in java. In: Tarr, P.L., Cook, W.R. (eds.) OOPSLA 2006, Portland, Oregon, USA, pp. 855–865. ACM (2006). https://doi.org/10.1145/1176617.1176735

20. Hamza, J., Felix, S., Kuncak, V., Nussbaumer, I., Schramka, F.: From verified scala to STIX file system embedded code using stainless. In: Deshmukh, J.V., Havelund, K., Perez, I. (eds.) NFM 2022, Pasadena, CA, USA. LNCS, vol. 13260, pp. 393–410. Springer (2022). https://doi.org/10.1007/978-3-031-06773-0_21
21. Kraus, S.: Using sourcery to automatically generate mocks (2019). https://medium.com/iqoqo-engineering/this-library-uses-your-jest-tests-to-generate-mocks-c07c322c58e3
22. Lahiri, S.K., Lal, A., Gopinath, S., Nutz, A., Levin, V., Kumar, R., Deisinger, N., Lichtenberg, J., Bansal, C.: Angelic checking within static driver verifier: Towards high-precision defects without (modeling) cost. In: FMCAD 2020, Haifa, Israel, pp. 169–178. IEEE (2020). https://doi.org/10.34727/2020/isbn.978-3-85448-042-6_24
23. Lattner, C., Adve, V.: LLVM: a compilation framework for lifelong program analysis and transformation, pp. 75–88. San Jose, CA, USA, March 2004
24. LLC., G.: Googletest user's guide (2023). https://google.github.io/googletest/
25. Munir, H., Wnuk, K., Petersen, K., Moayyed, M.: An experimental evaluation of test driven development vs. test-last development with industry professionals. In: Shepperd, M.J., Hall, T., Myrtveit, I. (eds.) EASE '14, London, United Kingdom, May 13-14, 2014, pp. 50:1–50:10. ACM (2014). https://doi.org/10.1145/2601248.2601267
26. Nagappan, N., Maximilien, E.M., Bhat, T., Williams, L.A.: Realizing quality improvement through test driven development: results and experiences of four industrial teams. Empir. Softw. Eng. **13**(3), 289–302 (2008). https://doi.org/10.1007/s10664-008-9062-z
27. Priya, S., Gurfinkel, A., Kahsai, T.: verify-mbedtls-artifact, June 2024. https://doi.org/10.6084/m9.figshare.26122222. https://figshare.com/articles/dataset/verify-mbedtls-artifact/26122222/1
28. Priya, S., Kahsai, T., Gurfinkel, A.: Unlocking the power of environment assumptions for unit proofs (extended) (2024). https://github.com/seahorn/seamock/blob/main/paper.md
29. Priya, S., Su, Y., Bao, Y., Zhou, X., Vizel, Y., Gurfinkel, A.: Bounded model checking for LLVM. In: Griggio, A., Rungta, N. (eds.) FMCAD 2022, Trento, Italy, pp. 214–224. IEEE (2022). https://doi.org/10.34727/2022/isbn.978-3-85448-053-2_28
30. Priya, S., Zhou, X., Su, Y., Vizel, Y., Bao, Y., Gurfinkel, A.: Verifying verified code. Innov. Syst. Softw. Eng. **18**(3), 335–346 (2022). https://doi.org/10.1007/s11334-022-00443-9
31. Rakamarić, Z., Emmi, M.: SMACK: decoupling source language details from verifier implementations. In: Biere, A., Bloem, R. (eds.) CAV 2014. LNCS, vol. 8559, pp. 106–113. Springer, Cham (2014). https://doi.org/10.1007/978-3-319-08867-9_7
32. Romano, S., Zampetti, F., Baldassarre, M.T., Penta, M.D., Scanniello, G.: Do static analysis tools affect software quality when using test-driven development? In: Madeiral, F., Lassenius, C., Conte, T., Männistö, T. (eds.) ESEM '22: ACM/IEEE Helsinki, Finland, pp. 80–91. ACM (2022). https://doi.org/10.1145/3544902.3546233
33. Wright, H., Winters, T.D., Manshreck, T.: Software Engineering at Google. O'Reilly (2020)

Towards Quantum Multiparty Session Types

Ivan Lanese(✉), Ugo Dal Lago(✉), and Vikraman Choudhury(✉)

OLAS Team, University of Bologna and INRIA, Bologna, Italy
{ivan.lanese,vikraman.choudhury}@gmail.com, ugo.dallago@unibo.it

Abstract. Multiparty Session Types (MPSTs) offer a structured way of specifying communication protocols and guarantee relevant communication properties, such as deadlock-freedom. In this paper, we extend a minimal MPST system with quantum data and operations, enabling the specification of quantum protocols. Quantum MPSTs (QMPSTs) provide a formal notation to describe quantum protocols, both at the abstract level of global types, describing which communications can take place in the system and their dependencies, and at the concrete level of local types and quantum processes, describing the expected behavior of each participant in the protocol. Type-checking relates these two levels formally, ensuring that processes behave as prescribed by the global type. Beyond usual communication properties, QMPSTs also allow us to prove that qubits are owned by a single process at any time, capturing the quantum no-cloning and no-deleting theorems. We use our approach to verify four quantum protocols from the literature, respectively Teleportation, Secret Sharing, Bit-Commitment, and Key Distribution.

Keywords: Multiparty Session Types · Linear Types · Quantum Protocols · Quantum Processes · Quantum Computing

1 Introduction

Quantum protocols involve the exchange of (quantum) information between multiple parties in (quantum) networks, giving rise to complex interaction patterns, interleaved with manipulations of quantum states. This raises the need for tools and techniques to specify, analyse, and verify such protocols. However, while many languages, notations, and formal calculi exist to describe quantum circuits, fewer options exist for formally describing quantum multiparty protocols (see the discussion in the recent systematic survey [15]). In fact, there does

Partially supported by the EU Marie Skłodowska-Curie action ReGraDe-CS (№: 101106046), by French ANR project SmartCloud ANR-23-CE25-0012, by INdAM - GNCS 2024 project MARVEL, code CUP E53C23001670001, and by the Italian Ministry of University and Research under PNRR - M4C2 - I1.4 Project CN00000013 "National Centre for HPC, Big Data and Quantum Computing".

A. Madeira and A. Knapp (Eds.): SEFM 2024, LNCS 15280, pp. 385–403, 2025.
https://doi.org/10.1007/978-3-031-77382-2_22

not exist a mainstream formal way to describe quantum protocols. This is witnessed by the fact that the Quantum Protocol Zoo [32], a well-known library of quantum protocols, relies on natural language—hence ambiguous—descriptions, paired with Python implementations.

Existing formalisms for quantum protocols include imperative languages such as LanQ [27] and QMCLANG [14,29], and process calculi such as CQP [16], $\mathrm{CCS^q}$ [2] and lqCCS [10]. The former do not allow for an abstract representation of the protocol, while the latter are not easy to understand (see the discussion in Sect. 6 for details). The analysis in [16] on the shortcomings of their CQP approach reports: "The proliferation of channels is a consequence of the fact that our type system associates a unique type with each channel. Introducing session types would allow a single channel to be used for the entire protocol".

Following this hint in [16], we propose a quantum extension to Multiparty Session Types (MPSTs) [22,24], dubbed Quantum MPSTs (QMPSTs), as a formal session-typed language to describe quantum protocols. QMPSTs provide both an abstract view—the *global type*, and a concrete view—a multiparty system made of named *quantum processes*. The global type describes the expected pattern of interactions from a global viewpoint, clarifying which communications take place, between which participants, and in which order. QMPST processes describe the sequence of actions taken by each participant inside the protocol, including quantum actions such as the application of unitary transformations or the measurement of qubits. The two views are formally related—*type checking* ensures that processes actually behave as prescribed by the global type (Theorem 3). The framework of MPSTs also ensures relevant communication properties by construction, such as progress (Theorem 5). Further, in our approach, messages will directly target participants, denoted by their name, avoiding the proliferation of channels (as in CQP), and clarifying the expected sender and receiver of each message (cf. Example 5).

Outline and Contributions. The main contribution of this paper is a novel framework for specifying quantum protocols using MPSTs, building on classical approaches, but extending them with quantum features. There is no other extension of MPSTs for quantum protocols in the literature, to the best of our knowledge.

- In Sect. 2, we introduce our calculus for QMPSTs. At the level of types, the main novelty is that data include references to qubits, and such references need to be treated in a linear way (cf. Theorem 7) due to the no-cloning and no-deleting theorems [34] of quantum computing. At the level of processes, as mentioned before, we introduce quantum operations such as unitary transformations and measurement.
- In Sect. 3, we provide a concrete operational semantics for QMPSTs. We define a labelled transition system for quantum multiparty systems, that is both non-deterministic and probabilistic, to account for multiparty system communication, and the probabilistic nature of quantum measurements.

- In Sect. 4, we establish meta-theoretical results for our calculus. We prove the usual communication safety properties of MPSTs, namely, subject reduction (Theorem 3), session fidelity (Theorem 4), progress (Theorem 5), and type safety (Theorem 6), and quantum safety properties, namely, unique ownership of qubits (Theorem 7) and qubit safety (Theorem 8).
- In Sect. 5, we show the expressive power and clarity of our approach by applying it to four quantum protocols from the literature, namely Teleportation (used as a running example), Secret Sharing (Example 5, in Sect. 5), Bit-Commitment (Example 6, in Sect. 5), and Key Distribution (see technical report [26]).

We remark that some familiarity with quantum computing is needed to understand the paper—for standard notions, we refer to [28]. For details of proofs, auxiliary results, and additional examples, we refer the reader to the extended technical report [26].

2 Type System

We start from a minimal MPSTs paradigm (such as the one in [35]) to avoid cluttering the work with technicalities that are not related to the interplay between MPSTs and quantum computing and which would spoil the cleanliness of the language. This approach is also useful in understanding which advanced features of MPSTs are useful in the quantum setting, and which ones are unnecessary.

We follow the usual top-down approach to MPSTs, whereby we first give a global type describing the interactions in the system from a global point of view. We then project the global type into local types, describing the required behavior of each participant. Local types are used to type check the processes describing participants. The main novelty of our type system is that basic types include qubits (**qbit**), and qubit variables are treated linearly.

Amongst the common features in approaches to MPSTs (such as [22,30]), we drop support for multiple sessions and delegation, and only use a single channel. These features are not useful for our case studies in Sect. 5, nor in other examples of quantum protocols we have looked at (see, e.g., the library of quantum protocols mentioned above [32]). The most important feature of MPSTs that we use is the notion of internal and external choice (or send and receive, respectively), and selection and branching constructs in processes, which allows processes to exchange both classical and quantum data. Hence, following Selinger's famous slogan *"quantum data + classical control"* for quantum lambda-calculus [31], the slogan for our quantum process calculus is *"quantum data + classical control + classical choice"*.

We first define the syntax of types. In the following definition, $(q_i)_{i\in I}$ and $\{\, q_i \,\}_{i\in I}$ denote indexed tuples and indexed sets, respectively. We also denote tuples as $\tilde{q}$, leaving the indexing implicit. We also write $\widetilde{x{:}B}$ to mean a tuple $\tilde{x}$ of typed variables, each of type B.

$$
\begin{array}{rcll}
G & ::= & \mathtt{p}{\to}\mathtt{q}\colon \{\ell_i(B_i).G_i\}_{i\in I} & \text{Transmission or Interaction} \\
& | & \mu\mathbf{t}.G \quad | \quad \mathbf{t} \quad | \quad \mathbf{end} & \text{Recursion, Type variable, Termination} \\
T & ::= & \mathtt{p}\&\{\ell_i(B_i).T_i\}_{i\in I} & \text{External choice (receive)} \\
& | & \mathtt{p}\oplus\{\ell_i(B_i).T_i\}_{i\in I} & \text{Internal choice (send)} \\
& | & \mu\mathbf{t}.T \quad | \quad \mathbf{t} \quad | \quad \mathbf{end} & \text{Recursion, Type variable, Termination} \\
B & ::= & \mathbf{bit} \mid \mathbf{qbit} \mid \mathbf{unit} \mid \ldots & \text{Basic types}
\end{array}
$$

Fig. 1. Syntax of types.

Definition 1 (Syntax of Types). *The syntax of* global types, local types, *and* basic types, *ranged over respectively by G, T and B, is defined in Fig. 1, where* $\mathtt{p}, \mathtt{q}$ *are* participants *(or roles) and ℓ_i denote* labels. *Labels in a global type are assumed to be disjoint, and label sets are non-empty. Basic types include at least* **bit***s,* **unit***, integers, and* references to qubits.

In choices we may drop braces when the index set is a singleton. References to qubits are needed since, due to entanglement, allowing values of distinct qubits to be related (indeed measuring one of them may impact the value of the other), it is not possible to provide separate descriptions of single qubits. Following [13, 31], we hence rely on a global qubit register, abstracting away from the actual physical location of the qubits, to describe the whole quantum state of a system. References are pointers (or names) to quantum states inside this register.

Labels are used as usual to communicate which branch is taken in a choice. We drop labels when the choice has a single branch, and the type of it, if it is **unit**. Global recursive types are contractive, that is, each occurence of the recursive type variable inside the body of the recursive definition is guarded. We also assume the equi-recursive equation: $\mu\mathbf{t}.G = G\{^{\mu\mathbf{t}.G}/_{\mathbf{t}}\}$ holds.

Example 1 (Quantum Teleportation [2, Fig. 14] *- Description and Global Type).* The quantum teleportation protocol [7] allows one to transmit a quantum state via a *non-quantum* medium. A slightly different version of the protocol is reported in [16, Fig. 5] under the name of "Quantum teleportation with EPR source".

In order to more easily model the example we extend our data types with n-uples of bits, denoted $\mathbf{bit}^n$. We can then write the global type below. We use a dedicated participant called `Env`, for environment, where other participants can take input from and send output to. This avoids the need for specific input and output primitives as in [2].

$$
\begin{aligned}
G = {} & \mathtt{Env} \to \mathtt{Alice} : (\mathbf{qbit}) \,.\, \mathtt{Source} \to \mathtt{Alice} : (\mathbf{qbit}) \,.\, \mathtt{Source} \to \mathtt{Bob} : (\mathbf{qbit}). \\
& \mathtt{Alice} \to \mathtt{Bob} : (\mathbf{bit}^2) \,.\, \mathtt{Bob}{\to}\mathtt{Env}{:}(\mathbf{qbit}).\mathbf{end}
\end{aligned}
$$

The idea is that `Alice` takes a **qbit** from `Env`, and wants to send it to `Bob` via a classical communication channel (indeed `Alice` only sends to `Bob` two classical

bits). Bob can then give the **qbit** to Env. In order to do so, Alice and Bob take from some Source two entangled qubits. ◇

The set of roles or participants in a global type G is given by $\text{pt}(G)$:

$$\text{pt}(\mathtt{p}{\to}\mathtt{q}\colon \{\ell_{\mathtt{i}}(B_i).G_i\}_{i\in I}) = \{\,\mathtt{p},\mathtt{q}\,\} \cup \bigcup_{i\in I} \text{pt}(G_i)$$
$$\text{pt}(\mu\mathbf{t}.G) = \text{pt}(G)$$
$$\text{pt}(\mathbf{t}) = \text{pt}(\mathbf{end}) = \emptyset$$

Projection allows one to derive which local type each participant needs to follow in order for their composition to behave as prescribed by the global type. We take the notion of projection below from [30].

Definition 2 (Global Type Projection). *The* projection of a global type G onto a role $\mathtt{p}$, *written* $G\upharpoonright\mathtt{p}$, *is:*

$$(\mathtt{q}{\to}\mathtt{r}\colon \{\ell_{\mathtt{i}}(B_i).G_i\}_{i\in I})\upharpoonright\mathtt{p} = \begin{cases} \mathtt{r}\oplus\{\ell_{\mathtt{i}}(B_i).(G_i\upharpoonright\mathtt{p})\}_{i\in I} & \textit{if } \mathtt{p}=\mathtt{q} \\ \mathtt{q}\&\{\ell_{\mathtt{i}}(B_i).(G_i\upharpoonright\mathtt{p})\}_{i\in I} & \textit{if } \mathtt{p}=\mathtt{r} \\ \bigsqcap_{i\in I} G_i\upharpoonright\mathtt{p} & \textit{if } \mathtt{p}\neq\mathtt{q} \textit{ and } \mathtt{p}\neq\mathtt{r} \end{cases}$$

$$(\mu\mathbf{t}.G)\upharpoonright\mathtt{p} = \begin{cases} \mu\mathbf{t}.(G\upharpoonright\mathtt{p}) & \textit{if } \mathtt{p}\in\text{pt}(G) \textit{ or } \mathsf{fv}(\mu\mathbf{t}.G)\neq\emptyset \\ \mathbf{end} & \textit{otherwise} \end{cases} \qquad \mathbf{t}\upharpoonright\mathtt{p}=\mathbf{t} \quad \mathbf{end}\upharpoonright\mathtt{p}=\mathbf{end}$$

where $\bigsqcap$ *is the full-merging operation, defined as:*

$$\mathtt{p}\oplus\{\ell_{\mathtt{i}}(B_i).T_i\}_{i\in I} \sqcap \mathtt{p}\oplus\{\ell_{\mathtt{i}}(B_i).T'_i\}_{i\in I} = \mathtt{p}\oplus\{\ell_{\mathtt{i}}(B_i).(T_i\sqcap T'_i)\}_{i\in I}$$
$$\mu\mathbf{t}.T \sqcap \mu\mathbf{t}.T' = \mu\mathbf{t}.(T\sqcap T') \quad \mathbf{t}\sqcap\mathbf{t} = \mathbf{t} \quad \mathbf{end}\sqcap\mathbf{end} = \mathbf{end}$$
$$\mathtt{p}\&\{\ell_{\mathtt{i}}(B_i).T_i\}_{i\in I} \sqcap \mathtt{p}\&\{\ell_{\mathtt{j}}(B_j).T'_j\}_{j\in J} = \mathtt{p}\&\{\ell_{\mathtt{k}}(B_k).T''_k\}_{k\in I\cup J}$$
$$\textit{where} \quad T''_k = \begin{cases} T_k\sqcap T'_k & \textit{if } k\in I\cap J \\ T_k & \textit{if } k\in I\setminus J \\ T'_k & \textit{if } k\in J\setminus I \end{cases}$$

Intuitively, participants involved in a choice act as prescribed by the choice. Participants which are not involved need either to behave the same in the two branches, or to receive messages with distinct labels telling them how to behave.

Example 2 (Quantum Teleportation - Local types). We can obtain the local types by projecting the global type in Example 1 on the different participants:

$$G\upharpoonright\mathtt{Alice} = \mathtt{Env}\&(\mathbf{qbit}).\mathtt{Source}\&(\mathbf{qbit}).\mathtt{Bob}\oplus(\mathbf{bit}^2).\mathbf{end}$$
$$G\upharpoonright\mathtt{Bob} = \mathtt{Source}\&(\mathbf{qbit}).\mathtt{Alice}\&(\mathbf{bit}^2).\mathtt{Env}\oplus(\mathbf{qbit}).\mathbf{end}$$
$$G\upharpoonright\mathtt{Source} = \mathtt{Alice}\oplus(\mathbf{qbit}).\mathtt{Bob}\oplus(\mathbf{qbit}).\mathbf{end}$$
$$G\upharpoonright\mathtt{Env} = \mathtt{Alice}\oplus(\mathbf{qbit}).\mathtt{Bob}\&(\mathbf{qbit}).\mathbf{end}$$

◇

A global type is well-formed if it is contractive, and can be projected onto all its roles. We implicitly assume that all global types are well-formed.

$$\frac{j \in I}{\mathtt{p}\rightarrow\mathtt{q}\colon \{\ell_i(B_i).G'_i\}_{i\in I} \xrightarrow{\mathtt{p}\rightarrow\mathtt{q}:\ell_j(B_j)} G'_j}\ [\text{GT-}\oplus\&]$$

$$\frac{\forall i \in I\ G'_i \xrightarrow{\alpha} G''_i \quad \mathtt{pt}(\alpha) \cap \{\mathtt{p},\mathtt{q}\} = \emptyset}{\mathtt{p}\rightarrow\mathtt{q}\colon \{\ell_i(B_i).G'_i\}_{i\in I} \xrightarrow{\alpha} \mathtt{p}\rightarrow\mathtt{q}\colon \{\ell_i(B_i).G''_i\}_{i\in I}}\ [\text{GT-Ctx}]$$

Fig. 2. Global type transitions

Definition 3 (Global Type Transitions). *The* global type transition *relation* $\xrightarrow{\alpha}$ *is defined in Fig. 2. We write* $G \longrightarrow G'$ *if there exists* α *such that* $G \xrightarrow{\alpha} G'$*. We also write* $G \longrightarrow$ *if there exists* G' *such that* $G \longrightarrow G'$*;* $\longrightarrow^*$ *denotes the reflexive and transitive closure of* $\longrightarrow$*.*

Rule GT-$\oplus$& in Fig. 2 just allows one to execute the first interaction. Rule GT-Ctx allows one to execute an interaction α available in all the continuations provided that it has disjoint participants from the first one. Sets of local types projected from a global type can be used to type programs. We extend the type system in [2, Fig. 12], which however requires channels to carry uniform values. Like in [16], qubits are treated linearly.

The syntax of systems, processes and expressions is in Fig. 3. We take inspiration from the syntax in [2, Fig. 11], with a few changes to fit MPSTs. First, for us a system is a parallel composition of processes with roles, and, send and receive actions explicitly refer to the target role $\mathtt{p}$. This makes the protocol clearer than using channels, and helps the technical development as well. Then, as customary for session types, we have input choice to allow a participant to wait for several input messages, and accept the first one that arrives. We use labels to clarify which branch of a choice is selected. Finally, we avoid the input/output constructs in [2, Fig. 11] (we model them as interactions with some Environment role, as done in our running example).

We assume a set $\mathcal{V}$ for variables, which may contain either classical values, or references to the qubit register which contains actual quantum information. We assume that operators in expressions only work on classical data, operations on **qbit**s are explicitly modeled as unitary operations. We assume to have a library of unitary operations (e.g., controlled not, Hadamard, ...), ranged over by $\mathtt{U}$. Process $\mathbf{0}_{\tilde{q}}$ is labelled with the tuple $\tilde{q}$ of **qbit**s it owns. This is needed to ensure linearity of **qbit**s, and to clarify which participant owns which **qbit**. This is relevant since due to entanglment (s)he (in a follow up protocol) may influence other **qbit**s entangled with its own. We write just $\mathbf{0}$ when $\tilde{q}$ is empty.

Note that $\prod_{i\in I} \mathtt{p}_i \triangleright P_i$ is shorthand for $\mathtt{p}_1 \triangleright P_1 \mid \ldots \mid \mathtt{p}_n \triangleright P_n$, where $\mid$ is the parallel composition operator, which is associative and commutative. For simplicity, we frequently assume that the tuples of formal parameters $\tilde{x}$ in process definitions and the tuples of expressions for actual parameters $\tilde{e}$ in process calls are split into standard and quantum ones.

$$
\begin{array}{rcll}
\mathtt{e} & ::= & x & \text{(variable)} \\
& | & q & \text{(reference inside the qubit register)} \\
& | & c & \text{(constant)} \\
& | & \mathbf{e}\,\mathbf{op}\,\mathbf{e} & \text{(operation)} \\
\mathbf{z} & ::= & x & \text{(variable)} \\
& | & q & \text{(reference inside the qubit register)} \\
P, Q & ::= & \mathbf{0}_{\tilde{z}} & \text{(inaction, owning qubits in } \tilde{z}\text{)} \\
& | & \mathtt{p}\oplus\ell\langle e\rangle.P & \text{(selection/send towards role p)} \\
& | & \mathtt{p}\&\{\ell_i(x_i).P_i\}_{i\in I} & \text{(branching/receive from role p with } I \neq \emptyset\text{)} \\
& | & \mathbf{def}\ X(\tilde{x}) = P\ \mathbf{in}\ Q & \text{(process definition)} \\
& | & X\langle\tilde{e}\rangle & \text{(process call)} \\
& | & \mathbf{if}\ e\ \mathbf{then}\ P\ \mathbf{else}\ Q & \text{(conditional)} \\
& | & x := \mathtt{meas}\ z.P & \text{(measurement)} \\
& | & \mathtt{new}\,x.P & \text{(new qubit generation)} \\
& | & \mathtt{U}(\tilde{z}).P & \text{(unitary operation)} \\
\mathcal{M} & ::= & \prod_{i\in I} \mathtt{p}_i \triangleright P_i & \text{(multiparty system)}
\end{array}
$$

Fig. 3. Syntax of expressions, processes, and systems

Example 3 (Quantum Teleportation - Processes). We can now write an actual system implementing the quantum teleportation protocol:

$$\mathcal{M} = \mathtt{Alice} \triangleright P_A \mid \mathtt{Bob} \triangleright P_B \mid \mathtt{Source} \triangleright P_S \mid \mathtt{Env} \triangleright P_E$$

where:

$$
\begin{aligned}
P_A &= \mathtt{Env}\&(w).\mathtt{Source}\&(x).\mathtt{CNot}(w,x).\mathtt{H}(w).\tilde{r} := \mathtt{meas}\,(w,x).\mathtt{Bob}\oplus\langle\tilde{r}\rangle.\mathbf{0} \\
P_B &= \mathtt{Source}\&(y).\mathtt{Alice}\&(\tilde{r}).\boldsymbol{\sigma}_{\tilde{\mathtt{r}}}(y).\mathtt{Env}\oplus\langle y\rangle.\mathbf{0} \\
P_S &= \mathtt{new}\,x_s, y_s.\mathtt{H}(x_s).\mathtt{CNot}(x_s,y_s).\mathtt{Alice}\oplus\langle x_s\rangle.\mathtt{Bob}\oplus\langle y_s\rangle.\mathbf{0} \\
P_E &= \mathtt{Alice}\oplus\langle q\rangle.\mathtt{Bob}\&(y).\mathbf{0}_y
\end{aligned}
$$

`Alice` takes the desired **qbits**, then applies to them two unitary transformations: a controlled not `CNot` (which negates the second **qbit** if the first one is true, just propagates it otherwise—and acts linearly if the states of the qubits are not classical states but a superposition of them) and a Hadamard gate H (which turns classical states into a superposition), measures the two resulting **qbits** obtaining two classical **bits** in r (here we extended the `meas` operator to work on pairs) and sends them to `Bob`.

`Bob` gets the two **bits** and uses them to select which of the 4 Pauli transformations $\boldsymbol{\sigma}_0, \ldots, \boldsymbol{\sigma}_3$ to apply to y, where $\boldsymbol{\sigma}_0$ is the identity matrix, and $\boldsymbol{\sigma}_1, \boldsymbol{\sigma}_2, \boldsymbol{\sigma}_3$

are the three 2×2 Pauli matrices[1]. `Source` just creates a pair of entangled **qbit**s, and sends its components to, respectively, `Alice` and `Bob`. `Env` just gives the initial **qbit** to `Alice` and gets the result from `Bob`. ◇

Now we describe the typing of processes and systems.

Definition 4 (Typing Contexts). *Θ (used for process definitions and calls) maps process variables to session types prefixed by the types of the parameters, Γ maps variables to basic types (except* **qbit***s), and Δ maps variables and references to (only) the* **qbit** *type.*

$$\Theta ::= \emptyset \mid \Theta, X{:}(\widetilde{B};T) \quad \Gamma ::= \emptyset \mid \Gamma, x{:}B \ (B \neq \mathbf{qbit}) \quad \Delta ::= \emptyset \mid \Delta, z{:}\mathbf{qbit}$$

Notably, following DILL [5], we use dual contexts for intuitionistic (classical data) variables and linear (quantum data) variables. Since we omit delegation, there are no channel variables in contexts Γ or Δ. We write Δ_q when Δ contains only qubit references, and omit contexts in judgements when empty and unambiguous.

Definition 5 (Typing Judgements). *Typing judgements are of the form:*

$$\Gamma;\Delta \vdash e : B \qquad \Theta \cdot \Gamma;\Delta \vdash P : T \qquad \Gamma;\Delta \vdash \mathcal{M} : G$$

Definition 6 (Typing Rules). *The typing rules are defined in Fig. 4. Typing rules for operators and constants are standard and omitted (but for 0 and 1). The Δ used in the conclusion of each typing rule in Fig. 4 is the concatenation of the (different) Δ_is used in the premises.*

The rules are mostly self-explanatory. Notably, due to linearity of **qbit**s, when a process sends a **qbit** (rule T-$\oplus$) it loses the ownership (indeed, Δ is split into Δ_1 used to type the payload of the message and Δ_2 used to type the continuation). Dually, when a process receives a **qbit** (rule T-&) it gains ownership on it. Indeed, it can be used to type the continuation. Note that the two sets of premises are needed to cover two cases depending on whether the received value is classical (first case, added to Γ) or quantum (second case, added to Δ). We have two rules for conditional, T-**if** applies when the two branches follow the same local type while T-$\oplus$-**if** when they contribute with different message send. In both the cases, both the premises use the same Δ_2 since in each computation only one of the branches is executed. In rule T-**def**, Θ stores the type of the defined function so that it can then be checked against the invocation in rule T-Call. There $\tilde{B}$ is shorthand for $B_1, \ldots, B_n$, and $\tilde{e}$ is shorthand for $e_1, \ldots, e_n$.

Example 4 (Quantum Teleportation - Typing). Using the typing rules we can derive the judgment:

$$q{:}\mathbf{qbit} \vdash \mathcal{M} : G$$

We show the typing of `Alice` as an example in Fig. 5. ◇

[1] We slightly abuse notation here, we could have modeled this choice in more details using conditionals to actually select one of the transformations.

$$\frac{x{:}B \in \Gamma}{\Gamma \vdash x : B}\;[\text{T-Var}] \qquad \frac{}{\Gamma\,;\, z{:}\mathbf{qbit} \vdash z : \mathbf{qbit}}\;[\text{T-QVar}] \qquad \frac{}{\Gamma \vdash 0, 1 : \mathbf{bit}}\;[\text{T-}\mathit{bit}]$$

$$\frac{\Theta \cdot \Gamma\,;\, \Delta, x{:}\mathbf{qbit} \vdash P : T}{\Theta \cdot \Gamma\,;\, \Delta \vdash \mathtt{new}\, x.P : T}\;[\text{T-}\mathit{qbit}] \qquad \frac{\Gamma\,;\, \Delta_1 \vdash z : \mathbf{qbit} \quad \Theta \cdot \Gamma, x{:}\mathbf{bit}\,;\, \Delta_2 \vdash P : T}{\Theta \cdot \Gamma\,;\, \Delta \vdash x := \mathtt{meas}\, z.P : T}\;[\text{T-}\mathit{meas}]$$

$$\frac{\Theta \cdot \Gamma\,;\, \Delta, \widetilde{z{:}\mathbf{qbit}} \vdash P : T}{\Theta \cdot \Gamma\,;\, \Delta, \widetilde{z{:}\mathbf{qbit}} \vdash \mathtt{U}(\tilde{z}).P : T}\;[\text{T-}U] \qquad \frac{}{\Theta \cdot \Gamma\,;\, \widetilde{z{:}\mathbf{qbit}} \vdash \mathbf{0}_{\tilde{z}} : \mathbf{end}}\;[\text{T-}\mathbf{end}]$$

$$\frac{\Gamma\,;\, \Delta_1 \vdash e : B \quad \Theta \cdot \Gamma\,;\, \Delta_2 \vdash P : T}{\Theta \cdot \Gamma\,;\, \Delta \vdash \mathtt{p}\oplus\ell\langle e\rangle.P : \mathtt{p}\oplus\{\ell(B).T\}}\;[\text{T-}\oplus]$$

$$\frac{\forall i \in I\ \Theta \cdot \Gamma, x_i{:}B_i\,;\, \Delta \vdash P_i : T_i \quad \forall j \in J\ \Theta \cdot \Gamma\,;\, \Delta, x_j{:}B_j \vdash P_j : T_j}{\Theta \cdot \Gamma\,;\, \Delta \vdash \mathtt{p}\&\{\ell_i(x_i).P_i\}_{i \in I \uplus J} : \mathtt{p}\&\{\ell_i(B_i).T_i\}_{i \in I \uplus J}}\;[\text{T-}\&]$$

$$\frac{\Gamma\,;\, \Delta_1 \vdash e : \mathbf{bit} \quad \Theta \cdot \Gamma\,;\, \Delta_2 \vdash P : T \quad \Theta \cdot \Gamma\,;\, \Delta_2 \vdash Q : T}{\Theta \cdot \Gamma\,;\, \Delta \vdash \mathbf{if}\, e\, \mathbf{then}\, P\, \mathbf{else}\, Q : T}\;[\text{T-}\mathbf{if}]$$

$$\frac{\Gamma\,;\, \Delta_1 \vdash e : \mathbf{bit} \quad \Theta \cdot \Gamma\,;\, \Delta_2 \vdash P : \mathtt{p}\oplus\{\ell_i(B_i).T_i\}_{i \in I} \quad \Theta \cdot \Gamma\,;\, \Delta_2 \vdash Q : \mathtt{p}\oplus\{\ell_i(B_i).T_i\}_{i \in J}}{\Theta \cdot \Gamma\,;\, \Delta \vdash \mathbf{if}\, e\, \mathbf{then}\, P\, \mathbf{else}\, Q : \mathtt{p}\oplus\{\ell_i(B_i).T_i\}_{i \in I \uplus J}}\;[\text{T-}\oplus\text{-}\mathbf{if}]$$

$$\frac{\Theta, X{:}(\tilde{B}, \tilde{B}'; T_1) \cdot \Gamma, \widetilde{x{:}B}\,;\, \Delta_1, \widetilde{x'{:}B'} \vdash P : T_1 \quad \Theta, X{:}(\tilde{B}, \tilde{B}'; T_1) \cdot \Gamma\,;\, \Delta_2 \vdash Q : T_2}{\Theta \cdot \Gamma\,;\, \Delta \vdash \mathbf{def}\ X(\tilde{x}, \tilde{x}') = P\ \mathbf{in}\ Q : \mu X.T_2}\;[\text{T-}\mathbf{def}]$$

$$\frac{\forall i \in [n] \quad \Gamma\,;\, \Delta_i \vdash e_i : B_i}{\Theta, X{:}(\widetilde{B}; T) \cdot \Gamma\,;\, \Delta \vdash X\langle\tilde{e}\rangle : T}\;[\text{T-Call}] \qquad \frac{\forall \mathtt{p}_i \in \mathtt{pt}(G) \qquad \Gamma\,;\, \Delta_i \vdash P_i : G \upharpoonright \mathtt{p}_i}{\Gamma\,;\, \Delta \vdash \prod_{\mathtt{p}_i \in \mathtt{pt}(G)} \mathtt{p}_i \triangleright P_i : G}\;[\text{T-Sys}]$$

Fig. 4. Typing rules for expressions, processes, and systems

$$\dfrac{\dfrac{\dfrac{\dfrac{\dfrac{\dfrac{\tilde{r}{:}\mathbf{bit}^2 \vdash \tilde{r} : \mathbf{bit}^2 \qquad \emptyset \cdot \tilde{r}{:}\mathbf{bit}^2 \vdash \mathbf{0} : \mathbf{end}}{\emptyset \cdot \tilde{r}{:}\mathbf{bit}^2 \vdash \mathtt{Bob}\oplus\langle\tilde{r}\rangle.\mathbf{0} : \mathtt{Bob}\oplus(\mathbf{bit}^2).\mathbf{end}}}{\emptyset \cdot w{:}\mathbf{qbit}, x{:}\mathbf{qbit} \vdash \tilde{r} := \mathtt{meas}\,(w, x).\mathtt{Bob}\oplus\langle\tilde{r}\rangle.\mathbf{0} : \mathtt{Bob}\oplus(\mathbf{bit}^2).\mathbf{end}}}{\emptyset \cdot w{:}\mathbf{qbit}, x{:}\mathbf{qbit} \vdash \mathtt{H}(w).\tilde{r} := \mathtt{meas}\,(w, x).\mathtt{Bob}\oplus\langle\tilde{r}\rangle.\mathbf{0} : \mathtt{Bob}\oplus(\mathbf{bit}^2).\mathbf{end}}}{\emptyset \cdot w{:}\mathbf{qbit}, x{:}\mathbf{qbit} \vdash \mathtt{CNot}(w, x).\mathtt{H}(w).\tilde{r} := \mathtt{meas}\,(w, x).\mathtt{Bob}\oplus\langle\tilde{r}\rangle.\mathbf{0} : \mathtt{Bob}\oplus(\mathbf{bit}^2).\mathbf{end}}}{\emptyset \cdot w{:}\mathbf{qbit} \vdash \mathtt{Source}\&(x).\mathtt{CNot}(w, x).\mathtt{H}(w).\tilde{r} := \mathtt{meas}\,(w, x).\mathtt{Bob}\oplus\langle\tilde{r}\rangle.\mathbf{0} : \mathtt{Source}\&(\mathbf{qbit}).\mathtt{Bob}\oplus(\mathbf{bit}^2).\mathbf{end}}}{\emptyset \cdot \emptyset \vdash \mathtt{Env}\&(w).\mathtt{Source}\&(x).\mathtt{CNot}(w, x).\mathtt{H}(w).\tilde{r} := \mathtt{meas}\,(w, x).\mathtt{Bob}\oplus\langle\tilde{r}\rangle.\mathbf{0} : G \upharpoonright \mathtt{Alice}}$$

Fig. 5. Typing for Alice in Quantum Teleportation

3 Semantics

The semantics that we present combines the management of quantum state following the approach in [13,31] (for a quantum λ-calculus), with classical semantics for MPST systems, such as in [30,35]. A main novelty is that we need to combine non-determinism (typical of process calculi but absent in λ-calculi) with probabilities originating from measurements of quantum states.

Given a finite set of qubit variables Q, called a quantum register, we denote with $\mathcal{H}[\mathsf{Q}]$ the Hilbert space generated by all functions $\mathsf{Q} \rightarrow \{0, 1\}$, denoted as $\mathcal{B}[\mathsf{Q}]$, which is the computational basis for $\mathcal{H}[\mathsf{Q}]$. Elements of $\mathcal{B}[\mathsf{Q}]$, are of the form

$|q_1 \leftarrow b_1, \ldots, q_n \leftarrow b_n\rangle$ and ranged over by $|\eta\rangle$, for every $q_i \in \mathsf{Q}$ and $b_i \in \{0, 1\}$. Hence, elements of $\mathcal{H}[\mathsf{Q}]$ are elements of Hilbert spaces with a chosen basis, that is, linear combinations of elements of $\mathcal{B}[\mathsf{Q}]$, written $\mathscr{Q} = \sum_{|\eta\rangle \in \mathcal{B}[\mathsf{Q}]} \alpha_\eta |\eta\rangle$, where $\alpha_\eta \in \mathbb{C}$ are complex probability amplitudes satisfying $\sum_{|\eta\rangle \in \mathcal{B}[\mathsf{Q}]} |\alpha_\eta|^2 = 1$. The probability operator $\mathbb{P}^q_b \colon \mathcal{H}[\mathsf{Q}] \to [0, 1]$ is given by $\mathbb{P}^q_b(\mathscr{Q}) = \sum_{\eta(q)=b} |\alpha_\eta|^2$. For $q \in \mathsf{Q}$, the projection operator $\hat{\mathsf{P}}^q_b \colon \mathcal{H}[\mathsf{Q}] \to \mathcal{H}[\mathsf{Q}\backslash\{q\}]$ is given by $\hat{\mathsf{P}}^q_b(\mathscr{Q}) = {}^1/\sqrt{\mathbb{P}^q_b(\mathscr{Q})} \sum_{|\eta\rangle \in \mathcal{B}[\mathsf{Q}\backslash\{q\}]} \alpha_{\eta\{q \leftarrow b\}} |\eta\rangle$. For $q \notin \mathsf{Q}$, the new operator $\mathsf{N}_q \colon \mathcal{H}[\mathsf{Q}] \to \mathcal{H}[\mathsf{Q} \cup \{q\}]$ is given by $\mathsf{N}_q(\mathscr{Q}) = \mathscr{Q} \otimes |q \leftarrow 0\rangle$ which assigns $|0\rangle$ to q. Qubits can be modified by unitary operations, written as $U_{\tilde{q}} \colon \mathcal{H}[\mathsf{Q}] \to \mathcal{H}[\mathsf{Q}]$, where $\tilde{q}$ is a sequence of distinct qubit variables.

The semantics, defined in Fig. 6, is a transition system over configurations of the form $\langle \mathscr{Q}, \mathcal{M} \rangle$, where $\mathscr{Q}$ is the quantum state associated to the underlying quantum register Q, and $\mathcal{M}$ is a multiparty session-typed system. The semantics is both non-deterministic and probabilistic (it forms a GPLTS, in the sense of [8, Definition 2.5])—the multiparty process behavior is non-deterministic (in the choice of redex for single processes which do some computation, or pairs of processes that communicate), and the quantum operations are probabilistic (in the choice of measurement outcome). The transition relation is: $\longrightarrow \subseteq \langle \mathscr{Q}, \mathcal{M} \rangle \times \mathsf{L} \times [0, 1] \times \langle \mathscr{Q}, \mathcal{M} \rangle$, where L is the set of labels: either $\mathsf{p} \to \mathsf{q} : v$ denoting a communication step, or p denoting a computation step (for role names p and q). We use π to range over probabilities. The semantics relies on a semantics of expressions as well. We do not present it since it is classical, and write $e \downarrow v$ to denote that expression e evaluates to value v. The evaluation relation on tuples $\tilde{e} \downarrow \tilde{d}$ is taken pointwise.

Rule [R-Comm] allows processes to communicate. Rules [R-Meas-0] and [R-Meas-1] define measurements, and are the only rules defining transitions with non-1 probability. They also consume the measured qubit. Dually, rule [R-New] extends the register with a new qubit. Note that there are no transitions for $\mathbf{0}_{\tilde{q}}$ processes.

The transition system satisfies the following properties (expected for GPLTS):

Proposition 1. *For any* $\mathscr{Q}, \mathcal{M}, \mathscr{Q}', \mathcal{M}', \alpha$,

1. *if* $\langle \mathscr{Q}, \mathcal{M} \rangle \xrightarrow{\alpha}_{\pi_1} \langle \mathscr{Q}', \mathcal{M}' \rangle$ *and* $\langle \mathscr{Q}, \mathcal{M} \rangle \xrightarrow{\alpha}_{\pi_2} \langle \mathscr{Q}', \mathcal{M}' \rangle$, *then* $\pi_1 = \pi_2$, *and*
2. *it holds that* $\sum \{ \pi \in [0, 1] \mid \langle \mathscr{Q}, \mathcal{M} \rangle \xrightarrow{\alpha}_{\pi} \langle \mathscr{Q}', \mathcal{M}' \rangle \} = 1$.

Proof. One can notice that the only probabilities which are not 1 originate from measurements. However, the first part holds since the two transitions corresponding to the two outcomes of a given measurement always lead to different states. This is also the only case where there are two transitions from the same state with the same label, and since the probabilities sum up to 1 also the second part holds.

We remark that labels in our semantics are just decorations to simplify the statement of the results in the next section, hence the semantics can be seen as an annotated reduction semantics.

$$\frac{j \in I \qquad \ell = \ell_j \qquad e \downarrow v}{\langle \mathscr{Q}, \mathtt{p} \triangleright \mathtt{q} \oplus \ell(e).P \mid \mathtt{q} \triangleright \mathtt{p} \& \{\ell_i(x_i).Q_i\}_{i \in I}\rangle \xrightarrow{\mathtt{p} \to \mathtt{q}:v}_1 \langle \mathscr{Q}, \mathtt{p} \triangleright P \mid \mathtt{q} \triangleright Q_j\{^v/_{x_j}\}\rangle} \text{[R-COMM]}$$

$$\frac{\tilde{e} \downarrow \tilde{d}}{\langle \mathscr{Q}, \mathtt{p} \triangleright \mathbf{def}\ X(\tilde{x}) = P\ \mathbf{in}\ Q\rangle \xrightarrow{\mathtt{p}}_1 \langle \mathscr{Q}, \mathtt{p} \triangleright Q\{^{P\{\tilde{d}/\tilde{x}\}}/_{X(\tilde{e})}\}\rangle} \text{[R-def]}$$

$$\frac{x \notin \mathsf{Q}}{\langle \mathscr{Q}, \mathtt{p} \triangleright \mathtt{new}\, x.P\rangle \xrightarrow{\mathtt{p}}_1 \langle \mathsf{N}_x(\mathscr{Q}), \mathtt{p} \triangleright P\rangle} \text{[R-NEW]} \qquad \frac{\tilde{z} \subseteq \mathsf{Q}}{\langle \mathscr{Q}, \mathtt{p} \triangleright \mathtt{U}(\tilde{z}).P\rangle \xrightarrow{\mathtt{p}}_1 \langle \mathtt{U}_{\tilde{z}}(\mathscr{Q}), \mathtt{p} \triangleright P\rangle} \text{[R-U]}$$

$$\frac{z \in \mathsf{Q} \qquad \pi = \mathbb{P}_0^z(\mathscr{Q})}{\langle \mathscr{Q}, \mathtt{p} \triangleright x := \mathtt{meas}\, z.P\rangle \xrightarrow{\mathtt{p}}_\pi \langle \hat{\mathsf{P}}_0^z(\mathscr{Q}), \mathtt{p} \triangleright P\{^0/_x\}\rangle} \text{[R-MEAS-0]}$$

$$\frac{z \in \mathsf{Q} \qquad \pi = \mathbb{P}_1^z(\mathscr{Q})}{\langle \mathscr{Q}, \mathtt{p} \triangleright x := \mathtt{meas}\, z.P\rangle \xrightarrow{\mathtt{p}}_\pi \langle \hat{\mathsf{P}}_1^z(\mathscr{Q}), \mathtt{p} \triangleright P\{^1/_x\}\rangle} \text{[R-MEAS-1]}$$

$$\frac{e \downarrow 1}{\langle \mathscr{Q}, \mathtt{p} \triangleright \mathbf{if}\, e\, \mathbf{then}\, P\, \mathbf{else}\, Q\rangle \xrightarrow{\mathtt{p}}_1 \langle \mathscr{Q}, \mathtt{p} \triangleright P\rangle} \text{[R-if-1]} \qquad \frac{e \downarrow 0}{\langle \mathscr{Q}, \mathtt{p} \triangleright \mathbf{if}\, e\, \mathbf{then}\, P\, \mathbf{else}\, Q\rangle \xrightarrow{\mathtt{p}}_1 \langle \mathscr{Q}, \mathtt{p} \triangleright Q\rangle} \text{[R-if-0]}$$

$$\frac{\langle \mathscr{Q}, \mathcal{M}\rangle \xrightarrow{\alpha}_\pi \langle \mathscr{Q}', \mathcal{M}'\rangle}{\langle \mathscr{Q}, \mathcal{M} \mid P\rangle \xrightarrow{\alpha}_\pi \langle \mathscr{Q}', \mathcal{M}' \mid P\rangle} \text{[R-CONG]}$$

Fig. 6. Semantic Rules

Note that we could also give a more abstract description of the semantics, disregarding the qubit register and probabilities. In this setting, actions from a single participant are to be considered as invisible τ steps. This allows one to more easily relate with MPSTs which indeed only describe communications, but we choose to work with the more concrete *quantum* semantics, showing the quantum state and probabilities.

Definition 7 (Multiparty System Transitions). *We say $\mathcal{M} \xrightarrow{\alpha} \mathcal{M}'$ if $\exists \mathscr{Q}, \mathscr{Q}', \pi \neq 0$ such that $\langle \mathscr{Q}, \mathcal{M}\rangle \xrightarrow{\alpha}_\pi \langle \mathscr{Q}, \mathcal{M}'\rangle$. We say $\mathcal{M} \xrightarrow{\tau} \mathcal{M}'$ if $\exists \mathtt{p}$, such that $\mathcal{M} \xrightarrow{\mathtt{p}} \mathcal{M}'$. We say $\mathcal{M} \stackrel{\alpha}{\Rightarrow} \mathcal{M}'$ if $\mathcal{M}\ (\xrightarrow{\tau})^* \xrightarrow{\alpha} (\xrightarrow{\tau})^*\ \mathcal{M}'$.*

4 Results

We prove two kinds of results—the first kind are classical results adapted from MPSTs theory, such as Subject Reduction and Session Fidelity (see, e.g., [9,30, 35]), to the quantum extension. Such results hold for *closed* terms, namely terms with no free variables, but, notably, they *can have references* to the qubit register. Hence the judgments in these statements have the form $\Delta_q \vdash \mathcal{M} : G$. The other kind of results show that **qbit**s are treated correctly, linearly in particular.

First, any global type which is not **end** can perform at least a transition.

Lemma 2 (Progress for Global Types). *If $G \neq$ **end**, then $G \longrightarrow$.*

Subject reduction, stated below, ensures that transitions preserve typability for systems with no free variables (which may however have references to the qubit register). We write $\exists\, \Delta \supseteq \Delta'$ to mean that there exists a context Δ' such that Δ is a weakening of Δ'.

Theorem 3 (Subject Reduction).

1. *If* $\Delta_q \vdash \mathcal{M} : G$ *and* $\mathcal{M} \xrightarrow{\mathtt{p}} \mathcal{M}'$*, then* $\exists \Delta_q'$ *such that* $\Delta_q' \vdash \mathcal{M}' : G$.
2. *If* $\Delta_q \vdash \mathcal{M} : G$ *and* $\mathcal{M} \xrightarrow{\mathtt{p}\to\mathtt{q}:\ell(v)} \mathcal{M}'$*, then* $\exists \Delta_q \supseteq \Delta_q', B, G'$ *such that* $\Delta_q' \vdash v : B$*,* $G \xrightarrow{\mathtt{p}\to\mathtt{q}:\ell(B)} G'$*, and* $\Delta_q \vdash \mathcal{M}' : G'$.

Note that the environment Δ_q never changes during communication steps: ownership can move from one process to the other, but **qbit**s are neither created nor destroyed. They can only be created and destroyed in computational steps, using, respectively, new qubit generation and measurement.

Session fidelity shows that transitions of global types and of systems do agree. Notice however that global types abstract away from non-communication steps, which are instead present in systems.

Theorem 4 (Session Fidelity).

1. *If* $\Delta_q \vdash \mathcal{M} : G$ *and* $G \xrightarrow{\mathtt{p}\to\mathtt{q}:\ell(B)} G'$*, then* $\exists \Delta_q', \Delta_q'', \mathcal{M}', v,$ *such that* $\Delta_q' \vdash v : B$*,* $\mathcal{M} \xRightarrow{\mathtt{p}\to\mathtt{q}:\ell(v)} \mathcal{M}'$*, and* $\Delta_q'' \vdash \mathcal{M}' : G'$.
2. *If* $\Delta_q \vdash \mathcal{M} : G$*,* $\mathcal{M} \xRightarrow{\mathtt{p}\to\mathtt{q}:\ell(v)} \mathcal{M}'$*, and* $G \xrightarrow{\mathtt{p}\to\mathtt{q}:\ell(B)} G'$*, then* $\exists \Delta_q', \Delta_q''$*, such that* $\Delta_q' \vdash v : B$*, and* $\Delta_q'' \vdash \mathcal{M}' : G'$.

We can now show that well-typed systems have progress and never get stuck.

Theorem 5 (Progress). *If* $\Delta_q \vdash \mathcal{M} : G$*, then either* $G = \mathbf{end}$*, or* $\mathcal{M} \longrightarrow$.

Definition 8. *A system* $\mathcal{M}$ *is stuck if it is not of the form* $\prod_{i\in I} \mathtt{p}_i \triangleright \mathbf{0}_{\tilde{z}_i}$*, and* $\mathcal{M} \not\longrightarrow$ *. A system* $\mathcal{M}$ *gets stuck, written* $\mathcal{M}\lightning$*, if it reduces to a stuck system.*

Theorem 6 (Type Safety). *If* $\Delta_q \vdash \mathcal{M} : G$*, then* $\mathcal{M}\lightning$ *does not hold.*

Given a well-typed process $\Gamma ; \Delta \vdash P : T$, the free qubits of p, written $\mathsf{fq}(P)$ are exactly the qubit variables in Δ. The typing rule [T-Sys] ensures unique ownership of qubits in a multiparty system. Alternatively, given a well-typed multiparty system $\Gamma ; \Delta \vdash \prod_{\mathtt{p}_i \in \mathrm{pt}(G)} \mathtt{p}_i \triangleright P_i : G$, $\mathsf{fq}(P_i)$ can be computed as $\Delta \cap \mathsf{fv}(P_i)$, which is exactly Δ_i, by inverting the typing rule [T-Sys]. We can rephrase in our setting the result in [16, Theorem 2].

Theorem 7 (Unique Ownership of Qubits). *If* $\Gamma ; \Delta \vdash \prod_{i\in I} \mathtt{p}_i \triangleright P_i : G$*, then for any* $j, k \in I$ *such that* $j \neq k$*, we have* $\mathsf{fq}(P_j) \cap \mathsf{fq}(P_k) = \emptyset$.

By safety, we can extend the transitions to typed systems as follows.

Definition 9 (Typed Multiparty System Transitions). *We say that* $\Delta_q \vdash \mathcal{M} : G \overset{\alpha}{\Rrightarrow} \Delta_q' \vdash \mathcal{M}' : G'$ *if* $\mathcal{M} \overset{\alpha}{\Rrightarrow} \mathcal{M}'$ *and* $G \xrightarrow{\beta} G'$ *and* $\Delta_q' \vdash \mathcal{M}' : G'$.

We can thus show that the **qbit**s needed at runtime are only the ones prescribed by the typing judgment.

Theorem 8 (Qubit Safety). *If* $\Delta_q \vdash \mathcal{M} : G \overset{\alpha}{\Rrightarrow} \Delta_q' \vdash \mathcal{M}' : G'$*, then* $\langle \mathcal{H}[\mathsf{qu}(\Delta_q)], \mathcal{M}\rangle \overset{\alpha}{\Rrightarrow} \langle \mathcal{H}[\mathsf{qu}(\Delta_q')], \mathcal{M}'\rangle$*, where* $\mathsf{qu}(\Delta) = \{ q \mid q{:}\mathbf{qbit} \in \Delta \}$.

5 Case Studies

We now put the theory developed in the previous sections to work on some sample quantum protocols from the literature, to complement Quantum Teleportation described in the previous sections. All the protocols mix communications of classical values and communications of references to qubits.

Example 5 (Quantum Secret Sharing [2, Fig. 21]*).* The problem of secret sharing [21] involves an agent `Alice` sending a **qbit** to two agents `Bob` and `Charlie`, one of whom is dishonest. `Alice` does not know which is the dishonest agent, so she encodes the **qbit** in a way that requires `Bob` and `Charlie` to collaborate to retrieve it. In order to do this, they need to have each a **qbit** which is part of a maximally entangled triple, provided by `Source`. As in the running example, we introduce `Env` to model input/output operations.

$$\texttt{Env} \to \texttt{Alice} : \mathbf{qbit} \,.\, \texttt{Source} \to \texttt{Alice} : \mathbf{qbit} \,.\, \texttt{Source} \to \texttt{Bob} : \mathbf{qbit}. \\ \texttt{Source} \to \texttt{Charlie} : \mathbf{qbit} \,.\, \texttt{Alice} \to \texttt{Charlie} : \mathbf{bit}^2. \\ \texttt{Bob} \to \texttt{Charlie} : \mathbf{bit} \,.\, \texttt{Charlie} \to \texttt{Env} : \mathbf{qbit}$$

We can now write an actual system implementing this multiparty global type:

$$\mathcal{M} = \texttt{Alice} \triangleright P_A \mid \texttt{Bob} \triangleright P_B \mid \texttt{Charlie} \triangleright P_C \mid \texttt{Source} \triangleright P_S \mid \texttt{Env} \triangleright P_E$$

where

$$\begin{aligned} P_A &= \texttt{Env}\&(x).\texttt{Source}\&(a).\texttt{CNot}(x,a).\texttt{H}(x).m := \texttt{meas}\, x. \\ &\qquad n := \texttt{meas}\, a.\texttt{Charlie}\oplus\langle m,n\rangle.\mathbf{0} \\ P_B &= \texttt{Source}\&(b).\texttt{H}(b).o := \texttt{meas}\, b.\texttt{Charlie}\oplus\langle o\rangle.\mathbf{0} \\ P_C &= \texttt{Source}\&(c).\texttt{Alice}\&(m,n).\texttt{Bob}\&(o).(\mathbf{if}\, o\, \mathbf{then}\, \boldsymbol{\sigma}_2(c)). \\ &\qquad (\mathbf{if}\, m\, \mathbf{then}\, \boldsymbol{\sigma}_1(c)).(\mathbf{if}\, n\, \mathbf{then}\, \boldsymbol{\sigma}_2(c)).\texttt{Env}\oplus\langle c\rangle.\mathbf{0} \\ P_S &= \texttt{new}\, a,b,c.\texttt{H}(a).\texttt{CNot}(a,b).\texttt{H}(a).\texttt{CNot}(b,c). \\ &\qquad \texttt{Alice}\oplus\langle a\rangle.\texttt{Bob}\oplus\langle b\rangle.\texttt{Charlie}\oplus\langle c\rangle.\mathbf{0} \\ P_E &= \texttt{Alice}\oplus\langle x\rangle.\texttt{Charlie}\&(c).\mathbf{0}_c \end{aligned}$$

We sometimes use conditional $(\mathbf{if}\, e\, \mathbf{then}\, P).Q$ as prefix. This can be seen as a shortcut for **if** e **then** $P\{Q/o\}$ **else** Q or easily added to the theory. We also consider tuples as data types.

We refer to [2] for a detailed description of the protocol, while we prefer to contrast the clarity of our notation against theirs. For instance, the process for `Charlie` in [2, Fig. 21] is as follows:

$$f?c.t?m.w?n.u?o. \\ (\mathbf{if}\, o\, \mathbf{then}\, \boldsymbol{\sigma}_2(c)).(\mathbf{if}\, m\, \mathbf{then}\, \boldsymbol{\sigma}_1(c)).(\mathbf{if}\, n\, \mathbf{then}\, \boldsymbol{\sigma}_2(c)).\mathbf{output}\, c.\mathbf{0}$$

While there is a direct correspondence between the two terms, we argue that the use of participant names instead of channel names makes our notation easier to understand. Also, local and global types provide abstract descriptions with no correspondence in their framework.

The typing of the participants is very close to the one of the running example, hence we do not detail it. ◇

Example 6 (Quantum Bit-Commitment [16, Fig. 6]*).* The quantum bit-commitment problem [6] requires `Alice` to choose a **bit** value which `Bob` then attempts to guess. The key issue is that `Alice` must evaluate `Bob`'s guess with respect to her original choice of **bit**, without changing her mind. Similarly, `Bob` must not find out `Alice`'s choice before making his guess.

The code in [16, Fig. 6] would roughly correspond to the QMPST below:

$$\begin{aligned}&\texttt{Alice} \to \texttt{Bob} : (\textbf{int}) \,.\, \mu t \,.\\&\qquad (\texttt{Alice} \to \texttt{Bob} : (\textbf{qbit}) \,.\, \texttt{Rnd} \to \texttt{Bob} : (\textbf{bit}) \,.\, \texttt{t}) +\\&\qquad (\texttt{Rnd} \to \texttt{Bob} : (\textbf{bit}) \,.\, \texttt{Bob} \to \texttt{Alice} : (\textbf{bit}) \,.\\&\qquad\qquad \texttt{Alice} \to \texttt{Bob} : (\textbf{bit}) \,.\, \texttt{Alice} \to \texttt{Bob} : ([\textbf{bit}]))\end{aligned}$$

The key idea is that `Alice` in order to encode a **bit** x chooses a sequence of **bit**s xs, and encodes each of them into a **qbit** using the standard basis if x is 0, and the diagonal basis otherwise. `Bob` measures each **qbit** using a random basis (he gets random values from a random number generator `Rnd`). If the random basis matches `Alice` base, it will get the corresponding bit from xs, otherwise a random bit (evenly distributed). After having done this, `Bob` sends to `Alice` his guess g, and `Alice` checks whether `Bob` guessed correctly. In order to certify her answer, she sends xs to `Bob`.

The global type above will not capture the fact that the number of iterations of the recursive behavior depends on the integer value sent by `Alice` to `Bob` in the first interaction, namely the length of xs. To capture this dependency one would need to introduce dependent types, which are outside the scope of the present work (we will come back to this point in the final discussion, in Sect. 6).

Additionally, `Rnd` does not know when the protocol should end (`Alice` and `Bob` both know the desired number of iterations), indeed actually the code for `Rnd` in [16, Fig. 6] is just an infinite loop. Since this may be a problem (`Rnd` is not of the form $\mathbf{0}_{\tilde{q}}$ for some $\tilde{q}$ when the protocol ends, falsifying type safety (Theorem 6)), most MPST approaches forbid this behavior (we will come back to this point as well in the final discussion, in Sect. 6).

We can instead formalize the protocol in a different form, that does not require dependent types, by having `Alice` telling `Bob` using distinct labels `data` and `stop` whether there are further data or not. We also solve the issue of `Rnd` by having `Bob` telling him when the protocol is about to finish. This results in the global type in Fig. 7.

We can then write the corresponding system (participants are defined in Fig. 8):

$$\mathcal{M} = \texttt{Alice} \triangleright P_A \mid \texttt{Bob} \triangleright P_B \mid \texttt{Rnd} \triangleright P_R$$

$$\mu t.\left\{ \texttt{Rnd}\!\to\!\texttt{Bob}{:}(\mathbf{bit})\,.\,\texttt{Alice}\!\to\!\texttt{Bob}{:}\left\{ \begin{array}{l} \mathsf{data}(\mathbf{qbit})\,.\,\texttt{Bob}\!\to\!\texttt{Rnd}{:}\mathsf{loop}\,.\,\mathbf{t},\\ \mathsf{stop}\,.\,\texttt{Bob}\!\to\!\texttt{Rnd}{:}\mathsf{stop}\,.\,\texttt{Bob}\!\to\!\texttt{Alice}{:}(\mathbf{bit}).\\ \quad \texttt{Alice}\!\to\!\texttt{Bob}{:}(\mathbf{bit},[\mathbf{bit}])\,.\,\texttt{Bob}\!\to\!\texttt{Env}{:}\left\{ \begin{array}{l}\mathsf{verified},\\ \mathsf{notVerified}\end{array}\right\} \end{array}\right\}\right\}$$

Fig. 7. Global type for Quantum Bit Commitment

$$\begin{array}{l}
P_A = \mathbf{def}\ X(x, xs, ys) = \\
\qquad \mathbf{if}\ xs \neq [\,]\ \mathbf{then}\ \mathbf{new}\,x_q.(\mathbf{if}\ \mathbf{hd}(xs) = 1\,\mathbf{then}\,\sigma_1(x_q)). \\
\qquad\quad (\mathbf{if}\ x = 1\,\mathbf{then}\,H(x_q)).\texttt{Bob}\oplus\mathsf{data}\langle x_q\rangle.X\langle x, \mathbf{tl}(xs), ys\rangle \\
\qquad \mathbf{else}\ \texttt{Bob}\oplus\mathsf{stop}.\texttt{Bob}\&\{(g).\texttt{Bob}\oplus\langle(x, ys)\rangle.\mathbf{0}\} \\
\quad \mathbf{in}\ X\langle x, xs, xs\rangle \\
P_B = \mathbf{def}\ X_V(ms, vs, a) = \\
\qquad \mathbf{if}\ ms = [\,]\ \mathbf{then}\ \texttt{Env}\oplus\mathsf{verified}.\mathbf{0} \\
\qquad \mathbf{else\ if}\ \mathbf{fst}(\mathbf{hd}(ms))\,!= a \vee \mathbf{snd}(\mathbf{hd}(ms)) = \mathbf{hd}(vs)\ \mathbf{then}\ X_V\langle \mathbf{tl}(ms), \mathbf{tl}(vs), a\rangle \\
\qquad\quad \mathbf{else}\ \texttt{Env}\oplus\mathsf{notVerified}.\mathbf{0} \\
\quad \mathbf{in\ def}\ X(ms) = \\
\qquad \texttt{Rnd}\&y.\texttt{Alice}\&\left\{ \begin{array}{l} \mathsf{data}(x).\texttt{Rnd}\oplus\mathsf{loop}.(\mathbf{if}\ y = 1\,\mathbf{then}\,\mathtt{H}(x))).z := \mathtt{meas}\ x.X\langle ms@(y,z)\rangle \\ \mathsf{stop}.\texttt{Rnd}\oplus\mathsf{stop}.\texttt{Alice}\oplus\langle g\rangle.\texttt{Alice}\&(a, vs).X_V\langle ms, vs, a\rangle \end{array}\right\} \\
\quad \mathbf{in}\ X\langle[\,]\rangle \\
P_R = \mathbf{def}\ X = \mathbf{new}\,x_q.\mathtt{H}(x_q).r := \mathtt{meas}\ x_q.\texttt{Bob}\oplus\langle r\rangle.\texttt{Bob}\&\left\{ \begin{array}{l}\mathsf{loop}.X\langle\rangle\\ \mathsf{stop}.\mathbf{0}\end{array}\right\}\ \mathbf{in}\ X\langle\rangle
\end{array}$$

Fig. 8. Processes for Quantum Bit-Commitment

$$\begin{array}{l}
G\!\restriction\!\texttt{Alice} = \mu\mathbf{t}.\texttt{Bob}\oplus\mathsf{data}(\mathbf{qbit}).\mathbf{t}, \mathsf{stop}.\texttt{Bob}\&(\mathbf{bit}).\texttt{Bob}\oplus(\mathbf{bit},[\mathbf{bit}]).\mathbf{end} \\
G\!\restriction\!\texttt{Bob} = \mu\mathbf{t}.\texttt{Rnd}\&(\mathbf{bit}).\texttt{Alice}\&\left\{ \begin{array}{l} \mathsf{data}(\mathbf{qbit}).\texttt{Rnd}\oplus(\mathsf{loop}).\mathbf{t} \\ \mathsf{stop}.\texttt{Rnd}\oplus(\mathsf{stop}).\texttt{Alice}\oplus(\mathbf{bit}).\texttt{Alice}\&(\mathbf{bit},[\mathbf{bit}]).\texttt{Env}\oplus\left\{ \begin{array}{l}\mathsf{verified}.\mathbf{end}\\ \mathsf{notVerified}.\mathbf{end}\end{array}\right\} \end{array}\right\} \\
G\!\restriction\!\texttt{Rnd} = \mu\mathbf{t}.\texttt{Bob}\oplus\left\{ (\mathbf{bit}).\texttt{Bob}\& \begin{array}{l}\mathsf{loop}.\mathbf{t}\\ \mathsf{stop}.\mathbf{end}\end{array}\right\}
\end{array}$$

Fig. 9. Projections for Quantum Bit-Commitment

$$\dfrac{\dfrac{\dfrac{\dfrac{\dfrac{\dfrac{X : (\emptyset, G\!\restriction\!\texttt{Rnd})\cdot r{:}\mathbf{bit} \vdash X\langle\rangle : G\!\restriction\!\texttt{Rnd} \qquad X : (\emptyset, G\!\restriction\!\texttt{Rnd})\cdot r{:}\mathbf{bit} \vdash \mathbf{0} : \mathbf{end}}{X : (\emptyset, G\!\restriction\!\texttt{Rnd})\cdot r{:}\mathbf{bit} \vdash \texttt{Bob}\&\left\{\begin{array}{l}\mathsf{loop}.X\langle\rangle\\ \mathsf{stop}.\mathbf{0}\end{array}\right\} : \texttt{Bob}\&\left\{\begin{array}{l}\mathsf{loop}.G\!\restriction\!\texttt{Rnd}\\ \mathsf{stop}.\mathbf{end}\end{array}\right\}}}{X : (\emptyset, G\!\restriction\!\texttt{Rnd})\cdot r{:}\mathbf{bit} \vdash \texttt{Bob}\oplus\langle r\rangle.\texttt{Bob}\&\left\{\begin{array}{l}\mathsf{loop}.X\langle\rangle\\ \mathsf{stop}.\mathbf{0}\end{array}\right\} : G\!\restriction\!\texttt{Rnd}}}{X : (\emptyset, G\!\restriction\!\texttt{Rnd})\cdot\emptyset\,; x_q{:}\mathbf{qbit} \vdash r := \mathtt{meas}\ x_q.\texttt{Bob}\oplus\langle r\rangle.\texttt{Bob}\&\left\{\begin{array}{l}\mathsf{loop}.X\langle\rangle\\ \mathsf{stop}.\mathbf{0}\end{array}\right\} : G\!\restriction\!\texttt{Rnd}}}{X : (\emptyset, G\!\restriction\!\texttt{Rnd})\cdot\emptyset\,; x_q{:}\mathbf{qbit} \vdash \mathtt{H}(x_q).r := \mathtt{meas}\ x_q.\texttt{Bob}\oplus\langle r\rangle.\texttt{Bob}\&\left\{\begin{array}{l}\mathsf{loop}.X\langle\rangle\\ \mathsf{stop}.\mathbf{0}\end{array}\right\} : G\!\restriction\!\texttt{Rnd}}}{X : (\emptyset, G\!\restriction\!\texttt{Rnd})\cdot\emptyset \vdash \mathbf{new}\,x_q.\mathtt{H}(x_q).r := \mathtt{meas}\ x_q.\texttt{Bob}\oplus\langle r\rangle.\texttt{Bob}\&\left\{\begin{array}{l}\mathsf{loop}.X\langle\rangle\\ \mathsf{stop}.\mathbf{0}\end{array}\right\} : G\!\restriction\!\texttt{Rnd} \qquad \Phi}}{\emptyset\cdot\emptyset \vdash \mathbf{def}\ X = \mathbf{new}\,x_q.\mathtt{H}(x_q).r := \mathtt{meas}\ x_q.\texttt{Bob}\oplus\langle r\rangle.\texttt{Bob}\&\left\{\begin{array}{l}\mathsf{loop}.X\langle\rangle\\ \mathsf{stop}.\mathbf{0}\end{array}\right\}\ \mathbf{in}\ X\langle\rangle : G\!\restriction\!\texttt{Rnd}}$$

where $\Phi = X : (\emptyset, G\!\restriction\!\texttt{Rnd})\cdot\emptyset \vdash X\langle\rangle : G\!\restriction\!\texttt{Rnd}$.

Fig. 10. Typing of `Rnd` in Quantum Bit-Commitment

Using the typing rules we can derive: $\vdash \mathcal{M} : G$, provided that x and xs in the initial invocation of `Alice` recursive behavior are replaced by concrete values (to have a closed term). As first step, we project the global type on the different participants, obtaining the result in Fig. 9. For simplicity, we show the typing of Rnd only, in Fig. 10. ◇

A further case study, discussing Gottesman and Chuang's Quantum Digital Signature [19], is available in the extended report [20].

6 Discussion

We have extended MPSTs so to provide a clean formalism to describe and reason about quantum protocols. There are other languages for describing quantum protocols, such as imperative languages like LanQ [27] and QMCLANG [14, 29], and process calculi such as CQP [16] and CCS^q [2]. *All* of them rely on named channels for communication, and channels are typed with the type of their payload (and linear in some approaches), hence multiple channels are needed between the same participants. We believe our approach of specifying in send (resp. receive) operations the target (resp. sender) of the message makes for a clearer description. All the approaches above are also based on classical types, not behavioral types, hence do not provide a global type as abstract description of the protocol.

Quantum Session Types. We purposefully based our approach on a minimal MPST system (taking inspiration from [18,35]), to highlight the interplay between MPSTs and quantum computing, and to understand which advanced features of session types are useful to type protocols in the area. While we have found no need for multiple sessions or delegation, Example 6 could be modeled in a way closer to the specification in [16, Fig. 6] by relying on value-dependent session types (see [33]). Indeed, one would like to specify that the number of iterations depends on an integer exchanged beforehand.

The same example has also shown that sometimes requiring all the processes to complete their program is too restrictive. In Example 6, Rnd could be more easily modeled as an infinite loop generating random numbers, and the fact that it could generate further random numbers after the end of the protocol is not an issue from the practical point of view. However, to type such a formalisation of the protocol one would need, beyond changing the typing rules, to weaken type safety (Theorem 6). One could specify that some participants do not need to terminate their behaviour. Such a kind of approach has been studied in [4]. Note that selective participation (as discussed in [17,20,23]), allowing a participant to join only in some branches of a protocol, would not be helpful here, since indeed Rnd is needed in all the executions.

In the future we want to tackle the two limitations discussed above It would also be interesting to consider refinement types. While not needed from the modeling point of view, they would allow proving stronger properties, e.g., about possible results of measure operations. This would need however to combine refinement types with probabilities (the result of a measurement operation is probabilistic) and to capture the phenomenon of entanglement, which relates the behavior of different qubits.

Quantum Processes. The particular abstraction of quantum processes we have chosen is based on CQP [16], where processes can perform quantum operations on quantum data, and exchange messages on *channels* with other processes—these channels allow for classical communication with *quantum* references, which are pointers to qubits in a *global* quantum register. Ergo, these are not *quantum channels* in the sense of quantum information theory (see [28, Ch.12]), because processes do not have *local* quantum state—however, having a global quantum state with local quantum references appears to be expressive enough—whether this is a limitation or a feature of our approach remains to be investigated.

There exist rigorous mathematical frameworks for quantum networks [11] and quantum protocols [1] (to name a few). We do not know any formal calculi for quantum processes and quantum channels based on these frameworks, and it is not yet clear how our approach of extending MPSTs to quantum computing could be related to them. Session types are a completely syntactic approach, but there are recent attempts to give them denotational semantics in terms of event structures [9], or using category theory [3,12,25]. In fact, the categorical structure of session types is the same as the categorical structure of quantum processes (compact closure or star-autonomy)—they both require a notion of strong duality. This suggests, on the one hand, a way to use session types to build a type theory for quantum processes, and on the other hand, a way to verify correctness of typed quantum processes using denotational semantics, which we hope to explore in future work.

References

1. Abramsky, S., Coecke, B.: A categorical semantics of quantum protocols. In: Proceedings of the 19th Annual IEEE Symposium on Logic in Computer Science, 2004, pp. 415–425. IEEE (2004). https://doi.org/10.1109/LICS.2004.1319636
2. Ardeshir-Larijani, E., Gay, S.J., Nagarajan, R.: Automated equivalence checking of concurrent quantum systems. ACM Trans. Comput. Log. **19**(4), 28:1–28:32 (2018). https://doi.org/10.1145/3231597
3. Atkey, R.: Observed communication semantics for classical processes. In: Yang, H. (ed.) ESOP 2017. LNCS, vol. 10201, pp. 56–82. Springer, Heidelberg (2017). https://doi.org/10.1007/978-3-662-54434-1_3
4. Barbanera, F., Dezani-Ciancaglini, M.: Partially typed multiparty sessions. In: 16th Interaction and Concurrency Experience, ICE 2023. EPTCS, pp. 15–34 (2023).https://doi.org/10.4204/EPTCS.383.2
5. Barber, A., Plotkin, G.: Dual intuitionistic linear logic. University of Edinburgh, Laboratory for Foundations of Computer Science (1996)
6. Bennett, C.H., Brassard, G.: Quantum cryptography: public key distribution and coin tossing. Theoret. Comput. Sci. **560**, 7–11 (2014)
7. Bennett, C.H., et al.: Teleporting an unknown quantum state via dual classical and Einstein-Podolsky-Rosen channels. Phys. Rev. Lett. **70**(13), 1895 (1993)

8. Bernardo, M., De Nicola, R., Loreti, M.: A uniform framework for modeling non-deterministic, probabilistic, stochastic, or mixed processes and their behavioral equivalences. Inf. Comput. **225**, 29–82 (2013)
9. Castellani, I., Dezani-Ciancaglini, M., Giannini, P.: Event structure semantics for multiparty sessions. J. Logic. Algeb. Methods Program. **131**, 100844 (2023). https://doi.org/10.1016/j.jlamp.2022.100844
10. Ceragioli, L., et al.: Quantum bisimilarity via barbs and contexts: curbing the power of non-deterministic observers. Proc. ACM Program. Lang. **8**(POPL), 1269–1297 (2024). https://doi.org/10.1145/3632885
11. Chiribella, G., D'Ariano, G.M., Perinotti, P.: Theoretical framework for quantum networks. Phys. Rev. A **80**, 022339 (2009). https://doi.org/10.1103/PhysRevA.80.022339
12. Choudhury, V.: Classical processes in modern dress (ST30 - SPLASH 2023). https://2023.splashcon.org/details/st-anniversary-30-papers/9/Classical-Processes-in-modern-dress
13. Dal Lago, U., Rioli, A.: Applicative bisimulation and quantum λ-calculi. In: Dastani, M., Sirjani, M.: FSEN 2015. LNCS, vol. 9392, pp. 54–68. Springer, Heidelberg (2015). https://doi.org/10.1007/978-3-319-24644-4_4
14. Davidson, T.A.S., et al.: Model checking for communicating quantum processes. Int. J. Unconv. Comput. **8**(1), 73–98 (2012)
15. Garhwal, S., Ghorani, M., Ahmad, A.: Quantum programming language: a systematic review of research topic and top cited languages. Archiv. Comput. Methods Eng. **28**, 289–310 (2021)
16. Gay, S.J., Nagarajan, R.: Communicating quantum processes. In: 32nd ACM SIGPLAN-SIGACT Symposium on Principles of Programming Languages, POPL 2005, pp. 145–157. ACM (2005). https://doi.org/10.1145/1040305.1040318
17. Gheri, L., et al.: Design-by-contract for flexible multiparty session protocols. In: Ali, K., Vitek, J.: 36th European Conference on Object-Oriented Programming (ECOOP 2022). Leibniz International Proceedings in Informatics (LIPIcs), pp. 8:1–8:28. Schloss Dagstuhl - Leibniz-Zentrum für Informatik, Dagstuhl (2022). https://doi.org/10.4230/LIPIcs.ECOOP.2022.8
18. van Glabbeek, R., Höfner, P., Horne, R.: Assuming just enough fairness to make session types complete for lock-freedom. In: LICS, pp. 1–13. IEEE (2021). https://doi.org/10.1109/LICS52264.2021.9470531
19. MISCGottesman, D., Chuang, I.: Quantum digital signatures. arXiv preprint arXiv:quantph/0105032 (2001)
20. Harvey, P., et al.: Multiparty session types for safe runtime adaptation in an actor language. In: ECOOP, LIPIcs, pp. 10:1–10:30. Schloss Dagstuhl - Leibniz-Zentrum für Informatik (2021). https://doi.org/10.4230/LIPICS.ECOOP.2021.10
21. Hillery, M., Bužek, V., Berthiaume, A.: Quantum secret sharing. Phys. Rev. A **59**(3), 1829 (1999)
22. Honda, K., Yoshida, N., Carbone, M.: Multiparty asynchronous session types. J. ACM **63**(1), 9:1–9:67 (2016). https://doi.org/10.1145/2827695
23. Hu, R., Yoshida, N.: Explicit connection actions in multiparty session types. In: FASE. LNCS, vol. 10202, pp. 116–133. Springer, Heidelberg (2017). https://doi.org/10.1007/978-3-662-54494-5_7
24. Hüttel, H., et al.: Foundations of session types and behavioural contracts. ACM Comput. Surv. **49**(1), 3:1–3:36 (2016). https://doi.org/10.1145/2873052
25. Kavanagh, R.: A domain semantics for higher-order recursive processes. arXiv preprint arXiv:2002.01960 (2020)

26. Lanese, I., Dal Lago, U., Choudhury, V.: Towards quantum multiparty session types. arXiv preprint arXiv:2409.11133 (2024)
27. Mlnarik, H.: Introduction to LanQ–an Imperative quantum programming language (2006). https://lanq.sourceforge.net/doc/introToLanQ.pdf
28. Nielsen, M., Chuang, I.: Quantum Computation and Quantum Information: 10th Anniversary Edition. Cambridge University Press (2010)
29. Papanikolaou, N.: Model checking quantum protocols. Ph.D. thesis, University of Warwick, Coventry (2009)
30. Scalas, A., Yoshida, N.: Less is more: multiparty session types revisited. Proc. ACM Program. Lang. **3**(POPL), 30:1–30:29 (2019). https://doi.org/10.1145/3290343
31. Selinger, P., Valiron, B.: A lambda calculus for quantum computation with classical control. MSCS **16**(3), 527–552 (2006). https://doi.org/10.1017/S0960129506005238
32. The Quantum Protocol Zoo (2024). https://wiki.veriqloud.fr/
33. Toninho, B., Caires, L., Pfenning, F.: Dependent session types via intuitionistic linear type theory. In: PPDP, pp. 161–172. Association for Computing Machinery, New York (2011). https://doi.org/10.1145/2003476.2003499
34. Wootters, W.K., Zurek, W.H.: A single quantum cannot be cloned. Nature **299**, 802–803 (1982). https://doi.org/10.1038/299802a0
35. Yoshida, N., Gheri, L.: A very gentle introduction to multiparty session types. In: ICDCIT. LNCS, vol. 11969, pp. 73–93. Springer, Heidelberg (2020). https://doi.org/10.1007/978-3-030-36987-3_5

Automated Invariant Generation for Efficient Deductive Reasoning About Embedded Systems

Philip Tasche[1(✉)], Paula Herber[1,2], and Marieke Huisman[1]

[1] University of Twente, Enschede, The Netherlands
{p.b.h.tasche,m.huisman}@utwente.nl
[2] University of Münster, Münster, Germany
paula.herber@uni-muenster.de

Abstract. Deductive verification is often more efficient than alternative techniques like model checking at reasoning about functional properties of programs. This is especially true when the program under verification contains very large or unbounded data ranges that model checkers struggle with. However, modular deductive verifiers struggle with verifying global properties, which are often crucial in concurrent and reactive embedded systems. Embedded systems often require complex user-defined invariants to capture the global state for the verification of local annotations, demanding high effort and expertise from the user. In this paper, we propose a method to automatically generate compact invariants that are sufficiently strong to enable effective deductive verification of global properties in embedded systems. Our key idea is that a good level of abstraction can be found automatically by choosing variables for refinement that influence relevant events and process interactions. We use this idea together with abstract interpretation to build a system's state space, abstracted to the relevant part for a given global property. We demonstrate the effectiveness of our approach on a SystemC design of an automotive control system that has in the past proved challenging to verify.

Keywords: Abstraction refinement · Deductive verification · Embedded systems · Invariant generation

1 Introduction

In our daily world, we are surrounded by embedded systems. They are present in transportation, medical instruments, power plants, and many more applications. The reliance on these systems for critical aspects of our lives raises the importance of techniques to ensure their correct functioning. System design languages for embedded systems, such as SystemC [24], are widely used to model embedded system designs early on in the development process. Since these designs are the basis for the subsequent development process, formal verification for such languages is highly desirable.

A. Madeira and A. Knapp (Eds.): SEFM 2024, LNCS 15280, pp. 404–422, 2025.
https://doi.org/10.1007/978-3-031-77382-2_23

There exist a variety of formal verification approaches for SystemC, including [12,19,20,23,25,26]. However, these are based on model checking, which does not scale well for programs with large state spaces and for data-dependent functional properties. To the best of our knowledge, our own previous work [32] is currently the only approach using deductive verification. It builds on the VerCors verifier and uses an abstract state enumeration technique to allow reasoning about global properties of the system. In particular, a key concept in [32] is the construction of a Reachable Abstract States Invariant (RASI), which builds an abstract state space based on process and event status variables but abstracts from data variables. While this approach is theoretically flexible in the level of abstraction, potentially allowing very high verification performance for a given property, it does not provide a way to automatically adjust the level of abstraction to make use of this flexibility. This can cause an infeasibly large state space by including unnecessary information, or it can cause overapproximation by abstracting from data variables that heavily influence process interactions.

In this paper, we present an approach to efficiently and automatically generate compact and sufficiently strong invariants for auto-active deductive verification of global properties in embedded systems. In particular, we propose a method based on abstract interpretation and abstraction refinement to automatically select an abstraction that allows efficient verification of a given global property in concurrent, reactive systems. Our underlying key idea is to refine variables that can weaken the invariant by introducing a blow-up in the state space due to an overapproximation of the reachable states. This overapproximation occurs whenever branching on abstract variables induces spurious paths in the abstract state space, and is especially expensive if it expands the set of interleavings between concurrent processes to consider. To overcome this problem, we propose a method to systematically choose variables for refinement that influence relevant events and process interactions. With that, we reduce the overapproximations in the RASI and thus can compute an abstraction that is specifically tailored to the relevant part for a given global property.

We demonstrate the applicability and effectiveness of our approach using an automotive control system that has in the past proved challenging to verify, namely an anti-lock braking system, which could not be verified with existing approaches based on model checking [20–22]. The same system was successfully verified in [32]. However, manual variable refinements were necessary to keep the verification effort at an acceptable level. In this paper, we improve on our work from [32] by selecting abstractions and refinements automatically.

Our main contributions are threefold:

- We present a method to automatically find good abstractions by selecting a minimal set of variables to include in the global invariant such that a given property can still be verified and overapproximation is mitigated.
- We discuss the integration of this method into our tool VeSUV (Verification of SystemC Using VerCors) as an extension of the VerCors deductive verifier.
- We demonstrate the effectiveness of our approach and analyze its scalability with experiments on an automotive control system.

The paper is structured as follows. Section 2 explains preliminaries, Sect. 3 presents our approach for the generation of reachable abstract state invariants and Sect. 4 implementation details and practical challenges, Sect. 5 describes our experimental evaluation, Sect. 6 related work and Sect. 7 concludes the paper.

2 Preliminaries

In this section, we introduce the necessary preliminaries to understand the remainder of the paper, namely abstract interpretation [14], SystemC [24], VerCors [3,8], and our encoding of the SystemC semantics in VerCors from [32].

2.1 Abstract Interpretation

Abstract interpretation [14] is a static analysis technique based on the idea to create an abstract model of a given program that simplifies its behavior while preserving essential properties. Rather than executing the program under verification, it applies an abstraction to the program state that reduces it to a usually very small representation, and applies an appropriate abstract semantics on the abstract representation to explore the behavior of the program. To ensure soundness, the abstract semantics must be an overapproximation of the underlying concrete program semantics.

Abstract interpretation is able to find conditions that must hold at a certain point in the program execution, though it is incomplete in the sense that not all such conditions can be found for a given abstraction. This incompleteness means that it might not be possible to verify a given property with a given abstraction. Abstraction refinement is a method to strategically improve the abstraction level to tailor it to the property of interest. Therefore, abstract interpretation is often used in conjunction with abstraction refinement techniques such as counterexample-guided abstraction refinement (CEGAR) [13].

2.2 Embedded System Design with SystemC

SystemC is a modeling language for hardware/software co-design and frequently used in the design stage of embedded systems. It is defined in an IEEE standard [24] and implemented as a C++ library. Its core philosophy is to support modelling and simulation at different levels of abstraction, from functional down to register transfer level. SystemC designs are organized into *modules*, representing either hardware or software components, that are connected by *channels*. Modules define *processes* that run concurrently and synchronize via discrete-time *events*. SystemC uses non-preemptive scheduling, which means that processes run until they terminate or voluntarily give up control with a `wait` statement. Processes can wait for events or for a fixed amount of simulation time. The SystemC library implements its own simulation kernel, which controls the scheduling of processes and handles events.

```
1  SC_MODULE(Sensor) {
2     sc_fifo_out<int> fifo;
3     void sns() {
4        while(true) {
5           wait(1, SC_MS);
6           fifo.write(read_sensor());
7        }
8     }
9     SC_CTOR(Sensor) {
10       SC_THREAD(sns);
11    }
12 };
13 SC_MODULE(Controller) {
14    sc_fifo_in<int> fifo;
15    int sens_val = -1;
16    void rcv(){
17       while(true)
18          sens_val = fifo.read();
19    }
20    void ctrl() {
21       while (true) {
22          wait(5, SC_MS);
23          calc_action(sens_val);
24       }
25    }
26    SC_CTOR(Controller) {
27       SC_THREAD(rcv);
28       SC_THREAD(ctrl);
29    }
30 };
```

Fig. 1. Running example of a simple robot in SystemC

Figure 1 shows a SystemC design we use as a running example in this paper. Its structure is shown in Fig. 3a. Blue rectangles indicate modules, white rectangles processes and arrows channels that the indicated processes communicate through. The example system consists of two modules, a `Sensor` and a `Controller`. The `Sensor` contains one process `sns`, defined as a method and declared as a thread process in lines 3 and 10. It periodically reads sensor values every 1 ms and writes them to the first-in first-out channel (`fifo`) connecting it with the `Controller` (line 4–7). The `Controller` contains two processes `rcv` and `ctrl`. `rcv` reads the sensor values from the `fifo` channel (lines 17–18). `ctrl` calculates a new action from the current sensor value every 5 ms (lines 21–24).

2.3 Deductive Verification with VerCors

Deductive verification is a powerful technique for mathematical reasoning about programs. For annotation-based deductive verification, the user annotates a program with specifications that encode desired properties and auxiliary invariants to guide the verifier. Given the user-defined annotations, the verifier automatically applies proof rules based on an underlying logic, often a variant of separation logic, to prove these annotations. In contrast to interactive theorem provers, deductive verifiers require no user interaction after providing the annotations.

VerCors is a deductive program verifier for concurrent programs [3,8]. It supports subsets of Java and C as well as PVL, its own Prototypal Verification Language, an object-oriented language similar to Java with built-in specification directives. In the following, we focus on PVL programs. Verification with VerCors is based on permission-based separation logic (PBSL) [2], i.e. a thread requires sufficient permission to access heap fields. The user-defined annotations must specify the permissions owned by a thread, which allows VerCors to verify data race freedom, memory safety and functional correctness of concurrent programs.

VerCors uses *contract-Based Reasoning*. Each method is annotated by the user with pre- and postconditions and automatically verified in isolation. Other methods called by the method under verification are replaced by their contracts. If information needs to be exchanged with other threads for verification, this

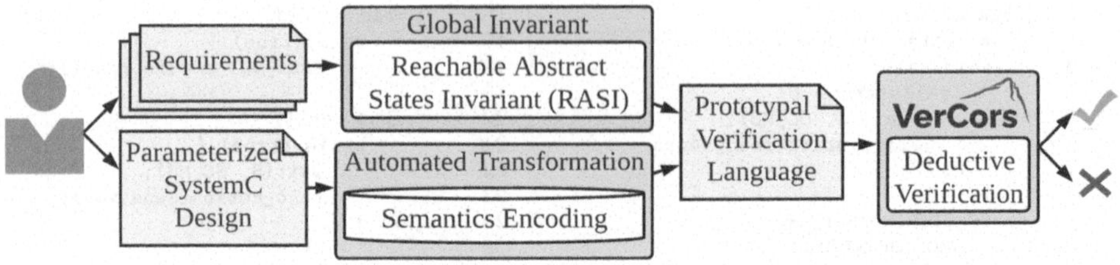

Fig. 2. Verification approach of the VeSUV tool, taken from [32]

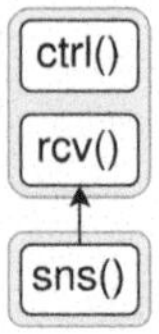

(a) System

```
(p_state == [READY,READY,READY] && e_state == [IDLE,IDLE,IDLE,IDLE]) ||
(p_state == [READY,READY,3] && e_state == [IDLE,IDLE,IDLE,5] ||
(p_state == [2,READY,READY] && e_state == [IDLE,DELTA,1,IDLE] ||
                              ...
(p_state == [2,1,3] && e_state == [IDLE,DELTA,1,5] ||
(p_state == [2,READY,3] && e_state == [IDLE,IDLE,1,5] ||
                              ...
```

(b) RASI excerpt

Fig. 3. Example use of the RASI

can occur at synchronization points. VerCors supports a variety of concurrency models, of which we focus on threads synchronizing via locks in this paper. Locks in PVL are annotated with *lock invariants* [28], which can be assumed when locking the lock and must be established again when releasing it. This allows the verification of properties across multiple threads.

2.4 Verification of SystemC Using VerCors

VeSUV is a tool for the **Ve**rification of **S**ystemC **U**sing **V**erCors [32]. As shown in Fig. 2, it works by encoding a SystemC design, along with user-specified properties, into PVL and verifying the design with VerCors.

VeSUV transforms each process in the SystemC design to a runnable class and each module to a shared data class in PVL. It encodes the scheduling semantics of SystemC in a central `Main` class that keeps track of every process and data variable in the system. It encodes waiting processes as well as the event and timing mechanism with global variables `p_state` and `e_state`, which we call the scheduling variables. The scheduling variables map process and event IDs to the current status of the respective process or event. The `Main` class encodes the SystemC scheduler in abstract methods, i.e. methods without implementation that are solely specified via their contracts. Further, to encode the non-preemptive scheduling semantics and allow for synchronization between the processes, it provides a global lock each process needs to hold to execute.

To enable the verification of global properties, a global invariant is associated with the global lock, so that it must hold at every interleaving point between processes. The idea behind this invariant is to specify the global behavior of the system, so that the prover can, at a local level within a method, reason about global properties that go beyond this scope. In order to reduce user effort for finding such an invariant, [32] proposes a Reachable Abstract States Invariant (RASI). This invariant consists of a disjunction of reachable states, abstracting from all data variables and tracking only the process and event states. Each state is represented by a conjunction of variable valuations.

As an example of this, consider our running example in Fig. 3. The RASI for this system captures the states of processes and events [32]. An excerpt is shown in Fig. 3b. Line 1 represents the initial state in which all processes are ready to execute and no event has been scheduled yet. Line 2 represents the state where `ctrl` (process ID 2) has been non-deterministically chosen for initialization first and waits for its timeout event (event ID 3), which is scheduled to be notified after 5 ms. Line 3 represents the state where `sns` (process ID 0) has been scheduled first, triggered the FIFO write event with a delta delay, and waits for 1 ms to be rescheduled. Line 5 represents the state where all processes have been initialized, and Line 6 the state where the delta-delayed notification of the write event has triggered `rcv` (process ID 1) again. This pattern continues until all reachable states with regard to the scheduling variables are enumerated.

3 Abstraction Refinement for Compact RASI Generation

A central motivation of the RASI is to reduce user effort when verifying global properties about embedded systems by automatically enumerating the state space with regard to global variables that abstractly describe the possible timing and scheduling of the system under verification. In principle, this approach allows for a flexible level of abstraction that can generate invariants that are both small and sufficiently restrictive to aid in the verification of certain global properties. However, [32] merely introduces this type of invariant. It does not provide a fully automated method for generating such invariants or selecting the appropriate level of abstraction. This is left to the user to manually decide.

The abstraction level should be selected such that the invariant remains manageable while retaining the necessary information to reason about the desired property. However, it is not trivial to decide which variables should be tracked to achieve this. In general, tracking a variable increases the invariant size – and verification time – since the invariant must store more information. On the other hand, to preserve soundness, untracked variables must be overapproximated, which can increase the set of program behaviors that must be considered. In such a case, the strength of the invariant can be increased and its size decreased by tracking more variables rather than fewer.

This trade-off makes it difficult to find a good level of abstraction, and variable refinements that have the potential to reduce the state space are difficult to identify. For this reason, [32] simply includes all scheduling-relevant variables in the global invariant by default. This is not ideal: Many of the included scheduling variables might be unnecessary for a given property, while data variables that might induce overapproximation are not included by default.

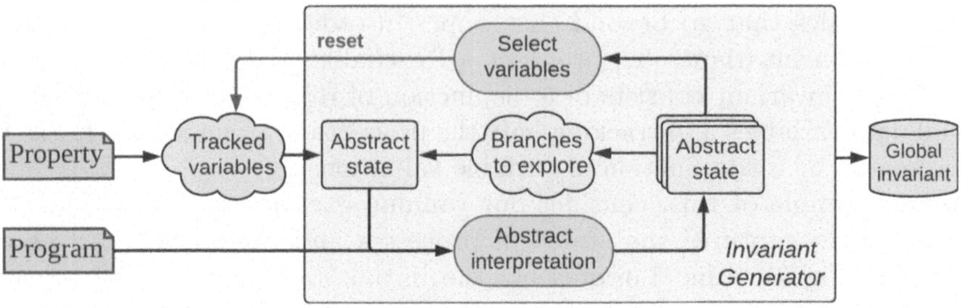

Fig. 4. Approach for the invariant generation

In this paper, we present an approach to automatically select a small set of variables to include in the RASI such that a given property can still be verified and overapproximation is mitigated. Figure 4 shows our approach. We start by extracting relevant scheduling variables from a given global property and exploring the state space of the program, abstracted to the tracked variables. If we encounter a conditional branch on an untracked variable that splits the state space and thus indicates an overapproximation, we select the variables that could affect the branch condition and add them to the tracked variable set. We then restart the exploration with the new variable set. Once the exploration terminates without detecting overapproximation, the abstract states form a global invariant that contains the information necessary to prove the given property.

The rest of this section explains the invariant generation process. Section 3.1 provides a motivating example, Sect. 3.2 explains the selection of the initial tracked variables and Sect. 3.3 our algorithms for exploration and variable selection.

3.1 Motivating Example

For our running example of a sensor communicating with a controller, a crucial property is that the controller always receives new sensor values within a given time limit. In [32], we have proposed to encode such timing properties by adding a new event, notifying this event with the desired delay to start measuring time, and checking that it has not yet occurred at the goal location.

To prove the timing property that sensor values are received within 1 ms for our running example, we introduce a new event (ID 4), which is notified with a 1 ms delay whenever a new sensor value is sent. The property we then aim to verify is that `e_state[4] > 0` whenever `recv` receives a value. This property can be verified using a RASI as proposed in [32]. However, if the RASI is generated from all scheduling and no data variables, the state space suffers from an unnecessary combinatorial explosion from considering all possible interleavings with the `ctrl` process, even though it is not relevant for this property. Furthermore, by abstracting from the number of entries in the FIFO, the naive RASI implementation will always consider that the `rcv` process might wait for a write event, even if a new sensor value has just been written. This overapproximation

Algorithm 1. Exploration procedure

Input: initial variables V_t, program *prg*
Output: ideal abstraction level V_t, abstract state space S_{found}
1: $S_{found} \leftarrow \emptyset$
2: $S_{unexplored} \leftarrow \{\text{initialState}(V_t)\}$
3: **while** $S_{unexplored} \neq \emptyset$ **do**
4:     $s \leftarrow \text{dequeue}(S_{unexplored})$
5:     $S_{unexplored} \leftarrow S_{unexplored} \setminus \{s\}$
6:     **for** each ready process p in *prg* **do**
7:         $S_{new} \leftarrow \text{takeStep}(p, s, V_t)$
8:         $S_{found} \leftarrow S_{found} \cup (S_{new} \setminus S_{found})$
9:         $S_{unexplored} \leftarrow S_{unexplored} \cup (S_{new} \setminus S_{found})$
10:         **if** $|S_{new}| > 1$ **then**
11:             $V_c \leftarrow \text{findCandidateVariables}(S_{new}, V_t)$
12:             $V_a \leftarrow \text{filterCandidateVariables}(V_c, S_{new})$
13:             **if** $V_a \neq \emptyset$ **then**
14:                 $V_t \leftarrow V_t \cup V_a$
15:                 **go to** 1
16:             **end if**
17:         **end if**
18:     **end for**
19: **end while**

could be reduced by including the number of entries in the FIFO into the RASI, thus strengthening the invariant and reducing verification time.

3.2 Initial Variable Selection

As initially tracked variables, we propose to use only those variables that directly influence the property we want to prove. These variables must be manually defined. Our automated abstraction refinement method will then automatically add further variables for refinement that help to tailor the state space to the part relevant for the chosen property.

Running Example. In our example, the considered property concerns timing constraints between the write and read operations of `sns` and `rcv`. Since the timing is encoded in the events, sensible starting variables are the states of the property event, `sns`'s timeout event and the FIFO channel's read and write events. Other necessary variables can be found automatically by the RASI generator.

3.3 Reachable Abstract State Space Exploration

To explore the abstract state space of a given PVL program that represents a SystemC design, we use a breadth-first search algorithm as shown in Algorithm 1. Its input is the program *prg* and the initial variable set V_t. In each iteration of the search, we select an unexplored state from $S_{unexplored}$ and compute its

```
1 ensures ((\old(p_state[0]) >= 0 && \old(e_state[p_state[0]]) == 0) ==> p_state[0] == -1)
2   && ((\old(p_state[1]) >= 0 && \old(e_state[p_state[1]]) == 0) ==> p_state[1] == -1)
3   && (p_state[0] != -1 ==> p_state[0] == \old(p_state[0])
4   && (p_state[1] != -1 ==> p_state[1] == \old(p_state[1]);
5 void immediate_wakeup();
```

Fig. 5. Postcondition of the abstract method `immediate_wakeup`

abstract successor states S_{new} that may result from executing any runnable process until the next `wait` statement. If the newly found states have not been explored before, we add them to the work list of unexplored states $S_{unexplored}$. If there are multiple successor states, e.g. because a branch in the control flow or an abstract method's postcondition cannot be precisely resolved, we check whether an overapproximation of one or more variables that influence the control condition or postcondition might be responsible for the split in the state space. If it (potentially) is, we refine the abstraction by adding the responsible variables to V_t and restart the exploration. The following describes how we identify candidate variables and check whether they are responsible for a split in the state space.

Candidate Selection. There are two possibilities for the state space to split, which is a necessary condition for overapproximation. The first possibility occurs if a control condition evaluates to *unknown*. Variables that could prevent such an overapproximation if tracked are those that distinguish between the condition being true or false. The second possibility occurs if the postcondition of an abstract method (see Sect. 4.3) does not precisely describe only one successor state, but allows multiple possibilities. In this case, distinguishing variables are those that make the postcondition true for some post-states and false for others.

To identify such variables, we consider the abstract successor states after a split in the state space, as well as the condition of either a branching statement or a method postcondition. For each successor state, we calculate the condition required to reach this state, and for each untracked variable that occurs in this condition, we calculate the possible values the variable can take on to make the required condition true. If the possible values for one variable differ between the different successor states, then it is a variable that can distinguish between these possibilities and, if the split represents an overapproximation, potentially prevent this overapproximation. Therefore, this variable would be a candidate.

Running Example. As an example, consider the method shown in Fig. 5 in a situation in which `p_state[0]` is the only tracked variable and has the value 5 in the method's pre-state. In this case, the postcondition allows two separate options. Either `\old(e_state[5]) == 0` and therefore `p_state[0] == -1`, or `p_state[0]` remains at its old value 5. The abstraction to only `p_state[0]` does not distinguish between these two possibilities, so a split in the state space occurs. To reach the state `p_state[0] == -1`, line 1 must evaluate to `true`, and to reach `p_state[0] == 5`, it must evaluate to `false`. The values that `e_state[5]` can take to reach the former are $\{0\}$, the values to reach the latter $\mathbb{Z} \cap ((-\infty, -1] \cup [1, \infty))$.

Since these sets are not equal, `e_state[5]` becomes a candidate variable to include in V_t. For all other variables, including `p_state[1]`, the sets of possible values are $\mathbb{Z}$ for both cases, so `e_state[5]` is the only candidate variable.

Filtering Candidate Variables. A local split in the state space is a necessary, but not a sufficient condition for overapproximation. It could be the case that, if all branches have the same effect on the tracked variables, they converge again without producing any excess states in the meantime. Only if the initial state of a branch cannot be reached by any other branch does the split cause overapproximation. Thus, variables responsible for a temporary split in the state space that ultimately does not cause overapproximation do not need to be included in the tracked variables. The problem with this observation is that the reachability argument cannot be reliably evaluated until the entire state space has been built, since a path that reaches a state might only be revealed later on. This makes it impossible to select new variables on the fly, instead requiring iterative executions of the entire exploration algorithm.

To overcome this problem, we partition process executions into atomic blocks (see Sect. 4.5), which end if the process releases control or if the global invariant is checked with changed variables, and check for overapproximation only at the end of *one atomic process step*. If there are multiple distinct post-states, this indicates that the branches had a distinct effect on the tracked variables or on possible process interleavings, e.g. if one branch encounters a `wait` statement and the other does not. In some cases, this algorithm falsely detects overapproximation, e.g. if both branches of an `if` statement encounter the same `wait` statement, but such cases are rare in practice. Since even in such cases, we only refine a possibly unnecessary variable, our approach remains sound. We accept this slight loss in accuracy in exchange for the increased efficiency of on-the-fly filtering.

Running Example. In our running example, if the FIFO read/write events are tracked, but the number of elements in the FIFO buffer is not, this results in an overapproximation. In that case, when `rcv` reads from the channel, both the possibility of waiting for the write event and the possibility of reading and thereby scheduling the read event must always be taken into account, even if the buffer is not empty. Therefore, the number of elements in the buffer, which is a candidate variable for disambiguating this split, should be added to V_t. On the other hand, as an example where no overapproximation is induced, consider a split caused by a branching statement within `ctrl`'s calculations. In this case, branches only affect data variables, which does not have any effect on the global state. Thus, all branches will converge again within the same atomic block, so the variables responsible should not be added to V_t.

4 Implementation

This section describes some of the considerations that are relevant for the implementation of the algorithms described in Sect. 3. Section 4.1 explains the assumptions made by the implementation. Section 4.2 explains the implementation of abstract interpretation we use, Sect. 4.3 describes how we deal with assumptions and postconditions that alter the state, Sect. 4.4 explains how we incorporate information from path conditions to avoid inconsistent paths and Sect. 4.5 discusses optimizations we make in our exploration procedure.

4.1 Assumptions and Limitations

To simplify the generation process, we make some assumptions about the layout of the program. We assume a design structured like the one generated by the SystemC-to-PVL transformation of [32], with a main scheduler process, a number of child processes, and a global lock held by each process when executing. We assume that there are no further locks used in the system. We also assume, without loss of generality, that every class has only one instance, that every field has a unique name and that all system parameters are referenced in a `parameter_invariant`. Method postconditions should precisely describe the post-state and specify only variables to which the method has write permission.

4.2 Abstract Representation

To implement abstract interpretation, we compute abstract representations of all tracked variables. As types, we consider booleans and integers. We use interval abstraction for integers and a three-valued abstraction for booleans, i.e. they can be true, false, or unknown. For both types, we additionally allow the empty value to keep track of unreachable states. Booleans can be combined with all operators supported by VerCors. For integers, we have implemented interval arithmetic for addition and subtraction. Multiplication is overapproximated to the interval between the maximum and minimum element of the result. All other operations, including bitwise operations, are overapproximated to an unknown value in our current implementation.

Sequences are currently the only type of collection that is supported, though other types could easily be added. They are represented by an integer indicating their length and a set of index-value pairs to represent their entries. All these values are themselves abstract and represented as described above. Abstract sequences support all sequence operations supported by VerCors.

4.3 Handling of Assumptions and Postconditions

One challenge for a state space exploration program designed for use with deductive verification is that it needs to handle both regular program statements and state-altering specifications. In VerCors, such specifications come in the form of assumptions (using the keywords `assume` or `inhale`) or postconditions of abstract methods. Since the generated invariant should be used in conjunction with the deductive verification, it must take into account the effect these specifications have on the possible values of the tracked variables.

Resolving such a specification requires to extract all possible valuations that satisfy its condition, restricted to the tracked variables. To the best of our knowledge, this is as of yet an unsolved problem. It is similar to the All-SMT problem in that it attempts to find a superset of all valuations that satisfy the given condition, but solving it with iterative calls to an SMT solver and blocking clauses, as is typically done in All-SMT [29,33], is not feasible for potentially unbounded result intervals. Instead, any given assumption is broken up into its set of atomic conditions. These are then converted into valuations of the affected variables in the abstract interval domain, and recombined according to the boolean operators in the assumption. For example, the condition `x >= 0 && x < 5` would be split into its atomic constraints $\texttt{x} \in [0, \infty)$ and $\texttt{x} \in (-\infty, 4]$. These would then be combined according to the boolean operator; in this case with an intersection, leaving $\texttt{x} \in [0, 4]$. This approach does not take dependencies between variables into account, but since our abstraction model does not track variable dependencies and we take steps to mitigate the overapproximation caused by this (see Sect. 4.5), this downside is acceptable.

4.4 Path Condition Tracking

During the exploration process, only the values of the tracked variables are stored in the encountered abstract states. However, in parameterized designs, this is insufficient for restricting the possible execution paths, since parameters are constant throughout the execution. Thus, while the concrete values of parameters are unknown, assumptions made about their values, e.g. by taking a certain branch whose condition depends on the parameter, must be consistent throughout an execution path. To achieve this, we enrich the abstract states with the constraints on parameter values that the path assumed along the way.

Path conditions can also be useful in assumptions and postconditions. If, due to abstraction, the left side of an implication in such specifications evaluates to unknown, the resulting state set after its incorporation will contain both states that assume the right side of the implication was taken into account and states that assume the opposite. Each of these rely on assumptions on whether the left side could be satisfied. Thus, we refine such states with path conditions that reflect these assumptions to increase the precision of our analysis.

4.5 Optimizations

A naive implementation of Algorithm 1 risks running into an explosion of the exploration space, especially as the size of the design and the number of processes grow. This is true even if the resulting state space invariant is relatively small due to a high level of abstraction, since the number of process interleavings to explore cannot be reduced by variable abstraction alone. For this reason, we implement a range of optimizations that keep the size of the exploration space approximately in line with the size of the resulting abstract state space.

Atomic Process Steps. Not every intermediate process step is interesting for the state space. Since a process in SystemC will execute until it voluntarily gives up control, we only need to track the behavior at such interleaving points. In the transformation designed by [32], such points are marked by releasing the global lock. Additionally, the global invariant is checked at some intermediate points, such as loop invariants. If the tracked variables have changed at such a check, this needs to also be recorded. As such, we split the execution of each process into atomic blocks that run until they encounter either a release of the global lock or, if the tracked variables have changed, a check on the global invariant.

Process Pruning. Considering all processes, including those that cannot change the tracked variables, leads to an exponential explosion in exploration branches for the same abstract state - one for each interleaving of these processes. For this reason, we statically check all processes before execution and only consider those processes that can influence the tracked variables for the actual exploration. This approach is sound, since all indirect dependencies between the tracked variables and such processes, e.g. through another variable that is not tracked, are lost to the abstraction regardless of whether the processes are explored. If a process does not influence tracked variables directly, it will not have an influence at all in the abstract interpretation.

State Splitting. Path conditions for postconditions with unknown parameter values are difficult to take into account, since they have implications not for the resulting state, but for the previous one. However, ignoring such path conditions would reduce accuracy. To mitigate this problem, we split states with unknown variables that are bounded to a small range into multiple states with a certain value each. For example, if an exploration step results in a state in which one variable's valuation is unknown, but bounded between 1 and 3, we split this state into three separate states with the concrete values 1, 2, and 3. Any subsequent calculation can then work with a precise value, avoiding overapproximations.

5 Evaluation

In [32], we have evaluated our approach for deductive verification of SystemC designs using a SystemC encoding in PVL and the RASI on several case studies, of which the largest by far is an automotive control system containing an anti-lock braking system (ABS) and an anti-slip regulation (ASR). Earlier verification approaches using, for example, the UPPAAL model checker [4] or the CPAchecker [7] were not able to verify this case study [20–22,32]. However, due to limited scalability of the RASI, even with our deductive approach, we were forced to make some simplifications to make verification feasible. To demonstrate the applicability of our novel RASI generation approach, we evaluate it on the original ABS/ASR system without simplifications, as well as modified versions in which we vary the number of wheels between 1 and 8 to test scalability. At the extreme, this effectively doubles the number of processes and events to consider compared to the original system, and nearly triples the number of processes

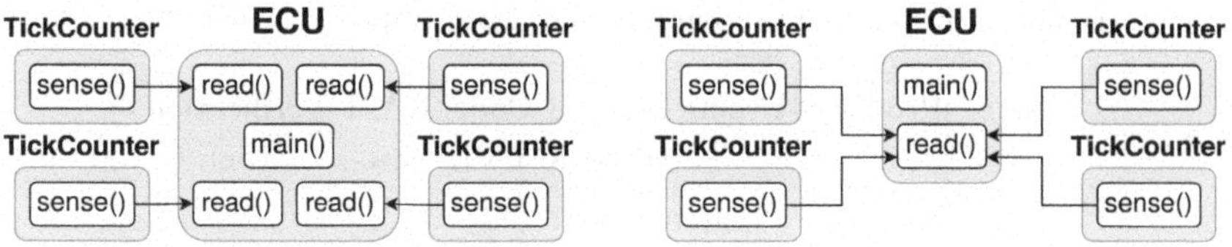

(a) Original ABS/ASR (b) ABS/ASR from [32]

Fig. 6. Different ABS/ASR versions

compared to the simplified system from [32]. All our results, the source code, the case studies and their translations can be found in our artifact [1].

Case Studies. The ABS/ASR design is based on a student implementation of an automotive control system in compliance with the Bosch specification [30]. Figure 6 shows its layout in its original form (in Fig. 6a) and the simplification used in [32] (in Fig. 6b). Each wheel contains a sensor that counts wheel rotations ("tick counter"). This data is sent to an electronic control unit (ECU) that runs the ABS and ASR algorithms to determine whether an intervention is necessary.

For our evaluation, we verify the original version of the ABS/ASR case study shown in Fig. 6, as well as a scaled-up version that contains eight wheels to test scalability. We compare the results to those from [32]. However, since the state space of these examples is too large for that approach due to the many independent processes, we restrict this comparison to the simplified ABS/ASR example. This version consolidates all read processes into one, which eliminates interleavings between these processes and thus greatly underapproximates the performance on the original version.

On all versions of the case study, we verify the same properties as in [32], namely correct initialization and function of the ABS/ASR algorithms in the ECU, deadlock freedom and, for each wheel, that data sent to the ECU is received correctly and within a given time limit. In contrast to [32], we use a more precise encoding of the SystemC scheduler and we use a newer version of VerCors (2.1.1 instead of 1.4.0).

Results. Our results can be seen in Table 1. We characterize the complexity of each case study by the number of processes and events it contains as well as the size of the code base, both in SystemC and, since the SystemC code can hide the underlying complexity, in the PVL encoding. The table columns describe, from left to right, the version of the ABS/ASR case study, the complexity of the case study by process and event count and lines of code in SystemC and PVL, the resulting size of the RASI and the verification time where applicable. Additionally, we explored the scalability of our approach by varying the case study size, as shown in Fig. 7. The experiments were measured running on an i7-8700 6-core 3.2 GHz CPU with 64 GB of main memory available.

Table 1. Experimental comparison of our approach with [32]

Design	Processes	Events	Lines of Code		RASI	Verification
			SystemC	PVL	size	time
Approach from [32]						
Simplified	6	17	394	1575	1×247	02:22:48
Original	9	17	369	1772	1×737	>72:00:00
Approach from this paper						
Original	9	17	369	1772	4×11	00:07:58

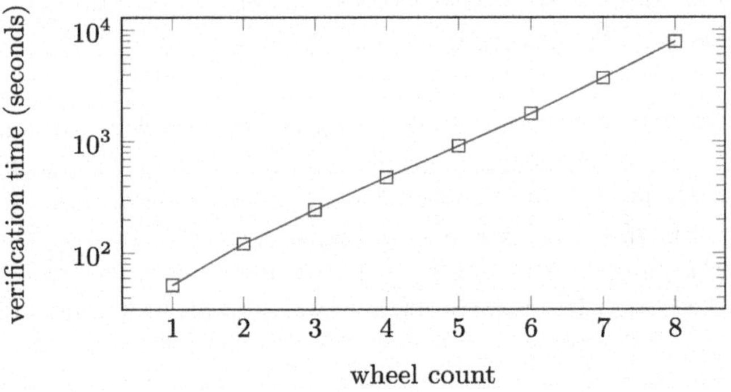

Fig. 7. Experiments with varying case study size

Discussion. The results shown in Table 1 demonstrate a significant improvement of our new RASI generation approach over our previous approach from [32]. Like previously, we were able to verify both functional and global safety properties about a complex parameterized SystemC design. However, our new abstraction finding algorithm was able to find much smaller invariants specifically tailored to each global property. As such, we were able to greatly reduce verification time. While the original ABS/ASR design was completely out of reach for our old technique, we were now able to verify it in a fraction of the time previously taken for even the simplified system. Furthermore, we were able to use our new approach on scaled versions of our case study that we used to test its scalability. While the experiments reveal an exponential scaling, the approach remains feasible even for our largest design (8 wheels, 17 processes, 33 events). This is promising for scaling our approach to industrial designs.

Besides the performance benefit in terms of reduced verification time, our approach also significantly reduced the user effort involved in the verification process. Since variables are now automatically selected for inclusion in the RASI by the generator, the user no longer has to experiment with different configurations to find the proper variables to include. Additionally, since the new RASI scales so much better, we do not need to rely on manual optimizations to make verification feasible. This reduces the manual effort in preparing the program for verification. The manual effort for each approach is further detailed in the step-by-step replication instructions in our artifact [1].

Overall, these results demonstrate the effectiveness of our approach. By automatically selecting an appropriate abstraction level for the RASI, we reduce both verification time and user effort and allow the application of deductive verification to embedded system at a greater scale.

6 Related Work

Invariant generation is a rich field, since many verification approaches rely on inferring invariants to either establish a given proof goal or support the proof by restricting the state space a prover must consider. There are several approaches to generate inductive invariants for model checking [6,9–11,16,27], using techniques such as Craig interpolation [15], data-flow analysis or abstract interpretation [14]. Many works in these fields also rely on abstraction refinement. A common technique is counterexample-guided abstraction refinement [13].

In contrast to approaches that use invariant generation directly for verification, we support deductive verification by providing a link between local and global state. Furthermore, rather than guessing refinements in a loop until successful verification in a general setting, we exploit domain knowledge in SystemC verification to tailor our refinement to variables that influence global behavior.

Existing work on invariant generation in deductive verification typically provides general procedures to derive invariants from postconditions [17,18], to generalize or propagate formulas locally for one loop or method [5], or generates invariants automatically by capturing general information such as data dependencies [31]. In contrast, we consider global properties in concurrent, reactive systems, and exploit the domain knowledge that these properties typically depend on process-event-interactions.

There exist several approaches to enable formal verification for SystemC, such as [12,19,20,23,25,26]. However, these are all based on model checking, making them difficult to apply to systems with large and complex state spaces or to verifying data-dependent functional properties. To the best of our knowledge, [32] is the only deductive approach to SystemC verification, but its invariant generation approach does not scale well, also limiting its applicability. This paper combines deductive verification suitable for functional properties and complex systems with an efficient and highly automatic invariant generation technique that greatly increases performance.

7 Conclusion

In this paper, we present an invariant generation approach for deductively proving global properties about embedded systems. Our approach allows us to generate invariants that capture those aspects of the state space that are relevant for a given global property. In contrast to our previous work, this approach leverages abstract interpretation to automate the generation process and abstraction refinement to automatically detect the ideal abstraction level for the invariant. This enables the use of much smaller invariants at a much higher level of abstraction than previously, without increasing the requirement for user effort. Thus, it allows the verification of much larger systems with much more complex behavior than before, and it brings this verification approach closer to being applicable to even larger industrial designs.

For future work, we want to relax the assumptions that are currently restricting the system under verification and investigate what other types of system can be verified with a global invariant in the style of the RASI. We also plan to investigate how to further refine our abstraction, e.g. using predicate abstraction.

References

1. Artifact. https://doi.org/10.4121/86963fe3-cc3f-45c3-b252-00d8780c4a1a
2. Amighi, A., Haack, C., Huisman, M., Hurlin, C.: Permission-based separation logic for multithreaded Java programs. Log. Methods Comput. Sci. **11**(1) (2015). https://doi.org/10.2168/LMCS-11(1:2)2015
3. Armborst, L., et al.: The VerCors verifier: a progress report. In: Gurfinkel, A., Ganesh, V. (eds.) CAV 2024. LNCS, vol. 14682, pp. 3–18. Springer, Cham (2024). https://doi.org/10.1007/978-3-031-65630-9_1
4. Behrmann, G., David, A., Larsen, K.G.: A tutorial on UPPAAL. In: Bernardo, M., Corradini, F. (eds.) SFM-RT 2004. LNCS, vol. 3185, pp. 200–236. Springer, Heidelberg (2004). https://doi.org/10.1007/978-3-540-30080-9_7
5. Bensalem, S., Lakhnech, Y.: Automatic generation of invariants. Form. Methods Syst. Des. **15**, 75–92 (1999). https://doi.org/10.1023/A:1008744030390
6. Beyer, D., Chien, P.C., Lee, N.Z.: Augmenting interpolation-based model checking with auxiliary invariants (2024). https://doi.org/10.48550/arXiv.2403.07821
7. Beyer, D., Keremoglu, M.E.: CPACHECKER: a tool for configurable software verification. In: Gopalakrishnan, G., Qadeer, S. (eds.) CAV 2011. LNCS, vol. 6806, pp. 184–190. Springer, Heidelberg (2011). https://doi.org/10.1007/978-3-642-22110-1_16
8. Blom, S., Darabi, S., Huisman, M., Oortwijn, W.: The VerCors tool set: verification of parallel and concurrent software. In: Polikarpova, N., Schneider, S. (eds.) IFM 2017. LNCS, vol. 10510, pp. 102–110. Springer, Cham (2017). https://doi.org/10.1007/978-3-319-66845-1_7
9. Bradley, A.R.: SAT-based model checking without unrolling. In: Jhala, R., Schmidt, D. (eds.) VMCAI 2011. LNCS, vol. 6538, pp. 70–87. Springer, Heidelberg (2011). https://doi.org/10.1007/978-3-642-18275-4_7
10. Case, M.L., Mishchenko, A., Brayton, R.K.: Automated extraction of inductive invariants to aid model checking. In: Formal Methods in Computer-Aided Design, pp. 165–172. IEEE (2007). https://doi.org/10.1109/FAMCAD.2007.12
11. Cimatti, A., Griggio, A.: Software model checking via IC3. In: Madhusudan, P., Seshia, S.A. (eds.) CAV 2012. LNCS, vol. 7358, pp. 277–293. Springer, Heidelberg (2012). https://doi.org/10.1007/978-3-642-31424-7_23
12. Cimatti, A., Narasamdya, I., Roveri, M.: Software model checking SystemC. IEEE Trans. Comput. Aided Des. Integr. Circuits Syst. **32**(5), 774–787 (2013). https://doi.org/10.1109/TCAD.2012.2232351

13. Clarke, E., Grumberg, O., Jha, S., Lu, Y., Veith, H.: Counterexample-guided abstraction refinement. In: Emerson, E.A., Sistla, A.P. (eds.) CAV 2000. LNCS, vol. 1855, pp. 154–169. Springer, Heidelberg (2000). https://doi.org/10.1007/10722167_15
14. Cousot, P., Cousot, R.: Abstract interpretation: a unified lattice model for static analysis of programs by construction or approximation of fixpoints. In: ACM SIGACT-SIGPLAN Symposium on Principles of Programming Languages, pp. 238–252. ACM Press (1977). https://doi.org/10.1145/512950.512973
15. Craig, W.: Linear reasoning. A new form of the Herbrand-Gentzen theorem. J. Symb. Logic **22**, 250–268 (1957). https://doi.org/10.2307/2963593
16. Fedyukovich, G., Bodík, R.: Accelerating syntax-guided invariant synthesis. In: Beyer, D., Huisman, M. (eds.) TACAS 2018. LNCS, vol. 10805, pp. 251–269. Springer, Cham (2018). https://doi.org/10.1007/978-3-319-89960-2_14
17. Furia, C.A., Meyer, B., Velder, S.: Loop invariants: analysis, classification, and examples. ACM Comput. Surv. (CSUR) **46**(3), 1–51 (2014). https://doi.org/10.1145/2506375
18. Galeotti, J.P., Furia, C.A., May, E., Fraser, G., Zeller, A.: DynaMate: dynamically inferring loop invariants for automatic full functional verification. In: Yahav, E. (ed.) HVC 2014. LNCS, vol. 8855, pp. 48–53. Springer, Cham (2014). https://doi.org/10.1007/978-3-319-13338-6_4
19. Große, D., Le, H.M., Drechsler, R.: Formal verification of SystemC-based cyber components. In: Jeschke, S., Brecher, C., Song, H., Rawat, D.B. (eds.) Industrial Internet of Things. SSWT, pp. 137–167. Springer, Cham (2017). https://doi.org/10.1007/978-3-319-42559-7_6
20. Herber, P., Glesner, S.: A HW/SW co-verification framework for SystemC. ACM Trans. Embed. Comput. Syst. (TECS) **12**(1s), 1–23 (2013). https://doi.org/10.1145/2435227.2435257
21. Herber, P., Hünnemeyer, B.: Formal verification of SystemC designs using the BLAST software model checker. In: ACESMB@ MoDELS, pp. 44–53 (2014). https://dblp.org/rec/conf/models/HerberH14
22. Herber, P., Liebrenz, T.: Dependence analysis and automated partitioning for scalable formal analysis of SystemC designs. In: ACM-IEEE International Conference on Formal Methods and Models for System Design, pp. 1–6. IEEE (2020). https://doi.org/10.1109/MEMOCODE51338.2020.9314998
23. Herdt, V., Große, D., Drechsler, R.: Formal verification of SystemC-based designs using symbolic simulation. In: Enhanced Virtual Prototyping, pp. 59–117. Springer, Cham (2021). https://doi.org/10.1007/978-3-030-54828-5_4
24. IEEE Standards Association: IEEE Std. 1666–2011, SystemC Language Reference Manual. IEEE Press (2011). https://doi.org/10.1109/IEEESTD.2012.6134619
25. Karlsson, D., Eles, P., Peng, Z.: Formal verification of SystemC designs using a Petri-net based representation. In: Design, Automation and Test in Europe, pp. 1228–1233. IEEE Press (2006). https://doi.org/10.1109/DATE.2006.244076
26. Man, K.L., Fedeli, A., Mercaldi, M., Boubekeur, M., Schellekens, M.: SC2SCFL: automated SystemC to $SystemC^{\mathbb{FL}}$ translation. In: Vassiliadis, S., Bereković, M., Hämäläinen, T.D. (eds.) SAMOS 2007. LNCS, vol. 4599, pp. 34–45. Springer, Heidelberg (2007). https://doi.org/10.1007/978-3-540-73625-7_6
27. McMillan, K.L.: Interpolation and SAT-based model checking. In: International Conference on Computer Aided Verification, pp. 1–13 (2003). https://doi.org/10.1007/978-3-540-45069-6_1
28. O'Hearn, P.W.: Resources, concurrency and local reasoning. Theor. Comput. Sci. **375**(1–3), 271–307 (2007). https://doi.org/10.1016/j.tcs.2006.12.035

29. Phan, Q.S., Malacaria, P.: All-solution satisfiability modulo theories: applications, algorithms and benchmarks. In: International Conference on Availability, Reliability and Security, pp. 100–109. IEEE (2015). https://doi.org/10.1109/ARES.2015.14
30. Reif, K.: Bremsen und Bremsregelsysteme [Brakes and brake control systems]. Bosch Fachinformation Automobil, Vieweg+Teubner Verlag Wiesbaden (2010). https://doi.org/10.1007/978-3-8348-9714-5
31. Tabar, A.H., Bubel, R., Hähnle, R.: Automatic loop invariant generation for data dependence analysis. In: IEEE/ACM International Conference on Formal Methods in Software Engineering, pp. 34–45 (2022). https://doi.org/10.1145/3524482.3527649
32. Tasche, P., Monti, R.E., Drerup, S.E., Blohm, P., Herber, P., Huisman, M.: Deductive verification of parameterized embedded systems modeled in SystemC. In: Dimitrova, R., Lahav, O., Wolff, S. (eds.) VMCAI 2024. LNCS, vol. 14500, pp. 187–209. Springer, Cham (2024). https://doi.org/10.1007/978-3-031-50521-8_9
33. Yu, Y., Subramanyan, P., Tsiskaridze, N., Malik, S.: All-SAT using minimal blocking clauses. In: International Conference on VLSI Design, pp. 86–91. IEEE (2014). https://doi.org/10.1109/VLSID.2014.22

Formal Analysis of Multi-Factor Authentication Schemes in Digital Identity Cards

Matteo Paier[1,2](✉), Roberto Van Eeden[1], and Marino Miculan[1]

[1] University of Udine, Udine, Italy
matteo.paier@imtlucca.it
[2] IMT School for Advanced Studies, Lucca, Italy

Abstract. We present a methodology for formally modelling and verifying multi-factor authentication (MFA) schemes employed in eIDAS digital identity cards. This methodology adopts an *interface-based threat model* to comprehensively analyse potential vulnerabilities and enumerate threat scenarios based on an attacker's capabilities. Using CIE, Italy's eIDAS-compliant digital identity card, as guiding example, we show how to automatically generate ProVerif models of these scenarios. Our analysis exposes some vulnerabilities; e.g., an attacker with Level 1 credentials can gain Level 2 authentication, even without compromising any interface. To address these vulnerabilities, we propose minor modifications to the protocols, whose correctness is proved by further formal analysis.

Keywords: Formal modelling · Formal specification · Multi-factor authentication · Security · Privacy · Threat models

1 Introduction

A strong digital identity (eID) infrastructure is essential for the success of today's digital transformation. Recognizing this, the European Commission adopted the eIDAS regulation in June 2014 [9], establishing standards for eIDs, digital certificates, Single Sign-On (SSO), and trust services across the EU. However, only a few countries have currently adopted eIDAS-compliant digital identity cards, because implementing such a nationwide service is a complex task [11, 14, 18].

In particular, designing and implementing secure multi-factor authentication (MFA) schemes is challenging and error-prone. SAML-based single sign-on (SSO) systems have often exhibited vulnerabilities in the past [2, 15, 16, 20]. Therefore, formal modelling, specification, and verification offer a powerful and valuable approach to designing and analysing these schemes.

In this paper, we propose a methodology for formally modelling and verifying multi-factor authentication schemes employed in eIDAS digital identity cards.

Analysing these schemes is complex due to the multitude of potential vulnerabilities. These include compromised passwords (the very reason for MFA),

A. Madeira and A. Knapp (Eds.): SEFM 2024, LNCS 15280, pp. 423–440, 2025.
https://doi.org/10.1007/978-3-031-77382-2_24

network disruptions, human error induced by phishing, and malware compromising devices. To address this complexity, following the approach presented in [12] we adopt an abstract view of an eID architecture as a distributed system whose components interact through well-defined *input and output interfaces*. Then, a *threat scenario* is defined in terms of the level of access (read or write) an attacker can gain to these interfaces. Consequently, depending on the attacker's capabilities, many combinations arise, yielding a plethora of threat scenarios. We show how, assuming a "strength ordering" between access levels, these scenarios can be reduced and automatically generated by means of suitable scripts. The resulting models can be analysed using the ProVerif security protocol verifier [6].

As a practical example, we consider the case of Italian *Carta di Identità Elettronica* (CIE), which is issued to any Italian citizen and has been replacing the paper-based identity card since July 2016. In particular, we focus on the security of CIE's Level 2 MFA, the most commonly used level for applications. Level 2 MFA offers three methods. The first, which we call *L2SMS*, sends a one-time passcode (OTP) via SMS; this methods suits users without smartphones. The other two methods require both a smartphone and the dedicated CieID app: *L2QRC* involves scanning a QR code with the app, while *L2PSH* prompts the user to authorize a request directly within the CieID app.

Our analysis exposes vulnerabilities in CIE's Level 2 mechanisms across various attack scenarios. For example, L2SMS is susceptible when an attacker can read the target's computer screen. Even more concerning, L2PSH possesses an inherent weakness: an attacker can achieve a Level 2 authentication using only Level 1 credentials, through a carefully timed attack.

Encouragingly, by analysing attack traces identified by ProVerif, we propose minor modifications to both L2SMS and L2PSH that significantly enhance their security. Further formal analysis confirms the effectiveness of these adjustments.

Summarizing, this work provides several contributions:

1. We propose a methodology for formal modelling and analysis of MFA schemes of eIDAS digital identity cards, adapting previous work [12] and using Italian CIE as a case study (Sect. 2).
2. We provide a threat model for CIE that covers vulnerabilities based on an attacker's access to interfaces of the system architecture. From this threat model we can automatically enumerate a reduced yet comprehensive family of potential attack scenarios (Sect. 3).
3. We provide a complete formalization of CIE's Level 2 authentication schemes using both sequence diagrams (Sect. 2) and ProVerif code (Sect. 4).
4. We conduct an extensive analysis of these schemes in ProVerif, under the attack scenarios identified by the threat model. This analysis exposes specific security vulnerabilities within L2SMS and L2PSH protocols (Sect. 5).
5. We propose targeted modifications to both L2SMS and L2PSH, effectively bringing the latter's security posture on par with L2QRC (Sect. 6).

Sect. 7 draws some conclusions and suggests directions for future work.

The interface-based modelling and analysis methodology used in this work can be adapted to other eIDAS digital identity cards, thus complementing the security analysis of cross-country eIDAS authentication scheme provided in [10].

All scripts, ProVerif formal models, verification outputs, etc., are available in the accompanying reusable artefact [17].

2 CIE Architecture and Protocols

As for others eIDAS compliant cards, CIE authentication relies on the SAML 2.0 standard to securely exchange authentication and authorization data across security domains. This process involves both the CIE Identity Provider (IdP) and the federated public administration Service Providers (SPs).

All communications between the IdP server and the devices participating in the login procedure utilize TLS (with exceptions documented as necessary).

The CIE identity provider offers three distinct authentication levels for secure online access. Level 1 authentication adopts a single factor, i.e., basic username and password. Level 2 authentication adds a second factor using a registered device: the user is required to either type a one-time passcode (OTP) received via SMS, or to authorize the login on the CieID app. In the second case, a PIN specific to the app must be entered after receiving a push notification or scanning a QR code. Finally, Level 3 authentication still uses two factors, but it requires the access to the physical CIE smartcard, and typing the corresponding PIN. The CIE smartcard can be accessed either using a dedicated USB (NFC) card reader or using the CieID app on an NFC-enabled smartphone.

To ensure a stronger security posture, service providers typically mandate Level 2 or 3 multi-factor authentication, relegating Level 1 to situations deemed low-risk and involving minimal access to personal information.

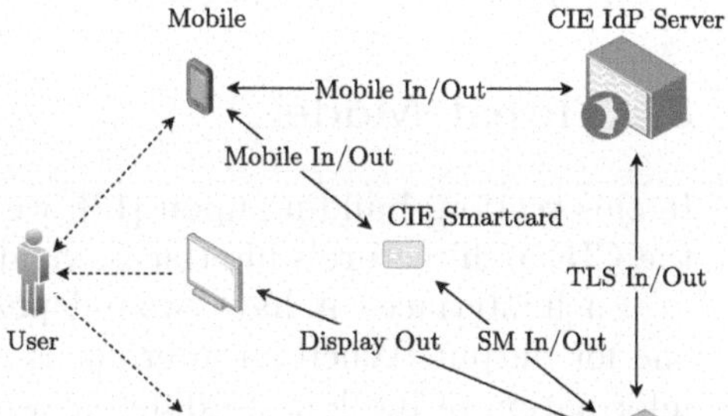

In line with the methodology established in [12], we give a model where entities like devices, computers, and servers are abstracted as collections of interfaces enabling data ingress and egress, as shown in the figure aside. Each interface can be independently compromised, thereby generating a multifaceted threat landscape.

The user's computer is modelled through the following interfaces:

Display Represents the user's PC screen, only capable of data output;
Keyboard Represents user input via the keyboard;
TLS Represents encrypted communication channels with remote entities like the IdP server. This interface offers simultaneous input and output functionality

because compromising one direction (e.g., sending data) also compromises the other (receiving data) due to the nature of protocols like TLS.

SM Represents bidirectional communication with the CIE smartcard, using the *Secure Message* protocol. This communication is encrypted and authenticated independently of the connection between the card reader and the PC (USB, Bluetooth, etc.); hence we need to model SM as a distinct interface.

To facilitate comparisons of attack vectors targeting various protocols, *mobile devices* involved in CIE authentication are consolidated into a single interface, encompassing both input and output functionalities.

The *Smartcard* itself is modelled with two interfaces: one for Secure Messaging (SM) In/Out with the PC and another for NFC In/Out with the mobile device. While authentication schemes utilizing the smartcard are beyond the scope of this paper, we included it for the sake of completeness.

The *IdP server* is represented as the TLS interface for communication with the computer, and the additional interface (either SMS or TLS) for communication with the mobile device.

Given this architecture the three protocols for CIE's Level 2 MFA are:

L2SMS The authentication scheme using SMS OTP requires both possession of the login credentials and control of the SIM card associated with the account; see Fig. 1 for the corresponding sequence diagram.

L2QRC The authentication scheme using QR code scanning requires both possession of the registered smartphone running the CieID app and knowledge of the app's 6-digit device pin (Fig. 2).

L2PSH The authentication scheme using a push notification requires knowledge of the CIE credentials and of the CieID app device PIN, and possession of the device running the CieID app (Fig. 3).

3 Threat Model

In this section, building upon [12], we discuss how an attacker can compromise the CIE architecture's interfaces, yielding many possible threat scenarios.

Each interface can have two independent information flows, one for input and one for output. When an interface is compromised, the attacker can access the information of its flows in different ways: they could be able to read data (i.e., a *passive* attack), write data (i.e., when the attacker can produce messages), or both. In an uncompromised system, the attacker has no access to any interface, neither for reading nor writing. Conversely, a completely compromised system gives the attacker full read-write access to all interfaces.

More formally, we denote by $\mathcal{A}^{if}_{d:a}$ the level of control exercised by the attacker over an interface if, where:

- $d \in \{\mathsf{in}, \mathsf{out}, \mathsf{io}\}$ denotes the direction which the attacker gains control over: the input (in), the output (out), or both (io);
- $a \in \{\mathsf{RO}, \mathsf{WO}, \mathsf{RW}\}$ represents the access control acquired by the attacker: read-only (RO), write-only (WO) or read-write (RW).

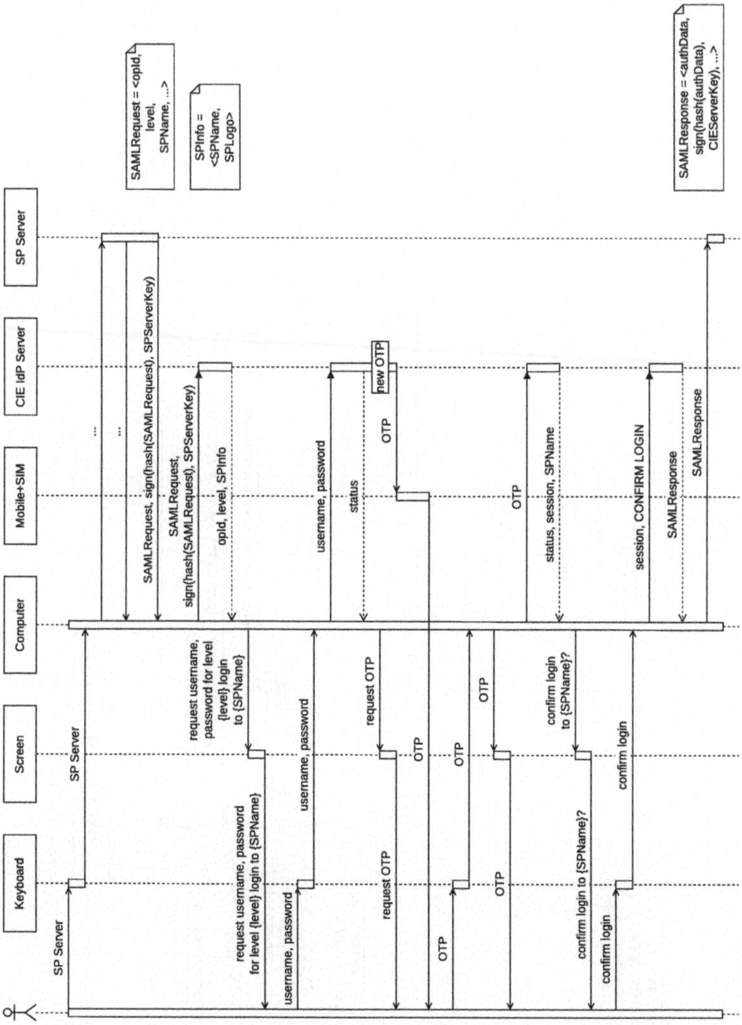

Fig. 1. Sequence diagram of L2SMS, Level 2 authentication via SMS OTP protocol. After having requested to connect to a given Service Provider server (SP Server), the user is prompted by the IdP server to enter their level 1 username and password. Following successful verification, the IdP server creates a unique OTP code specifically linked to the login attempt, which is then sent via SMS to the registered phone number on the user's account. Then, the user retrieves the OTP code from their mobile device and enters it on their computer. The computer transmits the code back to the IdP server for comparison. If the OTPs match, the IdP server grants access to the account, concluding the two-factor authentication.

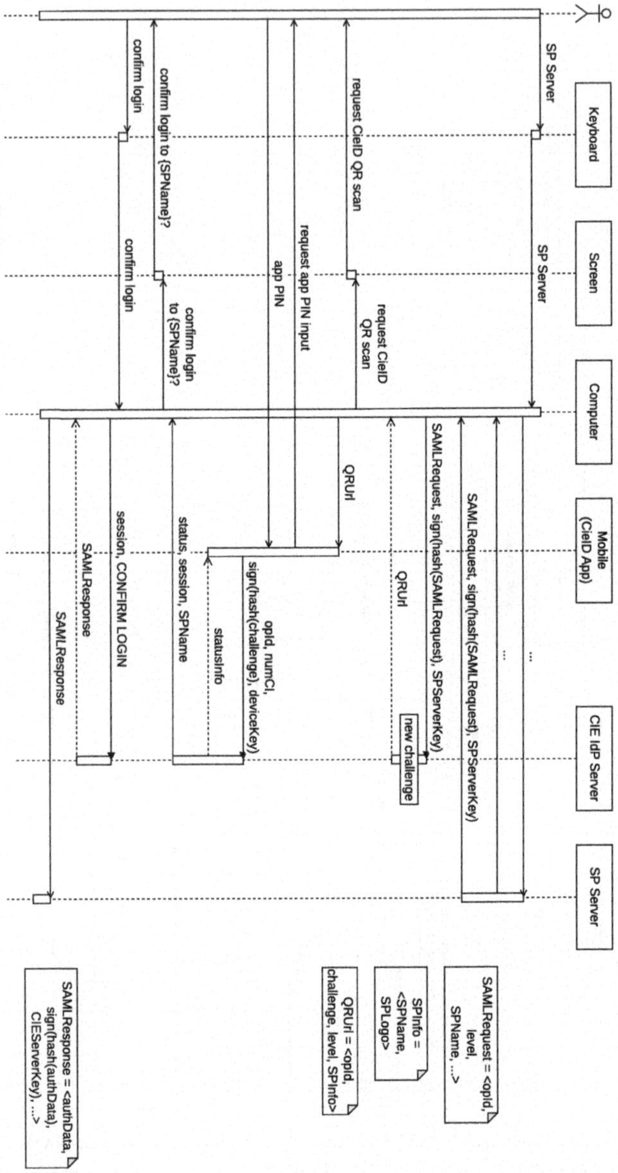

Fig. 2. Sequence diagram of L2QRC, Level 2 authentication via QR code recognition. The process begins with the user initiating a login on SP Server from their computer, which prompts the IdP server to generate a unique challenge associated with the login operation. This challenge is presented as a QR code, containing information like the operation ID and service provider details. The user scans the QR code with the CieID app, enters their device pin, and authorizes the login. The app then signs a hash of the challenge using the private key of the device and sends it, along with the CIE card number of the user, to the IdP server. The server validates the signature using the registered device certificates, and if successful, grants access to the account. The challenge expires within two minutes if validation does not occur.

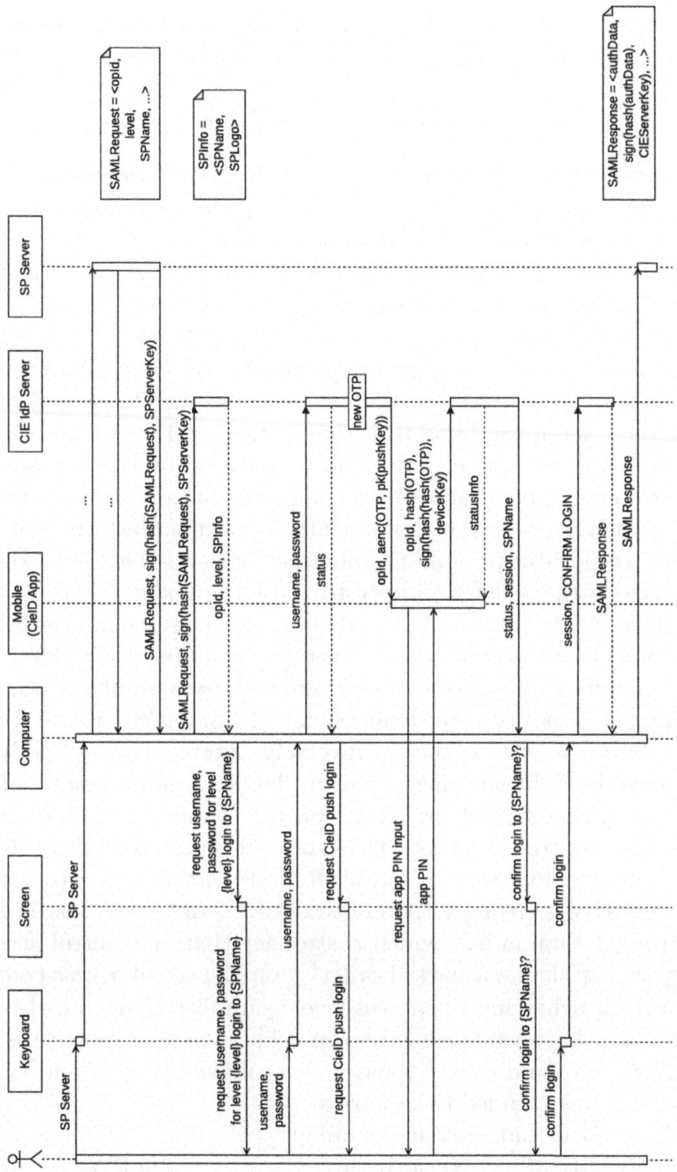

Fig. 3. Sequence diagram of L2PSH, Level 2 authentication via app push notification. Upon initiating login, a unique access token is generated by the IdP server. The user subsequently authenticates with their login credentials and selects the push notification option. The server then generates a 4-digit OTP code, encrypted using the user's device public key, and transmits it along with the access token via a secure notification service to the registered smartphone. Decryption and user verification occur on the device, requiring the 6-digi1t CieID app PIN for authorization. Subsequently, the CieID app signs a hash of the OTP code and transmits it, along with the access token and signature, back to the IdP server for verification. Successful validation by the server grants access to the requested service. It is important to note that this process is subject to time constraints, imposing a timely response for security purposes.

Then, a *threat scenario* $\mathcal{S}$ where the attacker acquires *access control levels* $d_1{:}a_1, \ldots, d_n{:}a_n$ on interfaces $\mathit{if}_1, \ldots, \mathit{if}_n$ respectively, is represented by the set

$$\mathcal{S} = \{\mathcal{A}^{\mathit{if}_1}_{d_1:a_1}, \ldots, \mathcal{A}^{\mathit{if}_n}_{d_n:a_n}\}.$$

Thus, the empty scenario $\{\}$ represents the uncompromised system.

For instance, the set $\{\mathcal{A}^{\mathsf{displ}}_{\mathsf{out:RW}}, \mathcal{A}^{\mathsf{mobile}}_{\mathsf{in:RO}}\}$ represents a scenario where the attacker has full control over the computer's display, allowing them to both read and manipulate what is shown on the screen, and can also passively monitor messages received by the mobile device.

In principle, all combinations of none/RO/WO/RW access on both directions of all interfaces are possible, yielding a large number of potential attack scenarios. For our CIE architecture (Sect. 2), we have 8 flows overall (since Keyboard and Display have only one meaningful direction), yielding $4^8 = 65536$ combinations. This large number of attack scenarios can be reduced by two key observations.

First, we observe that in general, seizing write access to a system interface requires higher privileges or the exploitation of specific platform vulnerabilities; such situation would also provide the attacker with read access. Consequently, write-only access attacks do not apply to the CIE model, where gaining write access inherently grants the attacker read access to the same interface. Therefore, we can limit ourselves to three access control levels: none, RO, RW.

Secondly, usually gaining control over an interface's input is easier than controlling its output. For instance, reading data from a USB port typically only requires user-mode code execution. Conversely, intercepting or modifying data transmitted over USB by another program demands administrator-level privileges or exploiting specific vulnerabilities on the system. Therefore, an attacker that achieves RW control of an interface's output, can also control its input.

From this observation, we can establish a *strength ordering* over the control access levels: out:RW is stronger than both out:RO, and in:RW; both out:RO and in:RW are stronger than in:RO, which is stronger than no control access at all.

Formally, we can define a partial order $\preceq$ on the set of access control levels: $\ell_1 \preceq \ell_2$ means that achieving the access level ℓ_1 implies achieving also the access level ℓ_2. This order between levels is shown aside, where $\top$ represents no access, $\ell_1 = \ell_2$ means $\ell_1 \preceq \ell_2$ and $\ell_2 \preceq \ell_1$, and $\ell_1 \prec \ell_2$ means $\ell_1 \preceq \ell_2$ and $\ell_1 \neq \ell_2$.

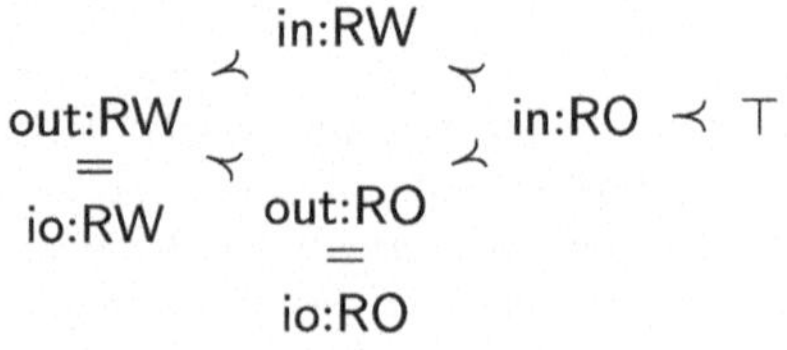

This order can be extended to scenarios pointwise: $\mathcal{S}_1 \preceq \mathcal{S}_2$ if and only if, for all $\mathcal{A}^{\mathit{if}}_{\ell_2} \in \mathcal{S}_2$ there exists $\mathcal{A}^{\mathit{if}}_{\ell_1} \in \mathcal{S}_1$ such that $\ell_1 \preceq \ell_2$. The order is strict, denoted as $\mathcal{S}_1 \prec \mathcal{S}_2$, when $\mathcal{S}_1 \preceq \mathcal{S}_2$ and $\mathcal{S}_2 \npreceq \mathcal{S}_1$.

As a consequence, we have that if a given protocol is proved secure in an attack scenario $\mathcal{S}$, then it is secure in every scenario $\mathcal{S}'$ such that $\mathcal{S} \preceq \mathcal{S}'$; in this case we say that the security of the protocol in $\mathcal{S}'$ is *implied by a stronger scenario*. Conversely, if a protocol is vulnerable in scenario $\mathcal{S}$, then it is vulnerable in every scenario $\mathcal{S}' \preceq \mathcal{S}$; in this case we say that the vulnerability of the protocol in

S' is *implied by a weaker scenario*. Therefore, if an attack is found in a given scenario, we can skip analysing stronger ones; conversely, a verified secure protocol in a scenario does not require checking in weaker ones. By leveraging these implications, we can reduce the number of scenarios to analyse 3 cases for both keyboard and display, since they encompass a single direction; 5 for the other three interfaces, yielding $3 \cdot 3 \cdot 5 \cdot 5 \cdot 5 = 1125$ scenarios.

We can further reduce this search space by recognizing that for TLS channels, the only relevant access levels are io:RO and io:RW, since gaining access to one direction of a TLS channel inherently grants access to the other direction as well. Here, we utilize a simplified model that captures the core properties of TLS (confidentiality, authentication, and message order) while acknowledging that attackers might be able to block or delay messages. A detailed formalization of TLS is beyond the scope of this paper; see e.g. [5].

A similar consideration applies to the SM channel between computer and the smartcard. However, the protocols considered in this paper do not need to access the smartcard, and hence attacks to the SM channel can be effectively ignored.

Overall, this allow us to reduce the analysis to $3 \cdot 3 \cdot 5 \cdot 3 = 135$ scenarios, since SM is not considered and TLS direction is only io.

Concerning phishing, even MFA systems are not immune to human error and social engineering attacks. Therefore, assessing how well CIE's multi-factor authentication can withstand these challenges is important. Our phishing attack model aligns with [12], but given the absence of fingerprint-related data in the CIE login process, we excluded fingerprint bypass from our analysis.

Under a phishing attack, users might be tricked into granting access to fake versions of legitimate services or unknowingly reveal sensitive information like OTPs. To model this attack in our scenarios, we assume the adversary has control over the targeted server, i.e. the server the user attempts to authenticate with.

Formally, to represent a phishing attack scenario we use the symbol PH in the attack scenario notation. This leads to double the number of scenarios to analyse, for a total amount of 270.

4 Formal Analysis of CIE Level 2 Authentication

We analyse the CieID Level 2 protocols against various security threats. We consider scenarios where the user's password is already compromised, attackers have varying degrees of control over user devices through malware, and phishing attempts can be successful. By simulating these threats, our analysis comprehensively assesses the effectiveness of the CieID multi-factor approach in protecting user accounts. The formal analysis is carried out using the ProVerif tool [6], a state-of-the-art security protocol verifier in the symbolic Dolev-Yao model.

We model each interface as two private channels: one for input and one for output. To simulate an attacker gaining read-only access to an interface, we reveal all message names transmitted on the corresponding private channels during protocol execution on a public channel. Formally, let `iface` represent a secret interface channel and `public` represent a public channel accessible to the attacker. To model the fact that the attacker has acquired read-only access to the interface, each instance of `out(iface, message)` is transformed into `out(public, message); out(iface, message)` and each instance of `in(iface, message)` into `in(iface, message); out(public, message)`. Conversely, to grant the attacker read-write access to a channel we provide them with the private channel name, allowing for a complete control of the communication channel itself.

We model the secure and authenticated communication via TLS channels using the `TLS(id, id):channel` function. To guarantee the integrity of the system, only authorized parties can invoke this function to acquire unique channel names. When establishing a TLS connection, one of the participating hosts generates a fresh session identifier, which is then attached to all subsequent messages, safeguarding against distinct sessions data mixing.

Since ProVerif's channels operate synchronously, the attacker would not be able to block or delay messages. In order to allow for this kind of attacks, we render each TLS channel as an asynchronous communication, by detaching communication using the "parallel" operator from the π-calculus.

Furthermore, to allow the attacker to consistently initiate TLS sessions with the IdP server, an auxiliary TLS manager process is used to reveal the channel names where the attacker maintains control over one of the parties involved.

In order to simulate phishing attacks, the model fetches the target server URL from a publicly available channel, mirroring potentially compromised online sources that could be tampered with. In a real-world scenario, a cautious user would compare the so obtained URL with the known and legitimate address of the IdP server. However, in scenarios contemplating phishing attacks, the model assumes that the human target bypasses this verification step.

The main property we consider is the *injective correspondence* of login attempts and successful logins. In other words: every successful access from a user's computer must correspond to a unique login attempt initiated by the user on the very same computer. In ProVerif this is rendered by a query as follows:
`query x:id;inj-event(Login(x)) ==> inj-event(UserLoginRequest(x)).`
where the `Login(x)` event is raised by the IdP Server when it successfully concludes a login attempt, and `UserLoginRequest(x)` is generated by the user when they initiate a login attempt.

The CieID level 2 protocols have been tested under every conceivable combination of platform compromise and human-induced threats. As discussed in Sect. 3, this testing resulted in a total of 270 distinct scenarios per protocol, each of them is modeled by a different ProVerif formalization.

To automate the generation of these ProVerif models, we have defined a general *model template* and employed the m4 macro processor [13]. Each possible attacker control and human threat is associated with a set of preprocessor definitions inside this template. We have developed a Python script to iterate over the entire set of possible scenarios: for each scenario, we use m4 to produce the corresponding model instance, which is then verified by ProVerif.

Table 1. Analysis results under different threat scenarios.

Threat Scenario				L2SMS	L2QRC	L2PSH
				✓	✓	✗
			$\mathcal{A}^{\mathsf{mobile}}_{\mathsf{in:RO}}$	✗	✓	✗
			$\mathcal{A}^{\mathsf{mobile}}_{\mathsf{in:RW}}$	✗	✗	✗
		$\mathcal{A}^{\mathsf{displ}}_{\mathsf{out:RO}}$		✗	✓	✗
		$\mathcal{A}^{\mathsf{displ}}_{\mathsf{out:RW}}$		✗	✗	✗
	$\mathcal{A}^{\mathsf{kbd}}_{\mathsf{in:RO}}$			✗	✓	✗
	$\mathcal{A}^{\mathsf{kbd}}_{\mathsf{in:RW}}$			✗	✗	✗
$\mathcal{A}^{\mathsf{tls}}_{\mathsf{io:RO}}$				✗	✓	✗
$\mathcal{A}^{\mathsf{tls}}_{\mathsf{io:RO}}$	$\mathcal{A}^{\mathsf{kbd}}_{\mathsf{in:RO}}$	$\mathcal{A}^{\mathsf{displ}}_{\mathsf{out:RO}}$	$\mathcal{A}^{\mathsf{mobile}}_{\mathsf{io:RO}}$	✗	✓	✗
$\mathcal{A}^{\mathsf{tls}}_{\mathsf{io:RW}}$				✗	✗	✗
PH				✗	✗	✗

Results:

- ✓ security proven
- ✓ security proven in a stronger scenario
- ✗ attack found
- ✗ attack found in a weaker scenario

Scenarios:

- PH: Phishing Attack
- $\mathcal{A}^{if}_{d:a}$: Attacker control over a system interface, where:
  - *if* is the name of the system interface
  - *d* represents control over interface's inputs (in), outputs (out) or both (io)
  - *a* is the access control over the interface: read-only (RO) or read-write (RW)

5 Analysis Results

Although CIE level 2 protocols provide a stronger defense against unauthorized access than passwords alone, their security is not without vulnerabilities. Table 1 reports the findings of our formal analysis of these authentication schemes.

While L2SMS may impede brute-force attacks leveraging stolen credentials, it remains susceptible to more advanced techniques. Malware, like USB keyloggers, can pose a significant threat by capturing the one-time passcodes delivered via SMS. Any attacker who intercepts these codes effectively bypasses L2SMS authentication, rendering it powerless against such threats.

L2SMS suffers from inherent transport-level weaknesses compared to protocols that leverage TLS channels. SIM swapping attacks, where an attacker redirects a victim's phone number to a different SIM card, pose a serious threat. Additionally, L2SMS might be susceptible to SS7 attacks on older UMTS and GSM networks. These attacks exploit weaknesses in the signaling system and potentially weaker encryption used in these networks, as highlighted in [21].

Our analysis revealed a particular problematic aspect of L2SMS: while it eliminates the need to scan codes on the computer screen (relying solely on SMS), the one-time passcode is still displayed on the computer's screen, making it vulnerable to malware that can capture the display output.

Currently, CIE users cannot disable L2SMS logins even after registering CieID devices to enable stronger Level 2 protocols. This creates a potential attack path, even if users prefer stronger protocols. Additionally, enrolling new L2QRC devices relies on an authentication scheme similar to L2SMS, raising concerns about its effectiveness as an upgrade. The possibility to bypass the security enhancements offered by other protocols is the most critical issue of L2SMS, leaving the entire system significantly more vulnerable.

L2QRC offers stronger security compared to L2SMS. It successfully avoids attacks passively extracting data from nearly all interfaces examined in the analysis, as demonstrated by the scenario $\{\mathcal{A}^{\mathsf{tls}}_{\mathsf{io:RO}}, \mathcal{A}^{\mathsf{usb}}_{\mathsf{in:RO}}, \mathcal{A}^{\mathsf{displ}}_{\mathsf{out:RO}}, \mathcal{A}^{\mathsf{mobile}}_{\mathsf{io:RO}}\}$. However, L2QRC struggles against active attackers. Many identified attacks involve substituting (through direct or indirect control of available system interfaces) the login operation identifiers presented to the CieID app. These attacks exploit the fact that the CieID app does not show to the user any element to identify the login session (such as device fingerprints [1]) during the L2QRC authentication phase: this prevents security-conscious users to recognise suspicious operations (like concurrent login attempts) and abort the authentication.

Our analysis identified an interesting attack applicable in scenario $\{\mathcal{A}^{\mathsf{kbd}}_{\mathsf{in:RW}}\}$. By modifying the keyboard input, an attacker can manipulate the URL a user intends to visit, essentially redirecting them to a malicious webpage. While similar to phishing attacks, this method operates on a lower level. Phishing deceives users into visiting malicious websites by exploiting human behaviour, whereas this attack directly alters user input, bypassing the user's awareness.

From our analysis, L2PSH is the protocol with the weakest security properties: an attack trace in the empty scenario has been found by ProVerif; see Fig. 4 for the sequence diagram. This attack requires only Level 1 login credentials and network control, resembling the timing attack on Google's G2OT found in [12]. In fact, L2PSH might be even more susceptible due to the way concurrent access attempts are handled: the CieID app overwrites earlier notifications, hindering the user's ability to detect fraudulent duplicate login attempts.

Additionally, L2PSH does not provide the user with any information regarding the device fingerprint or the attempted operation within the login request.

Therefore, in order to bypass L2PSH authentication, an attacker only needs to monitor the network waiting for a legitimate access attempt by the user; once such attempt is detected, they quickly initiate a malicious access attempt using level 1 credentials. Then, the legit access notification displayed to the user will be subtly replaced with the one from the malicious access attempt. The user proceeds to complete what they perceive as their login attempt using the notification, but actually grants the attacker access to the account.

The lack of any clear anomaly during this process makes it highly deceptive. The only symptom of the attack is a brief moment where the original notification is replaced with an identical-looking one; however, this is unlikely to be noticed by most users, including security-conscious ones.

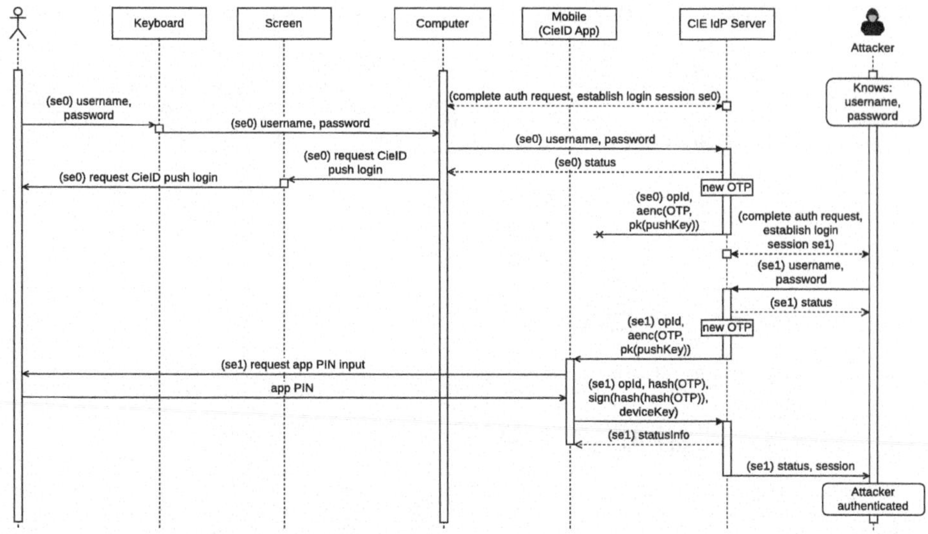

Fig. 4. Overview of the L2PSH attack in the empty scenario.

6 Protocol Improvement

From the analysis above, we can see that all protocols present some weakness. For example, in L2SMS, if the telephone number is under the attacker's control (e.g. via a SIM swap attack), the SMS code may be intercepted; in L2PSH if the smartphone has been compromised by a malware, the attacker can forward their own push notification to the user; in L2QRC if the attacker can display arbitrary data on the user's PC screen, they can show their QR code, and so on.

It should be noticed that most of these vulnerabilities are proper of the communication channels and the devices, and not due to logical flaws in the protocols; therefore, addressing these vulnerabilities would require a complete redesign of the architecture. Nevertheless, considering these attacks in our threat model allows us to analyse the protocols even when the channels or the platform have been attacked; for instance, our analysis points out that L2QRC is secure even if an attacker can decipher TLS traffic or intercept the keyboard input.

Still, certain weaknesses are intrinsic to the design of the protocols, and these can potentially be mitigated by minor changes. We propose an improvement of L2SMS and L2PSH protocols, in order to address the display channel vulnerability of the former and the "notification overwrite" of the latter.

L2SMS*: L2SMS Improvement. The ProVerif trace from our analysis shows that L2SMS vulnerability is that the OTP code is shown on the user's screen, exposing it to attackers with read-only screen access methods like screen sharing software or "shoulder surfing".

Table 2. Comparison with the improved protocols. See Table 1 for the rest of legend.

Threat Scenario	L2SMS	L2SMS*	L2PSH	L2PSH*	L2QRC
	✓	✓	✗	✓	✓
$\mathcal{A}^{\text{mobile}}_{\text{in:RO}}$	✗	✗	✗	✓	✓
$\mathcal{A}^{\text{mobile}}_{\text{in:RW}}$	✗	✗	✗	?	✗
$\mathcal{A}^{\text{mobile}}_{\text{io:RW}}$	✗	✗	✗	✗	✗
$\mathcal{A}^{\text{displ}}_{\text{out:RO}}$	✗	✓	✗	✓	✓
$\mathcal{A}^{\text{displ}}_{\text{out:RW}}$	✗	✓	✗	✗	✗
$\mathcal{A}^{\text{kbd}}_{\text{in:RO}}$	✗	✗	✗	✓	✓
$\mathcal{A}^{\text{kbd}}_{\text{in:RW}}$	✗	✗	✗	✗	✗
$\mathcal{A}^{\text{tls}}_{\text{io:RO}}$	✗	✗	✗	✓	✓
$\mathcal{A}^{\text{tls}}_{\text{io:RO}}$ $\mathcal{A}^{\text{kbd}}_{\text{in:RO}}$ $\mathcal{A}^{\text{displ}}_{\text{out:RO}}$ $\mathcal{A}^{\text{mobile}}_{\text{io:RO}}$	✗	✗	✗	✓	✓
$\mathcal{A}^{\text{tls}}_{\text{io:RW}}$	✗	✗	✗	✗	✗
NC	✱	✱	✱	✗	✱
PH	✗	✗	✗	✗	✗

Results:

- ? ProVerif does not reach a conclusive answer, failing with "Cannot be proven" (but it is safe to assume it is ✗)
- ✱ threat scenario not applicable to the protocol

Scenarios:

- NC: no-check scenario (the user skips the verification of the session identifier)

To rectify this vulnerability, it is enough to eliminate the step of displaying the OTP code on the display after keyboard input. The formal verification of this variant, which we call L2SMS*, confirms that the vulnerability has been effectively mitigated (see Table 2). This means an attacker with read-only or read-write access to the display channel can no longer gain unauthorized access.

To prevent attackers from observing the OTP during user input, a possibility is to give no feedback at all, by eliminating any character display on the screen while typing the code. Alternatively, characters can be masked, by replacing the actual digits with asterisks or bullets as they are typed. This keeps the actual code hidden from view, while providing some basic user confirmation.

L2PSH*: L2PSH Improvement. The attack trace visualized in Fig. 4 exposes a critical vulnerability inherent to the protocol itself, since it is susceptible to attack even in the absence of any compromised interfaces by an attacker.

In order to mitigate this vulnerability and elevate the protocol's security, we recommend the implementation of a mechanism empowering the user to verify the correspondence of a push notification with their own login attempt; in the case this verification fails, the user ought not continue the login procedure.

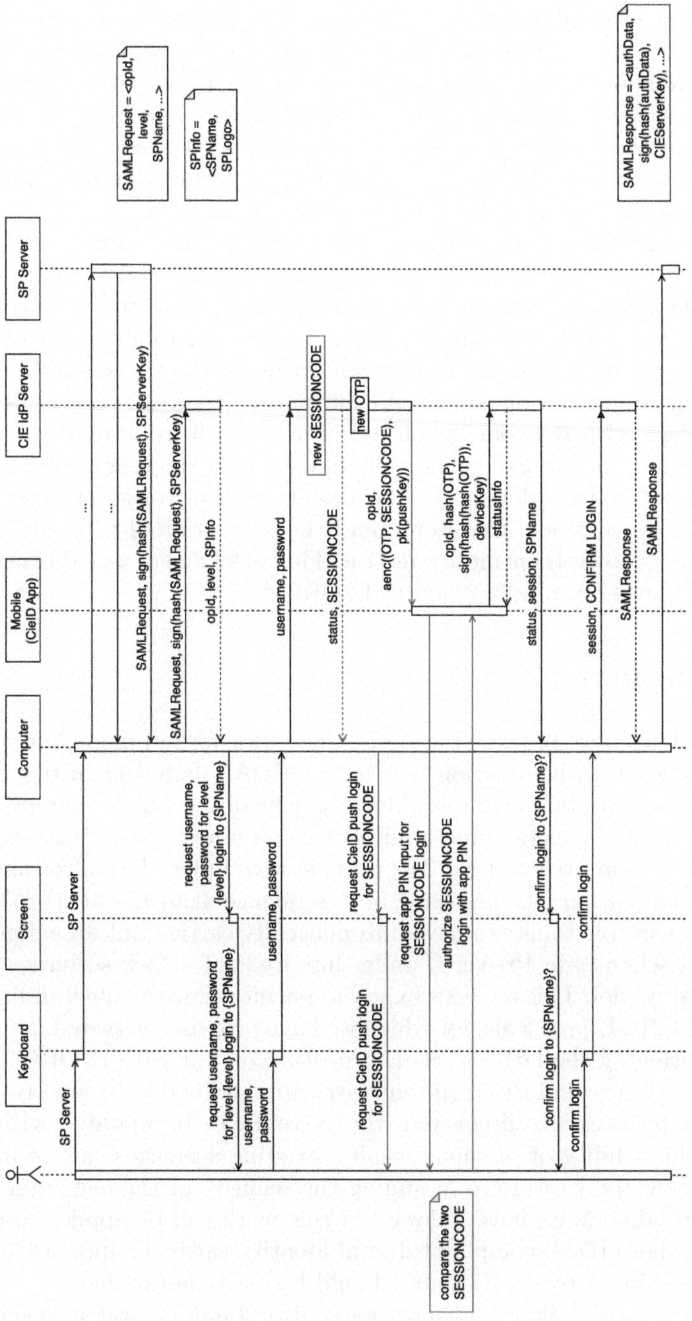

Fig. 5. Sequence diagram of L2PSH*, Level 2 authentication via app push notification improved with unique session code. In blue the exchange steps that have been added or modified. During the login process, the code (e.g. a number or a short passphrase) is generated by the IdP server and displayed on the user's computer screen. Simultaneously, the same code is sent along within the push notification and shown to the user on the mobile device. The user should then check that the two codes match, before proceeding with authorizing the login on the CieID mobile app. (Color figure online)

To address this vulnerability and elevate the protocol's security, we propose implementing a user verification mechanism for push notifications. This mechanism would allow users to check that the push notification on their device matches their login attempt; if the verification fails, the user should be able to cancel the login attempt to prevent unauthorized access. This new protocol L2PSH*, a variant of L2PSH incorporating a verification mechanism implemented by means of a unique session code, is shown in Fig. 5.

As shown in Table 2, the formal analysis of L2PSH* confirms that the vulnerability has been effectively mitigated, putting L2PSH* on a par with L2QRC.

While the proposed session code mechanism significantly enhances the protocol's security, it adds a potential human factor vulnerability: users can ignore the verification step, authorizing logins even when the session codes shown on the screen and on the mobile device do not match. In order to compel the user to actively engage with the code, a selection-based verification mechanism, can be adopted. This would involve generating and show on the user's computer screen a unique code, and displaying on the mobile device a grid of possible codes, including the correct one; the user would then be required to locate and select the matching code on their mobile device. This mechanism would bring L2PSH* to a security level essentially equal to L2QRC's.

7 Conclusions

In this paper we have proposed a methodology for formal modelling and analysis of multi-factor authentication schemes of eIDAS digital identity cards, using Italian CIE as a guiding example. More specifically, we have provided a threat model for CIE that covers vulnerabilities based on an attacker's access to interfaces of the system architecture. We provide a complete formalization of CIE's Level 2 authentication schemes using both sequence diagrams and ProVerif code. Then, using suitable tools, we have automatically carried out an extensive analysis of MFA schemes in ProVerif, under hundreds of attack scenarios identified by the threat model. This analysis exposes specific security vulnerabilities within L2SMS and L2PSH protocols, for which we have proposed targeted modifications effectively bringing the latter's security posture on par with L2QRC.

Our architecture and ProVerif templates are designed to be adaptable. If new attackable interfaces are discovered, the system can be updated without compromising the validity of previous results: existing scenarios can be interpreted within the new architecture as assuming the security of the new interfaces.

The methodology we have followed in this work can be applied also to MFA schemes of other eIDAS-compliant digital identity cards. Scripts are available in the accompanying artefact [17], and should be easily adaptable.

In previous work [19], the idea of aggregating fundamental attacker capabilities to simulate various attack scenarios for MFA in online banking was explored. Besides for the applicative context, our approach distinguishes itself also by employing automated tools to generate formal (ProVerif) models of these scenarios, thereby streamlining the process significantly.

We have contacted the Italian National Cybersecurity Authority (ACN) about the results of this research. We are collaborating to suggest improvements and formally verify the effectiveness of the solutions under development.
Future Work. We plan to formalize and verify the Level 3 CIE multi-factor authentication protocols. First, we aim to assess the resilience of smartphone-based login protocols against attacks, considering the distinct security paradigms employed by popular mobile platforms. Second, we plan to evaluate the susceptibility of existing CIE smartcards to side-channel attacks, which exploit unintended information leakage. Finally, investigating the implementation of official CIE authentication for adherence to security best practices holds promise as a research topic. By verifying such adherence, we can minimize potential attack vectors.

The interface-access threat model could be applied in other domains. A captivating case pertains to *containers*, which inherently possess well-defined interfaces for interaction. We envision integrating the interface-access threat model with formal models of container compositions, such as that from [7].

Another future work is to consider position-sensitive security protocols [8]. To this end, we need models of processes in continuous space, as in [3,4].

Acknowledgments. This research has been partially supported by the Department Strategic Project on Artificial Intelligence of the University of Udine (2020–25), and the project SERICS (PE00000014) under the NRRP MUR program funded by EU-NGEU.

Data and Artifact Availability. The artefact [17] includes ProVerif templates for all three Level 2 CieID protocols, scripts to instantiate them into formal models for all threat scenarios, and the complete results of the verification process.

Disclosure of Interests. The authors have no competing interests to declare that are relevant to the content of this article.

References

1. Alaca, F., van Oorschot, P.C.: Device fingerprinting for augmenting web authentication: classification and analysis of methods. In: Proceedings of the 32nd Conference on Computer Security Applications, pp. 289–301. ACM (2016)
2. Armando, A., Carbone, R., Compagna, L., Cuellar, J., Tobarra, L.: Formal analysis of SAML 2.0 web browser single sign-on: breaking the SAML-based single sign-on for Google apps. In: Proceedings of the 6th ACM Workshop on Formal Methods in Security Engineering, pp. 1–10 (2008)
3. Bacci, G., Miculan, M.: Structural operational semantics for continuous state probabilistic processes. In: Pattinson, D., Schröder, L. (eds.) CMCS 2012. LNCS, vol. 7399, pp. 71–89. Springer, Heidelberg (2012). https://doi.org/10.1007/978-3-642-32784-1_5
4. Bacci, G., Miculan, M.: Structural operational semantics for continuous state stochastic transition systems. J. Comput. Syst. Sci. **81**(5), 834–858 (2015)
5. Bhargavan, K., Blanchet, B., Kobeissi, N.: Verified models and reference implementations for the TLS 1.3 standard candidate. In: 2017 IEEE Symposium on Security and Privacy (S&P), pp. 483–502 (2017)

6. Blanchet, B., et al.: Modeling and verifying security protocols with the applied pi calculus and ProVerif. Found. Trends Priv. Secur. **1**, 1–135 (2016)
7. Burco, F., Miculan, M., Peressotti, M.: Towards a formal model for composable container systems. In: Proceedings of the 35th Annual ACM Symposium on Applied Computing, pp. 173–175 (2020)
8. Cook, A., Viganò, L.: Formal analysis of security protocols with movement. In: Proceedings of the Italian Conference on Cyber Security (ITASEC 2023). CEUR Workshop Proceedings, vol. 3488. CEUR-WS.org (2023)
9. Dumortier, J.: Regulation EU no 910/2014 on electronic identification and trust services for electronic transactions in the internal market (eIDAS regulation). In: EU Regulation of E-Commerce, pp. 256–289. Edward Elgar Publishing (2017)
10. Engelbertz, N., Erinola, N., Herring, D., Somorovsky, J., Mladenov, V., Schwenk, J.: Security analysis of eIDAS — the Cross-Country authentication scheme in Europe. In: 12th USENIX Workshop on Offensive Technologies (2018)
11. Gregušová, D., Halásová, Z., Peráček, T.: eIDAS regulation and its impact on national legislation: the case of the Slovak republic. Admin. Sci. **12**(4), 187 (2022)
12. Jacomme, C., Kremer, S.: An extensive formal analysis of multi-factor authentication protocols. ACM Trans. Priv. Secur. **24**, 1–34 (2021)
13. Kernighan, B., Ritchie, D.: The M4 macro processor. Technical report, Bell Laboratories Murray Hill (1977)
14. Lips, S., Bharosa, N., Draheim, D.: eIDAS implementation challenges: the case of Estonia and the Netherlands. In: Chugunov, A., Khodachek, I., Misnikov, Y., Trutnev, D. (eds.) EGOSE 2020. CCIS, vol. 1349, pp. 75–89. Springer, Cham (2020). https://doi.org/10.1007/978-3-030-67238-6_6
15. Mainka, C., Mladenov, V., Feldmann, F., Krautwald, J., Schwenk, J.: Your software at my service: security analysis of SaaS single sign-on solutions in the cloud. In: Proceedings of the 6th ACM Workshop on Cloud Computing Security, pp. 93–104 (2014)
16. Miculan, M., Urban, C.: Formal analysis of Facebook Connect single sign-on authentication protocol. In: SofSem 2011, Proceedings of Student Research Forum, pp. 99–116. OKAT (2011)
17. Paier, M., Van Eeden, R., Miculan, M.: Formal Analysis of Multi-Factor Authentication Schemes in Digital Identity Cards - Artifact (2024). https://doi.org/10.5281/zenodo.12586055
18. Sharif, A., Ranzi, M., Carbone, R., Sciarretta, G., Marino, F.A., Ranise, S.: The eIDAS regulation: a survey of technological trends for European electronic identity schemes. Appl. Sci. **12**(24), 12679 (2022)
19. Sinigaglia, F., Carbone, R., Costa, G., Zannone, N.: A survey on multi-factor authentication for online banking in the wild. Comput. Secur. **95**, 101745 (2020)
20. Somorovsky, J., Heiderich, M., Jensen, M., Schwenk, J., Gruschka, N., Lo Iacono, L.: All your clouds are belong to us: security analysis of cloud management interfaces. In: Proceedings of the 3rd ACM Workshop on Cloud Computing Security Workshop, pp. 3–14 (2011)
21. Ullah, K., Rashid, I., Afzal, H., Iqbal, M.M.W., Bangash, Y.A., Abbas, H.: SS7 vulnerabilities-a survey and implementation of machine learning vs rule based filtering for detection of SS7 network attacks. IEEE Commun. Surv. Tutor. . **22**(2), 1337–1371 (2020)

Leveraging Contracts for Failure Monitoring and Identification in Automated Driving Systems

Srajan Goyal[1,2](✉), Alberto Griggio[1](✉), and Stefano Tonetta[1](✉)

[1] Fondazione Bruno Kessler, Trento, Italy
{sgoyal,griggio,tonettas}@fbk.eu
[2] University of Trento, Trento, Italy

Abstract. As the deployment of AI agents in Automated Driving Systems (ADS) becomes increasingly prevalent, ensuring their safety and reliability is of paramount importance. This paper presents a novel approach to enhance the safety assurance of automated driving systems by employing formal contracts to specify and refine system-level properties. The proposed framework leverages formal methods to specify contracts that capture the expected behavior of perception and control components in ADS. These contracts serve as a basis for systematically validating system behavior against safety requirements during design and testing phases. We demonstrate the efficacy of our approach using the CARLA simulator and an off-the-shelf AI agent. By monitoring the components contracts on the ADS simulation, we could identify not only the cause of system failures, but also the situations which could lead to a system failure, facilitating the debugging and maintenance of the AI agents.

Keywords: Formal properties · Runtime verification · Test case generation · Autonomous systems · Assume-guarantee reasoning

1 Introduction

Automated Driving Systems (ADS) represent a technological innovation that is revolutionizing traditional transportation, potentially improving the traffic flow and increasing overall road safety. A central role in the success of ADS is played by AI agents, which may be responsible for various perception and control tasks. However, as ADS deployment accelerates, ensuring the safety and reliability of these AI agents becomes increasingly challenging.

Various formal verification techniques have been proposed to prove properties of AI-based autonomous systems. Much work in the literature [11,13,15,19,27]

This work has been supported by: the "AI@TN" project funded by the Autonomous Province of Trento; the PNRR project FAIR - Future AI Research (PE00000013), under the NRRP MUR program funded by the NextGenerationEU; and the PNRR MUR project VITALITY (ECS00000041), Spoke 2 ASTRA - Advanced Space Technologies and Research Alliance.

A. Madeira and A. Knapp (Eds.): SEFM 2024, LNCS 15280, pp. 441–460, 2025.
https://doi.org/10.1007/978-3-031-77382-2_25

focuses on system-level simulation-based testing using formal methods to specify formal properties and coverage criteria, and to generate automatically test cases. In this line of work, AI agents can be seen as black-boxes integrated into the simulator of the autonomous system, while formal properties can rely on the simulation data of the environment that is considered the ground truth and can be used to compare it with the agents' knowledge.

The VIVAS project [12], funded by ESA, developed a generic framework for system-level simulation-based Verification and Validation (V&V) of autonomous systems. This approach uses a simulation model, an abstract model to symbolically describe the system behavior, and formal methods to generate scenarios and verify simulation executions. It permits the specification of diverse coverage criteria, thereby guiding automated scenario creation and verification of formal properties. The framework has been evaluated on space and automotive applications [15]. For the latter, the simulation uses CARLA [10], a popular platform for simulating complex driving scenarios. Various AI-based solutions (e.g., [4,25,28]) for car perception and control components are validated with CARLA, which also hosts a competition to rank such solutions [2]. In [15], we demonstrated the integration of the VIVAS framework with CARLA to effectively generate interesting highway scenarios and evaluate AI-based agents in ADS.

However, one of the issues with these approaches is that the system-level verification focuses on system-level properties, mainly car crashes in the automotive case study. This has the limit of not being able, first, to identify the component that is failing in case of a crash and, second, to monitor component failures that may lead to a crash without an actual occurrence of a crash.

In this paper, we propose to integrate the simulation-based V&V framework with a contract-based design of the perception and control components of the autonomous system. The design-level verification ensures that the assumptions formalized on the environment model, used to generate the test cases, are sufficient to provide the system-level guarantees. Component properties are then monitored on the simulation traces. These two phases are iterated to tune the property specifications, as they may end up being either too strong, failing in the runtime monitoring, or too weak, failing in the contract refinement verification.

We evaluated the approach on the ADS case study using the CARLA simulator and the InterFuser AI agent [25], operating on a highway. The iterations led us to fine-tune challenging formal properties, for example, to formalize the safety conditions on the bounding boxes generated by the perception, and formalizing the safe states for AI-based planner. Through the evaluation, we were able to localize the faults in case of a crash, and monitor the component failures that could have led to a crash, but did not. Moreover, we could pinpoint interesting cases in which the ADS could have avoided the crash, if it acted in time.

2 Related Work and Contributions

There has been much recent work on compositional verification approaches using contract reasoning to achieve design-time assurance guarantees for autonomous systems [18,24,26]. These approaches leverage the robustness properties of DNNs to verify closed-loop systems. However, reducing the closed-loop safety properties into I/O properties for DNN is often quite challenging. Other methods approximate sensor models to prove safety properties based on low-dimensional sensor data [16]. However, when applied to systems dependent on rich sensors generating high-dimensional inputs, these methods become impractical.

Recent work has also focused on automatically synthesizing perception contracts to ensure closed-loop safety, using symbolic learning algorithms [1], and on bottom-up approaches such as [23] to generate weak assumptions for DNNs. However, these methodologies lack consideration for dynamic environments and face significant scalability challenges when dealing with multiple DNNs (e.g., both camera and lidar inputs). At some level, all this work relies on the internal structure of DNNs to specify or synthesize the contracts. In contrast, we focus on functional contracts for perception and control components, and their interaction with the environment contracts which specify the assumptions about the dynamic behaviors of objects.

A considerable body of work also addresses the repair of components' specifications when system-level properties are violated. For example, [14] proposes algorithms that synthesize model predictive controllers for ADS by identifying reasons for system-level contract infeasibility and suggesting repairs to the controller specification. [20] automatically searches and repairs contracts based on refinements from a contract library (and implementations) to formalize robotic mission planning specifications when new requirements or inconsistencies arise. [9] presents a simulation-based falsification framework that iteratively constructs contracts as constraints to synthesize safe controllers. However, none of this work considers ML components in their closed-loop analysis or validates the approaches in high-fidelity simulators. In our approach, we manually write the contracts, which could, in principle, be complemented by these methods to repair component contracts when system-level properties are violated. Nevertheless, due to the black-box nature of ML components, repairing their contracts without an implementation remains a significant challenge.

Contributions: Although the proposed methodology contains various elements studied in the literature as summarized above, it integrates them in a unique flow that presents various novel aspects:

- the contract-based design of autonomous systems is supported with contract reasoning that formally ensures specification correctness, while many previous works monitor properties without verifying contract refinement.
- the contracts are monitored on off-the-shelf AI solutions interfacing with perception and control components, while in the many previous works the monitors were applied at the system level.
- formalization of contracts on concrete perception and control components by specifying safety conditions on bounding box representations of cars.
- to the best of our knowledge, this is the first end-to-end methodology for the simulation-based verification of autonomous systems that starts from the design of the components to their monitoring.

3 Background

Transition Systems. Given a finite set V of variables with a (potentially infinite) domain D, we denote with $\Sigma(V)$ the set of assignments to V, i.e. mapping from V to D. Let V' denote a copy of the variables V, which are used to represent the values of V after a transition. A *Transition System* (TS), S is a tuple $S = \langle V, I, T \rangle$, where V is a set of (state) variables, I is a formula over V representing the set of initial states, and T is a formula over $V \cup V'$ representing the set of transitions. A state $s \in \Sigma(V)$ of S is an assignment to the variables V.

A trace σ of S is an infinite sequence of states $\sigma = s_0, s_1, \cdots$, where each s_i is an assignment to V, such that s_0 satisfies I and for all $i \geq 0$, the pair $\langle s_i, s_{i+1} \rangle$ satisfies T, i.e., $T(V, V')$ holds when V is assigned according to s_i and V' according to s_{i+1}. Given two transition systems $S_1 = \langle V_1, I_1, T_1 \rangle$ and $S_2 = \langle V_2, I_2, T_2 \rangle$, we define the synchronous product $S_1 \times S_2$ as $\langle V_1 \cup V_2, I_1 \wedge I_2, T_1 \wedge T_2 \rangle$. Since the product is commutative and associative, it can be generalized to a set of transitions systems.

LTL. Given a set of variables V, we assume to be given a set $Expr(V)$ of Boolean expressions over V as in [21]. In particular, in this paper, we consider standard arithmetic predicates $(<, \leq, >, \geq, \ldots)$ and functions $(+, -, \ldots)$ over integer and real variables. We define the set of LTL formulas over the variables V with the following grammar rule:

$$\phi := p \mid \phi \wedge \phi \mid \phi \vee \phi \mid \neg\phi \mid X\phi \mid \phi U \phi$$

where p ranges over $Expr(V)$. We use the following standard abbreviations: $\top := p \vee \neg p$, $\bot := \neg\top$, $\phi \rightarrow \psi := (\neg\phi) \vee \psi$, $F\phi := \top U \phi$, $G\phi := \neg F \neg \phi$.

LTL formulas are interpreted over traces over V, which are infinite sequences of assignments to V. We refer the reader to [8] for a formal definition of the semantics.

Given a transition system $S = \langle V, I, T \rangle$ and an LTL formula ϕ over V, $S \models \phi$ if and only if for all traces σ of S, $\sigma \models \phi$. Note that we are considering in general infinite-state transition systems for which the problem is undecidable. Our methods are based on SMT-based algorithms as those implemented in nuXmv [3].

At runtime, we evaluate a formula over the prefix of an infinite execution trace using the standard semantics of runtime verification [17]. In particular, a finite trace π violates a formula ϕ iff, for any suffix π', the concatenation of π and π' violates ϕ.

Contract Refinement. To simplify the presentation, in this paper, we define a contract refinement independently from the component interfaces. In practice, in OCRA [6], contracts are specified in terms of component input/output ports and the refinement has to take into account the connections among ports in component decomposition.

A contract C over the variables V is a pair $\langle \mathsf{A}, \mathsf{G} \rangle$ of LTL formulas over V representing respectively an *assumption* and a *guarantee*. We also denote A by

$\mathcal{A}(C)$, G by $\mathcal{G}(C)$, and $\neg\mathsf{A}\vee\mathsf{G}$ by $nf(C)$. Let $C = \langle\mathsf{A},\mathsf{G}\rangle$ be a contract over V. Let J and E be the two TSs over V. We say that J is a correct implementation of C iff $J \models \mathsf{A} \rightarrow \mathsf{G}$. We say that E is a correct environment of C iff $E \models \mathsf{A}$. We denote by $\mathcal{I}(C)$ and $\mathcal{E}(C)$, respectively, the set of correct implementations and the set of correct environments of C. Given two contracts C and C' over V, we say that C refines C' (denoted by $C \preceq C'$) iff $\mathcal{I}(C') \subseteq \mathcal{I}(C)$ and $\mathcal{E}(C) \subseteq \mathcal{E}(C')$.

Given a contract C and a set of contracts $Sub = \{C_1, \ldots, C_n\}$, we say that Sub is a refinement of C, written $Sub \preceq C$, iff the following conditions hold:

1. the correct implementations of the sub-contracts form a correct implementation of C: let V be the variables of C, $\{S_1 \times \ldots \times S_n \mid S_1 \in \mathcal{I}(C_1), \ldots, S_n \in \mathcal{I}(C_n)\} \subseteq \mathcal{I}(C)$;
2. for every $C_i \in Sub$, the correct implementation of the other sub-contracts and a correct environment of C form a correct environment of C_i: let V_i be the variables of C_i, $\{E \times S_1 \times \ldots \times S_{j\neq i} \times \ldots \times S_n \mid E \in \mathcal{E}(C),$ for all $j, 1 \leq j \leq n, j \neq i, S_j \in \mathcal{I}(C_j)\} \subseteq \mathcal{E}(C_i)$.

In [5,7], it was proved that the refinement is correct if and only if the following proof obligations ($PO(Sub, C)$) are valid temporal formulas:

$$nf(C_1) \wedge \ldots \wedge nf(C_n) \rightarrow nf(C)$$

$$\mathsf{A} \wedge \bigwedge_{1\leq j\leq n, j\neq i} nf(C_j) \rightarrow \mathsf{A}_i \text{ (for every } i, 1 \leq i \leq n)$$

4 Contract-Based Methodology

4.1 VIVAS Methodology

VIVAS is a V&V framework for generating test cases for autonomous systems (possibly using AI/ML components) via a combination of system-level simulation and symbolic model checking. VIVAS makes use of a symbolic model of the system under verification. This is inherently a transition system, written in the SMV language, which defines an abstract representation of the system behavior. On top of such model, the coverage criteria for the tests and the properties to verify are specified. The approach follows the flow depicted in Fig. 1 (right part): abstract test scenarios are generated from the symbolic model with model checking techniques based on the coverage criteria; the abstract test scenarios are then instantiated by the concretization of the abstract parameters to provide concrete scenarios to be executed on a system-level simulator encompassing AI/ML models; the simulation traces are in turn analyzed to check the properties defined on the symbolic model. The output of the framework is a V&V result consisting of coverage statistics of the executed traces with respect to the symbolic models, and quantitative and qualitative information for each use case.

An important observation is that the simulation traces can be instrumented to contain information on the autonomous system internal state as well as the

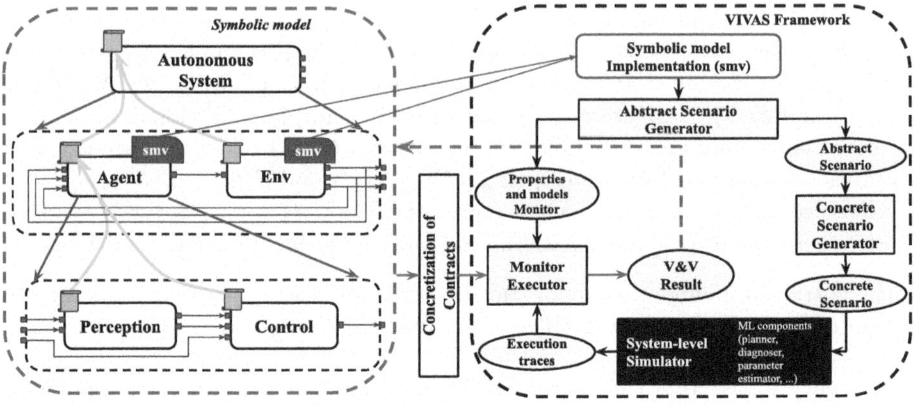

Fig. 1. V&V framework. (Color figure online)

environment state. Thus, the properties that are evaluated on such traces can compare the internal representation of the autonomous system with the ground truth provided by the simulator.

4.2 Contract-Based Extension

We extend the VIVAS framework with contract-based design of an autonomous system. We start from an OCRA specification of the system, as depicted in the left part of Fig. 1. The autonomous system (AS) is decomposed into an environment (Env) and an agent (Agent) component. The environment represents the physical world, including external and internal parts of the autonomous system (e.g., road structure, autonomous car, and other cars) and their dynamics. It models the evolution of the actual physical system states, henceforth called the ground truth, in response to control signals it receives from the agent. The agent receives the ground truth data from the environment (e.g., positions of other cars) and provides commands (e.g., steering and acceleration data).

The agent is in turn decomposed into a perception and a control component. The interfaces of such components are detailed based on the specific application and depend on the actual internal representation that the control has of the environment (e.g., position of the objects). They can also be further decomposed based on the internal structure of the agent.

Specific requirements of the autonomous system are formalized as LTL properties and structured into contracts. Each component in the hierarchy is associated with a set of contracts (depicted in green), specifying the acceptable behaviors for the component and its environment. Both the environment and the agent have a high-level description of their behavior, modeled as transition systems in SMV (depicted in purple), which can be composed to generate the system's behavior. This is verified compositionally against the top-level contracts. Given the above contract-based design, the verification is enhanced with the following checks:

- The contract refinement is proved correct for each decomposition level.
- The SMV implementations of Env and Agent are proved correct with respect to the local contracts.
- The contracts are checked at runtime on the finite simulation traces.

The verification of the last point can fail for various reasons, leading to the changes in the contract specification or to actual bugs in the Agent code as discussed in the following section.

4.3 Analyses of Monitoring Failures

We first focus on the Env component. If one or more Env contracts fail regardless of the system level contracts result, either of the following reasons would apply:

- e.1: the contracts are too strong and a realistic behavior in the simulation violates them; thus, we need to weaken them to allow such behavior.
- e.2: the contracts are violated by a behavior that we indeed discarded with the contracts because we excluded that from that verification (e.g., dangerous situations created by other agents); in this case, the result is accepted.
- e.3: the contracts are violated because of some constants used in the model of the dynamics; in this case, the model must be fixed adjusting such constants.

Focusing on the Autonomous system, agent and other subcomponents, the following outcomes are possible for each decomposition level:

- a.1: the parent contract is satisfied, but a child contract violated; in this case, we may have different causes:
  - a.1.1: the child component is indeed buggy, but the fault did not lead to the failure of parent component; we report this as a problem.
  - a.1.2: the contract of the child components are too strong and the behavior seen in the simulation could be actually accepted; thus, the contract must be weakened to allow such behavior.
  - a.1.3: the contracts are violated because of some constants used in the contracts (e.g., to specify safety margins); in this case, the model must be fixed adjusting such constants.
- a.2: the parent contract is violated as well as one or more child contracts; in this case, we identified the faulty components, and we report it as a problem.
- a.3: the parent contract is violated and all child contracts are satisfied; this must not happen, else there is a mistake in the framework, in the symbolic model (e.g., some connections), or in the concretization.
- a.4: finally, orthogonally to previous points, if a leaf component is failing in several simulation traces, we may want to decompose further to have a better localization of the fault; in this case, we may analyze the Agent's code to identify subcomponents and their contracts.

5 Automated Driving Use Case

In this section, we present a case study that applies our compositional approach, outlined in the previous section, to an automated driving system (ADS) using the CARLA simulation platform.

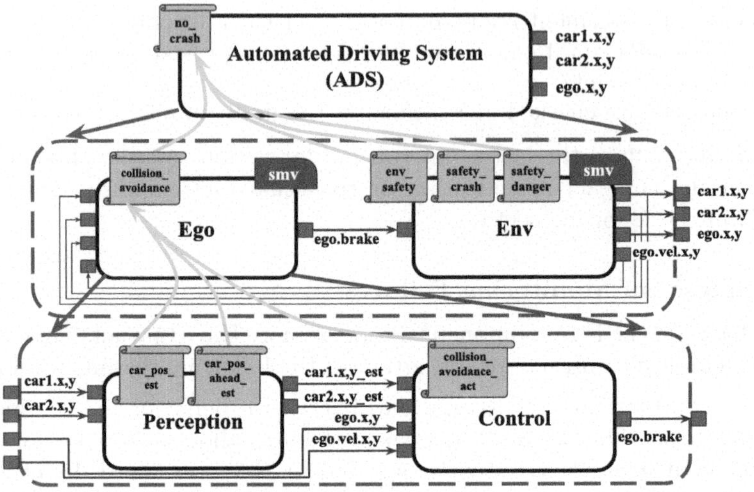

Fig. 2. Contract-based system architecture of Automated Driving System. (Color figure online)

5.1 Contract Based Design

We use OCRA [6], an extension of nuXmv for contract-based specification and reasoning, to partition our symbolic model into components equipped with assume-guarantee contracts. Figure 2 shows the decomposition of ADS into different components and subcomponents. These components communicate through input and output ports, depicted in red. For simplicity, we have combined the x and y coordinate ports into a single port. In the following, we describe such decomposition, providing the main details of the contracts for each component. For the contract specifications, here we only show the guarantees provided by the contracts. All assumptions are considered True unless stated otherwise.

ADS. The top level system component has an interface with no inputs and six output ports, which are mapped from its Env component. These ports provide the x, y (longitudinal and lateral) positions of the two non-ego vehicles and an ego at the ground truth level, with all vehicles represented point-wise. The top-level system contract `no_crash` (Eq. (1)) guarantees the absence of crashes, and is further refined by the contracts of Env and Ego (`Env.env_safety`, `Env.safety_danger`, `Env.safety_crash`, `Ego.collision_avoidance`). The predicate `crash` (Eq. (2)) is True only when the ego vehicle collides with any non-ego vehicle in front.

$$\texttt{no\_crash} : \mathbf{G}(\neg crash); \tag{1}$$

$$\begin{aligned} crash := & \bigvee_{i=1,2} (car[i].x > ego.x) \wedge (car[i].y = ego.y) \\ & \wedge (ego.velocity.x > 0) \wedge (car[i].y = \mathbf{X}(car[i].y)) \\ & \wedge (ego.y = \mathbf{X}(ego.y)) \wedge (\mathbf{X}(car[i].x \leq ego.x \wedge car[i].y = ego.y)) \end{aligned} \tag{2}$$

Ego. This component models the key properties for the autonomous vehicle to navigate safely in the environment. It takes as inputs from Env the current positions of non-ego and ego vehicles along with ego's speed, and produces a boolean brake command as output. The `collision_avoidance` contract (Eq. (3)) guarantees the brake application whenever ego is in a dangerous condition (Eq. (4)).

$$\texttt{collision\_avoidance} : \mathbf{G}(danger\_gt \rightarrow ego.brake); \tag{3}$$

$$\begin{aligned} danger\_gt := & ((car\_ahead\_gt) \wedge (ego.velocity.x > 0) \wedge \\ & (d_{min} \leq (braking\_distance + danger\_threshold))) \end{aligned} \tag{4}$$

$$car\_ahead\_gt := \bigvee_{i=1,2} (car[i].x > ego.x \ \wedge \ car[i].y = ego.y) \tag{5}$$

$$braking\_distance := (ego.velocity.x)^2/(2 * Max\_Braking) \tag{6}$$

where d_{min} is the distance to the closest car ahead of ego in its lane, *braking_distance* is the distance covered by ego while braking with Max_Braking[1] from its current position, computed using Newtonian physics in Eq. (6). The Ego is further decomposed into perception and control components, and its contract is therefore refined by the corresponding contracts of these subcomponents.

Perception. The perception component represents the ego's knowledge of the environment. It takes as input the ground truth positions of the non-ego vehicles, and provides as output their estimated positions. It has two contracts, `car_pos_est` and `car_pos_ahead_est` in Eq. (7) and (8) respectively, providing bounds on the estimate errors.[2]

$$\texttt{car\_pos\_est} : \mathbf{G}(\bigwedge_{i=1,2} (car[i].x - car[i].x\_est \leq \varepsilon) \wedge (car[i].y = car[i].y\_est)) \tag{7}$$

$$\texttt{car\_pos\_ahead\_est} : \mathbf{G}(\bigwedge_{i=1,2} ((car[i].x \geq ego.x) \rightarrow (car[i].x\_est \geq ego.x))) \tag{8}$$

Control. The control component takes as input the current estimated positions of the non-ego vehicles from the perception, and the current position and speed of ego vehicle from the environment at the ground truth level. Its contract (Eq. (9)) guarantees the application of brake whenever a dangerous situation is detected.

$$\texttt{collision\_avoidance\_act} : \mathbf{G}(danger\_est \rightarrow ego.brake) \tag{9}$$

---

[1] Max_Braking $= 4.6$ m/s^2, averaged (eyeballed) from literature.

[2] the ε parameter in (7) is the estimation error (in meters), which is set to 2 in the actual implementation when using InterFuser.

$$danger\_est := (car\_ahead\_est \wedge (ego.velocity.x > 0) \wedge (d_{min}\_est \leq (braking\_distance + danger\_threshold))) \tag{10}$$

$$car\_ahead\_est := \bigvee_{i=1,2} (car[i].x\_est > ego.x \wedge car[i].y\_est = ego.y) \tag{11}$$

where $d_{min}\_est = min_{i=1,2}\{(car[i].x\_est - ego.x - \varepsilon)\}$.

Env. This component represents the physical world, providing as output the ground truth positions and speeds of all the vehicles in the environment. The component has one input port, *ego.brake*, which is an output of the Ego component. We define three contracts for Env. The first, `env_safety` (Eq. (12)), ensures that if the ego starts in a safe condition and applies the brake, it cannot reach an unsafe condition:

$$\texttt{env\_safety} : safe\_condition \wedge \mathbf{G}(((safe\_condition) \wedge (ego.brake > 0)) \rightarrow \mathbf{X}(safe\_condition)) \tag{12}$$

$$safe\_condition := (car\_ahead\_gt \rightarrow (d_{min} > braking\_distance)) \tag{13}$$

Figure 3 shows the difference between safe_condition, danger_gt and braking_distance. In Ego's contract reasoning, $ego.brake = \top$ when $danger\_gt = \top$. Due to the presence of *danger_treshold* (set to 1 m), the model checker produces a counterexample of the system level contract in which there is a transition from $safe\_condition \wedge \neg danger\_gt$ to $\neg safe\_condition$. To avoid this situation, we formulate another contract for the Env, `safety_danger` in Eq. (14) which guarantees that the above situation does not occur. The last Env contract, `safety_crash` in Eq. (15), connects *safe_condition* with the *crash* predicate, guaranteeing that if the ego is in a safe condition, it is not involved in a crash.

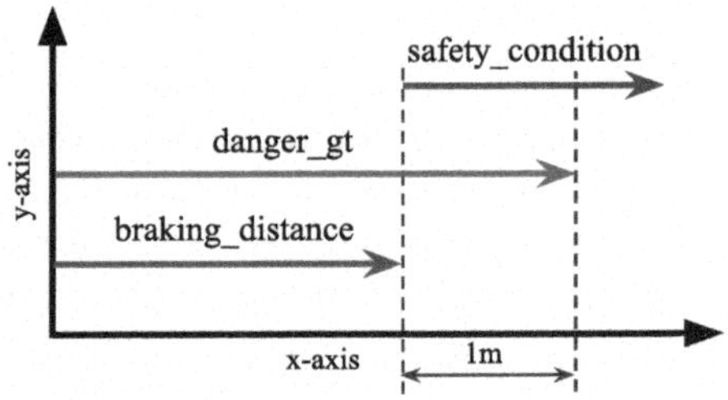

Fig. 3. Safe and dangerous conditions.

$$\texttt{safety\_danger} : \mathbf{G}((safe\_condition \wedge \neg danger\_gt) \rightarrow \mathbf{X}(env\_safety)) \tag{14}$$

$$\texttt{safety\_crash} : \mathbf{G}(safe\_condition \rightarrow \neg crash) \tag{15}$$

5.2 Implementation in SMV

We specify the abstract model of the ADS as a synchronous symbolic transition system, written in the language of the nuXmv [3] model checker. The system consists of two key components: the environment (Env) and the ego vehicle (Ego), as shown in Fig. 2. For abstract scenario generation, the Env implementation consists of 3 vehicles (one "ego" car, representing the autonomous agent under test, and two other cars) moving on a highway with 3 lanes, in which all the vehicles drive in the same direction. The two "non-ego" cars can move freely on the highway, with arbitrary accelerations, braking, and lane change maneuvers (subject to physical constraints about min/max acceleration rates and speed limits), but are not allowed to crash into each other or the ego. The Ego, on the other hand, always drives in the middle lane, aiming to maintain a set cruise speed. It brakes when necessary to avoid collisions with other vehicles and may accelerate when needed to reach the target speed. We are interested in generating test cases to check whether the ego can reach a given destination without crashing into other vehicles.

We use a discrete model of time, where each transition of the system corresponds to a time-lapse of 1 s. A shorter time step would improve the precision of generated abstract scenarios, however, at the cost of computational overhead. We found the choice of 1 s time step to be adequate enough for an effective concretization of the abstract scenarios on the real system. We use the theory of real arithmetic to encode the transition relation of the system, using mostly linear constraints to compute the updates to the speed and locations of the vehicles (thanks to the discretization of time). The concrete implementation of the AI-based vehicle under test in CARLA, instead, is based on the InterFuser agent [25], taken from CARLA autonomous driving leaderboard database [2].

5.3 Concretizing the Contracts on the Real System

When checking the contracts defined above on the simulation traces produced by CARLA, we must take into account the fact that the symbolic model provides an abstract view of the system, in which several details have been omitted. From the point of view of contract satisfaction, one key difference between our symbolic model and the ground truth is that CARLA gives as output the positions and dimensions of the bounding boxes of all the agents in the environment at every time instant in x-y coordinate plane (the vehicle navigation plane), with the ego always centered at the origin. In contrast, our symbolic model represents the agents' positions as single points in an absolute coordinate system (with the origin at the beginning of the road). If we compare only the center of estimated bounding boxes with the ground truth ones, the contract satisfaction may be dubious in some cases, e.g. when one or more vertices of the car are in ego's lane and the center lies in another lane.

In the following, we describe how the high-level contracts are mapped to those verified on concrete executions. First, the crash is evaluated by using the crash sensor mounted on the ego vehicle in CARLA for detecting collisions, considering only the instances where the ego vehicle collides with a non-ego vehicle in front. We opt for this method over defining collisions using ground-truth bounding boxes, as the latter caused many false positives due to simulator inaccuracies. Furthermore, we modify the definitions of car_ahead_gt (Eq. (5)), *car_ahead_est* (Eq. (11)) and the variables d_{min} and d_{min}_est introduced in Sect. 5.1 to account for the change of coordinates and the use of bounding boxes.

Closest Distance. The center of the ego vehicle is taken at origin of the 2D plane, with ego being oriented longitudinally towards positive x-axis. Let $v_i(j) = (x_{i,j}, y_{i,j})$ denote the jth bounding-box vertex of the ith non-ego vehicle; the closest distance d_{min} of the ego vehicle from the non-ego vehicles is defined as:

$$(-lane\_width/2 \leq y_{i,j} \leq lane\_width/2) \wedge (x_{i,j} \geq 0) \tag{16}$$

$$d_{min} = min\{x_{i,j} \mid (x_{i,j}, y_{i,j}) \texttt{ satisfies } (16)\} \tag{17}$$

Car Ahead of Ego. Let nc be the nearest car to ego, defined by:

$$\begin{aligned} \forall i(i = nc) \implies ((\exists j(x_{i,j}, y_{i,j}) \texttt{ satisfies } (16) \wedge \\ \forall i, j' \ (x_{i,j'}, y_{i,j'}) \texttt{ satisfies } (16)) \implies x_{i,j} \leq x_{i,j'}) \end{aligned} \tag{18}$$

then the distance to the closest vertex is given by $d_{v_{min}} = d(nc)$, where the distance $d(i)$ for the i-th car is defined as:

$$\begin{aligned} \forall i, j \ . \ x_{i,j} = d(i) \implies \exists j'(x_{i,j'}, y_{i,j'}) \texttt{ satisfies } (16) \wedge \\ x_{i,j} \geq 0 \ \wedge \forall j'' \ (x_{i,j''} \geq 0 \rightarrow x_{i,j} \leq x_{i,j''}) \end{aligned} \tag{19}$$

We then define the predicate *car_ahead_gt* as follows:

$$(0 \leq d_{v_{min}} \leq \delta) \leftrightarrow car\_ahead\_gt \tag{20}$$

where δ is the look-ahead distance of the AI-based perception module, beyond which it does not detect anything in the environment.[3]

Closest Estimated Distance. The definition of d_{min}_est is similar to the one of d_{min} (Eq. (17)), except that we use the coordinates of the estimated bounding boxes $(x_{est_{i,j}}, y_{est_{i,j}})$ and take into account the estimation error ε:

$$(-lane\_width/2 \leq y_{est_{i,j}} \leq lane\_width/2) \wedge (0 \leq x_{est_{i,j}} \leq d_{v_{min}} + \varepsilon) \tag{21}$$

$$d_{min}\_est = min\{x_{est_{i,j}} \mid (x_{est_{i,j}}, y_{est_{i,j}}) \texttt{ satisfies } (21)\} \tag{22}$$

Car Estimate Ahead of Ego. For all the bounding boxes estimated by the perception module, if there exists a vertex satisfying Eq. (21), while $0 \leq d_{v_{min}} \leq \delta$, then the predicate $car\_ahead\_est = \top$.

[3] For InterFuser, this distance is 20 m, so $\delta = 20$.

6 Experimental Evaluation

In this section, we evaluate our methodology on the ADS application, leveraging the VIVAS framework within the CARLA simulator, as detailed in [15]. We have expanded this framework with contract models, refinement checks, and monitoring, as discussed earlier. Contract refinement is checked using OCRA, employing nuXmv for LTL model checking. Refinement checks for the specified contracts and implementations of the Env and Ego components are conducted using the ic3 algorithm, taking only a few seconds. For abstract scenario generation, we use Bounded Model Checking (BMC) algorithm of the nuXmv [3] symbolic model checker. Due to the presence of non-linear constraints in our symbolic model, specifically in computing ego's braking distance, we leverage the z3 SMT solver [22] for checking the satisfiability of the BMC queries.

Experimentation was carried out on an Intel i7 with NVIDIA GeForce RTX 2080 8 GB GPU, meeting the minimum requirements for running CARLA simulations with AI models. All experiments required approximately 22 h to complete. Model checking completed in under 25 s on average per abstract scenario instance, with a timeout of 200 s being never reached during our experiments. However, the main performance bottleneck arose from concrete scenario instantiation in CARLA and subsequent simulations, averaging 4.5 min per scenario. The code and data necessary for reproducing our experiments are available at https://es-static.fbk.eu/people/sgoyal/sefm24.

6.1 Scenario Generation

In order to enumerate abstract scenarios, we followed the same specification defined in [15], which we report here for completeness. We define for each non-ego car a set of predicates specifying its position relative to the ego, in terms of occupation of cells of an abstract 3×3 "grid" centered on the ego. We then define an abstract scenario as a combination of constraints about the different positions of the non-ego cars on the grid at different points in time (ref. Figure 3 in [15]). More specifically, each abstract scenario is specified as an LTL property of the following form:

$$\begin{aligned} &\neg \mathbf{F}(\text{car1\_grid\_pos} = \text{CELL\_A1} \wedge \text{car2\_grid\_pos} = \text{CELL\_A2} \wedge \\ &\quad \mathbf{X}(\mathbf{F}(\text{car1\_grid\_pos} = \text{CELL\_B1} \wedge \text{car2\_grid\_pos} = \text{CELL\_B2}))) \end{aligned} \tag{23}$$

where car$i$_grid_pos encodes the position of the i-th non-ego car in the grid corresponding its cell number. We define our coverage criterion by selecting a subset of abstract scenarios of interest, consisting of various combinations of the traffic situations that can be modeled by positioning the non-ego cars in the grid around the ego. In total, for the experiments, we defined 144 such scenarios, concretizing them on two weather conditions.

In order to generate a concrete traffic scenario for the simulator, the abstract counterexample trace generated by the model checker is parsed for relevant information to be fed as input to the simulator. As an interface to the CARLA simulator, we used the CARLA module ScenarioRunner. It takes as input the route that needs to be followed by AI-based ego and a traffic scenario composed of non-egos' behaviors. Every state of the abstract scenario trace is concretized into the corresponding behavior of every non-ego agent. We do not need to extract ego's behavior from the abstract trace, since it is expected to make decisions autonomously in the simulator. Only its initial spawn position and destination need to be extracted to follow the route. For more details on the experimental setup for the scenario generation, please refer Sec. 5.1 of [15].

6.2 Evaluating Contracts at Runtime

The number of contract violations are reported in Table 1, column "Contract Violations". In total, we evaluate 288 simulation traces. In case of a crash, the results are saved only up to its first occurrence while rest of the trace is discarded. We will refer to the methodology in Sect. 4.3 to analyze the results from here on.

Table 1. Analysis of contract violations.

Composite component	**Sub component**	**Contracts**	**Contract count ($\bot$)**	**Crash Sequence ($\bot$)**
ADS		no-crash	62	62
ADS	Env	env_safety	10	0
		safety_danger	146	0
		safety_crash	2	0
	Ego	collision_avoidance	151	57
ADS.Ego	Perception	(7)$\wedge$(8)	169	58
	Control	collision_avoidance_act	127	52
Sequence leading to Crash (Total crashes = 62)				
Analysis class (Sect. 4.3)	**Perception**	**Control**	**Perception $\wedge$ Control**	
a.1 ($Ego \wedge \neg Child$)	2	0	0	
a.2 ($\neg Ego \wedge \neg Child$)	56	52	51	
a.3 ($\neg Ego \wedge \bigwedge Child$)	–	–	0	
Avoidable Crashes			1	

ADS. The system level contract, i.e., `no_crash` is violated 62 times. In 3 of these cases, ego's and all its subcomponents' contracts are true. These cases belong to the analyses class *a.3*, implying a mistake in our framework. These scenarios involve a non-ego unexpectedly rear-ending the ego while attempting to change lanes, then dragging ego forward from the side. This leads to $car\_ahead\_gt = \bot$ since none of the non-ego's vertices are in front of ego, yet its center moves ahead of ego (which is not aligned with the driving direction), triggering crash detection. The issue stems from an incorrect concretization of the crash condition in the simulator, unaccounted for in our symbolic framework. We should only consider the cases where the ego crashes from the front without any prior collisions.

Env. All the Env's contracts are violated in multiple executions. Since the Env contracts guarantee the physical laws, we need further analyses: all the violations belong to the class *e.2*, where, (a) non-egos cut in front of ego in unsafe conditions, violating `env_safety` and `safety_danger`, (b) they first hit ego from behind, violating `safety_crash`. One could add the predicate, *car_ahead_gt* in the assumption of former two Env contracts (following *e.1*), however, that will weaken the environment guarantees. We leave the contracts of the environment as they are (without the *car_ahead_gt* assumption), as they require non-ego cars to not cut in violating the safety conditions; this can happen in the ground truth and the monitoring tells us if we are in these violations.

Each simulation trace is at least 30 s long. As our formulations necessitate contract satisfaction throughout execution (using the "Globally" LTL operator), one single violation would signify a contract violation. Given that a scenario encompasses various traffic configurations around the ego vehicle, monitoring child components across the entire simulation trace becomes impractical, especially in crash scenarios. Our focus lies in identifying the specific situations leading to a crash and attributing failure to the responsible component(s).

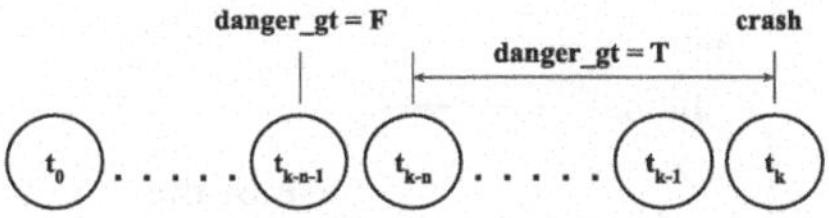

Fig. 4. Sequence leading to a crash.

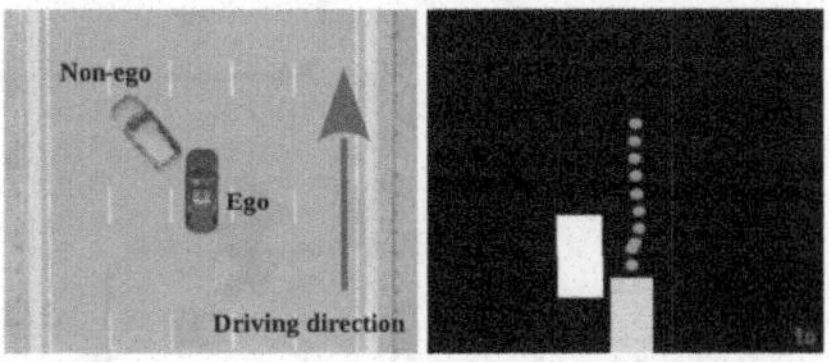

Fig. 5. Avoidable crash; (left): Bird's-eye view in CARLA; (right) AI-based ego's perception component's output.

Evaluating Contracts Violated in the Sequence Leading up to Crash. Many component violations are not linked to crash situations. In order to better localize the cause of crashes, we consider the contract violations only during the last sequence of time instances before the crash where $danger\_gt = \top$ consecutively. To be more precise, we consider the conditions inside the **G** operator of contracts and check their violation on the time sequence from t_{k-n} to t_k, where t_k is the crash state and t_{k-n} is the first danger state in the sequence (see Fig. 4). The results are reported in column "Crash Sequence" of Table 1. None of the Env contracts are violated during this sequence, implying that our assumptions on the environment are correct. Note that two global contract violations of `safety_crash` are not taken in account since $danger\_gt = \bot$ in those cases.

Ego. We further analyze contract violations of Ego and its subcomponents according to our classes, shown in Table 1. Class *a.1*: two cases of perception failure, not resulting in ego's violation; *a.2*: pinpoints the bug in both the *perception* and *control* subcomponents; *a.3*: implies no fault in the framework.

Avoidable Crashes. If $safe\_condition = \top$ (Eq. (13)) at any time instant in any sequence leading to a crash, ego vehicle has the possibility to brake and avoid the crash. Out of 62 crashes, we found 1 case where ego had this possibility. Figure 5 shows snapshot of crash from Carla simulator, with wrongly estimated non-ego's location and safe trajectory by InterFuser on the right.

6.3 Updating Refinements

In Table 1, the control contract is violated in the majority of situations, though not at the same time instants as the perception's violations, since danger situation is a conjunction of the correct detection of non-egos in front and their closest distance from the ego. We need to further analyze such erratic behavior of the controller, since it bases its decision on the AI module's state estimations.

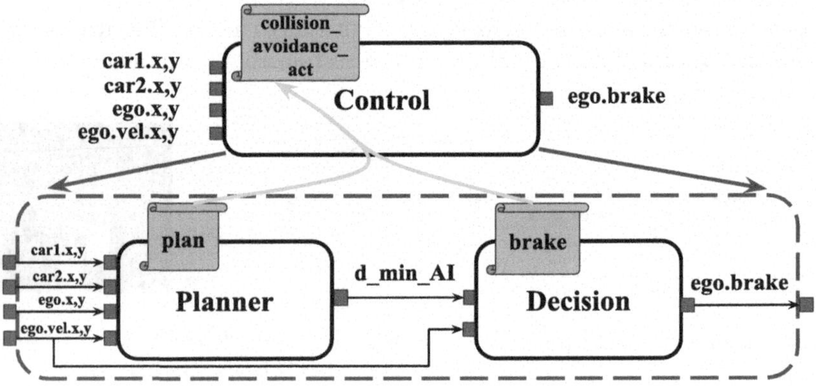

Fig. 6. Refinement of Control component.

Further analysis of the AI module revealed its role in predicting the ego's next 10 waypoints based on a coarse input route, estimating a collision-free distance (called "safe distance" by its designers) for the ego to drive forward. This distance guides the ego's collision avoidance maneuvers. However, the AI may predict a collision-free trajectory in situations where, for example, a non-ego is between two lanes. Despite this conservative approach, we argue that an autonomous vehicle should still apply the brakes in such scenarios. While violations of the Ego's contract may not always result in a system-level crash, if they do, we can identify the failure source. To formalize this, we decompose the ego's control component into planner and decision subcomponents (Fig. 6). Therefore, the contract `collision_avoidance_act` is further refined by the contracts of planner and decision (`Planner.plan` and `Decision.brake`, respectively).

Planner: The role of the planner is to mimic the black-box of AI-based ego's module which computes the "safe distance", d_{min}_AI. At the symbolic level, this distance is computed by the model checker in such a way that its value satisfies the contract `plan` in Eq. (25), always guaranteeing the detection of a dangerous situation, *danger_AI*, if *danger_est* $= \top$.

$$\begin{aligned} danger\_AI &:= d_{min}\_AI <= (braking\_distance + 1) \\ danger\_est &:= ((car\_ahead\_est) \wedge (ego.velocity.x > 0) \wedge \\ &\quad (d_{min}\_est <= (braking\_distance + 1))) \end{aligned} \tag{24}$$

$$\texttt{plan} : \mathbf{G}(danger\_est \rightarrow danger\_AI) \tag{25}$$

$$\texttt{brake} : \mathbf{G}(danger\_AI \rightarrow ego.brake) \tag{26}$$

Decision: Input to this component is d_{min}_AI computed by the planner component. The output is *ego.brake* which is subsequently propagated upstream to its composite component, control, and then further up to the level of Ego and Env. This contract (Eq. (26)) always guarantees that the braking occurs whenever *danger_AI* $= \top$.

6.4 Pinpointing Failure

Table 2 shows the violations of control contract's refinements, across all executions and crash sequences. Analyzing these based on our classification, *a.1*: no violations (empty set); *a.2*: pinpoints the source of failure to (a) the decision component, which failed to apply brakes despite the AI module detecting a dangerous situation, and (b) the planner component, implying incorrect computation of d_{min}_AI by the AI module, despite correctly estimating the objects ahead in the ego vehicle's lane. These errors occur when the lateral positions and/or orientations of non-egos are not estimated correctly, particularly when only part of the non-ego vehicle is within the ego's lane.

Table 2. Analysis of Control contract violations.

Composite component	**Sub component**	**Contracts**	**Contract count($\perp$)**	**Crash Sequence($\perp$)**
ADS.Ego.Control	Planner	plan	123	50
	Decision	brake	105	45
Sequence leading to Crash (Total crashes = 62)				
Analysis class (Sect. 4.3)	**Planner**	**Decision**	**Planner $\wedge$Decision**	
a.1: ($Control \wedge \neg Child$)	0	0	0	
a.2: ($\neg Control \wedge \neg Child$)	49	44	41	
a.3: ($\neg Control \wedge \bigwedge Child$)	–	–	0	

7 Conclusions and Future Work

In this paper, we have proposed an integration of contract-based design with test case generation for the system-level simulation-based verification of automated driving systems. System-level properties of the automated cars are decomposed into contracts of the ego components and assumptions on the environment. We introduced a methodology that leverages formal methods for contract reasoning to monitor the properties on the simulation executions to better diagnose issues in the autonomous system, and iteratively refine the contracts specification. Our experiments, conducted using the CARLA simulator and off-the-shelf AI agents, have provided empirical evidence of the effectiveness of contract-based refinement and runtime monitoring in enhancing the verification of ADS components.

There are several directions for future research and development. For example, we will explore the scalability and applicability of our approach to more complex ADS architectures and scenarios. Moreover, we will explore ways to incorporate uncertainty quantification methods into the contracts specification.

References

1. Astorga, A., Hsieh, C., Madhusudan, P., Mitra, S.: Perception contracts for safety of ML-enabled systems. Proc. ACM Program. Lang. **7**(OOPSLA2) (2023). https://doi.org/10.1145/3622875
2. CARLA Team: CARLA Autonomous Driving Leaderboard. https://leaderboard.carla.org/leaderboard/. Accessed 30 Aug 2023
3. Cavada, R., et al.: The NUXMV symbolic model checker. In: Biere, A., Bloem, R. (eds.) CAV 2014. LNCS, vol. 8559, pp. 334–342. Springer, Cham (2014). https://doi.org/10.1007/978-3-319-08867-9_22
4. Chen, D., Krahenbuhl, P.: Learning from all vehicles. In: CVPR, pp. 17201–17210. IEEE, June 2022. https://doi.org/10.1109/CVPR52688.2022.01671
5. Cimatti, A., Tonetta, S.: Contracts-refinement proof system for component-based embedded systems. Sci. Comput. Program. **97**, 333–348 (2015). https://doi.org/10.1016/j.scico.2014.06.011
6. Cimatti, A., Dorigatti, M., Tonetta, S.: OCRA: a tool for checking the refinement of temporal contracts. In: ASE, vol. 4144, pp. 702–705. IEEE/ACM, November 2013. https://doi.org/10.1109/ase.2013.6693137
7. Cimatti, A., Tonetta, S.: A property-based proof system for contract-based design. In: 2012 38th Euromicro Conference on Software Engineering and Advanced Applications, pp. 21–28. IEEE, September 2012. https://doi.org/10.1109/seaa.2012.68
8. Clarke, E.M., Grumberg, O., Peled, D.A.: Model Checking. MIT Press, Cambridge (2000)
9. DeCastro, J., Liebenwein, L., Vasile, C.-I., Tedrake, R., Karaman, S., Rus, D.: Counterexample-guided safety contracts for autonomous driving. In: Morales, M., Tapia, L., Sánchez-Ante, G., Hutchinson, S. (eds.) WAFR 2018. SPAR, vol. 14, pp. 939–955. Springer, Cham (2020). https://doi.org/10.1007/978-3-030-44051-0_54
10. Dosovitskiy, A., Ros, G., Codevilla, F., Lopez, A., Koltun, V.: CARLA: an open urban driving simulator. In: Levine, S., Vanhoucke, V., Goldberg, K. (eds.) Proceedings of the 1st Annual Conference on Robot Learning. PMLR, vol. 78, pp. 1–16, 13–15 November 2017. https://doi.org/10.48550/arXiv.1711.03938

11. Dreossi, T., et al.: VerifAI: a toolkit for the formal design and analysis of artificial intelligence-based systems. In: Dillig, I., Tasiran, S. (eds.) CAV 2019. LNCS, vol. 11561, pp. 432–442. Springer, Cham (2019). https://doi.org/10.1007/978-3-030-25540-4_25
12. Fratini, S., et al.: Verification and validation of autonomous systems with embedded AI: the VIVAS approach. In: ASTRA. ESA (2023). https://az659834.vo.msecnd.net/eventsairwesteuprod/production-atpi-public/070740b67e5b4a32a9be94228c9ac40d
13. Fremont, D.J., et al.: Scenic: a language for scenario specification and data generation. machine learning **112**(10), 3805–3849 (2022). https://doi.org/10.1007/s10994-021-06120-5
14. Ghosh, S., et al.: Diagnosis and repair for synthesis from signal temporal logic specifications. In: HSCC, HSCC 2016, pp. 31–40. ACM, April 2016. https://doi.org/10.1145/2883817.2883847
15. Goyal, S., Griggio, A., Kimblad, J., Tonetta, S.: Automatic generation of scenarios for system-level simulation-based verification of autonomous driving systems. In: FMAS@iFM. EPTCS, vol. 395, pp. 113–129 (2023). https://doi.org/10.4204/EPTCS.395.8
16. Ivanov, R., Jothimurugan, K., Hsu, S., Vaidya, S., Alur, R., Bastani, O.: Compositional learning and verification of neural network controllers. ACM Trans. Embed. Comput. Syst. **20**(5s), 1–26 (2021). https://doi.org/10.1145/3477023
17. Leucker, M., Schallhart, C.: A brief account of runtime verification. J. Logic Algebraic Program. **78**(5), 293–303 (2009). https://doi.org/10.1016/j.jlap.2008.08.004
18. Liu, S., Saoud, A., Jagtap, P., Dimarogonas, D.V., Zamani, M.: Compositional synthesis of signal temporal logic tasks via assume-guarantee contracts. In: CDC. IEEE, December 2022. https://doi.org/10.1109/cdc51059.2022.9992715
19. Majumdar, R., Mathur, A., Pirron, M., Stegner, L., Zufferey, D.: Paracosm: a test framework for autonomous driving simulations. In: FASE 2021. LNCS, vol. 12649, pp. 172–195. Springer, Cham (2021). https://doi.org/10.1007/978-3-030-71500-7_9
20. Mallozzi, P., Incer, I., Nuzzo, P., Sangiovanni-Vincentelli, A.: Contract-based specification refinement and repair for mission planning. In: FormaliSE, vol. 45, pp. 29–38. IEEE, May 2023. https://doi.org/10.1109/formalise58978.2023.00011
21. Manna, Z., Pnueli, A.: The Temporal Logic of Reactive and Concurrent Systems. Springer, New York (1992). https://doi.org/10.1007/978-1-4612-0931-7
22. de Moura, L., Bjørner, N.: Z3: an efficient SMT solver. In: Ramakrishnan, C.R., Rehof, J. (eds.) TACAS 2008. LNCS, vol. 4963, pp. 337–340. Springer, Heidelberg (2008). https://doi.org/10.1007/978-3-540-78800-3_24
23. Păsăreanu, C.S., et al.: Closed-loop analysis of vision-based autonomous systems: a case study. In: Enea, C., Lal, A. (eds.) CAV 2023. LNCS, pp. 289–303, vol. 13964, Springer, Cham (2023). https://doi.org/10.1007/978-3-031-37706-8_15
24. Phan-Minh, T.: Contract-based design: theories and applications. Ph.D. thesis, California Institute of Technology (2021)
25. Shao, H., Wang, L., Chen, R., Li, H., Liu, Y.: Safety-enhanced autonomous driving using interpretable sensor fusion transformer. In: Liu, K., Kulic, D., Ichnowski, J. (eds.) Proceedings of The 6th Conference on Robot Learning, PMLR, vol. 205, pp. 726–737, 14–18 December 2023. https://doi.org/10.48550/arXiv.2207.14024

26. Sharf, M., Besselink, B., Molin, A., Zhao, Q., Henrik Johansson, K.: Assume/guarantee contracts for dynamical systems: theory and computational tools. IFAC-PapersOnLine **54**(5), 25–30 (2021). https://doi.org/10.1016/j.ifacol.2021.08.469. 7th IFAC Conference on Analysis and Design of Hybrid Systems ADHS 2021
27. Vin, E., et al.: 3D environment modeling for falsification and beyond with scenic 3.0. In: Enea, C., Lal, A. (eds.) CAV 2023. LNCS, vol. 13964, pp. 253–265, Springer, Cham (2023). https://doi.org/10.1007/978-3-031-37706-8_13
28. Wu, P., Jia, X., Chen, L., Yan, J., Li, H., Qiao, Y.: Trajectory-guided control prediction for end-to-end autonomous driving: a simple yet strong baseline. In: Koyejo, S., Mohamed, S., Agarwal, A., Belgrave, D., Cho, K., Oh, A. (eds.) Advances in NeurIPS, vol. 35, pp. 6119–6132. Curran Associates, Inc. (2022). https://doi.org/10.48550/arXiv.2206.0812

Author Index

A. Madeira and A. Knapp (Eds.): SEFM 2024, LNCS 15280, pp. 461–462, 2025.
https://doi.org/10.1007/978-3-031-77382-2

S

T

V

W

Y

Z

GPSR Compliance

The European Union's (EU) General Product Safety Regulation (GPSR) is a set of rules that requires consumer products to be safe and our obligations to ensure this.

If you have any concerns about our products, you can contact us on ProductSafety@springernature.com

In case Publisher is established outside the EU, the EU authorized representative is:

Springer Nature Customer Service Center GmbH
Europaplatz 3
69115 Heidelberg, Germany

The manufacturer's authorised representative in the EU is Springer Nature Customer Service Centre GmbH, Europaplatz 3, 69115 Heidelberg, Germany. If you have any concerns regarding our products, please contact ProductSafety@springernature.com

Printed and bound by CPI Group (UK) Ltd, Croydon, CR0 4YY
01/10/2026
02225908-0016